A Special Issue of
Language and Cognitive Processes

Current issues in Morphological Processing

Edited by

Ram Frost
The Hebrew University, Jerusalem

Jonathan Grainger
Université d'Aix, France

and

Kathleen Rastle
University of London, UK

 Psychology Press
Taylor & Francis Group
HOVE AND NEW YORK

Published in 2005 by Psychology Press Ltd
27 Church Road, Hove, East Sussex, BN3 2FA

Simultaneously published in the USA and Canada
by Psychology Press Inc.,
711 Third Avenue, New York, NY 10017

First issued in paperback 2015

*Psychology Press is an imprint of the Taylor & Francis Group,
an informa business*

British Library Cataloguing in Publication Data
A catalogue record for this book is available from the British Library

ISBN 13: 978-1-138-87804-4 (pbk)
ISBN 13: 978-1-8416-9984-4 (hbk)

ISSN 0169-0965

Cover design by Jim Wilkie
Typeset in the UK by MFK Mendip, Frome, Somerset

Contents

LANGUAGE AND COGNITIVE PROCESSES
2005, 20 (1/2), 1–5

Current issues in morphological processing: An introduction

Ram Frost

Department of Psychology, The Hebrew University, Israel

Jonathan Grainger

CNRS and University of Provence, France

Kathleen Rastle

Department of Psychology, Royal Holloway, University of London, UK

That morphological considerations need to be introduced into any model of the mental lexicon is now the prevalent view in the field of word recognition. For several decades we have witnessed a virtual split between research on word recognition that focused on orthographic and/or phonological processing, and research that focused exclusively on the investigation of morphological structure. This split is well demonstrated by the classical models of the mental lexicon, which have not considered morphology as a necessary theoretical construct (e.g., Forster, 1976; McClelland & Rumelhart, 1981). From this perspective, however, it seems that the tide is turning. Whether the theoretical approach is distributed-connectionist or classical-localist, the role of morphologically defined variables is central in current attempts to explain linguistic behaviour. It remains to be seen, however, whether morphology needs to be explicitly represented in the system or whether morphological effects emerge from interactions within and between units representing form and meaning.

The present special issue is the third volume produced by a group of researchers who convene every two years to discuss the role of morphology in word recognition. It includes a series of experimental papers, all devoted to morphological processing. The experimental work outlined in the 13 papers of this volume is diverse. The volume explores a variety of

© 2005 Psychology Press Ltd

http://www.tandf.co.uk/journals/pp/01690965.html   DOI: 10.1080/01690960444000287

languages such as Arabic, Dutch, English, Finnish, French, German, Hebrew, Serbo-Croatian, and Spanish. The methods of investigations are diverse as well, and include single-word recognition, masked, cross-modal, and long-term priming, the monitoring of eye movements, or the use of computer simulations, with both the processing of speech and print being explored. However, most importantly, the present volume, being the third consecutive one on morphology, provides a longitudinal perspective on the theoretical issues currently under debate in this relatively young domain.

A brief overview of the papers appearing in the special issue suggests that the main theoretical controversies which were outlined a few decades ago by the pioneering experimental work on morphology, are still under debate. Current research is still focused on understanding how morphological information is stored in long-term memory and how it is used during the process of language comprehension and production. Central to this more general goal is the question of morphological decomposition, first raised in the seminal work of Taft and Forster (1975), and reflected in most of the volume's papers. How morphological structure interacts with the lexical system is indeed a central issue, since it bears on the representational architecture of the mental lexicon. However, the starting point for any reflection on this central issue is to provide evidence that morphologically defined variables do indeed influence language processing. Most articles in the volume provide clear behavioural evidence in this direction, emerging across different languages and methodologies.

The pervasiveness of morphological influences on word recognition is perhaps most plain in the article by Dijkstra and colleagues, who investigated effects of morphological family size (MFS) on the recognition of interlingual homographs in Dutch-English bilinguals. In a Dutch lexical decision task, they observed facilitatory effects of Dutch MFS accompanied by simultaneous inhibitory effects of English MFS—and the reverse was true when the language of the task was English. Dutch and English were also used by Kemps and her colleagues. Their paper explored the impact of prosodic information on the auditory recognition of morphologically complex words, showing that word-specific intonational information is lexically stored and assists morphological processing.

Given the cumulative evidence demonstrating morphological influences on lexical processing, a vast majority of articles in this volume seek to uncover the locus of these influences—evaluating key theories advanced over the past decade, be they single route (e.g., Taft, 1994) or dual-route (e.g., Schreuder & Baayen, 1995), sublexical (e.g., Frost, Forster, & Deutsch, 1997) or supralexical (e.g., Giraudo & Grainger, 2000), classical-localist (e.g., Marslen-Wilson, Tyler, Waksler, & Older, 1994) or distributed-connectionist (e.g., Rueckl, Mikolinski, Raveh, Miner, & Mars, 1997).

The sublexical and the supralexical accounts were examined by Diependael and colleagues in both Dutch and French using masked cross-modal priming. Whereas the results from Dutch provided support for a supralexical architecture, some of the results from French were not so obviously accommodated by such an approach. The paper by Rueckl and Galantucci explored the locus and time-course of long-term morphological priming using the fragment completion task (Weldon, 1993). Their results demonstrate that morphological priming has a modality-specific component early in the time course of processing.

A particularly topical issue, reflected in a number of the articles contained in this volume, concerns the extent to which morphological decomposition is influenced by semantic transparency. Though first raised in relation to classical-localist theories of lexical organization (Marslen-Wilson et al., 1994) this issue is central to more recent parallel-distributed processing (PDP) theories, proponents of which (e.g., Plaut & Gonnerman, 2000; Rueckl et al., 1997) postulate that morphological effects emerge as a consequence of learned statistical regularities that morphology brings to the form-meaning mapping. Mirkovic and her colleagues develop this account further in their examination of gender representation in Serbo-Croatian, which demonstrates that gender information results from systematic correlations between phonological structure and semantic features. Velan and her colleagues also evaluate this account in light of their observation that masked morphological priming in Hebrew is resistant to the orthographic changes seen in weak and defective roots.

In contrast to the data reported by Marslen-Wilson et al. (1994), a number of articles in this volume find morphological effects on word recognition that are uninfluenced by semantic transparency. Boudelaa and Marslen-Wilson demonstrate morphological priming effects in Arabic that do not appear to depend on the semantic similarity between prime and target; Diependaele and colleagues observe clear masked cross-modal morphological priming effects in spite of semantic opacity in French (although they find suggestive evidence for a semantic transparency effect at very short exposure durations); and Pollatsek and Hyönä fail to find any reliable difference in readers' eye fixation durations on Finnish compound words as a function of semantic transparency, while finding reliable constituent frequency effects for both transparent and opaque compounds.

These articles thus appear broadly consistent with recent arguments that favour a morphological decomposition process, blind to semantic transparency, which characterises early visual word processing. In the extreme case, it seems that pseudo-complex words such as 'corner' may well be initially processed as the combination of the (pseudo-) stem 'corn' and the (pseudo-) affix 'er' (Longtin, Segui, & Halle, 2003; Rastle, Davis, & New, in press). However, the characteristics of morphological decomposition may depend crucially on time, with effects of semantic transparency dominating later stages of processing (Rastle, Davis, Marslen-Wilson, & Tyler, 2000). This account fits nicely with the eye movement data presented by Juhasz and colleagues. They found that spaces inserted in non-normally spaced compound words (e.g., 'softball' → 'soft ball') facilitated early visual word recognition (gauged by first fixation durations), but disrupted later recognition (gauged by total gaze durations that include refixations) to the extent that spacing hampered meaning specification. By contrast, evidence against prelexical morphological decomposition is presented by Carreiras and his colleagues. They demonstrate in a series of experiments that the stem-homograph effect which has been traditionally regarded as providing support for the decompositional view (e.g., Allen & Badecker, 1999) is not a reliable effect in Spanish. Therefore, further research is needed, both to explore the suggestive, and potentially critical evidence for early effects of semantic transparency observed by Diependaele et al. with French stimuli, and to understand better why the Semitic languages such as Arabic depart so clearly from this pattern, as described by Boudelaa & Marslen-Wilson.

Finally, this special issue not only provides an overview of current work on morphological processing, but also sets the scene for future work in this field. One promising future direction is likely to concern the link between morphology and syntax and semantics at the sentence level. This direction is well represented in the work of Deutsch et al., and De Almeida and Libben. Both these papers show contextual influences on the way morphologically complex words are processed in sentences. Also, Zwitserlood and her colleagues examined priming by sentence context of dominant and subordinate meanings of particle verbs in Dutch, that were either semantically transparent or opaque. They demonstrate a clear dissociation between the lexical and the conceptual/semantic systems. Thus, one critical issue for future cross-linguistic investigations of morphological processing is to determine how lexical processing of morphological information interacts with sentence-level processing, and how this might vary as a function of factors such as word length and agglutination. Just as for isolated word recognition, morphologically complex words are likely to play a key role in developing our understanding of the architecture of the processing system that maps form onto meaning at the sentence level.

REFERENCES

Allen, M., & Badecker, W. (1999). Stem homograph inhibition and stem allomorphy: Representing and processing inflected forms in a multi-level lexical system. *Journal of Memory and Language.*

Forster, K. I. (1976). Accessing the mental lexicon. In R. Wales and E. Walker (Eds.), *New approaches to language mechanisms* (pp. 257–287). Amsterdam: North-Holland.

Frost, R., Forster, K. I., & Deutsch, A. (1997). What can we learn from the morphology of Hebrew: A masked priming investigation of morphological representation. *Journal of Experimental Psychology: Learning, Memory, and Cognition, 23*, 829–856.

Giraudo, H., & Grainger, J. (2000). Effects of prime word frequency and cumulative root frequency in masked morphological priming. *Language and Cognitive Processes, 15*, 421–444.

Longtin, C. M., Segui, J., & Halle, P. (2003). Morphological priming without morphological relationship. *Language and Cognitive Processes, 18*, 313–334.

Marslen-Wilson, W. D, Tyler, L. K., Waksler, R., & Older, L. (1994). Morphology and meaning in the English mental lexicon. *Psychological Review, 101*, 3–33.

McClelland, J. L., & Rumelhart, D. E. (1981). An interactive activation model of context effects in letter perception: Part 1. An account of basic findings. *Psychological Review, 88*, 375–407.

Plaut, D., & Gonnerman, L. (2000). Are non-semantic morphological effects incompatible with a distributed connectionist approach to lexical processing? *Language and Cognitive Processes, 15*, 445–485.

Rastle, K., Davis, M., Marslen-Wilson, W., & Tyler, L. K. (2000). Morphological and semantic effects in visual word recognition: A time-course study. *Language and Cognitive Processes, 15*, 507–537.

Rastle, K., Davis, M., & New, B. (in press). The broth in my brother's brothel: Morpho-orthographic segmentation in visual word recognition. *Psychonomic Bulletin and Review*.

Rueckl, J. G., Mikolinski, M., Raveh, M., Miner, C. S., & Mars, F. (1997). Morphological priming, fragment completion and connectionist networks. *Journal of Memory and Language, 36*, 382–405.

Schreuder, R., & Baayen, R. H. (1995). Modeling morphological processing. In L. B. Feldman (Ed.), *Morphological aspects of language processing*. Hillsdale, NJ: Lawrence Erlbaum Associates Inc.

Taft, M. (1994). Interactive activation as a framework for understanding morphological processing. *Language and Cognitive Processes, 9*, 271–294.

Taft, M., & Forster, K. I. (1975). Lexical storage and retrieval of prefixed words. *Journal of Verbal Learning and Verbal Behavior, 14*, 638–647.

Weldon, (1993). The time course of perceptual and conceptual contributions to word fragment completion priming. *Journal of Experimental Psychology: Learning, Memory, and Cognition, 19*, 1010–1023.

LANGUAGE AND COGNITIVE PROCESSES
2005, 20 (1/2), 7–41

A roommate in cream: Morphological family size effects on interlingual homograph recognition

Ton Dijkstra

Nijmegen Institute for Cognition and Information, Nijmegen,
The Netherlands

Fermín Moscoso del Prado Martín

Interfaculty Research Unit for Language and Speech, Nijmegen,
The Netherlands
Max Planck Institute for Psycholinguistics, Nijmegen, The Netherlands
MRC Cognition and Brain Sciences Unit, Cambridge, UK

Béryl Schulpen

Nijmegen Institute for Cognition and Information, Nijmegen,
The Netherlands

Robert Schreuder

Interfaculty Research Unit for Language and Speech, Nijmegen,
The Netherlands

R. Harald Baayen

Interfaculty Research Unit for Language and Speech, Nijmegen,
The Netherlands
Max Planck Institute for Psycholinguistics, Nijmegen, The Netherlands

Correspondence should be addressed to Ton Dijkstra, NICI, University of Nijmegen, P.O. Box 9104, 6500 HE Nijmegen, The Netherlands. Email: dijkstra@nici.kun.nl

The authors wish to thank Marc Brysbaert and one anonymous reviewer for helpful comments and suggestions on a previous version of this manuscript. The second, fourth, and fifth authors have been supported by the Dutch Research Council (NWO) through a PIONIER grant to R. H. Baayen. During the last stages of preparation of the manuscript, the second author received additional support from the Medical Research Council (UK) and the European Community, under the 'Information Society Technologies Programme' (IST-2001-35282).

http://www.tandf.co.uk/journals/pp/01690965.html   DOI: 10.1080/0169096044000124

In monolingual studies, target word recognition is affected by the number of words that are morphologically related to the target. Larger morphological families lead to faster recognition. We investigated the role of the morphological family size (MFS) effect in bilingual word recognition. First, re-analysis of available English lexical decision data from Dutch–English bilinguals reported by Schulpen, Dijkstra, and Schriefers (2003) revealed a facilitatory English MFS effect in purely English words and in Dutch–English interlingual homographs (such as ROOM, a word that exists both in English and in Dutch, where it means 'cream'). For interlingual homographs, the Dutch MFS simultaneously induced inhibitory effects, supporting a language non-selective access process. The MFS effect was independent of the relative frequency of the two readings of the homographs. Task-dependence of the MFS effect was demonstrated in generalized Dutch–English lexical decision data, which led to facilitatory effects of both families. Finally, the pervasiveness of the MFS effect was demonstrated in a Dutch lexical decision task performed by the same type of bilinguals. Facilitatory effects of Dutch MFS were found for Dutch monolingual words and interlingual homographs, which were also affected by inhibitory effects of English MFS. The results are discussed in relation to the task-sensitive BIA+ model of bilingual word recognition.

INTRODUCTION

A large number of reaction time (RT) studies in the last decade have provided evidence that the recognition of visually presented words by bilinguals proceeds in a language non-selective way. Thus, Dutch–English bilinguals reading a book in their second language (L2), English, will be affected by the lexical knowledge of their first language (L1), Dutch, even when they are not aware of it (Van Heuven, Dijkstra, & Grainger, 1998; Van Hell & Dijkstra, 2002). To the extent that Dutch words are orthographically similar to the English words that the bilinguals are reading, they will be coactivated and may affect item selection. More surprisingly, the bilinguals will even be affected by the knowledge of similar English words when they are reading in Dutch (Van Hell & Dijkstra, 2002). This indicates that the architecture of the lexical processing system is fundamentally non-selective in nature, although the actual effects of course depend on the degree of cross-language similarity of the involved items. A consequence of this theoretical position is that word recognition in L1 and L2 is open to effects of a variety of variables found to affect monolingual word recognition. In this paper, we will argue that this is indeed the case for a recently discovered independent variable in monolingual word recognition, morphological family size (MFS).

So far, the available evidence supporting language non-selective access has been collected in studies basically manipulating the degree of cross-language similarity of items in one of two ways (see Dijkstra & Van Heuven, 2002, for a review of studies). A first type of item manipulation has been to compare the RTs to words existing in one language only to words that share their orthographic, phonological, and/or semantic characteristics across languages. For instance, an item like LIST shares its orthography but not its meaning across Dutch and English (in Dutch, LIST means 'trick'). In contrast to such interlingual homographs, cognates like FILM share (most of) their meaning and orthography across languages. Studies have generally found facilitatory effects for cognates relative to one-language control items under various circumstances (Lemhöfer, Dijkstra, & Michel, 2004). The direction and size of RT effects for interlingual homographs appears to be dependent on task demands, stimulus list composition, and the relative frequency of the homograph readings in the two languages (e.g., Dijkstra, Grainger, & Van Heuven, 1999; Dijkstra, Van Jaarsveld, & Ten Brinke, 1998). Most studies have focused on homograph effects for bilinguals reading in their L2, but significant (inhibitory) effects have also been obtained in the L1 (De Groot et al., 2000). Note that interlingual homographs are words in two languages, even though they differ in meaning across these languages.

In a second type of manipulation, the number of orthographically or phonologically similar items to the target word from the same and the other language has been varied. As an example, words that are orthographically similar to WORK (called neighbours) are CORK and WORD in English, and VORK and WERK in Dutch. Intralingual and interlingual neighbourhood density have been found to affect the RT patterns observed for target words in a number of tasks (Van Heuven et al., 1998). For lexical decision, inhibitory effects of neighbourhood density have often been reported, but the mechanisms underlying the effects are not well understood and may be sensitive to a variety of factors (such as differences between languages, participants, and stimulus materials; Carreiras, Perea, & Grainger, 1997). Nevertheless, the manipulation of interlingual neighbourhood density provides convincing evidence in support of language non-selective access into an integrated lexicon, because it is concerned with 'on-line' effects for 'normal' words existing in only one language, in contrast to 'special' words like homographs and cognates.

The effects of neighbourhood density were first reported in monolingual studies before they were also demonstrated in bilingual studies. Recent monolingual studies have shown that the RTs in various word identification tasks are affected by yet another variable, called a word's 'morphological family size' (MFS; Baayen, Lieber, & Schreuder, 1997b; Bertram, Baayen, & Schreuder, 2000; de Jong, 2002; Schreuder & Baayen, 1997). For instance, a Dutch word like WERK (meaning 'work') is a constituent of many morphologically complex words, among which are HUISWERK ('homework'), WERKBAAR ('workable'), and VERWER-KEN ('to process'). Experiments have revealed that words with larger morphological families are processed faster and more accurately than those with smaller families. This effect is independent of other lexical effects such as word frequency or length (De Jong, Schreuder, & Baayen, 2000), and available evidence indicates that it is at least partially semantic in nature. First, the effect of MFS appears for both regular and irregular past participles (e.g., GEROEID, 'rowed' vs. GEVOCHTEN, 'fought'), even though the irregular past participles do not share the exact orthographic or phonological form across family members (e.g., ROEIER, 'rower', vs. VECHTER, 'fighter'). This suggests that morphological and/or semantic sources underlie the MFS effect. Second, only morphologically related words that are also semantically related contribute to the MFS (Bertram et al., 2000; Schreuder & Baayen, 1997). For instance, GEMEENTE ('municipality') is morphologically but not semantically related to GEMEEN ('nasty') and the correlation between RTs and family size decreases if GEMEENTE is included in the MFS count for GEMEEN.

Moscoso del Prado Martín, Deutsch, Frost, Schreuder, De Jong, and Baayen (2004) report an additional semantic characteristic of the MFS effect in Hebrew. The MFS of Hebrew words for which the morphological root is active in two semantic fields needs to be split into two different subfamilies, one for each semantic field. Both subfamilies show effects of a similar magnitude on the RTs to a particular Hebrew word. However, the direction of the effect is reversed for the subfamily that contains the words that are in a semantic field different from that of the target. For instance, the Hebrew root R-G-L can form words whose meaning is related to 'foot' (REGEL), and words whose meaning is related to 'spy' (MERAGGEL). Response latencies to REGEL are facilitated by the MFS containing those members of the family of R-G-L that are more related in meaning to 'foot' and inhibited by the MFS containing the members of the R-G-L family that are more related in meaning to 'spy'.

It is likely that bilinguals acquiring a second language will start to develop the morphological and semantic relations between words from their second language as well. Of course, the MFS in L2 may initially be smaller than in L1, but it should develop with vocabulary size. Therefore, just like an effect of interlingual neighbours can arise in bilingual word recognition (in spite of a smaller number of known L2 words), the MFS of a word would be expected to start playing a role in L2 as well. In other words, English word recognition in Dutch–English bilinguals should be affected by the English MFS of the target item. Even more interestingly, both the English and the Dutch MFS should play a role in the recognition of interlingual homographs, because these items belong to both English and Dutch families. Additionally, one might expect to find inhibition effects akin to those reported by Moscoso del Prado Martín et al. (2004) for Hebrew. For interlingual homographs, participants performing a lexical decision task in L2 might show a facilitatory effect of the MFS of the target in L2, and an inhibition effect of the MFS of the target in L1. Conversely, participants making lexical decisions in their L1 might show facilitation of the MFS of the word in L1, and for interlingual homographs, they might also show inhibition caused by the MFS of the word in L2.

These predictions follow straightforwardly from the basic assumptions of a recent model for bilingual word recognition, the BIA+ model (Dijkstra & Van Heuven, 2002). According to this language non-selective access model, word recognition entails parallel activation of words from different languages in an integrated word identification system. A task/ decision system monitors lexical activity and uses it in accordance with the demands of the task at hand, allowing for context sensitive performance patterns. For instance, let us assume that a Dutch–English bilingual is performing an English (L2) lexical decision task, in which an English word must be accepted ('yes' response), while other words and nonwords must be rejected ('no' response). According to the model, interlingual homographs are represented by means of two orthographic lexical representations, one for each reading of the homograph (e.g., ROOM has one orthographic representation linked to the phonological and semantic characteristics of the English item, and another linked to those of its Dutch counterpart). In the task situation at hand, recognising an interlingual homograph involves a 'race to recognition' between its two readings, with an ensuing response competition (one reading is connected to a 'yes' response, the other to the 'no' response). This whole process is modulated by the relative frequencies of the two readings of the interlingual homograph (because in the model a word's resting level activation depends on its frequency). When a homograph has a higher word frequency in the non-target language (Dutch) than in the target language (English), this induces extra competition resulting in inhibition relative to a one-language (English) control word (Dijkstra et al., 1998).

If the MFS behaves like word frequency, a large English MFS of the homograph should also exert a facilitatory effect in English lexical decision, because in this task it would support the selection of the target item and be indirectly linked to the correct response. At the same time, a large Dutch MFS, associated with the competitor item, should exert an inhibitory effect. This prediction can be contrasted to that for generalised lexical decision, in which participants give a 'yes' response to both English and Dutch words. In this task situation, both English and Dutch MFS should have a facilitatory effect on the RTs.

In sum, in the present study we will investigate a number of issues with respect to morphological families in L1 and L2. First, we will search for the expected MFS effects in the L1 and L2 of bilinguals. Second, we will test if in L2 MFS effects of both L1 and L2 occur for interlingual homographs differing in their relative frequency in L1 and L2. More specifically, we will test the prediction of BIA+ that in an English lexical decision task the MFS effects of Dutch (L1) on English (L2) are inhibitory in nature, while in a generalised lexical decision task they are facilitatory. Finally, we will go even further and try to demonstrate effects of the English (L2) morphological family size of interlingual homographs in a Dutch (L1) lexical decision task. Finding MFS effects would provide additional independent evidence supporting the language non-selective access hypothesis, because it would demonstrate that it is not just the stronger L1 that is affecting the weaker L2, but that there is a mutual effect between the two languages.

These predictions will be tested in two steps. In the first part of the paper, we will test the first two predictions by re-analysing some recent experiments reported by Schulpen et al. (2003). As part of a larger study, these authors conducted two lexical decision experiments with Dutch–English bilingual university students. In the first experiment, the participants responded by pressing a 'yes' or a 'no' button depending on whether they encountered English target words or non-words (English lexical decision task). No Dutch words were present in the experiment. Reaction times for interlingual homographs were compared to those for English control words, revealing only small non-significant latency differences (as observed in earlier studies by Dijkstra et al., 1998; and De Groot et al., 2000). In the second experiment, they pressed a 'yes' button when they encountered a word from English or Dutch, and a 'no' button otherwise (generalised Dutch–English lexical decision task). Now interlingual homographs were recognised faster than English control words. We will investigate if the difference in RT patterns between the two experiments is accompanied by a difference in the MFS effect.

In the second part, we will conduct a new Dutch léxical decision experiment with Dutch–English bilinguals involving largely the same test materials to test the third prediction, i.e., the presence of L2 on L1 effects in the interlingual homographs. This experiment is similar to that by De Groot et al. (2000, Experiment 2), who observed slower RTs to interlingual homographs than to purely Dutch control words. Note that the effects of morphological family size were examined in neither of the earlier studies.

PART I: REANALYSES OF TWO EARLIER STUDIES

Experiment 1: English Visual Lexical Decision

Method

Participants.   Nineteen students of the University of Nijmegen (mean age: 22.5 years) were paid to participate in the experiment. All were native speakers of Dutch. All had begun to acquire English at school when they were 11 or 12 years old.

Materials.   In total, the stimulus set consisted of 420 items of which 210 were words and 210 nonwords. All word items were selected from the CELEX database (Baayen, Piepenbrock, & Van Rijn, 1993) and had a length of 3–6 letters. Table 1 describes the characteristics of the relevant words in the three experiments of our study. The actual test words can be found in Appendices A and B. Experiments 1 and 2 correspond with Experiments 1 and 2 in Schulpen et al. (2003), while Experiment 3 refers to the present study only. The experiment included 42 interlingual homographs, i.e., words that are legal both in Dutch and English. Homographs were chosen from three frequency categories (high English frequency—high Dutch frequency, high English frequency—low Dutch frequency, and low English frequency—high Dutch frequency). The experiment also included 84 monolingual English words (note that the 84 Dutch words mentioned in Table 1 were only included in Experiments 2 and 3). These monolingual words were divided in four groups. Three groups of 14 words each (English Controls) were matched in English frequency with the three groups of interlingual homographs. The fourth group consisted of 42 words (English Open Range), chosen from English low, middle, and high frequency ranges (14 of each). Finally, 294 filler items (84 words and 210 nonwords with a legal English orthography) were included that do not concern us here.

Procedure.   The design consisted of item blocks that were rotated across participants. The presentation order of items within a block was randomised individually with the restriction that no more than three words or nonwords were presented in a row. Each participant was tested individually. The presentation of the visual stimuli and the recordings of the RTs were controlled by an Apple Powerbook G3 400 MHz with 128 megabytes of working memory, with an external Multiplescan 15AV Display and using experimentation software was developed by the technical group of the University in Nijmegen. The participants were seated at a table with the computer monitor at a 60 cm distance. The visual stimuli were presented in capital letters (24 points) in font New Courier in

TABLE 1
Materials present in Experiments 1, 2, and 3

Materials	Frequency range	Number of words	Dutch freq.	English freq.	Experiment	Appendix
English-Dutch homographs	HF English–HF Dutch	14	104	233		
	HF English–LF Dutch	14	9	244	1, 2, 3	A
	LF English–HF Dutch	14	114	32		
English monolingual words	HF English (HF Dutch)	14	–	233		
	HF English (LF Dutch)	14	–	244	1, 2	B
	LF English (HF Dutch)	14	–	32		
	Open range	42	–	5, 48, 415		
Dutch monolingual words	(HF English) HF Dutch	14	104	–		
	(HF English) LF Dutch	14	9	–	2, 3	C
	(LF English) HF Dutch	14	114	–		
	Open range	42	5, 40, 489	–		

The word frequency counts are in occurrences per million. The frequency conditions shown in parentheses in the monolingual words indicate the homograph frequency condition to which each group was matched. The three numbers in the frequency column of the Dutch and English open range monolingual words indicate the average frequency of the low, middle, and high frequency words in the group.

the middle of the screen on a white background. The participants performed an English visual lexical decision task. They first read an English instruction, telling them that they would see a letter string to which they were supposed to react by pressing the 'yes' button when it was an English word or the 'no' button when the letter string was a nonword. The participants were told to react as quickly as possible without making too many errors. Each trial started with the visual presentation of a fixation dot for 500 ms followed after 150 ms by the target letter string in the middle of the screen. The target letter string remained on the screen until the participant responded or until a maximum of 2000 ms. When the button was pressed, the visual target stimulus disappeared and a new trial was triggered immediately.

The experiment was divided in three parts of equal length. The first part was preceded by 24 practice trials. After the practice set the participant could ask questions. All communication between participant and experimentator was conducted in Dutch. After the experiment, the participants were asked to fill out two questionnaires, one on paper about their level of proficiency in the English language, and one on the computer evaluating their knowledge of the stimulus words used in the experiment on a 7-point scale. In total, each experimental session lasted about 45 minutes.

Results and discussion

Data cleaning procedures were based on error rates for items and participants. All incorrect responses were removed from the data (8.14% of all trials). All participants performed with an error rate of less than 20%. Eleven items elicited errors in more than 30% of the trials, and were removed from the analyses. After removing these, 74 trials with RTs that were outside the range of two standard deviations from the mean RT were considered as outliers and were discarded (3.56% of the remaining trials). Note here that our procedure for determining outliers is slightly different than the one reported by Schulpen et al. (2003) for this dataset (and also for the dataset in Experiment 2). Schulpen and colleagues also provide analyses of the monolingual English or Dutch fillers, which they analyse together with the English and Dutch open range words and controls. In our case, the analyses of the monolingual words is restricted to the controls and the open range monolingual words.

Table 2 provides the means, standard deviations, and ranges of the frequency counts, family size counts, and RTs after the data cleaning procedures had been applied.

For this dataset, Schulpen et al. (2003) report results using the traditional ANOVAs on different frequency conditions from a factorial design contrasting high and low Dutch and English frequency. However,

TABLE 2

Means, standard deviations, and ranges for the different counts in the data set from Experiment 1 (EVLD), and in the subsets of interlingual homographs and English monolingual words (after removing outliers)

	Total 115 items		Interlingual homographs 37 items		English monolingual words 78 items	
English frequency	179.63 ± 312.06	[1, 1981]	190.13 ± 297.78	[3, 1351]	174.65 ± 320.38	[1, 1981]
English family size	16.41 ± 21.76	[0, 112]	12.27 ± 14.99	[1, 70]	18.37 ± 24.16	[0, 112]
Dutch frequency	26.17 ± 85.23	[0, 724]	81.32 ± 135.62	[2, 724]	–	
Dutch family size	10.45 ± 25.11	[0, 134]	32.49 ± 35.50	[0, 134]	–	
Response latency (ms)	590 ± 65	[481, 875]	585 ± 48	[500, 710]	591 ± 72	[481, 875]

The word frequency counts are in occurrences per million.

we intend to assess the influence of an additional variable (morphological family size) that the original experimental design did not control for. Furthermore, the word frequency and morphological family size variables for both languages in this dataset follow smooth lognormal distributions according to Shapiro–Wilk normality tests (Royston, 1982) of the log counts ($W = 0.99$, $p = .40$, for English frequency, $W = 0.98$, $p = .13$ for English family size, $W = 0.98$, $p = .58$ for Dutch frequency of the homographs, and $W = 0.95$, $p = .08$ for Dutch family size of the homographs). Given these considerations, we decided to report regression analyses on the experimental results, which are more adequate for analysing this sort of data. In all cases, we report sequential analyses of variance on stepwise multilevel linear regression models (Alegre & Gordon, 1999; Baayen, Tweedie, & Schreuder, 2002; Lorch & Myers, 1990; Pinheiro & Bates, 2000).

We begin by assessing whether English word frequency and morphological family size have a significant influence on the response latencies to the remaining 76 English monolingual words in our dataset. A stepwise multilevel regression model with RT as the dependent variable and English word frequency and English morphological family size as independent variables showed facilitatory main effects of English word frequency, $F(1, 1313) = 112.28$, $p < .001$, and English morphological family size, $F(1, 1313) = 7.80$, $p < .01$, after having partialled out the effect of English word frequency), with the interaction between frequency and family size approaching but not reaching significance, $F(1, 1312) = 3.62$, $p = .06$.

In order to analyse the results for the interlingual homographs in this experiment, we investigate the possible influences of the different variables on the response latencies by means of correlations. As all variables are lognormally distributed, we will report correlations on their logarithms. Both English counts show negative correlation coefficients with RTs ($r = -.21$, $p = .21$ for English word frequency, and $r = -.36$, $p = .03$ for English morphological family size), for which we note that the correlation is not significant for English word frequency. In contrast, both Dutch counts show significant positive correlations with the response latencies ($r = .38$, $p = .02$ for Dutch frequency, and $r = .36$, $p = .03$ for Dutch family size). This indicates that while English word frequency and English family size exert more or less facilitatory influences, Dutch frequency and Dutch family size have inhibitory effects on the response latencies. This is in line with Schulpen et al. (2003) who report opposite effects of English frequency and Dutch frequency for this dataset in an ANOVA on the factorial design.

Note that the magnitude of the correlation coefficient of both family size counts is similar, differing mainly in the direction of the effect. This is reminiscent of the pattern reported by Moscoso del Prado Martín et al. (2004) for Hebrew, in which the semantically close and semantically distant family sizes appear to have effects that are equal in magnitude but different in direction. Moscoso del Prado Martín and colleagues operationalised this in their analyses by taking the difference between the two logarithmic counts as the predictor variable. Note here that a difference in logarithmic scale is equivalent to the logarithm of the ratio (in non-logarithmic scale). This log-transformed ratio, henceforth the family size ratio, turned out to be the crucial predictor for the Hebrew data.

In our regression analyses, we will make use of a similar approach, by which we consider the English counts to have a facilitatory effect on the task (given that English was the relevant language in the experiment), and the Dutch counts to have an inhibitory effect of the same magnitude as their English counterparts. More specifically, we will use two ratio variables for the interlingual homographs: the English–Dutch frequency ratio, i.e., the difference between the log of the English frequency and the log of the Dutch frequency, and the English–Dutch family size ratio, i.e., the difference between the logarithm of the English family size and the logarithm of the Dutch family size. The usage of these ratios allows us to jointly analyse the effects of these four highly correlated variables, and it significantly reduces the collinearity in the data matrix.

A stepwise multilevel regression analysis with the RTs as the dependent variable and the English–Dutch frequency ratio and the English–Dutch family size ratio as independent variables revealed facilitatory main effects for the frequency ratio, $F(1, 612) = 18.47$, $p < .001$, and the family size ratio, $F(1, 612) = 5.95$, $p = .02$, after having partialled out the effect of the frequency ratio, and no significant interaction, $F(1, 611) = 1.45$, $p = .23$.

Taken together, the analyses reported here clearly show effects of word frequency for both the English monolingual words and the English–Dutch interlingual homographs. In the later case, as illustrated by the effect of the frequency ratio, the effect of word frequency seems to be a composite effect, which consists of a facilitation effect caused by English word frequency (words with a high frequency in English are recognised faster), and an equivalent inhibitory effect due to the Dutch frequency count (homographs with a high Dutch frequency are recognised slower). These frequency effects confirm the results reported by Schulpen et al. (2003). Additionally, the regression analyses reveal an MFS effect for both the English monolingual words and the interlingual homographs. This effect shows characteristics similar to that of frequency, in that the size of the morphological paradigm of a word in the relevant language (i.e., English) facilitates the recognition of the word. Thus, words from large English morphological paradigms are recognised faster, while at the same time, the size of the morphological paradigm in the language that is not relevant for the task inhibits target recognition. In the next experiment, we will examine if the size and/or direction of MFS effects changes if the task is modified into a Generalised Lexical Decision task.

Experiment 2: Generalised Visual Lexical Decision

Method

Participants.   Eighteen students of the University of Nijmegen (mean age: 22.5 years) were paid to participate in the experiment. All were native speakers of Dutch who began to acquire English when they were 11 or 12 years old.

Materials.   The stimulus set consisted of 420 items of which 210 were words and 210 nonwords. The current experiment included the same 42 interlingual homographs and the 84 monolingual English words from Experiment 1. Additionally, the 84 monolingual Dutch words charac- terised in Table 1 were included in the experiment. Appendices A–C contain the test words themselves. As was the case for the English words, the set of monolingual Dutch words consisted of three groups of 14 words, each matched in frequency to one of the groups of interlingual homographs (Dutch Controls), plus 42 words in the low, medium, and high Dutch frequency ranges (Dutch Open Range). The experiment further contained 126 nonwords with a legal English orthography and 84 nonwords obtained by changing a letter in low and middle frequency Dutch words.

Procedure.   The procedure was identical to that of Experiment 1, except that this time participants were instructed to react by pressing the 'yes' button when the stimulus on the screen was either a legal English word or a legal Dutch word, and the 'no' button when the letter string was not a word in Dutch or English. All communication between participant and experimentator was conducted in Dutch. In total, each experimental session lasted about 60 minutes.

Results and discussion

All participants performed with an error rate of less than 20%. Ten items elicited errors in more than 30% of the trials, and were removed from further analyses. All incorrect responses were removed from the data (7.57% of all trials). After removing the errors, 166 trials with RTs that were outside the range of 2.5 standard deviations from the mean RT were considered as outliers and were thus discarded (4.75% of the remaining trials). Table 3 provides the means, standard deviations, and ranges of the frequency counts, family size counts, and RTs after the data cleaning procedures had been applied.

As in the previous experiment, the word frequency and morphological family size variables in this dataset followed smooth lognormal distributions according to conservative Shapiro–Wilk normality tests of the log counts ($W = 0.99, p = .27$, for frequency, $W = 0.98, p = .14$ for family size in the English words, and $W = 0.98, p = .12$ for Dutch family size of the Dutch words).[1] Therefore, we report once more analyses of variance on stepwise multilevel linear regression models.

We first assessed whether word frequency and morphological family size have a significant influence on the response latencies to the monolingual English and Dutch words in our dataset. A stepwise multilevel regression model with RT as the dependent variable and English word frequency and English morphological family size as independent variables showed main facilitatory effects of English word frequency, $F(1, 1166) = 98.22, p < .001$, and English morphological family size, $F(1, 1166) = 18.51, p < .001$, after having partialled out the effect of English word frequency, as well as a significant interaction between frequency and family size, $F(1, 1166) = 4.11, p = .04$.

With respect to the monolingual Dutch words, a stepwise multilevel regression model with RT as the dependent variable, and Dutch word frequency and Dutch morphological family size as independent variables showed a main facilitatory effect of Dutch word frequency, $F(1, 1412) = 74.40, p < .001$, but no significant effect of Dutch morphological family size, $F(1, 1410) = 2.29, p = .13$, after having partialled out the effect of Dutch word frequency, nor any interaction between frequency and family size ($F < 1$).

As for the English visual lexical decision experiment, we analysed the results for the interlingual homographs by using correlations on the log counts to provide an overview of the influences of the different variables on the response latencies. Both English counts showed significant negative correlation coefficients with RTs ($r = -.41, p < .001$ for English word frequency, and $r = -.30, p < .001$ for English morphological family size). In contrast to what we observed in English lexical decision, both Dutch counts in the present generalised lexical decision experiment show significant correlations with the response latencies ($r = -.38, p < .001$

---

[1] Dutch frequency appeared to be significantly non-lognormally distributed according to the very conservative Shapiro–Wilk test ($W = 0.97, p = .02$). However, inspection of a quantile-quantile plot showed that this deviation was quite small.

TABLE 3

Means, standard deviations, and ranges for the different counts in the data set from Experiment 2 (GVLD), and in the subsets of interlingual homographs and English monolingual words (after removing outliers)

	Total 200 items		Interlingual homographs 42 items		English monolingual words 74 items		Dutch monolingual words 84 items	
English frequency	103.52 ± 252.33	[0, 1981]	169.78 ± 284.63	[3, 1351]	183.43 ± 326.71	[1, 1981]	–	–
English family size	9.42 ± 18.33	[0, 112]	11.40 ± 14.28	[1, 70]	18.99 ± 24.58	[0, 112]	–	–
Dutch frequency	69.27 ± 177.22	[0, 1370]	75.90 ± 128.39	[2, 724]	–	–	126.97 ± 243.90	[1, 1370]
Dutch family size	22.80 ± 40.23	[0, 283]	31.71 ± 34.12	[0, 134]	–	–	38.43 ± 51.87	[0, 283]
Response latency (ms)	542 ± 48	[454, 716]	525 ± 29	[472, 598]	574 ± 49	[484, 716]	522 ± 37	[454, 606]

The word frequency counts are in occurrences per million.

21

for Dutch frequency, and $r = -.40, p < .001$ for Dutch family size), which are now also negative. This indicates that both English and Dutch word frequency and family size counts have facilitatory influences on the response latencies. This finding was predicted by the BIA+ model, which assumes that the two readings of an interlingual homograph are activated and processed in parallel. In other words, the English and Dutch readings are engaged in a 'race' to recognition and the fastest of them to be recognised in a particular trial determines the 'yes' response in the Generalised Lexical Decision task. We can operationalise this account by taking as independent variables in our regression analyses the maximum frequency of a word, i.e., the largest of the Dutch and the English frequency counts for a homograph, and the maximum family size of a word, i.e., the largest of the Dutch and the English family size counts for a given word, all of them in logarithmic scale. This operationalisation allows us to keep the collinearity in the data matrix under control while at the same time testing the predictions of the BIA+ model.

A stepwise multilevel regression analysis with the RTs as the dependent variable and the maximum logarithmic frequency and maximum logarithmic family size as independent variables revealed facilitatory main effects for the maximum frequency, $F(1, 690) = 11.28, p < .001$, and the maximum family size, $F(1, 690) = 5.23, p = .02$, after having partialled out the effect of the maximum frequency, and no significant interaction, $F < 1$. The effects of the maximum frequency and family size are consistent with the predictions of the BIA+ model. However, other analyses also reveal a similar pattern. For instance, the summed frequencies and summed family sizes of both readings of a homograph are also excellent predictors of the RTs, just as the maximum frequency and family size are. This shows that the pattern in the data is robust and independent of the specific theoretical framework of the BIA+ model.

These analyses showed effects of word frequency, for both the English and Dutch monolingual words, while in the case of the English-Dutch interlingual homographs it was the maximum of the frequency of the Dutch reading and the frequency of the English reading of the homograph that predicts response latencies. This effect of the maximum frequency confirms the predictions of models of bilingual word recognition that postulate the existence of a race between the two readings of a homograph in this task. Additionally, the analyses reveal the presence of family size effects for the English monolingual words and the interlingual homographs. Again, in line with the predictions of the BIA+ model, it is the maximum of the two family size counts that exerts an influence on the response latencies.

Discussion of Experiments 1 and 2

Our reanalyses of the two earlier experiments confirm and extend the original results of Schulpen et al. (2003). In bilingual participants, the frequency of the L1 reading of an interlingual homograph can affect the response latencies in a visual lexical decision task where L2 is the target language. This supports the predictions of the BIA+ model that both readings of the homograph are activated simultaneously. The presence of a 'race' between both readings of the homograph entails that, in cases of words with a high L1 frequency, it is the L1 reading of the homograph that 'wins' the race. This results in inhibition relative to an English control condition when the L1 reading of the homograph is not relevant for the task (English visual lexical decision), and in facilitation when either of the two readings represents a valid word and can be used for responding (generalised visual lexical decision).

The regression analyses document for the first time the presence of a morphological family size effect in the processing of L2. This is an indication that the family size effect is a fundamental characteristic of human lexical processing that is already present quickly after a morphological paradigm or group of paradigms is acquired. Crucially, the morphological family size effect in L2 shows very similar character-istics to its counterpart in L1. The analyses have shown that the morphologically related words that are related in meaning to the target provide facilitation, while those of which the meanings are not related to a relevant possible reading of the target for a given task produce inhibition. This inhibitory effect is very similar to the inhibitory effect caused by semantically opaque Hebrew words (Moscoso del Prado Martín et al., 2004).

PART II: A NEW EXPERIMENT

The finding of cross-lingual effects of MFS, reported in the previous section, provides new and independent evidence that during the processing of interlingual homographs, both their L1 and L2 readings are activated. As in earlier papers, this finding can be interpreted as evidence for language non-selective access. However, in the English lexical decision task, the response must be based upon the English reading of the homograph, so the evidence relates only to the effect of the strong L1 on the weaker L2. Furthermore, the bilingual participants are Dutch native speakers immersed in a Dutch environment. It is therefore possible that, although there are L1 effects of morphological family size in L2 processing, the opposite is not true. This would be the case, for instance, if L1, being the participant's native language, has a special status relative to L2. In other words, language non-selective access would not be general, but restricted to the native language. To investigate this possibility, we conducted an additional experiment testing if the contrasting effects of frequency and family size of the L2 (English) reading of a homograph also arise when participants make visual lexical decisions in their L1 (Dutch). We tested this in the strongest way possible by ensuring that the participants were not aware of the relevance of their second language while they were performing in their native language: the data from all participants who noticed the bilingual nature of interlingual homographs were excluded from analysis.

Experiment 3: Dutch Visual Lexical Decision

Method

Participants. Twenty-nine students of the University of Nijmegen (mean age: 22.5 years) were paid to participate in the experiment. All were native speakers of Dutch who learned English from age 11 or 12 onwards.

Materials. The stimulus set consisted of 252 items of which 126 were Dutch words and 126 were nonwords. As specified in Table 1, this experiment included the same 42 interlingual homographs used in Experiments 1 and 2, and the 84 monolingual Dutch words from Experiment 2. Appendices A and C contain the test words themselves. As nonwords we included the 84 Dutch nonwords from Experiment 2, and 42 nonwords with a pattern valid both in English and Dutch that were used in Experiments 1 and 2.

Procedure. The procedure was very similar to that employed in Experiments 1 and 2. Participants received their instructions in Dutch and were instructed to react by pressing the 'yes' button when the stimulus on the screen was a legal Dutch word, and the 'no' button when the letter string was not a word in Dutch. Words were presented on a NEC Multisync color monitor in white lowercase 24 point Arial letters. After the experiment, the participants were asked if they had noticed anything special about the experiment. Five participants reported having noticed the presence of some English words in the experiment and their data were excluded from the analyses to ensure that the results were not affected by any conscious strategies of the participants. In total, the experimental session lasted about 45 minutes.

Results and discussion

The remaining 24 participants performed with an error rate of less than 20%. Two items elicited errors in more than 30% of the trials and were removed from the analyses. All incorrect responses were removed from the data (3.72% of all trials). After removing the errors, 24 trials with RTs that were outside the range of 2.5 standard deviations from the mean RT were considered as outliers and were discarded (0.82% of the remaining trials). Table 4 provides the means, standard deviations, and ranges of the frequency counts, family size counts, and RTs after the data cleaning procedures had been applied.

In order to compare our results with those reported by Schulpen et al. (2003), we begin by analysing the results of the interlingual homographs and their frequency matched Dutch controls (excluding the Dutch open frequency range items) in terms of the original orthogonal design contrasting the English and Dutch frequencies of the homographs. Table 5 describes the reaction times, standard deviations, and errors in each frequency condition after applying the data cleaning procedures. By-participant and by-item analyses of variance revealed significant effects of Frequency Category: High English–High Dutch, High English–Low Dutch, or Low English–High Dutch; $F_1(2, 46) = 25.24$, $p < .001$; $F_2(2, 76) = 6.81$, $p < .01$; a less clear effect of Type of Target: Interlingual homograph vs. Dutch control, $F_1(1, 23) = 4.77$, $p = .04$; $F_2(1, 76) = 2.80$, $p = .09$; and an interaction reaching significance in the by-participant analysis, $F_1(2, 46) = 5.15$, $p < .01$; $F_2(2, 76) = 1.41$, $p = .25$. When we analysed the effect of Frequency Category in more detail, only the words in the High English frequency–Low Dutch frequency condition were significantly slower than the rest ($t = 2.17$, $p = .03$).

A logistic regression[2] on the ratio of incorrect to correct responses revealed significant effects of both Type of Target, $\chi^2(1, 80) = 28.76$, $p < .001$, and Frequency Category, $\chi^2(1, 78) = 20.37$, $p < .001$, with no significant interaction, $\chi^2(2, 76) = 0.83$, $p = .66$. As in the analyses of RTs, the only frequency category that differed from the rest was the high English frequency–low Dutch frequency category that gave rise to significantly more errors ($Z = 3.17$, $p < .01$).

On the whole, interlingual homographs were processed significantly slower and with more errors than their frequency matched controls. Table 5 and the reported t-test show that this was mostly due to the slow RT to homographs that had a low Dutch frequency and a high English frequency. The result pattern replicates that by De Groot et al. (2000, Experiment 2) in a directly comparable study. Thus, one might expect an interaction between Type of Target and Frequency Category, such that homographs

---

[2] Error data from lexical decision experiments are strongly non-normally distributed, due to the very small numbers of incorrect responses provided by participants. This violates the normality precondition for a traditional ANOVA. Instead, we use a logistic regression analysis which is less sensitive to the deviation from normality.

TABLE 4

Means, standard deviations, and ranges for the different counts in the data set from Experiment 3 (DVLD), and in the subsets of interlingual homographs and English monolingual words (after removing outliers)

	Total 124 items		Interlingual homographs 40 items		Dutch monolingual words 84 items	
English frequency	55.63 ± 182.71	[0, 1351]	172.45 ± 290.90	[3, 1351]	–	–
English family size	3.57 ± 9.70	[0, 70]	11.07 ± 14.53	[1, 70]	–	–
Dutch frequency	111.35 ± 214.71	[0, 1370]	78.52 ± 131.00	[2, 724]	126.98 ± 243.90	[0, 1370]
Dutch family size	36.77 ± 46.83	[0, 283]	33.27 ± 34.22	[0, 134]	38.43 ± 51.87	[0, 283]
Response latency (ms)	530 ± 36	[460, 657]	537 ± 41	[460, 657]	527 ± 33	[469, 636]

The word frequency counts are in occurrences per million.

TABLE 5

Means and standard deviations of the reaction times, and error percentages for the different frequency categories of interlingual homographs and their frequency matched Dutch controls from Experiment 3 (DVLD), after applying data cleaning procedures

| | RT (ms) | | SD (ms) | | Errors (per cent) | |
	Homographs	Controls	Homographs	Controls	Homographs	Controls
HFE-HFD	535	526	43	28	3.66	1.20
LFE-HFD	514	515	29	24	2.61	0.60
HFE-LFD	562	534	41	31	10.34	1.84

with a higher English frequency (or a lower Dutch to English frequency ratio) would show more inhibition than their corresponding Dutch controls. This interaction was indeed found in the by-participant analysis, but did not become significant in the by-item analysis. This suggests that the inhibition effect depends on both the English and the Dutch frequency of the homographs.

Having completed the factorial analysis of the frequency effects, we now turn to correlational and regression analysis of the data, including family size as independent variable. As in the previous experiments, the word frequency and morphological family size variables for both languages in this dataset follow lognormal distributions ($W = 0.96$, $p = .14$, for English frequency of the homographs, $W = 0.95$, $p = .08$ for English family size of the homographs, $W = 0.97$, $p = .02$ for Dutch frequency,[3] and $W = 0.99$, $p = .23$ for Dutch family size).

Both Dutch counts showed negative correlation coefficients with RTs ($r = -.40$, $p < .001$ for Dutch word frequency, and $r = -.43$, $p < .001$ for Dutch morphological family size). In contrast, both English counts showed positive correlations with the response latencies ($r = .29$, $p = .07$ for English frequency, and $r = .45$,[4] $p < .01$ for English family size). This pattern is precisely the opposite of that observed in the English visual lexical decision task. While Dutch word frequency and Dutch family size have facilitatory influences on the response latencies, English frequency and English family size exert inhibitory influences on the response latencies. Note that the correlation coefficients for English and Dutch are again similar.

---

[3] Although Dutch frequency appeared to be significantly non-lognormally distributed, visual inspection of a quantile-quantile plot showed that the deviation from lognormality was very small. Moreover, separate normality tests revealed that neither the subset of interlingual homographs ($W = 0.97$, $p > .05$), nor the subset of Dutch monolingual words ($W = 0.98$, $p = .60$), deviated significantly from lognormality.

[4] Although this correlation was only marginally significant, it reached full significance by a non-parametric Spearman correlation ($r_s = .37$, $p = .02$).

The correlation analyses indicate that there is an effect of the English frequency of the homographs. Figure 1 provides further evidence for this English frequency effect, using non-parametric regression (robust locally weighted regression; Cleveland, 1979). The horizontal axis displays log frequency. The vertical axis plots the pairwise difference in the response latencies for the homographs and their controls. The solid line represents the effect of English frequency on this difference, the dashed line the effect of Dutch frequency. Note that as the English frequency increases, the difference in response latency between homograph and control word increases as well, with perhaps a ceiling effect for the highest frequencies. Conversely, the difference in response latency decreases steadily with increasing Dutch frequency. The crossover of the two regression lines bears elegant witness to the inverse effects of English and Dutch frequency for interlingual homographs in Dutch visual lexical decision.

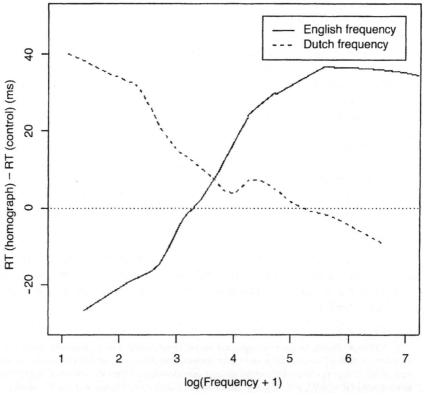

Figure 1. Nonparametric regression lines showing the effects of English word frequency (solid line) and Dutch word frequency (dashed line) on the average difference in RT between a homograph and its frequency-matched control. Frequency counts are in logarithmic scale.

Figure 2 shows a similar crossover between the effects of Dutch and English family size counts on the difference of RTs between homographs and controls. The horizontal axis now plots the logarithm of the family size counts, the vertical axis again displays the difference between the response latencies to a homograph and its control. The solid line representing the correlation between English family size and the difference in response latencies increases steadily with increasing family size. The greater the English family size is, the more time it takes to respond to a homograph relative to its control. The dashed line representing the correlation for Dutch family size suggests a floor effect for the words with larger families.

Having studied the correlations between frequency and family size with the difference in response latencies between the homographs and their controls, we now return to the response latencies to the homographs by themselves. As a first step, we fitted a stepwise multilevel regression model

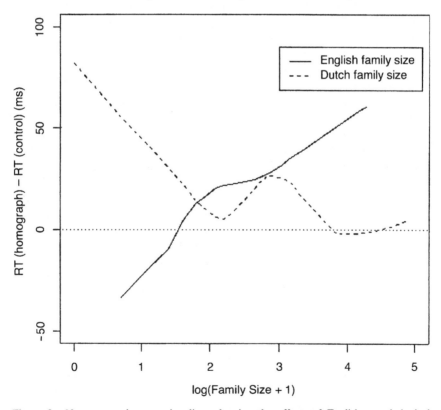

Figure 2. Nonparametric regression lines showing the effects of English morphological family size (solid line) and Dutch morphological family size (dashed line) on the average difference in RT between a homograph and its frequency-matched control. Family size counts are in logarithmic scale.

to the Dutch monolingual words with RT as the dependent variable, and log Dutch word frequency and log Dutch morphological family size as independent variables. We obtained facilitatory main effects of Dutch word frequency, $F(1, 1925) = 48.87, p < .001$, and Dutch morphological family size, $F(1, 1925) = 8.42, p < .01$, after having partialled out the effect of Dutch word frequency, with a small inhibitory interaction, $F(1, 1925) = 8.05, p < .01$.

As in the preceding analyses, we extend the model to take account of English frequency and family size by means of frequency and family size ratios. The Dutch–English frequency ratio captures the difference between the log of the Dutch frequency and the log of the English frequency. Similarly, the Dutch–English family size ratio accounts for the difference between the logarithm of the Dutch family size and the logarithm of the English family size. A stepwise multilevel regression analysis with the RTs of the interlingual homographs as the dependent variable and the Dutch–English frequency ratio and the Dutch–English family size ratio as independent variables revealed facilitatory main effects for the frequency ratio, $F(1, 847) = 43.06, p < .001$, and the family size ratio, $F(1, 847) = 20.20, p < .001$, after having partialled out the effect of the frequency ratio, and no significant interaction $(F < 1)$.

The effects of the frequency and family size ratios can be graphically depicted by comparing the RTs to homographs with those to controls. In Figure 3, the horizontal axis plots the two types of ratios on a logarithmic scale that positions them on a range from −4 to +4. The vertical axis plots the observed difference in RTs between a homograph and its control. The solid line in the figure thus visualizes the correlation between the latency difference and the frequency ratio, whereas the dashed line represents this correlation for the family size ratio. Note that for both ratios, the relation with latency difference is roughly linear with a negative slope that is perhaps slightly larger for the family size ratio. A linear regression with the average difference between RTs to the homographs and RTs to their control, and the Dutch–English frequency ratio and the Dutch–English family size ratio as independent variables, confirmed this linear relation. The frequency ratio had a significant effect on the magnitude of this difference, $F(1, 37) = 5.19, p = .03$, and so did the family size ratio, $F(1, 37) = 4.16, p < .05$, after partialling out the effect of the frequency ratio, with no significant interaction between them $(F < 1)$.

The pattern of results obtained for the Dutch visual lexical decision data is consistent with that obtained for the English visual lexical decision data of Experiment 1. In both experiments, the frequency and family size ratios are key predictors of the response latencies for interlingual homographs. Crucially, however, the ratios are defined with the English measures in the numerator and the Dutch measures in the denominator for Experiment 1,

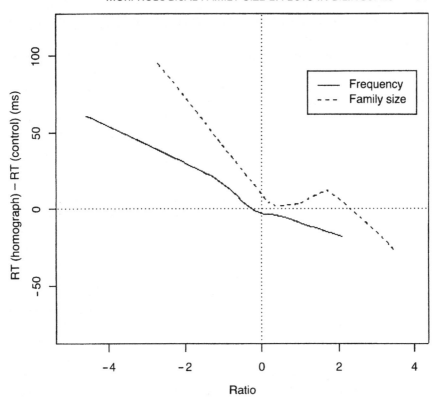

Figure 3. Nonparametric regression lines showing the combined effects of Dutch and English frequency (solid line), and Dutch and English morphological family size (dashed line) on the average difference in RT between a homograph and its frequency-matched control. English and Dutch counts are combined using the Dutch–English frequency and family size ratios.

while for Experiment 3, the Dutch measures are in the numerator and the English measures in the denominator. In other words, the effects are reversed when the task is changed from English lexical decision to Dutch lexical decision.

GENERAL DISCUSSION

The present study shows that neither words nor languages as a whole should be considered as isolated building blocks in the organisation of the mental lexicon. The recognition of words does not just depend on the characteristics of the items themselves (e.g., their frequency, length, or language membership), but also on lexical context, in our case the number of morphologically complex words that the word is related to. For words that exist in two languages, the morphological family sizes (MFS) in both languages play a role.

The experiments we presented led to several important new findings. First, in bilinguals, the MFS in L1 and L2 both affect lexical processing. Second, for interlingual homographs, (partially semantic) MFS effects from both languages are present simultaneously. This does not only indicate that lexical access is language non-selective, but also that the effects must arise in an integrated lexicon. Third, the direction of these effects is task dependent. In the English-specific lexical decision experiment, English family size was facilitatory for homographs, whereas Dutch family size was inhibitory. In contrast, in the generalised (Dutch–English) lexical decision task, both English and Dutch family size had a facilitatory effect.

The pervasiveness of the MFS was revealed by a Dutch lexical decision task. Participants performing in their native language, and unaware of the importance of their second language (English), nevertheless suffered from inhibitory effects of the non-target language MFS on the RTs to the target language reading of interlingual homographs.

A striking finding is that the direction of the MFS effects is in line with that of word frequency effects. In accordance with earlier studies by Dijkstra et al. (1998) and Schulpen et al. (2003), we reported that in the present English specific lexical decision study (Experiment 1), the RTs to interlingual homographs were inhibited to an extent that depended on the relative frequency of the two readings of these items. If the items had a low word frequency in English and a high word frequency in Dutch, RTs were slower than in a one-language control condition consisting of purely English words. In contrast, in the generalised Dutch–English lexical decision experiment (Experiment 2), word frequency in both languages exerted a facilitatory effect on the RTs.

Analogously to the English specific lexical decision experiment, in Experiment 3 (Dutch lexical decision) the RTs to the Dutch reading of interlingual homographs were faster when word frequency was higher in Dutch (LFE–HFD condition), and slower when it was higher in English (HFE–HFD and HFE–LFD conditions). These findings are in agreement with the data from the Dutch lexical decision experiment (Experiment 2) by De Groot et al. (2000).

Although the direction of MFS and word frequency effects was generally the same, the MFS effect in our data was not a mere frequency effect. The effects of the MFS remained significant after partialling out the word frequency effects. Still, the origin of both types of effects may to some extent be comparable. Word frequency effects have been attributed to both orthographic and conceptually semantic levels (e.g., Bradley and Forster, 1987, Morton, 1969, attribute frequency effects to the orthographic level, while Becker, 1979, Stanovich & West, 1981, Borowsky &

Besner, 1993, Plaut & Booth, 2001, argue for it being a conceptual-semantic effect), and the same may hold for MFS effects. In the introduction, we already reviewed the empirical evidence supporting the view that the MFS effect has a strong semantic component (Bertram et al., 2000; De Jong et al., 2000; Moscoso del Prado Martín, Bertram, Häikiö, Schreuder, & Baayen, in press; Moscoso del Prado Martín et al., 2004).

These findings and conclusions are compatible with both the mono-lingual model for the recognition of morphologically complex words that has been proposed to account for MFS effects by De Jong, Schreuder, & Baayen (2003) and with the BIA+ model of bilingual word recognition (Dijkstra & Van Heuven, 2002). Indeed, they suggest that an optimal integration of both models can easily be established.

The model accounting for morphological family size effects proposed by De Jong et al. (2003), the morphological family resonance model (FMRM), is an interactive activation (IA) model in which there is a cumulative build-up of activation resonating between lemmas (Levelt, 1989; Schreuder & Baayen, 1995) and the semantic and syntactic representations to which these lemmas are linked. If a lemma is linked to a semantic representation that itself is linked to a great many other lemmas, as is the case for a word with a large morphological family, this semantic representation will co-activate its associated lemmas, which in turn will contribute to the activation level of this semantic representation. Over time, this resonance within the morphological family speeds up the rate at which the activation of the target lemma increases. The greater the morphological family, the greater the rate will be with which the target lemma is activated. In the FMRM, a lexical decision response is initiated once a lemma has reached a threshold activation level. For a formal definition of the FMRM and some simulation studies, the reader is referred to De Jong et al. (2003).

The MFS effects documented for the bilingual lexicon can be explained in the MFRM framework along the following lines. Given a homograph as orthographic input, e.g., ROOM, two lemmas are activated in parallel: the English lemma 'room' (meaning 'chamber'), and the Dutch lemma 'room' (meaning 'cream'). Both lemmas activate their families simultaneously through the resonance mechanism. Consequently, depending on their respective family sizes, the activation levels of the two lemmas increase exponentially over time. If the task is language-specific visual lexical decision, the appropriate lemma has to be selected. This might be accomplished by means of, for instance, the Luce choice rule. If the task is generalised visual lexical decision, the lexical decision can be made at the time the first representation reaches the threshold activation level. Extended in this way, the MFRM becomes very similar in spirit to the BIA+ model.

The BIA+ model is also an IA model assuming interactive links between orthography and meaning levels within the lexicon, but it has focused on the bilingual recognition of monomorphemic words. The BIA+ model has successfully modelled a range of word frequency and neighbourhood effects in the bilingual lexicon, an area that the MFRM has not addressed at all. By assuming the more complex linkage system between lemmas and meaning that the MFRM proposes, the BIA+ model can be extended to account for the findings of the present study with respect to the MFS effects.

By incorporating the MFRM within the BIA+ architecture, a richer modelling framework is obtained that has interesting consequences for the processing of those interlingual homographs that share their meaning across languages, namely the homographs known as 'cognates'. An example of a form-identical cognate is the word FILM that shares its orthography, and to a large extent its semantics and phonology across languages. Non-identical cognates such as TOMAAT (Dutch)–TOMATO (English) also exist.

In the past, researchers such as Kirsner (e.g., Lalor & Kirsner, 2000) and Sánchez-Casas (e.g., Sánchez-Casas, Davis, & García-Albea, 1992) have proposed that cognates can be considered as morphological representations that are shared between languages. The extended BIA+ model provides a clear account of how this could work. The members of word pairs such as FILM/FILM and TOMATO/TOMAAT share most of their links to conceptual, semantic, and (partially) orthographic representations across languages. Given the process of morphological resonance we discussed above, the overlap may lead to the 'semantic' facilitation effects that are so often observed for these types of items (e.g., due to shared MF members; Van Hell & Dijkstra, 2002). As in the monolingual domain, the strength of the effect will depend on the transparency of the mappings between orthography and meaning within and across languages. It follows that cross-linguistic morphological priming effects should be obtained for items such as REGENACHTIG (Dutch for 'rainy') and RAIN (REGEN in Dutch).

To conclude, starting from the strong assumption of language non-selective lexical access into an integrated lexicon and the recent findings of morphological family size effects in the monolingual domain, we predicted analogous within-language and between-language effects with respect to bilingual word recognition. We did not only find the expected effects in a reanalysis of two experiments that had been performed with a completely different aim, but also in a new study that specifically investigated the effect of the L2 family size on L1 homograph recognition under circumstances where the participants were processing in their strongest language and were unaware of the bilingual nature of the experiment. Stated differently, the word recognition process of bilinguals is different from that of monolinguals, even when they are processing in their L1 and are unaware of the relevance of their L2 (Brysbaert, 2003). It further turned out that these empirically innovative data could be interpreted in an interesting theoretical integration of a monolingual model for the recognition of morphologically complex words and a bilingual model for monomorphemic word recognition. The new modelling framework, furthermore, allows a reinterpretation of earlier proposals about the representation of cross-linguistically ambiguous words such as interlingual homographs and cognates.

REFERENCES

Alegre, M., & Gordon, P. (1999). Frequency effects and the representational status of regular inflections. *Journal of Memory and Language, 40*, 41–61.

Baayen, R. H., Dijkstra, A., & Schreuder, R. (1997a). Singulars and plurals in Dutch: Evidence for a parallel dual route model. *Journal of Memory and Language, 37*, 94–117.

Baayen, R. H., Lieber, R., & Schreuder, R. (1997b). The morphological complexity of simplex nouns. *Linguistics, 35*, 861–877.

Baayen, R. H., Tweedie, F. J., & Schreuder, R. (2002). The subjects as a simple random effect fallacy: Subject variability and morphological family effects in the mental lexicon. *Brain and Language, 81*, 55–65.

Becker, C. A. (1979). Semantic context and word frequency effects in visual word recognition. *Journal of Experimental Psychology: Human Perception and Performance, 5*, 252–259.

Bertram, R., Schreuder, R., & Baayen, R. H. (2000). The balance of storage and computation in morphological processing: The role of word formation type, affixal homonymy, and productivity. *Journal of Experimental Psychology: Learning, Memory, and Cognition, 26*, 419–511.

Borowsky, R., & Besner, D. (1993). Visual word recognition: A multistage activation model. *Journal of Experimental Psychology: Learning, Memory, and Cognition, 19*, 813–840.

Bradley, D. C., & Forster, K. I. (1987). A reader's view of listening. *Cognition, 25*, 103–134.

Brysbaert, M. (2003). Bilingual visual word recognition: Evidence from masked phonological priming. In S. Kinoshita, and S. J. Lupker (Eds), *Masked priming: State-of-the-art*. Hove, UK: Psychology Press.

Carreiras, M., Perea, M., & Grainger, J. (1997). Effects of orthographic neighborhood in visual word recognition: Cross-task comparisons. *Journal of Experimental Psychology: Learning, Memory, and Cognition, 23*, 857–871.

De Groot, A. M. B., Delmaar, P., & Lupker, S. J. (2000). The processing of interlexical homographs in a bilingual and a monolingual task: Support for nonselective access to bilingual memory. *Quarterly Journal of Experimental Psychology, 53A*, 397–428.

De Jong, N. H. (2002). *Morphological families in the mental lexicon*. Max Planck Institute for Psycholinguistics, Nijmegen, The Netherlands.

De Jong, N. H., Schreuder, R., & Baayen, R. H. (2000). The morphological family size effect and morphology. *Language and Cognitive Processes, 15*, 329–365.

De Jong, N. H., Schreuder, R., & Baayen, R. H. (in press). Morphological resonance in the mental lexicon. In R. H. Baayen & R. Schreuder (Eds.), *Morphological structure in language processing* (pp. 65–88). Berlin: Mouton de Gruyter.

Dijkstra, A., Grainger, J., & Van Heuven, W. J. B. (1999). Recognition of cognates and interlingual homographs: The neglected role of phonology. *Journal of Memory and Language, 41*, 496–518.

Dijkstra, A. & Van Heuven, W. J. B. (2002). The architecture of the bilingual word recognition system: From identification to decision. *Bilingualism: Language and Cognition, 5*, 175–197.

Dijkstra, A., Van Jaarsveld, H., & Ten Brinke, S. (1998). Interlingual homograph recognition: Effects of task demands and language intermixing. *Bilingualism: Language and Cognition, 1*, 51–66.

Lalor, E., & Kirsner, K. (2000). Cross-lingual transfer effects between English and Italian cognates and noncognates. *International Journal of Bilingualism, 4*, 385–398.

Lemhöfer, K., & Dijkstra, A. (2004). Recognizing cognates and interlingual homographs: Effects of code similarity in language specific and generalized lexical decision. *Memory and Cognition, 32*, 533–550.

Lemhöfer, K., Dijkstra, A., & Michel, M. (2004). Three languages, one ECHO: Cognate effects in trilingual word recognition. *Language and Cognitive Processes, 19*, 585–611.

Levelt, W. J. M. (1989). *Speaking. From intention to articulation.* Cambridge, MA: The MIT Press.

Lorch, R. F., & Myers, J. L. (1990). Regression analyses of repeated measures data in cognitive research. *Journal of Experimental Psychology: Learning, Memory, and Cognition, 16*, 149–157.

Morton, J. (1969). The interaction of information in word recognition. *Psychological Review, 76*, 165–178.

Moscoso del Prado Martín, F., Bertram, R., Häikiö, T., Schreuder, R., & Baayen, R. H. (in press). Morphological family size in a morphologically rich language: The case of Finnish compared to Dutch and Hebrew. *Journal of Experimental Psychology: Learning, Memory, and Cognition.*

Moscoso del Prado Martín, F., Deutsch, A., Frost, R., Schreuder, R., De Jong, N. H., & Baayen, R. H. (2004). *Changing places: A cross-language perspective on frequency and family size in Hebrew and Dutch.* Manuscript submitted for publication.

Pinheiro, J. C., & Bates, D. M. (2000). *Mixed-effects models in S and S-PLUS.* Statistics and Computing. New York: Springer.

Plaut, D. C., & Booth, J. R. (2000). Individual and developmental differences in semantic priming: Empirical and computational support for a single mechanism account of lexical processing. *Psychological Review, 107*, 786–823.

Royston, P. (1982). An extension of Shapiro and Wilk's W Test for Normality to large samples. *Applied Statistics, 31*, 115–124.

Sánchez-Casas, R., Davis, C. W., & García-Albea, J. E. (1992). Bilingual lexical processing: Exploring the cognate/non-cognate distinction. *European Journal of Cognitive Psychology, 4*, 311–322.

Schreuder, R., & Baayen, R. H. (1995). Modeling morphological processing. In L. B. Feldman (Ed.), *Morphological aspects of language processing* (pp. 131–154). Hillsdale, NJ: Lawrence Erlbaum.

Schreuder, R., & Baayen, R. H. (1997). How complex simplex words can be. *Journal of Memory and Language, 37*, 118–139.

Schulpen, B., Dijkstra, A., & Schriefers, H. J. (2003). *L2 proficiency and task effects on interlingual homograph recognition by Dutch-English bilinguals.* Unpublished manuscript, University of Nijmegen.

Stanovich, K. E., & West, R. F. (1981). The effect of sentence context on ongoing word recognition: Test of a two-process theory. *Journal of Experimental Psychology: Human Perception and Performance, 7*, 658–672.

Van Hell, J. G., & Dijkstra, A. (2002). Foreign language knowledge can influence native language performance. *Psychonomic Bulletin & Review, 9(4)*, 780–789.

Van Heuven, W. J. B., Dijkstra, A., & Grainger, J. (1998). Orthographic neighborhood effects in bilingual word recognition. *Journal of Memory and Language, 39*, 458–483.

Appendix A: Interlingual Homographs
The superscript numbers indicate in which experiments a word has been excluded
from the analyses for eliciting more than 30% errors.

Item	Frequency		Family Size		Frequency condition
	English	Dutch	English	Dutch	
angel[3]	24	5	4	1	HELD
arts[1]	38	93	3	55	LEHD
bad	332	24	6	59	HELD
beer	51	23	1	14	HEHD
big	397	3	9	0	HELD
boom	27	137	2	96	LEHD
brand	16	45	4	123	LEHD
breed	26	131	9	32	LEHD
brief	54	200	7	77	LEHD
even	1351	724	13	38	HEHD
glad	64	37	3	13	HEHD
last	684	72	8	102	HEHD
lever	11	13	2	40	HEHD
list	114	6	20	4	HELD
long	1052	20	70	26	HELD
loom[1]	12	8	5	2	HEHD
lot	290	55	3	16	HEHD
map	45	9	4	6	HELD
mate	30	155	14	0	LEHD
nut	24	26	22	15	HEHD
peer	41	10	6	9	HELD
pet	22	19	4	5	HEHD
pink	52	6	3	4	HELD
pool[3]	49	29	4	23	HEHD
rest	263	115	16	8	HEHD
roof	60	2	6	39	HELD
room	542	5	63	21	HELD
rose	29	43	14	0	LEHD
rot[1]	16	14	7	21	HEHD
slang	3	27	4	26	LEHD
slap[1]	21	27	9	7	HEHD
slim	14	26	4	6	LEHD
slot	8	72	2	50	LEHD
spot	79	11	16	25	HELD
star	110	12	27	7	HELD
trap	51	116	16	49	LEHD
tree	204	4	22	1	HELD
vast	69	332	2	74	LEHD
vet[1]	9	37	1	45	LEHD
war	369	14	24	14	HELD
week	408	294	15	45	HEHD
wet	70	187	5	134	LEHD

Appendix B: English Monolingual Words
The superscript numbers indicate in which experiments a
word has been excluded from the analyses for eliciting more
than 30% errors

Item	Frequency	Family size	Frequency condition
aid	70	3	LE(HD)
area	333	1	HE(LD)
army	125	2	Open Range
attic[1,2]	8	0	Open Range
bike	11	0	HE(HD)
bird	108	32	HE(LD)
bless	19	0	Open Range
book	424	60	HE(HD)
candy	8	4	Open Range
cave	40	6	HE(LD)
chair	145	15	Open Range
chest	51	6	LE(HD)
child	1097	16	HE(LD)
chord[1,2]	5	0	Open Range
cloud	59	11	Open Range
coat	65	23	Open Range
cough	24	2	HE(HD)
cream	38	9	LE(HD)
crow	9	8	Open Range
doll	27	2	LE(HD)
duck	14	9	Open Range
eagle	10	5	Open Range
face	486	53	Open Range
far	687	16	HE(HD)
fear	155	8	Open Range
fish	204	37	HE(LD)
food	312	3	Open Range
foot	344	65	HE(LD)
force	191	18	Open Range
giant	47	1	HE(HD)
glue	7	2	Open Range
hate	111	4	HE(LD)
hiker	1	4	Open Range
hood	7	28	Open Range
horse	139	42	Open Range
house	616	112	Open Range
isle[1,2]	14	1	Open Range
itch[1,2]	1	4	Open Range
judge	98	7	Open Range
king	104	11	Open Range
kite[1,2]	5	2	Open Range
knife	49	16	HE(HD)
lawn	29	1	LE(HD)

Appendix B: *(continued)*

Item	Frequency	Family size	Frequency condition
liar	9	11	LE(HD)
lion	25	6	HE(LD)
lyric[2]	3	5	Open Range
mill[2]	22	21	Open Range
mind	401	69	HE(LD)
money	390	21	Open Range
movie	47	0	Open Range
nuts	1	1	Open Range
owner	64	12	HE(HD)
peace	92	19	Open Range
peach	6	2	Open Range
pig	46	28	HE(LD)
play	538	48	HE(LD)
proof	36	16	Open Range
quake	2	4	Open Range
razor[1,2]	9	6	Open Range
sail	26	11	LE(HD)
seed	52	16	HE(LD)
shark	21	1	HE(HD)
shift	79	11	HE(LD)
ship	80	110	Open Range
sir	284	1	HE(HD)
skin	113	32	Open Range
skirt	30	4	Open Range
smile	262	1	HE(HD)
snow	68	23	LE(HD)
soul	57	10	Open Range
spoon	16	9	HE(HD)
steam	30	14	LE(HD)
sugar	60	15	HE(LD)
tail	38	27	Open Range
theft[2]	8	0	Open Range
thief	12	6	HE(HD)
time	1981	77	Open Range
towel	24	5	Open Range
value	172	18	Open Range
way	1310	83	HE(HD)
weird	8	4	LE(HD)
whine[2]	16	2	Open Range
woman	876	46	Open Range
wound	54	2	LE(HD)

Appendix C: Dutch Monolingual Words

Item	Frequency	Family size	Frequency condition
berg	55	73	(HE)HD
bijl	10	4	(HE)LD
blauw	133	55	(LE)HD
bloem	94	102	(LE)HD
boog	46	29	Open Range
bril	36	17	Open Range
broer	128	6	Open Range
bron	64	43	Open Range
buis	9	30	Open Range
buurt	109	18	Open Range
darm	14	30	(HE)HD
deuk	3	4	Open Range
dier	188	100	(LE)HD
ding	365	15	Open Range
doel	165	40	Open Range
dorp	137	38	(LE)HD
dorst	14	11	(HE)LD
duif	19	13	(HE)HD
enkel	596	9	Open Range
feest	60	67	Open Range
fiets	48	37	Open Range
fooi	6	1	(HE)LD
fout	71	30	(HE)HD
geit	11	17	(HE)LD
gids	22	8	Open Range
gil	8	5	(HE)HD
gips	5	8	(HE)LD
grap	24	5	(HE)LD
griep	7	7	Open Range
haas	9	16	(HE)LD
hagel	4	12	Open Range
hitte	30	15	Open Range
hoofd	544	283	Open Range
hulp	116	92	(LE)HD
jaar	1143	190	Open Range
jacht	26	40	(LE)HD
kans	202	34	(LE)HD
kant	294	50	(HE)HD
kat	72	35	(LE)HD
kern	43	65	(LE)HD
kleur	155	118	(LE)HD
klok	37	39	(LE)HD
klomp	13	11	(HE)HD
kooi	23	11	(HE)HD
korst	13	6	Open Range
krat	4	1	(HE)LD

Appendix C: *(continued)*

Item	Frequency	Family size	Frequency condition
kust	52	24	Open Range
kwal	2	1	(HE)LD
laat	735	63	(HE)HD
maal	115	60	(HE)HD
mens	1370	103	Open Range
mond	228	39	Open Range
moord	45	42	(LE)HD
niets	864	8	Open Range
pand	11	17	Open Range
pijl	16	7	Open Range
reep	6	1	Open Range
rijst	6	20	Open Range
roet	3	5	(HE)LD
rund	5	6	Open Range
schep	2	37	Open Range
sfeer	65	42	Open Range
slok	26	5	(HE)HD
smoes	6	2	(HE)LD
snik	5	5	(HE)LD
snoek	2	3	Open Range
speld	5	14	Open Range
spuit	3	24	Open Range
stuk	282	135	Open Range
taak	147	12	Open Range
traan	77	14	Open Range
trui	20	5	(HE)LD
uier	1	0	Open Range
verf	27	34	(LE)HD
vlag	29	12	(HE)HD
vlek	27	30	(HE)HD
vlieg	18	130	Open Range
vork	12	7	(HE)LD
vorm	332	255	(LE)HD
vraag	475	85	Open Range
vuist	37	7	(HE)HD
wrok	8	2	Open Range
zaak	423	117	Open Range
zwaai	4	15	Open Range

LANGUAGE AND COGNITIVE PROCESSES
2005, 20 (1/2), 43–73

Psychology Press
Taylor & Francis Group

Prosodic cues for morphological complexity in Dutch and English

Rachel J. J. K. Kemps

Max Planck Institute for Psycholinguistics, Nijmegen, The Netherlands

Lee H. Wurm

Wayne State University, Detroit, MI, USA

Mirjam Ernestus

Max Planck Institute for Psycholinguistics, Nijmegen, The Netherlands

Robert Schreuder

Interfaculty Research Unit for Language and Speech, University of Nijmegen, The Netherlands

Harald Baayen

Max Planck Institute for Psycholinguistics, Nijmegen and Interfaculty Research Unit for Language and Speech, University of Nijmegen, The Netherlands

Previous work has shown that Dutch listeners use prosodic information in the speech signal to optimise morphological processing: Listeners are sensitive to prosodic differences between a noun stem realised in isolation and a noun stem realised as part of a plural form (in which the stem is followed by an unstressed syllable). The present study, employing a lexical decision task, provides an additional demonstration of listeners' sensitivity to prosodic cues

Correspondence should be addressed to R. J. J. K. Kemps, 4–32 Assiniboia Hall, Department of Linguistics, University of Alberta, Edmonton, Alberta, Canada, T6G 2E7. Email: rkemps@ualberta.ca

Part of this work has been made possible by the support of a Major Collaborative Research Initiative (MCRI) grant of the Social Sciences and Humanities Research Council of Canada awarded to Gary Libben.

http://www.tandf.co.uk/journals/pp/01690965.html   DOI: 10.1080/01690960444000223

in the stem. This sensitivity is shown for two languages that differ in morphological productivity: Dutch and English. The degree of morphological productivity does not correlate with listeners' sensitivity to prosodic cues in the stem, but it is reflected in differential sensitivities to the word-specific log odds ratio of encountering an unshortened stem (i.e., a stem in isolation) versus encountering a shortened stem (i.e., a stem followed by a suffix consisting of one or more unstressed syllables). In addition to being sensitive to the prosodic cues themselves, listeners are also sensitive to the probabilities of occurrence of these prosodic cues.

In languages with a concatenative morphological system, such as Dutch and English, morphologically complex words consist of (combinations of) stems preceded by one or more prefixes and/or followed by one or more suffixes. The orthographic representations of morphologically complex words suggest that these stems, prefixes, and suffixes are strung together as beads on a string. Acoustically, however, the realisations of morphemes that are concatenated to form a morphologically complex word are different from the realisations of these morphemes when produced in isolation, even when the morphemes are phonemically unchanged after concatenation. One of the reasons for this is that, in stress-timed languages, the duration of a stressed vowel reduces as a function of the number of unstressed syllables that follow (Nooteboom, 1972, for Dutch; Fowler, 1977, Lehiste, 1972, for English; Lindblom & Rapp, 1973, for Swedish). In other words, the duration of the vowel in a syllable is shorter when this syllable is followed by one or more unstressed syllables than when it is produced in isolation. For example, the vowel in the first syllable of *walking* is shorter than the vowel in *walk*.

Previous studies have shown that listeners are very sensitive to such acoustic differences. It has been shown that listeners can use these differences as cues to distinguish strings that are initially phonemically ambiguous between a word and a morphologically unrelated continuation form of that word. Salverda, Dahan, and McQueen (2003) recorded participants' eye movements while they listened to Dutch sentences including a word with a morphologically unrelated onset-embedded word (e.g., *hamster* containing *ham*). The participants saw four pictures of objects on a computer screen and were instructed to use the computer mouse to move the picture of the object that was mentioned in the sentence. There were more fixations to a picture representing the embedded word (*ham*) when the first syllable of the target word (*hamster*) had been replaced by a recording of the embedded word than when it came from a different recording of the target word. This demonstrates that segmentally ambiguous sequences can contain acoustic cues (in this case, the duration of the embedded word (*ham*) relative to the duration of its corresponding syllable in the target word (*hamster*)), that modulate its lexical interpretation.

Similar results were obtained by Davis, Marslen-Wilson, and Gaskell (2002). In a gating task, participants were presented with sentence fragments. In one condition (long-word condition), the sentence fragments ended in a long carrier word of which the initial syllable formed an onset-embedded word (e.g., *captain* containing *cap*). In the other condition (short-word condition), the fragments ended in the short word corresponding to the initial syllable of the carrier word followed by a word with an onset that matched the continuation of the longer carrier word (e.g., *cap tucked* versus *captain*). The first syllable in the short-word condition was significantly longer than the first syllable in the long-word condition, and there was a marginally significant difference in average fundamental frequency (average fundamental frequency was higher in the long-word condition than in the short-word condition). Significantly more short-word responses were made to gates from short-word stimuli than to gates from long-word stimuli, suggesting that listeners take advantage of the acoustic differences that exist between short and long word sequences. Similar results were obtained in a cross-modal priming task. The stimuli from the gating task were presented up to the offset of the first syllable of the target word (e.g., *cap* from either *cap* or *captain*) as auditory primes, and were followed by a visual target that was either the short word (*cap*) or the long word (*captain*). Greater facilitation occurred when prime syllables came from the same word as the target.

More recently, it has been shown that listeners are also sensitive to acoustic differences between phoneme strings that are initially ambiguous between a stem and a morphologically *related* continuation form of that stem, in particular, between a singular and a plural form of a noun (Kemps, Ernestus, Schreuder, & Baayen, in press). In Dutch, the regular plural form of many nouns consists of the noun stem and the plural suffix -*en*, which is usually realised as just a schwa (e.g., *boek* [buk] 'book'—*boeken* [bukə] 'books'). As a result of the addition of the schwa, the stem of the plural form is durationally and intonationally different from the stem realised in isolation (the singular form). In what follows, we will refer to such non-segmental differences in duration and intonation as prosodic differences. Such differences partly reflect differences in syllable structure. For instance, in the plural *boe-ken* [bukə], the suffix -*en* [ə] induces resyllabification of the stem-final obstruent ([k]) as onset of the next syllable and, as a consequence, the stem vowel is syllable-final in the plural [bukə] as opposed to syllable-medial in the singular *boek* [buk]. Listeners were presented with singular forms and with stems that were spliced out of plural forms. These stimuli were segmentally identical, but the stems of the plural forms carried mismatching prosodic information: The absence of a plural suffix pointed to the singular form, whereas the prosodic information pointed to the plural form. When presented with the mismatching forms, listeners were significantly delayed, both in a number decision task as well as in a lexical decision task. Similar results were obtained when listeners were presented with plural forms of which the stems carried either matching or mismatching prosodic information (i.e., plurals of which the stems originated either from another token of the plural form or from a realisation of the singular form), and also when listeners were presented with pseudowords of which the 'stems' carried either matching or mismatching prosodic information (i.e., pseudowords of which the stems were originally realised in isolation or in combination with a plural suffix). Importantly, the magnitude of this prosodic mismatch effect, that is, the magnitude of the delay in response latencies, correlated with the magnitude of the durational mismatch: The larger the durational difference between the stem realised in isolation and the stem realised as part of the plural form, the larger the delay. This correlation was stronger for words than for pseudowords.

The prosodic differences between uninflected forms and the stems of their corresponding inflected forms reduce the ambiguity between these forms. The observed sensitivity of listeners to these prosodic differences suggests that these acoustic cues help the perceptual system in determining early in the signal whether an inflected (bisyllabic) or an uninflected (monosyllabic) form is likely to be heard. Plurals are not singulars with an additional suffix. The precise acoustic realisation of the stem provides crucial information to the listener about the morphological context in which the stem appears.

The present study, employing a lexical decision task, aims at replicating these findings for different types of morphologically complex forms in Dutch, and at extending the investigation of listeners' sensitivity to prosodic cues for morphological complexity to another language, English. The morphologically complex forms under investigation in the present study are comparatives (inflection) and agent nouns (derivation). Studying the effects of prosodic mismatch in the processing of stems of agent nouns and of comparatives in both Dutch and English enables us to determine whether the effects observed in the processing of singular and plural forms in Dutch are specific to plural formation in Dutch, or whether they generalise to a different type of inflection, to derivation, and to a different language.

In Dutch and English, many agent nouns are formed by adding the suffix *-er* (Dutch: [ər]; English: [ɚ]) to the stem, which is a verb stem. For example, the English agent noun *worker* [wɝkɚ] consists of the verb stem *work* [wɝkə] and the deverbal agentive suffix *-er* [ɚ]. Similarly, the Dutch agent noun *werker* [wɛrkər] consists of the verb stem *werk* [wɛrk] and the deverbal agentive suffix *-er* [ər]. The suffix *-er* is homonymous (see Booij,

1979, for the many meanings of the suffix -er in Dutch): Many comparatives are also formed by adding the suffix -er to the stem, which in this case is an adjective. Thus, the English comparative *fatter* [fætɚ] consists of the adjective *fat* [fætə] and the comparative suffix -er [ɚ]. The Dutch comparative *vetter* [vɛtəʀ] consists of the adjective *vet* [vɛt] and the comparative suffix -er [əʀ]. The affixation of the suffix -er leads to shortening of the preceding stem and to changes in syllable structure. In the present study, employing a lexical decision task, we investigated whether listeners are sensitive to such prosodic differences between monosyllabic stems and the stems of bisyllabic complex forms. We presented listeners with stems of agent nouns and comparatives that carried either matching or mismatching prosodic information. If listeners are sensitive to the prosodic cues in the stem, they are expected to be slowed down in their responses when there is a mismatch between the number of syllables on the one hand, and the prosodic information in the acoustic signal on the other hand. If not, in other words, if listeners attend to segmental information only, mismatching prosodic information should not affect response latencies. Note that information about the identity of the complex forms that the stems originated from was not available to our listeners. The stem *werk* ('work'), for instance, originating from the agent noun *werker* ('worker') could just as well have originated from the infinitive verbal form *werken* ('to work'). We were therefore not interested in potential effects of the type of complex form that the stems originated from, but purely in the question of whether the prosodic mismatch effect observed in earlier work would generalize to different materials, and to a different language.

Dutch and English differ in morphological richness, in particular in the number of continuation forms that are possible given a certain monomorphemic stem. For example, whereas the verbal inflectional paradigm of the Dutch word *wandelen* ('to walk') consists of the forms *wandel, wandelt, wandelen, wandelde, wandelden, gewandeld, wandelend,* and *wandelende*, the verbal inflectional paradigm of the English word 'walk' contains only *walk, walks, walked,* and *walking*. In other words, the stem *wandel* is followed by an unstressed syllable in five inflectional forms, whereas the stem *walk* is followed by an unstressed syllable in only one form. In general, the number of continuation forms in which a stem is followed by an unstressed syllable is considerably smaller in English than in Dutch: Besides the richer verbal paradigm, Dutch also exhibits prenominal contextual inflection of adjectives (which consists of the addition of a schwa to the stem, e.g., *een groot boek* 'a big book (neuter gender)' versus *een grote auto* 'a big car (common gender)'), whereas English does not. Furthermore, in Dutch, most noun inflections consist of the addition of an unstressed syllable to the stem: Many plurals are formed by adding the suffix -en [ə(n)] to the stem. In English, on the other hand, many plurals are formed by adding the plural suffix *-s* ([s] or [z]) to the stem (no additional syllable, except for stems ending in sibilants). Finally, Dutch has more unstressed derivational suffixes than English. For example, diminutives in Dutch are formed by adding (an allomorph of) the diminutive suffix *-tje* [cə] to the stem, whereas diminutive derivation is not productive in English. It is conceivable that, as a consequence of these differences in the number of possible continuation forms in which a stem is followed by one or more unstressed syllables, Dutch and English listeners are not equally sensitive to prosodic cues in the stem that signal whether or not the stem will be followed by unstressed syllables. Possibly, English listeners are less sensitive to such prosodic cues, as, in English, a stem is relatively infrequently followed by an unstressed syllable.

We not only investigated the effect of prosodic mismatch on reaction times, but we also investigated the predictive value of two covariates that are word-specific indications of the prevalence of possible continuation forms: Syllable Ratio and Cohort Entropy.

Syllable Ratio gives a word-specific indication of the likelihood of observing an unshortened versus a shortened stem. It is defined as the log of the ratio which has as the numerator the Surface Frequency of a stem in isolation, and as the denominator the summed Surface Frequencies of words in which this stem is followed by an inflectional or derivational suffix consisting of one or more unstressed syllables (i.e., words in which the stem occurs in shortened form). We only considered inflectional and derivational suffixes that consist of one or more syllables containing schwa, so that the phonological shortening process in the stem is maximally comparable to that in the comparative stems and in the agent noun stems. For example, for the stem *strict*, the numerator of the Syllable Ratio would consist of the surface frequency of *strict* (i.e., 362), and the denominator would consist of the summed surface frequencies of *stricter*, *strictest*, and *strictness* (i.e., 69). All instances of the stem, irrespective of grammatical category, are included in the numerator of Syllable Ratio. Note that when the numerator is smaller than the denominator, the Syllable Ratio will be negative, as the log of reals between 0 and 1 is negative. Compounds were not included in the denominator, as little is known about phonological shortening within left constituents of compounds.

Syllable Ratio is the log odds ratio of observing an unshortened form versus observing a shortened form. All words occurred in monosyllabic form in the experiment. We therefore expected a facilitatory effect of Syllable Ratio: if Syllable Ratio was high for a given word (i.e., if a word occurs relatively often as a monosyllabic stem), faster response latencies were expected. A facilitatory effect of Syllable Ratio would constitute evidence for listeners' sensitivity to the likelihood of occurrence of a certain prosodic manifestation of a stem.

Syllable Ratio only considers specific types of continuation forms, namely, the continuation forms that are morphologically related to the stem and in which the stem has undergone a shortening process as a result of the addition of one or more unstressed syllables. However, given a certain stem, many types of continuation forms are possible, including continuation forms that are not morphologically related. In order to rule out the possibility that an effect of Syllable Ratio is in fact just an effect of whatever is still present in the cohort at the final position in the stem, we need an index of the latter. We therefore introduce another covariate: the Cohort Entropy. Entropy is an information-theoretical measure, indicating the amount of uncertainty about the outcome of a selection process (Shannon, 1948, see also Moscoso del Prado Martín, Kostíc, & Baayen, 2004). Cohort Entropy (H) is defined as:

$$H = -\sum_{i=1}^{n} p_i \log p_i$$

in which pi is the probability of a word given the n words that are still present in the cohort at the point in time when the stem-final segment of the target word has been perceived. In other words:

$$p_i = \frac{\text{Surface Frequency of Word}_i}{\substack{\text{Summed Surface Frequencies of } n \text{ Cohort Members at} \\ \text{stem-final segment of target word}}}$$

To illustrate, suppose that by the time that the final segment of Stem X has been perceived, the cohort consists of two word candidates: Word X_a and Word X_b Word X_a has a surface frequency of 80 and Word X_b has a surface frequency of 20. For Stem Y, the stem-final cohort also consists of two word candidates (Word Y_a and Word Y_b), both of which have a surface frequency of 50. The Cohort Entropies for Stem X and Stem Y are calculated as follows (note that the Cohort Entropy is larger for Stem Y):

$$p_{X_a} = \frac{80}{80+20} = 0.80 \qquad p_{X_b} = \frac{20}{80+20} = 0.20$$

$$H_X = -(0.80^* log(0.80) + 0.20^* log(0.20)) = 0.50$$

$$p_{Y_a} = \frac{50}{50+50} = 0.50 \qquad p_{Y_b} = \frac{50}{50+50} = 0.50$$

$$H_Y = -(0.50^* log(0.50) + 0.50^* log(0.50)) = 0.69$$

Cohort Entropy is calculated at the stem-final segment as only stems (with either matching or mismatching prosodic information) were presented to our listeners. Included in the cohort are *all* possible continuation forms, that is, both morphologically related and morphologically unrelated continuation forms. For example, the cohort for the stem *bake* consists of *bake, bakes, baked, baking, baker, bakers, bakery, bakeries*, but also *bacon* and *bakelite*. Cohort Entropy is a non-phonologically and non-morphologically based measure, defined purely in terms of lexical competition. Note however that for monomorphemic stems (the type of stems used in the present study), morphologically related continuation forms (i.e., inflections, derivations, and compounds) are more prevalent than morphologically unrelated continuation forms, both type-wise and token-wise. (Counts are presented below.) We expect an inhibitory effect of Cohort Entropy: The more uncertainty, the longer the response latencies.

EXPERIMENT

Part A: Dutch

Method

Participants.   Twenty participants, mostly students at the University of Nijmegen, were paid to participate in the experiment. All were native speakers of Dutch.

Materials.   From the CELEX lexical database (Baayen, Piepenbrock, & Van Rijn, 1993) we selected all Dutch comparatives and agent nouns that contained a monomorphemic and monosyllabic stem, in which the stem ended in a voiceless plosive. In Dutch, underlyingly voiced obstruents are devoiced in syllable-final position and all stems realised in isolation therefore end in voiceless obstruents (final devoicing). The suffix *-er* [ər] induces resyllabification of the stem-final obstruent as onset of the next syllable, and hence an underlyingly voiced stem-final obstruent remains voiced before *-er* (e.g., Booij, 1995). As a consequence, stems ending in underlyingly voiced obstruents do not have the same segments in isolation as before *-er* (e.g., [fiɑʀt]—[fiɑʀdəʀ] 'hard'—'harder'). We therefore only selected agent nouns and comparatives with stems ending in an underlying voiceless plosive, so that there is no change of the voicing characteristics of the plosive when the stems occur in isolation.

Furthermore, the comparatives and agent nouns in our initial data set occurred with surface frequencies larger than zero. (Token counts in CELEX are based on a corpus of 42.4 million words of written text for Dutch, and on a corpus of 17.9 million words of written and spoken text for

English.) From this initial data set of comparatives and agent nouns, we selected those forms that could subsequently be matched to English comparatives or agent nouns that met all the above criteria, and that, in addition, carried the same onset and coda characteristics (simplex versus complex), and that carried the same vowel characteristics (long versus short). The English set of items was used in Part B of this experiment. This selection procedure resulted in a set of 35 Dutch agent nouns and 27 Dutch comparatives (see Appendix A for a list of all Dutch items). Pseudowords were created from these words by changing several phonemes in the stem, while largely respecting the status of onset and coda (simplex versus complex), the vowel length (long versus short), and the restriction that the stem-final consonant is a voiceless plosive.[1] Due to errors, one word (comparative) and one pseudoword eventually had to be removed from the design.

Separate reading lists were created for the comparatives (e.g., *vetter*), the agent nouns (e.g., *werker*), the stems of the comparatives (e.g., *vet*), the stems of the agent nouns (e.g., *werk*), and their pseudoword counterparts. The lists were recorded in a soundproof recording booth by a native male speaker of Dutch, who was naïve regarding the purpose of the experiment. Each pseudoword list was read aloud for practice once before recording. The recordings were digitised at 18.9 kHz.

The forms were spliced out of their list using the PRAAT speech editing software (Boersma & Weenink, 1996). The stems that were produced in isolation functioned as the first type of stimulus in the experiment ('normal' stems, see top panel of Figure 2 for an example). From the complex forms, a second type of stimulus was created: the 'constructed' stems. The constructed stem consisted of the stem of the complex form – in other words, it was the complex form without the suffix *-er* [əʀ]. The point of splicing was located at the onset of the voicing of the schwa following the stem-final consonant. The point of splicing was always located at a zero-crossing. Figure 1 shows an example of a complex form (top panel) and the stem spliced out of that complex form (bottom panel).

As a result of the splicing manipulation, the constructed stem's prosodic information mismatched its number of syllables: Its prosodic characteristics signalled a bisyllabic form, whereas in fact the acoustic signal contained only one syllable. In the normal stem, there was no such mismatch. Duration was measured for the two types of stems, for both words and pseudowords. As expected, the constructed stems were

---

[1] This word-pseudoword matching in our materials was not perfect: We failed to match for the status of the coda for two Dutch items, we failed to match for the status of the onset for one Dutch item, and we failed to match for the length of the vowel for one Dutch item. For one English item, we failed to match for the status of the coda.

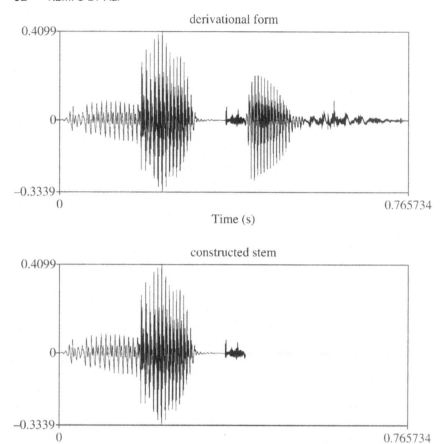

Figure 1. The complex form [natəʀ] (top panel) and the constructed stem [nat] spliced out of the complex form (bottom panel).

significantly shorter (161 ms on average) than the normal stems, $F(1, 119)$ = 486.1, $p < .0001$. The magnitude of this durational difference between normal and constructed stems was not significantly different for words and pseudowords (interaction of Stem Type (normal versus constructed stem) by Word Status (word versus pseudoword): $F(1, 119) = 1.6, p = .21$. For the words, we also measured the duration of the vowel, the duration of the closure of the stem-final obstruent, and the duration of the release noise of the stem-final obstruent. Analyses of variance with these durations as the dependent variable, and with Stem Type (normal versus constructed) and the Syllable Structure of the bisyllabic form (with an ambisyllabic stem-final obstruent, as in *gok-ker*, 'gambler'; with a syllable-initial stem-final obstruent and non-empty coda of the first syllable, as in *hel-per*, 'helper';

with a syllable-initial stem-final obstruent and an empty coda of the first syllable, as in *ma-ker*, 'maker') as predictors, revealed significant main effects of Stem Type and Syllable Structure for all three analyses ($p < .05$), but never an interaction of these factors ($p > .1$). Thus, the manipulation of Stem Type is independent of Syllable Structure.

The normal and constructed stems differed in prosodic structure. The normal and the constructed stems differed in yet another respect, however. The manipulation of interest (the manipulation of prosodic structure) was achieved through and therefore systematically confounded with a splicing manipulation: Splicing had occurred in the constructed stems (at the offset of the release noise of the stem-final consonant), whereas no splicing had occurred in the normal stems. We eliminated this confound by applying a splicing manipulation to the normal stems as well: We spliced away the last 25% of the release noise of the stem-final consonants (see Figure 2).

As a consequence, both stimulus types ended rather abruptly, the only difference remaining between normal and constructed stems being the difference in prosodic structure. Note that, by applying this splicing manipulation to the normal stems, we put the stimuli that we expected to be most easily processed at a disadvantage. This should make it harder for us to observe an effect of prosodic mismatch. The durational difference between the normal stems and the constructed stems after splicing away 25% of the release noises of the stem-final consonants of the normal stems was 131 ms on average, $F(1, 119) = 1391.3$, $p < .0001$. The interaction between Stem Type and Word Status remained non-significant, $F(1, 119) = 0.15$, $p = .70$. Table 1 lists the mean durations with their standard deviations for the two kinds of stems of words and pseudowords, before as well as after splicing away 25% of the release noise of the normal stems. In the following, the term 'normal stem' refers to the stem that carries matching prosodic information *and* of which 25% of the release noise of the stem-final consonant has been spliced away.

The total number of experimental trials amounted to 122 (35 agent noun stems and their matched pseudoword stems, and 26 comparative stems and

TABLE 1

Part A—Mean durations (in ms) with SD for normal stems and constructed stems in Dutch, before and after splicing away 25% of the release noise of the normal stems

Type of stem	Before		After	
	Duration	SD	Duration	SD
Normal word	635	91	597	91
Constructed word	465	79	465	79
Normal pseudoword	593	124	570	97
Constructed pseudoword	441	98	441	98

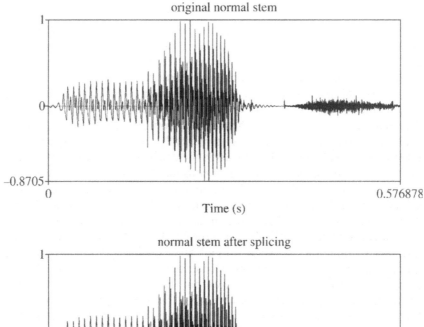

Figure 2. The original normal stem [nɑt] (top panel) and the normal stem [nɑt] after splicing away 25% of the stem-final release noise (bottom panel).

their matched pseudoword stems). So that participants would never be presented with both the normal and the constructed variant of a single stem, complementary versions of trial lists were created. If the normal form of a stem occurred in one version of a list, then the constructed form of that stem would occur in its complementary version. The composition of these lists (i.e., which items occurred in their normal stem variant and which items occurred in their constructed stem variant) was varied three times, resulting in six experimental trial lists (three 'compositions' with two complementary versions each). The order of presentation of the stimuli was pseudo-randomised within the three lists: no more than three words or pseudowords occurred successively. Orders were identical in the lists that were each other's complements. Participants were randomly assigned to experimental trial lists. Practice trials were presented prior to the actual experiment. The practice set consisted of 16 trials: 4 normal pseudoword stems, 4 constructed pseudoword stems, 4 normal word stems (2 comparative stems and 2 agent noun stems), and 4 constructed word stems (2 comparative stems and 2 agent noun stems). None of the stems in the practice set was presented in the actual experiment.

Procedure. Participants performed a lexical decision task. They were instructed to decide as quickly as possible whether or not the form that they heard was an existing word of Dutch. They responded by pressing one of two buttons on a button box. Each trial consisted of the presentation of a warning tone (189 Hz) for 500 ms, followed after an interval of 200 ms by the auditory stimulus. Stimuli were presented through Sennheiser headphones. Reaction times were measured from stimulus offset. Each new trial was initiated 2500 ms after offset of the previous stimulus. When a participant did not respond within 2000 ms post-offset, a time-out response was recorded. Prior to the actual experiment, the set of practice trials was presented, followed by a short pause. The total duration of the experimental session was approximately 10 minutes.

Part B: English

Method

Participants. Thirty-nine participants, students at Wayne State University, received course credit to participate in the experiment. All were native speakers of English.

Materials. The selection procedure described above for the Dutch materials resulted in a set of 35 English agent nouns and 27 English comparatives (see Appendix B for a list of all English items). Also for these words, pseudowords were created by changing several phonemes in the stem, while respecting the status of onset and coda (simplex versus complex), the length of the vowel (long versus short), and the restriction that the stem-final consonant is a voiceless plosive.

Reading lists were created in the same manner as in Part A of the experiment. The lists were recorded in a soundproof recording booth by a native male speaker of English.[2] Each pseudoword list was read aloud for practice once before recording. The recordings were digitised at 20 kHz.

---

[2] In American English, a stem-final /t/ typically becomes flapped in intervocalic position. Our speaker retained the non-flapped pronunciation in intervocalic position, which may be considered overly careful speech. Note, however, that the presence of unflapped stimuli in our experiment should work against our effect, as the unflapped /t/ in the constructed stem might be considered a strong cue for the monosyllabic form.

Normal and constructed stems were created in the same manner as in Part A of the experiment. As expected, the constructed stems were again significantly shorter (146 ms) than the normal stems, $F(1, 121) = 937.0$, $p < .0001$. The effect of Stem Type on duration was significantly larger for words than for pseudowords: Interaction of Stem Type by Word Status, $F(1, 121) = 7.3$, $p < .01$. Recall that, for Dutch, this interaction of Stem Type by Word Status was not significant, although it did show the same pattern (larger effect of Stem Type for words than for pseudowords). In the overall analysis, the interaction of Stem Type by Word Status was significant, $F(1, 141) = 6.5$, $p < .05$, and there was no significant three-way interaction of Stem Type by Word Status by Language, $F(1, 241) = 0.18$, $p = .67$. We will return to this issue below. Furthermore, the effect of Stem Type on duration was marginally smaller in English than in Dutch: interaction of Stem Type by Language, $F(1, 242) = 3.2$, $p = .07$. As for the Dutch words, we also measured the duration of the vowel, the duration of the closure of the stem-final obstruent, and the duration of the release noise of the stem-final obstruent for the English words. Analyses of variance with these durations as the dependent variable, and with Stem Type (normal versus constructed) and the Syllable Structure of the bisyllabic form as predictors, revealed only a main effect of Stem Type for the duration of the vowel ($p < .01$) and no effect of Syllable Structure nor an interaction of Syllable Structure with Stem Type ($p > .1$). None of these factors was predictive for the duration of the release noise. For the duration of the closure, Stem Type was predictive ($p < .01$), and there was an interaction of Syllable Structure with Stem Type ($p < .01$): For words such as *hel-per*, the difference in closure duration was somewhat less pronounced than for words such as *ma-ker* and *cut-ter*. Thus, the manipulation of Stem Type was independent of Syllable Structure, except for a small difference for one syllable type with respect to closure duration.

The difference in duration between normal and constructed stems remained significant after splicing away 25% of the release noise of the stem-final plosive for the normal stems (121 ms on average, $F(1, 121) = 837.7$, $p < .0001$. Table 2 lists the mean durations with their standard deviations for the two kinds of stems of words and pseudowords, before as well as after splicing away 25% of the release noise of the normal stems. The interaction of Stem Type by Word Status was now only marginally significant, $F(1, 242) = 2.9$, $p = .09$, and the three-way interaction of Stem Type, Word Status, and Language remained non-significant, $F(1, 242) = 1.4$, $p = .24$. The effect of Stem Type on duration was still marginally smaller in English than in Dutch: Interaction of Stem Type by Language, $F(1, 242) = 2.0$, $p = .09$.

Three experimental trial lists and their complements were created in the same manner as in Part A of the experiment. The total number of

TABLE 2

Part B—Mean durations (in ms) with SD for normal stems and constructed stems in English, before and after splicing away 25% of the release noise of the normal stems

	Before		After	
Type of stem	Duration	SD	Duration	SD
Normal word	506	101	475	97
Constructed word	347	84	347	84
Normal pseudoword	497	91	478	91
Constructed pseudoword	364	89	364	89

experimental trials amounted to 124. The practice set consisted of 16 trials: 4 normal pseudoword stems, 4 constructed pseudoword stems, 4 normal word stems (2 comparative stems and 2 agent noun stems), and 4 constructed word stems (2 comparative stems and 2 agent noun stems). None of the stems in the practice set was presented in the actual experiment.

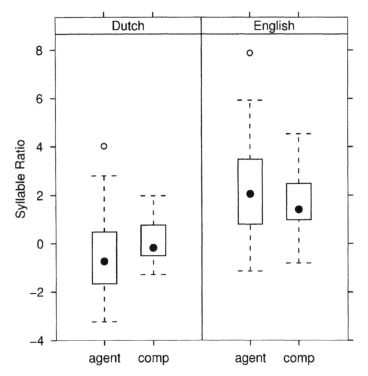

Figure 3. Syllable Ratio as a function of Word Type (stem of agent noun versus stem of comparative) and Language (Dutch versus English).

Syllable Ratio and Cohort Entropy were calculated for both the Dutch and the English words. Figures 3 and 4 summarise the distributions of Syllable Ratio and Cohort Entropy for the agent noun stems and the comparative stems in the Dutch and English part of the experiment, by means of boxplots. Each box shows the interquartile range, the filled circle in the box denotes the median, and the 'whiskers' extend to the observations within 1.5 times the interquartile range. Outliers beyond this range are represented by individual open circles.

Syllable Ratio was significantly higher for English than for Dutch, $F(1, 119) = 68.9$, $p < .0001$. This is what we expected, as there are fewer continuation forms with unstressed syllables in English than in Dutch. Word Type (agent noun versus comparative) had a stronger effect in Dutch than in English (with slightly higher Syllable Ratios for comparative stems than for agent noun stems), but this effect failed to reach significance in both languages; Dutch, $F(1, 59) = 2.1$, $p = .15$; English, $F(1, 60) = 2.2$, $p = .15$; interaction of Word Type by Language, $F(1, 119) = 10.1$, $p < .05$. Cohort Entropy was significantly lower for English than for Dutch, $F(1,$

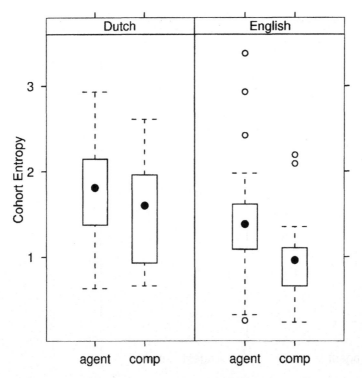

Figure 4. Cohort Entropy as a function of Word Type (stem of agent noun versus stem of comparative) and Language (Dutch versus English).

119) $= 20.2, p < .0001$. This was also expected, since there are fewer continuation forms in general in English than in Dutch. Cohort Entropy was significantly lower for comparative stems than for agent noun stems, $F(1, 119) = 11.0, p < .01$. This effect of Word Type on Cohort Entropy was similar for English and Dutch: Interaction of Word Type by Language, $F(1, 119) = 0.6, p = .42$. Furthermore, it turned out that Syllable Ratio and Cohort Entropy were correlated in English (Pearson's $r = -.24, p = .06$), but not in Dutch (Pearson's $r = -.14, p = .29$). Apparently, Cohort Entropy and Syllable Ratio consider largely the same continuation forms in English, but not in Dutch. In English, most continuation forms have unstressed syllables, whereas, in Dutch, many types of continuation forms are possible.

Procedure.   Participants performed English lexical decision. The same procedure was followed as in Part A of the experiment.

Results and discussion

For Dutch (Part A), no participants were excluded from the analyses, since they all showed error rates below 20%. Appendix A lists the mean reaction times and the error rates for the Dutch words and pseudowords. Fifteen items (10 existing words and 5 pseudowords) were excluded from subsequent analyses, as they showed error rates above 20%. Of these 15 items, 6 items had high error rates in both stem variants (i.e., normal versus constructed), 6 items had high error rates in the normal variant, and 3 items had high error rates in the constructed variant. Furthermore, trials eliciting incorrect responses were excluded (3% of the trials that remained after removal of the 15 items with high error rates), as well as trials eliciting reaction times faster than 150 ms (3% of all remaining correct trials).

For English (Part B), two participants were excluded from the analyses, since they performed with error rates above 20%. Appendix B lists the mean reaction times and the error rates for the English words and pseudowords, calculated over the trials remaining after removal of the two participants with high error rates. Twenty-five items (8 existing words and 17 pseudowords) were excluded from subsequent analyses, as they showed error rates above 20%. Of these 25 items, 6 items had high error rates in both stem variants, 9 items had high error rates in the normal variant, and 10 items had high error rates in the constructed variant. Finally, trials eliciting incorrect responses (5% of the trials that remained after removal of the two participants and the 25 items with high error rates) and trials eliciting reaction times faster than 150 ms were also excluded (4% of all remaining correct trials).

TABLE 3

Mean reaction times from word offset (in ms) with SD and error percentages for normal stems and constructed stems in Dutch and English

Type of stem	Reaction time	SD	Error
Dutch normal word	464	230	6%
Dutch constructed word	515	218	8%
Dutch normal pseudoword	526	238	6%
Dutch constructed pseudoword	596	226	6%
English normal word	335	160	2%
English constructed word	403	184	4%
English normal pseudoword	428	200	7%
English constructed pseudoword	488	215	7%

The mean response latencies (measured from word offset and calculated over the remaining correct trials only), their standard deviations, and the error percentages for the different types of stems for English and Dutch are summarised in Table 3. In general, incorrect responses occurred more often for pseudowords than for words ($z = -6.8$, $p < .0001$), and more often for constructed stems than for normal stems ($z = -3.0$, $p < .01$). The effect of Word Status on performance interacted with Language, however ($z = 4.6$, $p < .0001$): It was significant for English ($z = -6.8$, $p < .0001$), but not for Dutch ($z = 1.1$, $p = .29$).

In the following, we will report on an overall analysis, as well as on analyses of several subsets of the data. We will start with the overall analysis of the dataset including words as well as pseudowords, for Dutch as well as for English. Next, we will report on an analysis of only the pseudoword data for Dutch and English, and on a similar analysis of only the word data for Dutch and English. Finally, we will report on separate analyses for the Dutch and the English word data. The reasons for analysing each of these different subsets of the data will be clarified as we proceed.

In an initial, overall analysis, the data for Dutch and English words and pseudowords were analysed together. We fitted a multi-level covariance model (Pinheiro & Bates, 2000) to the data, with log reaction times[3] as the dependent variable, and Stem Type (normal versus constructed stem), Word Status (word versus pseudoword), Duration (the duration of the

---

[3] Here and in the following analyses, reaction times were logarithmically transformed in order to normalise their distribution.

form that was actually presented to the participants),[4] and Language (Dutch versus English) as predictors.[5] Note that in this analysis, we used only a subset of the available predictors. Syllable Ratio was not included as a predictor as it is not possible to calculate this ratio for pseudowords. It is possible to calculate Cohort Entropy for both words and pseudowords, but because Cohort Entropy exhibited very different distributions for words and pseudowords, we did not include Cohort Entropy as a predictor in this overall analysis. We will return to this issue below.

This analysis revealed significant effects of all predictors: Constructed stems were responded to slower than normal stems (56 ms on average for Dutch and 64 ms on average for English), $F(1, 5149) = 306.9, p < .0001$; pseudowords were responded to slower than words (91 ms on average for Dutch and 89 ms on average for English), $F(1, 5149) = 529.1, p < .0001$; duration was facilitatory (the longer the word, the faster the response latencies), $t(5149) = -8.7, p < .0001$; and the Dutch participants were slower than the English participants (100 ms on average), $F(1, 55) = 10.8, p < .01$. Furthermore, there were significant interactions of Word Status by Language (the effect of Word Status was less strong in Dutch than in English), $F(1, 5149) = 4.2, p < .05$; and of Stem Type by Duration (Duration was more facilitatory for the constructed stems), $t(5149) = 2.9, p < .01$. To understand the latter interaction, consider that the longer a given constructed stem is, the more it resembles its normal stem variant. Apparently, the less abnormal a form is, the faster listeners can respond to it.

---

[4] As reaction times were measured from word offset, we expect a facilitatory effect of Duration: At word offset, the listener has been exposed to more information when the duration of the word is long than when the duration of the word is short, facilitating the response. In order to establish whether Stem Type has an effect *independently* of Duration (normal stems have longer durations than constructed stems), we included Duration as a covariate in our analyses.

[5] In our multi-level covariance models, subject variability is accounted for by using subject as a grouping factor. In the analyses of word data exclusively, item variability is accounted for by including item-specific covariates in the regression model. However, in all our analyses involving both word and pseudoword data, and in all analyses involving pseudoword data exclusively, item variability has not been accounted for, as no item-specific covariates are available for pseudowords. Therefore, in all analyses involving pseudowords, Stem Type has been treated as a between-items factor even though we would have liked to treat it as a within-items factor. Nevertheless, even without the extra power of the within-items analysis, we obtained very robust effects of Stem Type. Furthermore, an analysis on Dutch and English words and pseudowords with *item* as the grouping factor yielded largely the same pattern of results as the analysis with *subject* as the grouping factor: Stem Type, $F(1, 203) = 117.3, p < .0001$; Word Status, $F(1, 203) = 130.2, p < .0001$; Duration, $t(203) = -5.2, p < .0001$; Language, $F(1, 203) = 138.4, p < .0001$; Stem Type by Duration, $t(203) = 2.9, p < .01$. The interaction of Word Status by Language was not significant in this analysis, $F(1, 5149) = 4.2, p = .67$.

To conclude, we have replicated the prosodic mismatch effect for stems of agent nouns and comparatives, in both Dutch and English. The prosodic mismatch effect emerged both in words and in pseudowords. Now the question remains: Do Cohort Entropy and Syllable Ratio have any predictive value? This question calls for separate analyses for words and pseudowords, for two reasons. First, Cohort Entropy (calculated at the stem-final segment) turned out to be normally distributed for Dutch and English words, but not for Dutch and English pseudowords: For the majority of pseudoword items, the cohorts were empty at the stem-final segment, and thus, the Cohort Entropy for these items was zero. For only a small number of pseudoword items (14 out of 56 Dutch pseudowords, and 9 out of 45 English pseudowords), the cohort at the stem-final segment was not empty. Second, the predictor Syllable Ratio can not be calculated for pseudowords.

We first turn to an analysis of the pseudoword data only. Because of the non-normal distribution of Cohort Entropy, we decided to treat Cohort Entropy as a factor with two levels (Entropy Zero versus Entropy Non-Zero), instead of as a covariate. In a multi-level covariance analysis, log reaction times were analysed as a linear function of Stem Type (normal versus constructed stem), Cohort Entropy (Entropy Zero versus Entropy Non-Zero), Duration, and Language (Dutch versus English). This analysis revealed significant effects of all predictors: Constructed stems were responded to slower than normal stems, $F(1, 2486) = 152.9, p < .0001$; Duration had a facilitatory effect, $t(2486) = -6.5, p < .0001$; English reaction times were faster than Dutch reaction times, $F(1, 55) = 7.0, p < .05$; and, importantly, items with empty cohorts (Entropy Zero) were responded to faster than items with non-empty cohorts: Entropy Non-Zero, $F(1, 2486) = 41.8, p < .0001$. Furthermore, there was a significant interaction of Cohort Entropy with Language: The effect of Cohort Entropy was less strong for English than for Dutch, $F(1, 2486) = 4.4, p < .05$. The effect of Cohort Entropy was significant in both languages, however: Dutch, $F(1, 1040) = 36.7, p < .0001$; English, $F(1, 1444) = 10.5, p < .01$.

We now turn to the word data. Log reaction times to the words were predicted by the same variables as log reaction times to the pseudowords: Stem Type (normal versus constructed stem), Duration, Cohort Entropy, and Language (Dutch versus English). In addition, Word Type (agent noun versus comparative) and Syllable Ratio were introduced as predictors. For the words (as opposed to the pseudowords), the Cohort Entropy values were normally distributed. Therefore, Cohort Entropy was now treated as a covariate (as opposed to as a factor).

A multi-level covariance analysis revealed significant effects of Stem Type: Constructed stems were responded to slower than normal stems,

$F(1, 2597) = 194.9, p < .0001$; Duration, facilitatory effect, $t(2597) = -5.9$, $p < .0001$; Language (English participants were faster than Dutch participants), $F(1, 55) = 11.5, p < .01$; and Word Type (adjectives were responded to faster than verb stems), $F(1, 2597) = 9.4, p < .01$. Furthermore, there was a significant inhibitory main effect of Cohort Entropy, $t(2597) = 3.1, p < .01$, whereas there was no significant main effect of Syllable Ratio, $t(2597) = 1.7, p = .08$. In addition, however, there was a significant second-order interaction of Cohort Entropy by Language, $t(2597) = -2.1, p < .05$, and a significant third-order interaction of Syllable Ratio by Cohort Entropy by Language, $F(2, 2597) = 9.1, p < .0001$. We will return to this issue below. Finally, we observed a significant interaction of Stem Type by Duration: Duration was more facilitatory for the constructed stems, $t(2597) = 3.2, p < .01$. This interaction had already been observed in the overall analysis described above (words and pseudowords in Dutch and English): The longer a given constructed stem is, the more it resembles its normal stem variant, and the faster listeners can respond to it.

As mentioned above, Syllable Ratio and Cohort Entropy were correlated in English (Pearson's $r = -.34, p < .05$), but not in Dutch (Pearson's $r = -.16, p = .26$).[6] This, in combination with the fact that we observed a second-order interaction of Cohort Entropy by Language, and a third-order interaction of Syllable Ratio by Cohort Entropy by Language, calls for separate analyses for the Dutch and the English word data. These separate analyses yielded the following results.

For Dutch, significant effects were again obtained for Stem Type, $F(1, 910) = 10.4, p < .01$; for Duration, $t(910) = -3.4, p < .001$; and for Word Type, $F(1, 910) = 4.6, p < .05$. Syllable Ratio had a significant facilitatory effect, $t(910) = -3.3, p < .01$, but there was no effect of Cohort Entropy, $t(910) = 0.1, p = .88$. Interestingly, there was a marginally significant interaction of Syllable Ratio by Stem Type, $t(910) = 1.9, p = .06$: The effect of Syllable Ratio was highly significant for the constructed stems, $t(458) = -3.5, p < .001$, but non-significant for the normal stems, $t(430) = -0.8, p = .40$. In other words, listeners only profited from a high Syllable Ratio when the monosyllabic form they were listening to was abnormal. This suggests that when the mapping of the acoustic signal on the representation of a stem is less effective as a result of the prosodic characteristics of the acoustic signal, the long-term probability of hearing an unshortened stem is more influential than when the bottom-up signal is unambiguous.

---

[6] The correlation coefficients reported here are calculated over the items that remained after removing the items with high error percentages, and are therefore numerically different from the correlation coefficients reported in the Materials section (which were calculated over all items that were presented to the participants).

For English, a different pattern emerged. We observed the usual effects of Stem Type, $F(1, 1686) = 159.8$, $p < .0001$; Duration, $t(1686) = -3.7$, $p < .001$; and Word Type, $F(1, 1686) = 4.7$, $p < .05$. Syllable Ratio, however, did not have a significant effect, $t(1686) = -0.8$, $p = .45$, whereas there was a significant inhibitory effect of Cohort Entropy, $t(1686) = 2.2$, $p < .05$. This effect of Cohort Entropy is an interesting finding, given the fact that the cohorts over which the Cohort Entropy values were calculated consist mainly of morphologically related continuation forms (i.e., inflections, derivations, and compounds). For English, of all 1,488 possible continuation forms (counted over all word stems), 1,280 forms (113,748 tokens) were morphologically related, and 208 forms (12,539 tokens) were morphologically unrelated. Of the morphologically related forms, 990 forms (110,234 tokens) were inflectional or derivational forms, and 290 forms (3,514 tokens) were compounds. In the cohort literature, it is generally assumed that morphological (inflectional and derivational) continuation forms should be excluded from the cohort (e.g., Marslen-Wilson, 1984; Tyler, Marslen-Wilson, Rentoul, & Hanney, 1988). Our finding shows that for a more realistic indication of the amount of competition in the mental lexicon, morphological continuation forms should be counted as cohort members. Unlike Syllable Ratio in Dutch, Cohort Entropy in English did not interact with Stem Type, $t(1685) = 0.17$, $p = .86$.

For completeness, we note that when Cohort Entropy is not included in the model, Syllable Ratio *is* predictive in English, $t(1687) = -2.0$, $p < .05$. However, when both correlated predictors Syllable Ratio and Cohort Entropy are entered into the model, only the latter is significant. In contrast, Cohort Entropy never showed an effect for Dutch, neither in a model with both Cohort Entropy and Syllable Ratio as predictors, nor in a model that included Cohort Entropy but not Syllable Ratio, $t(912) = 0.5$, $p = .61$.

To conclude, Syllable Ratio (a phonologically motivated measure) emerged as the superior predictor for Dutch reaction times, whereas Cohort Entropy (a non-phonologically motivated measure) emerged as the superior predictor for English reaction times. Apparently, in a language in which word stems are frequently followed by unstressed syllables, that is, in which stems frequently occur in shortened form, listeners develop a sensitivity for the likelihood of observing a shortened or an unshortened stem. In a language in which word stems occur relatively infrequently in shortened form, listeners are less sensitive to the likelihood of observing a shortened or an unshortened stem, but are instead sensitive to the contents of the cohort at stem-final position in general.

GENERAL DISCUSSION

In this study, we replicated the prosodic mismatch effect that was originally observed for plural inflection in Dutch (Kemps et al., in press) for another type of inflection (the formation of comparatives) and for derivation (the formation of agent nouns), in both Dutch and English. Listeners were presented with monosyllabic stems of comparatives (adjectives) and monosyllabic stems of agent nouns (verbs) that carried prosodic information that either matched or mismatched the number of syllables: The matching prosodic information pointed to a monosyllabic form, whereas the mismatching prosodic information pointed to a bisyllabic form. Lexical decision latencies were significantly slower for the items with mismatching prosodic information. This prosodic mismatch effect emerged for words as well as for pseudowords.

English is a morphologically less productive language than Dutch. As a consequence, a stem in English occurs less often in shortened form than a stem in Dutch. Nevertheless, our experiments show that Dutch and English listeners are equally sensitive to prosodic cues in the stem that signal whether or not the stem will be followed by one or more unstressed syllables. The difference in morphological richness between Dutch and English is however reflected in the predictive values of Syllable Ratio relative to Cohort Entropy. Dutch listeners are sensitive to Syllable Ratio, the log odds ratio of observing an unshortened form versus observing a shortened form: In the morphologically richer language, listeners are sensitive to the item-specific distribution of shortened and unshortened stems within the lexicon. In the morphologically poorer language, Cohort Entropy (the entropy of the distribution of cohort members at stem-final position) emerged as the superior predictor, and Syllable Ratio did not have any additional predictive value. Apparently, in a language such as English, in which stems occur relatively infrequently in shortened form, listeners are less sensitive to the item-specific distribution of shortened and unshortened stems within the lexicon. Instead, the contents of the (phonologically and morphologically non-restricted) cohort codetermine response latencies.

Our experiments also show that, in Dutch, Syllable Ratio is facilitatory for the constructed stems only. Apparently, when the mapping of the acoustic signal on the representation of a stem is less effective as a result of the prosodic characteristics of the acoustic signal, the long-term probability of hearing an unshortened stem has a larger role to play than when the bottom-up signal is unambiguous.

It might be argued that the prosodic mismatch effect arises purely due to a mismatch with syllable frame information. Consider the situation in which a listener hears the constructed form of *helper* (i.e., *help*). The prosodic cues of the stem might guide the listener to posit a syllable boundary before the stem-final plosive. Assuming that syllable frames are part of the lexical representations of *help* and *hel-per*, the inferred syllable boundary before the *p* in the constructed stem of *helper* would lead to a mismatch with the lexical representation of the stem (*hel-p* mismatches *help*). This line of reasoning predicts that a greater mismatch in syllabic structure should correspond with a greater prosodic mismatch effect. To test this prediction, we considered the three syllable structures exemplified by the words *ma-ker*, *hel-per*, and *cut-ter*. For words of the last type, the mismatch with a potential syllable frame is minimal, since the ambisyllabic stem-final plosive is both stem-final and syllable-final. Hence, the prosodic mismatch effect should be smallest for *cut-ter*, and larger for *ma-ker* and *hel-per* due to the misalignment of morphological and prosodic structure. Analyses of covariance of the response latencies in Dutch and English with Syllable Structure as an additional predictor revealed the following. In Dutch, an interaction of Syllable Structure with Stem Type emerged ($p <$ .05), indicating that the words with an ambisyllabic stem-final plosive suffered most instead of least from the Stem Type manipulation, contrary to the above prediction. In English, no interaction was present ($p >$ .6). We conclude that the prosodic mismatch effect cannot be reduced to a syllable frame mismatch effect.

The subsegmental durational effects documented in the present study probably arise during the mapping of the acoustic signal onto the lexicon. It is less clear at what level the effect of Syllable Ratio should be located. One possibility is to assume that it arises post-lexically. In that case, the inflected and derived words containing a given stem as the first constituent would form the sample space over which the (token-frequency based) probability for that stem of being followed by a syllable with a schwa would be estimated. This estimation, which can be conceptualised either as an on-line generalisation over stored exemplars (the inflectional and derivational types), or as an implicit generalisation represented in the weights of the connections between morphologically related lexical entries, would then take place after the mapping of the acoustic signal onto the lexical entries is completed. This is a way in which the present results might be incorporated in a model such as Shortlist (Norris, 1994).

To our mind, a post-lexical explanation of the effect of Syllable Ratio has the disadvantage that different aspects of what may well be the same morpho-phonological phenomenon are spread out over different levels of representation and processing. We view the subsegmental durational differences as providing subtle acoustic cues for the probability of particular syllable structures and of the likelihood of a following phonologically weak suffix. We interpret Syllable Ratio as a complementary frequency-based estimate of the same probabilities. Although it is technically possible to allocate the subsegmental and Syllable Ratio effects to different levels, we feel that this would lead to a generalisation being missed.

There is an alternative way in which the Syllable Ratio effect can be understood, namely, as an intrinsic part of the process mapping the acoustic input onto the lexicon. In this view, the fact that the inflectional and derivational types in the CELEX lexical database over which Syllable Ratio is calculated probably also have lexical representations would be irrelevant. What would be relevant is that the frequency with which the auditory system encounters these forms leaves its traces in the mapping of the acoustic input onto these lexical representations. This mapping operation would then be sensitive to both frequency and subsegmental duration.

This way of thinking is compatible with the results of Goldinger's study (1998) which suggest that perceptual details of speech are stored in memory and are integral to later perception. In this study, shadowers showed a tendency to spontaneously imitate the acoustic patterns (speakers' voice characteristics) of words and nonwords. Goldinger simulated these data with the strictly episodic MINERVA 2 model (Hintzman, 1986). In this model, which includes a mechanism of random forgetting necessary to avoid an exponential increase in the costs of storage and retrieval, spoken words were represented by vectors of simple elements. Each vector (i.e., each word token) contained 200 elements, of which 50 elements coded details of the speaker's voice that had produced the word. The model correctly predicted the tendency for shadowers to imitate the idiosyncratic acoustic details of speech, and it successfully predicted the response times in the shadowing task. These results strongly suggest the storage of detailed episodes in the mental lexicon. In the Goldinger study, the vector elements coded – among other things – voice characteristics. Vectors with elements coding other acoustic details, like segment durations, fit well within this approach.

Another subsymbolic, exemplar-based model that allows perceptual detail to be stored in memory, is discussed by Johnson (1997). Word-specific prosodic information was implicitly incorporated in a connectionist model. Johnson trained his model on vector-quantized speech data, which contained—among other things—information regarding the durations of the segments. This model correctly anticipated whether the incoming syllable was followed by another (unstressed) syllable or not. The connection weights in this model applied to our data would be higher between relatively *long* stem exemplars and the stem node than between relative *short* stem exemplars and the stem node. In this model, a constructed stem (with relatively short segment durations) would therefore less effectively activate the stem node than a normal stem (with relatively long segment durations). Similarly, more frequently encountered patterns would lead to enhanced performance.

The probabilistic, exemplar-based framework by Pierrehumbert (2001, 2003) offers a symbolic account of the representation of word-specific phonetic detail in the mental lexicon. In this framework, phonetic categories have probability distributions over a parametric phonetic space. These probability distributions consist of memory traces (exemplars), and are gradually built up as speech tokens are encountered and encoded. Word-forms, in turn, are viewed as sequences of phonetic categories, and also have probability distributions over temporal sequences of events in the phonetic space: Individual words have exemplar clouds associated with them. Extending this approach, we might imagine that morphologically complex forms will be associated with exemplars with relatively short stem segments, whereas isolated stems will be associated with exemplars with relatively long segments. Constructed stems are further away from the center of the distribution of stem exemplars than normal stems, and will therefore less effectively activate the representation of the stem.

To conclude, the present study provides more evidence for the role of prosodic information in morphological processing: Detailed acoustic information in the stem reveals whether the stem is realised in isolation or as part of a morphologically complex form. In a morphologically rich language like Dutch (compared to English), listeners are in addition sensitive to the likelihood within the morphological paradigm of a word of encountering a specific prosodic manifestation of that word. Although the data that we have presented in the present paper do not allow us to force a choice between different rival theoretical explanations, the most parsimonious interpretations seem to point to theories in which the mapping of the acoustic input onto the lexical representations is sensitive to both duration and probability of occurrence.

REFERENCES

Baayen, R. H., Piepenbrock, R., & van Rijn, H. (1993). *The CELEX lexical database (CD-ROM)*. Linguistic Data Consortium, University of Pennsylvania, Philadelphia, PA.

Boersma, P., & Weenink, D. J. M. (1996). PRAAT, a system for doing phonetics by computer, version 3.4. Institute of Phonetic Sciences of the University of Amsterdam, *Report 132*. Available at http://www.fon.hum.uva.nl/praat/.

Booij, G. E. (1979). Semantic regularities in word formation. *Linguistics, 17*, 985–1001.

Booij, G. E. (1995). *The phonology of Dutch*. Oxford: Clarendon Press.

Davis, M. H., Marslen-Wilson, W. D., & Gaskell, M. G. (2002). Leading up the lexical garden-path: Segmentation and ambiguity in spoken word recognition. *Journal of Experimental Psychology: Human Perception and Performance, 28*, 218–244.

Fowler, C. A. (1977). *Timing control in speech production*. Bloomington, IN: Indiana University Linguistics Club.

Goldinger, S. D. (1998). Echoes of echoes? An episodic theory of lexical access. *Psychological Review, 105*, 251–279.

Hintzman, D. (1986). 'Schema extraction' in a multiple-trace memory model. *Psychological Review, 95*, 528–551.

Johnson, K. (1997). The auditory/perceptual basis for speech segmentation. *Ohio State University Working Papers in Linguistics, 50*, 101–113.

Kemps, R. J. J. K., Ernestus, M., Schreuder, R., & Baayen, R. H. (in press). Subsegmental and suprasegmental cues for morphological complexity: The case of Dutch plural nouns. *Memory and Cognition.*

Lehiste, I. (1972). *Suprasegmentals.* Cambridge, MA: MIT Press.

Lindblom, B., & Rapp, K. (1973). Some temporal regularities of spoken Swedish. *PILUS, 21*, 1–59.

Marslen-Wilson, W. D. (1984). Function and process in spoken word recognition. A tutorial overview. In H. Bouma, & D. G. Bouwhuis (Eds.), *Attention and performance X: Control of language processes*, (pp. 125–150). Hove, UK: Lawrence Erlbaum Associates Ltd.

Moscoso del Prado Martín, F., Kostíc, A., & Baayen, R. H. (in press). Putting the bits together: An information theoretical perspective on morphological processing. *Cognition, 94*, 1–18.

Nooteboom, S. G. (1972). *Production and perception of vowel duration: A study of the durational properties of vowels in Dutch.* Unpublished doctoral dissertation, University of Utrecht, Utrecht.

Norris, D. (1994). Shortlist: A connectionist model of continuous speech recognition. *Cognition, 52*, 189–234.

Pierrehumbert, J. (2001). Exemplar dynamics: Word frequency, lenition and contrast. In J. Bybee & P. Hopper, (Eds.), *Frequency and the emergence of linguistic structure* (pp. 137–157. Amsterdam: John Benjamins Publishing Company.

Pierrehumbert, J. B. (2003). Probabilistic phonology: Discrimination and robustness. In R. Bod, J. Hay, and S. Jannedy, (Eds.), *Probability theory in linguistics* (pp. 177–228. Cambridge, MA: MIT Press.

Salverda, A., Dahan, D., & McQueen, J. (2003). The role of prosodic boundaries in the resolution of lexical embedding in speech comprehension. *Cognition, 90*, 51–89.

Shannon, C. E. (1948). A mathematical theory of communication. *Bell System Technical Journal, 27*, 379–423.

Tyler, L. K., Marslen-Wilson, W., Rentoul, J., & Hanney, P. (1988). Continuous and discontinuous access in spoken word-recognition: The role of derivational prefixes. *Journal of Memory and Language, 27*, 368–381.

APPENDIX A

Dutch materials

Dutch agent noun stem and matched pseudowords

Word	Cohort Entropy	Syllable Ratio	Normal Stem		Constructed Stem		Pseudoword	Cohort Entropy	Normal Stem		Constructed Stem	
			RT	Error	RT	Error			RT	Error	RT	Error
1. breuk	2.10	-0.99	513	11.11%	489	0.00%	veek	0.43	730	18.18%	662	0.00%
2. bijt	1.95	-0.73	492	27.27%	664	11.11%	peut	2.06	690	11.11%	734	9.09%
3. breek	1.41	-2.66	507	30.00%	695	0.00%	krook	1.75	507	20.00%	562	0.00%
4. denk	1.33	-0.49	437	0.00%	556	10.00%	lart	0.00	578	20.00%	751	30.00%
5. doop	2.46	0.79	692	22.22%	647	54.55%	book	0.70	468	0.00%	560	0.00%
6. dop	1.73	0.64	922	36.36%	639	0.00%	terp	0.00	694	11.11%	638	0.00%
7. drink	1.12	-1.13	578	0.00%	456	0.00%	plink	0.00	487	18.18%	579	0.00%
8. duik	2.07	-1.00	430	0.00%	480	0.00%	ponk	0.00	464	0.00%	615	0.00%
9. dweep	2.49	-2.68	696	44.44%	663	54.55%	smep	0.00	650	0.00%	591	0.00%
10. eet	2.41	-1.34	514	0.00%	726	11.11%	oot	1.65	642	0.00%	686	0.00%
11. fluit	1.89	-0.62	332	0.00%	447	0.00%	skoot	0.00	411	0.00%	512	0.00%
12. fok	2.31	-1.27	421	0.00%	732	30.00%	guk	0.00	379	10.00%	499	0.00%
13. gok	1.81	-0.37	390	0.00%	558	0.00%	fot	0.00	696	33.33%	734	36.36%
14. haat	1.05	0.75	378	0.00%	457	0.00%	gaak	0.00	467	0.00%	608	0.00%
15. help	0.97	-2.41	418	0.00%	425	0.00%	relt	0.00	671	22.22%	665	9.09%
16. kaart	1.45	2.69	299	0.00%	418	0.00%	peelt	0.00	553	10.00%	723	0.00%
17. kijk	1.31	-0.89	398	0.00%	584	18.18%	liek	2.25	637	0.00%	624	0.00%
18. kraak	2.20	-3.23	396	0.00%	537	11.11%	plook	0.00	472	0.00%	488	0.00%
19. kweek	2.07	-1.96	505	0.00%	534	0.10%	bleet	0.00	607	11.11%	557	0.00%
20. lok	1.81	-2.01	470	20.00%	825	20.00%	taft	0.00	497	10.00%	643	20.00%
21. maak	1.24	-2.85	612	11.11%	653	27.27%	naap	1.32	613	0.00%	599	0.00%
22. melk	1.75	2.81	292	0.00%	387	0.00%	bork	0.00	474	0.00%	551	0.00%
23. muit	1.66	-1.41	772	60.00%	813	90.00%	beep	0.00	712	11.11%	563	0.00%
24. plant	1.92	0.75	374	10.00%	448	0.00%	krint	0.00	642	18.18%	645	11.11%
25. pleit	0.98	-0.44	636	22.22%	652	9.09%	kleip	0.00	504	0.00%	602	0.00%
26. pluk	1.46	-1.92	435	0.00%	665	11.11%	klek	0.00	505	0.00%	572	0.00%
27. rook	1.79	0.36	461	0.00%	416	0.00%	biek	0.73	439	0.00%	634	10.00%
28. schep	2.34	-2.49	365	10.00%	521	0.00%	spik	1.49	727	9.09%	628	11.11%
29. slaap	2.19	-0.14	413	0.00%	421	0.00%	breep	0.00	395	0.00%	590	10.00%
30. spit	2.30	0.22	518	0.00%	694	0.00%	spep	0.00	500	0.00%	486	0.00%
31. sprint	1.47	0.14	366	0.00%	431	0.00%	skrump	0.00	516	0.00%	457	0.00%
32. strip	2.04	2.56	467	0.00%	504	0.00%	strok	0.00	444	0.00%	546	0.00%
33. vent	1.13	4.02	552	11.11%	426	0.00%	benk	0.00	581	9.09%	592	0.00%
34. werk	2.93	0.60	321	0.00%	492	0.00%	birk	0.00	441	10.00%	601	0.00%
35. zet	0.63	-1.41	642	20.00%	576	10.00%	wuk	0.00	541	10.00%	637	10.00%

Dutch comparative stems and matched pseudowords

Word	Cohort Entropy	Syllable Ratio	Normal Stem RT	Normal Stem Error	Constructed Stem RT	Constructed Stem Error	Pseudoword	Cohort Entropy	Normal Stem RT	Normal Stem Error	Constructed Stem RT	Constructed Stem Error
1. bleek	0.73	-0.50	552	0.00%	474	18.18%	vroot	0.00	473	11.11%	592	0.00%
2. bloot	1.77	-0.39	352	9.09%	464	11.11%	snook	0.00	460	0.00%	495	0.00%
3. dik	1.73	-1.00	436	0.00%	605	10.00%	det	0.00	695	0.00%	592	0.00%
4. flink	0.79	0.31	333	0.00%	427	0.00%	vrunt	0.00	428	0.00%	484	0.00%
5. gek	0.96	1.75	404	0.00%	476	0.00%	gip	1.12	458	10.00%	643	0.00%
6. groot	1.67	-0.80	411	9.09%	388	0.00%	glaat	0.00	535	0.00%	739	20.00%
7. heet	1.19	-0.08	475	0.00%	475	0.00%	wuut	0.00	419	0.00%	578	0.00%
8. juist	0.66	1.28	332	0.00%	346	0.00%	paagt	0.00	456	22.22%	407	54.55%
9. kort	1.67	-0.01	419	0.00%	474	9.09%	firt	0.00	414	0.00%	579	0.00%
10. laat	1.62	-1.28	429	0.00%	546	0.00%	voot	0.69	627	0.00%	768	11.11%
11. mat	2.51	-0.82	480	0.00%	578	20.00%	tup	0.00	619	0.00%	685	0.00%
12. nat	2.07	-0.26	281	0.00%	439	0.00%	plik	0.00	579	18.18%	695	0.00%
13. rank	1.58	-1.21	633	22.22%	594	9.09%	wink	2.12	764	22.22%	740	36.36%
14. rijk	2.44	0.91	416	0.00%	458	11.11%	leep	2.14	661	20.00%	584	10.00%
15. rijp	1.99	-0.41	405	0.00%	472	0.00%	tiek	1.06	562	0.00%	796	20.00%
16. scherp	1.50	-0.01	228	0.00%	429	0.00%	stimp	0.00	497	0.00%	519	0.00%
17. sterk	1.33	0.07	521	11.11%	383	0.00%	blask	0.00	410	0.00%	718	11.11%
18. stomp	2.07	-0.41	528	0.00%	487	0.00%	krunt	0.00	445	9.09%	467	0.00%
19. stout	1.80	-0.14	403	0.00%	477	0.00%	praak	0.00	501	0.00%	705	0.00%
20. strikt	0.68	0.76	527	0.00%	657	0.00%	sprent	0.00	434	0.00%	554	0.00%
21. vast	2.61	1.21	488	0.00%	394	0.00%	mork	0.00	397	0.00%	647	0.00%
22. vlak	0.83	1.21	336	0.00%	518	0.00%	blek	0.60	549	0.00%	751	10.00%
23. wit	0.93	-0.89	451	0.00%	537	0.00%	bup	0.00	482	0.00%	643	0.00%
24. zout	1.26	1.98	335	0.00%	427	0.00%	beut	0.00	508	0.00%	647	0.00%
25. zwak	1.96	-0.44	423	0.00%	445	0.00%	slek	0.00	535	10.00%	613	0.00%
26. zwart	0.89	-0.21	362	0.00%	461	0.00%	knesp	0.00	518	0.00%	633	9.09%

APPENDIX B

English materials

English agent nouns and matched pseudowords

Word	Cohort Entropy	Syllable Ratio	Normal Stem RT	Normal Stem Error	Constructed Stem RT	Constructed Stem Error	Pseudoword	Cohort Entropy	Normal Stem RT	Normal Stem Error	Constructed Stem RT	Constructed Stem Error
1. book	1.28	7.88	298	0.00%	471	0.00%	nop	0.00	488	9.52%	531	25.00%
2. doubt	1.11	1.93	339	6.25%	386	28.57%	doyp	0.00	416	5.26%	419	0.00%
3. smoke	1.43	2.01	249	0.00%	296	0.00%	shweep	0.00	316	0.00%	421	4.76%
4. bank	1.38	2.24	200	0.00%	428	5.56%	gailt	0.00	487	0.00%	495	43.75%
5. reap	2.42	0.90	438	27.78%	493	10.53%	layp	0.00	449	33.33%	481	12.50%
6. hop	1.74	0.67	490	14.29%	397	6.25%	wep	0.87	541	44.44%	572	63.16%
7. drink	1.06	2.06	228	0.00%	426	15.79%	dromp	0.00	425	5.56%	433	36.84%
8. fake	1.12	2.55	288	0.00%	335	0.00%	veet	1.01	376	23.81%	430	6.25%
9. creep	1.54	0.70	315	10.53%	501	0.00%	klope	0.00	584	10.53%	505	16.67%
10. eat	1.19	3.52	281	5.26%	504	11.11%	ope	1.43	602	10.53%	624	11.11%
11. float	1.47	0.40	279	12.50%	471	33.33%	frukc	0.00	464	31.25%	549	4.76%
12. kick	1.48	2.32	321	0.00%	362	0.00%	kak	1.81	393	6.25%	513	9.32%
13. mock	1.98	3.61	370	16.67%	474	15.79%	nep	0.69	492	12.50%	471	9.52%
14. boat	0.81	4.83	331	0.00%	353	0.00%	doot	0.00	431	4.76%	534	6.25%
15. help	1.31	2.58	340	0.00%	402	0.00%	walp	0.00	460	36.84%	555	22.22%
16. sort	0.49	3.76	419	15.79%	513	5.56%	zaylt	0.00	412	0.00%	412	0.00%
17. make	1.00	4.23	409	0.00%	360	0.00%	neek	0.67	497	27.78%	468	15.79%
18. stalk	2.93	0.63	292	6.25%	403	0.00%	stip	1.67	532	4.76%	488	6.25%
19. break	1.60	3.43	239	0.00%	313	0.00%	ploot	0.76	403	0.00%	462	15.79%
20. pack	0.25	0.00	376	10.53%	609	16.67%	tep	0.24	545	16.67%	555	31.58%
21. bake	1.88	-1.13	354	0.00%	414	0.00%	kvck	0.00	396	0.00%	514	0.00%
22. milk	0.55	5.93	269	0.00%	351	0.00%	malp	0.00	371	10.53%	523	16.67%
23. beat	1.67	0.24	391	0.00%	497	0.00%	toop	1.27	412	0.00%	550	0.00%
24. plant	1.20	1.33	287	0.00%	333	0.00%	krent	0.00	374	11.76%	465	10.33%
25. skate	0.94	1.75	219	0.00%	383	0.00%	spote	0.00	496	18.75%	505	0.00%
26. track	1.70	3.45	379	5.26%	523	44.44%	brip	0.00	361	6.25%	503	14.29%
27. hike	1.60	0.97	375	0.00%	523	16.67%	hewt	2.37	530	22.22%	583	63.16%
28. snap	1.56	3.44	285	5.26%	383	0.00%	smik	0.00	402	10.53%	487	11.11%
29. sleep	1.17	2.75	301	0.00%	340	12.50%	shrape	0.00	366	0.00%	420	6.25%
30. quit	0.64	3.90	366	0.00%	478	4.76%	kwop	0.00	383	6.25%	469	9.52%
31. sprint	0.32	0.25	296	4.76%	302	0.00%	strent	0.00	433	15.79%	500	11.11%
32. strip	3.38	1.94	392	0.00%	495	0.00%	splik	0.00	438	0.00%	500	26.32%
33. hunt	1.63	-0.41	299	0.00%	353	0.00%	yamp	0.00	370	0.00%	424	4.76%
34. work	1.48	1.39	267	0.00%	330	0.00%	yert	0.00	361	0.00%	453	0.00%
35. cut	1.15	3.97	345	0.00%	329	0.00%	gak	0.00	471	21.05%	488	11.11%

English comparative stems and matched pseudowords

Word	Cohort Entropy	Syllable Ratio	Normal Stem RT	Normal Stem Error	Constructed Stem RT	Constructed Stem Error	Pseudoword	Cohort Entropy	Normal Stem RT	Normal Stem Error	Constructed Stem RT	Constructed Stem Error
1. bleak	0.54	2.83	441	28.57%	408	25.00%	gloop	0.00	402	5.56%	537	10.53%
2. cute	0.90	1.81	342	0.00%	512	36.84%	goip	0.00	338	12.50%	438	4.76%
3. thick	1.25	1.33	301	0.00%	394	5.56%	thep	0.00	431	5.56%	503	10.53%
4. drunk	1.13	-0.18	279	0.00%	282	0.00%	klunt	0.00	405	4.76%	528	0.00%
5. sick	2.19	1.27	304	0.00%	350	12.50%	zek	0.00	395	0.00%	375	5.56%
6. great	1.06	1.11	256	0.00%	519	4.76%	bluke	0.51	450	4.76%	625	0.00%
7. tight	2.09	0.53	475	0.00%	565	10.53%	powk	0.00	395	12.50%	470	0.00%
8. moist	0.23	1.10	242	0.00%	279	0.00%	newsk	0.00	369	11.11%	457	15.79%
9. dark	1.01	0.87	272	6.25%	386	0.00%	barp	0.00	431	12.50%	548	14.29%
10. late	0.95	-0.80	353	0.00%	446	5.56%	roke	0.00	504	33.33%	662	25.00%
11. fat	0.89	2.37	347	11.11%	572	42.11%	fik	1.73	585	26.32%	583	44.44%
12. wet	0.66	2.75	231	0.00%	400	0.00%	lup	0.00	509	15.79%	529	5.56%
13. pink	0.55	4.53	223	0.00%	319	0.00%	gont	0.00	532	14.29%	502	12.50%
14. weak	1.35	-0.28	348	0.00%	385	0.00%	yate	0.00	474	12.50%	515	14.29%
15. ripe	1.22	0.73	291	0.00%	360	0.00%	loik	0.00	432	0.00%	578	0.00%
16. sharp	1.26	1.32	231	0.00%	356	4.76%	shelk	0.00	549	5.26%	419	5.56%
17. stark	0.61	2.62	505	31.25%	619	38.10%	spelk	0.00	383	9.52%	540	0.00%
18. plump	0.65	1.78	325	4.76%	428	12.50%	krump	0.66	434	27.78%	453	52.63%
19. bright	1.07	1.30	252	0.00%	332	5.56%	kloik	0.00	304	6.25%	451	4.76%
20. strict	1.01	1.65	305	4.76%	403	12.50%	splekt	0.00	376	5.26%	362	0.00%
21. fast	0.79	0.67	175	0.00%	351	0.00%	hesk	0.00	427	5.26%	551	0.00%
22. black	0.96	3.23	241	6.25%	412	14.29%	kret	1.37	322	5.26%	501	0.00%
23. hot	0.39	3.21	242	0.00%	491	6.25%	yek	0.00	377	20.05%	583	0.00%
24. white	0.56	4.06	267	0.00%	428	5.56%	howk	0.00	461	0.00%	464	5.26%
25. quick	1.04	1.41	338	0.00%	410	5.56%	kwep	0.00	379	12.50%	508	0.00%
26. slick	0.71	2.10	384	0.00%	451	0.00%	slek	0.00	409	11.11%	487	15.79%
27. smart	0.98	1.78	193	0.00%	277	0.00%	snalk	0.68	379	6.25%	363	0.00%

LANGUAGE AND COGNITIVE PROCESSES
2005, 20 (1/2), 75–114

Masked cross-modal morphological priming: Unravelling morpho-orthographic and morpho-semantic influences in early word recognition

Kevin Diependaele and Dominiek Sandra

University of Antwerp, Antwerp, Belgium

Jonathan Grainger

CNRS and Université de Provence, Aix-en-Provence, France

Two experiments examined priming from semantically transparent and opaque suffix-derivations (including pseudo-derived words such as *corner*), using the masked cross-modal priming technique. Experiment 1 showed that in a Dutch lexical decision task, latencies to root targets were facilitated when visually presented primes were transparent derivations of the target, regardless of whether targets were presented visually or auditorily. Pseudo-derivations only provided weak evidence for priming and only when targets were presented visually. In Experiment 2 we tested transparent and opaque priming more thoroughly in a French lexical decision task by using the incremental priming technique in combination with a psychophysical approach. The results showed that opaque as well as transparent derivations facilitated the visual and auditory processing of their (pseudo-) root. However, transparent priming occurred earlier than opaque priming in the visual modality. Moreover, when facilitation from opaque derivations appeared in the visual modality, transparent derivations produced a larger facilitation effect. We argue that our findings illustrate the existence of two distinct processing systems underlying early morphological processing: a *morpho-orthographic system* and a *morpho-semantic system*.

Correspondence should be addressed to Kevin Diependaele, Centre for Psycholinguistics, University of Antwerp, Prinsstraat 13, 2000 Antwerpen, Belgium.
Email: kevin.diependaele@ua.ac.be
Kevin Diependaele was supported by a research grant of the Fund for Scientific Research Flanders. The authors would like to thank Ram Frost, Cristina Burani and Len Katz for their helpful comments on earlier versions of this article.

http://www.tandf.co.uk/journals/pp/01690965.html   DOI: 10.1080/01690960444000197

Over the past decades a growing set of empirical data on the recognition of morphologically complex words has suggested that morphemic information plays a crucial role in the processing and representation of these words. Despite the many attestations of morphological effects, collected with a variety of techniques (see McQueen & Cutler, 1998, for a review), there is no consensus among researchers as to the representational architecture underlying these effects. Within the visual word recognition domain, three broad theoretical approaches can be distinguished in this regard. These approaches differ mainly in terms of where morphemic representations are hypothesised to be located in the processing hierarchy that moves from sensory features to semantic representations.

In a single-route prelexical decomposition model (e.g., Taft, 1994; Taft & Forster, 1975) an obligatory morphological parsing mechanism is assumed to isolate potential roots in letter strings, with the purpose of enabling lexical access to morphologically complex words, which are built from this root. By definition, such a prelexical process is purely form-based, as it can rely only on the orthographic pattern of morphemes. As a result, in quite a few cases it will make an unsuccessful access attempt, using a letter sequence that matches the spelling pattern of a morpheme but does not correspond to a real morpheme in the word being processed (i.e., a pseudomorpheme such as -er in *finger*). It follows that, in principle, this parsing mechanism can be regarded as being blind to the morphological status of the whole word. Dual-route models of morphological processing (e.g., Caramazza, Laudanna, & Romani, 1988; Schreuder & Baayen, 1995) also have a prelexical decomposition route as part of the word recognition process, and, as in the single-route model, its operation is automatic. However, in this type of model decomposition is not a prerequisite for the recognition of each morphologically complex word. For instance, in race models (e.g., Schreuder & Baayen, 1995) the decomposition route competes with a whole-word recognition route, which attempts to match the entire letter sequence with a stored orthographic representation. If the whole-word route achieves access faster than the decomposition route, the morphological structure of the word has played no decisive role in the recognition process. Despite the difference between single and dual-route models of morphological processing, they have one important feature in common: in both approaches morphological effects originate from a sublexical or prelexical decomposition process.

In a recent alternative proposal, however, morphological effects are situated at a level beyond whole-word representations: the so-called supralexical model of morphology (Giraudo & Grainger, 2000, 2001, 2003). This model has been conceived within the general framework of a hierarchical interactive-activation model (McClelland & Rumelhart,

1981), where word recognition is seen as an activation process that proceeds from low-level sensory codes, over whole-word form (lexical) representations, to higher-level semantic representations. In the supralexical architecture, morphemic representations are located between whole-word form and higher-level semantic representations. Thus, morphemic representations can only become active after they have been contacted by whole-word form representations. In turn, an active morphemic unit sends back activation to all form representations that are compatible with it. For the present purposes it is important to note that, in contrast to what is the case in the sublexical models described above, morphological codes are defined as abstract, form-independent representations. We will return to this issue after reviewing the critical evidence favouring the supralexical model.

The data that have been gathered in support of the supralexical model come from masked priming experiments. In this technique (Forster & Davis, 1984), a briefly presented (usually around 50 ms) visual prime word is immediately followed by a visual target word. The prime is both forward masked by a row of hash marks (#####; presented for about 500 ms) and backward masked by the target. Since the brief prime duration and the masking procedure make the primes unavailable for conscious report, effects of the prime on responses to targets are assumed to reflect the automatic preactivation of representations shared by prime and target. Using the masked priming technique in combination with a French lexical decision task (i.e., a speeded word-nonword decision task), Giraudo and Grainger reported several results that are hard to explain within the sublexical framework. In a first study they tested for the effect of surface frequency and cumulative root frequency on the size of morphological priming (Giraudo & Grainger, 2000). In both cases, primes were a suffixed-derived form of the free root target. Contrary to what would be expected on the basis of the sublexical decomposition hypothesis, they found that the magnitude of morphological priming was not modulated by the cumulative root frequency of the prime words. Instead, the surface frequency of the primes determined the effect, which is compatible with the view that information about a word's morphology only becomes available after its whole-word representation has been activated. Giraudo and Grainger (2001) also found that suffixed derivations and their free roots are equally good primes for other derivations of the same root. This contradicts the notion of a time-consuming decomposition mechanism, since one would expect derivational primes to have had less opportunity to facilitate target processing than the free roots. In the same study, priming was not obtained when primes were monomorphemic words containing a pseudo-root at their beginning (e.g., *brothel-BROTH*), which is at odds with a blind morphological decomposition.

However, despite the evidence provided by Giraudo and Grainger, recent masked priming studies in French and English challenge the supralexical hypothesis (Longtin, Segui, & Hallé, 2003; Rastle, Davis, & New, in press). In these studies, priming of free root targets was obtained by suffixed primes with a semantically opaque relation to the target (e.g. *department-DEPART*) and by monomorphemic primes that consisted of a pseudo-root and a pseudo-suffix (so-called pseudo-derived primes; e.g., *brother-BROTH*). Both these prime types can be considered as semantically opaque, since their meaning is not predictable from the meaning of their constituent morphemes. Henceforth, we will therefore speak of *opaque derivations* when referring to these primes. In line with Giraudo and Grainger (2001) the above studies found no evidence for priming when monomorphemic primes contained a pseudo-root but no pseudo-suffix. Taken together, these results seem to suggest that as soon as a given letter sequence is fully decomposable into (pseudo-) morphemes, parsing will take place (see also Frost, Forster, & Deutsch, 1997, for similar findings in Hebrew). Clearly, this pattern can be readily accounted for by the sublexical approach to morphological representation, since it suggests that only the morphological surface structure determines morphological priming effects.

In the present paper we report two experiments that were designed as a further test of the supralexical and sublexical accounts. As noted before, a major difference between these approaches is the nature of morphemic representations. Whereas these representations are purely form-based in a sublexical framework, they are situated at an abstract, form-independent level in the supralexical architecture. In such a supralexical architecture, morphological representations receive input from both whole-word orthographic and phonological representations. These morphemic representations can therefore be considered as amodal representations (i.e., independent of processing in the visual and auditory modality), that reflect learned regularities between word forms and their meaning. As a consequence, the supralexical account predicts that morphological priming effects should not be restricted to an intra-modal priming situation, but should also occur in a cross-modal priming setting.

One widely used paradigm in the literature on morphological processing is the so-called cross-modal immediate priming paradigm (Marslen-Wilson, Tyler, Waksler, & Older, 1994), where an overt (i.e., conscious) auditory prime word is immediately followed by a visually presented target word. Several studies reported significant effects of prime-target morphological overlap with this paradigm (e.g., Frost, Deutsch, Gilboa, Tannenbaum, & Marslen-Wilson, 2000; Longtin et al., 2003; Marslen-Wilson et al., 1994; Meunier & Segui, 2002). However, since prime stimuli are unmasked and easily identifiable with this procedure, participants are able to develop hypotheses regarding the manipulated prime-target relationship. Therefore, this technique is susceptible to strategic biases and the results obtained with it might not reflect automatic processes evoked by the primes.

Recently, Kouider and Dupoux (2001) and Grainger, Diependaele, Spinelli, Ferrand and Farioli (2003) developed a masked prime version of cross-modal priming. In this procedure, a visual masked prime is followed by either a visual or an auditory target. When a target is presented auditorily, a visual backward mask is displayed. Kouider and Dupoux (2001) found that in a lexical decision task, cross-modal identity priming (i.e., priming with identical primes and targets) only became reliable with prime exposures of 67 ms, a duration at which they obtained a significant result in a prime visibility test. However, Grainger et al. (2003) demonstrated that by adopting a stronger backward masking procedure (i.e., a random string of uppercase consonants instead of a fixed string of ampersands) significant cross-modal identity priming can already be observed with a 53 ms prime exposure in the absence of conscious processing of the primes. They interpreted this result within the framework of a bi-modal interactive-activation model (Grainger & Ferrand, 1994). In this architecture, parallel routes for visual and auditory word recognition are heavily interconnected both at the sublexical and lexical level. Interestingly, Grainger et al.'s (2003) backward masking procedure was inspired by an unpublished study by Ford and Marslen-Wilson (2001) in which mixed evidence was found for masked cross-modal morphological priming.

Within the bi-modal framework, masked cross-modal morphological priming effects could reflect a level of amodal morphological representation that mediates between whole-word orthographic and phonological representations and semantics. Nevertheless, the framework could also capture these cross-modal morphological effects at a sublexical level of representation, in terms of mappings between sublexical orthographic and phonological morphemic representations. However, the fact that the morphological structure of a word becomes available through a blind parsing routine in the sublexical account, whereas it is retrieved through a lexical representation in the supralexical account, leads to distinct predictions concerning the nature of cross-modal morphological priming effects. According to the sublexical account, these should be found whenever a prime and a target share (pseudo-) morphemes. It thus follows that there should be no differences between semantically transparent and opaque prime-target pairs. The supralexical account, however, predicts that cross-modal morphological priming should only be obtained with primes and targets that have a semantically transparent relationship, since only these will share representations at the morphemic level. A suggestive outcome in the study by Longtin et al. (2003) is that opaque derivations did not produce significant effects in a cross-modal immediate priming situation. However, as noted above, it is uncertain whether this result truly reflects the underlying representational architecture.

When taken together, the masked cross-modal priming paradigm and the contrast between morphologically structured words that are semantically transparent and those that are opaque, offer us the necessary tools to provide a critical test of the sublexical and supralexical approaches to morphological processing. In our first experiment we used transparent Dutch suffixed-derivations and pseudo-derivations as the critical prime types and their (pseudo-) root as targets. We evaluated priming against both an unrelated and an orthographic priming condition. The critical question was whether masked cross-modal priming would occur with derived primes and whether or not this would also be true for pseudo-derived primes. Our second experiment provided a more detailed investigation of these issues using several prime exposure durations and French stimulus materials. The design and stimulus set were largely identical to those used in the study by Longtin et al. (2003) where robust priming was found for both transparent and opaque items. In order to obtain information about the time-course of the different priming effects, we tested (pseudo-) root priming at three different prime exposure durations, using the incremental priming technique (Jacobs, Grainger, & Ferrand, 1995) in combination with a psychophysical approach. The critical primes were transparent suffix-derivations and opaque suffix-derivations (including pseudo-derivations).

EXPERIMENT 1

Method

Participants.   Thirty-six undergraduate students at the University of Antwerp took part in Experiment 1 for course credit. All were native speakers of Dutch, and had normal or corrected-to-normal vision, and reported having no hearing impairment.

Stimuli and design.   Word stimuli were selected from the CELEX Dutch database (Baayen, Piepenbrock, & Gulikers, 1995). All word items are listed in Appendix 1.

Ninety words and ninety nonwords served as target items in the derived priming block. All word targets were free roots. They had an average printed frequency of 146 occurrences per million (range = 3–2040, SD = 314) and an average length of 4.19 letters (range = 3–7, SD = 0.97). For each target three types of prime were selected, defining the levels of the

Prime Type factor: (a) a suffix-derived prime: a semantically transparent derived word whose root matched the target (e.g., *domheid-DOM*, "stupidity-stupid"), (b) an orthographic control prime: a semantically unrelated monomorphemic word whose word beginning matched the target (e.g., *dominee-DOM*, "preacher-stupid"), and (c) an unrelated prime: a semantically unrelated monomorphemic word with no formal overlap with the target (e.g., *paprika-DOM*, "pepper-stupid"). The derived primes had an average printed frequency of 16 occurrences per million (range = 1–428, SD = 46.90) and were on average 6.94 letters long (range = 4–10, SD = 1.13). Orthographic and unrelated control primes were matched for frequency and length with the morphologically related primes on an item-by-item basis (this was confirmed by means of pair-wise t-tests; all ts < 1). For each word target, a nonword was constructed that shared the same consonant-vowel structure and that did not violate the phonotactic rules of Dutch. In order to have nonword conditions that were comparable to those in the word set, three types of nonword primes were selected for each nonword target. In the "morphologically related" condition, a real suffix was added to the nonword target (e.g., *jumheid-JUM*). This suffix always matched the suffix of the derived word prime, with which the particular nonword item was paired. For the construction of the orthographic and unrelated control primes, the same criteria regarding form overlap were used as with the word items. Again, care was taken that all nonword primes were orthographically regular and pronounceable in Dutch.

In the pseudo-derived priming block, 72 words and 72 nonwords were used as targets. Word targets were free roots and had an average printed frequency of 312 occurrences per million (range = 2–4956, SD = 966) and an average length of 3.72 letters (range = 2–6, SD = 0.77). Except for the morphologically related prime condition, the levels of the Prime Type factor were defined as in the derived priming block. Critical primes were now pseudo-derivations of the targets, i.e., semantically unrelated monomorphemic words whose orthographic pattern was the concatenation of a pseudo-root and a pseudo-suffix (e.g., *branding-BRAND*, "surf-fire"). Pseudo-derived primes had an average printed frequency of 40 occurrences per million (range = 1–575, SD = 91) and an average length of 6.11 letters (range = 4–8, SD = 1.11). As in the derived priming block, matching for surface frequency and length between the different prime categories was done on an item-by-item basis (all ts < 1). The nonword items were obtained in exactly the same manner as in the derived priming block.

For both the derived priming and the pseudo-derived priming block, six experimental lists were constructed by rotating the factors Prime Type (related–orthographic control–unrelated control) and Target Modality (visual–auditory) over participants and materials, using a Latin Square design. Each participant received one list in the derived priming and the pseudo-derived priming block, with the order of blocks counterbalanced over participants.

Procedure. The experimental session began with a practice block, followed by the two experimental blocks and finally, a prime visibility test. The practice block consisted of 24 trials. The stimulus types and the procedure in the practice block were similar to those used in the experimental blocks.

In the derived priming block 180 trials were presented, and in the pseudo-derived priming block 144 trials were presented, both in random order. Within each block, half of the word and nonword targets were presented visually and the other half auditorily. All visual stimuli appeared in white fixed-width font (Courier New) against a black background on a monitor with a 75Hz refresh rate (a 13.33ms refresh cycle). Auditory stimuli were recorded by a female Dutch native speaker. They were presented during the experiment via a "Sennheiser HD 280" headset, connected to a "Creative Sound Blaster AudioPCI (WDM)" soundboard.

At the beginning of each trial a forward mask (11 hash marks) was presented for 493 ms, together with two vertical lines, one above and one beneath the centre of the forward mask. This was immediately followed by the presentation of the prime. The prime stayed on the screen for 53 ms (4 refresh cycles of a 75Hz video monitor) and was printed in lowercase (Courier New 12 point). After the prime presentation, a backward mask immediately followed on the screen. This mask was composed of a pseudo-random string of 11 uppercase consonants (e.g., WCXPLSTHNZD). For each target a separate backward mask was constructed that was used with this target in all six conditions. Care was taken that the backward mask did not contain any consonants from the target or one of its primes. In case of visual target presentations, the backward mask was replaced by the visual target after 13 ms. Visual targets then stayed on the screen until the end of the trial. They were printed in uppercase letters and were one and a half times bigger than the primes and masks (Courier New 18 point). On auditory trials, the target was also presented after exactly 13 ms, but here the mask stayed on the screen until the end of the trial. All visual stimuli were centred on the screen. Participants were asked to decide as quickly and accurately as possible whether the target stimulus was a Dutch word or not, regardless of the modality it was presented in. No mention was made of the prior presentation of the prime stimuli. Participants gave their responses by pressing one of the two front buttons on a "Microsoft SideWinder game pad", connected to the game port of the computer. Participants gave word-nonword responses with their preferred hands. As soon as a response was given, the screen was cleared for 533 ms before the next trial began. The response deadline was set to 4000 ms. The experiment was controlled using DMDX (Forster & Forster, 2003).

The visibility test consisted of 48 trials. Contrary to the main experiment, here, all targets were words and were primed by either an unrelated word or an unrelated nonword. Again, on half of the trials a visual target was presented and on the other half an auditory target. In each modality, half of the targets were paired with an unrelated word prime and half with an unrelated nonword prime. All stimuli were selected in an equal proportion from each of the experimental blocks. The structure of the trials in the visibility test consisted of the same sequence of events as in the experimental trials, with the exception that there was no response deadline. Participants were informed about the presentation of primes prior to the targets. They were asked to decide whether a prime consisted of a Dutch word or not, and to guess if they had no idea. Responses were given in the same way as in the experimental session. Six versions were constructed of the visibility test to make sure that participants received no prime-target pairings that they had encountered in the experiment itself. Additionally, targets were always presented in the opposite modality to that of the main experiment.

Results

Prior to the analyses, error responses (6.6% of the data) and outliers (RTs faster than 400 ms or slower than 1500 ms; 0.6% of the data) were removed from the RT data. Because some items produced error scores above 50% in some conditions, we removed the data from one word item and six nonword items in the derived priming block, and those of seven words and four nonwords in the pseudo-derived priming block (see Appendix 1). Mean RTs and error data per experimental condition are shown in Table 1 for the derived priming block, and in Table 2 for the pseudo-derived priming block.

The data were analysed separately for derived priming and pseudo-derived priming blocks, and for word and nonword targets. We ran ANOVAs on the RT data for correct responses, and the error rates, with Target Modality (visual–auditory) and Prime Type (related–orthographic control–unrelated) as main independent variables. Additionally, we included the factors Latin-Square Group and Presentation Order (the order in which the two experimental blocks were presented to a particular participant) in the analysis by participants, in order to account for the variance associated with these variables. In the analysis by items we only included Latin-Square Group as an extra factor, since the inclusion of Presentation Order generated too many empty cells. For both experiments reported here, all F values were calculated by participants (F_1) and by items (F_2). Unless stated otherwise, there always was a significant main effect of the Target Modality factor (with $p < .05$ for both F_1 and F_2), indicating slower RTs and less accuracy for auditory targets compared with visual targets. For reasons of parsimony, we will report the details of significant effects only.

TABLE 1

Mean reaction times (in ms) and percent errors in the derived priming block in Experiment 1

	Primes	Within modality		Between modality	
		Mean RT	Errors	Mean RT	Errors
Words	Derived	602	1%	856	5%
	Orthographic control	626	4%	871	4%
	Unrelated	628	3%	876	5%
	effect against orthographic baseline:	24**	3%**	15*	−1%
	effect against unrelated baseline:	26**	2%*	20*	0%
Nonwords	Derived	736	5%	932	5%
	Orthographic control	737	6%	955	4%
	Unrelated	751	7%	941	6%
	effect against orthographic baseline:	1	1%	23*	−1%
	effect against unrelated baseline:	15(*)	2%	9	1%

(*) $p < .10$; * $p < .05$; ** $p < .01$. $n = 36$.

TABLE 2

Mean reaction times (in ms) and percent errors in the pseudo-derived priming block in Experiment 1

	Primes	Within modality		Between modality	
		Mean RT	Errors	Mean RT	Errors
Words	Pseudo-derived	625	4%	858	5%
	Orthographic control	640	4%	845	4%
	Unrelated	623	3%	856	5%
	effect against orthographic baseline:	15(*)	0%	−13	−1%
	effect against unrelated baseline:	−2	−1%	−2	0%
Nonwords	Pseudo-derived	734	4%	972	4%
	Orthographic control	731	4%	966	6%
	Unrelated	728	3%	972	5%
	effect against orthographic baseline:	−3	0%	−6	2%
	effect against unrelated baseline:	−6	−1%	0	1%

(*) $p < .10$.

Derived priming. In the RT analysis for word targets, the main effect of Prime Type was significant, $F_1(2, 48) = 10.65$, $p < .001$; $F_2(2, 166) = 12.06$, $p < .001$. There was no interaction of Prime Type with Modality (both Fs < 1). Planned comparisons showed reliable priming against both the orthographic baseline, $F_1(1, 24) = 15.50$, $p < .001$; $F_2(1, 83) = 12.17$, $p < .001$; a 23 ms advantage for morphologically related primes, and the unrelated baseline, $F_1(1, 24) = 15.09$, $p < .001$; $F_2(1, 83) = 19.83$, $p < .001$; a 20ms advantage for morphologically related primes. The partial interaction of these effects with Target Modality was not significant (all Fs < 1). All individual priming effects (i.e., per modality and per baseline condition) were significant with $p < .05$ for both F_1 and F_2. In the error scores for words, there was only a significant interaction between priming against the orthographic baseline and Target Modality, $F_1(1, 24) = 6.20$, $p < .03$; $F_2(1, 83) = 5.27$, $p < .03$. Priming was significant for visual targets, $F_1(1, 24) = 8.53$, $p < .008$; $F_2(1, 83) = 8.85$, $p < .004$; 3% fewer errors with related primes, but not for auditory targets (both Fs < 1).

The RTs for nonwords showed significant facilitation for related primes against both the orthographic baseline (although only marginally in the F_2 analysis) and the unrelated baseline: orthographic, $F_1(1, 24) = 4.37$, $p < .05$; $F_2(1, 78) = 3.40$, $p = .07$; a 12 ms advantage; unrelated, $F_1(1, 24) = 4.53$, $p < .05$; $F_2(1, 78) = 4.89$, $p < .03$; a 12 ms advantage. However, priming against the orthographic baseline interacted marginally with Target Modality, $F_1(1, 24) = 3.54$, $p = .07$; $F_2(1, 78) = 3.70$, $p = .06$. An inspection of the individual priming effects revealed a significant facilitation only for auditory targets and only against the orthographic baseline, $F_1(1, 24) = 7.74$, $p < .02$; $F_2(1, 78) = 7.49$, $p < .008$; a 23 ms advantage. The error analysis for nonwords showed no main effect of Target Modality (both Fs < 1) and no other significant effects.

Pseudo-derived priming. For words, the RT analysis showed a significant interaction between Target Modality and Prime Type, $F_1(2, 48) = 4.36$, $p < .02$; $F_2(2, 118) = 4.46$, $p < .02$. The effect of priming against the orthographic baseline interacted significantly with Target Modality, $F_1(1, 24) = 5.66$, $p < .03$; $F_2(1, 59) = 5.66$, $p < .02$. Priming seemed only evident for visual targets. However, the facilitation effect was only marginally significant, $F_1(1, 24) = 3.53$, $p = .07$; $F_2(1, 59) = 3.13$, $p = .08$; a 15 ms advantage. The difference between the orthographic and the unrelated baseline also interacted significantly with Target Modality, $F_1(1, 24) = 8.44$, $p < .008$; $F_2(1, 59) = 6.91$, $p < .02$. Further investigation of this interaction indicated significantly longer RTs with orthographic control primes in the visual condition only, $F_1(1, 24) = 4.55$, $p < .05$; $F_2(1, 59) = 6.16$, $p < .02$; a 17 ms disadvantage. The error scores for words yielded no significant results.

There were also no significant results in the RT and the error analysis for nonwords.

Interactions across experimental blocks.   In order to examine interactions across the two experimental blocks, we conducted an additional analysis on the combined data, including Priming Block (derived–pseudo-derived) as an independent variable.

In the RT analysis for word targets, Priming Block interacted significantly with Prime Type, $F_1(2, 48) = 5.97, p < .005; F_2(2, 284) = 5.98, p < .003$. The planned comparisons showed that the facilitation of related primes interacted significantly across blocks, both against the orthographic baseline, $F_1(1, 24) = 6.44, p < .02; F_2(1, 142) = 4.44, p < .04$, and the unrelated baseline, $F_1(1, 24) = 10.26, p < .004; F_2(1, 142) = 11.32$, $p < .001$. None of these partial interactions were further modified by Target Modality. In the error analysis for words, there were no significant interactions with Priming Block. No such interactions were found in the RT and error analysis of the nonword data either.

Prime visibility.   Finally, we calculated a d' measure for every participant, based on their forced choice data in the visibility test. The average d' value was 0.08 for visual targets and 0.03 for auditory targets. Both means were not significantly different from zero, $t(35) = 0.94, p = .35$ and $t(35) = 0.33, p = .75$, respectively. Neither did the means for visual and auditory targets differ significantly from each other, $t(35) = 0.48, p = .63$. There were no significant correlations between the d' values and the size of any of the priming effects.

Discussion

In our first experiment we investigated masked visual–visual and visual–auditory priming of free root targets by suffix-derived primes and pseudo-derived primes in Dutch. The results of Experiment 1 can be summarised as follows: lexical decision latencies were facilitated by derived primes both when targets were presented visually and auditorily. This facilitation was significant relative to an orthographic and an unrelated baseline condition. Pseudo-derived primes provided a marginally significant facilitation with visual targets and only when measured against the orthographic priming condition. However, since orthographic control primes showed a significant inhibitory effect relative to the unrelated baseline, the facilitatory trend with pseudo-derived primes may actually have been due to inhibition from these orthographic controls. In short, the above pattern shows that only priming with transparent morphologically complex words resulted in robust facilitation of visual and auditory target processing, as confirmed by the significant interaction of the priming effects across blocks. The results of Experiment 1 therefore match the predictions of the supralexical model that were outlined in the introduction section.

Interestingly, Experiment 1 only provides a weak replication of the opaque priming effects that have been previously reported in the visual domain (Longtin et al., 2003; Rastle et al., in press). While these studies found reliable priming effects against both an orthographic and an unrelated baseline, we only found a trend towards facilitation relative to our orthographic priming condition. Moreover, as noted above, it appears that we have observed inhibition from the orthographic control primes rather than facilitation from the pseudo-derived primes. A potentially critical difference between our orthographic controls and those used by Longtin et al. (2003) and Rastle et al. (in press), relates to the fact that we were not always able to select words that had a pseudo-root at their beginning (i.e., the *brothel-BROTH* type items). This was due to the within-items manipulation of the priming conditions in our design. Therefore, we were sometimes forced to select primes that were not perfect orthographic controls in terms of letter positions and number of shared letters (e.g., *hengel-HELD*). As a result, there was a bias towards a greater orthographic overlap between targets and (pseudo-) derived primes, than between targets and orthographic primes for approximately 50% of the items. Although our within-items design is arguably superior to the between-items design used by Longtin et al. (2003) and Rastle et al. (in press), it is clear that this issue might hamper a straightforward interpretation of the results of Experiment 1. Additionally, it could also be argued that, especially in case of cross-modal priming, a close matching for the phonological overlap between the (pseudo-) derived primes and the targets is of great importance. A further inspection of the materials reveals that in several cases the orthographic controls also differed from the test primes on properties such as number of syllables and syllabic parsing (e.g., *dom/heid-*do/mi/nee-*DOM*).

Our second experiment was therefore primarily designed to eliminate all potentially critical biases in our first stimulus set in order to obtain more directly comparable intra-modal and cross-modal priming with transparent and opaque derivations. Our first goal was to provide orthographic controls that would take into account the problems mentioned above.[1] On the other hand, we were also concerned with some unbalanced factors between the two types of priming in Experiment 1. These factors were: the specific suffixes that were used, the prime-target frequencies, and the number of items in each set. Since most of the above issues were due to item restrictions, imposed by the within-items design in Experiment 1, we

---

[1] We thank Cristina Burani for pointing out such potential problems.

decided to shift our design to a between items comparison of the priming conditions. As such, the design became directly comparable with that of Longtin et al. (2003) for French, and that of Rastle et al. (in press) for English. In order to obtain an even more direct comparability with these studies, we also decided to use French materials that were largely identical to those tested in the study by Longtin et al. (2003). Opaque derivations now consisted of both pseudo-derivations and genuine-derivations that were semantically opaque. Henceforth, we will refer to this condition as the 'opaque priming condition'.

However, regardless of the differences in materials, there could be another critical factor in our design determining our failure to replicate the visual pseudo-derived priming effect. Namely, Experiment 1 applied a longer prime duration and prime-target stimulus onset asynchrony (SOA) than the experiments of Longtin et al. (2003) and Rastle et al. (in press). While our prime duration and SOA were set to 53 ms and 67 ms respectively, these studies typically used a prime duration and SOA of around 40 ms. In particular a study by Rastle, Davis, Marslen-Wilson, and Tyler (2000) suggests that this procedural difference might be of great importance. These authors showed that while priming from opaque derivations yielded a significant facilitation (against unrelated controls) at a prime duration and SOA of 43 ms, there was a gradual decrease in priming when prime duration was increased to 72 ms and 230 ms. Specifically, it might be that the prime duration and SOA in Experiment 1 were too long to observe facilitation from opaque primes. Needless to say that in that case the possibility still remains that cross-modal priming also occurs for opaque primes, but at shorter prime durations and/or SOAs.

Hence, as an additional objective in Experiment 2 we also wanted to obtain information regarding the specific time-course of the different priming effects at study. We therefore chose to use the incremental priming technique as proposed by Jacobs et al. (1995). The technique involves the gradual increase of prime intensity/duration starting from a level that is too low to influence target processing. As such, priming can be evaluated not only against a different priming condition (the *across-condition* baseline; e.g., an unrelated priming condition), but also against the starting point (the *within-condition* baseline). As argued by Jacobs et al. (1995), this double-baseline allows for a more reliable measurement of priming effects. In Experiment 2 derived, opaque and orthographic priming were evaluated against an unrelated baseline at 40 ms and 67 ms prime exposures (53 ms and 80 ms SOA, respectively). A prime duration of 13ms (26 ms SOA) provided us with the within-condition baseline. Finally, we also adopted a psychophysical approach in Experiment 2 (e.g., Frost, Ahissar, Gotesman, & Tayeb, 2003; Jacobs et al., 1995) in which we presented participants with primes and targets repeatedly, once for each prime duration. By using this procedure we could prevent the possible interaction of subject variability with the prime exposure conditions. The large number of trials that are presented to each participant also ensured a more stable measurement of priming effects.

EXPERIMENT 2

Method

Participants.   Thirty-eight undergraduate students at Université de Provence took part in Experiment 2 for course credit. All participants were native speakers of French and reported having normal or corrected-to-normal vision, and no hearing impairment.

Stimuli and design.   Our set of word items was largely based on the primes and targets tested in the Longtin et al. (2003) study. However, in order to complete our design and to replace unfavourable items in the Longtin et al. selection, we selected additional items. The complete set of word items used in Experiment 2 is given in Appendix 2. Word frequency counts were retrieved from the LEXIQUE French database (New, Pallier, Ferrand, & Matos, 2001).

We selected 144 words and 144 nonwords to serve as target items in the experiment. All word targets were free roots. They were divided into three sets, each consisting of 48 items. Each set corresponded to one of three priming conditions (i.e., the three levels of the Priming factor): the transparent condition, the opaque condition, and the orthographic control condition. Within each condition, a related and an unrelated prime were selected for every target (defining the two levels of the Relatedness factor). In the transparent condition, related primes were semantically transparent suffix-derived words whose root matched the target (e.g., *clochette-CLOCHE*, "small bell-bell"). The related primes in the opaque condition were also words with a surface structure that consisted of an existing root (that matched the target) and an existing suffix. However, contrary to the transparent condition there was no obvious semantic relationship between the prime and the target. More specifically, primes in the opaque condition consisted of pseudo-derivations (e.g., *baguette-BAGUE*, "French bread-ring"; 30 items) and opaque derivations (e.g., *vignette-VIGNE*, "vignette-vine"; 18 items).[2] Across the transparent and the opaque condition, primes

---

[2] We included both word types since there is no theoretical reason to distinguish these word types from each other in the present context (see Rastle et al., 2000, Rastle and Davis, 2003, Rastle et al., in press, for a similar approach). As stated in the introduction, both types can be considered as semantically opaque (i.e., their meaning is not predictable from the meaning of their constituent morphemes). The amount of pseudo-derived items was higher in this condition, since we could not select an equal number of both types that met the specific demands of our selection procedure.

were matched for suffixes on an item-by-item basis. Finally, in the orthographic control condition related primes and targets were chosen so that they matched the transparent and opaque condition as closely as possible in terms of prime-target orthographic and phonological overlap (see Table 3).

Across all three priming conditions we matched related primes and targets on length and frequency in a list-wise fashion (all $ts < 1$; see Table 3 for details). For each target, an unrelated prime was chosen that showed no clear formal and semantic overlap with it. The unrelated primes were matched on length and frequency with the related primes on an item-by-item basis (all pair-wise $ts < 1$). As in Experiment 1, the nonword items were presented in the same priming conditions as the word items. We therefore constructed a "transparent", "opaque" and "orthographic" priming condition, each consisting of 48 targets. In accordance with Longtin et al. (2003) all primes were words. Instead of pairing each nonword target with both a related and an unrelated prime, we paired one half of the targets with a related prime and the other half with an unrelated prime (in each priming condition). So each nonword target was always accompanied by the same prime in our design. In the "transparent" condition related primes were suffix-derived forms and targets were formed by substituting one or more letters of the root (e.g., *totalité-TUTAL* from *totalité-TOTAL*). In the "opaque" condition targets were constructed in an identical way, but here the primes were opaque derivations (e.g., *aversion-IVERSE* from *aversion-AVERSE*). The related

TABLE 3
Stimulus characteristics for the word items in Experiment 2

	Priming condition								
	Transparent (n = 48)			Opaque (n = 48)			Orthographic (n = 48)		
	Mean	Range	SD	Mean	Range	SD	Mean	Range	SD
Target length	5.27	3–8	1.07	4.79	3–7	1.01	4.42	3–7	0.92
Prime length	7.56	5–10	1.17	7.08	5–9	1.07	7.13	5–10	1.16
Target frequency*	36.17	0.42–260.97	58.65	32.55	0.23–351.19	67.84	31.87	1.29–216.03	38.74
Prime frequency*	10.80	0.13–126.16	21.11	10.35	0.16–100.23	16.03	10.40	0.13–41.84	10.01
Graphemic overlap**	5.04	3–7	1.01	4.56	3–6	0.90	4.25	3–6	0.89
Phonetic overlap***	3.27	1–5	0.79	3.04	1–5	0.85	3.15	1–5	0.95
Syllabic overlap****	0.50	0–2	0.55	0.38	0–2	0.57	0.58	0–2	0.65

* number of occurrences per million.
** number of shared letters in the same order
*** number of shared phonemes in the same order
**** number of shared syllables in the same order.

items in the "orthographic" condition consisted of nonword targets that were fully or partially embedded at the beginning of the word primes (e.g., *mercredi-MERCRE*). All primes and targets in the nonword conditions were matched on average length with the primes and targets in the word conditions (all list-wise *ts* < 1). Care was taken that all nonword targets were orthographically regular and pronounceable in French.

Due to the limited amount of different suffixes that appeared in the transparent and opaque word conditions (i.e., *-eau, -elle, -er, -et, -ette, -on, -ure, -ier, -able, -age, -eur, -oir,* and *-ial*) there was a high amount of repetition for orthographic word endings in the case of related transparent and opaque primes, compared to the related orthographic primes for word targets. Therefore, we avoided using any of these suffixes in the "transparent" and "opaque" primes for nonword targets. Moreover, the related "orthographic" primes and the unrelated primes for nonword targets were selected so that they shared orthographic endings with the related orthographic primes for word targets (e.g., *haricot* was selected in the nonword set for *abricot* in the word set). This resulted in the fact that orthographic word endings of all the related primes for word targets were repeated on average four times over the entire stimulus set.

For the word targets, four lists were constructed by rotating the factors Relatedness (related—unrelated) and Target Modality (visual—auditory) within each level of the Priming factor (transparent—opaque—orthographic control) using a Latin Square design. For the nonword set, two lists were obtained through the rotation of the Target Modality factor within each level of the Priming factor and the Relatedness factor. Every word list was tied to one of the two nonword lists. For each of the four resulting experimental lists, three versions were created by rotating the Exposure Duration factor (13 ms—40 ms—67 ms) within each cell of the design. So across these three versions, prime-target pairs were repeated, however, at different prime durations. By rotating prime duration levels within each cell, we avoided any systematic confound with the other factors defining the design. A participant received all three versions of a given experimental list. In order to minimise the impact of target repetition effects, each participant received the entire set of targets once as practice trials. These trials were taken evenly from each of the three versions of the experimental list. In line with Frost et al. (2003) we argue that, although target repetition was not systematically confounded with any of our experimental conditions, these dummy trials allow to minimise error variance induced by repetition by bringing the impact of repetition closer to the asymptote.

Procedure.   In the experimental session each participant received a practice block, three experimental blocks and a prime visibility test, in that order. During the practice block a participant was presented with each of the 144 word and 144 nonword targets for the first time. Half of the word and nonword targets were presented visually, and the other half auditorily. The same targets were then repeated three times, once in each experimental block. In both the practice block and the experimental blocks, one third of the primes were presented for 13 ms, one third for 40 ms and one third for 67 ms (respectively 1, 3 and 5 refresh cycles of a 75Hz video monitor). A given prime-target pair appeared at each of these prime durations, across the experimental blocks. The presentations within each block and the order of the experimental blocks were randomised over participants. After each block the participants were allowed to take a short break. They restarted the experiment by pressing the space bar on a standard PC keyboard.

The visibility test was constructed following the same principles as in Experiment 1. We created four lists, each consisting of 72 prime-target pairs. However, as for the main experiment, three versions of each list were obtained by rotating the three prime exposure levels within each cell. Every participant thus received a given list three times with a different prime exposure configuration. Participants completed all 216 trials in random order and without a break.

Auditory stimuli were recorded by a female French native speaker and word/nonword responses were now given via the two front buttons on a "Logitec Wingman Precision game pad". All further procedural characteristics were identical to those of Experiment 1.

Results

We cleaned the RT data by removing error responses (4.2% of the data) and outliers (1.4%). The data of two participants were also removed since they made errors on more than 10% of the trials. Finally, we removed the data of three words and two nonwords (see Appendix 2) because of error scores that exceeded 50% in some conditions. Table 4 gives an overview of the mean RTs and error data for words in each of the conditions.

Preliminary analyses indicated that apart from the main effect of Target Modality, there were no significant results in the RT and error analysis for nonwords. In what follows we will therefore only report the analyses for word items. We first analysed the RTs of correct responses and the error rates in an ANOVA with, as main factors, Target Modality (visual–auditory), Prime Type (transparent–opaque–orthographic control), Relatedness (related–unrelated) and Prime Duration (13 ms–40 ms–67 ms). In order to test our hypotheses regarding the between-condition priming effect (i.e., priming as measured against the unrelated baseline), we then performed a series of planned comparisons on the RT and error data. The

TABLE 4
Mean reaction times (in ms) and percent errors for words in Experiment 2

Priming type		Within modality						Between modality					
		Mean RT			Errors			Mean RT			Errors		
		13 ms	40 ms	67 ms	13 ms	40 ms	67 ms	13 ms	40 ms	67 ms	13 ms	40 ms	67 ms
Transparent	Related	576	560	544	3%	2%	1%	796	796	776	4%	4%	2%
	Unrelated	574	581	587	3%	1%	3%	790	803	806	4%	3%	2%
	effect:	-2	21(*)	43***	0%	-1%	2%**	-6	7	30***	0%	-1%	0%
Opaque	Related	572	574	563	3%	3%	1%	793	799	784	5%	4%	4%
	Unrelated	583	566	583	5%	3%	5%	797	795	805	6%	3%	4%
	effect:	11	-8	20***	0%	0%	4%***	4	-4	21***	0%	-1%	0%
Orthographic	Related	579	579	581	4%	6%	5%	815	808	822	3%	2%	5%
	Unrelated	577	583	592	3%	4%	5%	816	795	806	5%	8%	6%
	effect:	-2	4	11*	0%	-2%	0%**	1	-13	-16*	0%	6%***	1%
	average d' value	-0.04	-0.11	0.07				-0.02	0.04	0.04			

(*) p < .10; * p < .05; ** p < .01; *** p < .001.

within-condition priming effects were assessed via separate ANOVAs (for each level of the Prime Type and Relatedness factor) with Target Modality and Prime Duration as main factors. These analyses tested whether RTs and error scores increased or decreased as a function of prime duration. In all analyses Latin-Square Group was included as an additional factor.

Main analysis.   The RT analysis showed a main effect of Relatedness in both analyses, $F_1(1, 32) = 12.15$, $p < .002$; $F_2(1, 129) = 9.56$, $p < .003$, indicating faster responses following related primes. This effect significantly interacted with Target Modality in the analysis by participants $F_1(1, 32) = 4.43$, $p < .05$; $F_2(1, 129) = 2.20$, $p = .14$. As can be seen in Figure 1, the overall effect of Relatedness tended to be larger for visual target processing. The main effect of Prime Type was significant by participants, $F_1(2, 64) = 15.39$, $p < .001$, but not by items, $F_2(2, 129) = 1.19$, $p = .31$. There was a significant interaction between Prime Type and Relatedness, $F_1(2, 64) = 5.55$, $p < .006$; $F_2(2, 129) = 3.79$, $p < .03$, and between Prime Duration and Relatedness, $F_1(2, 64) = 9.43$, $p < .001$; $F_2(2, 258) = 6.74$, $p < .002$. The former interaction shows that the overall effect of Relatedness was highest in the transparent condition, less pronounced in the opaque condition and close to zero in the orthographic condition. The latter interaction indicates an overall increase in the effect of Relatedness as prime duration increased. Finally, the analysis showed a significant three-way interaction of Relatedness with Prime Type and Duration, $F_1(4, 128) = 4.37$, $p < .003$; $F_2(4, 258) = 4.18$, $p < .003$. This interaction was analysed more closely by means of planned comparisons (see next sections).

In the error analysis, the main effect of Relatedness was significant by both participants and items, $F_1(1, 32) = 5.33$, $p < .03$; $F_2(1, 129) = 4.84$, $p < .03$, indicating less errors after related primes. The main effect of Prime Type was significant by participants, $F_1(2, 64) = 9.68$, $p < .001$, and marginally significant by items, $F_2(2, 129) = 2.76$, $p = .07$. Prime Type interacted significantly with Prime Duration, $F_1(4, 128) = 5.25$, $p < .001$; $F_2(4, 258) = 4.61$, $p < .002$. While error scores tended to decrease with higher prime durations in the transparent and opaque conditions, they increased in the orthographic condition. There were also significant three-way interactions of Target Modality, Prime Type and Relatedness, $F_1(2, 64) = 4.99$, $p < .01$; $F_2(2, 129) = 3.20$, $p < .04$, and Target Modality, Prime Duration and Relatedness, $F_1(2, 64) = 4.47$, $p < .02$; $F_2(2, 258) = 4.35$, $p < .02$. As for the latency data, we will further analyse these interactions using planned comparisons.

Transparent priming.   The RT data showed that transparent primes already yielded a significant facilitation effect (21 ms) at the 40 ms prime duration, but only in case of visual targets (although marginally by

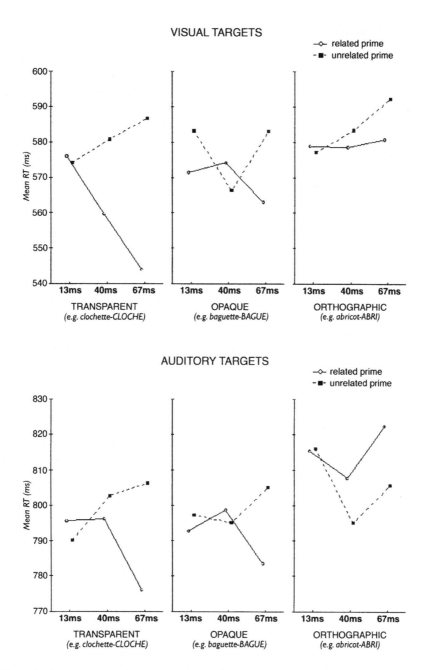

Figure 1. Mean reaction times in Experiment 2 as a function of Target Modality (visual–auditory), Prime Type (transparent–opaque–orthographic), Relatedness (related–unrelated), and Prime Duration (13 ms–40 ms–67 ms).

participants), $F_1(1, 32) = 3.89, p = .06; F_2(1, 129) = 5.70, p < .02$. Priming at 67 ms yielded a significant facilitation in both modalities, $F_1(1, 32) = 42.31, p < .001; F_2(1, 129) = 27.34, p < .001$; a 36 ms advantage. There was a significant interaction between priming at 40 ms and 67 ms, indicating a larger effect at 67 ms, $F_1(1, 32) = 7.36, p < .02; F_2(1, 129) = 7.31, p < .008$; a 22 ms difference. The within-condition priming effect, i.e., the evolution of the effect over the three different prime durations, was significant for related primes, $F_1(2, 64) = 9.40, p < .001; F_2(2, 88) = 12.03, p < .001$. There was a clear decrease in RTs with increasing prime duration. This effect was also significant for unrelated primes, although here RTs increased with increasing prime duration (only marginally by items), $F_1(2, 64) = 3.38, p < .05; F_2(2, 88) = 2.74, p = .07$. Neither effect interacted with Target Modality.

The error scores showed a significant facilitation effect (2%) at the 67ms prime duration in the case of visual targets (although marginally significant by items), $F_1(1, 32) = 8.10, p < .008; F_2(1, 129) = 2.88, p = .10$. This effect was significantly larger than the visual effect at 40 ms (although, again only marginally significant by items), $F_1(1, 32) = 8.45, p < .007; F_2(1, 129) = 3.82, p = .06$. The within-condition effect was only significant in the case of related primes, $F_1(2, 64) = 4.66, p < .02; F_2(2, 88) = 4.98, p < .009$. This reflected the presence of fewer errors at longer prime durations. This effect did not interact with Target Modality.

Opaque priming.   A facilitation effect from opaque primes occurred in the RTs at the 67 ms prime duration only and did not interact with modalities, $F_1(1, 32) = 16.32, p < .001; F_2(1, 129) = 8.70, p < .004$; a 21 ms advantage. This effect was significantly different from priming at 40 ms $F_1(1, 32) = 12.24, p < .002; F_2(1, 129) = 9.18, p < .003$; a 26 ms difference. Within-condition priming was marginally significant for related primes, but only by participants, $F_1(2, 64) = 3.11, p = .05; F_2(2, 86) = 1.93, p = .15$. This reflected a trend towards shorter RTs at longer prime durations. For unrelated primes, within-condition priming was marginally significant in both analyses, $F_1(2, 64) = 3.07, p = .05; F_2(2, 86) = 3.07, p = .05$, but this time the trend was towards longer RTs with increasing prime duration. Neither effect interacted with modality.

The errors showed significant visual priming at the 67 ms duration, $F_1(1, 32) = 15.97, p < .001; F_2(1, 129) = 8.02, p < .006$, reflecting 4% fewer errors in the related condition. This effect differed significantly from priming at the 40 ms condition, $F_1(1, 32) = 8.43, p < .007; F_2(1, 129) = 6.74, p < .02$. The within-condition effect was significant for unrelated primes, $F_1(2, 64) = 6.77, p < .003; F_2(2, 86) = 6.54, p < .003$, indicating a trend towards less errors at longer prime durations. This effect did not interact with Target Modality.

Orthographic priming. The RTs showed that orthographic priming interacted with Target Modality at the 67 ms prime duration. This interaction was significant by participants, $F_1(1, 32) = 9.03, p < .006$, and marginally significant by items, $F_2(1, 129) = 3.63, p = .06$. A closer investigation of the interaction revealed a significant facilitation by participants for visual targets, $F_1(1, 32) = 4.66, p < .04; F_2 < 1$; an 11 ms advantage, and a significant inhibitory effect by participants for auditory targets, $F_1(1, 32) = 4.24, p < .05; F_2(1, 129) = 2.60, p = .11$; a 16 ms disadvantage.

The error scores showed an interaction with Target Modality at 40 ms, $F_1(1, 32) = 11.64, p < .002; F_2(1, 129) = 14.78, p < .001$. Further comparisons showed a significant facilitation for auditory targets only, $F_1(1, 32) = 14.42, p < .001; F_2(1, 129) = 14.00, p < .001$; 6% less errors in case of a related prime. The within-condition priming effect interacted significantly with Target Modality for related primes, $F_1(2, 64) = 4.47, p < .02; F_2(2, 84) = 4.22, p < .02$. There was a trend towards higher error scores with increasing prime duration, but only for auditory targets.

Prime visibility. The average d' value per modality and per prime duration is given in Table 4. None of the means were significantly different from zero and from each other. There were no significant correlations between the d' values and the observed priming effects.

Discussion

A comparison between the related and unrelated conditions in Experiment 2 yields the following picture. Visual target processing was already facilitated by transparent derivations at a 40 ms prime exposure. At 67 ms both transparent and opaque derivations showed a robust facilitation, but transparent primes caused a larger effect than opaque primes. Auditory targets showed a different pattern: significant facilitation effects emerged only at the 67 ms duration, both for transparent and opaque primes and without significant differences between these two prime types. Orthographic primes produced opposite priming effects as a function of target modality at the 67 ms prime duration. While they facilitated visual target processing, they had an inhibitory effect on auditory target processing. These effects were, however, only significant in the analysis by participants. A comparison of the evolution of RTs within conditions, i.e., using the within-condition baseline, supports the distinction between transparent and opaque priming. They show in particular that the facilitatory linear trend in the related conditions was reliable for transparent primes, but only marginally so for opaque primes. Finally, priming from transparent and opaque primes also emerged at 67 ms in the error scores for visual targets.

These results show important differences relative to those obtained in Experiment 1, the most important being that we now obtained significant priming with opaque derivations in both target modalities. This is at odds with the predictions of the supralexical model. However, an even more important finding in Experiment 2 is that the facilitation effect from transparent derivations emerged earlier and was systematically larger than the effect of opaque derivations when the root targets were presented visually. This effect of semantic transparency can not be accounted for by the sublexical account of morphological processing, since it predicts that both transparent and opaque words are treated equally in initial processing stages. The outcome of Experiment 2 thus challenges both the supralexical and the sublexical accounts. Hence, we believe that this pattern of results poses strong constraints for theories of morphological processing.

Note that the results of Experiment 2 also contradict the hypothesis that prime duration and/or SOA was too high in Experiment 1 in order to allow for facilitation from opaque primes. On the contrary, it seems that the pattern in Experiment 1 might reflect the situation in which prime intensity was too low for opaque priming to emerge. We will return to this issue in the general discussion.

Finally, we examined whether a difference in the construction of the opaque conditions in Experiment 1 and 2 might have affected the results. In Experiment 1 all items in this condition were pseudo-derivations, while in Experiment 2 this category consisted of both genuine-derivations that were semantically opaque (18 items) and pseudo-derivations (30 items). We addressed this question via post-hoc comparisons of the priming effects of each type of opaque primes. None of these comparisons showed significant differences.

GENERAL DISCUSSION

The present research aimed at testing the contrasting predictions of the sublexical and supralexical accounts of morphological processing regarding the effects of transparent and opaque suffix-derived (including pseudo-derived) primes in the masked cross-modal priming paradigm.

In Experiment 1 we showed that the subliminal visual presentation (53 ms) of Dutch transparent suffix-derivations facilitated subsequent lexical decision responses to their free root, regardless of whether the root was presented visually or auditorily. Pseudo-derivations only provided a weak priming effect against orthographic control primes and only when their pseudo-root was presented visually. This pattern is readily accounted for by the supralexical account, which predicts that only true morphologically related primes and targets can provide robust intra-modal and cross-modal priming effects under masking conditions. This is because the hypothesised sources of morphological priming effects are supralexical morphological representations that are connected to the lexical representations of prime and target. These supralexical representations can only be accessed by whole-word lexical representations of polymorphemic words that are semantically transparent with regard to their morphemes. In such an architecture, morphological representations form an amodal interface between form and meaning. However, as we argued in detail in the discussion of Experiment 1, some aspects of the experiment prevented us from drawing firm conclusions.

Experiment 2 provided a more thorough investigation of transparent and opaque priming in the masked cross-modal paradigm. We now studied priming effects in a French lexical decision task, using the incremental priming technique in combination with a psychophysical approach. More specifically, each participant encountered a given prime-target pair at three different levels of prime duration (13 ms, 40 ms and 67 ms). The critical prime types corresponded to the ones tested in Experiment 1, however, opaque primes now consisted of pseudo-derivations as well as genuine-derivations that were semantically opaque. In contrast to Experiment 1, the results showed evidence of priming with opaque as well as transparent prime-target pairs in both modalities. Specifically, both prime types showed reliable intra-modal and cross-modal facilitation of their (pseudo-) root at the 67 ms duration. However, priming with transparent derivations already facilitated the visual processing of their roots at a prime duration of 40 ms. There were no effects of opaque derivations at this duration. Moreover, even at the longest prime duration, the visual processing of (pseudo-) roots benefited more from the prior presentation of a transparent prime than from an opaque prime containing that (pseudo-) root. This dissociation between transparent and opaque priming was also confirmed by the fact that the general trend to facilitate target processing with increasing prime duration (i.e., the within-condition priming effect) was reliable in the case of transparent primes, but only marginally so for opaque primes. Thus, while both transparent and opaque primes produced significant priming of their visual or auditorily presented (pseudo-)roots, transparent primes showed both an earlier and a stronger effect on visual targets. Note that, even though Experiment 2 did not include a prime duration condition of 53 ms (i.e., the duration used in Experiment 1), the evidence for facilitation from opaque derivations occurred at a longer duration than the one used in Experiment 1. The results of Experiment 2 thus provide a broader picture that is compatible with the results of Experiment 1.

It is important to emphasise that the present results did not depend on conscious prime processing. We evaluated prime visibility through a forced-choice word-nonword detection task (performed on the primes). This allowed us to calculate d-prime values for each participant via a signal detection analysis. As argued by Grainger et al. (2003), a word-nonword detection task is preferable to a letter-pseudo-letter detection task (as proposed by Kouider and Dupoux, 2001), since the latter may be too conservative and could lead to unfounded claims of conscious prime processing. In the present experiments, none of the observed d-prime values differed significantly from zero, nor did they correlate significantly with any of the observed priming effects. We are therefore confident that primes were not consciously processed in our experiments and that our cross-modal priming effects should be interpreted as a product of a functional interconnection between the visual and auditory processing modalities.

Before considering the theoretical ramifications of our results, we need to discuss their relation to the earlier studies that addressed priming from transparent and opaque derivations in the visual masked priming paradigm (i.e., Longtin et al., 2003; Rastle et al., in press). These studies reported equally large priming effects from transparent and opaque derivations, using a prime duration of approximately 40 ms. Our findings seem to contradict these results,[3] since the 40 ms prime duration only yielded an effect of transparent derivations. Our effect for opaque items only appeared with a 67 ms prime duration. We believe that the reason for this dissociation lies in the backward masking procedure adopted here. In the masked cross-modal priming paradigm (as proposed by Grainger et al., 2003) an extra backward mask is inserted between the prime and the target. This mask consists of a random string of consonants. Grainger et al. (2003) argued that such a backward mask produces higher amounts of interference at low-level letter coding stages, leading to a slower accumulation of the activation induced by the primes. It would therefore be interesting to see whether the use of shorter prime durations (e.g., around 30 ms) in the designs of Longtin et al. (2003) and Rastle et al. (in press) would also show an effect of transparent derivations in the absence of an effect of opaque derivations.

---

[3] Note that the word items used in Experiment 2 were largely identical to those tested in the study by Longtin et al. (2003).

In sum, the data presented here form one of the first clear demonstrations of masked cross-modal morphological priming (see also Ford and Marslen-Wilson, 2001). The most striking consequence of our results, however, is that if we try to link them to any of the two accounts of morphological processing at test here, we come to the conclusion that they fall in between the predictions made by each account. On the one hand, they indicate that as soon as a masked visual prime consists of the concatenation of a (pseudo-) root and a (pseudo-) suffix, both intra-modal and cross-modal priming of the (pseudo-) root occurs. Proponents of the sublexical account can easily interpret this as the result of a purely form-based mechanism which isolates potential morphemes whenever the visual input is fully decomposable. The fact that cross-modal priming was also found shows that the results of this mechanism are amodal. Thus from this perspective, our findings not only add support for the existence of such a form-based mechanism, they also provide further insight in the specific nature of this 'prelexical morphological decomposition' process. On the other hand our results also show a clear dissociation between the effect of primes that are truly complex and the effect of primes that are only seemingly so (from the point of view of the language user). More specifically, we observed a clear effect of semantic transparency. The finding that semantic transparency influenced our priming effects is in line with the general tenets of the supralexical account. Therefore, our results could be taken as evidence for the existence of a representational level that captures the systematic co-occurrence of form and meaning that arises with transparent complex words.

The present results thus support a view in which morphological processing is governed by a system that is both sensitive to the formal (morpho-orthographic) properties of a complex word and to its semantic (morpho-semantic) properties. This makes it obvious that no model that explains morphological processing exclusively in terms of either morpho-orthographic or morpho-semantic properties can provide an adequate explanation of the present results. Our findings therefore impose strong constraints on the modelling of morphological processing. The critically constraining findings can be summarised as follows: (1) the effect of semantic transparency appears in the absence of the effect of morphological surface structure in the visual modality (i.e., the early visual effect for transparent derivations), (2) the effect of morphological surface structure appears in the absence of semantic transparency (i.e., the opaque priming effect), (3) the effect of semantic transparency occurs earlier than the effect of morphological structure, (4) when the effect of morphological surface structure appears in the visual modality, the presence of semantic transparency increases the effect (i.e., the larger effect for transparent primes at the longest prime duration in the visual modality) and (5) when the effect of morphological surface structure appears, it does so in both modalities at the same time (i.e., the cross-modal effects with transparent and opaque primes at the longest prime duration).

To our knowledge, there is currently no model of morphological processing that can account for the present results. Any model that assumes a full morphological segmentation as a prerequisite for lexical access (for instance, the prelexical decomposition model of Taft and Forster, 1975) cannot explain why we observed priming from transparent primes in the absence of an opaque priming effect (i.e., the first finding listed above). On the other hand, the supralexical model as presented in the work of Giraudo and Grainger (2000, 2001, 2003), has serious difficulties in accounting for the effects of opaque derivations reported here and elsewhere (i.e., the second finding). Although the morphological race model of Schreuder and Baayen (1995), could in principle account for the first two findings mentioned above, it is hard to see how it would explain the third finding (i.e., the early effect of transparency in the visual modality). Indeed, the race model predicts that lexical access can be established both with and without a morphological segmentation of the input. However, it situates effects of semantic transparency at the level of central semantic representations. Therefore, it is far from plausible that such an effect would occur with a prime duration as short as 40 ms (and before the decomposition route has activated the lexical representation of the root). As demonstrated by Rastle et al. (2000), masked semantic priming effects only tend to influence target processing with fairly high (and arguably, conscious) levels of prime duration (at 230 ms in their study).

We believe that our findings, as summarised above, imply the existence of at least two distinct processing mechanisms, underlying morphological processing of transparent suffix-derivations: (1) a purely form-based mechanism that activates the root whenever the visual input is fully decomposable into a root and a suffix (we refer to this system as the *morpho-orthographic system*), and (2) a mechanism that activates the root whenever the visual input is fully decomposable and shares semantic features with its root (i.e., the *morpho-semantic system*). Furthermore, our findings indicate that these mechanisms operate with different speeds. More specifically, the morpho-semantic system activates the root faster than the morpho-orthographic system does.

In what follows we will illustrate how these mechanisms could be tentatively incorporated in the bi-modal interactive-activation framework (as proposed by Grainger et al., 2003). This framework describes two hierarchically organised localist connectionist networks: one for visual (orthographic) language processing and one for auditory (phonological) language processing. Within each network, activation flows from low-level sensory (sublexical) codes towards whole-word (lexical) form representations. Once orthographic and/or phonological lexical representations have become active, they will in turn activate higher-level amodal semantic representations. Critically, visual and auditory processing are heavily interconnected. This is realised through direct mappings between the orthographic and the phonological lexicon and through an amodal sublexical interface. This interface receives input from lower-level orthographic and phonological codes, and sends activation to both the orthographic and phonological lexicons to an equal extent.

The bi-modal framework could account for the modality-independent nature of the morpho-orthographic system, by assuming that it is located at the amodal sublexical interface. This would mean that this level contains sublexical codes that correspond to morphemes. Upon the presentation of a transparent or an opaque suffix-derivation, these codes would become activated and would in turn activate both the orthographic and phonological representations of the (pseudo-) root. However, at present the model does not allow us to hypothesise why these morphemic codes are only contacted when the (visual) input is exhaustively decomposable into (pseudo-) morphemes. A suggestion on this part was made by the early connectionist accounts of sublexical orthographic processing (Seidenberg, 1987, see also Rastle et al., in press, for a discussion). In short, it could be argued that the morpho-orthographic system can rely on the transitional bigram and trigram frequencies within words. Since these frequencies are typically lower between (pseudo-) morphemes (i.e. at the morpheme boundaries) than within (pseudo-) morphemes, the activation pattern induced by a fully decomposable visual word could fall apart into separate segments that correspond to the (pseudo-) morphemes.

It is less obvious how the bi-modal framework with supralexical morphology could account for the apparent modality-specific nature of the morpho-semantic system, since there is no obvious reason why such a supralexical level would be modality-specific. Here we propose a very tentative solution to this apparent paradox. This solution is based on the idea that cross-modal facilitation with transparent primes is absent at the 40 ms prime duration because the supralexical facilitation component is cancelled out by an inhibitory component. Evidence for such an inhibition process in the auditory modality comes from a finding in Experiment 2 that we did not comment thus far: the inhibitory cross-modal effect of orthographically related primes (which was, admittedly, only significant in the analysis by participants). These orthographic primes were French words that carried a pseudo-root at their beginning and had a non-suffix ending (e.g., *abricot-ABRI*). The fact that these same primes facilitated visual target processing, suggests that the locus of the observed cross-modal inhibition lies in the auditory word processing system itself.

Moreover, findings reported by Slowiaczek and Hamburger (1992) suggest that the interference is located at the lexical level. These authors demonstrated an inhibition in an auditory single-word shadowing task when target words were preceded by visually or auditory presented primes that shared three initial phonemes with it. However, this inhibition was only evident when primes were words. In line with Slowiaczek and Hamburger (1992), we suggest that the observed inhibition reflects the specific nature of the lexical selection process in auditory word recognition. Indeed, given the strictly serial nature of auditory stimulus input, the selection process for a given auditory word is most likely to be troubled if another form has been pre-activated (within the auditory lexicon) that has a certain degree of initial phonological overlap with it.

In order to explain the early visual effect of semantic transparency we first need to assume that a visual word prime rapidly activates its own orthographic lexical representation but also the representations of orthographically similar words (although to a lesser extent) including embedded words. However, this co-activation quickly decays if it is not maintained by additional sources of activation. Finally, we need to assume that the relative activation levels of co-activated words are a function of both morpho-semantic transparency and of modality. The presence of a morpho-semantic relationship makes it possible to maintain the co-activation of the root by means of top-down facilitation from the supralexical level. This will happen in the case of transparent suffix-derived primes only. In the case of opaque primes, initial co-activation of the root will not be able to influence target processing since the root representation cannot benefit from any extra activation at this duration, neither from a supralexical level (with which it has no connection) nor from the arguably slower operating morpho-orthographic system. In the auditory modality, the co-activated roots of derived primes do not only receive facilitation from the supralexical level, but are also subject to the inhibitory effect that is due to the word-initial overlap between the derived prime and its root. In the case of transparent primes, the trade-off between these facilitatory and inhibitory components would lead to a null effect at short prime durations. At later durations the slower morpho-orthographic system will increase the activation levels of the root in the two modalities.

We want to emphasise that the sequence of activation patterns, tentatively described above, should await further empirical evidence. Nevertheless, an important hypothesis regarding the morpho-orthographic system is that it is situated at an amodal sublexical processing level. This leads to the prediction that if nón-word primes were to be used that are built from a pseudo-root and a pseudo-suffix, pseudo-root priming should occur in both modalities. On the other hand, our tentative proposal to account for the apparent modality-specific nature of the morpho-semantic system could be put to the test by using prefix-derived primes instead of suffix-derivations. If word-initial overlap is the reason why we did not observe an early effect of transparency in the auditory modality, clearly, this factor would be eliminated with prefix-derived primes. Finally, we think that reversing our prime and targets, i.e., using (pseudo-) roots as primes and transparent and opaque derivations as targets, provides a useful way to further establish the distinction between the morpho-orthographic and morpho-semantic systems. More precisely, in this situation the morpho-orthographic system could be bypassed. We predict that in this case, no priming should occur with opaque derivations.

In conclusion, the present results reconcile the general tenets of the sublexical and supralexical accounts of morphological processing. More precisely, they show evidence for the existence of two independent processing systems underlying masked morphological priming effects: one that takes the morpho-orthographic properties of a complex word into consideration and one that takes its morpho-semantic properties into consideration. The former system allows pseudo- or genuine-root priming to occur whenever a visual prime is fully decomposable into pseudo- or genuine-morphemes, whereas the latter system will produce root priming whenever a visual prime is decomposable into genuine-morphemes and has a semantically transparent relationship with those morphemes. Our data show that the morpho-orthographic system causes a modality-independent priming effect, in that it will facilitate the subsequent processing of both a visual and an auditory presentation of the (pseudo-) root. The morpho-semantic system only seems to influence visual target processing, but this could be due to the use of suffixed primes in the present experiments. Our data indicate that this morpho-semantic system is not only qualitatively different from the morpho-orthographic system, but also operates faster. When taken together, the present results impose strong constraints on theories of morphological processing. We have shown how these constraints could be integrated into the general framework of the bi-modal interactive-activation model. From a more general point of view, our findings are also in line with a series of studies demonstrating the importance of morpho-semantic properties in the word recognition process. One type of study in which this has been done concerns the demonstration of processing differences between semantically transparent and opaque morphologically complex forms, with different experimental paradigms (e.g., Feldman, Soltano, Pastizzo, & Francis, 2004; Marslen-Wilson et al., 1994; Sandra, 1990). Another type of study concerns the morphological family size effect (e.g., Schreuder & Baayen, 1997; De Jong, Schreuder, & Baayen, 2000), an effect that has been shown to be rooted in the morpho-semantic relationships between words. A critical outcome in the present study is, however, that such morpho-semantic influences already occur in the early phases of word recognition.

REFERENCES

Baayen, R. H., Piepenbrock, R., & Gulikers, L. (1995). *The CELEX lexical database* (CD-ROM). Philadelphia, PA: Linguistic Data Consortium, University of Pennsylvania.

Caramazza, A., Laudanna, A., & Romani, C. (1988). Lexical access and inflectional morphology. *Cognition, 28*, 297–332.

De Jong, N. H., Schreuder, R., & Baayen, R. H. (2000). The morphological family size effect and morphology. *Language and Cognitive Processes, 15*, 329–365.

Feldman, L. B., Soltano, E. G., Pastizzo, M. J., & Francis, S. E. (2004). What do graded effects of semantic transparency reveal about morphological processing? *Brain and Language, 90*, 17–30.

Ford, M. A., & Marslen-Wilson, W. D. (2001). Morphological effects in lexical access: Evidence from cross-modal masked priming. *Abstracts of the 12th Conference of the European Society for Cognitive Psychology*, Edinburgh, Scotland.

Forster, K. I., & Davis, C. (1984). Repetition priming and frequency attenuation in lexical access. *Journal of Experimental Psychology: Learning, Memory and Cognition, 10*, 680–698.

Forster, K. I., & Forster, J. (2003). DMDX: A Windows display program with millisecond accuracy. *Behavioral Research Methods, Instruments and Computers, 35*, 116–124.

Frost, R., Ahissar, M., Gotesman, R., & Tayeb, S. (2003). Are phonological effects fragile? The effect of luminance and exposure duration on form priming and phonological priming. *Journal of Memory and Language, 48*, 346–378.

Frost, R., Deutsch, A., Gilboa, O., Tannenbaum, M., & Marslen-Wilson, W. (2000). Morphological priming: Dissociation of phonological, semantic, and morphological factors. *Memory and Cognition, 28*, 1277–1288.

Frost, R., Forster, K. I., & Deutsch, A. (1997). What can we learn from the morphology of Hebrew? A masked-priming investigation of morphological representation. *Journal of Experimental Psychology: Learning, Memory, and Cognition, 23*, 829–856.

Giraudo, H., & Grainger, J. (2000). Effects of prime word frequency and cumulative root frequency in masked morphological priming. *Language and Cognitive Processes, 15*, 421–444.

Giraudo, H., & Grainger, J. (2001). Priming complex words: Evidence for supralexical representation of morphology. *Psychonomic Bulletin and Review, 8*, 127–131.

Giraudo, H., & Grainger, J. (2003). A supralexical model for French derivational morphology. In E. M. H. Assink and D. Sandra (Eds.), *Reading complex words: Cross-language studies* (pp. 139–157). New York: Kluwer Academic.

Grainger, J., & Ferrand, L. (1994). Phonology and orthography in visual word recognition: Effects of masked homophone primes. *Journal of Memory and Language, 33*, 218–233.

Grainger, J., Diependaele, K., Spinelli, E., Ferrand, L., & Farioli, F. (2003). Masked repetition and phonological priming within and across modalities. *Journal of Experimental Psychology: Learning, Memory and Cognition, 29*, 1256–1269.

Jacobs, A. M., Grainger, J., & Ferrand, L. (1995). The incremental priming technique: A method for determining within-condition priming effects. *Perception and Psychophysics, 57*, 1101–1110.

Kouider, S., & Dupoux, E. (2001). A functional disconnection between spoken and visual word recognition: Evidence from unconscious priming. *Cognition, 82*, B35–B49.

Longtin, C.-M., Segui, J., & Hallé, P. A. (2003). Morphological priming without morphological relationship. *Language and Cognitive Processes, 18*, 313–334.

Marslen-Wilson, W., Tyler, L., Waksler, R., & Older, L. (1994). Morphology and meaning in the English mental lexicon. *Psychological Review, 101*, 3–33.

McClelland, J. L., & Rumelhart, D. E. (1981). An interactive activation model of context effects in letter perception: Part 1. An account of basic findings. *Psychological Review, 88*, 375–405.

McQueen, J. M., & Cutler, A. (1998). Morphology in word recognition. In A. Spencer and A. M. Zwicky (Eds.), *Handbook of morphology* (pp. 406–427). Oxford: Blackwell Publishers.

Meunier, F., & Segui, J. (2002). Cross-modal morphological priming in French. *Brain and Language, 81*, 89–102.

New, B., Pallier, C., Ferrand, L., & Matos, R. (2001). Une base de données lexicales du français contemporain sur internet: LEXIQUE [A lexical database on the internet for contemporary French: LEXIQUE]. *L'Année Psychologique, 101*, 447–462.

Rastle, K., & Davis, M. H. (2003). Reading morphologically complex words: Some thoughts from masked priming. In S. Kinoshita, & S. Lupker, (Eds.), *Masked priming: The state of the art* (pp. 279–305). Hove, UK: Psychology Press.

Rastle, K., Davis, M. H., & New, B. (in press). The broth in my brother's brothel: Morpho-orthographic segmentation in visual word recognition. *Psychonomic Bulletin and Review*.

Rastle, K., Davis, M. H., Marslen-Wilson, W. D., & Tyler, L. K. (2000). Morphological and semantic effects in visual word recognition: A time-course study. *Language and Cognitive Processes, 15*, 507–537.

Sandra, D. (1990). On the representation and processing of compound words: Automatic access of constituent morphemes does not occur. *Quarterly Journal of Experimental Psychology, 42A*, 529–567.

Schreuder, R., & Baayen, R. H. (1995). Modelling morphological processing. In L. B. Feldman (Ed.), *Morphological aspects of language processing* (pp. 131–154). Hillsdale, NJ: Lawrence Erlbaum Associates, Inc.

Schreuder, R., & Baayen, R. H. (1997). How complex simplex words can be. *Journal of Memory and Language, 37*, 118–139.

Seidenberg, M. S. (1987). Sublexical structures in visual word recognition: Access units or orthographic redundancy? In M. Coltheart, (Ed.), *Attention and Performance XII: The psychology of reading* (pp. 245–263). Hove, UK: Lawrence Erlbaum Associates Ltd.

Slowiaczek, L. M., & Hamburger, M. B. (1992). Prelexical facilitation and lexical interference in auditory word recognition. *Journal of Experimental Psychology: Learning, Memory, and Cognition, 18*, 1239–1250.

Taft, M. (1994). Interactive-activation as a framework for understanding morphological processing. *Language and Cognitive Processes, 9*, 271–294.

Taft, M., & Forster, K. I. (1975). Lexical storage and retrieval of prefixed words. *Journal of Verbal Learning and Verbal Behavior, 14*, 638–647.

APPENDIX 1

TABLE A1.1: Word stimuli used in the derived priming
block in Experiment 1

Targets	Derived prime	Orthographic control prime	Unrelated prime
TEL	teller	tempel	radijs
WOL	wollig	wortel	pastei
LUI	luiheid	lucifer	brutaal
DOM	domheid	dominee	paprika
KAT	kattig	katrol	poliep
PEES	pezig	peper	arena
WAAS	wazig	wagon	bloem
PARK	parking	parkiet	biscuit
MOED	moedig	moeite	chemie
RUST	rustend	rustiek	patrijs
ECHT	echtheid	echtpaar	piramide
ROND	ronding	rondeel	ambacht
STRAAL	straling	stramien	premiere
KOORTS	koortsig	klooster	papegaai
MUZIEK	musicus	muskiet	oordeel
REK	rekking	rekruut	paraplu
LAF	lafaard	lafenis	periode
DOF	dofheid	dolfijn	pinguin
ROT	rotting	rotonde	scepsis
VET	vettig	vector	jaguar
VOL	volheid	voltage	bliksem
BEEN	benig	bende	olijf
GESEL	geseling	geslacht	nicotine
SERIE	serieel	serieus	piccolo
APART	apartheid	aperitief	boemerang
ZONDE	zondig	zonder	premie
VREDE	vredig	vreemd	augurk
KLEUR	kleurig	kleuter	citroen
BLOED	bloedig	bloesem	diamant
SCHOOL	scholing	schommel	paradijs
REM	remming	remedie	patriot
RAS	racisme	rapport	schedel
GOD	godheid	gordijn	applaus
JAAG	jager	japon	riool
LAST	lastig	latent	blouse
SPEL	speler	spleet	poezie
PLAN	planner	planeet	echelon
OPEN	openlijk	operatie	district
DRAAG	drager	dragon	perzik
GENIE	geniaal	genesis	algebra
KROON	kroning	kroniek	papyrus
SPORT	sportief	spontaan	eekhoorn
MASSA	massief	massage	censuur
NACHT	nachtelijk	nachtegaal	delinquent
MARINE	marinier	marionet	pensioen
FEL	felheid	feodaal	chirurg
VIS	visser	visite	ravijn
MOE	moeheid	moesson	parasol

continued opposite

TABLE A1.1—*continued*

Targets	Derived prime	Orthographic control prime	Unrelated prime
WET	wettig	westen	bagage
PLAS	plasser	plastic	festijn
AMBT	ambtelijk	ambulance	procedure
GRAP	grappig	granaat	klimaat
GEEL	gelig	geluk	piano
DIER	dierlijk	dirigent	panorama
HAND	handig	handel	oorlog
SCHIM	schimmig	schimmel	parabool
PLANT	plantage	plankton	brochure
LUCHT	luchtig	luchter	akkoord
HUMAAN	humanisme	humaniora	pantoffel
CHARME	charmant	charisma	bisschop
VUL*	vulling	vulkaan	amazone
SAP	sappig	schaap	biljet
HEL	hels	helm	smid
ZON	zonnig	zombie	fazant
MAN	mannelijk	mandarijn	porselein
DUIK	duiker	duivel	asfalt
KAAL	kaalheid	kalender	bouillon
NOOD	nodig	noord	druif
BAAS	bazig	banjo	puree
SATAN	satanist	sanitair	ooievaar
OFFER	offeraar	officier	bulletin
STRAF	strafbaar	strategie	ceremonie
DROOM	dromerig	drommels	cassette
EINDE	eindig	eiland	putsch
MACHT	machtig	machete	ontwerp
ACT	acteur	affect	regime
NUT	nuttig	nudist	pagina
KOOK	kokend	krokus	pedaal
PRET	prettig	prefect	ontslag
PEIL	peiling	pelgrim	fortuin
ADEL	adellijk	adequaat	prognose
KOEL	koelheid	kolibrie	parochie
REDE	redelijk	redactie	advocaat
MAAK	maker	markt	clown
ORDE	ordening	orchidee	principe
WAAR	waarheid	waarborg	probleem
SPONS	sponzig	sponsor	perikel
VLEES	vlezig	vlecht	opinie
ANGST	angstig	angelus	ontbijt
PASTOOR	pastorie	paspoort	fantasie

*: removed from analysis

TABLE A1.2: Word stimuli used in the pseudo-derived
priming block in Experiment 1

Targets	Pseudo-derived prime	Orthographic control prime	Unrelated prime
STUIF*	stuiver	stupide	barbaar
GEN*	genade	genoot	risico
PIEK	pieker	pikant	balein
SCHILD	schilder	schilfer	parasiet
BOK	bokaal	boeket	nectar
PEN	penning	pension	collega
POST	poster	portie	bamboe
LEED	leder	ledig	tango
MES	mest	mens	galg
ACHT	achter	accent	beroep
KOP	koppel	kompas	crisis
KAN	kaneel	kanaal	scherf
DOK	dokter	donker	figuur
BIL	billijk	biljart	droesem
BAST*	bastaard	basiliek	relikwie
KAM	kameel	kamfer	reflex
BAN*	banaal	banaan	vizier
KOE	koester	koekoek	vanille
AS	aster	astma	prent
BRIL	briljant	broccoli	schouder
KAST	kasteel	kapstok	vervoer
BANK	banket	balkon	goeroe
TAAK	takel	tabak	rebus
BIJ	bijster	bijlage	trompet
VAAR	vaardig	vaarwel	tombola
HOON*	honing	honger	altaar
KARAF	karavaan	karakter	bioscoop
TEER	teerling	terminal	saffraan
PAAL	paling	paleis	schuim
RUIT	ruiter	ruimte	blanco
NEEF	nevel	netto	pluim
IJS	ijzer	ijdel	radar
VAL	vals	valk	gesp
LEEG	leger	legio	thuis
DIRECT	directie	discreet	imbeciel
PAAR	parel	pater	saldo
POOK*	poker	polka	ruine
PION	pionier	pistool	gazelle
ZOOM	zomer	zomin	agent
HAAS	hazelaar	handicap	populier
ENG	engel	eigen	robot
BOL	bolster	bioloog	grafiek
HELD	helder	hengel	parfum
TON	toneel	tonijn	arbeid
MAAG	mager	magma	plooi
BOOT	boter	boete	rebel
AARD	aardig	absurd	vrucht
PAS	passief	patrijs	tribune
MOL	molaar	moraal	antiek

continued opposite

TABLE A1.2—*continued*

Targets	Pseudo-derived prime	Orthographic control prime	Unrelated prime
NAAD	nader	naald	schip
GUL	gulzig	gulden	fresco
SCHAAR	schaars	schaats	vennoot
HEES	heester	hersens	bariton
SOM	soms	smog	plak
BEET	beter	beton	proef
WAND	wandel	wankel	orkest
BRAND	branding	brancard	polemiek
HAAR	haring	harnas	schelp
GANG	gangster	gangreen	prothese
KOM	kommer	komijn	narcis
BEEF*	bever	bezem	pruik
BUUR	bureel	burcht	plasma
LEK	lekker	lelijk	natuur
TACT	tactiek	tractor	congres
MAGIE	magister	magazine	huwelijk
LEEF	lever	leeuw	rijst
BAL	balling	ballast	verdict
PAN	paneel	paniek	schouw
BAR	barst	barok	poort
MIS	mist	mits	foto
KERK	kerker	kelder	nomade
OOG	oogst	orgel	slang

*: removed from analysis

APPENDIX 2

TABLE A2.1: Transparent word items
in Experiment 2

Targets	Related prime	Unrelated prime
CAVE	caveau	festin
RUE	ruelle	tricot
FOUDRE	foudroyer	héberger
COFFRE	coffret	aisselle
POIGNE	poignet	coutume
GAUFRE	gaufrette	kayak
HACHE	hachette	escargot
BUCHE	bûcheron	panthère
ARME	armature	cocktail
CASQUE	casquette	testament
LAIT	laitier	piscine
BLOUSE	blouson	dessein
PALPER	palpable	intensif
MASSER	massage	galopin
CARRE	carreau	pelouse
SAUT	sauter	fixer
SIGNAL	signaler	inventer
POULE	poulet	extase
CLOCHE	clochette	exode
CACHER	cachette	réservoir
BLANC	blancheur	interview
TABLE	tableau	heureux
DOUANE	douanier	fourneau
COUSSIN	coussinet	dépotoir
OLIVE	olivier	musique
FUMER	fumoir	ventouse
STATUE	statuette	confident
ROND	rondelle	enclave
ABUS	abuser	borner
MULE	mulet	venin
SAVON	savonnette	caméra
SONNER	sonnette	affiche
FILLE	fillette	triangle
HOTEL	hôtelier	vagabond
COMPTER	comptoir	marchand
LARD	lardon	coyote
DRAP	drapeau	licence
JUPE	jupon	cidre
COL	collier	ampoule
GLACE	glacial	complot
VARIER	variable	identité
CHAUFFER	chauffage	parcours
PLUME	plumeau	crampon
POUTRE	poutrelle	compote
SOUHAIT	souhaiter	préférer
MARQUE	marquer	enlever
JARDIN	jardinet	portique
POCHE	pochette	cavale

TABLE A2.2: Opaque word items
in Experiment 2

Targets	Related prime	Unrelated prime
ROSE	roseau	hublot
FLAN	flanelle	dortoir
CHAT	chatoyer	fignoler
FLEUR	fleuret	billot
FOU	fouet	globe
VIGNE	vignette	fichier
BAGUE	baguette	contexte
BOULE	boulon	signet
FOUR	fourrure	gendarme
BANQUE	banquette	marquise
PAPE	papier	matière
PAPILLE	papillon	garantie
MINER	minable	cocasse
SAUVER	sauvage	épais
PINCE	pinceau	candeur
RAT	rater	trotter
SOUDE	soudoyer	craqueler
VAL*	valet	neveu
TOILE	toilette	menton
MOQUER	moquette	nectar
TERRE	terreur	alcool
PANNE	panneau	horloge
PION	pionnier	navette
BRIQUE	briquet	corset
BERGE	berger	forcer
COULER	couloir	prison
CARPE	carpette	anchois
DENT	dentelle	cloison
LOUP	louper	chuter
COUPLE	couplet	parasol
LUNE	lunette	poignée
EPUISER	épuisette	périscope
CHOU	chouette	nomade
CHANT	chantier	argument
BOUGER	bougeoir	sondage
GAZ	gazon	idole
POTE	poteau	rétine
BAR	baron	frein
MORT	mortier	fission
CORDE	cordial	limpide
COUPER	coupable	sincère
RAVIR	ravage	tortue
RIDE	rideau	motif
CANNE	cannelle	nombril
GIGOT	gigoter	réviser
TRAIT	traiter	brûler
BROCHE	brochet	console
FAUVE	fauvette	neurone

*: removed from analysis

TABLE A2.3: Orthographic word items
in Experiment 2

Targets	Related prime	Unrelated prime
VAIN	vaincre	échelon
MODE	modeste	armoire
AVEU	aveugle	liquide
BOUC	boucan	piéger
PORC	porche	album
CHAMP	champagne	plastique
PAN	panorama	festival
RECUL	recueil	suspect
ORGUE	orgueil	chagrin
FER	fertile	trapèze
VERT	vertige	python
AVIS	avide	tuyau
JOIE	joindre	classer
PROMPT	promettre	magnitude
SEC	secte	furie
ESSAI	essaim	axiome
PIEU	pieuvre	soprano
PAROI	paroisse	offrande
CERF	cerfeuil	bottin
FOSSE	fossile	peluche
BOL	bolide	nymphe
CIME	ciment	navire
TRAC	tracteur	guidon
AUBE	auberge	planète
BOURG*	bourgogne	transfert
TORT	torpédo	sadisme
CASSER	casserole	manuscrit
REQUIN	requinquer	enrober
SAC	sacrifice	orchestre
CHIC	chiche	arcade
ABRI	abricot	locution
TEXTE	textile	guichet
DEFI	déficit	hostile
TOUR	tournoi	guérilla
CONTINU	continent	excellent
PRÊT	prêtre	minuit
DECADE*	décadent	albatros
CUIR	cuisse	amiral
TRIBU	tribune	hormone
DESIR	désert	bateau
FRIGO	frivole	morbide
ARCHE	archiduc	synonyme
VENDRE	vendredi	permanent
BAL	balai	gilet
BULLE	bulletin	répertoire
FRIC	friche	fourmi
AUTO	automne	magasin
TROU	troupe	jambe

*: removed from analysis

LANGUAGE AND COGNITIVE PROCESSES
2005, 20 (1/2), 115–138

The locus and time course of long-term morphological priming

Jay G. Rueckl and Bruno Galantucci

*University of Connecticut, Storrs, CT, and Haskins Laboratories,
New Haven, CT, USA*

Two experiments investigated the effects of long-term morphological priming in the fragment completion task. Completions for some of the fragments were presented visually during a preceding task, and others were presented auditorily. In addition, some of the target completions were morphologically related to words that were presented visually during the study task, while still others were unrelated to any of the study words. Fragments were most likely to be completed if either the completion or one of its morphological relatives was presented visually during the study task. Analyses of response latencies also indicated that the time course of morphological priming was similar to that of visual identity priming and that both morphological and visual identity priming had earlier influences than auditory identity priming. Overall, the results indicate that morphological priming includes a modality-specific component that reflects the operation of processes that occur relatively early in the time course of processing.

In a seminal paper, Murrell and Morton (1974) demonstrated that morphology plays an important role in visual word recognition. In the priming phase of their experiment, subjects studied a short list of words with the expectation that their memory for these words would later be tested. Shortly after the study phase, an identification task was administered. The accuracy with which words were identified during this task varied as a function of their relationships with words on the study list. Specifically, repeated words were identified more easily than unprimed

Correspondence should be addressed to Jay Rueckl, Department of Psychology, U-1020, University of Connecticut, Storrs, CT 06269. Email: jay.rueckl@uconn.edu.

This research was supported by Grant HD-01994 from the National Institute of Child Health and Development to Haskins Laboratories. We would like to thank Harald Baayen and an anonymous reviewer for their helpful comments

http://www.tandf.co.uk/journals/pp/01690965.html   DOI: 10.1080/01690960444000188

words (i.e., words that were not related to any of the study words), as were words that had been preceded by a morphologically related prime (e.g., *cars* at study, *car* at test). Thus, both identity (repetition) priming and morphological priming facilitated identification. In contrast, no priming was observed for words that were preceded by morphologically unrelated primes that were similar in spelling and pronunciation (e.g., *card-car*).

Murrell and Morton's (1974) findings have been extended in numerous ways over the last three decades. The influence of morphological structure on visual word recognition has been demonstrated with a variety of experimental measures (e.g., lexical decision latencies, tachistoscopic identification accuracy, fixation duration, fragment completion rate), in a variety of languages (e.g., English, Chinese, Dutch, Finnish, and Italian), and using a variety of experimental manipulations (e.g., prime-target relationship, family size, stem frequency, etc.). (See Feldman, 1991, Henderson, 1985, and Marslen-Wilson et al., 1994, for reviews; and the papers in the Feldman, 1995, and Frost & Grainger, 2000, volumes for representative examples.) Given this wealth of evidence, it is now widely agreed that readers are influenced by the morphological structure of the words that they read. However, the psychological underpinnings of this influence remain a matter of debate.

One issue concerns the manner in which words are represented. One view, often termed the *decompositional* approach, holds that words are represented in terms of the morphological constituents (e.g., Taft & Forster, 1975). In contrast, *whole-word* (or *full-listing*) accounts (e.g., Feldman & Fowler, 1987; Lukatela, Gligorijevic, Kostic, & Turvey, 1980) hold that each morphologically complex word has its own representation, and that these representations are organised such that morphological relationships affect processing. A third class of models, *dual-process* accounts, assume that some morphologically complex words are repre- sented in terms of their constituents and other are represented as whole words, with the choice of representation determined by factors such as the relative frequency of the word and its morphemes (Laudanna & Burani, 1995; Caramazza, Laudanna, & Romani, 1988) or the phonological and semantic transparency of the constituent morphemes (Baayen et al., 1997; Frauenfelder & Schreuder, 1991). Finally, a fourth class of models holds that words are represented by distributed patterns of activation, and that these representations are more-or-less componential in a way that reflects morphological structure (Plaut & Gonnerman, 2000; Rueckl & Raveh, 1999; Seidenberg & Gonnerman, 2000).

A second issue concerns the locus of morphological influences on the lexical processing system. One possibility is that morphological factors have a relatively early influence on word recognition. For example, some theories (e.g., Taft, 1994; Taft & Forster, 1975) hold that a word is decomposed into its morphemic constituents before lexical access occurs. For this sort of theory, morphological factors have their effects pre-lexically, and morphemes serve as the "access units" for word recognition. An alternative perspective is that the locus of morphological effects is the lexicon proper. On this view, morphological effects reflect the nature of the representations accessed in word identification, rather than the characteristics of the pre-lexical access units (Marslen-Wilson et al., 1994). A third theoretical perspective holds that morphological effects reflect neither the properties of the access units nor the organisation of lexical representations per se. Instead, on this view morphological effects reveal the operation of post-access processes that are sensitive to morphological structure (Giraudo & Grainger, 2001; Henderson et al., 1984; Manelis & Tharp, 1977).

Two points concerning the locus of morphological effects are worth noting. First, the theoretical alternatives are not necessarily mutually exclusive. It is perfectly conceivable that morphology influences more than one stage of lexical processing and that different morphological effects reflect the operation of different stages of processing (see Marslen-Wilson et al., 1994, for further discussion of this point). Second, it seems fair to say that questions about the locus of morphological effects have been somewhat neglected in the literature on morphology and word recognition. For example, in reviewing relevant papers in preparation for writing this article, we found that whereas virtually every theoretical proposal very carefully articulated a position about how morphological structure is represented, in a surprising number of cases it was difficult to ascertain what was being proposed about the processing locus of morphological effects. The same conclusion was reached by Marslen-Wilson et al. (1994, p. 4), who wrote that "psycholinguistic research into morphological complex words has often failed to maintain this distinction [between access units and lexical entries], making it hard to sort out whether claims and evidence for full-listing or morpheme-based accounts apply to the access representation, the lexical entry or both."

The purpose of the experiments reported in this paper was to investigate the processing locus of long-term morphological priming. Given that different morphological effects may have different processing loci, it is worth emphasising that we are specifically concerned with long-term priming, in which the presentation of a number of items (typically at least ten and often many more) intervenes between the presentation of the prime and target, and thus seconds, minutes, or even days pass between these two events. Morphological effects are also observed in "short-term" priming tasks, in which the target is usually presented immediately after the prime (e.g., at a lag of 0–1000 ms). Although morphological effects are evident in both paradigms, there is good reason to suppose that different mechanisms underlie short- and long-term priming. For example, while semantic relatedness usually results in substantial short-term priming, long-term priming based on semantic relatedness alone has rarely been reported (see Rueckl, 2002, for further discussion).

The approach we took to investigate the locus of long-term morphological effects was inspired by a body of research concerning the processes underlying a related phenomenon: long-term identity priming. In the next section we review this body of research. We then report two experiments suggesting a relatively early locus for long-term morphological priming.

MODALITY-SPECIFIC AND MODALITY-INDEPENDENT CONTRIBUTIONS TO IDENTITY PRIMING

One issue that has been carefully explored in studies of long-term identity priming is whether or not priming reflects the operation of processes that act at an abstract, modality-independent level. Early models of identity priming, most notably Morton's logogen model (Morton, 1969), answered in the affirmative. In Morton's model, words are represented by processing units called logogens, and word recognition occurs when enough perceptual evidence suggesting the presence of a particular word accumulates, causing that word's logogen to cross its threshold. One of the consequences of crossing threshold is that the threshold is then lowered, so that less evidence is needed for the logogen to cross the threshold again. Identity priming effects are a behavioral manifestation of this change in threshold.

In the original version of the logogen model (Morton, 1969), it was assumed that the same logogen was involved in reading a printed word, hearing a spoken word, or selecting a word when speaking. Because logogens are assumed to be modality-independent, Morton's model predicts that identity priming should transfer broadly across modalities and tasks. However, this turns out not to be the case. For example, Winnick and Daniel (1970) found that the recognition of a printed word was not primed as a result of naming that word aloud in response to either a picture or a definition. Morton (1979) replicated Winnick and Daniel's (1970) results and also found that hearing a word did not facilitate the subsequent recognition of its written form.

Based on evidence of this sort, Morton (1979) hypothesised that different cognitive processes draw on different sets of logogens. For example, to account for the Winnick and Daniel (1970) and Morton (1979) findings, the revised logogen model included distinct banks of logogens for visual word recognition, spoken word recognition, and speech production. Hence, hearing or producing a word doesn't facilitate the subsequent recognition of its visual form because the logogens activated during the former processes are not the same logogens responsible for visual word recognition. The revised logogen model thus places the locus of identity priming effects at a modality-specific level of representation. Moreover, based on Murrell and Morton's (1974) observation that the recognition of a word can be primed by prior exposure to a morphological relative of that word, logogens were thought to represent morphemes, rather than whole words. Thus, according to the logogen model identity priming and morphological priming have a common basis: changes in the thresholds of modality-specific access units.

Although the revised logogen model accounted for an impressive array of the empirical findings of its day, subsequent research has shown that it is wrong in several important ways. One problem is that it is based on the conclusion (drawn from the Winnick and Daniel, 1970, and Morton, 1979, results) that hearing or generating a word will have no effect on the subsequent identification of its written form. However, the results of a large number of more recent studies contradict this assumption. It is now generally accepted that changes in modality between the prime and the target reduce, but do not eliminate, repetition priming (see Kirsner, Dunn, & Standen, 1989, and Roediger & McDermott, 1993, for reviews). This pattern of results suggests that both modality-specific and modality-independent processes contribute to priming. The contribution of modality-specific processes gives rise to the advantage of same-modality priming; cross-modal priming reflects the contribution of more abstract, amodal processes involved in seeing, hearing, and perhaps producing a word (Kirsner et al., 1989; Weldon, 1993). (Substantial evidence points to both phonological and semantic loci for the modality-independent components of priming; see Rueckl and Mathew, 1999, and Weldon, 1991, 1993, for further discussion.)

In addition to failing to account for the modality-independent source of priming effects, a second problem for the revised logogen model is that it does not fully capture the characteristics of modality-specific priming effects. For example, in the logogen model priming should only occur when familiar words (or morphemes) are repeated. However, a variety of studies have demonstrated that priming facilitates the processing of unfamiliar pseudowords and nonwords (see Rueckl, 2002, and Tenpenny, 1995, for reviews), and under certain conditions priming transfers to orthographically similar items, suggesting that priming has a pre-lexical basis (see Rueckl, 2002, for a review). Similarly, whereas the logogen model assumes that modality-specific access units are perceptually abstract (across variations in font, size, and other perceptual characteristics), differences in the perceptual characteristics of the prime and target sometimes result in a reduction in the magnitude of priming (see Rueckl,

2002, and Tenpenny, 1995, for reviews). While their theoretical implications are a matter of some debate (cf. Bowers, 1996; Brown & Carr, 1993; Jacoby, 1983; Marsolek, Kosslyn, & Squire, 1992; Roediger, 1990; Rueckl, 2002), these results imply that the modality-specific component of priming cannot be ascribed solely to changes in modality-specific lexical/morphemic access units. Indeed, these results suggest that the modality-specific component may itself reflect the contribution of several distinct processes.

THE LOCUS AND TIME COURSE OF MORPHOLOGICAL PRIMING

Given the evidence that has emerged from the investigation of identity priming, several hypotheses about the locus of morphological priming can be formulated. On the one hand, theories that hold that morphological effects in reading arise from the organisation of the central lexicon suggest that morphological priming should be aligned with the modality-independent component of identity priming. Alternatively, theories that hold that words are decomposed into their morphological components prior to lexical access suggest a modality-specific basis for morphological priming. To be clear, these hypotheses about the locus of morphological priming are not mutually exclusive. As noted above, the influence of morphological factors at one level of processing does not preclude the possibility that morphology matters at other levels as well. Thus, just as long-term identity priming includes several components, so too might long-term morphological priming. Consequently, the goal of the present experiments was not to identify "the" locus of morphological priming. Instead, these experiments were designed to evaluate the hypothesis that morphological priming is due (at least in part) to processes involving modality-specific representations.

A second (and related) goal was to gain evidence about the time-course of morphological priming. The rationale for this aspect of our study was based on Weldon's (1993) observation that the contribution of modality-specific processes to identity priming occurs earlier than does the contribution of modality-independent processes. Because Weldon's study played an especially critical role in the design and interpretation of our experiments, we describe it in some detail here.

Weldon (1993) examined priming in a visual word-fragment completion task, in which participants are asked to complete a fragment such as ___l__p__a__t with the first word that comes to mind. (For this example, "elephant" is the only legal completion.) In addition to an unprimed baseline condition, there were three other priming conditions: During a seemingly unrelated task that preceded the fragment completion task, participants either saw a target word ("elephant"), heard it, or saw a corresponding picture. Whereas modality-independent priming might occur in all three of these conditions, only visual identity primes would be expected to give rise to modality-specific priming.

Weldon (1993) considered the test fragment to be a retrieval cue that sometimes elicits representations stored during the processing of a prime. She reasoned that, if modality-specific representations are accessed before modality-independent representations, these two components of identity priming should have different time courses. In Experiment 1, information about the time course of priming was obtained by varying how long each test fragment remained visible. With relatively brief fragment durations (500 ms and 1 s), only visual word primes increased the completion rate. However, at longer durations (5 and 12 s) spoken primes (and to a lesser extent, picture primes) also improved performance, although not as strongly as visual identity primes did. This pattern of results suggests that the modality-specific component has a faster time course, as would be expected if seeing a word primes relatively early, modality-specific processes while either hearing or seeing a word primes relatively late, modality-independent operations.

In a second experiment, Weldon (1993) looked at the time course in a different way: by measuring response latencies. She found that, when differences in the completion rate were taken into account, visually primed fragments were solved at a faster rate than either auditorily or pictorially primed fragments, again suggesting the modality-specific and modality-independent components of priming have different time courses.

In the experiments presented below, we adapted Weldon's (1993) methodology to examine the time course of morphological priming. Participants performed two tasks—a pleasantness judgement task (the study task), followed by a fragment completion task (the test task). As in Weldon's experiments, some of the target completions were presented visually during the study task, others were presented auditorily, and some were unrelated to any of the words presented during the study task. Unlike Weldon's experiments, however, there were no picture primes. Instead, some of the study words were morphological relatives of the target completions (e.g., *arrangement-arrange*). The morphological primes included both inflections and derivations and were always presented visually. As was the case in Weldon's (1993) study, the time course of priming was examined in two ways. In Experiment 1, the fragments were presented for varying durations. In Experiment 2, the fragments were presented for a fixed duration and response latencies were recorded.

In summary, the present experiments were designed to gain information about the locus and time course of morphological priming by comparing visual morphological priming to both visual and auditory identity priming. While the visual identity condition provides an estimate of the combined effects of modality-specific and modality-independent priming under these experimental circumstances, the auditory identity condition provides a benchmark for the maximal contribution of modality-independent processes[1]. Thus, if morphological priming is purely a consequence of processes with an amodal central lexicon, within-modality morphological priming and cross-modal identity priming should be similar in both magnitude and time course. In contrast, if morphological priming includes a modality-specific component, morphological and auditory identity priming should differ in both magnitude and time course, with morphological priming more closely resembling visual identity priming. (In the latter case, if morphological and visual identity priming differ in either magnitude or time course, these differences could reflect either modality-specific [visual or orthographic] or modality-independent [semantic, phonological, or lexical] factors. Converging evidence would be necessary to disentangle these possibilities.)

EXPERIMENT 1

Method

Participants. Seventy-two undergraduates from the University of Connecticut participated for course credit. All the participants were native speakers of English with normal or corrected vision.

Design. A 4 × 3 mixed design was used with priming condition manipulated within subjects and fragment exposure times manipulated between subjects. The four priming conditions were visual identity, auditory identity, visual morphological, and unrepeated (baseline). The three exposure times were 1, 5 and 12 s. The assignment of target words to study condition was completely counterbalanced so that, across participants, each item appeared in each priming condition an equal number of times.

Materials. The target items were the solutions of 60 word fragments. The targets were low- to moderate-frequency words (mean 86, range 0–465; Kucera & Francis, 1967) and ranged in length from 5 to 9 letters. The 60 test fragments were selected from a larger set of fragments whose level

---

[1] Note that we could have used cross-modal morphological priming, rather than cross-modal identity priming, as our index of the modality-independent contribution to priming. Also note that identity priming is a special case of morphological priming—one in which only the target morpheme is presented during the priming event. We chose to use cross-modal identity priming to maximise the magnitude of cross-modal priming, and thus provide a conservative test of the hypothesis that (visual-visual) morphological priming includes a modality-specific component.

of difficulty, in absence of priming, was assessed in a pilot experiment. The average percentage of correct solutions in a sample of ten subjects for the set of fragments selected was 25% (range: 10–40%). Fragments were formed by removing 25–50% of a target word's letters, with the constraint that the only legal completion for a given fragment was its target word.

In the morphological priming condition, the relationships between the primes and their targets were rather heterogeneous, including verbal inflections (e.g., *consumed/consume*), nominal inflections (*hammers/hammer*), and various types of derivations (e.g., *believer/believe*; *systematic/ system*; *arrangement/arrange*). The prime-target pairs were selected so that the morphological relationships were orthographically, phonologically, and semantically transparent.

The assignment of items to priming conditions was counterbalanced by partitioning the 60 target words into four sublists of 15 words each and rotating these sublists through the priming conditions. Across subjects, each word appeared in each priming condition an equal number of times.

Each participant was presented with the same list of fragments to complete. This list included the 60 critical fragments, along with 30 fillers. None of the completions for the filler fragments were presented during the study task. Thus, of the 90 fragments presented during the completion task, 45 were related to words presented during the study task, and 45 (the 15 items in the unprimed condition plus the 30 fillers) were not. The fillers were included to reduce the likelihood that participants would attempt to complete the fragments by consciously trying to recall words from the study task.

For the auditory condition a male native speaker of American English was recorded producing each of the target words. These recordings were digitised using the Sound Edit 16 software for the Macintosh. The intelligibility of these recordings was checked through the judgements of another native speaker of American English, who reported that each recording was clear and understandable. The visually presented stimuli in both tasks appeared in the centre of a computer screen in 18-point extended Courier font. (Courier is a fixed width font, and thus letter spacing provided no cues about the identity of the absent letters.)

Procedure.   Participants were tested individually or in pairs. They were told that they would perform several tasks concerning various aspects of their knowledge of words. The experiment included three distinct phases. During the first phase, the participants judged the pleasantness of each of a list of words on a scale from 1 to 5. The list included six buffer items (the first three and last three words in the series) and 45 target words (15 each in the visual, morphological, and auditory conditions). The words from the different priming conditions were intermixed and presented in a different random order for each subject. The words in the auditory condition were presented over headphones; the words in the visual and morphological conditions appeared in the centre of a computer screen

Immediately after the study phase, the participants completed an irrelevant filler task in which they were given three minutes to write down the names of as many magazines as they could remember. The filler task was then followed by the test phase, during which the participants performed a fragment completion task. The fragments of the 60 critical items and 30 filler items were intermixed and presented in a random order. Each fragment was visible for a maximum of 1, 5 or 12 s, depending on the duration condition to which the participant was assigned. In the 1-s and 5-s conditions the presentation of the fragment was followed by an additional 5-s response interval. Upon discovering the completion for a fragment, the participant clicked the computer mouse to terminate the trial, and then typed the solution when prompted. If no response was made before the end of the trial, the participant was encouraged (but not required) to guess.

The experiment was controlled by a HyperCard program running on Macintosh computers. After the test phase participants were briefly interviewed about their impressions on the tasks. They were asked if they noticed that some of the words repeated themselves in different tasks of the experiment and, if they answered yes, they were asked if they used memories from the study-phase to help themselves in the test-phase. Finally, they were debriefed and thanked.

Results

A response was scored as a target completion only if it exactly matched the target word. Thus, apparent misspellings and other responses were considered misses. The target completion rates for the various study conditions are presented in Figure 1. Inspection of the figure reveals that the results are broadly consistent with those of Weldon (1993): Completion rates increased with longer fragment exposure durations and as a result of exposure to a target word during the study task. This description of the data is consistent with the results of an analysis of variance (ANOVA) which revealed significant main effects of study condition, by participants, $F_1(3, 207) = 20.93, p < .0001$, and by items, $F_2 (3, 177) = 24.21 p < .0001$, and exposure duration, $F_1 (2, 69) = 4.75, p < .05, F_2 (2, 59) = 5.31 p < .01$. The interaction of these factors was not significant, $F_1 < 1, F_2 < 1$.

A set of planned comparisons was performed to examine the differences among the study conditions. These comparisons revealed significant priming effects—in the form of elevated target completion rates relative to the baseline condition—in the visual, $F_1(1, 71) = 56.18, p < .0001, F_2(1, 59) = 64.97, p < .0001$, morphological, $F_1(1, 71) = 33.52, p < .0001, F_2(1, 59) = 38.77, p < .0001$, and auditory, $F_1(1, 71) = 12.89, p < .001, F_2(1, 59)$

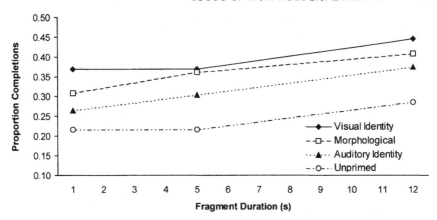

Figure 1. Target completion rates as a function of priming condition in Experiment 1.

$= 14.91, p < .001$, study conditions. Moreover, there were significantly more target completions in the visual priming condition than in the auditory condition, $F_1(1, 71) = 15.25, p < .0001, F_2(1, 59) = 17.63, p < .0001$, and similarly, more fragment completions in the morphological priming condition than in the auditory condition, $F_1(1, 71) = 4.84, p < .05; F_2(1, 59) = 5.6, p < .05$. Thus, there was a significant effect of cross-modal priming, but more priming occurred when both the study and test items were presented visually. Finally, although the target completion rate was somewhat higher in the visual condition than in the morphological condition, this difference was only marginally significant, $F_1(1, 71) = 2.91, p = .09; F_2(1, 59) = 3.36, p = .07$, and seemed to vary with presentation duration. (Post-hoc analyses revealed that the difference between the visual and morphological conditions was only significant in the 1-s duration condition.)

As a methodological aside, the short interviews of the participants at the end of the experiment revealed that most of the participants were aware of the fact that some words were present in two tasks. However, the impression most commonly reported by the participants about the effects of this repetition was that, during the process of looking for a solution for the target, the solutions "popped out" all of a sudden when they were words already encountered in the previous list. None of the participants claimed to have strategically used this knowledge about the repetition of some words in the two tasks. Consistent with the self-reports, the data from the baseline condition also suggest that participants did not adopt an explicit memory strategy. Such a strategy should be detrimental in the case of unprimed words, for which attempts to recall items from the study task would fail to generate a correct response. In fact, however, the completion rate in the unprimed rate was quite similar to what was found in the pilot experiment used to select the materials (24% in the experiment, 25% in the pilot experiment).

Discussion

Several aspects of the results are particularly noteworthy. First, a target word was more likely to be generated as a fragment completion if it was primed by a visually presented morphological relative than if it was primed by itself in the auditory identity condition. Because identity priming is, in a sense, the strongest possible case of morphological priming (one in which only the root morpheme is presented during the priming event), the auditory identity condition provides an upper limit for the contribution of the modality-independent component of priming under these conditions. The fact that priming was greater in the morphological condition than in the auditory condition thus provides strong evidence that morphological priming, like identity priming, includes a modality-specific component.

The evidence concerning the time course of morphological priming is less clear. The pattern of results suggests that morphological priming has an earlier influence on processing than does cross-modal identity priming, and that the effect of morphological priming is delayed slightly in comparison to visual identity priming. However, given the lack of a significant interaction of duration and priming condition and the differences among the priming conditions at the longest duration presentation, one could argue that the differences at the shortest duration are related to the magnitude of priming, rather than its time course. Because the results of the second experiment yield more definitive evidence about this point, we will not belabour it here.

EXPERIMENT 2

Like Experiment 1, Experiment 2 investigated the effects of visual identity, morphological, and auditory identity priming on visual fragment completion rates. In the second experiment fragment presentation duration was not manipulated. Each fragment was presented for a maximum of 16 s, and response latencies were measured along with target completion rates.

Method

Participants.   Thirty-two undergraduates from the University of Connecticut participated for course credit. All the participants were native speakers of English with normal or corrected vision.

Design and procedure.   The design and procedure of Experiment 2 were identical to those of Experiment 1, with three exceptions. First, fragment presentation duration was not manipulated. Each fragment was presented for 16 s or until the participant clicked the mouse to indicate that he or she had found a completion. Second, response latencies (defined as the length of the interval between the onset of the fragment and the mouse click that indicated that a solution had been found) were recorded. Third, only responses that were initiated before the end of the 16 s presentation duration were treated as possible target completions. (As in the first experiment, if the participant had not clicked the mouse by the end of the response interval, he or she was prompted to guess. However, because the response latencies of these late guesses are not well defined, they were treated as misses for all of the analyses. Late correct responses occurred on only 41 of 1920 total trials (2.13%), and the same pattern of effects were obtained whether or not they were included in the completion rate analyses.)

Results

Target completion rates.   As in Experiment 1, responses were scored as target completions only if they exactly matched a target word, and apparent misspellings were treated as misses. Table 1 presents the target completion rates in Experiment 2 as a function of study condition. The effect of study condition was significant by both subjects, $F_1(3, 93) = 5.59$, $p < .001$, and items, $F_2(3, 177) = 5.94$, $p < .001$. A set of planned comparisons was performed to examine the differences among the priming conditions. Relative to the baseline condition, significant priming effects were observed in both the visual identity, $F_1(1, 31) = 13.06, p < .001; F_2(1, 59) = 14.01, p < .001$, and morphological, $F_1(1, 31) = 9.08, p < .01; F_2(1, 59) = 5.94, p < .001$, study conditions. In addition, more fragments were completed in the visual identity condition than in the auditory identity condition, $F_1(1, 31) = 3.95, p = .056; F_2(1, 59) = 5.20, p < .05$. Finally, although the effects were numerically comparable to those of Experiment 1, the differences between the morphological and auditory conditions and between the auditory and baseline conditions were not statistically

TABLE 1
Fragment completion rates in Experiment 2

Priming condition	Completion rate
Visual identity	.41
Morphological	.39
Auditory identity	.34
Unprimed	.29

TABLE 2
Response times in Experiment 2

Priming condition	Mean	Median	SD	Skew	Kurtosis
Visual identity	4510	3100	3593	1.39	1.13
Morphological	4418	3183	3432	1.61	1.94
Auditory identity	5392	4150	3618	0.86	−0.24
Unrepeated baseline	5763	4367	4007	0.96	−0.15

significant. Presumably the lack of statistical significance for these comparisons is due to the smaller sample size in the present experiment.

Response times.   Table 2 displays the mean response times (along with other summary statistics) for trials on which the target completions were generated. As is typically done with response time data, ANOVAs were conducted to analyse the results. In contrast to the results of the analyses of completion rates, the main effect of study condition was only marginally significant, $F_1(3, 93) = 2.31$, $p = .082$; $F_2(3, 177) = 2.6$ $p = .10$. Consequently, no comparisons were performed to examine the differences among the priming conditions.

While it is certainly possible that a manipulation might have a stronger influence on completion rates than on response times, several considerations suggest that for this kind of experiment an ANOVA obscures, rather than reveals, the pattern in the data. First, the numerical differences among the conditions were often large and patterned as would be expected based on the completion rates. However, the variability in response times was substantial in comparison to typical results from other response time paradigms (e.g., lexical decision, speeded naming). The relatively large standard deviations observed in the present experiment do not reflect unusually small numbers of subjects or items, but instead are intrinsic to this form of the fragment completion task: Completions are often found within 1 or 2 seconds, but are also found after 10 or 15 seconds of search. A related concern is that, in addition to the high variability, the RT distributions in each of the four study conditions are positively skewed, and the distributions for the visual and morphological conditions are also substantially kurtotic (see Table 2). Thus, not only are the RT distributions non-normal (thus violating one of the assumptions of ANOVA),[2] but their shapes differ as a function of study condition (see Figure 2). Finally, in the ANOVA trials on which the target completion was not generated before the deadline (65% of the total) were excluded. Thus, the ANOVA failed

---

[2] Kolmogorov–Smirnov tests for normality confirmed that the four distributions are all non-normal ($p < .001$ for all four distributions).

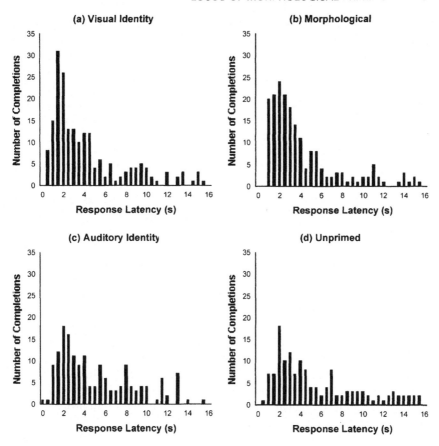

Figure 2. The distribution of target completion latencies in Experiment 2 as a function of priming condition.

to make use of the information that these trials provide. Moreover, the number of "missing" trials varied across study conditions: Trials were excluded most often in the unprimed condition and least often in the visual identity condition. Systematic differences in exclusion rates could easily give rise to potentially misleading results. (For example, if priming decreases the time needed to complete a fragment, some of the trials that would have been solved after the deadline in the baseline condition might have been solved before the deadline in a primed condition. Such trials would be excluded from the computation of the baseline RT, but would increase the mean RT in the primed condition, resulting in an artificially slow average RT in the primed condition relative to the unprimed condition.)

Cumulative proportion-of-asymptote. Together, the preceding considerations imply that analyses of the present data based on average response times are at best weak, and at worst, misleading. Clearly, a different type of analysis that addresses these considerations is desirable. One possibility was suggested by Weldon (1993). To analyse the time course of processing in her fragment completion experiment, Weldon plotted the cumulative frequency of target completions as a function of response latency. To address the fact that the cumulative frequency functions approached different asymptotes in the different study conditions, the cumulative frequency functions were transformed into cumulative proportion-of-asymptote functions. The results allowed Weldon to conclude that within-modality priming is not only larger in magnitude than cross-modal priming, but also that within-modality priming occurs earlier in the time course of fragment completion.

We applied the cumulative proportion-of-asymptote analysis to the results of Experiment 2. Response times were grouped into 1 s bins, and the cumulative frequency of target completions for each bin was plotted as a proportion of the total number of completions at the end of the 16-s response period (see Figure 3). Not surprisingly, the effect of response period was significant, $F(15, 465) = 418.13, p < .0001$.[3] More importantly, although the effect of priming condition was not significant $(F < 1)$, there was a significant interaction of priming condition and response period, $F(45, 1395) = 2.023, p < .0001$. Interaction contrasts confirmed what the pattern depicted in Figure 3 suggests: The time course of priming of visual identity and morphological priming differed from that of auditory identity priming; visual/auditory × response interval: $F(15, 465) = 2.283, p < .005$; morphological/auditory × response interval: $F(15, 465) = 4.086, p < .0001$. In contrast, neither the difference between morphological and visual identity priming nor the interaction with response period was significant. Similarly, there were no significant effects involving the contrast between the auditory priming and unprimed baseline conditions.

Survival analysis. Compared to ANOVA, the cumulative proportion-of-asymptote analysis is more revealing about the time course of processing. Nonetheless, it is less than ideal in several respects. One concern is that, given that the choice of a deadline is arbitrary, scaling the cumulative functions relative to a deadline-dependent measure is somewhat arbitrary as well. That is, to the degree to which different deadlines yield different estimates of asymptotic performance, the apparent relationships among

---

[3] Because there were only eight observations per item per condition, analyses with items treated as random variables were not conducted.

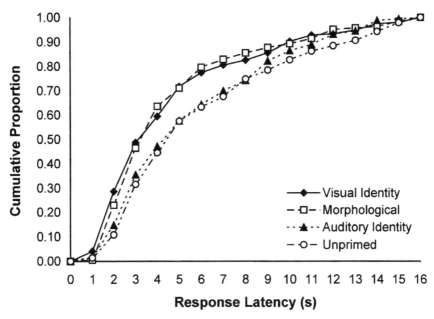

Figure 3. Cumulative-proportion-of-asymptote as a function of priming condition in Experiment 2.

the cumulative proportion-of-asymptote functions for the different study conditions will also tend to vary. A second concern is that the choice of bin size is also somewhat arbitrary, and while using too few bins could obscure real differences in the time course of priming, using too many bins could inappropriately magnify neglible differences among the conditions. A third and particularly important concern is that, because it is insensitive (by design) to differences in the asymptotic completion rate, the cumulative proportion-of-asymptote analysis fails to make use of the information provided by trials on which the target completion was not found. An approach that addresses these shortcomings is *survival analysis.*

Survival analysis, first developed as a tool for analysing data in actuarial mathematics, has become a common instrument of statistical investigation whenever the time course of a series of events as well as the distribution of lost observations (censored data) are of central interest. (For a general introduction to survival analysis see Lee, 1992 or Klein & Moeschberger, 1997.) Consider, for example, an experiment meant to compare the effectiveness of two cancer treatments. The critical observations in such an experiment are the "survival periods", the intervals between treatment and death for those patients that died during an observation period. However, some of the patients may survive until the end of the observation period, and some may die for reasons other than cancer (e.g., car accidents). The fact that a patient was alive at the end of the observation period or until an unrelated death provides information concerning the effectiveness of the treatment, but in neither case is it appropriate to consider the end of the observation to be the end of the survival period. The mathematical underpinnings of survival analysis allow it to take information from these censored cases into account.

In the case of the present experiment, the critical events (comparable to cancer-related deaths in the example) were responses indicating that a target completion had been found. Thus, only trials on which a target response was reported (as indicated by a mouse click) before the end of the 16-s response interval yielded an observable survival period. This occurred on 36% of the trials. The remaining trials were classified into two types. Trials on which a wrong or null answer was given before the end of the response interval (33% of the trials) were "left-censored". These trials are the analogue of car-accident victims in the cancer example. Trials on which the participant did not respond before the end of the response interval were "right-censored". These trials (31% of the total) are analogous to the patients who are still alive at the end of the observation period in the cancer example.

The nonparametric Kaplan–Meier survival function for each priming condition is presented in Figure 4. A Gehan's Wilcoxon test for the equality of the survival distributions revealed that the type of priming had a highly significant effect, $\chi^2(3) = 32.45, p < .0001$. A set of planned

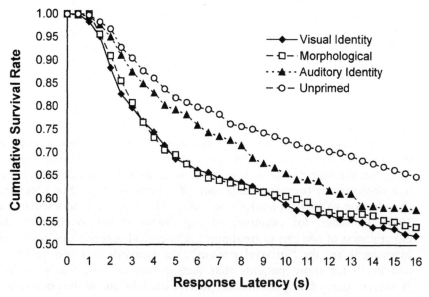

Figure 4. Survival functions for the priming conditions of Experiment 2.

pairwise Wilcoxon tests was performed to examine the differences among the priming conditions. All the priming conditions led to significantly lower survival rates than the baseline, $\chi^2(1) = 24.17$, $p < .0001$ for the visual identity condition; $\chi^2(1) = 20.52$, $p < .0001$ for morphological priming, and $\chi^2(1) = 4.23$, $p < .05$ for the auditory identity condition. Moreover, the survival rates for both the visual identity and morphological conditions differed significantly from that of the auditory identity condition, $\chi^2(1) = 9.39$, $p < .01$ for visual identity priming, $\chi^2(1) = 7.31$, $p < .01$, for morphological priming. The survival rates for the visual identity and morphological priming conditions were not significantly different, $\chi^2(1) < 1$.

Discussion

The target completion rates in Experiment 2 closely resembled those of the first experiment, providing additional evidence of a modality-specific contribution to morphological priming. Evidence concerning the time course of priming also supports this conclusion. The results indicate that morphological priming and visual identity priming have similar time courses, and that both forms of priming exert an earlier influence on fragment completion than does cross-modal priming.

As did Weldon (1993), we assume that fragment completion, like word recognition more generally, involves a variety of modality-specific (e.g., visual, orthographic) and modality-independent (e.g., lexical, semantic, phonological) processes. We further assume that these processes operate in a cascaded fashion, with the presentation of a word fragment initiating modality-specific processes, and these processes in turn driving other, modality-independent processes. Hearing a word leaves a lasting influence on one or more of the modality-independent processes, whereas seeing a word influences both modality-specific and modality-independent processes. The relatively early effect of visual identity and morphological priming (i.e., the greater likelihood of generating the target completion in the first few seconds after the fragment is presented) is a manifestation of this difference—it is in these conditions that priming has the largest impact on early-occurring, modality-specific processes.

GENERAL DISCUSSION

One goal of the present study was to determine whether long-term morphological priming involves a modality-specific level of representation, or if instead the only level at which morphological priming occurs is that of central, modality-independent representations. The results clearly demonstrate that morphological priming has a modality-specific component. In both experiments, target completions were more likely to be generated when they were preceded by visually presented morphological primes than by auditorily presented identity primes. Because the auditory identity condition provides an upper limit for the contribution of the modality-independent component of priming, the difference between the morphological and auditory primes can be taken as strong evidence that morphological priming has a modality-specific component.

Evidence concerning the time course of priming also supports this conclusion. The strongest time-course evidence comes from the results of Experiment 2, where both the survival analysis and the cumulative-proportion-of-asymptote analysis revealed that morphological priming had an earlier effect on fragment completion than did auditory identity priming. This difference between morphological and cross-modal priming, as well as the fact that the time course of morphological priming closely resembled that of visual identity priming, is what would be expected if morphological priming influences modality-specific processes that operate relatively early in processing.

This interpretation of the results assumes that priming in the morphological condition was truly a consequence of the fact that the primes and targets in that condition were morphologically related. However, given that morphologically related words are usually similar in form and in meaning, it is fair to ask whether our putative "morphological" priming effects were truly morphological in character. Could it be the case, for example, that the modality-specific component of priming in the morphological condition was actually a consequence of the orthographic similarity between the primes and targets?

While this possibility cannot be ruled out on the basis of the present results alone, the available evidence suggests that it is highly unlikely that it is the correct interpretation of our results. Although effects of orthographic similarity are often found in short-term priming paradigms, they are far less commonly observed in long-term priming studies. In a review of such studies, Rueckl (2002) concluded that priming based on orthographic similarity is unlikely to be observed unless there are (a) multiple repetitions of an orthographically related prime, (b) multiple related primes, (c) relatively unfamiliar targets (e.g., pseudowords), or (d) relatively unskilled readers (e.g., 3rd graders). When these conditions are not met (as is the case for the present experiments), priming is typically not observed for orthographically similar primes and targets unless they are morphologically related. (See, for example, Drews & Zwisterlood, 1995; Feldman, 2000; Murrell & Morton, 1974; Napps & Fowler, 1987; Ratcliff & McKoon, 1996; Rueckl & Mathew, 1999; Stolz & Feldman, 1995.) For present purposes, perhaps the most telling of these findings was reported by Rueckl, Mikolinski, Raveh, Miner, & Mars (1997), who also studied the effects of long-term morphological priming on fragment completion. In

Experiment 2 of that study morphologically related and unrelated primes were matched in terms of their orthographic similarity to their corresponding targets (e.g., *blanked-blank* vs. *blanket-blank*). While there was substantial priming in the morphologically related condition (comparable to the effects observed in the present study), there was no evidence of priming in the orthographic control condition.

Taken together, then, present and past results support the conclusion that morphological priming influences modality-specific processes. This conclusion is consistent with models of word recognition that hold that morphological structure is represented at a relatively early stage of processing (e.g., by modality-specific access units, Taft, 1994, or in the organisation of the distributed representations that mediate the mapping from visual input to meaning; Rueckl et al., 1997). Other findings provide converging evidence for an early influence of morphology. For example, Rueckl et al. (1997) found that morphological priming effects varied as a function of orthographic similarity. Similar prime-target pairs (*made-make, bit-bite*) produced more priming than dissimilar pairs (*took-take, bought-buy*). This interaction indicates a relatively early locus for morphological priming—early enough for orthography to be a relevant factor. An early influence of morphology is suggested by phenomena other than morphological priming, as well. For example, Prinzmetal et al. (1986) demonstrated a morphological influence on perceptual grouping—a process typically considered to be "too early" to be of direct interest to models of lexical processing.

As noted in the Introduction, evidence for a modality-specific locus for morphological priming does not imply that more central processes do not also contribute to morphological priming effects. However, attempts to isolate such a contribution—for example, by varying the semantic relatedness of morphologically related prime-target pairs—have generally proven unsuccessful (e.g., Bentin & Feldman, 1990; Raveh & Rueckl, 2000). Nevertheless, given the relative insensitivity of most priming measures to manipulations of this sort (see Weldon, 1991, 1993, for discussion), these null effects do not provide a compelling basis for concluding that morphological structure is only relevant at the level of, say, modality-specific access units. Indeed, given the nature of the evidence concerning morphological influences in other word recognition paradigms (e.g., Frost, Forster, & Deutsch, 1997; Gonnerman, Devlin, Andeersen, & Seidenberg, 1995; Marslen-Wilson et al., 1994), and the importance of morphology for various language comprehension and production processes more generally, it seems implausible to suppose that morphological structure is only represented at the level of the modality-specific representations involved in visual word recognition. In other words, our results are not inconsistent with claims that the "mental lexicon"—an amodal, abstract level of representation—is morphologically structured. However, our results do imply that such accounts are incomplete unless they allow for morphological influences at other levels of representation as well.

To conclude, the present results are generally consistent with accounts that hold that morphological structure influences relatively early ("pre-lexical") processes in word recognition. Because our results do not provide a strong basis for distinguishing among such accounts, we will not review the relative merits of them here. Instead, we close by pointing towards several broader theoretical issues that we believe are too often ignored, and yet will ultimately prove critical to the evaluation of these accounts. First, with rare exception, accounts of long-term morphological priming ignore the broader literature on repetition priming and implicit memory. This is unfortunate, as phenomena such as pseudoword priming and perceptual specificity effects are likely to provide interesting and valuable constraints for accounts of morphological priming (see Rueckl, 2002, for discussion). Second, more theoretical attention should be paid to the question of how word recognition processes come to be morphologically structured. To us, an account that attempts to describe the representations and processes employed in skilled reading without attempting to explain how those representations and processes came to be is an incomplete account at best. We agree that there is an important sense in which a model can account for the present results by positing *that* morphology has an early effect on word recognition. However, a more satisfying account would also explain *how* and *why* the word recognition process comes to be organised this way.

REFERENCES

Baayen, R. H., Dijkstra, T., & Schreuder, R., (1997). Singulars and plurals in Dutch: Evidence for a parallel dual route model. *Journal of Memory and Language, 37,* 94–117.

Bentin, S., & Feldman, L. B. (1990). The contribution of morphological and semantic relatedness to repetition priming at short and long lags: Evidence from Hebrew. *Quarterly Journal of Experimental Psychology, 42A* (4), 693–711.

Bowers, J. S. (1996). Different perceptual codes support priming for words and pseudowords: Was Morton right all along? *Journal of Experimental Psychology: Learning, Memory, and Cognition, 22,* 1336–1353.

Brown, J. S., & Carr, T. H. (1993). Limits on perceptual abstraction in reading: Asymmetric transfer between surface forms differing in typicality. *Journal of Experimental Psychology: Learning, Memory, and Cognition, 19,* 1277–1296.

Caramazza, A., Laudanna, A., & Romani, C. (1988). Lexical access and inflectional morphology. *Cognition, 28,* 297–332.

Drews, E., & Zwisterlood, P. (1995). Morphological and orthographic similarity in visual word recognition. *Journal of Experimental Psychology: Human Perception and Performance, 21,* 1098–1116.

Feldman, L. B. (1991). The contribution of morphology to word recognition. *Psychological Research, 53,* 33–41.

Feldman, L. B. (Ed.). (1995). *Morphological aspects of language processing.* Hillsdale, NJ: Lawrence Erlbaum Associates Inc.

Feldman, L. B. (2000). Are morphological effects distinguishable from the effects of shared meaning and shared form? *Journal of Experimental Psychology: Learning, Memory, and Cognition, 26,* 1431–1444.

Feldman, L. B. & Fowler, C. A. (1987). The inflected noun system in Serbo-Croatian: Lexical representation of morphological structure. *Memory and Cognition, 15* (1), 1–12.

Frauenfelder, U. H., & Schreuder, R. (1991). Constraining psycholinguistic models of morphological processing and representation: The role of productivity. In G. E. Booij & J. van Marle (Eds.), *Yearbook of morphology 1991* (pp. 165–183). Dordrecht: Kluwer.

Frost, R., Forster, K., & Deutsch, A. (1997). What can we learn from the morphology of Hebrew? A masked priming investigation of morphological representation. *Journal of Experimental Psychology: Learning, Memory, and Cognition, 23,* 1–28.

Frost, R., & Grainger, J. (Eds.). (2000). *Cross-linguistic perspectives on morphological processing.* [Special Issue of Language and Cognitive Processes.] Hove, UK: Psychology Press.

Giraudo, H., & Grainger, J. (2001). Priming complex words: Evidence for supralexical representation of morphology. *Psychonomic Bulletin and Review,* 127–131.

Gonnerman, L., Devlin, J., Andersen, E. S., & Seidenberg, M. S. (1995). "Morphological" priming without a morphological level of representation. *Journal of the International Neuropsychological Society, 1,* 142.

Henderson, L. (1985). Towards a psychology of morphemes. In A. W. Ellis (Ed.), *Progress in the psychology of language,* vol. 1 (pp. 15–72). Hove, UK: Lawrence Erlbaum Associates Ltd.

Henderson, L., Wallis, J., & Knight, K. (1984). Morphemic structure and lexical access. In H. Bouma & D. Bouwhuis (Eds.), *Attention and performance X: Control of language processes* (pp. 211–226). Hove, UK: Lawrence Erlbaum Associates Ltd.

Jacoby, L. (1983). Perceptual enhancement: Persistent effects of an experience. *Journal of Experimental Psychology: Learning, Memory, and Cognition, 9,* 21–38.

Kirsner, K., Dunn, J., & Standen, P. (1989). Domain-specific resources in word recognition. In S. Lewandowsky, J. C. Dunn, & K. Kirsner (Eds.), *Implicit memory: Theoretical issues* (pp. 99–122). Hillsdale, NJ: Lawrence Erlbaum Associates Inc.

Klein, J. P., & Moeschberger, M. L. (1997). *Survival analysis: Techniques for censored and truncated data.* Berlin: Springer.

Kucera, H., & Francis, W. (1967). *Computational analysis of present-day American English.* Providence, RI: Brown University Press.

Laudanna, A., & Burani, C. (1995). Distributional properties of derivational affixes: implications for processing. In L. B. Feldman (Ed.), *Morphological aspects of language processing* (pp. 345–364). Hillsdale, NJ: Lawrence Erlbaum Associates Inc.

Lee, E. T. (1992). *Statistical methods for survival data analysis.* New York: John Wiley & Sons.

Lukatela, G., Gligorijevic, B., Kostic, A., & Turvey, M. T. (1980). Representation of inflected nouns in the internal lexicon. *Memory and Cognition, 8,* 415–423.

Manelis, L., & Tharp, D. A. (1977). The processing of affixed words. *Memory and Cognition, 5,* 690–695.

Marslen-Wilson, W., Tyler, L. K., Waksler, R., & Older, L. (1994). Morphology and meaning in the English mental lexicon. *Psychological Review, 101,* 3–33.

Marsolek, C. J., Kosslyn, S. M., & Squire, L. R. (1992). Form-specific visual priming in the right cerebral hemisphere. *Journal of Experimental Psychology: Learning, Memory, and Cognition, 18,* 492–508.

Morton, J. (1969). Interaction of information in word identification. *Psychological Review, 76,* 165–178.

Morton, J. (1979). Facilitation in word recognition: Experiments causing a change in the logogen model. In P. A. Kolers, M. E. Wrostal, & H. Bouma (Eds.), *Processing visible language I* (pp. 259–268). New York: Plenum Press.

Murrell, G. A., & Morton, J. (1974). Word recognition and morphemic structure. *Journal of Experimental Psychology, 102,* 963–968.

Napps, S. E., & Fowler, C. A. (1987). Formal relationships among words and the organization of the mental lexicon. *Journal of Psycholinguistic Research, 16,* 257–272.

Plaut, D. C., & Gonnerman, L. M. (2000). Are non-semantic morphological effects incompatible with a distributed connectionist approach to lexical processing? *Language and Cognitive Processes, 15,* 445–485.

Prinzmetal, W., Treiman, R., & Rho, S. (1986). How to see a reading unit. *Journal of Memory and Language, 25,* 461–475.

Ratcliff, R., & McKoon, G. (1996). Bias effects in implicit memory tasks. *Journal of Experimental Psychology: Learning, Memory, and Cognition, 21,* 754–767.

Raveh, M. & Rueckl, J. (2000). Equivalent effects of inflected and derived primes: Long-term morphological priming in fragment completion and lexical decision. *Journal of Memory and Language, 42,* 103–119.

Roediger, H. L. (1990). Implicit memory: Retention without awareness. *American Psychologist, 45,* 1043–1056.

Roediger, H. L., & McDermott, K. B. (1993). Implicit memory in normal human subject. In H. Spinnler & F. Boller (Eds.), *Handbook of neuropsychology,* (Vol. 8, pp. 63–130). Amsterdam: Elsevier.

Rueckl, J. G. (2002). A connectionist perspective on repetition priming. In J. S. Bowers & C. Marsolek (Eds.), *Rethinking implicit memory* (pp. 67–104). Oxford: Oxford University Press.

Rueckl, J. G., & Mathew, S. (1999). Implicit memory for phonological processes in visual stem completion. *Memory and Cognition, 27,* 1–11.

Rueckl, J. G., & Raveh, M. (1999). The influence of morphological regularities on the dynamics of a connectionist network. *Brain and Language, 68,* 110–117.

Rueckl, J. G., Mikolinski, M., Raveh, M., Miner, C., & Mars, F. (1997). Morphological priming, fragment completion, and connectionist networks. *Journal of Memory and Language, 36,* 382–405

Seidenberg, M., & Gonnerman, L. (2000). Explaining derivational morphology as the convergence of codes *Trends in Cognitive Sciences, 4,* 353–361.

Stolz, J. A., & Feldman, L. B. (1995). The role of orthographic and semantic transparency of the base morpheme in morphological processing. In L. B. Feldman (Ed.). *Morphological aspects of language processing.* (pp. 109–130). Hillsdale, NJ: Lawrence Erlbaum Associates Inc.

Taft, M. (1994). Interactive-activation as a framework for understanding morphological processing. *Language and Cognitive Processes, 9,* 271–294.

Taft, M., & Forster, K. I. (1975). Lexical storage and retrieval of prefixed words. *Journal of Verbal Learning and Verbal Behavior, 14,* 638–647.

Tenpenny, P. L. (1995). Abstractionist vs. episodic theories of repetition priming and word identification. *Psychonomic Bulletin and Review, 2,* 339–363.

Weldon, M. S. (1991). Mechanisms underlying priming on perceptual tasks. *Journal of Experimental Psychology: Learning, Memory and Cognition, 17,* 526–541.

Weldon, M. S. (1993). The time course of perceptual and conceptual contributions to word fragment completion priming. *Journal of Experimental Psychology: Learning, Memory and Cognition, 19,* 1010–1023.

Winnick, W. A., & Daniel, S. A. (1970). Two kinds of response priming in tachistoscopic recognition. *Journal of Experimental Psychology, 84,* 74–81.

LANGUAGE AND COGNITIVE PROCESSES
2005, 20 (1/2), 139–167

Ψ Psychology Press
Taylor & Francis Group

Where does gender come from? Evidence from a complex inflectional system

Jelena Mirković, Maryellen C. MacDonald and
Mark S. Seidenberg

University of Wisconsin, Madison, WI, USA

Although inflectional morphology has been the focus of considerable debate in recent years, most research has focused on English, which has a much simpler inflectional system than in many other languages. We have been studying Serbian, which has a complex inflectional system that encodes gender, number, and case. The present study investigated the representation of gender. In standard theories of language production, gender is treated as an abstract syntactic feature segregated from semantic and phonological factors. However, we describe corpus analyses and computational models which indicate that gender is correlated with semantic and phonological information, consistent with other cross-linguistic studies. The research supports the idea that gender representations emerge in the course of learning to map from an intended message to a phonological representation. Implications for models of speech production are discussed.

Language production involves translating a conceptual representation, a message, into a phonological code that serves as the basis for an articulatory plan. Within this broad framework, there have been several proposals concerning the nature of the representations that mediate this

Correspondence should be addressed to Mark S. Seidenberg, Department of Psychology, University of Wisconsin, Madison WI 53706. Email: seidenberg@wisc.edu.

This research was supported by NIMH grant RO1 MH58723 and NIMH grant P50 MH64445. Mark Seidenberg was also supported by an NIMH research scientist development award. We would like to thank Marc Joanisse with whom we collaborated on developing the models used here, using software developed by Michael Harm, whom we also thank. We also thank Aleksandar Kostić for making available the electronic version of the Frequency Dictionary of Contemporary Serbian. This work benefited from the feedback of the attendees of the 3rd Workshop on Morphological Processing, held in Aix-en-Provence, France.

http://www.tandf.co.uk/journals/pp/01690965.html   DOI: 10.1080/01690960444000205

computation and the degree of interactivity among different types of representations. A complicating issue is the fact that words also encode information about the syntactic structures in which they participate, information that also influences a word's phonological form. Many languages employ inflectional affixes that convey largely grammatical information such as number, tense, case, and gender. Whereas English nouns encode only number inflectionally (e.g., *cat - cats*), many other Indo-European languages require that nouns (and often also adjectives and determiners) mark grammatical gender (as in the Spanish *el chico* (boy, masculine) vs. *la chica* (girl, feminine)). Some of these languages also mark case, indicating the grammatical role of a noun phrase in a sentence. One such language is Serbian, in which nouns are marked for case, number and gender.[1] For example, the suffix /u/ in /kravu/[cow] denotes that the noun is feminine accusative singular.[2]

Models of word production have traditionally assumed that gender and other grammatical features are represented independently from a word's semantics and phonological form. For example, although the word production models of Levelt and colleagues (Levelt, Roelofs, & Meyer, 1999) and Caramazza (1997) differ in some respects, they share two important assumptions. First, syntactic information, including grammatical gender, is represented by abstract features at a distinct syntactic level of representation. Second, processing at this syntactic level is independent of phonological and semantic processing (see Figure 1).

Evidence for the claim that gender is represented as an abstract syntactic feature has been obtained using two language production tasks, picture-word interference and fragment completion. In the former task (e.g., Glaser & Dungelhoff, 1984; Lupker, 1979; Schriefers, Meyer, & Levelt, 1990), the participant names a picture using a single word or, in some studies, a noun phrase (e.g., "dog", "a dog", "big dog"). A distractor word is presented on or near the picture (in case of auditory distractors, in close proximity or simultaneously with presentation of the picture). Depending on the timing of distractor presentation and other properties of the materials, the distractor word may interfere with picture naming, yielding longer naming latencies. Gender has been studied using this task by manipulating the genders of the pictured item and the distractor word. Several studies in Dutch found that picture naming latencies were longer when the distractor word had a different gender than the pictured item, compared with when they had the same gender (e.g., Schriefers, 1993).

---

[1] Languages referred to as Serbian, Croatian, and Bosnian were referred to as Serbo-Croatian in earlier literature.

[2] All Serbian examples are written in International Phonetic Alphabet, unless otherwise specified.

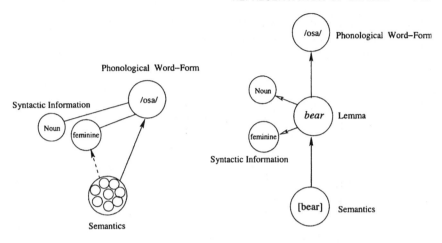

Figure 1. Word production models showing activation of the Spanish word /osa/[she-bear]. The model based on Caramazza (1997) is presented on the left, and the model based on Levelt et al. (1999) is presented on the right. Both models represent grammatical gender as an abstract syntactic node.

This result has been taken as evidence for priming of an abstract gender node, in that the gender of the distractor word interferes with activating the appropriate gender of the pictured item.

The fragment completion paradigm has been used to investigate agreement processes, whereby grammatical features on a noun (gender, number, and/or case) are also marked on other words in the sentence, as when a determiner or adjective agrees with the noun it modifies. In this paradigm (e.g., Bock, Eberhard, Cutting, Meyer, & Schriefers, 2001; Vigliocco, Hartsuiker, Jarema, & Kolk, 1996), participants are given a short sentence fragment and must generate a sentence that begins with this phrase. The dependent variable is the rate of agreement errors produced in the sentences. One focus of this research is whether semantic or phonological properties of the agreeing words influence the agreement process. In several studies these properties did not modulate the rate of agreement errors (e.g. Bock & Eberhard, 1993). These results have been taken as support for the view that agreement is an autonomous process in which abstract grammatical features such as gender or number are copied from a noun to the agreeing forms.

ALTERNATIVE VIEWS OF GENDER REPRESENTATION

Although these data are consistent with the view that word production involves activation of abstract gender and other grammatical features, other data raise questions about this approach. First, there is considerable linguistic research emphasising the extent to which grammatical gender is related to semantics and phonology (e.g., Corbett, 1991). In a comprehensive study of gender, Corbett (1991) argued that grammatical gender is predictable from various semantic and morphophonological regularities. He described the semantic and phonological correlates of gender across languages, attempted to describe them in terms of rules, and concluded that there may not be a need for a syntactic specification of gender. Corbett's view is that all gender systems have a semantic core; languages vary in the extent to which they make use of additional morphophonological information. In French, for example, a language whose gender system is often thought to be highly arbitrary, 94.2% of nouns ending in /ʒ/ are masculine, whereas 90% of nouns ending in /z/ are feminine (Corbett, 1991). Corbett (1991) also suggested that these language-specific correlates of gender are learned through exposure to a broad range of utterances.

Corbett (1991) offered similar observations about semantic regularities correlated with gender. He argued that gender has a semantic basis but not always the male–female distinction that is typical of Indo-European languages. Many languages, such as Ojibwa and other Algonquian languages, use an animate-inanimate distinction as a basis for the gender system. Moreover, even in Indo-European languages such as German, which incorporates clear male–female distinctions in the gender system, there are groups of same-gendered nouns that cluster on the basis of other semantic properties (e.g., Zubin & Köpcke, 1981, 1986). German nouns denoting superordinate categories are usually neuter, for example Obst (fruit), Instrument (instrument), Gemüse (vegetables); nouns denoting alcoholic drinks tend to be masculine; nouns denoting apes, mammals, and birds tend to be masculine, whereas nouns denoting reptiles and lower animals tend to be feminine. Corpus analyses supported these generalisations: for example, Zubin and Köpcke (1986) estimated that 70% of nouns denoting birds are masculine, whereas 76.9% of the nouns for lower animals are feminine (Zubin & Köpcke, 1986). Corbett (1991) identified gender systems based on semantic distinctions including animate–inanimate, natural gender, whether the word refers to something rational or non-rational, human vs. non-human, and augmentative vs. diminutive. These criteria vary in frequency across languages, with animacy and natural gender the most common.

These patterns appear to be part of a broader trend in which syntactic elements turn out to have semantic and/or phonological correlates. Grammatical categories such as noun and verb provide a salient example (e.g., Miller & Fellbaum, 1991; Kelly, 1992). The semantic correlates of these categories have been widely recognised (e.g., Gentner, 1981; Miller & Fellbaum, 1991); the phonological regularities associated with these classes have been investigated in recent years because of their roles in acquisition and processing. Kelly (1992) showed that phonological characteristics of English nouns and verbs vary in terms of factors such as stress, number of syllables, and word duration and that people make use of this information in processing. Similarly, Haskell, MacDonald, and Seidenberg (2003) identified phonological regularities among adjectives in English. These regularities were discovered by a simple connectionist model trained to distinguish adjectives from other open class words on the basis of phonological information alone. The model correctly classified 80% of the words in the training set. Cassidy, Kelly, and Sharoni (1999) showed that even in English, which codes grammatical gender only in pronouns, male and female names tend to have different phonological properties, which people use to infer the natural gender of the named individual (see also Cutler, McQueen, & Robinson, 1990). Studies of language acquisition suggest that these phonological cues play an important role in the acquisition of grammatical categories (Gerken, 2002). Thus the linguistic analyses indicate that there are strong correlations between grammatical features such as gender and semantic and phonological properties of words; the studies of acquisition and processing suggest that this information is utilised.

Some studies of language production also call into question the idea that gender is represented by a feature at an autonomous level of syntactic representation. Caramazza and colleagues observed that the gender interference effect in picture-word interference tasks, which has been taken as evidence for abstract gender nodes (e.g., Schriefers, 1993), does not occur in all languages. In Romance languages the form of a gender-marked determiner depends not only on the gender of the noun but also may depend on the phonological form of the noun (as in English, where the phonological form of the noun determines the choice between the *a* and *an* determiners). Caramazza, Miozzo, Costa, Schiller, and Alario (2001) interpreted this result to indicate that the architecture of the production system must afford different degrees of interactivity between different types of representations depending on the language. Thus syntax and phonology interact in Romance languages but not in Germanic languages, in which phonological form does not affect determiner selection. However, these results could equally be taken as evidence against autonomous gender nodes, in favour of a representation that integrates semantic and phonological information. Languages apparently differ in the extent to which gender relies on each of these factors. The same issue arises in connection with several studies using the fragment completion paradigm suggesting that both broad semantic factors beyond the conceptual representation of individual nouns (e.g., Thornton & MacDonald, 2003; Vigliocco et al., 1996) and morphophonological factors (e.g., Haskell & MacDonald, 2003; Vigliocco, Butterworth, & Semenza, 1995) influence the process of subject–verb number agreement.

In summary, considerable progress has been made within theories in which gender is treated as an abstract syntactic feature. At the same time, there is substantial evidence that gender is correlated with semantic and phonological factors that are segregated from syntactic representations in such theories, and that this information is used in acquisition and processing. Minimally these findings raise questions about how these correlations can be represented in models such as those illustrated in Figure 1. A further possibility is that the use of gender information in processes such as agreement is not merely influenced by semantic and phonological information; rather, that is *how gender is represented*. Gender, on this view, is an emergent property in lexical systems in which statistical relations between different types of information (principally semantics and phonology) within and across words are encoded. Note that on this view no single cue has to be entirely reliable, and indeed cross-linguistic analyses suggest that they are not. A given cue does not have to occur in all or even a majority of cases to be used in networks that encode probabilistic constraints (e.g., connectionist constraint satisfaction networks; Seidenberg & MacDonald, 1999). Such networks can make use of lower probability constraints; moreover, the interactions among constraints are nonlinear. Thus, two cues that are only mildly constraining in isolation may be highly constraining when taken together. Hence the existence of substantial though nonetheless imperfect cues to gender such as the ones discussed by Corbett (1991) and Zubin and Köpcke (1981, 1986) are significant.

In this article we investigate the role of semantic and phonological factors in gender representation and word production. We first present corpus analyses of gender in Serbian, a language with a complex inflectional system, including gender marking. These data indicate that semantic properties are highly but not perfectly correlated with gender in this language. Thus semantics provides strong probabilistic cues to gender. We then describe a computational model of noun production used to investigate the gender system. This model was developed by Mirković, Seidenberg, & Joanisse (2002) as a preliminary exploration of the capacity of connectionist networks to learn a complex inflectional system. The model (described further below) performed a simplified version of a production task: it was given information about a word (lemma, number, case, and sometimes gender) as input and had to produce its correct phonological form as output. The model succeeded in learning a large corpus of inflected words, generalised on the basis of this knowledge, and provided information about sources of complexity in the Serbian system. In the present research, we examined gender issues by comparing the performance of three versions of this basic model. In one condition the model included an explicit representation of a noun's gender as part of the input. In a second condition, the model did not receive any information about gender; it could therefore only produce correctly inflected forms by picking up on other types of information that are correlated with gender. In a third condition the model included a semantic cue that is strongly correlated with gender in Serbian. The comparisons between these conditions provide evidence concerning the extent to which gender marking can arise from correlated information.

SEMANTIC CORRELATES OF GENDER IN SERBIAN NOUNS

Serbian is a south Slavic language with a complex inflectional system (see Table 1). Nouns are coded for case (7 of them), number (singular-plural) and gender (masculine, feminine, and neuter). As the examples in Table 1 illustrate, because Serbian is a fusional language, these properties are coded with a single suffix. However, the relationship between the suffixes and the three properties is probabilistic. For example, with respect to gender, most masculine nouns in nominative singular end in a

TABLE 1
Inflectional forms of nouns /medved/ [bear], /krava/ [cow] and /selo/ [village]

case	Singular forms masculine	feminine	neuter
nominative	medved	krava	selo
genitive	medveda	krave	sela
dative	medvedu	kravi	selu
accusative	medveda	kravu	selo
instrumental	medvedom	kravom	selom
locative	medvedu	kravi	selu
vocative	medvede	kravo	selo

case	Plural forms masculine	feminine	neuter
nominative	medvedi	krave	sela
genitive	medveda	krava	sela
dative	medvedima	kravama	selima
accusative	medvede	krave	sela
instrumental	medvedima	kravama	selima
locative	medvedima	kravama	selima
vocative	medvedi	krave	sela

Note: All Serbian examples are written in the International Phonetic Alphabet.

TABLE 2
Examples of singular forms of a masculine (/sudija/[judge])
and a feminine noun /domatɕitsa/[housewife]) ending in /a/

case	masculine	feminine
nominative	sudija	domatɕitsa
genitive	sudije	domatɕitse
dative	sudiji	domatɕitsi
accusative	sudiju	domatɕitsu
instrumental	sudjom	domatɕitsom
locative	sudiji	domatɕitsi

consonant. However, there is a small group of masculine nouns that end in /a/ in this case/number form (e.g., /sudija/[judge], Table 2). Ambiguity is created by the fact that the /a/ ending is also used for the majority of feminine nouns in nominative singular. Interestingly, however, these masculine nouns are semantically similar: most of them refer to professions or actions that were traditionally performed by men, such as /sudija/ [judge], /vodʑa /[leader]. To complete the circle, some feminine nouns end in a consonant in this case/number form (e.g., /strast/[passion], Table 3).

As Corbett (1991) noted, in some languages a more reliable correlation between gender and form is obtained by looking at the whole set of inflectional forms a noun can take. That is, the gender of nouns ending in a consonant cannot be determined by looking only at the nominative singular (citation) form; however, a clear distinction between masculine and feminine nouns is observed if all inflectional forms are taken into account (Table 3). Because all inflectional forms of a noun have to be taken into consideration in order to find a reliable correspondence to grammatical gender, Corbett classifies the Serbian gender system as morphological (Corbett, 1988, 1991).

TABLE 3
Examples of singular forms of a masculine (/rast/[growth])
and a feminine noun (/strast/[passion]) ending in a consonant. Note the difference in the suffixes of the nouns of the
two genders

case	masculine	feminine
nominative	rast	strast
genitive	rasta	strasti
dative	rastu	strasti
accusative	rast	strast
instrumental	rastom	straʃtɕu
locative	rastu	strasti

In Serbian and other Slavic languages, gender systems are based on a male–female distinction for humans and for animals whose sex matters to humans (Corbett, 1988). For example, /lav/[lion] is masculine, whereas /lavitsa/[lioness] is feminine. Many neuter nouns refer to human or animal offspring, e.g., /devojtʃe/[young girl], /kutʃe/[puppy], /matʃe/[kitty], /lane/ [fawn]. Consistent with Zubin and Köpcke's results for German (Zubin & Köpcke, 1981, 1986), these examples suggest there may be strong semantic correlates of grammatical gender in Serbian nouns.

We investigated this possibility with respect to two potential semantic cues, animacy and abstractness, which were chosen because they are correlated with gender in other Indo-European languages (Corbett, 1991). We extracted a sample of 407 Serbian noun lemmas from the Frequency Dictionary of Contemporary Serbian (Kostić, 1999) to identify the distribution of the two possible gender cues. Approximately 74% of these nouns (300 lemmas) were randomly drawn from the Serbian frequency dictionary, and the rest were added to represent nouns that have relatively less frequent morphophonological patterns. The added items (107 lemmas) were randomly selected from the nouns with these lower frequency patterns. This corpus was also used in the simulation work presented below, and more details about the sample are provided there. Preliminary simulations run without these added items indicated that adding them had little impact on the model's learning of the training set; however, they do improve generalisation because the model cannot produce generalisations of lower frequency patterns unless it has been exposed to them. Each noun was coded for the two semantic features. Animacy was coded by the first author as a binary factor. Abstractness-concreteness is a graded dimension, but for the purpose of this work, we coded it in binary terms. To assign these values, we used English translations for Serbian nouns and the corresponding concreteness norms in the MRC Database (Coltheart, 1981). All nouns that had a concreteness rating higher than the mean concreteness rating in the database were coded as concrete, and the ones below were coded as abstract. In cases where the direct translation was not in the database, the closest semantic neighbour was used (e.g., *pound* was used instead of *kilo*).

The data presented in Figure 2 show that animacy, and to a lesser degree, abstractness, are strong cues to gender in Serbian. The vast majority of animate nouns in the sample (81.08%) are masculine, and the remaining are equally divided between feminine and neuter. Similarly, over half of the abstract nouns are feminine.

Given these positive results for abstractness and animacy, we next investigated a narrower semantic distinction. In some languages, food-related properties of words are taken as one of the criteria for gender classification (Corbett, 1991). For example, nouns that refer to edible and

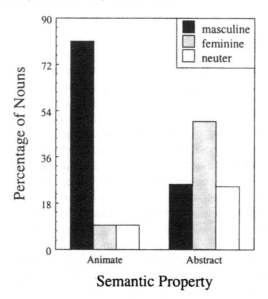

Figure 2. Animacy and abstractness as cues for gender in Serbian.

non-edible things may tend to belong to different genders (Corbett, 1991). In Dyirbal, an Australian language, an even narrower semantic distinction is informative: Dyirbal has a gender for non-flesh food. We investigated whether something similar occurred in Serbian, specifically whether the categories of fruit vs. vegetable co-vary with gender. The sample of nouns used above contained only one noun from these categories and so could not be used for this analysis. We therefore used Serbian translations of the English words that were unambiguously classified as a fruit or as a vegetable in the production norms of McRae, Cree, Seidenberg, and McNorgan (in press), which yielded 18 fruits and 20 vegetables. The data presented in Figure 3 show that nouns referring to fruits in Serbian tend to be feminine (72.22%) and nouns referring to vegetables tend to be masculine (65%). Thus at least some narrower semantic distinctions also co-vary with gender in Serbian.

In summary, these data suggest that, as in other languages, the Serbian gender system is at least partially determined by the morphophonological and semantic properties of nouns. Of course the cues we examined are probabilistic rather than absolute; given these semantic properties one cannot predict the gender of a word with certainty. However, we examined only two cues; the interesting possibility is that the system as a whole entails multiple probabilistic cues that together establish a word's gender with a high degree of certainty. This is a basic characteristic of constraint satisfaction processing systems. Cues that may be only partially reliable

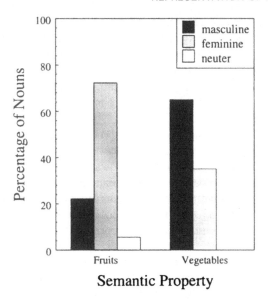

Figure 3. Fruits and vegetables as cues for gender in Serbian.

when taken individually become highly constraining when taken in
conjunction with other cues.

COMPUTATIONAL EVIDENCE

We then wanted to explore whether the representation of gender in terms
of semantic and phonological regularities could provide a basis for the
representation of gender in models of word production. As a tool, we used
a connectionist (PDP) model that was developed to address morphological
processing in Serbian nouns (Mirković et al., 2002). The earlier work had
two main goals. One was to determine, in a preliminary way, merely
whether a complex inflectional system such as in Serbian could be encoded
by a simple connectionist network. Traditional grammars of the language
describe the system in terms of a large number of complex rules with many
conditions attached to them. Such a system might better be described by a
set of simultaneous probabilistic constraints, and we built a model to
examine this. The other was to use the model as a tool for discovering
sources of consistency and complexity in the system that are otherwise
difficult to identify. The model took an explicit representation of lemma,
gender, number, and case as input and produced the correctly inflected
phonological form as output. Details are provided in the Mirković et al.
(2002) poster and below; the model was based on an architecture
developed by Joanisse (2000) to study Dutch inflectional morphology.
The model learned to produce correctly inflected forms for a large corpus

of Serbian nouns (over 3000 words). The model revealed some additional non-obvious facts about the system. One was that, in the model, the main source of complexity was learning about deformations of the stem (e.g., epenthesis, palatalisation) that are influenced by the inflection, rather than learning the inflections themselves. For example, if the phoneme preceding the suffixes /e/ or /i/ is /k/, /g/, or /x/, the consonant changes to /ts/, /z/, or /s/, respectively, in case of suffix /i/ and to /tʃ/, /ʒ/, /ʃ/ respectively in case of suffix /e/, as in /savetnik/[counselor]-MASC.NOM.SG., /savetnitsi/-NOM.PL, /savetnitʃe/-VOC.SG. The model also led to the discovery of a novel type of lexical neighbourhood that was shown to influence reading performance in native speakers of Serbian. In summary, this research represented a first attempt to model a complex inflectional system using principles that had been previously explored in work on the simpler English inflectional system and the representation of spelling-sound information.

The present research built on this work but focused on a different question: whether gender emerges from semantic and phonological regularities. The main data concern the performance of three versions of the Mirković et al. (2002) model that differed with respect to the way grammatical gender was represented.

Description of the models

The Mirković et al. (2002) model performed a simplified word production task (Figure 4, top). In the present study, three versions of the model were compared. One was the model described by Mirković et al. (2002), in which the gender of nouns was explicitly represented by three binary nodes, one for each gender (*Explicit Gender* condition). In the *Morphophonology Only* condition, gender was not represented on the input at all. In the *Animacy* condition, the model again did not have an explicit representation of gender; rather, the input included information about a probabilistic semantic cue, animacy. The principal research question concerned the extent to which a model of this type could produce correct output without an explicit gender feature on the input, using correlated semantic and phonological cues. It was beyond the scope of this research to develop full semantic representations for all words in the training corpus, and so the input did not represent all of the semantic features that may be correlated with gender. Instead we included only animacy, a highly salient feature identified in the corpus analysis described above. Given this limitation, we expected the model to perform worse than the condition in which gender is explicitly represented. However, this could be for either of two reasons. One is because gender really is represented in terms of an abstract syntactic feature, which the model

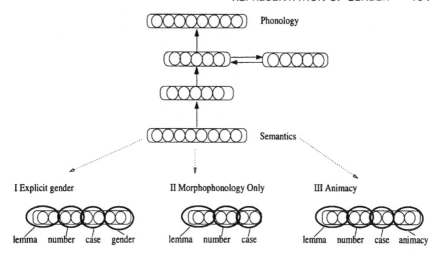

Figure 4. Architecture of the models. The general architecture relevant to all three models is at the top. The bottom row shows the semantic layer in the three types of models. Ellipses represent groups of units organised into layers. Arrows indicate directional weighted connections used to pass information among layers. The semantic layer is connected to the phonological output through two hidden layers with 250 and 100 nodes respectively. The second hidden layer has a layer of recurrence with 100 nodes.

lacked. The other is that the implemented model had limited semantic information with which to work: lemmas were encoded by localist nodes rather than distributed representations of their meanings, and the semantic condition included only one feature, animacy. Thus, the models with no explicit gender information had a built-in limitation on the extent to which correlates of gender could be discovered. Explicit gender nodes could be seen as standing in for these missing semantic representations, something that will need to be addressed in future research by developing models that use richer semantic representations. In this modelling we were mainly interested in examining the extent to which the model could pick up gender regularities given the information it had to work with, not whether performance would match that in the explicit gender condition.

Architecture of the models

The basic architecture of the models is presented in Figure 4. All models were fully recurrent networks that consisted of four layers of units with weighted connections between them. Each model's task was to produce the phonological form of a word given different types of input information described below. We refer to this input layer as "semantic" because in an ideal model it would consist of a distributed representation of the intended meaning (see Harm & Seidenberg, 2004, for a model using this type of representation). We have assigned specific functions to units for computational simplicity and labelled them for clarity. In reality we think these representations are also learned.

The output layer represents the word's phonology as a sequence of syllables that develops over time. The syllables are vowel centred within a CCVCC frame (C = consonant, V = vowel; /r/, /l/ and /n/ were coded as vowels in cases where they had a vocalic function; Stanojčić, Popović & Micić, 1989). Each phoneme in the syllable was represented by 16 binary phonetic features (Table 4), based on the standard description of Serbo-Croatian phonemes (Stanojčić et al., 1989). The use of recurrence allowed the network to generate a series of discrete outputs over time, which permitted simulating the production of multisyllabic words of varying lengths. Each syllable is produced on a different time step.

In all of the models, there were localist units representing a word's lemma, number and case. That yielded 407 lemma units, 2 number units (singular, plural), and 7 case nodes. Localist representations were used instead of distributed ones in order to keep the simulation computationally tractable. (Even in this simplified form, each model took several days to run.) To be clear, the use of localist representations here was a pragmatic choice, not a theoretical claim. In future research it will be important to determine whether, as we assume, the results replicate using distributed representations (e.g., semantic feature representations of the meaning associated with a given lemma rather than a lemma node). Ideally the input layer should reflect as closely as possible the nature of the production task, which involves starting with an intended message, not explicit representations of lemma, gender, number, and case.

In summary, the *Explicit Gender* condition included units encoding lemma, number, case, and also gender. In the *Morphophonology Only* condition, the input layer consisted of units representing lemma, number, and case, but not gender. Because gender is not explicitly represented and the semantics of the lemma was represented by localist units, the model could only derive the correct inflectional form based on morphophonological information. The *Animacy* model was identical to the *Morphophonology Only* condition except that one node that represented the animacy of the noun was added to the input layer.

Training

The training procedure was the same in all three conditions. The input was the representation of a word, which varied across conditions. For example, the model was presented with the word /krava/[cow] either as <krava>-NOM.SG.FEM. in the *Explicit Gender* condition, or as <krava>-NOM.SG. in the *Morphophonology Only* condition, or as

TABLE 4
Phonological representation used in the network

phoneme	consonant	vocalic	obstruent	sonorant	lateral	continuant	noncontin.	voiced	voiceless	nasal	labial	coronal	palatal	high	distribut.	dorsal
p	1	0	1	0	0	0	1	0	1	0	1	0	0	0	0	0
b	1	0	1	0	0	0	1	1	0	0	1	0	0	0	0	0
t	1	0	1	0	0	0	1	0	1	0	0	1	0	0	0	0
d	1	0	1	0	0	0	1	1	0	0	0	1	0	0	0	0
k	1	0	1	0	0	0	1	0	1	0	0	0	0	0	0	1
g	1	0	1	0	0	0	1	1	0	0	0	0	0	0	0	1
f	1	0	1	0	0	1	0	0	1	0	1	0	0	0	0	0
v	1	0	1	0	0	1	0	1	0	0	1	0	0	0	0	0
ts	1	0	1	0	0	0	1	0	1	0	0	1	0	0	0	0
s	1	0	1	0	0	1	0	0	1	0	0	1	0	0	0	0
z	1	0	1	0	0	1	0	1	0	0	0	1	0	0	0	0
ʒ	1	0	1	0	0	1	0	1	0	0	0	1	1	0	1	0
ʃ	1	0	1	0	0	1	0	0	1	0	0	1	1	0	1	0
dʒ	1	0	1	0	0	0	1	1	0	0	0	1	1	0	1	0
dz	1	0	1	0	0	0	1	1	0	0	0	1	0	0	0	0
tʃ	1	0	1	0	0	0	1	0	1	0	0	1	1	0	1	0
tɕ	1	0	1	0	0	0	1	0	1	0	0	1	1	0	1	0
x	1	0	1	0	0	1	0	0	1	0	0	0	0	0	0	1
m	1	0	0	1	0	0	1	1	0	1	1	0	0	0	0	0
n	1	0	0	1	0	0	1	1	0	1	0	1	0	0	0	0
ɲ	1	0	0	1	0	0	1	1	0	1	0	1	1	0	1	0
l	1	0	0	1	1	1	0	1	0	0	0	1	0	0	0	0
ʎ	1	0	0	1	1	1	0	1	0	0	0	1	1	0	1	0
r	1	0	0	1	0	1	0	1	0	0	0	1	0	0	0	0
j	1	0	0	1	0	1	0	1	0	0	0	0	1	1	0	0
i	0	1	0	1	0	1	0	1	0	0	0	0	1	1	0	0
e	0	1	0	1	0	1	0	1	0	0	0	0	0	0	0	0
a	0	1	0	1	0	1	0	1	0	0	0	0	0	0	0	1
o	0	1	0	1	0	1	0	1	0	0	1	0	0	0	0	1
u	0	1	0	1	0	1	0	1	0	0	1	0	0	1	0	1

<krava>-NOM.SG.ANIMATE in the *Animacy* condition. The model's task was to produce the correct phonological form of the word as output (in this example, the features representing the five phonemes in /krava/). On a training trial the representation of a word was activated on the input layer for a pre-set number of time steps. Activation propagated from the input to other layers. The first syllable was activated on the output layer starting from time step 3. For example, the features coding the phonemes in the syllable /kra/ would be active for time steps 3 and 4, and the features coding the syllable /va/ would be active for time steps 5 and 6. The models were trained using the backpropagation through time learning algorithm (Pearlmutter, 1995) which compares target activation values in the output layer to the obtained activations at each time step, and adjusts each connection weight in a way that gradually minimises differences between obtained and desired activations. Activation was compared using cross-entropy error (Bishop, 1995), which improves learning using backpropagation learning algorithm in periods of stagnation. The error radius was set to 0.1, meaning that errors less than this value were counted as zero, and the learning rate was 0.005. The network was initialised with small random weights.

Training corpus

The training corpus consisted of 3274 nouns generated from 407 lemmas taken from the Frequency Dictionary of Contemporary Serbian (Kostić, 1999). Each noun lemma in Serbian can have between 1 and 14 surface forms (7 cases × 2 numbers); for most lemmas, however, the model was exposed to only a subset of these forms. This reflects the fact that not all inflectional forms appear in the corpus of 2 million words on which the Serbian frequency dictionary was based. Also, we withheld 60 items (one inflectional form for each of 60 lemmas) to use in the generalisation test discussed below.

Several criteria were applied in the selection of words for the training corpus. The maximum length of words was six syllables and each syllable could not exceed the CCVCC frame. This did not require excluding many items; approximately 0.5% of the nouns in the Serbian frequency dictionary are more than 6 syllables long. All the words were in the Ekavian dialect. The final training corpus consisted of 42.26% masculine nouns, 36.85% feminine nouns, and 20.88% neuter nouns. These proportions are consistent with the proportions obtained in a larger corpus[3] (corpus: masculine–44.99%, feminine–40.43%, neuter–14.57% (Kostić, personal communication).

---

[3] This larger corpus consists of 2 million words from the 20th century daily press and poetry (Kostić, 1999, and http://www.serbian-corpus.edu.yu).

Word frequencies taken from the Serbian frequency dictionary were logarithmically transformed based on the equation

$$p = \frac{log(f + 1)}{log(f_{max})}$$

where f is the frequency of the word, and f_{max} is the frequency of the most frequent word in the corpus (/broj/(number)-MASC.NOM.SG., frequency of 1426 occurrences out of 2 million words). This type of frequency compression preserved the general statistical structure of Serbian, while assuring that the network was exposed to low frequency words without extensive sampling.

RESULTS

Learning

Five replications, corresponding to different "subjects", were run in each condition. The replications differed in terms of the initial random weight assignments, and because words were selected for training on a quasirandom basis (biased only by frequency), each model was trained on a different sample of words. All the models were trained for 3 million iterations (trials). Data were averaged across simulations, which yielded very similar results.

Performance of the model was assessed by a Euclidean distance nearest neighbour criterion, whereby an item was scored as correct if each computed phoneme was closer to the correct one than to any other one. It took the models approximately one million iterations to learn to produce 90% of the training corpus correctly (Figure 5). Importantly, the three models exhibited different learning curves. The Animacy model correctly produced an average of 92.35% of the items in the training corpus after 900,000 iterations, whereas it took an additional 100,000 iterations for the Morphophonology Only model to reach the same level of performance (as compared to the Explicit Gender model which took 800,000 iterations). For each run of the models a logistic function was fit to the learning curve, which in all cases yielded a good fit, with r^2 in the range .80–.91, and $p <$ .001. This procedure yielded estimates of the slope coefficient for each curve. The analysis of variance on the slope coefficients showed a significant main effect of model, $F(2, 12) = 18.781$, $p < .001$, with the Morphophonology Only model having the shallowest slope. Planned comparisons showed that the Animacy model had a steeper learning curve than the Morphophonology Only model, $t(12) = 3.527$, $p < .01$. This analysis shows that the Morphophonology Only model was slower than the Animacy model in learning the training corpus. Importantly, however, all

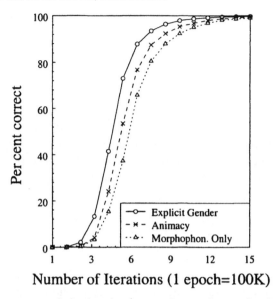

Number of Iterations (1 epoch=100K)

Figure 5. Per cent correct during learning (averaged across 5 runs of each of the models). The first 1.5 million trials are shown in the figure, the point at which all models correctly produced at least 99% of the training corpus correctly.

the models reached essentially perfect performance within 3 million iterations: the Morphophonology Only and the Animacy models produced on average 0.6 items incorrectly, whereas the Explicit Gender model produced no errors.

The items that were incorrectly produced across the five runs of the simulation in the Animacy and the Morphophonology Only models after 3 million iterations were very similar. The errors on the two items which both models missed were identical: /plemitɕ/[nobleman]-MASC.NOM.SG. produced as /plemits/, and /maʃtɕu/[lard]-FEM.INST.SG. produced as /mastɕu/. In the few items that were not learned correctly the errors were due to missing one or two features in a phoneme.

The results indicate that all the models, regardless of how gender was treated, successfully learned the training corpus, but at different rates. In order to examine this more closely, we performed an analysis of variance on the percentage of errors the models produced after 1.5 million iterations. The analysis of variance on the percentage of errors per gender showed significant main effects of model, $F(2, 12) = 31.591, p < .001$, and gender, $F(2, 24) = 39.745, p < .001$. Importantly, the Model × Gender interaction was also significant, $F(4, 24) = 3.886, p < .05$. In addition to being correlated with grammatical gender, animacy is relevant for determining the suffix of the accusative singular form of masculine nouns: in animate nouns the accusative singular form is the same as the genitive singular form whereas in inanimate nouns it is the same as the nominative singular form (e.g., /medved/[bear]-NOM.SG., /medveda/[bear]-ACC.SG. = GEN.SG.; /krompir/[potato]-NOM.SG. = ACC.SG., /krompira/[potato]-GEN.SG.). Thus, the difference between the models might have been carried by the accusative singular forms of masculine nouns. We therefore performed an additional analysis with the accusative singular forms of masculine nouns removed. The analysis showed the same effects: main effects of model, $F(2, 12) = 33.290, p < .001$, and gender, $F(2, 24) = 37.356$, $p < .001$, and a Model $\times$ Gender interaction, $F(4, 24) = 3.698, p < .05$. The significant interaction occurred because masculine nouns benefited most from the addition of the semantic cue, as expected (Figure 6).

The main effect of gender can be explained by the statistical structure of phonological properties of nouns of different genders. The largest number of errors in all three models is in masculine nouns and the majority of these (between 62% and 80%) are in the final phoneme of the nominative singular form. Whereas in the majority of feminine and neuter nouns the nominative singular ending is typical for that gender (/a/ and /o/ respectively), any consonant can appear in the nominative singular form of masculine nouns. For example, of the 25 consonants in Serbian only /dʒ/ does not appear as the nominative singular ending in masculine nouns in the Serbian frequency dictionary. Therefore, in terms of type frequency

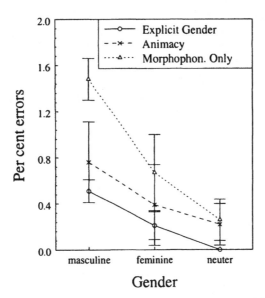

Figure 6. Percentage of incorrectly produced items in the three models after 1.5 million iterations.

any particular ending in the nominative singular of masculine nouns will be less frequent than the one for feminine or neuter nouns.

In summary, the analyses to this point show that grammatical gender in Serbian nouns is largely learnable from morphophonological and semantic regularities that exist in a substantial subset of words. Importantly, the simulations show that morphophonological cues are highly reliable in determining the correct inflectional forms of nouns: the Morphophonology Only model successfully learned more than 99% of the training corpus. However, if the performance of the model is more carefully examined, we can see that the model makes use of the additional semantic cue that was provided in the Animacy model, which speeds up learning.

One question raised by these results is whether the models achieved high levels of performance by merely memorising the training sets. With sufficient training the models could learn input-output mappings for all words without necessarily relying on statistical regularities that occur across words. In order to examine this possibility we conducted further tests of the models' capacities to generalise. Models that have merely memorised the training set would not be able to produce correctly inflected forms for items on which they had not been trained.

Generalisation

The generalisation stimuli consisted of 60 items. These words were derived from the lemmas the models were trained on (20 items per gender), but they were withheld from training. For example, the model was trained on all forms of the word /biʎka/[plant] except for the dative singular form, which was then used in the generalisation test.

The items in each gender were chosen to represent two broad sets: one consisted of nouns that are morphophonologically more typical for one of the genders in terms of type frequency, and the other consisted of nouns that are less typical of that particular gender. For example, approximately 70% of Serbian feminine nouns end in /a/ in nominative singular and their inflectional forms are made by changing the suffix, leaving the stem unchanged (Mirković et al., 2002). By contrast, approximately 10% of feminine nouns end in a consonant in nominative singular (cf. Table 3) and take a different set of suffixes than the rest of feminine nouns. This factor, referred to as category size, was shown to have an effect both in the performance of the model and in word naming in Serbian native speakers (Mirković et al., 2002), such that speakers were slower to name nouns from smaller categories compared with items from larger categories (with words equated in frequency and length). Similarly, the model performed worse on these items, both in learning and generalisation. Therefore the items in the generalisation test were matched across genders for this factor, such that half of the items in each gender were from the largest category and half were from smaller categories.

Testing involved presenting a generalisation item as the input and determining whether the model produced the correct phonological form. Generalisation was tested after every 100,000 learning trials (Figure 7). The Animacy model was always slightly better than the Morphophonology Only and slightly worse than the Explicit Gender model. At asymptote, the Animacy model produced 72.33% of the items correctly, whereas the Morphophonology Only model yielded 68.33% correct and the Explicit Gender model 78%. This performance indicates that the models had not simply memorised the training set. The absolute level of performance is difficult to assess because the model's training set was much smaller than a native speaker's vocabulary. The training corpus included only a subset of the nouns in the language. Perhaps more importantly, it did not include words from other grammatical categories, which is relevant because some morphophonological patterns such as jotatition occur more frequently in other categories (e.g., adjectives) than in nouns. Finally, as we have noted, the localist representations of the input did not allow the model to pick up on other correlations between form and meaning. Thus, it is relevant that the models were able to correctly produce many untrained forms using the restricted information in the training corpus, and there is a suggestion that higher levels could be achieved by using richer semantic representations and larger corpus.

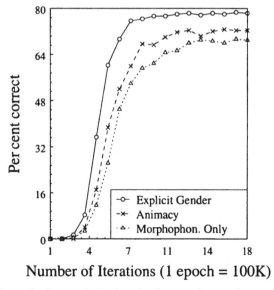

Number of Iterations (1 epoch = 100K)

Figure 7. Generalisation test during learning (averaged across 5 runs of each model).

We performed additional analyses on the number of errors in the generalisation test after 1.5 million iterations of learning (approximately 90% of the training corpus correctly produced in all three models) and after 3 million iterations (99–100% of the training corpus correctly produced). There was no significant difference in the pattern of results across the two analyses, so we will present data from the test ran after 1.5 million trials. The analysis of variance on the average number of errors per gender showed significant main effects of model, $F(2, 12) = 5.539, p < .05$, and gender, $F(2, 24) = 18.753, p < .001$; the Model × Gender interaction was not significant. Planned comparisons showed that the difference between the Morphophonology Only and Animacy models was not significant. This analysis shows that at asymptote morphophonological information was sufficient to derive novel inflected forms.

In summary, the generalisation test indicates that the models can generalise to new forms, indicating that they had not merely memorised the training sets. The model did not perform perfectly on the generalisation test, but it is difficult to know how this performance would compare to that of human subjects on a similar task (e.g., generating inflected forms for nonce words). The model's performance is likely to undershoot peoples', but the model was exposed to fewer forms and had less capacity to encode semantic regularities.

GENERAL DISCUSSION

The goal of this study was to examine the semantic and phonological correlates of gender in a highly inflected language. Consistent with previous studies of other languages, the corpus analyses indicated that such correlations exist. We identified several, such as the relationships between animacy and abstractness and the masculine and feminine genders shown in Figures 2 and 3. These findings suggest that gender distinctions are strongly correlated with various semantic features. In future research it will be necessary to determine whether there are other semantic correlates of gender, in order to assess the extent to which gender is predictable from multiple probabilistic constraints. This could be achieved by using a connectionist model similar to the one we described above to discover these correlations. For example, a large corpus of words could be assigned featural representations that capture main elements of meaning, as in the McRae et al. (2002) and Harm and Seidenberg (2004) studies. The model could be given these semantic representations as input and trained to classify words as masculine, feminine, or neuter, similar to the use of a connectionist model to discover phonological correlates of adjectives by Haskell et al. (2003). This exercise would provide stronger evidence concerning the extent to which gender is predictable from semantic factors.

The above modelling results are consistent with the corpus analyses insofar as a model lacking an explicit representation of gender both learned to produce correctly inflected forms and generalised to non-trained forms. In future research we anticipate developing models that can extract generalisations about both semantic and phonological correlates of gender and other inflections. We conjecture that the combination of these types of information is highly constraining, but this claim requires further research.

The best performance was achieved in the models that represented gender clearly and unambiguously using dedicated features. It is important not to overinterpret this result. It may be that models that, unlike the ones implemented here, provide a richer representation of lexical semantics would converge on a similar level of performance. The localist model performs better than other models (perhaps too well compared with people) but it cannot encode the correlations between semantics and gender that are present in the language and affect human performance.

Thus, the models provide preliminary data consistent with the hypothesis that grammatical gender can be learned and represented in terms of morphophonological and semantic regularities. This is in accordance with some linguistic analyses (e.g., Corbett, 1991) and with the general PDP approach in which a task such as production is construed in terms of mapping between semantic and phonological representations, with graded representations of gender, case, number and other lexical properties emerging out of learning to master this task.

Challenges for production models

Our research is preliminary and none of the results can be taken as definitive evidence against models in which information such as gender is represented by localist nodes at an autonomous level of syntactic representation. As we have noted, further research is needed to determine the extent to which a functional representation of gender arises from phonological and semantic information. That is the main challenge for our approach. However, our research also raises challenges for standard approaches to production. One thing that is prominent in our account and wholly absent from alternatives such as the Levelt et al. (1999) and Caramazza (1997) models is attention to how representations are learned. These representations must be learned because they are language-specific rather than universal. Thus a key question for theories that incorporate abstract syntactic nodes is the mechanism by which a child develops such representations given the information available in the input and facts about the capacities that children bring to the acquisition process. We know of no account of how a child would create the kinds of abstract, localist syntactic feature nodes that are prominent in standard theories of production. By contrast, in this paper and in other work (e.g., Haskell et al., 2003), we have examined how lexical representations could develop in a system that is learning to perform tasks such as comprehending and producing utterances. From this perspective it is easy to see how a learner would pick up on the semantic and phonological correlates of something like gender; moreover, there is growing evidence that young language learners are also encoding correlational information of this sort (Gerken, 2002). Although we have not demonstrated it here, our strong conjecture is that cross-linguistically, syntactic distinctions such as gender have substantial nonsyntactic correlates and that these are encoded in the course of learning to use language. This information may even prove to be sufficient to support processes such as producing and comprehending correctly inflected forms.

Further progress in deciding between competing accounts of production will require placing them on an even footing. Connectionist models need to address the wealth of behavioural evidence thought to implicate architectures like the ones proposed by Levelt or Caramazza. By the same token, these traditional theories need to consider how the representations incorporated in these architectures could be learned.

Further implications

Although the models presented here were not intended to capture the full range of processes underlying language production (and do not do so), they have implications for current accounts of how gender and other grammatical information is represented. Recall that the two dominant models of word production assume that grammatical information, including gender, number, case, and tense, are represented as abstract nodes that are separate from both semantic and phonological representations (Caramazza, 1997; Levelt et al., 1999). By contrast, we have suggested that these features may be emergent from semantic and phonological information. We presented data from Serbian nouns showing that gender identity is highly correlated with certain semantic properties, consistent with observations in several other languages (Corbett, 1991; Zubin & Köpcke, 1981). We incorporated animacy, the most general of these semantic features, into a model as a first attempt to illustrate how semantic information could guide the computation of a gender-marked phonological form. The clear effects of animacy in the model lead us to speculate that a richer semantic representation may obviate the need for explicit gender and other grammatical nodes in theories of production.

Of course, the viability of an emergent account of gender and other morphological features would not in itself be evidence that abstract grammatical nodes are not a part of the production architecture. That is, explicit nodes might seem rather superfluous, but theories incorporating them could still account for data of the sort that we have presented here. These accounts would have to address other questions to remain viable accounts of language use, however. First, there are now abundant demonstrations of correlations between grammatical features and semantic and phonological representations that affect language users' behaviours (Cassidy et al., 1999; Gerken, 2002; Kelly, 1992) and it is not clear how these correlations could be represented in systems in which gender and other grammatical features are represented through abstract nodes. Second, if gender is represented in terms of abstract syntactic features, how are they learned? Our own view is that gender arises out of semantics and phonology, information the child has to acquire in learning a language. If such information is not sufficient to account for facts about grammatical gender, then how does the child move from knowledge of form and meaning to this abstract level of syntactic representation? Models such as Levelt's and Caramazza's are silent on the issue of where these representations come from.

If gender information is emergent in the mapping between semantic and phonological forms, then it is possible to reconceptualise several important debates concerning the nature of inflectional processing during language production. To this point, we have considered inflectional processing only with regard to the production of individual nouns, but in many languages, features such as number, gender, and case also appear on determiners, adjectives and verbs. In these cases, the inflectional forms depend on the form of a noun; for example in French, a feminine singular noun such as *table* (table) will appear with a feminine singular determiner, any adjective that modifies this noun will also be inflected in the feminine/singular form, and if this noun phrase is the subject of the sentence, the verb will also be marked for singular, as in *La table est petite.* (The table is small.) The computation of agreement during production is typically viewed as a syntactic process in which the abstract grammatical features of the agreement controller (the noun) are passed to other words in the sentence (e.g., Bock et al., 2001). Within this view, a major question concerns interaction between syntax, semantics and phonological representations, specifically the extent to which the syntactic process of feature-passing is influenced by semantic and phonological information. Studies using the fragment completion paradigm have shown that the number of gender agreement errors on predicate adjectives (such as *petite* in the sentence above) is influenced by conceptual gender of nouns (Vigliocco & Franck, 1999, 2001). Vigliocco and Franck found lower error rates when the gender of the agreement controller had a conceptual basis (as in words for woman, man, nun, father, etc.) compared with the situation in which the noun's gender was more purely grammatical, as in the feminine French noun *table* above. They interpreted these results to indicate that conceptual features can influence the gender agreement process, and similar effects have been shown for number agreement (e.g., Bock, Nicol, & Cooper Cutting, 1999). Number information, like gender, has been assumed to be represented as an abstract syntactic feature. Accounts of agreement production have accommodated influences of conceptual properties of the noun agreement controller (Eberhard, 1999; Vigliocco et al., 1995) but have suggested that the agreement processes should be independent of broader semantic and morphophonological processes (Bock & Miller, 1991; Bock et al., 1999). The most interactive of these models is the Maximalist Input hypothesis (e.g., Vigliocco & Franck, 1999), which suggests that all the available information influences syntactic processes. Importantly, even though these models differ in crucial ways from the non-interactive word production models of Caramazza and Levelt, all of them incorporate the assumption that syntactic information, including grammatical gender and number, is represented on a level separate from semantic and morphophonological information. In this respect, the models differ only in the extent they allow the various levels of representation to interact.

By contrast, if grammatical information like gender emerges from phonological and semantic regularities that exist in the system, then the process of agreement takes on a very different character. The agreement process in this system could be construed in terms of semantic and phonological co-variations between the noun and the agreeing element (determiner, adjective, verb) (see Haskell & MacDonald, 2003; Thornton & MacDonald, 2003, for related discussion). This approach emphasises the important roles of learning and experience in the production process. That is, in the course of learning to comprehend and produce a language, the speaker is sensitive to phonological and semantic co-occurrences. Several previous studies suggest that co-occurrences of this type can modulate production processes. For example, Stallings, MacDonald, and O'Sheghdha (1998) found that the choice of syntactic structure during sentence production was modulated by properties of the main verb in the sentence, which they attributed to speakers' previous experience with verb-structure pairings. Similarly, Dell, Reed, Adams, and Meyer (2000) found that the distributional pattern of phonemes in four-syllable nonsense sequences affected the rate of speakers' speech errors in producing these syllable sequences, and the effects appeared within less than 100 trials.

Applying these general ideas to agreement, it is clear that co-occurrence between elements in a system that is sensitive to sequential patterns should have a powerful effect on production processes. Agreeing elements by definition co-occur, and a system sensitive to statistical structure will pick up these regularities. For example, in Spanish, the feminine determiner /la/ and nouns ending in /a/ tend to frequently co-occur. Similarly, in semantic terms, agreement controllers (nouns) tend to have a semantic relationship with their agreeing elements; for example subject nouns will tend to be plausible subjects of their agreeing verbs. Thornton and MacDonald (2003) investigated the role of this subject-verb semantic relationship in the production of noun-verb number agreement in English. They found that when another noun in the sentence was also a highly plausible subject, the rate of verb number agreement errors increased. They attributed this result to speakers' sensitivity to distributional patterns in the language, such that noun-verb plausibility relationships become a constraint during the computation of the number marking on the verb. We can speculate that a similar relationship could hold for noun-adjective relationships in languages with gender. On this view, masculine nouns will tend to co-occur with adjectives that denote more male qualities, and feminine nouns will tend to co-occur with more female qualities (e.g., Boroditsky, Schmidt, & Phillips, 2003). This fact can be used in production such that, if semantics is construed in terms of distributed representations, the semantic overlap between the adjective and the noun will facilitate the production of the correct gender-marked phonological forms of both words, because of previous experience of co-occurrence of these phonological patterns.

In summary, the models we have described partially instantiate an alternative perspective on the representation of gender and other grammatical features in language production. This approach emphasizes the acquisition and use of probabilistic information that seems to underlie distinctions such as gender that are treated categorically in most syntactic theories. The research raises several important issues. Are gender nodes necessary or is gender simply a convenient term for a network of probabilistic constraints involving other information, principally semantics and phonology? Are the latter types of information sufficient to account for language processes that involve gender or are other types of representations (e.g., explicit syntactic ones) required? If they are required, and they are not plausibly or demonstrably part of universal grammar, how are they learned? Does the emergentist account of gender extend to other types of grammatical representations, e.g., case, grammatical categories, and other syntactic elements? These questions are likely to be the focus of considerable future research.

REFERENCES

Bishop, C. (1995). Training with noise is equivalent to tikhonov regularization. *Neural Computation, 7*, 108–116.

Bock, K., & Eberhard, K. M. (1993). Meaning, sound, and syntax in English number agreement. *Language and Cognitive Processes, 8*, 57–99.

Bock, K., Eberhard, K. M., Cutting, C. J., Meyer, A. S., & Schriefers, H. (2001). Some attractions of verb agreement. *Cognitive Psychology, 43*, 83–128.

Bock, K., & Miller, C. A. (1991). Broken agreement. *Cognitive Psychology, 23*, 45–93.

Bock, K., Nicol, J., & Cooper Cutting, J. (1999). The ties that bind: Creating number agreement in speech. *Journal of Memory and Language, 40*, 330–346.

Boroditsky, L., Schmidt, L., & Phillips, W. (2003). Sex, syntax, and semantics. In D. Gentner & S. Goldin-Meadow (Eds.), *Language in mind: Advances in the study of language and cognition* (pp. 61–79). Cambridge, MA: MIT Press.

Caramazza, A. (1997). How many levels of processing are there in lexical access? *Cognitive Neuropsychology, 14*, 177–208.

Caramazza, A., Miozzo, M., Costa, A., Schiller, N., & Alario, F.-X. (2001). A crosslinguistic investigation of determiner production. In E. Dupoux (Ed.), *Language, brain, and cognitive development: Essays in honor of Jacques Mehler* (pp. 209–226). Cambridge, MA: MIT Press.

Cassidy, K. W., Kelly, M. H., & Sharoni, L. J. (1999). Inferring gender from name phonology. *Journal of Experimental Psychology: General, 128*, 362–381.

Coltheart, M. (1981). The MRC Psycholinguistic database. *Quarterly Journal of Experimental Psychology, 33A*, 497–505.

Corbett, G. G. (1988). Gender in Slavonic from the standpoint of a general typology of gender systems. *The Slavonic and East European Review, 66*, 1–20.

Corbett, G. G. (1991). *Gender.* Cambridge, UK: Cambridge University Press.

Cutler, A., McQueen, J., & Robinson, K. (1990). Elizabeth and John: Sound patterns of men's and women's names. *Journal of Linguistics, 26*, 471–482.

Dell, G. S., Reed, K. D., Adams, D. R., & Meyer, A. S. (2000). Speech errors, phonotactic constraints, and implicit learning: A study of the role of experience in language production. *Journal of Experimental Psychology: Learning, Memory and Cognition, 26*, 1355–1367.

Eberhard, K. M. (1999). The accessibility of conceptual number to the processes of subject-verb agreement in English. *Journal of Memory and Language, 41*, 560–578.

Gentner, D. (1981). Verb semantic structures in memory for sentences: Evidence for componential representation. *Cognitive Psychology, 13*, 56–83.

Gerken, L. A. (2002). Early sensitivity to linguistic form. *Annual Review of Language Acquisition, 2*, 1–36.

Glaser, W. R., & Dungelhoff, F.-J. (1984). The time-course of picture-word interference. *Journal of Experimental Psychology: Human Perception and Performance, 10*, 640–654.

Harm, M., & Seidenberg, M.S. (2004). Computing the meanings of words in reading: Cooperative division of labor between visual and phonological processes. *Psychological Review, 111*, 662–720.

Haskell, T. R., & MacDonald, M. C. (2003). Conflicting cues and competition in subject-verb agreement. *Journal of Memory and Language, 48*, 760–778.

Haskell, T. R., MacDonald, M. C., & Seidenberg, M. S. (2003). Language learning and innateness: Some implications of compounds research. *Cognitive Psychology, 47*, 119–163.

Joanisse, M. F. (2000). *Connectionist Phonology.* (Ph.D. Dissertation. University of Southern California.)

Kelly, M. H. (1992). Using sound to solve syntactic problems: The role of phonology in grammatical category assignments. *Psychological Review, 99*, 349–364.

Kostić, Đ. (1999). *Frekvencijski recnik savremenog srpskog jezika [Frequency dictionary of contemporary Serbian language].* Yugoslavia: Institute for Experimental Phonetics and Speech Pathology and Laboratory for Experimental Psychology, University of Belgrade.

Levelt, W. J. M., Roelofs, A., & Meyer, A. S. (1999). A theory of lexical access in speech production. *Behavioral and Brain Sciences, 22*, 1–75.

Lupker, S. J. (1979). The semantic nature of response competition in the picture-word interference task. *Memory and Cognition, 7*, 485–495.

McRae, K., Cree, G. S., Seidenberg, M. S., & McNorgan, C. (in press). Semantic feature production norms for a large set of living and nonliving things. *Behavioral Research Methods, Instruments, and Computers.*

Miller, G. A., & Fellbaum, C. (1991). Semantic networks of English. *Cognition, 41*, 197–229.

Mirković, J., Seidenberg, M. S., & Joanisse, M. F. (2002). *Morphology in an inflectionally rich language: Implications for the rules vs. connections debate.* Poster presented at the annual meeting of the Psychonomic Society, Kansas City.

Pearlmutter, B. A. (1995). Gradient calculations for dynamic recurrent neural networks: A survey. *IEEE Transactions on Neural Networks, 6*, 1212–1228.

Schriefers, H. (1993). Syntactic processes in the production of noun phrases. *Journal of Experimental Psychology: Learning, Memory and Cognition, 19*, 841–850.

Schriefers, H., Meyer, A. S., & Levelt, W. J. M. (1990). Exploring the time course of lexical access in language production: Picture-word interference studies. *Journal of Memory and Language, 29*, 86–102.

Seidenberg, M. S., & MacDonald, M. C. (1999). A probabilistic constraints approach to language acquisition and processing. *Cognitive Science, 23*, 569–588.

Stallings, L. M., MacDonald, M. C., & O'Sheghdha, P. G. (1998). Phrasal ordering constraints in sentence production: Phrase length and verb dispositions in heavy-NP shift. *Journal of Memory and Language, 39*, 392–417.

Stanojčić, Ž, Popović, L., & Micić, S. (1989). *Savremeni srpskohrvatski jezik i kultura izražavanja [Contemporary Serbo-Croatian grammar and style manual].* Belgrade, Novi Sad: The Institute for Textbooks and Teaching Aids.

Thornton, R., & MacDonald, M. C. (2003). Plausibility and grammatical agreement. *Journal of Memory and Language, 48*, 740–759.

Vigliocco, G., Butterworth, B., & Semenza, C. (1995). Constructing subject-verb agreement is speech: The role of semantic and morphological factors. *Journal of Memory and Language, 34*, 186–215.

Vigliocco, G., & Franck, J. (1999). When sex and syntax go hand in hand: Gender agreement in language production. *Journal of Memory and Language, 40*, 455–478.

Vigliocco, G., & Franck, J. (2001). When sex affects syntax: Contextual influences in sentence production. *Journal of Memory and Language, 45*, 368–390.

Vigliocco, G., Hartsuiker, R. J., Jarema, G., & Kolk, H. H. J. (1996). One or more labels on the bottles? Notional concord in Dutch and French. *Language and Cognitive Processes, 11*, 407–442.

Zubin, D. A., & Köpcke, K. M. (1981). Gender: A less than arbitrary grammatical category. In R. A. Hendrick, C. A. Masek, & M. F. Miller (Eds.), *Papers from the seventeenth regional meeting, Chicago Linguistic Society* (pp. 439–449). Chicago: Chicago Linguistic Society.

Zubin, D. A., & Köpcke, K. M. (1986). Gender and folk taxonomy: The indexical relation between grammatical and lexical categorization. In C. G. Craig (Ed.), *Noun classes and categorization: Proceedings of a symposium on categorization and noun classification, Eugene, Oregon, October 1983* (pp. 139–180). Amsterdam: Benjamins.

LANGUAGE AND COGNITIVE PROCESSES
2005, 20 (1/2), 169–206

The processing of root morphemes in Hebrew: Contrasting localist and distributed accounts

Hadas Velan, Ram Frost, and Avital Deutsch

The Hebrew University of Jerusalem, Jerusalem, Israel

David C. Plaut

Carnegie-Mellon University

The present paper investigates whether Semitic languages impose a rigid tri-consonantal structural principle on root-morpheme representation, by examining morphological priming effects obtained with primes consisting of weak roots. For weak roots, the complete three-consonantal structure is not kept in most of their derivations, and only two letters are consistently repeated in all derivations. In a series of masked priming experiments subjects were presented with primes consisting of the weak roots letters which are repeated in all derivations. The results showed that the two consistent letters of weak roots facilitated the recognition of targets derived from these roots. In contrast, any two letters of complete roots did not facilitate the recognition of complete root derivations. The implications of these results to Parallel-Distributed models and to localist-representational approaches, are discussed.

Although lexical structure is traditionally regarded as an interplay of orthographic, phonological, and semantic units, the view that morphological considerations need to be introduced into any model of the mental lexicon has been gaining increasing support. How morphological factors determine lexical organisation is, however, the focus of recent debates. Two contrasting approaches can be outlined to describe the present controversy. The Parallel-Distributed Processing (PDP) view of lexical

Correspondence should be addressed to Ram Frost, Department of Psychology, Hebrew University, Jerusalem 91905, Israel. Email: frost@mscc.huji.ac.il.

This study was supported in part by the Binational Science Foundation Grant 00-00056, and in part by National Institute of Child Health and Human Development Grant HD 01994 to Haskins Laboratories.

http://www.tandf.co.uk/journals/pp/01690965.html   DOI: 10.1080/01690960444000214

structure focuses on patterns of activation over processing units that correspond to the orthographic, phonological, and semantic sublexical features of a word. The PDP approach thus argues that there is no level of explicit and discrete representation that corresponds to morphological units. Rather, groups of intermediate or "hidden" units learn to mediate between phonology and semantics or orthography and semantics (e.g., Plaut & Gonnerman, 2000; Rueckl, Mikolinski, Raveh, Miner, & Mars, 1997; Seidenberg, 1987). Morphological effects, on this view, reflect a fine-tuning of the system to the statistical structure that exists among the phonological, orthographic, and semantic properties of words (see Plaut & Gonnerman, 2000, for a discussion).

In contrast to the present PDP models, the traditional localist framework posits that the lexicon should be modelled through representations at the level of meaningful units. Thus, localist models typically assume that morphemic units are explicitly represented in the mental lexicon, such that morphological representations are discrete and non-distributed. Although some investigators within a localist approach have suggested that all morphologically complex words are listed in the lexicon independently of the base forms from which they are derived (e.g., Butterworth, 1983; Henderson, Wallis, & Knight, 1984), current opinion is moving more strongly towards some form of morphemic account in which analysis and decomposition occurs for most morphologically complex words (e.g., Baayen, 1991; Burani & Laudanna, 1992; Caramazza, Laudanna, & Romani, 1988; Laudanna, Burani, & Cermele, 1994; Frauenfelder & Schreuder, 1991; Frost, Forster, & Deutsch, 1997; Marslen-Wilson, Tyler, Waksler, & Older, 1994; Schreuder & Baayen, 1995; Taft, 1994).

Distinguishing between localist and distributed approaches on the basis of pure empirical evidence is not a simple matter. When morphological processing is concerned, the two approaches often yield similar predictions. For example, localist models predict effects of morphological priming, expecting a facilitation that is due to the lexical interconnection between morphologically related words, or alternatively, to the mediation of morphemic units. In contrast, PDP models would predict the same effects, but describe them as a result of weight changes in the connections between the semantic, orthographic, and phonological layers, given the repeated exposure of the speaker to words having similar forms and meanings. Since PDP models focus on the amount of structure between surface forms and meaning, and this measure is continuous and non-discrete in character, languages having a rich and complex morphological system provide a natural ground for examining the validity of the distributed versus localist approaches.

Research on morphological processing in Hebrew is of special significance in the context of this debate, because of its great richness and unique characteristics. Morphological complexity is created in different languages according to different principles. As a rough approximation, the morphological structure of Indo-European languages can be characterised by a linear and sequential concatenation of morphemic units to form multimorphemic words. Thus, both inflectional and derivational morphology is based on appending prefixes or suffixes to a base morpheme, and as a general rule the orthographic integrity of the base form remains intact. In Hebrew, on the other hand, most words can be decomposed into two abstract morphemes: the root and the word pattern. Roots in most cases consist of three consonants, whereas word patterns can be either a sequence of vowels or a sequence consisting of both vowels and consonants. Roots and word patterns are abstract structures because only their joint combination results in specific phonemic word-forms with specific meanings.

The most salient feature of Semitic languages' morphology concerns, however, the special manner with which morphemic units are combined to form morphological complexity. Roots and word-patterns are not appended one to the other linearly, as in languages with concatenated morphology. Rather the consonants of the root are intertwined with the phonemes (and therefore, the corresponding letters) of the word-pattern (see Frost et al., 1997, for detailed description of Hebrew morphology). For example, the Hebrew word /**tirkovet**/ (meaning "combination"), consists of the combination of the root morpheme **r.k.v** (conveying the meaning of "combining") with the nominal pattern **ti--o-et** which conveys the syntactic information that the word is a feminine noun (the dashed lines stand for the places where the root's consonants are to be inserted). The same principle also applies to the verbal system. For example, the word /**hirkiv**/ (meaning "he combined") is formed by the same root **r.k.v** interwoven with the verbal pattern **hi--i-**.

Although Hebrew words are basically composed of two morphemes, these morphemic units play different linguistic roles in the derivational system of Hebrew. Whereas the root carries the core meaning of the words, the word-pattern provides mainly grammatical information such as definition of word class. A series of recent studies have employed both masked priming and cross-modal priming to examine the role of roots and word patterns in Hebrew lexical organisation and lexical access (Frost et al., 1997, 2000; Frost, Deutsch, & Forster, 2000; Deutsch, Frost & Forster, 1998; Frost, Deutsch, Gilboa, Tannenbaum, & Marslen-Wilson, 2000). Within the nominal system, when primes and targets shared an identical word-pattern, lexical decisions and naming of targets were not facilitated. In contrast, root primes facilitated both lexical decision and the naming of target words that were derived from these roots. In addition, in a further series of experiments within the verbal system, clear evidence was found for a facilitatory priming effect induced by the verbal word-patterns as well as by roots (Deutsch et al., 1998). These results suggest that roots as well as verbal patterns determine lexical organisation and govern lexical access. Thus, they are both recovered from the printed input. However, given the nonconcatenated nature of Hebrew morphology, morphemic units are, in most cases, represented by noncontiguous letters. How exactly are these units recognised in the very brief exposure durations of the masked priming paradigm?

At a first blush, it seems that a necessary condition for fast decomposition of printed words into their morphemic constituents requires a rigid structural system that provides native speakers with reliable cues regarding which letters (or phonemes) of a given word belong to the root and which belong to the word-pattern. For example, one possible cue could be a general constraint that roots in a Semitic language such as Hebrew necessarily include three consonants. When such a structural constraint is adopted, one can easily suggest an algorithm that separates the root letters from the other letters of the printed word with a reasonable error rate. This is because the distribution of the word-pattern letters is highly biased. For example, most word patterns begin with the letters H, M, T, or N. Many of them end with the letter T, etc. When the distributional properties of word-pattern letters are considered along with the requirement that three letters should be allocated to the root-morpheme, in most cases a single solution for parsing a printed word into a root and a word-pattern emerges.

To examine the possibility that Hebrew readers use constraints such as a tri-consonantal structure, Frost et al. (2000) employed a special subset of verbal forms that poses a genuine difficulty in parsing. These forms are labelled in Hebrew "weak roots". Weak roots are roots in which the complete three-consonantal structure is not kept in some of the derivations. These belong to two main classes: *defective* roots, charac-terised by an assimilation of one consonant in certain derivations, and *mute* roots, in which one consonant is almost never pronounced and becomes a quiescent letter in print. This is because of some linguistic processes (such as sound shifting analogies in derivation or conjugation, and phonetic assimilation). Although the phenomenon of weak roots seems to be a peculiar case anchored in phonetic and historical linguistic processes, we should emphasize that there are many weak roots in Hebrew (about 10% of the roots), and many of them form common, frequently used verbs.

In the defective roots, when the weak radical (usually the initial consonant /**n**/), has a zero vowel (a quiescent schwa), it is assimilated into the following phoneme. This phonetic process is systematic and occurs always at the same phonetic environment, i.e., it will always occur in the same word patterns whether they are nominal or verbal.[1] The only clue to this assimilation is the gemination of the following (second) consonant. The phonetic expression of the gemination is of an emphasised articulation. However, in Modern Hebrew, only three consonants have preserved this phonetic emphasis, the fricative consonants /v/, /x/, and /f/ (represented by the letters ב, כ, and פ respectively), which change to stops once geminated (namely change to /b/, /k/, and /p/ respectively). Orthographically, the gemination is marked by a diacritical point, which is inserted into the geminated consonant. Hence, in unpointed Hebrew the gemination remains unmarked (Berman, 1978; Blaue, 1971).

Since the phonetic and orthographic clues indicating the consonantal assimilation are not reliable in Modern Hebrew in both modalities (the change of articulation in the spoken form, and the diacritic mark in the written form), the end result is a "missing" consonant or letter in both the spoken and the visual modalities. Moreover, even if the gemination marking would have existed, the gemination by itself does not reveal the identity of the consonant which was assimilated. As a consequence, without specific training in linguistics, the existence of a defective root radical in the form is far from being obvious to any naïve speaker. However, the identity of the "missing" consonant could be revealed, by considering the quasi-regular appearance of the missing consonant. This is because the defective roots may appear as complete forms in some derivations, and readers may use this information to identify the consonant that is missing in the weak forms. For example, when the Hebrew root **n.p.l** (conveying the action of falling) is conjugated in the causative verbal pattern **hi- -i-**, the verbal form **/hinpil/** changes to **/hipil/**, and the identity of the missing consonant becomes obscure. However, since the conjugation of the same root with the reflexive verbal pattern **hit-a-e-** produces the form **/hitnapel/**, Hebrew speakers may gain some cues regarding the missing consonant in **/hipil/**.

The mute roots present an entirely different case. There are three different kinds of mute roots, and those are classified according to the specific radical and the position of the mute radical in the root (the first, the second, or the third phoneme of the root). The weak radicals are always one of the semi-vowel consonants /y/ or /w/ (the letters י / ו) or the plosive or fricative glottal consonant /ʔ/ or /h/ (the letters א / ה). Once a mute root is embedded in a word pattern (either verbal or nominal), the metric structure of the word pattern changes, because of the unpronounced radical. The scope of the metrical change may vary, depending on the

---

[1] For example, assimilation of the radical /n/ occurs in the following conjugations in Modern Hebrew: hif'il, huf'al, nif'al (in the past and present tense), and pa'al/kal (only in the future tense).

specific weak radical and the specific woɪ d-pattern. These metrical changes usually also entail some changes in the vowel structure of the word-pattern. For example, the regular form of the complete root **r.g.s** ("to feel") conjugated with the verbal pattern **hi- -i-** is a two syllabic CVC-CVC word, /**hirgish**/ ("he felt"). However when the same verbal pattern is conjugated with a mute root like **b.y.n** ("to understand") which has the weak radical 'y' in second position, the conjugated form is /**hebin**/ with the metric structure of CV-CVC, and a different vowel in the first syllable. The same verbal-pattern conjugated with the root **g.l.h**, ("to deport") in which the weak radical is the third radical, /**h**/, becomes /**higla**/ with the metric structure of CVC-CV, and a different vowel in the second syllable. The circumstances are even more complicated because in many cases there are alterations between the two semi-vowels /**y**/ and /**w**/ within one root so that the same root will appear in print in some occasions with the quiescence letter /**y**/ and in other occasions with the quiescent letter /**w**/. Similarly, in the few cases when the weak radical is pronounced and the derived form appears as a complete root, the weak radical can be pronounced sometimes as /**y**/ and sometimes as /**w**/. Thus unlike the defective roots, in which the specific identity of the weak radical can be unequivocally inferred from the cases in which the root appears in its complete form, the identification of the weak radical in the mute root is much more complicated and is not unequivocal. Another complication comes from the written manifestation of the mute roots. Apparently, the weak radical is explicitly presented in the written form of the word as a quiescent letter. However, the radicals of the mute roots, i.e., 'y' (י), 'w' (ו), '?' (א) and 'h' (ה) serve also as vowel letters in Hebrew to denote each of the five vowels (/i/, /e/, /o/, /u/, and /a/) that exist in Modern Hebrew. Consequently, the appearance of these letters in the mute root can be perceived by the naïve reader of the language as representing the vowel of the syllable rather than the mute radical. In sum, the existence of a weak radical in the mute root and its specific identification is a very vague matter, which is almost impossible to decipher for the native speaker of the language. This is because of three main reasons. First, the great variety in the metrical changes in the various root derivations given the location and identity of the specific weak phoneme of the root. Second, the alternations between the weak radical within one root, and third, the confounding with vowel letters in printed forms. These characteristics are in sharp contrast to the defective roots, in which the metrical changes are very consistent and thus probably more transparent (Berman, 1978; Blau, 1971).

To explore the process of morphological decomposition in Hebrew, Frost et al. (2000) used weak-root derivations in a series of experiments. These experiments revealed that the robust verbal-pattern priming effects in Hebrew (Deutsch et al., 1998), could not be obtained if primes and/or targets consisted of weak root derivations. Thus, when one consonantal letter was missing in the derived forms, subjects did not seem to be able to retrieve the verbal-pattern of the printed word. More importantly, once the weak forms were made to be complete by inserting a random consonant into their phonological structure thereby forming a pseudoverb, the verbal-priming effect re-emerged. These findings were interpreted to suggest that, in contrast to derivations composed of full forms, derivations composed of weak roots do not undergo morphological decomposition. Frost et al. (2000) thus argued that weak root forms present a genuine parsing problem to the native speaker. For if three consonants of the form are assigned to the root, there would be one missing for the verbal-pattern, and if all the correct consonants are assigned to the verbal-pattern morpheme, there would be only two consonants left for the root. This would violate the formal tri-consonantal structural representational constraint presumably adopted by the reader of Hebrew.

The present paper is thus concerned with the following question: Do Semitic languages indeed impose a rigid tri-consonantal structural principle on root-morpheme representations? Note that this question is not simply relevant for describing the psycholinguistic constraints imposed on any model of morphological processing of Hebrew. More importantly, it concerns whether distributed models will be able to account for the full range of morphological effects in languages with rich morphological systems (see Plaut & Gonnerman, 2000, for discussion). One major difference between distributed and localist approaches concerns whether behaviour is characterised as rule-based or not. Localist models typically regard the occurrence of morphological priming as a discrete cognitive event that reflects the existence or nonexistence of morphological connections. By contrast, PDP models focus on the amount of statistical structure between inputs and outputs, which is fundamentally continuous in nature. Thus, in general, any morphological effect that appears to have an all-or-none character constitutes an important, although not necessarily insurmountable challenge to the distributed approach (see also Marcus, Brinkmann, Clahsen, Weise, & Pinker, 1995). For example, returning to the context of Hebrew morphology, the fact that the robust verbal-pattern priming observed when stimuli have structurally intact three-consonant roots, totally collapses when primes or target contain only two root consonants, seems, on the face of it, more compatible with a rule-based processing system than with a distributed system.

This conclusion, however, may be premature and requires further empirical examination. The claims regarding distributed systems were based entirely on the failure to obtain a verbal-pattern priming effect with weak roots. The logic of this investigation was that the verbal-pattern priming effect necessarily reflects morphological decomposition, and if morphological decomposition cannot be demonstrated for weak roots then they are not represented as morphemic units in the Hebrew lexicon. It is possible, however, that although weak-root forms are not decomposed as fast as full forms, Hebrew speakers are nevertheless sensitive to the two consonants that are repeated in all of the weak-roots' derivations. The possibility that the two repeated letters of weak roots have a special lexical status relative to the other letters was not directly examined by Frost et al. (2000). The present research was aimed at conducting this investigation.

In a series of masked priming experiments, subjects were presented with primes consisting of the letters of mute and defective roots. We measured whether these letters facilitated the recognition of targets derived from those roots. The previous study on weak roots (Frost et al., 2000) did not differentiate between mute and defective roots. However, models of distributed representations have clear and differential predictions regarding their processing. First, PDP models suggest that the two consonants that are repeated in all derivations of mute and defective roots will reveal morphological priming effects. Similarly they suggest that the "formal" three consonants of mute roots will not reveal priming. This is because the third consonant does not have any consonantal (and therefore) explicit formal realisation. Finally, they predict that the three consonants of defective roots will reveal morphological priming effects, at least to some extent. This is because the third consonant appears in many of the derivations although not in all of them.

In contrast to prediction of the distributed approach, the view that Semitic languages impose a rigid structural constraint on the representation of root morphemes suggests that any primes consisting of two letters rather than three will not facilitate the recognition of derived targets. On this localist view, no difference is expected between mute and defective roots: none of them will reveal morphological priming.

EXPERIMENT 1

In Experiment 1, we investigated the processing of mute roots. The aim of the experiment was to examine whether a prime consisting of the two root-letters that are repeated in all of the root derivations can facilitate lexical decisions to the root derivations. Subjects were presented with target words, all mute-root derivations, which were paired with three different primes: in the related condition, the primes were the two repeated letters of the mute roots. In the orthographic control condition, the primes for the same targets were two letters contained in the targets, but not the two repeated root letters. Finally, in the identity condition the primes were identical to the targets. The purpose of the identity condition was to obtain a baseline for the maximal priming effect when the targets are primed by themselves. As in previous studies, facilitation in the related condition was assessed relative to the orthographic control condition in which an orthographic but not a morphological relationship existed between primes and targets. Greater facilitation for the two repeated root-letters would suggest that these letters have a special status relative to other letters of the targets.

Method

Participants.   The participants were 48 undergraduate students at the Hebrew University, all native speakers of Hebrew, who took part in the experiment for course credit or payment.

Stimuli and design.   The stimuli consisted of 48 target words. All targets were nouns which were derived from mute roots. Targets were four to six letters long, and contained two or three syllables with four to seven phonemes. Their mean number of letters was 4.73 and their mean number of phonemes was 5.46. The words were root derivations that were combined with a variety of common word patterns in Hebrew. The target words were paired with 48 primes to create three experimental conditions: in the identity condition, primes and targets were the same word. In the related condition, the primes consisted of the two letters of the root that are repeated across all the various derivations of the root, and the targets were the root derivations. In the control condition, the primes consisted of a sequence of two letters contained in the target, which were not the two letters of the root (although one root letter could be present). An example of the stimuli used in the experiment is presented in Table 1, the stimuli are presented in Appendix B. Similar to the word targets, the nonwords were also divided into three experimental conditions, identity, pseudo-related, and control.

TABLE 1

Examples of the stimuli used in Experiment 1 in the identity, related and control conditions. Stimuli are derived from mute roots

	Identity	*Related*	*Control*
Mask	#######	#######	#######
Prime	/hokara/ (respect) y.q.r (ר.ק.י) hwqrh הוקרה	qr קר	hq הק
Target	hwqrh הוקרה	hwqrh הוקרה	hwqrh הוקרה

The stimuli were divided into three lists. Each list contained 16 words and 16 nonwords in each of the three experimental conditions. The stimuli were rotated within the three conditions in each list in a Latin Square design. Sixteen different participants were tested in each list, performing a lexical decision task. This procedure allowed each participant to provide data points in each condition while avoiding stimulus repetition effects.

The stimuli in Experiment 1, as well as in all other experiments of the present study, were presented in unpointed Hebrew characters. Unpointed script was used because this is the way in which adults read Hebrew. Since we employed unpointed print, some of our letter-pairs in the related and the control conditions could be read as words. For example, the two letters 'QR' could have been read as /kar/ meaning "cold". Previous studies from our laboratory suggested that prime lexicality does not affect masked morphological priming in Hebrew (e.g., Frost et al., 1997, Expt 3). However, to ensure that prime lexicality did not introduce a confound in our study, we calculated the number of times the primes could be read as words in the related and the control conditions, for the purpose of conducting post hoc-analyses. The number of possible word readings was 41 in the related condition, and 19 in the control condition.

Procedure and apparatus.   The experiment was conducted on an IBM Pentium computer. The software used for presentation of stimuli and for measuring the reaction times was the DMDX display system developed by K. I. Forster and J. C. Forster at the University of Arizona. Each trial consisted of three visual events. The first was a forward mask consisting of a row of seven hash marks, which appeared for 500 ms. The mask was immediately followed by the prime, with an exposure duration of 40 ms. The prime was in turn immediately followed by the target word, which remained on the screen for an additional 1000 ms. The time lag between the subject's response and the next stimuli was 1000 ms. All visual stimuli were centred in the viewing screen and were superimposed on the preceding stimuli. Although only the Hebrew square font was used, two versions of this font, which differed in their relative size, were included. Targets were always presented in the larger font (20% larger than the primes). This guaranteed complete visual masking of the primes by the targets and made the primes and the targets physically distinct stimuli.

Results and discussion

The reaction times (RTs) were averaged for correct responses in the three experimental conditions across participants and across items. Within each participant, RTs that were outside a range of 2 SD from the participant's mean were curtailed. Establishing cutoffs of 2 SD above and below the mean for each participant minimised the effect of outliers. Any RTs exceeding these cutoffs were replaced by the appropriate cutoff value. Trials on which an error occurred were discarded. This procedure was repeated in all of the following experiments. The effect of the identity and related primes were assessed relative to the control baseline. The results are presented in Table 1a. Lexical decisions to targets were facilitated in the identity condition (32 ms) when the primes and the targets were the same word. The more interesting results, however, concern lexical decisions to target words with morphologically related primes. When primes consisted of the two letters repeated in all derivations, a significant facilitation of 13 ms was obtained.

The results were subjected to a two-way analysis of variance (ANOVA) in which the prime condition was one factor, and the word list was the other. This procedure was used in all of the following experiments, but only the main effect of the prime will be reported because the list variable was introduced merely to extract any variance due to counterbalancing.

The prime-condition factor was significant in both the participants and the item analyses, $F_1(2, 90) = 36.17$, $MSE = 348$, $p < .001$; $F_2(2, 90) = 20$, $MSE = 637$, $p < .001$. Planned comparisons revealed that the difference between the related and the control conditions was significant for both participants and items, $F_1(1, 45) = 14.29$, $MSE = 303$, $p < .001$; $F_2(1, 45) = 7.69$, $MSE = 604$, $p < .008$. The error analysis revealed a non-significant prime condition factor for both participants and items, $F_1(2, 90) = 1.46$, $MSE = 36$, $p < .238$; $F_2(2, 90) = 2.02$, $MSE = 26$, $p < .138$. The prime condition for nonwords revealed a significant effect for participants but not for items, $F_1(2, 90) = 3.18$, $MSE = 475$, $p < .046$; $F_2(2, 90) = 1.47$, $MSE = 814$, $p < .236$. No effect was found for errors for nonwords, $F_1(2, 90) = 2.4$, $MSE = 42$, $p < .096$; $F_2(2, 90) = 2.46$, $MSE = 42$, $p < .092$. In general, priming does not occur reliably for nonword targets under masked presentation. This is because facilitation in this paradigm is considered to reflect lexical processes, depending on the existence of a lexical representation (Forster, 1987; Forster & Davis, 1984; Forster et al. 1987).

TABLE 1a

Reaction times (RTs, in ms, and per cent errors for lexical decision to target words and nonwords in the identity, related and control conditions of Experiment 1

Words			Nonwords		
Identity	Related	Control	Identity	Related	Control
546	565	578	624	626	634
4.2%	5.6%	6.4%	8.4%	5.6%	7.5%
+32	+13		+10	+8	

To ensure that prime lexicality did not affect our results, we compared response latencies when the two-letter primes could be read as a word and when they could not. Planned comparisons revealed that lexical decisions to the targets did not differ significantly when the two-letter primes were words or not, in both the related and the control conditions, $t(46) = 0.5$, $p < .6$; $t(46) = 0.2$, $p < .8$; respectively. These results are similar to the findings reported by Frost et al. (1997).

The striking result of Experiment 1 is that primes consisting of the two letters of a mute root that are repeated in all of the root derivations facilitated the recognition of targets derived from these roots. This outcome demonstrates that the two repeated letters have acquired a lexical role that is different from all other letter combinations. From a representational perspective, the results of Experiment 1 suggest that, at least when mute roots are considered, a tri-consonantal structural principle is not necessarily imposed on root-morpheme representation.

EXPERIMENT 2

In Experiment 2, subjects were presented with primes consisting of the three formal letters of the mute roots. It should be emphasised that the linguistic origin of the three consonants of mute roots is well-defined in Hebrew grammar.[2] However, from a pure psychological perspective, since the weak radical of mute roots became a quiescent consonant, its exact identity is far from being transparent to native speakers of Hebrew. Note that some root derivations contain the "missing" letter in their printed forms. But since this letter is perceived as a vowel letter, it appears to belong to the word-pattern. The aim of Experiment 2 was to examine whether the presentation of all three root-letters of mute roots as primes facilitates lexical decisions to targets derived from them. Subjects were therefore presented with the same targets of Experiment 1, except that the primes contained the elusive quiescent letter, in addition to the repeated two letters of the roots.

Method

Participants. The participants were 48 undergraduate students at the Hebrew University, all native speakers of Hebrew, who took part in the experiment for course credit or payment. None of the participants had taken part in Experiment 1.

---

[2] Although for some mute roots there are arguments regarding whether the quiescent letter is a "y" or a "w".

TABLE 2A
Examples of the stimuli used in Experiment 2 in the identity,
related, and control conditions

	Identity	Related	Control
Mask	#######	#######	#######
Prime	/hokara/ (respect) y.q.r (י.ק.ר) hwqrh הוקרה	yqr יקר	hqr הקר
Target	hwqrh הוקרה	hwqrh הוקרה	hwqrh הוקרה

Stimuli and design. The stimuli consisted of the same 48 target words which were used in Experiment 1. As in Experiment 1, the target words were paired with 48 primes to create three experimental conditions: in the identity condition, primes and targets were the same word. In the related condition, the primes consisted of the three formal letters that form the root, and the targets were the root derivations. Note that because Experiment 2 deals with mute roots, one of the letters of the root does not necessarily appear in the target word. In the control condition, the primes consisted of a sequence of three letters contained in the target, which were not the root letters. The number of possible word readings was 38 in the related condition and 17 in the control condition. An example of the stimuli used in the experiment is presented in Table 2A, the stimuli are presented in Appendix C. As with the word targets, the nonwords were also divided into three experimental conditions. The stimuli were divided into three lists. Each list contained 16 words and 16 nonwords in each of the three experimental conditions. The stimuli were rotated within the three conditions in each list in a Latin Square design.

Procedure and apparatus. The procedure and apparatus were identical to those in Experiment 1.

Results and discussion

Response times were averaged for correct responses in the three experimental conditions across participants and across items. The results are presented in Table 2B. Lexical decisions to targets were facilitated in the identity condition (14 ms) when the primes and the targets were the same word. The interesting results, however, concern lexical decisions to target words with morphologically related primes. In the related condition no facilitation whatsoever was obtained.

TABLE 2B

Reaction Times (RTs, in ms) and per cent errors for lexical decision to target words and nonwords in the identity, related and control conditions of Experiment 2

Words			Nonwords		
Identity	*Related*	*Control*	*Identity*	*Related*	*Control*
569	583	583	638	647	642
5%	7.2%	8%	8.1%	7.7%	8.4%
+14	+0		+4	–5	

The results were subjected to a two-way ANOVA in which the prime condition was one factor and the word list was the other. The prime-condition factor was significant in both the participants and the item analyses, $F_1(2, 102) = 6.78$, $MSE = 529$, $p < .0017$; $F_2(2, 90) = 6.18$, $MSE = 653$, $p < .0031$, but this was due only to the faster latencies in the identity condition. The important result, however, was the identical latencies in the related and the control condition. The error analysis revealed a significant prime condition factor $F_1(2, 102) = 3.86$, $MSE = 34$, $p < .024$; $F_2(2, 90) = 3.42$, $MSE = 34$, $p < .037$. This was mainly due to fewer errors in the identity condition. The number of errors in the related and the control conditions did not differ significantly (F_1 and $F_2 < 1$). The prime effect for nonwords was not significant for both participants and items. $F_1(2, 102) = 2.24$, $MSE = 482$, $p < .112$; $F_2(2, 90) = 2.24$, $MSE = 575$, $p < .113$. No effect was found for errors to nonwords (F_1 and $F_2 < 1$).

Similar to Experiment 1, planned comparisons were conducted to assess whether prime lexicality had any effect on response latencies. As in the previous experiment, lexical decision latencies to the targets did not differ significantly when the three-letter primes could be read as words or not, in both the related and the control conditions, $t(46) = 0.7$, $p < .5$; $t(46) = 0.7$, $p < .5$; respectively).

The results of Experiment 2 show that, unlike complete roots, the formal tri-consonantal root of mute roots does not facilitate the recognition of forms derived from it. One possible explanation to consider is that the identity priming effect obtained in the Experiment was relatively small (14 ms only), whereas a larger effect (32 ms) was obtained in Experiment 1. By this view, perhaps the priming in the related condition was partly eliminated given the overall small priming effects obtained in the experiment (variations in the size of the identity priming are not uncommon in masked priming experiments). However, from a theoretical perspective, the lack of morphological priming is not surprising. In order to establish any form of root representation, or, alternatively, in order to pick up on the statistical structure between form and meaning, the three consonants of the root need be transparent to the speaker. In the case of mute roots, they are not. If this interpretation is indeed correct, then we should note that the two repeated letters of mute roots were present in the priming stimuli, as they were in Experiment 1. Thus, it seems that the mere presentation of the additional formal letter, which is missing in the derivations, was enough to eliminate the priming effect. We will refer to the implications of this finding in the General Discussion.

EXPERIMENT 3

In Experiment 3, the processing of defective roots was investigated. As described in the introduction, unlike mute roots, defective roots are characterised by an assimilation of one of the consonants of the root in certain derivations, whereas in other derivations all the letters and phonemes of the root are transparent. Readers of Hebrew are therefore exposed to the third consonant, although not to the same extent as they are with complete roots. The aim of Experiment 3 was to examine whether defective roots are processed by native readers as mute roots are. Thus, in Experiment 3 subjects were presented with primes consisting of the two letters of the defective root, which are repeated in all derivations. We examined whether the two repeated letters of defective roots facilitate lexical decisions to targets that are root derivations.

Method

Participants.   The participants were 48 undergraduate students at the Hebrew University, all native speakers of Hebrew, who took part in the experiment for course credit or payment.

Stimuli and design.   The stimuli consisted of 36 target words that were both verbal (past, singular, masculine) and nominal forms which were derived from defective roots. All the targets were words in the defective form, namely, the first letter of the root was opaque. Targets were three to six letters long and contained two or three syllables with five to seven phonemes. Their mean number of letters was 4.06 and their mean number of phonemes was 5.44. The target words were paired with 36 primes to create three experimental conditions, identity, related, and control. In the related condition, the primes consisted of the two letters of the root which are repeated across all the various derivations of the root, and the targets were the root derivations in their defective form. In the control condition, the primes consisted of a sequence of two letters contained in the target, which were not the two letters of the root. The number of possible word readings was 21 in the related condition and 16 in the control condition. An example of the stimuli used in the experiment is presented in Table 3A; the stimuli are presented in Appendix D. As with the word targets, the

TABLE 3A
Examples of the stimuli used in Experiment 3 in the identity, related
and control conditions

	Identity	*Related*	*Control*
Mask	#######	#######	#######
Prime	/mapolet/ (landslide) n.p.l (נ.פ.ל) mpwlt מפולת	pl פל	pt פת
Target	mpwlt מפולת	mpwlt מפולת	mpwlt מפולת

nonwords were also divided into three experimental conditions. The
stimuli were divided into three lists. Each list contained 12 words and 12
nonwords in each of the three experimental conditions. The stimuli were
rotated within the three conditions in each list in a Latin square design.

Procedure and apparatus.   The procedure and apparatus were identical
to those in Experiment 1.

Results and discussion

Response times were averaged for correct responses in the three
experimental conditions across participants and across items. The results
are presented in Table 3B. Lexical decisions to targets were facilitated in
the identity condition (29 ms) when the primes and the targets were the
same word. The interesting result, however, is that, similar to Experiment
1, there was a large priming effect in the related condition (19 ms).

The results were subjected to a two-way ANOVA in which the prime
condition was one factor and the word list was the other. The prime-
condition factor was significant in both the participants and the item
analyses, $F_1(2, 90) = 10.50, MSE = 959, p < .001; F_2(2, 66) = 11.55, MSE = 643, p < .001$. Planned comparisons revealed that the difference between

TABLE 3B
Response times and per cent errors for lexical decision to target words and nonwords
in the identity, related and control conditions of Experiment 3

Words			Nonwords		
Identity	*Related*	*Control*	*Identity*	*Related*	*Control*
601	611	630	683	685	679
8.7%	8.3%	11.8%	13%	12.3%	12%
+29	**+19**		**–4**	**–6**	

the related and the control conditions was significant for participants and for items, $F_1(1, 45) = 8.30$, $MSE = 976$, $p < .006$; $F_2(1, 33) = 18.06$, $MSE = 421$, $p < .001$. The error analysis was not significant in the participants analysis but reached significance in the item analysis, $F_1(2, 90) = 2.13$, $MSE = 82$, $p < .124$; $F_2(2, 66) = 3.25$, $MSE = 40$, $p < .045$. The number of errors in the related and the control conditions differed significantly for items but nor for participants. $F_1(1, 45) = 3.59$, $MSE = 80$, $p < .064$; $F_2(1, 33) = 7.68$, $MSE = 28$, $p < .009$. The prime effect for nonwords was not significant for participants and items (F_1 and $F_2 < 1$), nor was the effect for errors (F_1 and $F_2 < 1$). As in the previous experiments, planned comparisons revealed that lexical decision latencies to the targets did not differ significantly when the two-letter primes could be read as words or not, in both the related and the control conditions, $t(34) = 0.2$, $p < .8$; $t(34) = 1.1$, $p < .3$; respectively.

In essence, the results of Experiment 3 replicate those of Experiment 1. Primes consisting of the two letters of a defective root which are repeated in all the root derivations facilitate lexical decision to the respective derivations. This outcome suggests again that a tri-consonantal structural constraint is not imposed on the root morpheme representation.

EXPERIMENT 4

The main difference between mute and defective roots concerns the quasi-regular appearance of the third consonant. Thus, in defective roots one radical is assimilated into the following radical only in certain derivations, whereas for the rest of the derivations the three consonants of the defective root are entirely transparent. The aim of Experiment 4 was to examine whether the partial exposure to the assimilated radical in certain derivations is sufficient to establish a tri-consonantal representation for defective roots that is similar to that for complete and intact Hebrew roots. For this purpose, subjects were presented with the three root letters of defective roots as primes, while the targets consisted of root derivations which included the assimilated radical (i.e., targets appearing in their complete forms).

Method

Participants. The participants were 48 undergraduate students at the Hebrew University, all native speakers of Hebrew, who took part in the experiment for course credit or payment. None of the participants had taken part in Experiment 3.

Stimuli and design. The stimuli consisted of 36 target words that were both verbal and nominal forms, which were derived from the same defective roots employed in Experiment 3. *All the targets in Experiment 4,*

TABLE 4A

Examples of the stimuli used in Experiment 4 in the identity, related
and control conditions

	Identity	Related	Control
Mask	#######	#######	#######
Prime	/nefila/ (fall) n.p.l (נ.פ.ל) npylh נפילה	npl נפל	plh פלה
Target	npylh נפילה	npylh נפילה	npylh נפילה

*however, were derivations in which the three letters of the defective roots
were transparent.* Targets were four to six letters long, and contained two
or three syllables with five to eight phonemes. Their mean number of
letters was 4.64 and their mean number of phonemes was 5.92. The target
words were paired with 36 primes to create three experimental conditions,
identity, related, and control. In the related condition, the primes consisted
of the three letters of the root and the targets were the root derivations in
their complete form. In the control condition, the primes consisted of a
sequence of three letters contained in the target which were not the three
letters of the root. The number of possible word readings was 29 in the
related condition and 11 in the control condition. An example of the
stimuli used in the experiment is presented in Table 4A, the stimuli are
presented in Appendix E. As with the word targets, the nonwords were
also divided into three experimental conditions. The stimuli were divided
into three lists. Each list contained 12 words and 12 nonwords in each of
the three experimental conditions.

Procedure and apparatus.   The procedure and apparatus were identical
to those in the previous experiments.

Results and discussion

Response times were averaged for correct responses in the three
experimental conditions across participants and across items. The results
are presented in Table 4B. Lexical decisions to targets were facilitated in
the identity condition (22 ms) when the primes and the targets were the
same word. However, similar to the primes consisting of the two repeated
letters, but in sharp contrast to the results of Experiment 2 with mute roots,
there was a significant and robust priming effect in the related condition
(17 ms).

TABLE 4B
Response times and per cent errors for lexical decision to target words and nonwords
in the identity, related and control conditions of Experiment 4

Words			Nonwords		
Identity	Related	Control	Identity	Related	Control
618	623	640	689	699	688
8.2%	7.2%	11.6%	8.9%	10.8%	6.6%
+22	+17		−1	−11	

The results were subjected to a two-way ANOVA in which the prime condition was one factor and the word list was the other. The prime-condition factor was significant for both participants and items, $F_1(2, 108) = 5.94$, $MSE = 1265$, $p < .0036$; $F_2(2, 66) = 5.72$, $MSE = 1051$, $p < .005$. Planned comparisons revealed that the difference between the related and the control conditions was significant for both participants and items, $F_1(1, 54) = 6.50$, $MSE = 1285$, $p < .014$; $F_2(1, 33) = 5.42$, $MSE = 1215$, $p < .026$. The error analysis revealed a significant effect for participants and a significant effect for items. $F_1(2, 108) = 5.25$, $MSE = 57$, $p < .007$; $F_2(2, 66) = 4.13$, $MSE = 46$, $p < .020$. The number of errors in the related the control conditions differed significantly, $F_1(1, 54) = 10.17$, $MSE = 54$, $p < .002$; $F_2(1, 33) = 8.19$, $MSE = 42$, $p < .007$. RTs in the identity and the control conditions for nonwords were virtually identical. Once again, planned comparisons revealed that response latencies to the targets did not differ significantly when the three-letter primes could be read as words or not, in both the related and the control conditions, $t(34) = 0.4$, $p < .7$; $t(34) = 1.4$, $p < .2$; respectively).

The conclusions from Experiment 4 are straightforward. Primes that include the variably missing letter of defective roots facilitate the recognition of targets that are defective-root derivations.

EXPERIMENT 5

Experiment 4 yielded one interesting outcome: similar to complete roots (Frost et al., 1997), the three consonants of defective roots produced significant root priming. These results, however, do not concur with the findings obtained with mute roots in Experiment 2. The possible difference between the two experiments is that the targets employed in Experiment 2 did not include the third consonantal letter which appeared in the priming stimulus, whereas the targets employed in Experiment 4 included the three letters of the defective roots. Thus, the overall orthographic similarity between primes and targets may have been larger for the defective roots than for the mute roots. The aim of Experiment 5 was to examine whether root priming can be obtained when the three letters of defective roots are presented as primes but the weak radical is missing in the target. Any priming effect obtained in this experimental manipulation will emphasise the morphological origin of the priming effect, and will reinforce the conclusion that defective roots have acquired a tri-consonantal representation for readers of Hebrew. For this purpose, participants were presented with target words, all defective root derivations, in which the weak radical was missing. The targets in the related condition were primed by the three letters of the defective roots. This introduced an additional orthographic dissimilarity relative to the manipulation employed in the previous experiment.

Method

Participants.   The participants were 48 undergraduate students at the Hebrew University, all native speakers of Hebrew, who took part in the experiment for course credit or payment. None of the participants had taken part in Experiments 3 or 4.

Stimuli and design.   The stimuli consisted of the same 36 target words as in experiment 3 with slight changes. Like Experiment 3, the target words appeared in their defective form (one letter of the root was missing). Targets were three to six letters long, and contained two or three syllables with five to seven phonemes. Their mean number of letters was 4.11 and their mean number of phonemes was 5.47. The target words were paired with 36 primes to create three experimental conditions: identity related, and control. In the related condition, the primes consisted of the three letters of the root, whereas the targets were the root derivations in their defective form. In the control condition, the primes consisted of complete roots that contained two letters of the defective roots, the letters which are repeated in all of the roots' derivations, in addition to another letter which did not belong to the root. This ensured complete orthographic similarity between the related and the control conditions. The number of possible word readings was 31 in the related condition and 33 in the control condition. An example of the stimuli used in the experiment is presented in Table 5A, the stimuli are presented in Appendix F. The stimuli were divided into three lists, each list contained 12 words and 12 nonwords in each of the three experimental conditions. The procedure and apparatus were identical to those in the previous experiments.

Results and discussion

Response times for correct responses were averaged in the three experimental conditions across participants and across items. The results

TABLE 5A
Examples of the stimuli used in Experiment 5 in the identity, related
and control conditions

	Identity	Related	Control
Mask	#######	#######	#######
Prime	/mapolet/ (landslide) n.p.l (נ.פ.ל) mpwlt מפולת	npl נפל	kpl כפל
Target	mpwlt מפולת	mpwlt מפולת	mpwlt מפולת

are presented in Table 5B. Lexical decisions to targets were facilitated in
the identity condition (35 ms). The interesting result, however, is, that
similar to Experiment 4, there was a significant priming effect in the
related condition (19 ms) even though not all the three consonants of the
root were present in the targets.

The results were subjected to a two-way ANOVA in which the prime
condition was one factor and the word list was the other. The prime
condition factor was significant in both the participants and the item
analysis, $F_1(2, 90) = 15.49$, $MSE = 969$, $p < .001$; $F_2(2, 66) = 10.94$, $MSE = 866$, $p < .001$. Planned comparisons revealed that the difference between
the related and the control conditions was significant for both participants
and items. $F_1(1, 45) = 9.50$, $MSE = 944$, $p < .004$; $F_2(1, 33) = 7.48$, $MSE = 756$, $p < .001$. The error analysis revealed a nonsignificant effect for both
participants and items (F_1 and $F_2 < 1$). The number of errors in the related
and the control conditions did not differ significantly (F_1 and $F_2 < 1$). The
prime effect for nonwords revealed a significant effect for both participants
and items. $F_1(2, 90) = 8.87$, $MSE = 1057$, $p < .001$; $F_2(2, 66) = 5.93$, $MSE = 852$, $p < .005$. The error analysis of nonwords revealed a nonsignificant
effect for both participants and items $F_1(2, 90) = 2.27$, $MSE = 113$, $p < .109$; $F_2(2, 66) = 2.92$, $MSE = 66$, $p < .061$.[3] Since almost all primes had a
word reading in both the related and the control condition, we did not
assess the effect of lexicality.

The results of Experiment 5 clearly demonstrate the differences between
mute and defective roots. Unlike Experiment 2, the three letters of
defective roots facilitated the recognition of root derivations even though

---

[3] We have no explanation for the effect obtained for nonwords, since the printing obtained
under masked presentation is considered a lexical effect. We can only report that such effects
have sometimes been found and reported in our laboratory (e.g., Frost et al., 2000, Expt 3).

TABLE 5B
Response times and per cent errors for lexical decision to target words and nonwords
in the identity, related and control conditions of Experiment 5

Words			Nonwords		
Identity	*Related*	*Control*	*Identity*	*Related*	*Control*
570	586	605	634	653	662
9.2%	10.1%	11.1%	17.2%	13.4%	13%
+35	**+19**		**+28**	**+9**	

one of the letters of the root was missing in the target. From a
representational perspective, the results of Experiment 5 together with
Experiment 4 seem to suggest that defective roots have an allomorphic
representation. The priming effects obtained with the two repeated letters
of the root and with the full three letters are virtually identical.

EXPERIMENT 6A AND 6B

The priming effects obtained for both mute and defective roots suggest
that the two repeated letters of the root are sufficient to induce
morphological priming. The aim of Experiment 6a and 6b was to
investigate whether this finding extends to complete roots as well. None
of the previous experiments investigating root priming with complete roots
tested whether two root letters facilitate target recognition better than any
other letters of the word. If all three root letters yield robust priming but
any pair of root letters do not, it would implicate highly conjunctive,
nonlinear processing in morphology that would place strong constraints on
graded, distributed accounts. To avoid inferential problems related to
statistical power, two sets of participants as well as two sets of items were
tested in two independent experiments, 6a and 6b.

Method

Participants.   The participants were 48 undergraduate students at the
Hebrew University, all native speakers of Hebrew, who took part in the
experiment for course credit or payment.

Stimuli and design.   The stimuli consisted of 48 target words. All targets
were derived from complete roots. Targets were four to six letters long,
and contained two or three syllables with five to eight phonemes. Their
mean number of letters was 4.92 and their mean number of phonemes was
6.19. The target words were paired with 48 primes to create three
experimental conditions, identity, related, and control. In the related

TABLE 6A
Examples of the stimuli used in Experiment 6 in the identity, related
and control conditions

	Identity	*Related*	*Control*
Mask	#######	#######	#######
Prime	/maxberet/ (notebook) x.b.r (ר.ב.ח)		
	mxbrt	xr	mb
	מחברת	חר	מב
Target	mxbrt	mxbrt	mxbrt
	מחברת	מחברת	מחברת

condition, the primes consisted of two out of the three letters of the root.[4] In the control condition, the primes consisted of a sequence of two letters contained in the target, which were not the two letters of the root. In both the related and the control conditions, half of the trials involved the disruption of the prime's sequence within the target, and half of the trials did not. The number of possible word readings was 34 in the related condition and 22 in the control condition. An example of the stimuli used in the experiment is presented in Table 6A; the stimuli are presented in Appendix G. Forty-eight target nonwords were employed and similar to the words, they included three experimental conditions. The stimuli were divided into three lists. Each list contained 16 words and 16 nonwords in each of the three experimental conditions. The stimuli were rotated within the three conditions in each list in a Latin Square design. Sixteen different participants were tested in each list, performing a lexical decision task. The procedure and apparatus were identical to the previous experiments.

Results

Response times for correct responses were averaged in the three experimental conditions across participants and across items. The results are presented in Table 6B. Lexical decisions to targets were facilitated in the identity condition (26 ms) when the primes and the targets were the same word. The important result, however, concerns lexical decisions in the related condition: only a small facilitation was obtained (7 ms).

The prime-condition factor was significant in both the participants and the item analyses, $F_1(2, 90) = 23.86$, $MSE = 384$, $p < .001$; $F_2(2, 90) = 5.22$, $MSE = 1979$, $p < .008$. Planned comparisons revealed that the difference

---

[4] One third of the primes were the first and second letters of the root, a third were the first and last letters of the root, and a third were the second and third phoneme of the root.

TABLE 6B

Response times and per cent errors for lexical decision to target words and nonwords
in the identity, related and control conditions of Experiment 6a

Words			Nonwords		
Identity	Related	Control	Identity	Related	Control
536	555	562	606	604	613
6	8.3	7.8	5.2	7.1	5.9
+26	+7		1	+9	

between the related and the control conditions was not significant for both participants and items. $F_1(1, 45) = 2.89, MSE = 374, p < .096; F_2 < 1$. The error analysis revealed a non-significant prime condition factor for both participants and items. $F_1(2, 90) = 1.94, MSE = 38, p < .150; F_2 < 1$. The number of errors in both the related condition and the control condition did not differ significantly (F_1 and $F_2 < 1$). The prime effect for nonwords revealed a nonsignificant effect for participants and for items. $F_1(2, 90) = 2.96, MSE = 392, p < .057; F_2(2, 90) = 2.22, MSE = 752, p < .114$. No effect was found for errors to nonwords. $F_1(2, 90) = 1.94, MSE = 25, p < .15; F_2 < 1$. Similar to all previous experiments, planned comparisons revealed that response latencies to the targets did not differ significantly when the two-letter primes could be read as words or not, in both the related and the control conditions, $t(46) = 0.6, p < .6; t(46) = 1.5, p < .1$; respectively.

EXPERIMENT 6B

Since Experiment 6a presents a critical constraint on the distributed approach, the null-effect obtained in the experiment seems to offer non-conclusive evidence regarding the ability of two root letters to prime root derivations. This outcome may be due simply to a lack of power. The aim of Experiment 6b was to allow an operational replication of Experiment 6a. Thus, the design of the experiment was identical to that of Experiment 6a, while 48 different participants were tested with 48 novel stimuli, the stimuli are presented in Appendix H.

Results and discussion

The results are presented in Table 6C. Lexical decisions to targets were facilitated in the identity condition (25 ms) when the primes and the targets were the same word. However, while considering the related condition, no priming was observed whatsoever. In fact, the related condition was slightly slower than the control condition (−4 ms).

ANOVA revealed that the prime-condition factor was significant in both the participants and the item analyses, $F_1(2, 90) = 29.25, MSE = 398, p <$

TABLE 6C
Response times and per cent errors for lexical decision to target words and nonwords
in the identity, related and control conditions of Experiment 6b

Words			Nonwords		
Identity	*Related*	*Control*	*Identity*	*Related*	*Control*
547	576	572	615	621	622
5.6	8.3	7.9	9.4	9.1	8.1
+25	**–4**		**+7**	**+1**	

.001; $F_2(2, 90) = 8.63$, $MSE = 1434$, $p < .001$. Planned comparisons revealed that the small inhibition observed in the related condition was not significant for both participants and items, F_1 and $F_2 < 1$. The error analysis revealed a non-significant prime condition factor for both participants and items. $F_1(2, 90) = 2.65$, $MSE = 40$, $p < .076$; $F_2 < 1$. The prime effect for nonwords revealed a non-significant effect for participants and for items, $F_1(2, 90) = 1.49$, $MSE = 361$, $p < .231$; $F_2 < 1$. No effect was found for errors as well (F_1 and $F_2 < 1$). Planned comparisons revealed that response latencies to the targets did not differ significantly when the two-letter primes could be read as words or not, in both the related and the control conditions, $t(46) = 0.4$, $p < .7$; $t(46) = 0.6$, $p < .5$; respectively.

The striking result of Experiments 6a and 6b is that two letters of a complete root do not facilitate complete root derivations. In other words, unlike the mute and defective roots respectively, two letters of complete roots cannot prime the roots' derivations. This outcome suggests that morphological priming is not a linear product of increasing orthographic overlap. We will discuss the implications of this finding in the following General Discussion.

GENERAL DISCUSSION

The present study examined the processing of mute and defective Hebrew roots. Our experiments were motivated to a large extent by the two contrasting views of morphological representation and processing: the traditional localist view, which holds that the processing of morphologically complex words involves parsing the input into explicit morphemes and activating discrete units corresponding to these morphemes, and the PDP approach which holds that morphological processing reflects the learned sensitivity of internal distributed representations to the statistical structure among surface forms of words and their meanings. Although certain general characteristics of these theories as applied to morphology can be used to derive contrasting predictions (localist theories typically treat the derivation of component morphemes as an all-or-none event, whereas PDP theories treat morphological relatedness as a matter of degree), distinguishing between localist and distributed theories of cognitive processes is notoriously difficult (see, e.g., Schwartz, Martin, Saffran, & Gagnon, 1997). From this perspective, we assume that any given set of experiments may provide important constraints to any of the present approaches. Thus, our discussion of the results will focus on the implications to both the localist and the PDP theories.

From a representational perspective, the results of the present study provide novel data that need to be incorporated into our previous model of processing morphological information in Hebrew (Deutsch et al., 1998; Frost et al., 1997). According to this model, all words, whether nouns or verbs, which are derived from a given root, are linked to a shared morphological unit corresponding to the root. The Hebrew lexical system is regarded as consisting of multiple levels of representations; a level of lexical units (i.e., words) and a level of sub-word units of root morphemes. These two levels are interconnected, so that the root morpheme can be accessed via the lexical level from words containing that root or, alternatively, directly following a process of morphologically decomposing the orthographic structure. By this view, the recognition of printed words is often aided by access to their respective roots. Therefore, presenting the root information in a fast priming paradigm facilitates the recognition of the target derived from that root. Given the unique characteristic of Semitic morphologies, we suggested that Hebrew readers decompose a printed word into its morphemic constituents by using a general constraint that is structural in nature—mainly, that root morphemes are tri-consonantal entities (Frost et al., 2000).

The results of Experiment 1 and 2, which manipulated mute roots, do not support this assumption. Our findings clearly demonstrated that the two letters of mute roots which are repeated in all derivations facilitated the recognition of targets derived from these roots. Thus, our findings seem to compel localist models of Hebrew to accommodate morphemic units that are bi-consonantal as well. Note, however, that this may have implications for any word-parsing algorithm for Hebrew. Since root letters are not necessarily contiguous, relinquishing the tri-consonantal constraint may result in too many degrees of freedom regarding the possible identity of the root letters, rendering decomposition slow and inefficient. The only possible solution for such a stalemate would be to draw a demarcation line between our theory of representation and our theory of morphological decomposition. This solution would lead us to suggest that although morphemic units can, in principle, be bi-consonantal, the fast process of morphological decomposition still uses a tri-consonantal constraint for parsing the printed word. Hence, the reported absence of verbal-pattern priming for weak roots (Frost et al., 2000) reflects a simple decomposition failure rather than an absence of root-morpheme units for mute roots. In a nutshell, the tri-consonantal parsing constraint would work for most Hebrew words, but not for words derived from weak roots.

The findings of the experiments manipulating defective roots provide additional potential complications for the representational view. These experiments demonstrate that targets derived from defective roots can be primed either by a bi-consonantal or by a tri-consonantal root unit. This finding leads us to suggest that defective roots have an allomorphic representation. Thus, both the three consonants of the root and the two consonants which are repeated in all root derivations are represented at the morphemic level, and both units mediate the recognition of defective roots. Admittedly, this view lacks parsimony but it does accommodate all findings reported in Hebrew in a coherent framework.

An alternative explanation for the effects obtained with primes consisting of the three root letters of defective roots considers these priming effects as reflecting lexical priming rather than root priming. Since all defective roots in unpointed print can be read as nouns or verbs inflected in simple past tense, it is possible that the priming effects in this experiment resulted from the interconnections of morphologically related words at the lexical level rather than from connections between root-morpheme units and word units (see Frost et al., 1997; Experiment 3, for a discussion). On this view, defective roots, like mute roots, have only bi-consonantal representations.

On the PDP approach, lexical representations are not stipulated in advance but are derived in the process of learning internal representations that mediate among the written and spoken forms of words and their meanings. These internal representations are initially biased toward picking up direct correlations among input and output features. As a result, the network tends to map similar inputs to similar outputs, supporting effective generalisation. However, for those aspects of the mappings for which lower-order correlations are insufficient, the internal representations are pressured to develop sensitivity to higher-order structure. For example, internal units might learn to respond to conjunctions of input features but not to the features in isolation, as in the classic exclusive-OR (XOR) problem. It is important to emphasise, though, that such non-linear sensitivity generally arises only when lower-level structure is absent or misleading.

These properties are directly relevant to understanding the implications of the PDP approach for morphological processing. Morphology is the lowest level of linguistic structure for which similarity in form is (partially) predictive of similarity in meaning; for individual morphemes, the relationship among form and meaning is essentially arbitrary. As a consequence, correlations among lower-level features like letters or phonemes and semantic features are largely absent, and there is strong pressure for internal representations to develop sensitivity to higher-order structure at roughly the level of morphemes. Note, however, that the system retains its bias toward relying on lower-level structure whenever possible, so that internal representations would be expected to reflect sub-morphological structure when it is, in fact, predictive of semantic properties.

The results of the first five experiments in the current series can be understood as natural implications of this theoretical perspective. Although not a full, three-consonant root in their own right, two of the consonants of a weak root are nonetheless reliably present in the surface forms derived from them and also have equivalent semantic correlations with meaning as complete roots. Thus, a PDP system would be expected to learn to represent two-consonant forms of weak roots much like standard roots, and exhibit priming to forms derived from them (Experiments 1 and 3).

The PDP account can also explain the observed difference among mute versus defective roots; namely, that full tri-consonantal forms of defective but not mute roots serve as effective morphological primes (Experiments 2, 4, and 5). This is because only for defective roots is the tri-consonantal form unambiguously available in the input. For mute roots, by contrast, the system has had little opportunity to learn the relationship between the tri-consonantal form and the bi-consonantal form that actually occurs in derivations, even though, from a linguistic point of view, the former provides more complete evidence for the root morpheme.

The results of Experiment 6a and 6b, on the other hand, are less natural to account for within a PDP theory of Hebrew morphology, and thus place strong constraints on such a theory. These experiments showed that the priming from two-consonantal forms of weak roots does not generalise to complete roots; for the latter, two of three root consonants provided no greater priming of a derived form containing the root than did two non-root letters. This pattern of results implies a very strong degree of non-linearity in how the three consonants of standard roots are represented. Indeed, such fully conjunctive representations are, for all intents and purposes, functionally equivalent to localist representations of standard roots. On the PDP account, such conjunctive representations would be expected to develop through learning only when sensitivity to all lower-level structure is still insufficient to accomplish the mapping among forms and meanings. In fact, it is typically the case that any pair of consonants from a standard root also occur in many other roots. Thus, on its own, any given pair has little if any coherent implications for semantics. By contrast, although the two reliable consonants of a weak root may also occur in other roots, they do, on their own, have coherent semantic implications as a weak root.

In this way, the current findings provide evidence for sensitivity both to graded statistical structure and to "all-or-none" conjunctions in morphological processing. Although the PDP approach provides a theoretical basis for reconciling these properties, considerable work remains to develop an explicit implementation that accounts for all of the relevant findings. In addition, the approach must also account for existing empirical findings that suggest all-or-none, structure-dependent morphological parsing. In the current context, the clearest examples of such findings are the lack of word pattern priming for forms with weak roots and the reinstatement of such priming when the missing root letter is replaced by a random consonant (Frost et al., 2000). Such findings appear particularly problematic for PDP theories in that the presence or absence of morphological priming is tied, not to semantic or formal factors, but to the kinds of structural manipulations that would be expected to affect an all-or-none parsing mechanism.

However, Plaut and Frost (2001, in preparation) showed that a distributed connectionist network trained on an abstract version of Hebrew exhibited the same pattern of priming with weak roots, even though it lacked any explicit morphological parsing mechanism. Rather, over the course of learning, the system developed a high degree of sensitivity to the predominant tri-consonantal root structure of Hebrew, such that weak-root exceptions to this structure were represented very differently (and did not yield priming of words with the standard structure). Whether such a distributed approach can be extended to account for the more specific findings from the current set of studies remains to be demonstrated in future work.

REFERENCES

Baayen, H. (1991). Quantitative aspects of morphological productivity. In G. Booij & J. Van Marle (Eds.), *Yearbook of morphology* (pp. 109–149). Dordrecht, the Netherlands: Kluwer Academic.

Berman, R. A. (1978). *Modern Hebrew Structure*. Tel Aviv, Israel: University Publishing Projects.

Blau, Y. (1971). *Phonology and morphology*. Tel Aviv, Israel: Hakibbutz Hameuchad Press.

Butterworth, B. (1983). Lexical representation. In B. Butterworth (Ed.), *Language production* (Vol. 2, pp. 257–294). San Diego: Academic Press.

Burani, C., & Laudanna, A. (1992). Units of representation of derived words in the lexicon. In I. R. Froat & L. Katz (Eds.), *Advances in psychology: Orthography, phonology, morphology and meaning* (pp. 27–44). Amsterdam: Elsevier.

Caramazza, A., Laudanna, A., & Romani, C. (1988). Lexical access and inflectional morphology. *Cognition, 28*, 207–332.

Dell, G. S., Schwartz, M. F., Martin, N., Saffran, E. M., & Gagnon, D. A. (1997). Lexical access in normal and aphasic speakers. *Psychological Review, 104*, 801–838.

Deutsch, A., Frost, R., & Forster, K. I. (1998). Verbs and nouns are organized and accessed differently in the mental lexicon: Evidence from Hebrew. *Journal of Experimental Psychology: Learning, Memory and Cognition, 24,* 1238–1255.

Frauenfelder, U. H., & Schreuder, R. (1991). Constraining psycholinguistic models of morphological processing and representation: The role of productivity. In G. Booij & J. Van Marle (Eds.), *Yearbook of morphology* (pp. 165–183). Dordrecht, the Netherlands: Kluwer Academic.

Forster, K. I. (1987) Form priming with masked primes: The best match hypothesis. In M. Coltheart (Ed.), *Attention and performance: XII. The psychology of reading* (pp. 127–140). Hove, UK: Lawrence Erlbaum Associates Ltd.

Forster, K. I., & Davis, C. (1984). Repetition priming and frequency attenuation in lexical access. *Journal of Experimental Psychology: Learning, Memory, and Cognition, 10,* 680–698.

Forster, K. I., Davis, C., Schocknecht, C., & Carter, R. (1987). Masked priming with graphemically related forms: Repetition or partial activation? *Quarterly Journal of Experimental Psychology, 39A,* 211–251.

Frost, R., Deutsch, A., Gilboa, O., Tannenbaum, M., & Marslen-Wilson, W. (2000). Morphological priming: Dissociation of phonological, semantic and morphological factors. *Memory and Cognition, 28,* 1277–1288.

Frost, R., Deutsch, A., & Forster, K. I. (2000). Decomposing morphologically complex words in a nonlinear morphology. *Journal of Experimental Psychology: Learning, Memory and Cognition, 36,* 751–765.

Frost, R., Forster, K. I., & Deutsch, A. (1997). What can we learn from the morphology of Hebrew? A masked-priming investigation of morphological representation. *Journal of Experimental Psychology: Learning, Memory and Cognition, 23,* 829–856.

Henderson, L., Wallis, J., & Knight, K. (1984). Morphemic structure and lexical access. In H. Bouma & D. Bouwhuis (Eds.), *Attention and Performance X: Control of language process* (pp. 211–226). Hove, UK: Lawrence Erlbaum Associates Ltd.

Laudanna, A., Burani, C., & Cermele, A. (1994). Prefixes as processing units. *Language and Cognitive Processes, 9,* 295–316.

Marcus, G. F., Brinkmann, U., Clahsen, H., Weise, R., & Pinker, S. (1995). German inflection: The exception that proves the rule. *Cognitive Psychology, 29,* 189–256.

Marslen-Wilson, W., Tyler, L. K., Waksler, R., & Older, L. (1994). Morphology and meaning in English mental lexicon. *Psychological Review, 101,* 3–33.

Plaut, D. C., & Frost, R. (2001). Does morphological structure in Hebrew reduce to surface structure? *Paper presented at the 42nd annual meeting of the Psychonomic Society:* Orlando, November 2001.

Plaut, D. C., & Gonnerman, L. M. (2000). Are non-semantic morphological effects incompatible with a distributed connectionist approach to lexical processing? *Language and Cognitive Processes, 15*(4/5), 445–485.

Rueckl, J. G., Mikolinski, M., Raveh, M., Miner, C. S., & Mars, F. (1997). Morphological priming, fragment completion and connectionist networks. *Journal of Memory and Language, 36,* 382–405.

Schreuder, R., & Baayen, R. H. (1995). Modeling morphological processing. In L. B. Feldman (Ed.), *Morphological aspects of language processing* (pp. 131–154). Hillsdale, NJ: Lawrence Erlbaum Associates Inc.

Seidenberg, M. S. (1987). Sublexical structures in visual words recognition: access units or orthographic redundancy? In M. Coltheart (Ed.), *Attention and performance XII: The psychology of reading* (pp. 244–263). Hove, UK: Lawrence Erlbaum Associates Ltd.

Taft, M. (1994). Interactive activation as a framework for understanding morphological processing. *Language and Cognitive Processes, 9,* 271–294.

APPENDIX A

The Hebrew Alphabet

Hebrew Print	Orthographic Transcription	Phonetic Transcription
א	ʔ	ʔ
ב	b	b / v
ג	g	g
ד	d	d
ה	h	h
ו	w	o / u / v
ז	z	z
ח	x	x
ט	θ	t
י	y	i / y
כ	k	k / x
ךª	K	x
ל	l	l
מ	m	m
םª	M	m
נ	n	n
ןª	N	n
ס	S	s
ע	ʕ	ʔ
פ	p	p / f
ףª	P	f̱
צ	c	ṯs
ץª	C	ṯs
ק	q	k
ר	r	r
ש	s	s / s̱h
ת	t	t

ª The letters k, m, n, p, and c have different orthographic forms when they appear at the end of the word.

APPENDIX B

Stimuli used in Experiment 1

			Morphological Prime		Control	
Word	Ortho. Trans.	Phonetic Trans.	Letters	Ortho. Trans.	Letters	Ortho. Trans.
תאורה	t?wrh	/te?ura/	אר	?r	אה	?h
הוקרה	hwqrh	/hokara/	קר	qr	הק	hq
תוצאה	twc?h	/totsa?a/	צא	c?	תא	t?
ריצה	rich	/ritsa/	רצ	rc	צה	ch
תולדה	twldh	/tolada/	לד	ld	תל	tl
הורדה	hwrdh	/horada/	רד	rd	הר	hr
תמותה	tmwth	/tmuta/	מת	mt	תה	th
תודעה	twdçh	/toda?a/	דע	dç	דה	dh
מועצה	mwçch	/mo?atsa/	עצ	çc	מע	mç
תורשה	twrsh	/torasha/	רש	rs	רה	rh
מושבה	mwsbh	/moshava/	שב	sb	וש	ws
תקומה	tqwmh	/tkuma/	קמ	qm	ומ	wm
תגלית	tglit	/taglit/	גל	gl	לת	lt
תבונה	tbwnh	/tvuna/	בנ	bn	תנ	tn
תזונה	tzwnh	/tzuna/	זנ	zn	נה	nh
מטוס	mθwS	/matos/	טו	θS	מו	mw
תלונה	tlwnh	/tluna/	לנ	ln	תו	tw
הובלה	hwblh	/hovala/	בל	bl	הל	hl
תבואה	tbw?h	/tvu?a/	בא	b?	בה	bh
תמורה	tmwrh	/tmura/	מר	mr	מה	mh
מוסד	mwSd	/mosad/	סד	Sd	מס	mS
תועלת	twçlt	/to?elet/	על	çl	עת	çt
תקופה	tqwph	/tkufa/	קפ	qp	קה	qh
מוצג	mwcg	/mutsag/	צג	cg	וצ	wc
בושה	bwsh	/busha/	בש	bs	שה	sh
מוצר	mwcr	/mutsar/	צר	cr	מו	mw
מועד	mwçd	/mo?ed/	עד	çd	מע	mç
תכונה	tkwnh	/txuna/	כנ	kn	תכ	tk
הוכחה	hwkxh	/hoxaxa/	כח	kx	כה	kh
תעופה	tçwph	/te?ufa/	עפ	çp	פה	ph
נסיעה	nSyçh	/nesi?a/	סע	Sç	ען	çn
ריקנות	ryqnwt	/rekanot/	רק	rq	נק	nq
תוספת	twSpt	/tosefet/	סס	Sp	תפ	pt
הוזלה	hwzlh	/hozala/	זל	zl	לה	lh
מוצב	mwcb	/mutsav/	צב	cb	מב	mb
תנוחה	tnwxh	/tnuxa/	נח	nx	תח	tx
הפוגה	hpwgh	/hafuga/	פג	pg	פו	pw
מצוף	mcwP	/matsof/	צפ	cp	וצ	cw
תבוסה	tbwSh	/tvusa/	בס	bS	תס	tS
מוקש	mwqs	/mokesh/	קש	qs	וק	wq
מוצק	mwcq	/mutsak/	צק	cq	מצ	mc
מחוגה	mxwgh	/mxoga/	חג	xg	מג	mg
מחצית	mxcit	/maxatsit/	חצ	xc	צת	ct
מכולה	mkwlh	/mxola/	כל	kl	מל	ml
תופעה	twpçh	/tofa?a/	פע	pç	עה	çh
מותר	mwtr	/mutar/	תר	tr	ור	wr
מוקד	mwqd	/moked/	קד	qd	מו	mw
מוזר	mwzr	/muzar/	זר	zr	מז	mz

APPENDIX C

Stimuli used in Experiment 2

	Target		Morphological Prime		Control	
Word	Ortho. Trans.	Phonetic Trans.	Letters	Ortho. Trans.	Letters	Ortho. Trans.
הארה	hʔrh	/heʔara/	אור	ʔwr	ארה	ʔrh
הוקרה	hwqrh	/hokara/	יקר	yqr	הקר	hqr
תוצאה	twcʔh	/totsaʔa/	יצא	ycʔ	צאה	cʔh
מריץ	mryC	/merit͟s/	רוצ	rwc	מרצ	mrc
תולדה	twldh	/tolada/	ילד	yld	לדה	ldh
הורדה	hwrdh	/horada/	ירד	yrd	רדה	rdh
המתה	hmth	/hamata/	מות	mwt	התה	hth
תודעה	twdʕh	/todaʔa/	ידע	ydʕ	ודע	wdʕ
מועצה	mwʕch	/moʔat͟sa/	יעצ	yʕc	מעצ	mʕc
תורשה	twrsh	/torash͟a/	ירש	yrs	רשה	rsh
מושבה	mwsbh	/moshava/	ישב	ysb	משב	msb
הקמה	hqmh	/hakama/	קומ	qwm	המה	hmh
תגלית	tglyt	/taglit/	גלה	glh	גלת	glt
תבונה	tbwnh	/tvuna/	בינ	byn	בנה	bnh
הזנה	hznh	/hazana/	זונ	zwn	הזה	hzh
טיסן	θySN	/tisan/	טוס	θwS	יסנ	ySn
לינה	lynh	/lina/	לונ	lwn	ינה	ynh
הובלה	hwblh	/hovala/	יבל	ybl	בלה	blh
לקנות	lqnwt	/liknot/	קנה	qnh	לנת	lnt
ממיר	mmyr	/memir/	מור	mwr	ממי	mmy
מוסד	mwSd	/mosad/	יסד	ySd	מוס	mwS
תועלת	twʕlt	/toʔelet/	יעל	yʕl	תעל	tʕl
ערנות	ʕrnwt	/ʔeranut/	עור	ʕwr	רנו	rnw
תצוגה	tcwgh	/tet͟suga/	יצג	ycg	תוג	twg
ביישן	byysN	/baysh͟an/	בוש	bws	בשנ	bsn
מוצר	mwcr	/mut͟sar/	יצר	ycr	מצר	mcr
מועד	mwʕd	/moʔed/	יעד	yʕd	מעד	mʕd
הצבה	hcbh	/hat͟sava/	יצב	ycb	צבה	cbh
הוכחה	hwkxh	/hoxaxa/	יכח	ykx	הכח	hkx
עפיפון	ʕpypwN	/afifon/	עופ	ʕwp	עפנ	ʕpn
שייטת	syyθt	/sh͟ayetet/	שוט	swθ	יטת	yθt
שיחון	syxwN	/sixon/	שוח	swx	חונ	xwn
תוספת	twSpt	/tosefet/	יספ	ySp	תוס	twS
הוזלה	hwzlh	/hozala/	זול	zwl	זלה	zlh
מוצב	mwcb	/mut͟sav/	יצב	ycb	מוב	mwb
מונח	mwnx	/munax/	נוח	nwx	מנח	mnx
דירה	dyrh	/dira/	דור	dwr	דיה	dyh
מוצף	mwcP	/mut͟saf/	צופ	cwp	וצפ	wcp
מובס	mwbS	/muvas/	בוס	bwS	מבס	mbS
מוקש	mwqs	/moke͟sh/	יקש	yqs	מקש	mqs
מוצק	mwcq	/mut͟sak/	יצק	ycq	מוק	mwq
חייגן	xyygN	/xaygan/	חוג	xwg	חגנ	xgn
חצות	xcwt	/xat͟sot/	חצה	xch	צות	cwt
הכיל	hkyl	/hexil/	כול	kwl	הכי	hky
תופעה	twpʕh	/tofaʔa/	יפע	ypʕ	פעה	pʕh
השבה	hsbh	/hash͟ava/	שוב	swb	הבה	hbh
מוקד	mwqd	/moked/	יקד	yqd	מוד	mwd
לסטות	lSθwt	/listot/	סטה	Sθh	סות	Swt

APPENDIX D

Stimuli used in Experiment 3

	Target		Morphological Prime		Control	
Word	Ortho. Trans.	Phonetic Trans.	Letters	Ortho. Trans.	Letters	Ortho. Trans.
מתיז	mtyz	/matiz/	תז	tz	מז	mz
הגיע	hgyʕ	/higiʔa/	גע	gʕ	גי	gy
מושק	mwsq	/mushak/	שק	sq	מק	mq
הקיז	hqyz	/hikiz/	קז	qz	יז	yz
התיק	htyq	/hitik/	תק	tq	הת	ht
הכיש	hkys	/hikish/	כש	ks	יש	ys
השיר	hsyr	/hishir/	שר	sr	הש	hs
הקיש	hqys	/hikish/	קש	qs	קי	qy
הדיף	hdyP	/hidif/	דפ	dp	הפ	hp
הציל	hcyl	/hitsil/	צל	cl	הצ	hc
מביט	mbyθ	/mabit/	בט	bθ	מט	mθ
הזיל	hzyl	/hizil/	זל	zl	הל	hl
הסיג	hSyg	/hisig/	סג	Sg	הג	hg
הגיד	hgyd	/higid/	גד	gd	הד	hd
השיל	hsyl	/hishil/	של	sl	יל	yl
התיר	htyr	/hitir/	תר	tr	הר	hr
השיא	hsyʔ	/hisiʔ/	שא	sʔ	שי	sy
הדיר	hdyr	/hidir/	דר	dr	די	dy
מתכת	mtkt	/matexet/	תכ	tk	כת	kt
מגבת	mgbt	/magevet/	גב	gb	מב	mb
מפוחית	mpwxyt	/mapuxit/	פח	px	מו	mw
הסעה	hSʕh	/hasaʔa/	סע	Sʕ	סה	Sh
משיר	msyr	/mashir/	שר	sr	מר	mr
היכרות	hykrwt	/hekerut/	כר	kr	רו	rw
מסוק	mSwq	/masok/	סק	Sq	סמ	mS
הדחה	hdxh	/hadaxa/	דח	dx	הח	hx
מצור	mcwr	/matsor/	צר	cr	צו	cw
מתנה	mtnh	/matana/	תנ	tn	מת	mt
מטע	mθʕ	/mata/	טע	θʕ	מע	mʕ
משב	msb	/mashav/	שב	sb	מש	ms
הבעה	hbʕh	/habaʔa/	בע	bʕ	הב	hb
מפץ	mpC	/mapats/	פצ	pc	מצ	mc
הסחה	hSxh	/hasaxa/	סח	Sx	חה	xh
מזיק	mzyq	/mazik/	זק	zq	מי	my
הגשה	hgsh	/hagasha/	גש	gs	שה	sh

APPENDIX E

Stimuli used in Experiment 4

	Target		Morphological Prime		Control	
Word	Ortho. Trans.	Phonetic Trans.	Letters	Ortho. Trans.	Letters	Ortho. Trans.
ניתז	nytz	/nitaz/	נתז	ntz	נוז	nwz
נוגע	nwgç	/noge?a/	נגע	ngç	וגע	wgç
התנשק	htnsq	/hitnashek/	נשק	nsq	תנק	tnq
ניקז	nyqz	/nikez/	נקז	nqz	ניק	nyq
נותק	nwtq	/nutak/	נתק	ntq	ותק	wtq
מנקר	mnqr	/menaker/	נקר	nqr	מנק	mnq
נושר	nwsr	/nosher/	נשר	nsr	ושר	wsr
מתנקש	mtnqs	/mitnakesh/	נקש	nqs	מקש	mqs
נודף	nwdP	/nodef/	נדפ	ndp	ודפ	wdp
התנצל	htncl	/hitnatsel/	נצל	ncl	תנצ	tnc
נובט	nwbθ	/novet/	נבט	nbθ	ובט	wbθ
נוזל	nwzl	/nozel/	נזל	nzl	וזל	wzl
נסוג	nSwg	/nasog/	נסג	nSg	סוג	Swg
התנגד	htngd	/hitnaged/	נגד	ngd	תגד	tgd
נושל	nwsl	/nushal/	נשל	nsl	ושל	wsl
מנתר	mntr	/menater/	נתר	ntr	מתר	mtr
התנשא	htns?	/hitnase/	נשא	ns?	השא	hs?
נודר	nwdr	/noder/	נדר	ndr	ודר	wdr
נתיך	ntyK	/natix/	נתכ	ntk	תיכ	tyk
נפילה	npylh	/nefila/	נפל	npl	פלה	plh
ניגוב	nygwb	/niguv/	נגב	ngb	יגב	ygb
נפיחות	npyxwt	/nefixut/	נפח	npx	פחת	pxt
נסיעה	nSyçh	/nesi?a/	נסע	nSç	סעה	Sçh
נשורת	nswrt	/neshoret/	נשר	nsr	שרת	srt
נוכרי	nwkry	/noxri/	נכר	nkr	כרי	kry
נסיקה	nSyqh	/nesika/	נסק	nSq	סקה	Sqh
נידח	nydx	/nidax/	נדח	ndx	ניד	nyd
ניצרה	nycrh	/nitsra/	נצר	ncr	ניה	nyh
נתין	ntyN	/natin/	נתנ	ntn	תינ	tyn
נטיעה	nθyçh	/neti?a/	נטע	nθç	טיע	θyç
נשיבה	nsybh	/neshiva/	נשב	nsb	שיב	syb
נביעה	nbyçh	/nevi?a/	נבע	nbç	בעה	bçh
מנופץ	mnwpC	/menupats/	נפצ	npc	ופצ	wpc
נוסחה	nwSxh	/nusxa/	נסח	nSx	וסה	wSh
נזיקין	nzyqyN	/nezikin/	נזק	nzq	נקנ	nqn
נגישות	ngyswt	/negishut/	נגש	ngs	גשת	gst

APPENDIX F

Stimuli used in Experiment 5

	Target		Morphological Prime		Control	
Word	Ortho. Trans.	Phonetic Trans.	Letters	Ortho. Trans.	Letters	Ortho. Trans.
מתיז	mtyz	/matiz/	נתז	ntz	תעז	tçz
הגיע	hgyç	/higiʔa/	נגע	ngç	רגע	rgç
מושק	mwsq	/mushak/	נשק	nsq	חשק	xsq
הקיז	hqyz	/hikiz/	נקז	nqz	קזז	qzz
התיק	htyq	/hitik/	נתק	ntq	תקנ	tqn
הכיש	hkys	/hikish/	נכש	nks	רכש	rks
השיר	hsyr	/hishir/	נשר	nsr	פשר	psr
הקיש	hqys	/hikish/	נקש	nqs	קשר	qsr
הדיף	hdyP	/hidif/	נדפ	ndp	גדפ	gdp
הציל	hcyl	/hitsil/	נצל	ncl	אצל	ʔcl
מביט	mbyθ	/mabit/	נבט	nbθ	חבט	xbθ
הזיל	hzyl	/hizil/	נזל	nzl	אזל	ʔzl
הסיג	hSyg	/hisig/	נסג	nSg	סגר	Sgr
הגיד	hgyd	/higid/	נגד	ngd	בגד	bgd
משיל	msyl	/mashil/	נשל	nsl	כשל	ksl
התיר	htyr	/hitir/	נתר	ntr	בתר	btr
השיא	hsyʔ	/hisiʔ/	נשא	nsʔ	שאג	sʔg
הדיר	hdyr	/hidir/	נדר	ndr	גדר	gdr
מתכת	mtkt	/matexet/	נתכ	ntk	חתכ	xtk
מפולת	mpwlt	/mapolet/	נפל	npl	כפל	kpl
מגבת	mgbt	/magevet/	נגב	ngb	חגב	xgb
מפוחית	mpwxyt	/mapuxit/	נפח	npx	טפח	θpx
הסעה	hSçh	/hasaʔa/	נסע	nSç	פסע	pSç
השרה	hsrh	/hashara/	נשר	nsr	גשר	gsr
היכרות	hykrwt	/hekerut/	נכר	nkr	זכר	zkr
מסוק	mSwq	/masok/	נסק	nSq	פסק	pSq
הדחה	hdxh	/hadaxa/	נדח	ndx	קדח	qdx
מצור	mcwr	/matsor/	נצר	ncr	עצר	çcr
מתנה	mtnh	/matana/	נתנ	ntn	חתנ	xtn
מטע	mθç	/mata/	נטע	nθç	קטע	qθç
שבשבת	sbsbt	/shavshevet/	נשב	nsb	חשב	xsb
הבעה	hbçh	/habaʔa/	נבע	nbç	טבע	θbç
מפץ	mpC	/mapats/	נפצ	npc	חפצ	xpc
הסחה	hSxh	/hasaxa/	נסח	nSx	סחר	Sxr
מזיק	mzyq	/mazik/	נזק	nzq	חזק	xzq
הגשה	hgsh	/hagasha/	נגש	ngs	הגש	hgs

APPENDIX G

Stimuli used in Experiment 6a

	Target		Morphological Prime		Control	
Word	Ortho. Trans.	Phonetic Trans.	Letters	Ortho. Trans.	Letters	Ortho. Trans.
הליכה	hlykh	/halixa/	לכ	lk	הי	hy
מחברת	mxbrt	/maxberet/	חר	xr	מב	mb
התחנף	htxnP	/hitxanef/	חנ	xn	תפ	tp
מגדל	mgdl	/migdal/	דל	dl	מג	mg
מספרה	mSprh	/maspera/	סר	Sr	מה	nh
סליחה	Slyxh	/slixa/	סל	Sl	לי	ly
תזמורת	tzmwrt	/tizmoret/	מר	mr	מת	mt
קציר	qcyr	/katsir/	קר	qr	יר	yr
מחבט	mxbθ	/maxbet/	חב	xb	מט	mθ
הגביר	hgbyr	/higbir/	בר	br	הב	hb
סועד	Swçd	/soʔed/	סד	Sd	וע	wç
השקיף	hsqyP	/hishkif/	שק	sq	שי	sy
הכתבה	hktbh	/haxtava/	תב	tb	בה	bh
חיפוש	xypws	/xipus/	חש	xs	חו	xw
קמצן	qmcN	/kamtsan/	קמ	km	קנ	qn
בריחה	bryxh	/brixa/	רח	rx	רי	ry
משמרת	msmrt	/mishmeret/	שר	sr	מת	mt
משתלה	mstlh	/mishtala/	שת	st	מש	ms
מרכבה	mrkbh	/merkava/	כב	kb	רה	rh
מגרפה	mgrph	/magrefa/	גפ	gp	גה	gh
סחיטה	Sxyθh	/sxita/	סח	Sx	סי	Sy
מרדף	mrdP	/mirdaf/	דפ	dp	מפ	mp
שוקל	swql	/shokel/	של	sl	שו	sw
צילום	cylwM	/tsilum/	צל	cl	לו	lw
טבילה	θbylh	/tvila/	בל	bl	טי	θy
פתרון	ptrwN	/pitaron/	פר	pr	פנ	pn
מזבלה	mzblh	/mizbala/	זל	zl	מז	mz
הרעיש	hrçys	/hirʔish/	עש	çs	יש	ys
שליחות	slyxwt	/shlixut/	שח	sx	לת	lt
החמיר	hxmyr	/hixmir/	חמ	xm	הח	hx
קישר	qysr	/kisher/	קש	qs	קי	qy
התלבט	htlbθ	/hitlabet/	בט	bθ	תל	tl
התנהל	htnhl	/hitnahel/	נל	nl	תה	th
כניעה	knyçh	/kniʔa/	נע	nç	כה	kh
מכוער	mkwçr	/mexoʔar/	כע	kç	מכ	mk
הדפסה	hdPSh	/hadpasa/	פס	pS	הפ	hp
התמרח	htmrx	/hitmareax/	מח	mx	תמ	tm
חלוקה	xlwqh	/xaluka/	חל	xl	וק	wq
הרשמה	hrsmh	/harshama/	רש	rs	שה	sh
תלמיד	tlmyd	/talmid/	מד	md	תד	td
שידוך	sydwK	/shidux/	שכ	sk	יד	yd
התאים	htʔym	/hitʔim/	תא	tʔ	הת	ht
התרסק	htrSq	/hitrasek/	סק	Sq	תק	tq
רוקחות	rwqxwt	/rokxut/	רק	rq	חת	xt
פריחה	pryxh	/prixa/	פח	px	יח	yx
הקציף	hqcyP	/hiktsif/	צפ	cp	יפ	yp
דחיסה	dxySh	/dxisa/	דס	dS	די	dy
העתיק	hçtyq	/heʔetik/	עת	çt	הק	hq

APPENDIX H

Stimuli used in Experiment 6b

	Target		Morphological Prime		Control	
Word	Ortho. Trans.	Phonetic Trans.	Letters	Ortho. Trans.	Letters	Ortho. Trans.
מכבסה	mkbSh	/mixbasa/	בס	bS	מב	mb
הבריש	hbrys	/hivrish/	בש	bs	בי	by
התחדש	htxds	/hitxadesh/	חד	xd	הד	hd
בושם	bwsM	/bosem/	שמ	sm	וש	ws
מסגרת	mSgrt	/misgeret/	סר	Sr	סת	St
שאלה	s?lh	/she?ela/	שא	s?	אה	?h
משחה	msxh	/mishxa/	שח	sx	חה	xh
מקלט	mqlθ	/miklat/	קט	qθ	מל	ml
הועבר	hwçbr	/hu?avar/	עב	çb	הע	hç
תפירה	tpyrh	/tfira/	פר	pr	פה	ph
חשיפה	xsyph	/xasifa/	חפ	xp	חי	xy
מטריה	mθryh	/mitriya/	מט	mθ	רה	rh
הזכיר	hzkyr	/hizkir/	כר	kr	כי	ky
הקדים	hqdyM	/hikdim/	קמ	qm	ימ	ym
התלבש	htlbs	/hitlabesh/	לב	lb	תל	tl
ספינה	spynh	/sfina/	פנ	pn	פי	py
הזמנה	hzmnh	/hazmana/	זנ	zn	זה	zh
התפאר	htp?r	/hitpa?er/	פא	p?	תא	t?
צרבת	crbt	/tsarevet/	רב	rb	בת	bt
מאופר	M?wpr	/me?upar/	אר	?r	ור	wr
רכישה	rkysh	/rexisha/	רכ	rk	שה	sh
שריטה	sryθh	/srita/	רט	rθ	טה	θh
סכנה	Sknh	/sakana/	סנ	Sn	כה	kh
העליב	hçlyb	/he?eliv/	על	çl	יב	yb
הזריק	hzryq	/hizrik/	רק	rq	הז	hz
מפגש	mpgs	/mifgash/	פש	ps	מש	ms
התחרש	htxrs	/hitxaresh/	חר	xr	תח	tx
שיחק	syxq	/sixek/	חק	xq	יח	yx
ממלכה	mmlkh	/mamlaxa/	מכ	mk	לה	lh
ניגון	nygwn	/nigun/	נג	ng	גו	gw
מגלשה	mglsh	/maglesha/	לש	ls	גה	gh
מחרוזת	mxrwzt	/maxrozet/	חז	xz	זו	wz
הקפיץ	hqpyC	/hikpits/	קפ	qp	הפ	hp
מטפלת	mθplt	/metapelet/	פל	pl	לת	kt
הקלדה	hqldh	/haklada/	קד	qd	הל	hl
התחשב	htxsb	/hitxashev/	חש	xs	תש	ts
קריאה	qry?h	/kri?a/	רא	r?	קי	qy
סריקה	Sryqh	/srika/	סק	Sq	סה	Sh
בורג	bwrg	/boreg/	בר	br	בו	bw
הדליק	hdlyq	/hidlik/	לק	lq	הק	hq
הבריק	hbryq	/hivrik/	בק	bq	הב	hb
שיכון	sykwn	/shikun/	שכ	sk	ונ	wn
חתונה	xtwnh	/hatuna/	תנ	tn	תו	tw
מפתח	mptx	/mafteax/	פח	px	מפ	mp
מלחמה	mkxmh	/milxama/	לח	lx	מה	mh
התאמן	ht?mN	/hita?men/	מנ	mn	תמ	tm
עבדות	çbdwt	/?avdut/	עד	çd	עת	çt
שקרן	sqrn	/shakran/	שק	sq	רנ	rn

LANGUAGE AND COGNITIVE PROCESSES
2005, 20 (1/2), 207–260

Discontinuous morphology in time: Incremental masked priming in Arabic

Sami Boudelaa and William D. Marslen-Wilson

MRC Cognition and Brain Sciences Unit, Cambridge, UK

Semitic morphology is based on the combination of two abstract discontinuous morphemes, the word pattern and the root. The word pattern specifies the phonological structure and morpho-syntactic properties of the surface form, while the consonantal root conveys core semantic information. Both units play a crucial role in processing Semitic languages such as Arabic and Hebrew. Here we use incremental masked priming to probe the time-course of word pattern and root activation in reading Arabic deverbal nouns and verbs. The morphological (word pattern and root), orthographic, and semantic relationship between prime and targets is varied over four stimulus onset asynchronies (SOAs) (32, 48, 64, and 80 ms). Results show distinctive patterns of activation for the two morphemic entities. Word pattern effects are transient, and detectable only at SOAs 48 and 64 in deverbal nouns and SOA 48 in verbs. Root effects are strong at all SOAs. This may reflect differences in the timing with which word pattern and root information can be extracted from the orthographic input, as well as differences in the roles of these morphemes in building internal lexical representations. Both types of morphemic effect contrast strongly with the effects of orthographic and semantic primes, where reliable facilitation is only obtained at the longest SOA (80 ms). The general pattern of results is consistent with the view that morphological effects in Semitic languages represent distinct structural characteristics of the language.

Correspondence should be addressed to: Dr. Sami Boudelaa, MRC Cognition and Brain Sciences Unit, 15, Chaucer Road, Cambridge CB2 2EF, UK.
Email: sami.boudelaa@ mrc-cbu.cam.ac.uk; william.marslen-wilson@mrc-cbu.cam.ac.uk

We thank Mike Ford for his assistance in the preparation of the two experiments and Abdallah Megbli, headmaster of the High School in Tataouine, Tunisia for his generous help in providing testing facilities and access to participants for testing. We also thank Matt Davis, Dave Plaut, Kathy Rastle, and an anonymous reviewer for helpful comments on an earlier version of this work. This work was supported by the Medical Research Council (UK).

http://www.tandf.co.uk/journals/pp/01690965.html   DOI: 10.1080/01690960444000106

INTRODUCTION

The identification of morphemes in a language is based on the existence of consistent relationships, synchronically and diachronically, between phonological form, semantic meaning, and grammatical function (Aronoff, 1976; Scalise, 1986). A central concern of experimental research into morphology is whether morphemes play a role in the cognitive language system that is separable from phonological, orthographic, and semantic co-occurrence, so that morphological structure is a qualitatively distinct organising property of lexical representation and processing (Caramazza, Laudanna, & Romani, 1988; Clahsen, 1999; Feldman, Frost, & Pnini, 1995; Forster & Azuma, 2000; Marslen-Wilson, Tyler, Waksler, & Older 1994; Rueckl, Mikolinski, Raveh, Miner, & Mars, 1997; Schreuder & Baayen, 1995; Seidenberg & Gonnerman, 2000).

There are two aspects to this question that are not always kept separate. The first is the essentially methodological question of whether, given the likely correlation in a stimulus set between form-based, semantic, and morphological variables, any resulting effects can be safely attributed to morphological factors. In the English prime-target pairs *jumps/jumped* and *darkness/dark*, for example, experimental effects attributed to morphological relatedness can also reflect the other ways these stimuli are related. The second is the more complex question, given that unambiguously morphological effects might be observed, of what this means for the role of morphology in lexical representation and processing. The implications are straightforward for current localist models (Caramazza et al., 1988; Frost, Forster, & Deutsch, 1997; Schreuder & Baayen, 1995), where morphological structure is already an explicit and stipulated property of the model. Such a result would present more of a challenge, however, for connectionist learning models where morphology has no explicit representation (Plaut & Gonnerman, 2000, Seidenberg & Gonnerman, 2000), and has been viewed in the past as simply the interaction of form and meaning-based constraints.

The goal of this paper is to exploit the special properties of Semitic morphology, using the incremental masked priming task (Dominguez, Cuetos, & Segui, 2002; Rastle, Davis, Marslen-Wilson, & Tyler, 2000) to contribute to both these questions. Naturally, there is a great deal of research using other techniques which addresses these issues, and which overall provides substantial evidence for the separability of morphological effects from semantic and form-based factors. However, the advantage of incremental masked priming (and similar tasks) is that it allows us to track the time-course with which different types of processing information become available during visual word-recognition and lexical access, thereby providing an important dynamic perspective on the operations of the language system. For example, the research on English reported by Rastle et al. (2000) varied the morphological, semantic, and orthographic relationship between primes and targets over three Stimulus Onset Asynchronies (SOA), of 43, 72, and 230 ms. The observed pattern of activation over the three SOAs was clearly distinct for the three types of processing relationship, suggesting different time-courses for morphological, orthographic, and semantic effects, and therefore implying their separability as potential contributors to priming effects between morphologically related items.

There are two main reasons why it is of interest to apply these techniques to Semitic languages. The first is that arguably the strongest evidence for morphology as an organising principle of internal representation and processing comes from Semitic languages like Hebrew and Arabic (Boudelaa & Marslen-Wilson, 2000, 2001; Deutsch, Frost, & Forster, 1998; Deutsch, Frost, Pollatsek, & Rayner, 2000; Frost et al., 1997; Frost, Deutsch, Gilboa, Tannenbaum, & Marslen-Wilson, 2000), so that they should provide a fertile ground for studies of the temporal fine-structure of morphological processing. The second is that these languages separate out morphological functions in a very different way to languages with concatenative morphologies (such as English, French, and Finnish), providing a valuable cross-linguistic contrast. In Arabic, the building of surface word forms is standardly viewed as involving at least two bound morphemic units, a *root* and a *word pattern* (Holes, 1995; Versteegh, 1997; Wright, 1995). Roots and word patterns have a very different phonological make-up and distinct morphological functions. Roots consist solely of consonants and convey semantic meaning, while word patterns consist primarily of vowels but can be comprised of consonants as well, and act as a phonological structure that conveys syntactic information (Wright, 1995). These two units are interleaved and surface in a discontinuous way. For example, in the Modern Standard Arabic (hereafter MSA) verb form [xatama] *seal*, the consonants of the root {xtm}, which conveys the semantic load *sealing*, are discontinuous as a result of being interspersed with the vowels of the word pattern {faʕala},[1] which carries the syntactic meaning *active, perfective*.

Both roots and word patterns play a significant cognitive role in the processing of Arabic and Hebrew (Boudelaa & Marslen-Wilson, 2000, 2001; Deutsch et al., 1998; Frost et al., 1997). Importantly, facilitation among word pairs sharing a root morpheme is neither modulated by nor is dependent on the semantic relationships underlying the prime and target

---

[1] The letters fʕl are traditionally used as place holders indicating where the first, second and third letter of the root are to be inserted.

(Boudelaa & Marslen-Wilson, 2000; 2001; Frost et al., 1997).[2] The Arabic target [kaatibun] *writer* is facilitated by the morphologically and semantically related prime [kitaabun] *book*, where {ktb} has the same semantics in both prime and target, but also by the morphologically related but semantically unrelated prime [katiibatun] *squadron*, where the root {ktb} does not have its dominant writing-related meaning. Furthermore, word patterns, which are intrinsically non-semantic elements, show significant priming in Hebrew verbs (Deutsch et al., 1998), and in Arabic verbs and deverbal nouns (Boudelaa & Marslen-Wilson, 2000).

In the context of such languages, the question of whether morphology, semantics and phonology or orthography have differential time courses can be refined further by asking whether morphology-based effects have the same time course irrespective of the structural and functional characteristics of the morpheme in question. Will root and word pattern effects have the same time course and distribution during on-line processing, or will they differ as a function of the information being conveyed? Additionally, since the consonantal root conveys semantic meaning, and the word pattern conveys phonological information and syntactic meaning, it is possible that root effects over time will have commonalities with semantic effects, whereas word pattern effects may be analogous to form-based effects.

To approach these issues, we focus on Arabic deverbal nouns and verbs and assess how the prior presentation of a masked prime word affects lexical decision to a target as a function of (a) the relationship between prime and target, and (b) prime display duration. As regards (a), we vary morphological, orthographic, and semantic relationships between primes and targets such that the respective contributions of each of these properties can be examined. With respect to (b), we use four prime display durations, of 32, 48, 64, and 80 ms, to assess the dynamics of priming across these dimensions of similarity.

In an earlier masked priming investigations of Arabic morphology, we found reliable word pattern and root priming effects at a 48 ms SOA. Since both morphemic units seem to be active at this SOA, we included a shorter SOA of 32 ms, to determine whether word patterns and roots have different processing onsets. We included the two longer SOAs (64 and 80 ms) to monitor for the life span of the priming likely to be generated by these units. It should be stressed that at SOA 32 ms and 48 ms, participants

---

[2] This is true of masked priming in Arabic and Hebrew. However, cross-modal priming offers a different picture with a slight increase in the magnitude of priming among transparent pairs in Hebrew (Frost et al., 2000), but not in Arabic (Boudelaa & Marslen-Wilson, 2000).

are not aware of the presence of a prime at all, while at 64 and 80 ms, the presence of a prime may be detectable, though never reliably enough to be reported. This means that masked priming performance is relatively insensitive to episodic and strategic confounds. Furthermore, previous research using this paradigm has shown it to be well suited to the study of morphological and orthographic effects at short SOAs (Forster & Azuma, 2000; Frost et al., 1997; Rastle et al., 2000), and to the investigation of potential semantic effects at longer SOAs (Perea & Gotor, 1997; Sereno, 1991). Accordingly, apart from minimizing strategic behaviour, our choice of a small range of incremental steps in prime durations should allow us to track the dynamics of processing events as they unfold over time, and in a more fine-grained manner than earlier studies using this technique with larger SOAs (Feldman, 2000; Rastle et al., 2000).

If morphological structure in Arabic is playing a role that is genuinely distinct from that played by orthography and semantics, as our work on Arabic (Boudelaa & Marslen-Wilson, 2001) and Frost and colleagues' work on Hebrew suggest, then this should be reflected in differential priming effects in the morphological, orthographic, and semantic conditions across the four SOAs. In particular, word pattern and root effects should be able to emerge earlier than semantic effects, and should be stronger than orthography-driven effects.

EXPERIMENT 1

Arabic deverbal nouns, so called because they derive from the same stock of consonantal roots as verbs, draw on over a hundred different word patterns (Bohas & Guillaume, 1984). More importantly this set of Arabic nouns exhibits a relatively high degree of productivity and systematicity with respect to the word patterns and roots they involve. A root morpheme such as {ksr}, with the semantic field of 'breaking', is recruited many times to construct such deverbal nouns as [kasrun] *breaking*, [kasiirun] *broken*, [taksiirun] *shattering*, and [maksuurun] *fractured*. Similarly, a deverbal noun word pattern like {faaʕilun} meaning *agent noun* participates in the building of numerous forms such as [haaribun] *one who flees*, [kaatimun] *one who hides*, [faatiħun] *one who opens*.

In our previous research, where we found masked priming evidence for deverbal noun word patterns and roots as units subserving the process of mapping orthographic input onto central representations, we co-varied the morphological, orthographic, and semantic relationship between prime and target (Boudelaa & Marslen-Wilson, 2000). Here we follow to the same procedure, focusing on six experimental conditions where the relationship underlying prime and target is either morphological, orthographic, or semantic as illustrated in Table 1.

TABLE 1
Experiment 1: Experimental conditions with example stimulus set

Condition	Test	Prime Baseline	Target
1. **[+WP]**	خالد [xaalidun] *eternal*	نهوض [nuhuudˤun] *getting up*	حارس [ħaarisun] *guard*
2. **[+Orth1]**	طائرة [tˤaaʔiratun] *plane*	فتور [futuurun] *lassitude*	خالص [xaalisˤun] *pure*
3. **[+R +S]**	رئاسة [riʔaasa] *president*	عاقبة [ʕaaqɪbatun] *end*	رئيس [raʔiisun] *presidency*
4. **[+R −S]**	ظالم [ðˤalaamun] *oppressor*	حريق [ħariiqun] *fire*	ظلام [ðˤaalimun] *obscurity*
5. **[+Orth2]**	إبريق [ʔibriiqun] *jug*	تأميم [taʔmiimun] *nationalization*	تامّ [taammun] *complete*
6. **[−R +S]**	عمود [ʕamuudun] *post*	حكايه [ħikaajatun] *story*	قصّة [qisˤsˤatun] *novel*

In Condition 1, with pairs like [xaalidun]-[ħaarisun] *eternal-guard*, and [ħaziinun]-[kariimun] *sad-generous*, the prime and target are morphologically related in the sense of sharing a word pattern, which is {faaʕilun} in the first pair and {faʕiilun} in the second. Pairs sharing a word pattern have primarily a vocalic overlap, but may overlap in terms of consonants as well. Note that Arabic noun word patterns, unlike their Hebrew counterparts, do prime successfully provided that they occur in the context of productive roots, and have the same morpho-syntactic meaning in both prime and target (Boudelaa & Marslen-Wilson, 2000,). Priming among [xaalidun]/[ħaarisun]-like pairs will be compared with possible effects in Condition 2, designed to provide an orthographic control – although it should be noted that there is increasing evidence that purely orthographic effects are weak to non-existent in masked priming with Semitic languages (Frost, Kugler, Deutsch, & Forster, 2001). Here we use pairs like [ʃahwatun]-[manðˤarun] *desire-sight*, and [saħaabatun]-[tˤalaaqun] *cloud-divorce*, where primes and targets share an orthographic relationship that mimics as closely as possible the kind of form overlap (chiefly in vowels) found between word pairs sharing a word pattern. If the structural status of the vowels, as parts of a specific word pattern, bears on the mapping of Arabic orthographic forms onto internal representations, a differential pattern of facilitation should emerge across these two conditions. Note that because only long vowels are written in Arabic script, the overlap here is partly implicit, and has to be inferred from an orthographic input which does not spell out the phonetic properties of the word pattern in full.

Conditions 3 and 4 probe the effects of the consonantal root. In Condition 3, the prime and target pairs share a root and a transparent semantic relationship as illustrated by pairs such as [taħqiiqun]-[ħaqiiqatun] *investigation-truth*, and [riʔaasatun]-[raʔiisun]- *presidency-president*. In Condition 4, with pairs like [miʕtˤafun]-[ʕaatˤifatun] *coat-sentiment*, [ʃartˤun]-[ʃurtˤatun] *condition-police* the prime and target share a root, the same structural unit as in Condition 3, but their underlying semantic relationship is opaque (as judged by a panel of native Arabic speakers). One of the critical questions Conditions 3 and 4 are meant to address is whether root morpheme priming will evolve in the same way over time irrespective of the semantic transparency or opacity of the forms involved. Another question relates to whether root and the word pattern priming effects will have comparable profiles over time.

To provide a fuller context for interpreting possible root effects in Conditions 3 and 4, we also included Conditions 5 and 6. Condition 5 consisted of word pairs that are orthographically but not morphologically related, sharing two to three consonants that do not constitute a common root, as in [sulaħfaatun]-[silaaħun] *turtle-weapon*, and [muftin]-[mufat-tiʃun] *Islamic scholar-inspector*. If the priming effects hypothesised in Conditions 3 and 4 are due to the orthographic overlap necessarily obtaining for any two surface forms sharing a root unit, then the word pairs in Condition 5 should show facilitation effects comparable with those in Conditions 3 and 4. Note that because Arabic script codes all consonants, the form overlap between words sharing a root is fully specified in the orthography. Finally, Condition 6 consists of word pairs like [ʕarabatun]-[saɟɟaaratun] *vehicle-car*, and [qitaalun]-[ħarbun] *fight-war*, which are strongly semantically related but do not share either roots or word patterns. Such pairs fail to yield any facilitation in masked priming at short SOAs, but can prime at longer SOAs (Rastle et al., 2000). It will be of interest to determine the point at which meaning-based effects start to show, and how this relates to the time-course of word pattern and root effects.

Method

Participants. A group of 139 volunteers aged 16 to 20 took part in the experiment. They were pupils at the high school of Tataouine in South Tunisia, and used MSA on regular basis.

Material. Each of the six conditions described above was made up of 24 prime-target pairs. The target words were chosen to be orthographically unambiguous, as far as possible by including long vowels, which are written in the orthography. In a few cases, where targets were still orthographically ambiguous, we chose targets where the intended alternative was far more frequent than its homograph. In Condition 1, which we will refer to as [+WP], the prime and target share a word pattern (e.g., [xaalidun]-[ħaarisun] *eternal-guard*). These pairs had an average of 1.2 letters in common, computing orthographic units present in the written form of prime and target. To control for the overlap between prime and target pairs, Condition 2, [+Orth1], consisted of primes and targets that had an average of 0.9 letters in common, as illustrated by pairs like [saħaabatun]-[tˤalaaqun] *cloud-divorce*, but which had no morphological or semantic relationship.[3]

In Condition 3, labelled [+R +S], the prime and target pairs share a root morpheme and the root has the same semantically transparent interpretation in both (e.g., [riʔaasatun]-[raʔiisun] *presidency-president*). This contrasts with Condition 4, labelled [+R −S], where the prime and target share a root (as in [ðˤaalimun]-[ðˤalaamun] *oppressor-obscurity*) but the root does not have the same semantic interpretation in the target as in the prime, where the relationship between the meaning of the root and the meaning of the full form is opaque. Primes and targets shared 3.4 letters in both the [+R +S] condition and the [+R −S] condition.

Condition 5, labelled [+Orth 2], is the orthographic control for the two conditions sharing a root (e.g., [sulaħfaatun]-[silaaħun] *turtle-weapon*). Here the prime and target shared 2.5 letters on average.[4] The difference between [+Orth1] and [+Orth2] is that the orthographic overlap relates to the shared vowels across prime and target in the former, but to the shared consonants in the latter. Because of the nature of Arabic script, the actual orthographic overlap is greater for the consonantal case, underlining the need for different orthographic/form controls for the word patterns and for the roots. Finally Condition 6, [−R +S], consists of semantically but not morphologically related pairs, which share 0.6 letters on average (e.g., [ʕarabatun]-[sajjaaratun] *vehicle-car*).

---

[3] Conditions 1 and 2 were also matched in terms of their underlying phonological overlap (i.e., counting the short vowels not specified in the orthography), which averaged 2.3 and 2.1 phonemes in common, respectively. However, we assume that the critical factor here is orthographic overlap, since this is the overt form dimension directly shared by prime and target.

[4] As is generally the case in research with Semitic scripts, it is not possible to fully match orthographically without introducing morphological confounds. It is hard to find pairs of words that share three consonants that do not share a root as well, especially given the other constraints on the stimuli.

The transparency of the semantic relationship between primes and targets in each condition was determined in a pretest using a large set of potential stimuli where 15 participants were asked to judge the relatedness of the pairs on a 9-point scale, ranging from *very unrelated* (1) to *very related* (9). The mean ratings for the [+R +S] and [−R +S] conditions were equivalent at 7.11 and 7.14 respectively. The ratings for the [+R −S] condition were much lower, at 3.80, though not as low as in the conditions where there was no shared root – for [+WP], [+Orth1], and [+Orth2] the ratings were 1.78, 1.50, and 1.63, respectively. The reason for the intermediate rating in the [+R −S] condition is that Arabic raters treat words sharing a root as having some basic degree of relationship, even if there is no actual semantic overlap.

Each of the 144 test primes was matched as closely as possible in terms of familiarity and of length in letters and syllables to a baseline prime (see Appendix 1 for full list of materials). The mean length of the test primes was 4.43 letters and 3.36 syllables, while the baseline primes were on average 4.29 letters and 3.20 syllables in length. The targets were 4.15 letters and 3.17 syllables long on average. Familiarity was based on a pre-test in which native speakers of MSA were asked to rate a list of words on a five-point scale with 1 being *very unfamiliar* and 5 *very familiar*. The target words, the related primes, and the baseline primes were rated 3.88, 4.04, and 4.43 respectively on this scale. The baseline items were neither morphologically, semantically, or orthographically related to the target.

A similar number of word-pseudoword pairs were constructed so as to echo the form overlap between the test pairs. Some of the word-pseudoword pairs used overlapped in vowels only (e.g., [madiinatun]-*[ʔakiibun] *city*),[5] others in consonants only (e.g., [markabun]-*[muruu-kun] *boat*), and others in neither (e.g., [duxuulun]-*[maħʃafun] *entering*). Two experimental versions were constructed each containing 288 pairs of which 144 were word-word pairs and 144 word-pseudo word pairs, plus 40 practice trials consisting of 20 word-word responses and 20 word-pseudo-word responses.

Design and procedure.   The two versions were constructed such that all the targets appeared only once in each version, half preceded by a related prime and half by an unrelated prime. Each trial consisted of three visual events. The first was a forward pattern mask, in the form of a sequence of 28 vertical lines in a 30-point traditional Arabic font size, displayed for 500 ms. The choice of vertical lines as a mask instead of the more commonly used hash marks was made following a pretest session where we compared

---

[5] Asterisks indicate a pseudoword throughout.

the two masks and found the former to be more effective. The second event was a prime word written without diacritics in the same font but in 24-point font size. Four SOAs corresponding to a prime display duration of 32, 48, 64, and 80 ms were used. The third event was a target word or non-word written without diacritics in a 34 point font size. The target was displayed until participants responded or 2000 ms had elapsed. The larger font size of the target was used because MSA does not have the lower-case upper-case distinction.

Timing, stimulus display, and data collection were controlled by three laptop PCs running the DMDX package so that up to three participants could be tested simultaneously (Forster & Forster, 2003). Thirty-two participants were assigned to the first SOA, 40 to the second, 36 to the third, and 30 to the fourth SOA. Participants were asked to make as accurate and quick a lexical decision as possible about the target by pressing a YES or a NO key. The experiment started with the practice trials followed by the experimental items. There were two breaks in the test session; one after the practice session and the other halfway through the main test sequence. The experiment lasted about 15 minutes.

Results

Table 2 lists mean RTs and per cent error rate as a function of experimental condition and SOA. The data were pruned in two ways. First, by removing participants with error rates exceeding 30%. Second,

TABLE 2
Experiment 1: Mean RT (ms) and per cent error (in parentheses)

	Stimulus onset asynchrony (SOA)							
	32 ms		48 ms		64 ms		80 ms	
Condition	Test	Control	Test	Control	Test	Control	Test	Control
1. [+WP]	621	624	603	630	586	621	583	594
	(6.25)	(5.99)	(6.04)	(5.73)	(8.59)	(5.73)	(3.06)	(3.06)
2. [+Orth1]	610	632	636	634	623	627	599	591
	(5.47)	(5.21)	(2.92)	(4.17)	(4.95)	(5.73)	(3.89)	(5.28)
3. [+R +S]	605	626	600	625	595	618	568	591
	(5.99)	(6.77)	(5.63)	(7.81)	(5.47)	(5.99)	(3.89)	(3.61)
4. [+R –S]	604	627	617	648	599	630	571	599
	(4.95)	(4.69)	(4.79)	(6.77)	(6.77)	(5.99)	(5.56)	(4.17)
5. [+Orth2]	638	647	661	671	645	654	586	627
	(7.29)	(7.03)	(6.88)	(7.03)	(7.81)	(7.55)	(5.83)	(6.67)
6. [–R +S]	633	636	639	651	628	629	578	610
	(5.99)	(5.99)	(4.59)	(7.55)	(7.03)	(7.03)	(7.22)	(5.28)

by removing data points lying 2 standard deviations above or below the participant's mean. Together the two procedures eliminated one participant from version 1 of SOA 64, and 0.8% of the total data, which were not replaced. The results can best be appreciated by inspecting Figure 1, where the mean priming effects are plotted by condition and SOA.

The data were submitted to mixed-design analyses of variance (ANOVA) with four factors, Condition (six levels, +WP, +Orth1, +R +S, +R −S, +Orth2, −R +S), Prime Type (two levels, test, control), SOA (four levels 32, 48, 64, and 80 ms), and List (two levels), which was included to extract any variance due to counterbalancing. In the participants' analysis (F_1), Condition and Prime Type were treated as repeated factors and SOA and List as unrepeated. In the items' analysis (F_2), Prime Type and SOA were treated as repeated factors and Condition and List as unrepeated. The main effect of Condition was significant by participants and items, $F_1(5, 130) = 36.94, p < .001; F_2(5, 143) = 10.42, p < .001$, and so were the main effects of Prime Type, $F_1(1, 130) = 58.93, p < .001; F_2(1, 143) = 24.00, p < .001$, and SOA, $F_1(3, 130) = 23.50, p < .001; F_2(3, 143) = 26.93, p < .001$. The interaction between Condition and Prime Type was significant in the participants' analysis, $F_1(5, 130) = 4.61, p < .05$, but not in the items' analysis ($F_2 < 1$). The two-way interactions between Condition and SOA and between Prime and SOA were not significant

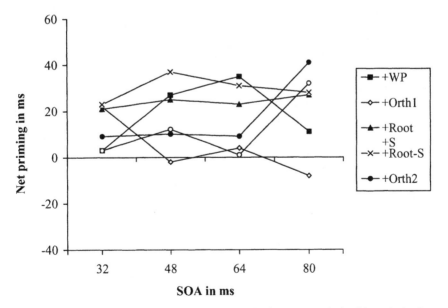

Figure 1. Priming in deverbal nouns as a function of prime-target relationship and stimulus onset asynchrony (SOA).

$(F_1 < 1, F_2 < 1)$. By contrast the three-way interaction between Condition, Prime Type and SOA was significant both by participants and items. $F_1(2, 130) = 2.42, p < .05; F_2(2, 143) = 4.21, p < .05$, suggesting that the amount of priming in the six conditions was not constant across the four SOAs. This three-way interaction was unpacked in a series of Bonferroni-corrected planned comparisons (Keppel, 1982).

The significant overall priming effect in the [+WP] condition, $F_1(1, 130) = 20.17, p < .001; F_2(1, 23) = 11.92, p < .001$, was exclusively driven by the strong word pattern facilitation at SOA 48, $F_1(1, 39) = 10.15, p < .003; F_2(1, 23) = 4.58, p < .044$, and SOA 64, $F_1(1, 35) = 19.46, p < .001; F_2(1, 23) = 11.67, p < .002$, with no effects at earlier or later SOAs. Priming in the [+Orth1] condition was not significant overall $(F_1 < 1), F_2 < 1$. The 22 ms facilitation at SOA 32 was marginally significant, $F_1(1, 31) = 7.10, p < .012; F_2(1, 23) = 4.084, p < .056$, but there was no significant [+Orth1] priming at any of the remaining SOAs.

The overall difference in magnitude of priming between the [+WP] condition and its orthographic control [+Orth1] proved to be significant, $F_1(1, 130) = 6.56, p < .05; F_2(1, 47) = 4.04, p < .046$. Looking at each SOA separately, the difference between [+WP] and [+Orth1] approached significance at SOA 48, $F_1(1, 39) = 6.15, p < .018; F_2(1, 47) = 1.31, p < .25$, and SOA 64, $F_1(1, 35) = 7.26, p < .011; F_2(1, 47) = 3.58, p < .065$, but there were no differences at SOA 32 or SOA 80.

Turning to the root conditions, priming was highly significant overall in the [+R +S] condition, $F_1(1, 130) = 31.20, p < .001; F_2(1, 23) = 62.86, p < .001$, averaging 23 ms, and also proved significant at each individual SOA. Similarly the [+R −S] condition yielded overall significant priming, averaging 28 ms, $F_1(1, 130) = 45.44, p < .001; F_2(1, 23) = 34.64, p < .001$, with significant effects at each SOA. Overall priming in the [+Orth2] condition was not significant $(F_1 < 1; F_2 < 1)$, with an average priming effect of 9 msec over SOAs 32 to 64, but with an unexpected facilitatory effect at SOA 80, $F_1(1, 130) = 11.41, p < .002; F_2(1, 23) = 11.44, p < .003$. The [−R +S] semantic condition showed a similar pattern, with no significant overall priming, an average effect of 5 ms over the first three SOAs, and significant priming emerging at SOA 80, $F_1(1, 29) = 15.48, p < .001; F_2(1, 23) = 6.07, p < .022$.

There was no difference in the amount of priming between the two root conditions, [+R +S] and [+R −S], with $F_1 < 1, F_2 < 1$. Despite the consistent differences between these two conditions and the two control conditions [+Orth2] and [−R +S] across the first three SOAs, we did not obtain robust statistical confirmation of this. Both in overall comparisons collapsing across SOAs, and in individual comparisons at each SOA, we found reliable differences by participants but not by items (under Bonferroni correction).

Given the absence of a clear-cut morphological effect for the root conditions, we conducted additional correlational analyses to check for the possibility of primarily orthographically driven effects in the two [+R] conditions and in the [+Orth2] condition. No correlation between size of priming effect and amount of orthographic overlap was found at any SOA, either for the three conditions individually, or for the three conditions taken together. In a further check, re-running our main analyses of variance with orthographic overlap as a co-variate, we found no modulation of the amount of morphological priming.

We also looked for parallel effects in the semantic domain, checking for possible correlations with semantic relatedness in the two [+R] conditions and in the [−R +S] condition, and again found only weak and inconsistent results. The only significant correlation, in 16 comparisons, was for the combined analysis of all three conditions, at SOA 48 ($r = .235, p = .047$), but with no reliable effects at other SOAs . There is little in these two sets of further analyses to support the view that either orthographic or semantic factors are important independent contributors to the priming effects observed here for the prime-target pairs sharing a root.

The error data were analysed in the same way as the RT data. The main effect of Condition was marginally significant by participants, $F_1(5, 130) = 2.14, p < .059$, but not by items, $F_2(5, 132) < 1$. The main effect of SOA was unreliable by participants, $F_1(3, 130) = 1.12, p < .34$, but reliable by items, $F_2(3, 132) = 12.41, p < .001$. None of the remaining effects or interactions reached significance.

Discussion

Experiment 1 asked two questions: whether morphology-based effects are dissociable from form-based and meaning-based effects over time, and whether morphemic units have distinct time signatures as a function of the kind of information they convey.

As regards the first query, the pattern of effects in the three morphological conditions, [+WP], [+R +S], and [+R −S] differs from their matched orthographic and semantic controls, [+Orth1], [+Orth2], and [−R +S]. This contrast is strongest for Conditions 1 and 2, where targets primed by a shared word pattern are significantly facilitated at SOAs 48 and 64 ms, while the matched orthographic control [+Orth1] generates only an early and transient priming effect at SOA 32. This is consistent with previous findings of effective priming by Arabic noun word patterns when these occur in the context of productive roots, and share the same morpho-syntactic interpretation across prime and target (Boudelaa & Marslen-Wilson, 2000). The two root conditions, [+R +S] and [+R −S], yield consistently robust priming across all four SOAs, contrasting not only with their matched form-based control condition, [+Orth2], which is facilitatory only at SOA 80 ms, but also with the meaning-based matched control condition, [−R +S], whose facilitatory effects are also limited to SOA 80. These contrasts with the root control conditions, however, were not fully statistically robust.

The second outcome of Experiment 1 relates to the differential time course underlying the processing of functionally distinct morphemic entities. Root morphemes, the semantic components of Arabic surface forms, generate priming very early in processing, at SOA 32, and this effect persists over the remaining three SOAs, possibly suggesting a dominant role for this morphemic entity in Arabic visual word recognition. By contrast, word patterns, the means of expressing morpho-syntactic and phonological information about Arabic surface form, seem to affect processing slightly later, and for a noticeably shorter interval of time, with priming being limited to SOAs 48 and 64. Thus, visual word processing in Arabic seems to involve, along with the broad distinction between orthographic, semantic, and morphemic entities, a more fine-grained distinction within the morphological domain, distinguishing word patterns from roots.

A further point relates to the early priming seen in the [+Orth1] vowel overlap condition and the late priming in the [+Orth2] consonant overlap condition. On the basis of our own research (Boudelaa & Marslen-Wilson, 2000, 2001), and research on Hebrew (Frost et al, 2001), where no masked orthographic priming was found at comparably short SOAs (48 ms in Arabic, and 50 ms in Hebrew), the [+Orth1] priming at SOA 32 was not expected. The late priming in the [+Orth2] condition was also not predicted. Since this latter effect (in contrast to the [+Orth1] effect) is replicated in Experiment 2, we will return to it in the later discussion.

In sum, morphological effects seem to dominate over form-driven and meaning-driven effects, and both word pattern and root morphemes are actively used early in processing, but with a temporal precedence for root effects. However, word pattern effects are distinctly transient, yielding facilitation only over two SOAs, while the effects of the root are more durable (Deutsch et al., 2000). This qualitative difference in the effects of word patterns and roots may reflect differences in the processing role of the information conveyed by these two units.

In Experiment 2, we seek to replicate and extend these findings, by asking whether similar patterns emerge from the other major subdivision of Arabic morphology, the Arabic verb.

EXPERIMENT 2

Verb forms are distinguished from deverbal nouns purely by virtue of the word pattern morpheme being used; the underlying root is the same across both syntactic categories. There are only 10 verb word patterns currently in common use. Ordered from 1 to 10 in keeping with the Western tradition, these are: {faʕala}, {faʕʕala}, {faaʕala}, {ʔafʕala}, {tafaʕʕala}, {tafaaʕala}, {ʔinfaʕala}, {ʔiftaʕala}, {ʔifʕalla}, and {ʔistafʕala}. Each of these word patterns has two to three morpho-syntactic interpretations associated with it, such as *causative, intensive, reciprocal* and so on.[6] To address the issue of when morphology-driven effects come into play as opposed to semantic and orthographic effects, we evaluated priming in six conditions built along exactly the same lines as in the previous experiment.

The first condition is again labelled [+WP] and consists of pairs of verbs sharing a word pattern, such as [laxxasˤa]-[fakkara] *sum up-think*, which share the word pattern [faʕʕala], or [laaħaðˤa]-[saafara] *notice-travel* which share the pattern [faaʕala]. In the [+Orth1] condition, where pairs like [qamarun]-[nasaʒa] *moon-weave*, [qalamun]-taraka] *pen-leave* are used, the prime and target share an orthographic overlap that closely mimics that underlying the pairs in condition 1. In the [+R +S] condition the prime and target share a root and a transparent semantic relationship as in [ʔanzala]-[nazala] *cause to go down-go down*, or [ʔistafaada]-[ʔafaada] *benefit-cause to benefit*, while in [+R −S] they share a root but an opaque semantic relationship as in [xallafa]-[ʔixtalafa] *leave behind-disagree*, or [naafaqa]-[ʔanfaqa] *dissimulate-spend*. In [+Orth2], the orthographic control for the [+R +S] and the [+R −S] conditions, the prime and target pairs are orthographically related. They share two to three consonants as illustrated by pairs such as [muʒaadalatun]-[ʒaada] *discussion-give generously* or [ʕafanun]-[ʕafaa] *decomposition-forgive*. Finally, the [−R +S] condition is one in which the prime and target share only a semantic relationship as in [ʔalqaa]-[ramaa] *throw-fling* or [ʔixtafaa]-[ɣaaba] *disappear-vanish*.

---

[6] A word pattern has a *causative* morpho-syntactic interpretation or meaning when the surface form where it appears is glossable as *cause someone to do X*, where X is the core semantic meaning associated with the root. For example, in the form [ʔaskata], where the root is {skt} *keeping quiet* and the word pattern is {ʔafʕal}, the latter is considered to have a *causative* meaning in the sense that [ʔaskata] is glossable as *cause someone to keep quiet*. Analogously, a word pattern is *intensive* when the surface form of which it is part has to be glossed as *do X with intensity*, and a *reciprocal* word pattern is one which entails a gloss like *X is done mutually by two agents* (Holes, 1995; Wright, 1995).

TABLE 3
Experiment 2: Experimental conditions with example stimulus set

| Condition | Prime | | Target |
	Test	Control	
1. **[+WP]**	لخّص [laxxasˁa] *sum up*	مسحة [mushatun] *tinge*	فكّر [fakkara] *think*
2. **[+Orth1]**	لجنة [laʒnatun] *committee*	خضوع [xudˁuuˁun] *submission*	أنكر [ʔankara] *deny*
3. **[+R +S]**	احترق [ʔiħtraqa] *burn*	تصديق [tasˁdiiqun] *believing*	أحرق [ʔaħraqa] set ablaze
4. **[+R −S]**	نظّر [naðˁðˁara] *theorize*	مجهول [maʒhuulun] *unknown*	انتظر [(intaðˁtara] *wait for*
5. **[+Orth2]**	بلعوم [bulˁuumun] *pharynx*	مجد [maʒdun] *glory*	بلّل [ballala] *moisten*
6. **[−R +S]**	أيقن [ʔajqana] *ascertain*	تحفة [tuħfatun] *masterpiece*	تأكّد [taʔakkada] *be confirmed*

Method

Participants.   Another group of 108 participants from the same age group and linguistic background as those in Experiment 1 took part in this experiment.

Material and design.   The design was analogous to that used in Experiment 1. The material consisted of prime and target verb forms which made up six experimental conditions with 24 pairs each as depicted in Table 3.

In Condition 1, [+WP], the prime and target share a word pattern (e.g., [ʔaħraza]-[ʔablaɣa] *acquire-cause to reach*), with orthographic overlap averaging 1.5 letters.[7] Condition 2, [+Orth 1], was again an orthographic

---

[7] Average underlying phonological overlap was 2.5 phonemes for Condition 1 and 2.0 phonemes for Condition 2.

control for condition 1 (e.g., [laʒnatun]-[ʔankara] *committee-deny*, averaging 0.9 letters overlap.[8]

In condition 3, [+R +S], prime and target share a root morpheme and a transparent semantic relationship (e.g., [ʔiħtaraqa]-[ʔaħraqa] *burn-set ablaze*), while in condition 4, [+R −S], they share a root but have an opaque semantic relationship (e.g., [naðˤðˤara]-[ʔintaðˤara] *theorise-wait for*). The number of shared letters across primes and targets were 3.1 and 3.3 in the [+R +S] and [+R −S] conditions respectively. Condition 5, labelled [+Orth 2], is the orthographic control for conditions 3 and 4 (e.g., [balaʕa]-[ballala]). Here the prime and target pairs share 2.1 letters on average. Condition 6, [−R +S], tests for purely semantic effects (e.g., [ʔayqana]-[taʔakkada] *ascertain-be confirmed*), and the number of letters shared by the prime and target pairs was only 0.4.

The strength of the semantic relationship between primes in targets was again assessed in a pre-test similar to that conducted in Experiment 1. The mean ratings for the [+R +S] and [−R +S] conditions were again equivalent, at 7.21 and 7.33 respectively, with the [+R −S] condition coming in at 3.10. Ratings were uniformly low for [+WP], [+Orth1], and [+Orth2], at 1.62, 1.59, and 1.77, respectively.

As in Experiment 1, each of the related primes was matched as closely as possible on number of letters, number of syllables and familiarity to a baseline prime that shared no relationship with the target (see Appendix 2 for the full stimulus set). The target probes were on average 3.73 letters and 3.08 syllables long, and were chosen to be orthographically unambiguous. The test primes were 4.18 letters and 3.36 syllables long while the baseline primes averaged 3.97 and 3.36 in letter and syllable length respectively. With regard to familiarity, which was determined in a similar pre-test as in Experiment 1, the target words received an average rating of 3.88 on the five-point scale. The test prime and the baseline prime received a rating of 3.97 and 4.46 respectively. A similar number of pseudoword-word pairs was constructed in such a way as to echo the form overlap between the word-word pairs.

Procedure.   The procedure was the same as in Experiment 1.

Results

Mean decision latencies and percentage of errors are given in Table 4. About 0.5% of the data were removed as a result of setting cutoffs at 2

---

[8] Because of the much more restricted range of word patterns in the verbal morphology (10 instead of hundreds), and because of the constraints imposed by the need to use long vowels where possible, it was not possible to fully match Condition 1 in number of overlapping letters without introducing potential morphological confounds.

TABLE 4
Experiment 2: Mean RTs (ms) and per cent error (in parentheses)

	Stimulus onset asynchrony (SOA)							
	32 ms		48 ms		64 ms		80 ms	
Condition	Test	Control	Test	Control	Test	Control	Test	Control
1. [+WP]	635	628	584	616	626	621	595	580
	(5.83)	(5.56)	(6.52)	(4.35)	(6.25)	(4.86)	(6.12)	(5.91)
2. [+Orth1]	670	672	654	654	644	657	615	605
	(7.22)	(6.94)	(6.88)	(6.52)	(6.94)	(7.29)	(7.26)	(6.18)
3. [+R +S]	588	622	584	623	577	623	544	586
	(5.56)	(5.00)	(7.25)	(6.16)	(3.82)	(5.56)	(3.23)	(6.99)
4. [+R −S]	610	638	586	616	595	634	564	592
	(6.94)	(5.83)	6.88)	(5.43)	8.33)	(6.35)	(5.65)	(5.91)
5. [+Orth2]	666	645	631	620	642	636	577	606
	(6.67)	(6.83)	(8.33)	(6.16)	(6.60)	(6.25)	(7.27)	(4.84)
6. [−R +S]	631	618	631	617	614	616	564	586
	(6.67)	(5.28)	(8.70)	(5.43)	(6.94)	(5.21)	(8.06)	(5.65)

standard deviations above or below the participant's own mean. These were not replaced. The mean priming effects are plotted by condition and SOA in Figure 2.

Latency and error data were submitted to separate mixed design ANOVAs with four factors: Condition, Prime Type, SOA, and List. In the by-participants analysis, Condition and Prime Type were treated as repeated factors, with SOA and List as unrepeated factors. In the by-items analysis, Prime Type and SOA were repeated factors, and Condition and List unrepeated. The results revealed the main effects of Condition, $F_1(5, 107) = 45.23$, $p < .001$; $F_2(5, 143) = 13.99$, $p < .001$, Prime Type, $F_1(1, 107) = 14.00$, $p < .001$; $F_2(1, 143) = 10.46$, $p < .002$, and SOA, $F_1(3, 107) = 3.49$, $p < .019$; $F_2(3, 143) = 16.08$, $p < .001$. Condition interacted significantly with Prime Type, $F_1(5, 107) = 14.39$, $p < .001$; $F_2(5, 143) = 4.05$, $p < .05$, and with SOA, $F_1(5, 107) = 4.97$, $p < .05$; $F_2(5, 143) = 3.51$, $p < .05$. There was no Prime Type by SOA interaction ($F_1 < 1$, $F_2 < 1$). The three-way interaction between Condition, Prime Type, and SOA was significant, $F_1(15, 107) = 2.37$, $p < .05$; $F_{21}(15, 143) = 2.56$; $p < .05$, and we took the same planned comparison approach as in the previous experiment to unpack it.

Overall, priming in the [+WP] condition was not significant ($F_1 < 1$, $F_2 < 1$). However, the 32 ms facilitation for word pairs sharing a word pattern at SOA 48 was significant by participants and items, $F_1(1, 22) = 4.49$, $p < .045$; $F_2(1, 23) = 13.51$; $p < .001$. No significant [+WP] effects were observed at any other SOAs. Priming in [+Orth1] failed to reach significance overall,

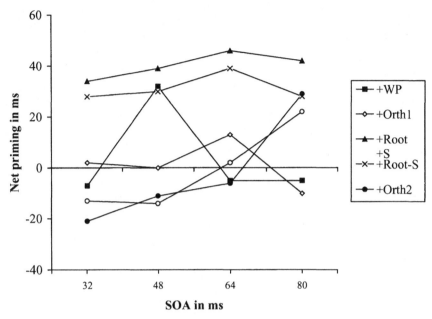

Figure 2. Priming in verbs as a function of prime-target-relationship and stimulus onset asynchrony (SOA).

or at each SOA individually. In particular, there was no sign of the early priming observed at SOA 32 in Experiment 1. The overall difference between the [+WP] and the [+Orth1] condition was not significant ($F_1 < 1$, $F_2 < 1$), but the two conditions did differ at SOA 48, $F_1(1, 29) = 3.64$, $p < .050$; $F_2(1, 23) = 4.67$; $p < .036$.

Turning to the two root conditions, priming in the [+R +S] condition was highly significant, $F_1(1, 107) = 69.83$, $p < .001$; $F_2(1, 23) = 62.86$; $p < .001$, and did not vary across SOA. Averaging 40 ms, the effects are generally stronger than in Experiment 1. A similar pattern held for the [+R −S] condition, $F_1(1, 107) = 28.32$, $p < .001$; $F_2(1, 23) = 34.64$; $p < .001$, with priming overall averaging 31 ms. Conversely, overall priming in the [+Orth2] and the [−R +S] conditions failed to reach significance ($F_1 < 1$, $F_2 < 1$). However, at SOA 80 both [+Orth2], with, $F_1(1, 107) = 28.32$, $p < .001$; $F_2(1, 23) = 4.77$; $p < .040$, and [−R +S], with $F_1(1, 30) = 4.98$, $p < .033$; $F_2(1, 23) = 6.30$; $p < .020$, again showed significant facilitation.

No difference in magnitude of priming was found between the two root conditions, [+R +S] and [+R −S]. In contrast to Experiment 1, there were robust differences with the two root control conditions, both overall and individually, over the first three SOAs. The overall priming for [+R +S] differed significantly from the [Orth2] condition, $F_1(1, 107) = 29.93$, $p < .001$; $F_2(1, 23) = 23.15$; $p < .001$. More specifically, these two conditions differed at SOA 32, $F_1(1, 29) = 21.72$, $p < .001$; $F_2(1, 23) = 11.05$; $p < .002$, SOA 48, $F_1(1, 22) = 5.75$, $p < .025$; $F_2(1, 23) = 6.84$; $p < .012$, and SOA 64, $F_1(1, 23) = 9.13$, $p < .006$; $F_2(1, 23) = 7.46$; $p < .009$, but not at SOA 80 ($F_1 < 1$, $F_2 < 1$). A similar pattern held for the comparison between [+R −S] and [−R +S], with a significant overall difference, $F_1(1, 107) = 28.43$, $p < .001$; $F_2(1, 23) = 25.66$; $p < .001$, accompanied by significant effects at SOA 32, $F_1(1, 29) = 16.83$, $p < .001$; $F_2(1, 23) = 10.95$; $p < .002$, SOA 48, $F_1(1, 22) = 7.93$, $p < .010$; $F_2(1, 23) = 8.14$; $p < .006$, and SOA 64, $F_1(1, 23) = 3.69$, $p < .050$; $F_2(1, 23) = 5.69$; $p < .021$, but not SOA 80.

Comparing [+R −S] and [+Orth2], an overall difference is also found, $F_1(1, 107) = 16.38$, $p < .001$; $F_2(1, 23) = 14.37$; $p = .001$, accompanied by significant differences at the three shortest SOAs (SOA 32, $F_1(1, 29) = 17.82$, $p < .001$; $F_2(1, 23) = 6.37$; $p < .015$, SOA 48, $F_1(1, 22) = 5.02$, $p < .035$; $F_2(1, 23) = 5.76$; $p < .020$, and SOA 64, $F_1(1, 23) = 6.77$, $p < .016$; $F_2(1, 23) = 5.50$; $p < .023$). Similarly for the overall comparison of [+R −S] and [−R +S], with $F_1(1, 107) = 21.48$, $p < .001$; $F_2(1, 23) = 15.33$; $p = .001$, and differences again observed at SOA 32, $F_1(1, 29) = 11.05$, $p < .002$; $F_2(1, 23) = 5.53$, $p < .023$, SOA 48, $F_1(1, 22) = 7.02$, $p < .015$; $F_2(1, 23) = 7.02$; $p < .011$, and SOA 64, $F_1(1, 23) = 7.29$, $p < .013$; $F_2(1, 23) = 4.83$; $p < .033$.

As in Experiment 1, we also ran correlational analyses to check for possible orthographic overlap effects, focusing on the two root conditions and [+Orth2]. No significant effects were found either for each condition separately or as a group, with the one exception of a correlation of .416 ($p = .043$) for [+Orth2] at SOA 32. Parallel analyses were also run on the same two [+R] conditions and the semantic condition [−R +S] to assess the effects of semantic relatedness. No significant effects were found at any SOA.

The error data were submitted to the same mixed design ANOVA, with SOA emerging as the only significant main effect, $F_1(3, 107) = 5.19$, $p < .002$; $F_2(5, 143) = 6.87$, $p < .05$. Weaker effects were seen for Condition, $F_1(5, 107) = 3.52$, $p < .004$; $F_2(5, 143) = < 1$, and for Prime Type, $F_1(1, 107) = 5.13$, $p < .025$; $F_2(1, 143) = 3.21$ $p < .075$. No other significant effects or interactions were found.

Discussion

The results of this experiment, tapping into the second major domain of Arabic word-formation, confirm the major features of Experiment 1, with a completely new set of materials. We again see a distinct time course for morphology-based effects in contrast to form-based and meaning-based effects, with essentially the same pattern of contrasts between the [+WP] and [+Orth1] conditions on the one hand, and the two root conditions, [+R +S], [+R −S], and their matched orthographic [+Orth2] and semantic [−R +S] controls on the other. In this second experiment, however, these root effects are now statistically very reliable.

We also replicate the marked differences in the patterns of activation over time for the two different types of morpheme involved. Root priming onsets very early, at SOA 32, at essentially full strength, and carries on through at equivalent levels until SOA 80. Word pattern priming again operates within a narrow temporal window, here restricted to SOA 48. Interestingly, this is similar to the 42 ms SOA at which verb word pattern priming was observed in Hebrew in a single SOA masked priming experiment (Deutsch et al., 1998). No word pattern effects are observed at SOAs earlier or later than 48 ms. This is all the more striking given that the effects of the word pattern in other priming tasks, such as cross-modal and auditory-auditory immediate repetition priming, seem just as durable as root priming effects (Boudelaa & Marslen-Wilson, 2004a).

Experiment 2 also replicates two features of the priming responses for the control conditions. Both the root orthographic control [+Orth2] and the purely semantic condition [−R +S] again show significant facilitatory effects at the longest SOA (80 ms), but no significant effects at shorter SOAs. The third control effect observed in Experiment 1, the significant priming at SOA 32 for the word pattern orthographic control [+Orth1], showed no signs of replication here, indicating that this is not a robust finding. We now turn to a discussion of the overall results for the two experiments.

GENERAL DISCUSSION

This study addressed two questions – whether morphological effects have a different time course from form-based and meaning-based effects, and whether functionally distinct morphemic entities have different effects over time. To do this we focused on the processing of discontinuous morphemes in Arabic deverbal nouns and verbs, using the incremental masked priming paradigm in combination with lexical decision. The combined results of the two experiments give a clear and consistent picture of the dynamics of morphological effects in Arabic visual word recognition. What are the implications of these results?

Are morphological effects separable from orthographic and semantic effects?

Semitic languages such as Arabic already provide some of the strongest evidence for separable morphological effects in psycholinguistic tasks. The experiments here, contrasting morphological, orthographic, and semantic relationships in the incremental masked priming task, reinforce this view.

There are two aspects of the results that contribute to this conclusion. These are the marked differences in the temporal patterning of the priming effects attributable to different sources, and, second, the apparent irrelevance of form-based and semantic factors to the presence or absence of a priming effect between words in Arabic sharing a morpheme.

Words sharing a root morpheme show reliable priming across all four SOAs, with little change from SOA 32 to SOA 80. This pattern of effects cannot be due to a confound with semantic factors. First, priming is equally strong regardless of whether primes and targets share a transparent (e.g., [taħqiiqun]-[ħaqiiqatun] *investigation-truth*) or an opaque semantic relationship (e.g., [miʕtˤafun]-[ʕaatˤifatun] *coat-sentiment*), at all SOAs. Second, significant priming effects for pairs that share a semantic relationship [−R +S] but no morphological relationship emerge only at SOA 80, and are undetectable at earlier SOAs, for both experiments. This is consistent with most earlier studies that have looked at semantic effects in masked priming at short SOAs. Third, there is no correlation for either root condition with degree of semantic relatedness.

Similar arguments hold for orthographic factors. Orthographically related words in [+Orth2], sharing two or more consonants that do not belong to the same root (e.g., [sulaħfaatun]-[silaaħun] *turtle-weapon*), generate reliable priming only at the longest SOA (80 ms). Correlational analyses for the two [+R] conditions together with [+Orth2], as well as analyses of covariance with orthographic overlap as a co-variate, consistently show no effects of orthographic factors on priming. The late effect for [+Orth2] may itself not be a purely orthographic effect – in scripts like English such effects are typically found at the shortest SOAs (e.g., Rastle et al, 2000). Instead, it may reflect a late interaction between the root consonants signalled in the target and the partial overlap with these in the prime. However, this is an effect that itself requires further research.

Turning to the word pattern results, with their distinctive transient effects peaking at the middle SOAs, it is even clearer that these are morphologically driven rather than reflecting semantic or orthographic confounds. Where semantics is concerned, words sharing just a word-pattern are viewed by native speakers as being wholly semantically unrelated (with the same low ratings as baseline unrelated prime-target pairs in pre-tests of semantic relatedness). In terms of conventional views of the conditions under which semantic priming occurs, there is simply no basis for such effects in the [+WP] pairs. For orthography, there is similarly very little basis for an effect based just on form overlap. Because of the nature of Arabic script, with most vowels not written, and with the surface phonetic content of word patterns being predominantly in the form of vowels, direct orthographic overlap was very low in the [+WP] conditions, averaging 1.3 letters for targets 4 letters long. Even if an orthographic priming effect could be generated on this minimal basis, there would be no grounds for expecting it to show the same pattern over SOAs as the [+WP] conditions – especially since neither the [+Orth1] condition, nor the [+Orth2] condition, with twice as much overlap in terms of letters, showed anything like this pattern.

More generally, orthographic effects in Semitic languages seem to be difficult to obtain (Frost et al., 2001), while morphological effects are robust and consistent even in cases of minimal form overlap (Boudelaa & Marslen-Wilson, 2001) and of allomorphic variation (Boudelaa & Marslen-Wilson, 2004b). Indeed, in a recent study (Boudelaa & Marslen-Wilson, 2004a), we found evidence for morphological priming between Arabic verbs with no orthographic overlap at all. These were prime-target pairs sharing the same CV-Skeleton, or abstract consonant-vowel (CV) sequence. The CV-Skeleton, viewed as a component of the word pattern, is an abstract prosodic morpheme which specifies the overall phonological structure of the surface word, as well as critical morpho-syntactic properties, but does not specify the exact phonological or orthographic identity of the consonants and vowels in the word (McCarthy, 1981, 1982). The prime-target pair [fuuʒiʔa]-[ʃaaraka] *be surprised-participate*, for example, share the reciprocal CV-Skeleton {CVVCVCV}, but have no orthographic content in common. Such pairs, nonetheless, prime consistently across a variety of tasks, including masked priming at an SOA of 48 ms (Boudelaa & Marslen-Wilson, 2004b).

Overall, these results demonstrate that morphological effects in Arabic visual word-recognition and lexical access can be conclusively separated from potential effects of form or meaning overlap. Priming for pairs sharing roots and word-patterns is robust, occurs at short SOAs, and is likely to reflect repeated access to the same underlying sub-lexical units in prime and target. There is little evidence at all for consistent orthographic priming, and semantic priming seems to reflect late effects, possibly based on the spread of activation between separate lexical representations.

Why is morphology different from orthography and semantics?

Morphology, orthography, and semantics are three distinct domains of knowledge. Each of them provides a different and independent type of information about lexical items, and exerts differential effects on the way words are processed and organised in lexical space. Since the lexical system seeks out patterns in the environment in order to acquire, store, and access linguistic knowledge in an efficient way, it is the domain of knowledge that is most consistent and regular that will gain more weight in determining the way the mental lexicon is organised. This will vary cross-linguistically since speakers of different languages make differential choices of the way they encode meaning. In Semitic languages the most consistent and recurrent patterns are those provided by the morphological domain.

Consider for example the notion of *causativity*. In Indo-European languages like English, causativity is encoded either lexically as in 'teach' *cause to learn*, or syntactically as in *make someone happy*, and occasionally through derivational morphology as in 'widen' *cause to become wide*. By contrast, in Semitic languages like Arabic, the idea of causativity is almost exclusively encoded morphologically by using such word patterns as {ʔafʕala} or {faʕʕala} to create causative verbs like [ʔaʕlama] *cause to know*, or [farraħa] *cause to become happy*. Now consider the following Arabic forms: [kataba], [kaataba], [kitaabun], [maktabun], and [kaatibun] and their respective English equivalents *write, correspond, book, office, author*. The broad meaning of *writing* inherent in all the Arabic forms above, is conveyed by the root {ktb}, which occurs in all the forms. The same general meaning of *writing* or *having to do with writing* is also present in the English translation. However, there is no clearly recurring element across all the English forms. In other words, the Arabic linguistic environment offers a generally more consistent relationship between the form of a word and its meaning than its English counterpart; and the crucial elements in this consistency are roots and word patterns. Every time a causative meaning is encountered, the pattern {ʔafʕala} or {faʕʕala} is more likely than not to be present, and every time the meaning of *writing* is encountered, the root {ktb} has a high probability of being present. Thus as language learning progresses a coherent system evolving around roots and word patterns emerges, and the extraction of these elements becomes the primary task of the language processor.

However if Arabic, and indeed Semitic, morphology derives its weight from the fact that it is the means of choice for expressing meaning, why is there no difference between [+R +S] and [+R −S]? What would the justification be for parsing a complex form like [katiibatun] *squadron* when its meaning is not the sum of its component morphemes? One suggestion is that the search for regular patterns that the lexical system undertakes is guided by consistency between form and meaning only at the outset. Later on in development the system would be looking for and using consistency wherever it can be found. The form commonality between [katiibatun], *squadron* [maktabun] *office*, [kitaabun] *book* and [kataba] *write* would be enough to build a morphological family around the root {ktb}. The end-state lexical processor in Semitic languages would thus be looking for morphological structure provided by roots and word patterns regardless of meaning.

Why do roots and word patterns have differential priming profiles?

This study demonstrates that the root morpheme has an earlier and more long-lived effect than the word pattern in the masked priming task. The earlier onset of root effects compared with word pattern effects may derive at least in part from the consonantal nature of Arabic orthography, where consonants but not vowels are fully specified. In other words, while the visual event presents fully specified information about the consonantal root, it presents only partial information about the word pattern. This means that while accessing the meaning of an orthographically presented root can be direct, the mapping of a visually presented word pattern onto its morpho-syntactic meaning is indirect and may require mediation through access to phonology. If this is correct, then it is phonological mediation that results in word pattern priming kicking in after root priming. Another factor underlying the differential priming onsets of word patterns and roots may be simply the nature of information conveyed by the two units. In particular, the meaning conveyed by the root is arguably more constraining than that conveyed by the word pattern. Surface forms sharing a root make up a more coherent morphological family than those sharing a word pattern, and this may also facilitate access (for evidence on morphological family size effects in Semitic languages, see Moscoso del Prado Martín, Bertram, Schreuder, & Baayen, in press). The emergence of root effects prior to word pattern effects is perhaps paralleled by Hebrew developmental data showing that the ability to identify and manipulate root morphemes (in offline tasks) is present even in 3- to 4-year-olds, while word pattern identification and manipulation takes place only after the child is 10 years old or more (Ravid & Malenky, 2001).

What is less straightforward to account for is why roots and word patterns have differential priming offsets. If priming by these two units is subserved by the same underlying mechanism, namely by access to a common morpheme in prime and target, why does word pattern priming have transient effects in this task, whereas in other priming tasks such as cross-modal and auditory-auditory priming, it has effects that seem as long-lasting as those of roots?

The transient effects may reflect the timing with which word pattern information is used in the dynamic processes of early visual word recognition and lexical access. At SOA 32, as sketched above, word pattern information about the prime may not yet be available to influence processing of the target. Twenty milliseconds later, at around SOA 48, prime word pattern information is available and interacts strongly with word pattern extraction processes in the analysis of the target. This window seems quite narrow, however, since by SOA 80 there is no longer any priming effect. This may reflect the genuine transience of word pattern activation for briefly exposed masked primes, or it may reflect transfer of information about word patterns to levels of the system that are not engaged by masked priming. An important issue for further research is to begin to probe the basis of these timing differences—whether they reflect differences in activation rate for different morpheme-types, for example, or whether they reflect specific properties of lexical architecture.

Theoretical implications

While previous investigations of Semitic languages (Boudelaa & Marslen-Wilson, 2001, 2004b; Frost et al., 1997) have established the importance of morphology in processing and representation, the current findings constitute a substantial step forward in understanding not only the dynamic unfolding of morphological, orthographic, and semantic effects over time, but also the more fine-grained unfolding of word pattern and root effects. Morphological effects, including root and word pattern effects, take precedence over orthographic and semantic effects, because morphological structure offers a more salient and consistent domain of analysis and processing in lexical access.

At this point, there are two possible directions one can take. The first is the class of dual route models such as the one put forward by Frost and his colleagues (Frost et al., 1997, 1998, 2000) for Hebrew. On this account, lexical units (words) and sub-lexical units (morphemes) are both represented, and processing of printed stimuli consists of a lexical retrieval process in which lexical units are located at the word level, and a morphological parsing process in which morphemic units are extracted and located at the sub-lexical level. The difference between word pattern priming in Hebrew verbs and nouns, where significant facilitation was observed for the former but not the latter is captured by allowing verb word patterns to be represented at the sub-lexical level and the lexical level, while the nominal word pattern is represented only at the lexical level (Deutsch et al., 1998; Frost et al., 1997). An Arabic version of such a model would thus need to feature deverbal noun word patterns, verb word patterns and roots, since they all prime successfully in this language. With this done, we can proceed to assess how such an architecture may accommodate the differential morphological, orthographic, and semantic effects on the one hand, and the differential effects of roots and word patterns on the other.

The earlier onset of morphological priming compared with orthographic and semantic effects can be modelled by assuming that the parsing route and the full form access route run in parallel and the fastest route wins the race. The time required to recognise a word via either route would be a stochastic variable with some overlap in the temporal distribution of the two routes. Thus under some circumstances both routes have a chance of winning. However, since most Arabic words are clearly made up of an identifiable root and an identifiable word pattern, the parsing route will often win the race and produce a successful parse as evidenced by the earliness and durability of root priming. Orthographic and semantic effects, may emerge at longer SOAs because the direct access route will have had enough time to deliver an output. As regards the differential onset of word pattern and root priming, it may be argued to derive, as mentioned above, from the consonantal nature of Arabic orthography which provides full information about roots but partial information at best about word patterns. An orthographically presented word pattern may need to be mapped onto a phonological representation before its morpho-syntactic interpretation can be contacted. This is not the case for the root, which can in principle be directly accessed from print without need for phonological mediation, hence its earlier priming effects. Finally, with respect to the different offsets of word pattern and root priming, one possibility is to model these in terms of differential decay functions.

The alternative direction to this dual route approach is to look at connectionist models (Plaut & Gonnerman, 2000; Rueckl et al., 1997; Rueckl & Raveh, 1999). On this account, morphological effects derive from the learned sensitivity of the language processor to the systematic relationships among the surface forms of words and their meanings, just as phonological representations themselves may derive from learned rela-tionships among acoustic, semantic, and articulatory information (Plaut & Kello, 1998). Recently, Plaut and Gonnerman (2000) carried out a simulation in which a set of morphologically related words varying in semantic transparency were embedded either in a morphologically rich language (intended to simulate Hebrew), or a morphologically impover-ished language (intended to simulate English). The network showed more priming as a function of semantic transparency in both languages, which is inconsistent with a number of masked priming experiments in Hebrew and Arabic where no difference in magnitude of priming between [+R +S] and [+R −S]-type pairs was found (Boudelaa & Marslen-Wilson, 2000, 2004a, 2004b; Frost et al., 1997). Furthermore, the network extended priming to the semantically opaque words (i.e., [+R −S]) only in the morphologically rich language. This, however, seems inconsistent with recent masked priming data showing equivalent priming among semantically transparent (e.g., driver/DRIVE) and semantically opaque forms (e.g., corner/CORN) in morphologically less rich languages such as English (Feldman & Soltano, 1999; Rastle et al., 2000), and French (Longtin, Segui, & Halle, 2003). Another challenge, although outside the scope of the Plaut and

Gonnerman network, would be to explain how cross-modal priming, with overt, auditorily presented primes, shows equivalent priming between morphologically related words regardless of semantics in Semitic languages (e.g., Boudelaa & Marslen-Wilson, 2000), but not in Indo-European languages (e.g., Marslen-Wilson et al., 1994).

The empirical weaknesses of the Plaut & Gonnerman's (2000) network do not, of course, entail the failure of the entire distributed connectionist approach. Networks trained on a more naturalistic input, and embodying more realistic assumptions about the impact of morphological factors on lexical organisation and lexical processing, may well show results more consistent with what natural language users do. Such a system should treat Arabic and English differently because regularities in the two types of languages lie in different places, as well as reflecting further differences in the functional and distributional properties of Arabic word pattern and root morphemes.

Conclusion

The present work presents new information on how the dynamics of the language processor are influenced by morphology, orthography, and semantics. Across languages, these three domains of knowledge have different impacts on the way visual input is mapped onto internal representations of lexical forms. The existing models of language processing and representation are mainly guided by what we know about Indo-European languages, and in particular English. If we are to build a viable theory of language processing that captures the universal properties of language without failing to acknowledge the idiosyncratic characteristics of different languages, we need to sample typologically different languages. The present study is a step in this direction.

REFERENCES

Aronoff, M. (1976). *Word formation in generative grammar*. Cambridge, MA: MIT Press.

Bertram, R., Laine, M., & Karvinen, K. (1999). The interplay of word formation type, affixal homonymy, and productivity in lexical processing: Evidence from a morphologically rich language. *Journal of Psycholinguistic Research, 28*, 213–226.

Bohas, G., & Guillaume, J.-P. (1984). *Etudes des Théories des grammairiens Arabes: I Morphologie et Phonologie*. Damascus, Syria.

Boudelaa, S., & Marslen-Wilson, W. D. (2000). Non-concatenative morphemes in language processing: Evidence from Modern Standard Arabic. *Proceedings of the Workshop on Spoken Word Access Processes, 1*, 23–26. Nijmegen, Netherlands.

Boudelaa, S., & Marslen-Wilson, W. D. (2001). Morphological units in the Arabic mental lexicon. *Cognition, 81*, 65–92.

Boudelaa, S., & Marslen-Wilson, W. D. (2004a). Abstract morphemes and lexical representation: The CV-Skeleton in Arabic. *Cognition, 92*, 271–303.

Boudelaa, S., & Marslen-Wilson, W. D. (2004b). Allomorphic variation in Arabic: Implications for lexical processing and representation. *Brain and Language, 90* 106–116.

Caramazza, A., Laudanna, A., & Romani, C. (1988). Lexical access and inflectional morphology. *Cognition, 28,* 297–332.

Clahsen, H. (1999). Lexical entries and rules of language: A multidisciplinary study of German inflection. *Behavioural and Brain Sciences, 22,* 991–1013.

Deutsch, A., Frost, R., & Forster, K. I. (1998). Verbs and nouns are organized and accessed differently in the mental lexicon: Evidence from Hebrew. *Journal of Experimental Psychology: Learning Memory, and Cognition, 24,* 1238–1255.

Deutsch, A., Frost, R., Pollatsek, A., & Rayner, K. (2000). Early morphological effects in word recognition in Hebrew: Evidence from parafoveal preview benefit. *Language and Cognitive Processes, 15,* 487–506.

Dominguez, A., Cuetos, F., & Segui, J. (2002). Representation and processing of inflected words in Spanish: Masked and unmasked evidence. *Linguistics, 40,* 235–259.

Drews, E., & Zwitserlood, P. (1995). Morphological and orthographic similarity in visual word recognition. *Journal of Experimental Psychology: Human Perception and Performance, 21,* 1098–1116..

Feldman, L. (2000). Are morphological effects distinguishable from the effects of shared meaning and shared form. *Journal of Experimental Psychology: Learning, Memory, and Cognition, 6,* 1431–1444.

Feldman, L., Frost, R., & Pnini, T. (1995). Decomposing words into their constituent morphemes: Evidence from English and Hebrew. *Journal of Experimental Psychology: Learning, Memory and Cognition, 21,* 947–960.

Feldman, L., & Soltano, E. G. (1999). Morphological priming: The role of prime duration, semantic transparency, and affix position. *Brain and Language, 68,* 33–39.

Forster, K. I., & Davis, C. (1984). Repetition priming and frequency attenuation in lexical access. *Journal of Experimental Psychology: learning Memory and Cognition, 10,* 680–698.

Forster, K. I., & Azuma, T. (2000). Masked priming for prefixed words with bound stems: Does submit prime permit? *Language and Cognitive Processes, 15,* 539–561.

Forster, K. I., & Forster, J. C. (2003). DMDX: A windows display program with millisecond accuracy. *Behavior Research Methods, Instruments, and Computers, 35,* 116–124.

Frost, R., Deutsch, A., Gilboa, O., Tannebaum, M., & Marslen-Wilson, W. D. (2000). Morphological priming: Dissociation of phonological, semantic and morphological factors. *Memory and Cognition, 28,* 1277–1288.

Frost, R., Forster, K. I., & Deutsch, A. (1997). What can we learn from the morphology of Hebrew? A masked priming investigation of morphological representation. *Journal of Experimental Psychology: Learning, Memory and Cognition, 23,* 829–856.

Frost, R., Kugler, T., Deutsch, A., & Forster, K. I. (2001). Orthographic structure versus morphological structure: Principles of lexical organization in a given language. paper presented at the 2nd Workshop on Morphology (June 11–14). Nijmegen, The Netherlands.

Grainger, J., Colé, P., & Segui, J. (1991). Masked morphological priming in visual word recognition. *Journal of Memory and Language, 30,* 370–384.

Holes, C. (1995). *Modern Arabic.* London: Longman.

Keppel, G. (1982). *Design and analysis: A researchers handbook.* Englewood Cliffs, NJ: Prentice Hall.

Longtin, C.-M., Segui, J., & Halle, P. (2003). Morphological priming without morphological relationship. *Language and Cognitive Processes, 18,* 313–334.

Marslen-Wilson, W. D., & Tyler, L. K. (1998). Rules, representations and the English past tense. *Trends in Cognitive Sciences, 2,* 428–435.

Marslen-Wilson, W. D., Tyler, L. K., Waksler, R., & Older, L. (1994). Morphology and meaning in the English mental lexicon. *Psychological Review, 101,* 3–33.

Marslen-Wilson, W. D., Zhou, X-L., & Ford, M. (1996). Morphology, modality, and lexical architecture. In G. Booij & J. Van Mark (Eds.), *Yearbook of morphology* (pp. 117–134). Dordrecht, the Netherlands: Kluwer Academic.

McCarthy, J. J. (1981). A prosodic theory of non-concatenative morphology. *Linguistic Inquiry, 12*, 373–418.

McCarthy, J. J. (1982). Prosodic templates, morphemic templates, and morphemic tiers. In H. V. der Hulst & N. Smith (Eds.), *The structure of phonological representations* (pp. 191–223). Dordrecht, the Netherlands: Foris Publications.

Moscoso del Prado Martín, F., Bertram, R., Schreuder, R., & Baayen, R. H. (in press). Morphological family size in a morphologically rich language: The case of Finnish compared to Dutch and Hebrew. *Journal of Experimental Psychology: Learning, Memory, and Cognition.*

Perea, M., & Gotor, A. (1997). Associative and semantic priming effects occur at very short stimulus-onset asynchronies in lexical decision and naming. *Cognition, 62*, 223–240.

Plaut, D., & Gonnerman, L. M. (2000). Are non-semantic morphological effects incompatible with a distributed connectionist approach to lexical processing? *Language and Cognitive Processes, 15*, 445–485.

Plaut, D., & Kello, C. (1998). The interplay of speech comprehension and production in phonological development: A forward modelling approach. In B. MacWhinney (Ed.), *The emergence of language* (pp. 381–415). Mahwah, NJ: Lawrence Erlbaum Associates Inc.

Rastle, K., Davis, M. H., Marslen-Wilson, W. D., & Tyler, L. K. (2000). Morphological and semantic effects in visual word recognition: A time-course study. *Language and Cognitive Processes, 15*, 507–537.

Ravid, D., & Malenky, D. (2001). Awareness of linear and nonlinear morphology in Hebrew: A developmental study. *First Language, 21*, 25–56.

Rueckl, J., & Raveh, M. (1999). The influence of morphological regularities on the dynamics of a connectionist network. *Brain and Language, 68*, 110–117.

Rueckl, J. G., Mikolinski, M., Raveh, M., Miner, C. S., & Mars, F. (1997). Morphological priming, fragment completion, and connectionist networks. *Journal of Memory and Language, 36*, 382–405.

Scalise, S. (1986). *Generative morphology.* Dordrecht, the Netherlands: Foris Publications.

Schreuder, R., & Baayen, H. (1995). Modelling morphological processing. In Feldman (Eds.), *Morphological aspects of language processing* (pp. 131–154). Hillsdale, NJ: Lawrence Erlbaum Associates Inc.

Seidenberg, M., & Gonnerman, L. (2000). Explaining derivational morphology as the convergence of codes. *Trends in Cognitive Sciences, 4*, 353–361.

Sereno, J. A. (1991). Graphemic, associative, and syntactic priming effects at brief stimulus onset asynchrony in lexical decision and naming. *Journal of Experimental Psychology: Learning, Memory and Cognition, 17*, 459–477.

Versteegh, K. (1997). The Arabic language. *Edinburgh: Edinburgh University Press.*

Wright, W. (1995). *A grammar of the Arabic language.* Cambridge: Cambridge University Press.

Appendix 1

Test items used in Experiment 1. For every item, the Arabic script, an IPA transcription and an English gloss are given.

Prime		Target
+WP	**Unrelated**	**Target**
خالد	غوض	حارس
[xaalidun]	[nuhuudˤun]	[ħaarisun]
eternal	getting up	guard
نشيط	جنون	صغير
[naʃiitˤun]	[ʒunuunun]	[sˤaɣiirun]
active	insanity	small
ضعيف	نقطة	أخير
[dˤaʕiifun]	[nuqtˤatun]	[ʔaxiirun]
weak	point	final
تجارة	حمولة	كتابة
[tiʒaaratun]	[ħumuulatun]	[kitaabatun]
trade	burden	writing
فقير	شهرة	بعيد
[faqiirun]	[ʃuhratun]	[baʕiidun]
poor	fame	remote
فاسد	هدنة	قادم
[faasidun]	[hudnatun]	[qaadimun]
corrupt	truce	coming
حزين	لعبة	كريم
[ħaziinun]	[luʕbatun]	[kariimun]
unhappy	game	generous
ثورة	حفرة	دعوة
[θawratun]	[ħufratun]	[daʕwatun]
rebellion	hole	invitation
كشّاف	غياب	فلّاح
[kaʃʃaafun]	[ɣijaabun]	[fallaaħun]
scout	absence	farmer
تهمة	فرار	سلطة
[tuhmatun]	[firaarun]	[sultˤatun]
allegation	departure	authority
وضوح	بلاغ	جلوس
[wudˤuuħun]	[balaaɣun]	[ʒuluusun]
clarity	bulletin	sitting
خلافة	صعوبة	دراسة
[xilaafatun]	[sˤuʕuubatun]	[diraasatun]
succession	difficulty	study

Prime		Target
+WP	**Unrelated**	**Target**
وقوع	رقيق	دخول
[wuquuʕun]	[raqiiqun]	[duxuulun]
happening	delicate	entering
سلوك	شبكة	حصول
[suluukun]	[ʃabakatun]	[ħusˤuulun]
behavior	net	coming about
خبيث	زينة	سريع
[xabiiθun]	[ziinatun]	[sariiʕun]
malicious	decoration	fast
عاقل	بؤس	خادم
[ʕaaqilun]	[buʔsun]	[xaadimun]
rational	wretchedness	servant
صامت	ممكن	لاجئ
[sˤaamitun]	[mumkinun]	[laaӡiʔun]
quiet	possible	refugee
خطيب	مبدع	شريف
[xatˤiibun]	[mubdiʕun]	[ʃariifun]
orator	innovator	noble
سقوط	دهشة	خروج
[suquutˤun]	[dahʃatun]	[xuruuӡun]
falling down	astonishment	coming out
سرور	خليّة	هجوم
[suruurun]	[xalijjatun]	[huӡuumun]
happiness	cell	attack
ثمين	فرصة	عجيب
[θamiinun]	[fursˤatun]	[ʕaӡiibun]
valuable	opportunity	wonderful
جريح	رؤية	نظيف
[ӡariiħun]	[ruʔjatun]	[naðˤiifun]
wounded	vision	clean
غليظ	مربّع	عميق
[ɣaliiðˤun]	[murabbaʕun]	[ʕamiiqun]
thick	square	profound
رحيل	ندرة	نصيب
[raħiilun]	[nudratun]	[nasˤiibun]
departure	scarceness	share

Prime		
+Orth1	**Unrelated**	**Target**
ثروة	عبور	مذهب
[θarwatun]	[ʕubuurun]	[maðhabun]
fortune	crossing	ideology
رياضة	خمود	كفاح
[riʒaadˤatun]	[xumuudun]	[kifaaħun]
sport	abatement	struggle
بطالة	نشوء	حصار
[bitˤaalatun]	[nuʃuuʕun]	[ħisˤaarun]
unemployment	emergence	embargo
شماتة	نبوغ	جبان
[ʃamaatatun]	[nubuɣuun]	[ʒabaanun]
gloating over others' grief	genius	coward
قسوة	هدوء	مركب
[qaswatun]	[huduuʔun]	[markabun]
hardness	quietude	boat
مائدة	سكون	ضابط
[maaʔidatun]	[sukuunun]	[dˤaabitˤun]
dining table	inactivity	officer
نقابة	رابطة	حنان
[naqaabatun]	[raabitˤatun]	[ħanaanun]
trade union	bond	compassion
غنيمة	هبوط	عديد
[ɣaniimatun]	[hubuutˤun]	[ʕadiidun]
spoils	landing	numerous
سباحة	شرود	صراع
[sibaaħatun]	[ʃuruudun]	[sˤiraaʕun]
swimming	roaming	conflict
سماحة	شروق	ذهاب
[samaaħatun]	[ʃuruuqun]	[ðahaabun]
kindness	sun rise	going away
دامية	بروز	رائع
[daamiʒatun]	[buruuzun]	[raaʔiʕun]
bloody	protrusion	marvelous
بضاعة	سكوت	جهاد
[bidˤaaʕatun]	[sukuutun]	[ʒihaadun]
commodity	silence	fight

Prime		Target
+Orth1	**Unrelated**	**Target**
شهوة [ʃahwatun] desire	مرور [muruurun] passing by	منظر [manðˤarun] sight
سحابة [saħaabatun] cloud	عصفور [ʕusˤfuurun] bird	طلاق [tˤalaaqun] divorce
تفاهة [tafaahatun] triviality	شروع [ʃuruuʕun] beginning	عناء [ʕanaaʔun] toil
حديقة [ħadiiqatun] garden	شحرور [ʃuħruurun] blackbird	عريض [ʕariidˤun] large
صرامة [sˤaraamatun] strictness	نزوح [nuzuuħun] exodus	جواد [ʒawaadun] horse
حماقة [ħamaaqatun] foolishness	صعود [sˤuʕuudun] going up	سماع [samaaʕun] hearing
زاوية [zaawiʒatun] corner	بلوغ [buluuɣun] reaching	قادر [qaadirun] capable of
طازجة [tˤaaziʒatun] fresh	خضوع [xudˤuuʕun] submission	ماهر [maahirun] skillful
طائرة [tˤaaʔiratun] plane	فتور [futuurun] tepidity	خالص [xaalisˤun] pure
ذريعة [ðariiʕatun] pretext	سهولة [suhuulatun] ease	خبير [xabiirun] expert
قبيلة [qabiilatun] tribe	ليونة [luʒuunatun] softness	عريق [ʕariiqun] deep rooted
عزيمة [ʕaziimatun] determination	مرونة [muruunatun] flexibility	شقيق [ʃaqiiqun] brother

Prime		Target
+R+S	**Unrelated**	**Target**
رئاسة	عاقبة	رئيس
[riʔaasatun]	[ʕaaqibatun]	[raʔiisun]
presidency	upshot	president
جماعة	وسيلة	اجتماع
[ʒamaaʕatun]	[wasiilatun]	[ʔiʒtimaaʕun]
company	means	gathering
مشترك	بنيان	شركة
[muʃtarikun]	[bunjaanun]	[ʃarikatun]
participant	edifice	partnership
أديب	لسان	أدب
[ʔadiibun]	[lisaanun]	[ʔadabun]
author	tongue	literature
تحقيق	موضوع	حقيقة
[taħqiiqun]	[mawdˤuuʕun]	[ħaqiiqatun]
investigation	subject	truth
تحرير	أسبوع	متحرّر
[taħriirun]	[ʔusbuuʕun]	[mutaħarrirun]
emancipation	week	emancipated
وظيفة	إلغاء	موظّف
[wadˤˤiifatun]	[ʔilɣaaʔun]	[muwadˤˤafun]
function	cancellation	functionary
سليم	جدير	سلام
[saliimun]	[ʒadiirun]	[salaamun]
safe	worthy of	safety
احتفال	انتداب	حفل
[ʔiħtifaalun]	[ʔintidaabun]	[ħaaflun]
celebration	assignment	party
مشاورة	إقامة	مشورة
[maʃaawaratun]	[ʔiqaamatun]	[maʃuuratun]
consultation	sojourn	counsel
وحدة	سؤال	توحيد
[wiħdatun]	[suʔaalun]	[tawħiidun]
union	question	unification
مستعمر	مفاجأة	استعمار
[mustaʕmirun]	[mufaaʒaʔatun]	[ʔistiʕmaarun]
coloniser	surprise	colonisation

Prime		Target
+R+S	**Unrelated**	**Target**
رسول [rasuulun] messenger	حصان [ħisʔaanun] horse	رسالة [risaalatun] message
سعيد [saʕiidun] happy	وكيل [wakiilun] representative	سعادة [saʕaadatun] happiness
تصحيح [tasħiiħun] correction	فرق [farqun] difference	صحيح [saħiiħun] correct
محبّة [maħabbatun] love	تيّار [tajjaarun] current	حبيب [ħabiibun] darling
ارتياح [ʔirtijaaħun] comfort	ابتزاز [ʔibtizaazun] extortion	مريح [muriiħun] comfortable
رحيم [raħiimun] pitiful	كيان [kijaanun] entity	رحمة [raħmatun] pity
شاهد [ʃaahidun] witness	كامل [kaamilun] complete	شهادة [ʃahaadatun] testimony
شجاع [ʃuʒaaʕun] courageous	خاتم [xaatimun] ring	شجاعة [ʃaʒaaʕatun] courage
توجيه [tawʒiihun] directing	توزيع [tawziiʕun] distribution	وجهة [wiʒhatun] direction
مهاجر [muhaʒirun] immigrant	عدالة [ʕadaalatun] justice	هجرة [hiʒratun] immigration
مبتدأ [mubtadiʔun] beginner	تعزيز [taʕziizun] consolidation	ابتداء [ʔibtidaaʔun] beginning
محسن [muħsinun] beneficent	مظهر [maðˤharun] appearance	إحسان [ʔiħsaanun] beneficence

Prime		Target
+R-S	**Unrelated**	**Target**
حكمة	شراء	حكومة
[ħikmatun]	[ʃiraaʔun]	[ħukuumatun]
wisdom	purchasing	government
مطرقة	حافلة	طريق
[mitˤraqatun]	[ħaafilatun]	[tˤariiqun]
hammer	coach	road
حدوث	جفاء	محادثة
[ħuduuθun]	[ʒafaaʔun]	[muħaadaθatun]
happening	repulsion	discussion
تقديم	واسطة	قديم
[taqdiimun]	[waasitˤatun]	[qadiimun]
introduction	mediator	old
طباعة	رقابة	طبيعة
[tˤibaaʕatun]	[raqaabatun]	[tˤabiiʕatun]
printing	surveillance	nature
سفير	بريد	سفر
[safiirun]	[bariidun]	[safarun]
ambassador	mail	travel
منطق	يتيم	منطقة
[mantˤiqun]	[jatiimun]	[mintˤaqatun]
logic	orphan	zone
منحرف	هذيان	حريف
[munħarifun]	[haðajaanun]	[ħariifun]
perverted	hallucination	customer
علامة	جارية	تعليم
[ʕalaamatun]	[ʒaarijatun]	[taʕliimun]
mark	bond-maid	education
غروب	كتلة	غريب
[ɣuruubun]	[kutlatun]	[ɣariibun]
sun set	lump	foreign
سكون	شمول	مسكين
[sukuunun]	[ʃumuulun]	[miskiinun]
tranquility	exhaustion	needy
قناع	حائط	قناعة
[qinaaʕun]	[ħaaʔitˤun]	[qanaaʕatun]
mask	wall	satisfaction

Prime		Target
+R-S	**Unrelated**	**Target**
سلبيّ [salbijjun] negative	نحوي [naħwijjun] grammatical	أسلوب [ʔusluubun] style
حرام [ħaraamun] illicit	جماد [ʒamaadun] inanimate	احترام [ʔiħtiraamun] respect
أغنية [ʔuɣnijatun] song	حقيقة [ħaqiiqatun] truth	غنيّ [ɣanijjun] rich
ظالم [ðˤaalimun] oppressor	حريق [ħariiqun] fire	ظلام [ðˤalaamun] obscurity
عقدة [ʕuqdatun] knot	محنة [miħnatun] afflication	اعتقاد [ʔiʕtiqaadun] belief
عذاب [ʕaðaabun] torture	فداء [fidaaʔun] sacrifice	عذب [ʕaðbun] sweet
منبسط [munbasitˤun] cheerful	منخرط [munxaritˤun] affiliated	بسيط [basiitˤun] simple
غيرة [ɣiiratun] envy	سطوة [satˤwatun] influence	تغيير [taɣjiirun] change
مجاوزة [muʒawaazatun] overtaking	نخاع [nuxaaʕun] spinal cord	جواز [ʒawaazun] admissibility
معطف [miʕtˤafun] overcoat	ملفوف [malfuufun] wrapped up	عاطفة [ʕaatˤifatun] sentiment
مراجعة [muraaʒaʕatun] revision	محافظة [muħaafaðˤatun] preservation	رجوع [ruʒuuʕun] coming back
شرط [ʃartˤun] condition	خطأ [xatˤaʔun] error	شرطة [ʃurtˤatun] police

Prime		Target
+Orth2	**Unrelated**	**Target**
محايد	مدافع	حياة
[muħaaɟidun]	[mudaafiʕun]	[ħaɟaatun]
neutral	defender	life
مستبدّ	تصوير	سبب
[mustabiddun]	[tasˤwiirun]	[sababun]
tyrant	portrayal	reason
تمساح	تجربة	مساء
[timsaaħun]	[taʒribatun]	[massaʔun]
crocodile	experience	evening
مدير	كثيف	دين
[mudiirun]	[kaθiifun]	[diinun]
director	dense	religion
تحدّ	تقريب	حدّ
[taħaddin]	[taqriibun]	[ħaddun]
challenge	approximation	frontier
مصافحة	معالجة	صفة
[musˤaafaħatun]	[muʕaalaʒatun]	[sˤifatun]
hand shake	treatment	attribute
تأميم	إبريق	تامّ
[taʔmiimn]	[ʔibriiqun]	[taammun]
nationalisation	jug	complete
مسرح	مصحف	سرّ
[masraħun]	[musˤħafun]	[sirrun]
theatre	Koran	secret
ثابت	شارع	ثواب
[θaabitun]	[ʃaariʕun]	[θawaabun]
firm	avenue	reward
سلحفاة	انتهاء	سلاح
[sulaħfaatun]	[ʔintihaaʔun]	[silaaħun]
turtle	radio	weapons
معبد	موسم	تعبير
[maʕbadun]	[mawsimun]	[taʕbiirun]
place of worship	season	expression
محراث	مذياع	حرارة
[miħraaθun]	[miðjaaʕun]	[ħaraaratun]
plow	radio	heat

Prime		
+Orth2	**Unrelated**	**Target**
مقعد	مهنة	قاعة
[maqʕadun]	[mihnatun]	[qaaʕatun]
seat	profession	room
موجب	مطرب	موجة
[muuʒibun]	[mutʕribun]	[mawʒatun]
motive	singer	wave
مفت	لقب	مفتّش
[muftin]	[laqabun]	[mufattiʃun]
casuist	title	inspector
تأجيل	إقليم	تاج
[taʕʒiilun]	[ʔiqliimun]	[taaʒun]
postponement	province	crown
ميلاد	بطاقة	ميل
[miilaadun]	[bitʕaaqatun]	[majlun]
birth	card	inclination
فضاء	يسار	فضيلة
[fadʕaaʕun]	[jasaarun]	[fadʕiilatun]
space	left	virtue
إمضاء	إحساس	ضئيل
[ʔimdʕaaʕun]	[ʔiħsaasun]	[dʕaʕiilun]
signature	feeling	scanty
إعراب	إفلاس	معركة
[ʔiʕraabun]	[ʔiflaasun]	[maʕrakatun]
inflection	bankruptcy	battle
ناجع	خاشع	منجد
[naaʒiʕun]	[xaaʃiʕun]	[munʒidun]
efficient	earnest	dictionary
لمجة	غرفة	مجرم
[lumʒatun]	[ɣurfatun]	[muʒrimun]
snack	chamber	criminal
دينار	إغراء	مدينة
[diinaarun]	[ʔiɣraaʕun]	[madiinatun]
monetary unit	seduction	metal
منتعل	قوّة	نعيم
[muntaʕilun]	[quwwatun]	[naʕiimun]
shod	power	amenity

Prime		Target
-R+S	**Unrelated**	**Target**
أزمة	قنصل	مشكلة
[ʕazmatun]	[qunsʕulun]	[muʃkilatun]
crisis	consul	problem
غوث	صاف	معونة
[ɣawθun]	[sˤaafin]	[maʕuunatun]
rescue	crystal	help
إضافة	قافلة	زيادة
[ʔidˤaafatun]	[qaafilatun]	[zijaadatun]
addition	caravan	increase
داء	كأس	مرض
[daaʔun]	[kaʔsun]	[maradˤun]
disease	cup	illness
عربة	إلقاء	سيّارة
[ʕarabatun]	[ʔilqaaʔun]	[sajjaaratun]
vehicle	addition	car
شبّاك	مرشّح	نافذة
[ʃubbaakun]	[muraʃʃaħun]	[naafiðatun]
window	candidate	window
غذاء	إبرة	طعام
[ɣiðaaʔun]	[ʔibratun]	[tˤaʕaamun]
nutrition	needle	food
فوز	شخص	نجاح
[fawzun]	[ʃaxsˤun]	[naaʒaaħun]
victory	individual	success
حكاية	عمود	قصّة
[ħikaajatun]	[ʕamuudun]	[qisˤsˤatun]
story	post	novel
زعيم	كثرة	قيادة
[zaʕiimun]	[kaθratun]	[qijaadatun]
leader	abundance	leadership
حلف	تنظيم	معاهدة
[ħilfun]	[tanðˤiimun]	[muʕaahadatun]
pact	organisation	treaty
عروس	قوت	زواج
[ʕaruusun]	[quutun]	[zawaaʒun]
bride	nutriment	marriage

Prime		
-R+S	**Unrelated**	**Target**
علوّ	موز	ارتفاع
[ʕuluwwun]	[mawzun]	[ʔirtifaaʕun]
rising	banana	going up
وفاة	قلعة	موت
[wafaatun]	[qalʕatun]	[mawtun]
death	tower	death
عائلة	نصيحة	أسرة
[ʕaaʔilatun]	[nasʕiiħatun]	[ʔusratun]
family	advice	family
أمانة	تدريب	ثقة
[ʔamaantun]	[tadriibun]	[θiqatun]
trustworthiness	training	trust
جولة	قصّاب	نزهة
[ʒawlatun]	[qasʕsʕaabun]	[nuzhatun]
excursion	butcher	promenade
قتال	خيال	حرب
[qitaalun]	[xaʃaalun]	[ħarbun]
fight	imagination	war
حجّة	صلة	دليل
[ħuʒʒatun]	[sʕilatun]	[daliilun]
evidence	link	proof
متعسف	تقسيم	جبّار
[mutaʕassifun]	[taqsiimun]	[ʒabbaarun]
despot	dividing	tyrant
متعب	مخيّم	شقاء
[mutʕibun]	[muxaʃʃamun]	[ʃaqaaʔun]
tiring	camp	toil
خير	جهد	بركة
[xaʃrun]	[ʒuhdun]	[barakatun]
fortune	effort	fortune
بيت	وعي	حجرة
[baʃtun]	[waʕʃun]	[ħuʒratun]
house	consciousness	room
عجوز	سرير	شيخ
[ʕaʒuuzun]	[sariirun]	[ʃaʃxun]
old woman	bed	old man

Appendix 2

Test items used in Experiment 2. For every item, the Arabic script, an IPA transcription and an English gloss are given.

Prime		Target
+WP	Unrelated	
لخّص [laxxasˤa] sum up	مسحة [musħatun] tinge	فكّر [fakkara] think
تخلّص [taxallasˤa] get rid of	منطفئ [muntˤafiʔun] extinguished	تعرّض [taʕarradˤa] deal with
لاحظ [laaħaðˤa] notice	منتج [muntiʒun] produces	سافر [saafara] travel
أحرز [ʔaħraza] acquire	برود [buruudun] frigidity	أبلغ [ʔablaɣa] cause to reach
ابتسم [ʔibtasama] smile	مغفّل [muɣaffalun] silly	التفت [ʔiltafata] look back
استأجر [ʔistaʔʒara] hire	مغازلة [muɣaazalatun] flirting	استغرق [ʔistaɣraqa] engross
حصل [ħasˤala] happen	دين [diinun] religion	جلس [ʒalasa] sit down
أنهمر [ʔinhamara] pour down	تهافت [tahaafutun] follow in succession	انقطع [ʔinqatˤaʕa] be cut
رتّب [rattaba] tidy up	كسب [kasbun] earning	مثّل [maθθala] act
تضمّن [tadˤammana] include	واجب [waaʒibun] duty	تذكّر [taðakkara] remember
ناقش [naaqaʃa] discuss	إكرام [ʔikraamun] deference	ساعد [saaʕada] help
أبصر [ʔabsˤara] see	رفيق [rafiiqun] companion	أغلق [ʔaɣlaqa] close

Prime		Target
+WP	**Unrelated**	**Target**
احتقر	نيابة	اجتمع
[ʔiħtaqara]	[niʝaabatun]	[ʔiʒtamaʕa]
despise	representation	meet
استأذن	دحرجة	استخدم
[ʔitaʔðana]	[daħraʒatun]	[ʔistaxdama]
seek permission	rolling	use
لمع	تامّ	صرخ
[lamaʕa]	[taammun]	[sˤaraxa]
glimmer	complete	shout
انفجر	تلقيح	انصرف
[ʔinfaʒara]	[talqiiħun]	[ʔinsˤarafa]
explode	vaccination	depart
بارك	مريض	خالف
[baaraka]	[mariidˤun]	[xaalafa]
congratulate	ill	disagree
أقفل	مخطئ	أصدر
[ʔaqfala]	[muxtˤiʔun]	[ʔasˤdara]
close	erroneous	issue
استخرج	مقاومة	استعمل
[ʔistaxraʒa]	[muqaawamatun]	[ʔistaʕmala]
extract	fight	utilize
تفضّل	مزمن	تعلّق
[tafadˤdˤala]	[muzminun]	[taʕallaqa]
oblige	chronic	stick to
أطعم	واسع	أخبر
[ʔatˤʕama]	[waasiʕun]	[ʔaxbara]
feed	wide	tell
استأنف	متأرجح	استقبل
[ʔistaʔnafa]	[mutaʔarʒiħun]	[ʔistaqbala]
resume	swinging	receive
انفرد	متخصّص	انقلب
[ʔinfarada]	[mutaxasˤsˤisˤun]	[ʔinqalaba]
isolate oneself	specialist	be overturned
تأخّر	قلعة	تمكّن
[taʔaxxara]	[qalʕatun]	[tamakkana]
be late	tower	manage to

Prime		
+Orth1	**Unrelated**	**Target**
غاية	شهوة	ثابر
[ɣaajatun]	[ʃahwatun]	[θaabara]
purpose	desire	persevere
بطة	نور	نصّب
[batˤtˤatun]	[nuurun]	[nasˤsˤaba]
duck	light	appoint
راية	بروز	عالج
[raajatun]	[buruuzun]	[ʕaalaʒa]
banner	appearing	treat
بدعة	هدوء	احترم
[bidʕatun]	[huduuʔun]	[ʔiħtarama]
novelty	quiet	respect
مرق	كوخ	ذبح
[maraqun]	[kuuxun]	[ðabaħa]
broth	hut	slay
محنة	وضوء	اندثر
[miħnatun]	[wudˤuuʔun]	[ʔindaθara]
ordeal	ablution	become extinct
طلقة	سوء	صرّح
[tˤalqatun]	[suuʔun]	[sˤarraħa]
shot	evil	declare
مجلة	سرور	تحرّك
[maʒallatun]	[sururun]	[taħarraka]
magazine	happiness	move
نادم	غروب	دافع
[naadimun]	[ɣuruubun]	[daafaʕa]
repentant	sun set	defend
عدد	ثبوت	لمس
[ʕadadun]	[θubuutun]	[lamasa]
number	stability	touch
عالة	طموح	صاهر
[ʕaalatun]	[tˤumuuħun]	[sˤaahara]
dependent	aspiration	become related by marriage
سهر	صوف	خلع
[saharun]	[sˤuufun]	[xalaʕa]
staying up	wool	remove

Prime		
+Orth1	**Unrelated**	**Target**
خلسة	وجوب	انتصر
[xilsatun]	[wuʒuubun]	[ʔintasˤara]
furtively	necessity	conquer
أسد	سور	كفل
[ʔasadun]	[suurun]	[kafala]
lion	fence	sponsor
شمعة	عزوف	أقلق
[ʃamʕatun]	[ʕuzuufun]	[ʔaqlaqa]
candle	turning away	pester
لجنة	خضوع	أنكر
[laʒnatun]	[xudˤuuʕun]	[ʔankara]
committee	submission	deny
بعثة	شرود	انخدع
[biʕθatun]	[ʃuruudun]	[ʔinxadaʕa]
delegation	straying	be deceived
صخرة	جمود	كلّف
[sˤaxratun]	[ʒumuudun]	[kallafa]
rock	solidity	entrust
سلّة	عضو	ضمّد
[sallatun]	[ʕudˤwun]	[dˤammada]
basket	limb	bandage
قامة	بزوغ	جامل
[qaamatun]	[buzuuɣun]	[ʒaamala]
stature	emergence	compliment
قمر	قوت	نسج
[qamarun]	[quutun]	[nasaʒa]
moon	subsistence	weave
رجّة	فول	حصّن
[raʒʒatun]	[fuulun]	[ħasˤsˤana]
shock	beans	fortify
بدن	غول	نقم
[badanun]	[ɣuulun]	[naqama]
body	ogre	begrudge
قلم	حوت	ترك
[qalamun]	[ħuutun]	[taraka]
pen	fish	leave behind

Prime		
+R+S	**Unrelated**	**Target**
نكوّن	معلّم	كوّن
[takawwana]	[muʕallimun]	[kawwana]
form	teacher	form
احترق	تصديق	أحرق
[ʔiħtaraqa]	[tasˁdiiqun]	[ʔaħraqa]
burn	believing	set ablaze
خالط	غدير	اختلط
[xaalatˁa]	[ɣadiirun]	[ʔixtalatˁa]
mix with	brook	be mixed with
أنزل	حرأة	نزل
[ʔanzala]	[ʒurʔatun]	[nazala]
lower	boldness	come down
انتقل	توديع	نقل
[ʔintaqala]	[tawdiiʕun]	[naqala]
move	leave taking	cause to move
ابتعد	مصيبة	أبعد
[ʔibtaʕada]	[musˁiibatun]	[ʔabʕada]
move away	calamity	put aside
استفاد	معاناة	أفاد
[ʔistafaada]	[muʕaanaatun]	[ʔafaada]
benefit	endurance	cause to benefit
ابتدأ	ممتاز	بدأ
[ʔibtadaʔa]	[mumtaazun]	[badaʔa]
begin	excellent	begin
ارتفع	مجتهد	رفع
[ʔirtafaʕa]	[muʒtahidun]	[rafaʕa]
rise	diligent	raise
أوجد	نزيف	وجد
[ʔawʒada]	[naziifun]	[waʒada]
create	hemorrhage	find
استمع	تأليف	سمع
[ʔistamaʕa]	[taʔliifun]	[samiʕa]
listen	composition	hear
تغلّب	شروع	غلب
[taɣallaba]	[ʃuruuʕun]	[ɣalaba]
overcome	starting	defeat

Prime		Target
+R+S	**Unrelated**	**Target**
استمتع	ازدهار	تمتّع
[ʔistamtaʕa]	[ʔizdihaarun]	[tamattaʕa]
enjoy	prosperity	savor
انتفع	تدبير	نفع
[ʔintafaʕa]	[tadbiirun]	[nafaʕa]
profit	arrangement	be beneficial
استحسن	مبادلة	أحسن
[ʔistaħsana]	[mubaadalatun]	[ʔaħsana]
find something to be good	exchange	do well
التقى	متشبّث	لقي
[ʔiltaqaa]	[mutaʃabbiθun]	[laqija]
meet	adhering	find
تفرّق	مهذّب	فارق
[tafarraaqa]	[muhaððabun]	[faaraqa]
become separated	well-mannered	leave
تشارك	مناسب	اشترك
[taʃaaraka]	[munaasibun]	[ʔiʃtaraka]
take part	convenient	participate
تعذّر	منقذ	اعتذر
[taʕaððara]	[munqiðun]	[ʔiʕtaðara]
be beneficial	rescuer	apologize
اكتشف	واسطة	كشف
[ʔiktaʃafa]	[waasʕitʕatun]	[kaʃafa]
discover	mediator	uncover
تعجّب	قصير	أعجب
[taʕaʒʒaba]	[qasʕiirun]	[ʔaʕʒaba]
marvel at	short	admire
أدخل	زواج	دخل
[ʔadxala]	[zawaaʒun]	[daxala]
insert	marriage	enter
عاون	صدفة	تعاون
[ʕaawana]	[sʕudfatun]	[taʕaawana]
help	coincidence	help each other
هاجم	وقوف	هجم
[haaʒama]	[wuquufun]	[haʒama]
raid	stopping	attack

Prime		Target
+R-S	**Unrelated**	**Target**
ناهض [naahad$^\varsigma$a] oppose	مصلح [mus$^\varsigma$lihun] reformer	نهض [nahad$^\varsigma$a] stand up
تفرّس [tafarrasa] stare	مهمل [muhmilun] negligent	افترس [ʔiftarasa] devour
غامر [ɣaamara] venture	ناقد [naaqidun] critic	غمر [ɣamara] overwhelm
استعمر [ʔista$^\varsigma$mara] colonize	لوم [lawmun] blame	اعتمر [ʔi$^\varsigma$tamara] visit
تعارف [ta$^\varsigma$aarafa] become acquainted	رخصة [ruxs$^\varsigma$atun] license	اعترف [ʔi$^\varsigma$tarafa] admit
عقّد [$^\varsigma$aqqada] complicate	صبح [s$^\varsigma$ubhun] morning	اعتقد [ʔi$^\varsigma$taqada] believe
تحوّل [tahawwala] become	عتاب [$^\varsigma$itaabun] admonition	حاول [haawala] try
واجه [waaʒaha] confront	مطبخ [mat$^\varsigma$baxun] kitchen	توجّه [tawaʒʒaha] head for
تقرّر [taqarrara] be decided	سكوت [sukuutun] silence	استقرّ [ʔistaqarra] settle
وقّع [waqqa$^\varsigma$a] sign	سند [sanadun] support	توقّع [tawaqqa$^\varsigma$a] expect
نافق [naafaqa] dissimulate	ممثل [mumaθθilun] actor	أنفق [ʔanfaqa] spend
تقاسم [taqaasama] share	إعارة [ʔi$^\varsigma$aaratun] loan	أقسم [ʔaqsama] take an oath

Prime		Target
+R-S	**Unrelated**	**Target**
نظّر	هبة	انتظر
[naðˤðˤara]	[hibatun]	[ʔintaðˤara]
theorise	gift	wait for
تقاعد	شتيمة	قعد
[taqaaʕada]	[ʃatiimatun]	[qaʕada]
resign	insult	sit down
استأثر	مجازفة	أثّر
[ʔistaʔθara]	[muʒaazafatun]	[ʔaθθara]
appropriate	hazard	influence
أضرب	متعب	اضطرب
[ʔadˤraba]	[mutʕibun]	[ʔidˤtˤraba]
go on strike	tiring	be disturbed
أحدث	طاعة	تحدّث
[ʔaħdaθa]	[tˤaaʕatun]	[taħaddaaθa]
cause to happen	obedience	talk
تشرّف	كفاح	أشرف
[taʃarrafa]	[kifaaħun]	[ʔaʃarafa]
be honored	struggle	supervise
احتضر	مفاجئ	أحضر
[ʔiħtadˤara]	[mufaaʒiʔun]	[ʔaħadˤara]
be in the throes of death	surprising	bring
ابتذل	مراقب	بذل
[ʔibtaðala]	[muraaqibun]	[baðala]
make trite	supervisor	sacrifice
خلّف	جريح	اختلف
[xallafa]	[ʒariiħun]	[ʔixtalafa]
leave behind	wounded	disagree
تقادم	مجهول	تقدّم
[taqaadama]	[maʒhuulun]	[taqaddama]
become old	unknown	advance
قبّل	شروق	تقابل
[qabbala]	[ʃuruuqun]	[taqaabala]
kiss	sun rise	meet
تنافس	ثمرة	تنفّس
[tanaafasa]	[θamratun]	[tanaffasa]
compete	fruit	breath

Prime		Target
+Orth2	**Unrelated**	**Target**
متراجع [mutaraaʒiʕun] retreating	اجنحناء [ʔinħinaaʔun] bending	ترجم [tarʒama] translate
اشمئزاز [ʔiʃmiʔzaazun] disgust	استفسار [ʔistifsaarun] inquiry	شمّ [ʃamma] smell
تكسير [taksiirun] breaking	تقليص [taqliisˤun] shrinking	كسا [kasaa] clothe
مربض [marbadˤun] fold	خفيف [xafiifun] light	ربّى [rabbaa] raise
حنق [ħanaqun] anger	يأس [jaʔsun] despair	حان [ħaana] be imminent
جرعة [ʒrʕatun] mouthful	وتر [watarun] string	جاع [ʒaaʕa] feel hungry
مفتوح [maftuuħun] open	منسحب [munsaħibun] withdrawing	فات [faata] elapse
مفروض [maafruudˤun] imposed	موضوع [mawdˤuuʕun] subject	فرّ [farra] flee
مطلع [matˤlaʕun] beginning	مسبح [masbaħun] swimming pool	طال [tˤaala] become long
إسقاط [ʔisqaatˤun] tumbling	إخلاص [ʔixlaasˤun] faithfulness	سقى [saqaa] water
هبوط [hubuutˤun] landing	عيش [ʕajʃun] way of life	هبّ [habba] blow
تقليد [taqliidun] imitation	تسمية [tasmijatun] nomination	قلّ [qalla] diminish

Prime		
+Orth2	**Unrelated**	**Target**
متلهّف	مطمئنّ	تلا
[mutalahhifun]	[mutˤmaʔinnun]	[talaa]
yearning for	serene	succeed
سعال	ذنب	سعى
[suʕaalun]	[ðanbun]	[saʕaa]
sneezing	wrong-doing	endeavor
إبعاد	إرسال	باع
[ʔibʕaadun]	[ʔirsaalun]	[baaʕa]
removal	sending	sell
بلعوم	مجد	بلّل
[bulʕuumun]	[maʒadun]	[ballala]
pharynx	glory	moisten
مجادلة	انصراف	جاد
[muʒaadalatun]	[ʔinsˤiraafun]	[ʒaada]
discussion	departure	give generously
مجلّد	مربّع	جال
[muʒalladun]	[murabbaʕun]	[ʒaala]
hardbound book	square	walk
مضحك	مسعف	ضحّى
[mudˤħikun]	[musaʕifun]	[dˤaħħaa]
humorous	rescuer	sacrifice
عفن	درج	عفا
[ʕafanun]	[daraʒun]	[ʕafaa]
decomposition	stairs	forgive
متشابه	متألّم	شبّ
[mutaʃaabihun]	[mutaʔallimun]	[ʃabba]
similar	suffering	grow up
تجريد	تخطيط	جرّ
[taʒriidun]	[taxtˤiitˤun]	[ʒarra]
dispossessing	planning	pull
صفعة	طور	صفا
[sˤafʕatun]	[tˤawrun]	[sˤafaa]
smack	period	become clear
مخبأ	معدن	خاب
[maxbaʔun]	[maʕdanun]	[xaaba]
hiding place	metal	fail

Prime		Target
-R+S	**Unrelated**	**Target**
أيقن	تحفة	تأكّد
[ʔajqana]	[tuħfatun]	[taʔakkada]
ascertain	masterpiece	be confirmed
هاج	نيّة	أغضب
[haaʒa]	[nijjatun]	[ʔaɣdˤaba]
become agitated	intention	cause to become angry
حذف	طيّب	ألغى
[ħaðafa]	[tˤajjibun]	[ʔalɣaa]
omit	good	cancel
أنجز	جبهة	وفى
[ʔanʒaza]	[ʒabhatun]	[wafaa]
carry out	front	fulfill
رحم	مزعج	أشفق
[raħima]	[muzʕiʒun]	[ʔaʃfaqa]
have mercy	annoying	pity
استغلّ	طريقة	انتهز
[ʔistaɣalla]	[tˤariiqatun]	[ʔintahaza]
exploit	method	seize the opportunity
اقتنص	مشاكس	اصطاد
[ʔiqtanasˤa]	[muʃaakisun]	[ʔisˤtˤaada]
hunt	quarrelsome	hunt
اقتفى	سيطرة	اتّبع
[ʔiqtafaa]	[sajtˤaratun]	[ʔittabaʕa]
track	dominion	follow
نظّف	ميز	غسل
[naðˤðˤafa]	[majzun]	[ɣasala]
clean	segregation	wash
اختفى	صيانة	غاب
[ʔixtafaa]	[sˤijaanatun]	[ɣaaba]
hide	upkeep	vanish
دنا	نيل	اقترب
[danaa]	[najlun]	[ʔiqtaraba]
become nearer	obtainment	draw closer
أنشد	واضح	غنّى
[ʔanʃada]	[waadˤiħun]	[ɣannaa]
chant	clear	sing

Prime		Target
-R+S	**Unrelated**	
صوّر	بيت	رسم
[sˤawwara]	[bajtun]	[rasama]
draw	house	paint
نما	شهر	ازداد
[namaa]	[ʃahrun]	[ʔizdaada]
grow	month	increase
ارتدى	ولاية	لبس
[ʔirtadaa]	[wilaajatun]	[labisa]
wear	state	wear
امتنع	منتشر	رفض
[ʔimtanaʕa]	[muntaʃirun]	[rafadˤa]
abstain	widespread	refuse
بيّن	سجلّ	أظهر
[bajjana]	[siʒillun]	[ʔaðˤhara]
show	register	display
قبض	خير	أمسك
[qabadˤa]	[xajrun]	[ʔamsaka]
grasp	good	seize
استدعى	ارتجال	نادى
[ʔistadʕaa]	[ʔirtiʒaalun]	[naada]
invite	improvisation	call
شيّد	مشي	بنى
[ʃajjada]	[maʃjun]	[banaa]
establish	walk	build
أجمع	منحة	اتّفق
[ʔaʒmaʕa]	[minħatun]	[ʔittafaqa]
concur	grant	agree
ألقى	ضياع	رمى
[ʔlqaa]	[dˤajaaʕun]	[ramaa]
fling	loss	throw
أدرك	ثقيل	فهم
[ʔadraka]	[θaqiilun]	[fahima]
understand	heavy	understand
رقد	سير	نام
[raqada]	[sajrun]	[naama]
slumber	marching	sleep

LANGUAGE AND COGNITIVE PROCESSES
2005, 20 (1/2), 261–290

The role of semantic transparency in the processing of Finnish compound words

Alexander Pollatsek

University of Massachusetts, Amherst, MA, USA

Jukka Hyönä

University of Turku, Finland

Three experiments examined whether the semantic transparency of a long Finnish compound word has any influence on how the compound word is encoded in reading. The frequency of the first constituent (as a separate word) was manipulated, while matching for the frequencies of the compound word and of the second constituent. The effect of this frequency manipulation on encoding time served as a 'marker' that the compound word was processed, at least in part, componentially. In Experiment 1, each high-frequency transparent compound was paired with a low-frequency transparent compound, and each high-frequency opaque compound was paired with a low-frequency opaque compound. A sentence frame was created for each pair that was identical up to the word following the target word. In Experiments 2 and 3, the matching was done between transparent and opaque word pairs. In addition, Experiment 3 had a display change manipulation in which most of the second constituent was not visible until it was fixated. Readers' eye fixation patterns on and immediately after the target word were examined. Reliable first constituent frequency effects were observed in the fixation duration measures on the target word, but there were no effects of transparency. In addition, a comparison of the display change condition to the standard condition indicated that the constituents of the compound word were processed sequentially. It thus appears that the

Correspondence should be addressed to: Alexander Pollatsek, Department of Psychology, University of Massachusetts, Amherst MA 01003, USA.
Email: pollatsek@psych.umass.edu.

The first author was supported by Grants HD17246 and HD26765 from the National Institutes of Health and the second author acknowledges the support of Suomen Akatemia (the Academy of Finland). We thank Jonathan Grainger, Gary Libben, and an anonymous reviewer for their comments on a previous version of this article. We are also grateful to Tuomo Häikiö for his help in analysing the data of Experiment 3.

© 2005 Psychology Press Ltd
http://www.tandf.co.uk/journals/pp/01690965.html   DOI: 10.1080/01690960444000098

identification of both transparent and opaque long compound words takes place, at least in part, by accessing the constituent lexemes and does not rely on constructing the meaning from the components.

The goal of the present study was to investigate the effect that the semantic transparency of a compound word has on processing a compound word when people are reading sentences. A compound word is usually defined as transparent when the meaning of the compound word is consistent with the meanings of the constituents (e.g., *carwash*). In contrast, a compound word is defined as semantically opaque, when its meaning cannot be constructed by directly combining the meanings of the individual constituents (e.g., *pineapple*).[1]

Our previous work (Bertram & Hyönä, 2003; Hyönä & Pollatsek, 1998, 2000; Pollatsek, Hyönä, & Bertram, 2000), examined the processing of semantically transparent compound words when they are embedded in a sentential context. The participants read the sentences silently for comprehension while their eye fixation patterns were recorded. This technique allowed us to obtain a detailed picture of the time-course of compound word processing during sentence processing. One of the key questions in this research was the extent to which compound words are recognised via their constituents. One way we studied this question was by manipulating the frequency of compound word constituents (i.e., their frequencies as separate words) while matching the compound words on their (whole-word) frequency. For the two-constituent compound words we studied, we observed large and reliable effects of the frequency of both constituents in the eye fixation patterns. The frequency of the first constituent exerted a large effect on the gaze duration on the word (i.e., the sum of the durations of the fixations on the word prior to the eyes leaving the word) and part of this effect was 'early', as the duration of the initial fixation on the compound word was influenced by this manipulation. The frequency of the second constituent also had a large and reliable effect on the gaze duration, but its effect did not appear until the second fixation on the word. These results, which have recently been replicated and extended to English (Andrews, Miller, & Rayner, 2004; Juhasz, Starr, Inhoff, & Placke, 2003), clearly show that compound words are identified, at least in part, via their constituents.

---

[1] Usually, for most transparent compound words, the meaning of the word cannot be uniquely computed from the constituents, as a *carwash* could be some sort of device that washes with a car; instead the meaning is usually a highly plausible combination of the constituent meanings.

The 'whole-word' frequency of the compound, however, also exerts a large and reliable effect on compound word processing. Pollatsek et al. (2000) observed a whole-word frequency effect that emerged relatively early in the eye movement records, and there was even a suggestion of an effect in the first fixation duration. On the basis of these results, Pollatsek et al. proposed a parallel dual-route model for processing compound words in text in which compounds are identified by simultaneously accessing the constituent lexemes and the whole-word representation. The access of the first constituent was assumed to occur prior to accessing either the second constituent or the whole-word representation. More recently, Bertram and Hyönä (2003) demonstrated that the length of a compound word determines which of the two routes (decomposition vs. whole word) is more influential in processing. They showed that with long compounds (about 13 letters), as those used in our previous work, the initial constituent gets a head-start, whereas with shorter compounds (7–9 letters) the whole-word representation receives an early activation. In Experiment 1, there was an early effect of first constituent frequency (as reflected in the first fixation duration) for long compounds, but not for short compounds. In contrast, when whole-word frequency was manipulated (Experiment 2), early processing stages were reliably affected for short compounds but not for long compounds. Bertram and Hyönä felt that their pattern of results was most parsimoniously explained by visual acuity constraints. That is, when a long compound word is initially fixated (usually not far from the middle of the initial constituent), the initial constituent is much easier to process than the entire compound, whereas with shorter compounds the entire word is readily perceivable during the initial eye fixation and thus the whole-word route is speeded relative to the compositional route.[2]

In the present study, we addressed the question of whether long compound words are accessed via their constituents in silent reading even when the meaning of the compound word is not readily constructed as a combination of the constituent meanings. To our knowledge, there are no previous reading studies that address this question. On the other hand, there is a lot of prior work on the role of transparency in compound word processing using the lexical decision paradigm. This research has examined whether transparency modulates the ability of components of compound words either to prime or to be primed using both constituent priming and

---

[2] Some recent attempts to model our data quantitatively (Pollatsek, Rayner, & Reichle, 2003) suggest that the two routes are not likely to be independent, as in a standard 'race' model. That is, the sizes of the frequency effects observed in the Finnish compound word experiments were virtually impossible to fit with any reasonable assumptions about processing times for the words or the constituents.

semantic priming techniques (for the effects of semantic opacity in processing inflected words, see Schreuder, Burani, & Baayen, 2003). We will first review the constituent priming studies and then the semantic priming studies.

In the constituent priming studies, a compound word constituent has either been employed as the prime or the target (the studies cited below used the immediate unmasked priming paradigm, except for Monsell (1985) who used long lag priming). Zwitserlood (1994, Experiment 1) used the compound word as the prime and either the first or second constituent as the target, and observed a constituent priming effect of similar magnitude for transparent and opaque Dutch compounds. Monsell (1985) and subsequently Libben and colleagues (Libben, Gibson, Yoon, & Sandra, 1997, 2003; Jarema, Busson, Nikolova, Tsapkini, & Libben, 1999) used one of the compound word constituents as the prime for the compound word and obtained similar results for English compounds. Monsell (1985) observed a healthy priming effect for both transparent and opaque compounds, and Libben et al. (1997, 2003) also observed equal priming effects for opaque and transparent compounds. Libben et al. also distinguished between *fully opaque* compounds such as *humbug* (where the meaning of neither constituent is related to the meaning of the compound) and *partially opaque* compounds such as *strawberry* (where the meaning of one of the constituents is related to the meaning of the compound) and found no difference in priming. Jarema et al. (1999) employed the same constituent priming paradigm to study the recognition of French compounds and found a strong priming effect of similar magnitude for transparent and opaque compounds. In a second experiment employing Bulgarian compounds, they observed a reliable priming effect for all compound word types except for the fully opaque ones.

In sum, constituent priming of similar magnitude was observed for transparent and opaque compounds with one exception: Jarema et al. (1999) did not observe constituent priming for fully opaque Bulgarian compounds. With this possible exception, the constituent priming studies thus indicate that, at some level, the lexical entries of constituents are activated for opaque compounds and are not suppressed. However, it is possible that a different pattern of results might emerge with a task such as semantic priming, which may tap the activation of the meanings of the constituents and not merely their lexical activation. To our knowledge, only two semantic priming studies have examined the effect of semantic transparency on compound word processing. Sandra (1990) primed a compound word (e.g., *milkbottle*) with a lexical item that was semantically associated with the compound word constituent (e.g., *cow*). He observed a reliable priming effect in Dutch for transparent compounds (e.g., *koe* → *melkfles* = cow → milkbottle) but not for opaque compounds (e.g., *koe* →

melkweg = cow → milky way). Zwitserlood (1994) used transparent and opaque Dutch compounds as primes and semantic associates of either the first or second constituent as targets (e.g., transparent: *kerkorgel* → *priester* = church organ → priest; opaque: *drankorgel* → *bier* = drunkard → beer). She found a semantic priming effect for transparent and partly opaque compounds but not for completely opaque compounds. Thus, the two semantic priming studies offer suggestive evidence that the meaning of constituents of opaque compound words may not be available during compound word processing, either because they are not activated or that they are quickly suppressed by the whole-word meaning.

Although the overall pattern of results emerging from the priming studies reviewed above is not totally consistent, one may tentatively conclude that compound word constituents are represented at the lexical level regardless of the semantic transparency of the compound, whereas constituent meanings may not be available for (fully) opaque compounds. In the model proposed by Libben (1998), the mental organisation of transparent and opaque compounds is worked out along these lines. The model distinguishes three levels of representation: stimulus, lexical, and conceptual. At the conceptual level, semantic transparency determines the extent to which constituent meanings are mentally represented. For example, at this level, *bird* in *jailbird* is not mentally represented, whereas *jail* in *jailbird* is. Although Libben's (1998) model posits a qualitative difference in the mental organisation of transparent and opaque compounds at the conceptual level, transparency is not assumed to matter at the lexical level. Both transparent and opaque compounds are assumed to be decomposed into their morphological constituents. Thus, at the lexical level both the constituents and the full-form are represented.

There are two key related questions that we hoped to address with the current research. The first is whether opaqueness produces a processing cost in identifying long Finnish compound words in reading. Although most of the above research suggests that transparency of a compound word did not have a significant role in its priming characteristics, we think it is at least reasonable to suspect that transparency may play a larger role in Finnish. That is because compounding is quite productive in Finnish, and furthermore, as in German, compounds must be written without spaces between the constituents. As a result, it is likely that the typical Finnish reader encounters 10–20 novel compound words a day. Moreover, logically, such novel compounds need to be comprehended by composing the meaning of the constituents, as there is no lexical entry for the word. Because readers cannot know, a priori, whether a letter string is a novel compound or not, it would seem reasonable that at least part of the process of encoding an existing compound would be encoding the meaning of the constituents, and to the degree to which the combination of these meanings differ from the meaning of the compounds, there should be some cost in encoding the word.

The related question is whether the frequency effects we had previously obtained with semantically transparent words would extend to semantically opaque words. At one extreme, if the compositional process in reading is completely at the conceptual level, one might expect the frequency of the initial constituent to be irrelevant for opaque words, as they would have to be recognised by a non-compositional process. Indeed, it is even possible, given this kind of model, that there could be a reverse frequency effect (i.e., longer recognition times when the first constituent is higher), especially if the first constituent is the opaque constituent. That is, it is possible that the higher the frequency of the first (opaque) constituent, the more it will interfere with the correct computation of the compound word's meaning. At the other extreme, if the compositional process is completely at the lexical level, then one might expect the transparency of the compound to have no effect on processing, and thus observe equal frequency effects for transparent and opaque compounds. Another possibility, of course, is that the compositional process is at both levels. If so, one might expect some initial constituent frequency effect for opaque compounds, but less of an effect than for transparent compounds.

In the present study, we examined the time course of compound word processing by examining readers' eye movements as they read both transparent and opaque compound words in sentential context. In three experiments, pairs of compound words, either opaque or transparent, were selected that differed in the frequency of the first constituent but were matched on their second-constituent frequency and whole-word frequency. A sentence frame was constructed for a pair of matched target words that was identical up to the word following the target word. In Experiment 1, either (a) a transparent word with a low-frequency first constituent was paired with a transparent word with a high-frequency first constituent or (b) an opaque word with a low-frequency first constituent was paired with an opaque word with a high-frequency first constituent. This was to assess whether both classes of words produced first-constituent frequency effects, and if so, whether they were of differing magnitudes. In Experiments 2 and 3, an opaque compound was directly matched with a transparent one of the same first constituent frequency class to provide a more sensitive test of whether transparency had any effect on reading. Participants read the sentences for comprehension, while their eye fixation patterns were registered. (We will describe other details of Experiment 3 later.)

Eye-movement measures provide the researcher with a detailed picture of the time-course of processing (for a review, see Rayner, 1998). This should be helpful in sorting out lexical and semantic effects, if one assumes that the lexical effects occur earlier. That is, if we find that both lexical and compositional effects occur, one might expect to find the effects due to the frequency of the first constituent early in processing, but not later in processing. We used as early processing measures the duration of initial fixation on the target word and the probability of making a second fixation on the word (the decision to refixate the word needs to be made during the initial fixation). As somewhat later processing measures, we employed the gaze duration on the target word, the durations of the second and third fixations, and the probability of making three fixations on the word. As measures of even later processing, we employed the probability of making a regression out of the target word and the probability of skipping word N + 1.

EXPERIMENT 1

Method

Participants.   Twenty-six students from the introductory psychology course at the University of Turku, all of whom were native speakers of Finnish, participated in the experiment as a part of the course requirement.

Apparatus.   Eye movements were collected by the EYELINK eye-tracker manufactured by SR Research Ltd. (Canada). The eyetracker is an infra-red video-based tracking system combined with hyperacuity image processing. There are two cameras mounted on a headband (one for each eye) including two infra-red LEDs for illuminating each eye. (The headband weighs 450 g.) The cameras sample pupil location and pupil size at the rate of 250 Hz. Registration is binocular and is performed for the selected eye(s) by placing the camera(s) and the two infra-red light sources 4–6 cm away from the eye. In the present study, registration was done monocularly using the right eye. The resolution of eye position is 15 seconds of arc and the average spatial accuracy approximately 0.5 degrees. Head position with respect to the computer screen is tracked with the help of a head-tracking camera mounted on the centre of the headband at the level of the forehead. Four LEDs are attached to the corners of the computer screen, which are viewed by the head-tracking camera, once the participant sits directly facing the screen. Possible head motion is detected as movements of the four LEDs and is compensated for on-line from the eye position records.

Materials and design.   A set of 40 semantically transparent and 40 opaque compounds was selected. All target words were 2-noun compound words (12–15 characters long). For both sets, the frequency of the first constituent was manipulated: one set had a frequent first constituent and the other set had an infrequent first constituent. There were 20 words of each kind both for transparent and opaque words (i.e., a total of 80 target items). The constituent frequency refers to the frequency the constituent has as a separate word in Finnish. The frequencies were computed on the basis of an unpublished 22.7 million word newspaper corpus of Laine and Virtanen (1996).

By definition, a semantically transparent compound is one whose approximate meaning can be derived from the constituent meanings by 'glueing' them together. On the other hand, a compound word is semantically opaque when its meaning cannot be computed by simply glueing together constituent meanings. In our set of opaque compounds either the meaning of the whole word was opaque (e.g., *kompastuskivi* = stumbling block), or the meaning of the first constituent was opaque (e.g., *verivihollinen* = blood enemy) and the meaning of the second constituent was transparent (none of the words was opaque only in its second constituent). In the former case, the compound word meaning was often metaphorical. An initial selection of the target words was done by intuition. To ensure that the words indeed differed in semantic transparency we asked a group of eight subjects to rate the words for transparency using a 7-point scale (1 = totally transparent, 7 = totally opaque). As the ratings indicated (see Table 1), the two word sets clearly differed in their perceived transparency.

TABLE 1
Characteristics of the target words used in Experiment 1, 2, and 3

	Transparent compounds		Opaque compounds	
Stimulus characteristic	Low frequency first constituent	High frequency first constituent	Low frequency first constituent	High frequency first constituent
Frequency of first constituent[a,b]	5	274	5.7	299.1
Frequency of compound word[a,c]	2	2.4	2.2	2.2
Frequency of second constituent[a,b]	229.5	189.3	168.9	59.5
Length of compound word (in characters)	12.9	12.8	13.2	12.9
Length of first constituent	7.2	6.1	6.6	5.9
Rated semantic transparency[d]	1.52	1.6	5.24	4.76

[a] These frequencies have been converted to frequencies per million.

[b] The frequencies are of the constituents as separate words in all their inflectional forms, including the nominative case.

[c] The frequencies are of the compound words in all their inflectional forms, including the nominative case.

[d] 1 = completely transparent, 7 = completely opaque.

Characteristics of the target words are presented in Table 1. There was a large difference in the frequency of the first constituent between the two word sets, whereas the whole-word frequency was closely matched. The target words were also matched for word length and for first constituent length.

The target words were near the beginning of sentences, but never in the initial word position. A target word with an infrequent first constituent was paired with one that had a frequent initial constituent, and a sentence frame was created for this word pair so that it was identical up through the word following the target word. The matching was done separately for transparent and opaque compounds. A typical sentence pair is as follows, with the target word in italics.

Low-frequency first constituent condition, transparent compound

Edessäni huomasin *alttaritaulun*, joka oli niin täynnä yksityiskohtia, etten jaksanut tutkia sitä sen tarkemmin.
(In front of me I saw an *altarpiece*, which was so full of detail so that I didn't have the energy to examine it any closer.)

High-frequency first constituent condition, transparent compound

Edessäni huomasin *yleisöjoukon*, joka oli varmaan menossa samaan konserttiin.
(In front of me I saw a *spectator group* that was presumably going to the same concert.)

To ensure that the two sentences of each pair were equally natural in meaning, we asked a separate group of eight subjects to compare the naturalness of the two sentences in each pair. The subjects were asked to choose between three alternatives: (1) the sentences are equally natural, (2) sentence A is more natural than sentence B, and (3) sentence B is more natural than sentence A. If the majority of subjects favoured one sentence over the other, that sentence pair was revised, and another group of three subjects performed the comparison for ten revised sentence pairs. The outcome of this procedure was that the final set of sentence pairs were equated for the perceived naturalness.

The target sentences were presented in Courier font starting from a point near the left of the computer screen. The sentences occupied a maximum of three lines of text, and the critical word never appeared as the initial or final word of a text line. With a viewing distance of about 65 cm, one character subtended approximately 0.5 degrees of visual angle in the horizontal direction. There were two blocks of sentences, with the sentence frames containing each word pair appearing in separate blocks. The order of the blocks was counterbalanced across participants. Thus, each participant saw all the critical target words. Within each block, the order of target sentences was randomised. There were 30 filler sentences among the critical sentences.

Procedure. The eye-tracker was first calibrated using a nine-point calibration grid which spanned the entire screen area. Ten practice sentences were presented before the actual experiment. Participants were instructed to read each sentence for comprehension. They were told that they would be occasionally asked to paraphrase the sentence they had just finished reading. Before the presentation of each sentence, they were required to gaze at a fixation point in the top left corner of the screen. In case of a calibration drift, the calibration was automatically corrected. Immediately after the fixation point was erased from the screen, a sentence, extending 1–3 lines of text, was presented left-justified and centred vertically on the screen. The experimental session took a maximum of 30 minutes.

Results and discussion

Gaze duration. The most common measure of global processing time on the target word is *gaze duration*, the sum of the durations of all fixations on the first encounter with the target word (i.e., prior to a saccade leaving the target word). As seen in Table 2, there was a 40 ms difference in gaze durations between the target words with high frequency first constituents and those with low frequency first constituents, $F_1(1, 24) = 28.3, p < .001$, $F_2(1, 38) = 6.02, p < .05$. Surprisingly, there was no effect of transparency; the overall difference between transparent and opaque compound words was 1 ms, and the interaction between transparency and frequency was very small, $Fs < 1$.

More detailed measures on the target word. A more detailed account of processing can be obtained by looking at individual fixations (see Table 2). First, consider the duration of the initial fixation on the word. Here (quite surprisingly in view of the above null result for transparency), there was an indication of a main effect of transparency, $F_1(1, 24) = 20.7, p < .001$, $F_2(1, 38) = 3.42, p < .10$. It should be noted that this effect may be a result of the different sentence frames used for transparent and opaque compounds (cf. Experiments 2 and 3). The small effect of the first constituent frequency was not significant overall, $F_1(1, 24) = 1.50, p > .20$, $F_2 < 1$, nor was the 5 ms frequency effect for the transparent compounds, $t_1(24) = 1.89, p < .10, t_2(24) = 1.05, p > .20$. There was a slight hint of a frequency effect in the duration of the second fixation, although all Fs in

TABLE 2
Experiment 1: Various reading indexes on the target word as a function of first
constituent frequency and semantic transparency

Eye movement measure	Transparent compounds		Opaque compounds	
	Low frequency first constituent	High frequency first constituent	Low frequency first constituent	High frequency first constituent
Gaze duration (in milliseconds)	538	492	540	493
First fixation duration (in milliseconds)	193	188	199	200
Second fixation duration (in milliseconds)	191	188	187	187
Third fixation duration (in milliseconds)	182	184	184	177
Probability of an initial fixation	1	0.98	0.98	0.98
Probability of refixating target word	0.93	0.9	0.92	0.88
Probability of refixating target word at least twice	0.51	0.46	0.55	0.45
Per cent of saccades leaving target word that are regressions	3.2	3.2	6	5.8
Per cent of forward saccades that skip word N + 1	3.3	3.4	6.2	6.2

the analyses were less than 1. Thus, little of the frequency effect in the gaze
duration is attributable to differences in individual fixation durations.
Instead, most of the frequency effect on the gaze durations appears to be
due to differing numbers of fixations made on the target word. The
probability of making a second fixation was 3.3% greater for the low
frequency words, $F_1(1, 24) = 7.73, p < .01, F_2(1, 38) = 5.59, p < .05$, and
the probability of making a third fixation was 5.2% greater for the low
frequency words, $F_1(1, 24) = 19.1, p < .001, F_2(1, 38) = 6.45, p < .05$.
None of the transparency effects on the probability of refixation were
significant.

Effects subsequent to processing the target word ('spillover'). As
transparency may have 'delayed' effects, we thought it would be of
interest to examine where the eyes went after leaving the target word.
Unfortunately, these data are not completely 'clean' as the text prior to
and after the target word were not the same for the transparent and
opaque words. We first examined the per cent of times that people left the
target word by regressing back to a prior word. In fact, the number of
regressions from opaque words was almost double the number of
regressions from transparent words (6.0% vs. 3.2%), $F_1(1, 24) = 8.77$,

$p < .01$, however, $F_2(1, 38) = 3.10, p < .10$. A second measure that was taken was the probability that the reader would skip the word after the target word when leaving the target word. Here, surprisingly, there appeared to be a difference in the 'wrong' direction, as there were more such skips for opaque words than for transparent words, $F_1(1, 24) = 8.79$, $p < .01$, however, $F_2(1, 38) = 3.12, p < .10$. However, again, these two differences could have been due to differences in the sentence frames.

EXPERIMENT 2

Although transparency clearly had no effect on the total 'first pass' processing time on the target word (as measured by the gaze duration) in Experiment 1, there were some suggestions that transparency might have had some subtle effects (e.g., on the duration of the first fixation). There is a problem with those comparisons, however, because the matched transparent and opaque words were in different sentence frames. Therefore, these transparency effects could merely have been due to uncontrolled differences in the sentence frames preceding the target words. As a result, in Experiment 2, we used matched transparent and opaque compound words in the same sentence frames to get a better measure of transparency effects.[3]

Method

Participants.   Twenty-four students from the introductory psychology course at the University of Turku, all of whom were native speakers of Finnish, participated in the experiment as a part of the course requirement. None of them took part in Experiment 1.

Apparatus.   The same apparatus was used as in Experiment 1.

Materials and design.   The same target words were used as in Experiment 1. However, the target words appeared in different sentence frames than in Experiment 1. The matching of sentence frames was performed by either pairing an opaque and transparent compound that had a high-frequency initial constituent or pairing an opaque and transparent compound that had a low-frequency initial constituent. This allowed us to make more reliable comparisons between opaque and

---

[3] The main reason we did not use a completely crossed design (which would have allowed transparency and frequency to both be within-item variables) is that the resulting sentences would have been much less natural. That is, it is quite difficult to construct a sentence frame such that four compound words can equally felicitously fit in. Further, in such a design, we would have had to construct four such frames for each quartet of target words.

transparent compounds. Each participant saw 120 sentences: the 80 experimental sentences containing the target words and 40 filler sentences.

A group of five subjects performed naturalness ratings for each sentence pair as described above for Experiment 1.

Procedure. The experimental procedure was identical to that of Experiment 1.

Results and discussion

Gaze duration. As in Experiment 1, we start with *gaze duration*, the sum of the durations of all fixations on the first encounter with the target word (i.e., prior to a saccade leaving the target word). As seen in Table 3, the pattern was quite similar to that in Experiment 1. There was a 36 ms difference in gaze durations between the target words with high frequency first constituents and those with low frequency first constituents, $F_1(1, 23) = 26.5, p < .001$, however, $F_2 < 1$. This frequency effect was not reliable across items largely because frequency was a 'between item' manipulation in this experiment in order to allow for the most reliable estimates of

TABLE 3

Experiment 2: Various reading indexes on the target word as a function of first constituent frequency and semantic transparency

	Transparent compounds		Opaque compounds	
Eye movement measure	Low frequency first constituent	High frequency first constituent	Low frequency first constituent	High frequency first constituent
Gaze duration (in milliseconds)	457	432	479	433
First fixation duration (in milliseconds)	205	203	209	206
Second fixation duration (in milliseconds)	196	181	189	183
Third fixation duration (in milliseconds)	199	177	180	179
Probability of an initial fixation	0.98	0.99	1	0.98
Probability of refixating target word	0.8	0.78	0.8	0.75
Probability of refixating target word at least twice	0.31	0.3	0.35	0.3
Per cent of saccades leaving target word that are regressions	4.5	8	5.6	6.7
Per cent of forward saccades that skip word N + 1	32.1	43.4	33.2	41.5
Duration of first fixation on Word N + 1 (in milliseconds)	196	199	204	205

transparency effects. Nonetheless, in spite of the greater power and control of the current experiment for analysing transparency, there was only a suggestion of a transparency effect (11 ms) which was not close to being significant, $F_1(1, 23) = 2.00, p > .10, F_2 < 1$. Unlike in Experiment 1, there was a suggestion of an interaction between transparency and frequency, but the effect was small, $F_1(1, 23) = 1.90, p > .10, F_2 < 1$, and it was in the opposite direction of what one might expect—with a larger first constituent frequency effect for the opaque words.

More detailed measures on the target word. The only significant effect of constituent frequency on individual fixation durations was the 11 ms difference in second fixation duration, $F_1(1, 23) = 9.34, p < .01, F_2(1, 38) = 4.52, p < .05$. None of the main effects of transparency on individual fixation durations was close to significant (all $ps > .20$ and most $Fs < 1$) and the only effect involving transparency that was close to significant was the interaction suggesting that the frequency effect was larger for transparent words, $F_1(1, 23) = 3.81, p < .10, F_2(1, 38) = 2.46, p > .10$, $F_1(1, 19) = 3.38, p < .10, F_2 < 1$, for second and third fixation durations, respectively.[4] There were no completely reliable frequency effects on the probability of refixating, possibly due to the fact that this was a 'between-item' variable. The only effect that was close to significant was that the probability of making a first refixation on the target word was 4.2% greater for the low frequency words, $F_1(1, 23) = 4.70, p < .05$, but $F_2 = 1$. No effect involving transparency was close to significant (again, all $ps > .20$ and most $Fs < 1$).

This general pattern thus differs somewhat from Experiment 1. In Experiment 1, little of the difference in gaze duration between high- and low-frequency first constituent words was attributable to differences in individual fixation durations and most of the difference was attributable to differences in refixation probabilities. In contrast, in Experiment 2, roughly half of the gaze duration difference appeared to be due to differences in the second and third fixation durations.

Measures after leaving the target word ('spillover'). The sentence frames containing the pairs of matched transparent and opaque words were identical up to the word following the target word. Thus, it is of interest to see whether transparency did have some effect immediately

---

[4] It is highly unlikely that the trend for the frequency effect being slightly larger in the duration of second and third fixation for transparent compounds is a result of the second constituent in the low-frequency opaque condition being of lower frequency than in the other conditions. This is because the trend is primarily due to relatively long fixations observed in the low-frequency transparent condition.

after leaving the target word. Perhaps the purest measure is the per cent of time that people initially left the target word with a regression back to prior text. Here, somewhat surprisingly, there was a suggestion of a frequency effect, $F_1(1, 23) = 3.94$, $p < .10$, but $F_2 < 1$, which was in the 'wrong' direction, with more regressions when the initial constituent was high frequency. However, there was no effect of transparency, with Fs close to zero. A second measure of 'where' the eyes landed after leaving the target word is the per cent of time people skipped word N + 1 and went immediately to word N + 2. In fact, people skipped word N + 1 almost 10% more in the high frequency condition, but this effect was not reliable over items, $F_1(1, 23) = 29.5$, $p < .001$, but $F_2(1, 38) = 1.20$, $p > .20$. Again, there was no effect of transparency, Fs < 1. A third measure to assess processing immediately after leaving the target word was the duration of the first fixation after leaving the target word for those fixations that landed on word N+1. Here was one of the few indications of a transparency effect, as the mean fixation duration was 7 ms less for transparent than for opaque words, $F_1(1, 23) = 3.79$, $p < .10$, but $F_2 < 1$.

Summary.   Experiment 2 replicated the main features of Experiment 1. Again, there was no significant transparency effect on gaze duration, and the few somewhat odd transparency effects that occurred on detailed measures in Experiment 1 disappeared, indicating that they were likely due to the differences in sentence frames in Experiment 1 between the opaque and transparent compound words. We observed a first constituent frequency effect in Experiment 2 that was only a little smaller than the one in Experiment 1 (36 ms vs. 45 ms), but it was not significant over items, most likely because constituent frequency was a between-item manipulation in Experiment 2. Finally, there was a marginal tendency (clearly non-significant in the item analysis) observed in the durations of the second and third fixation for the frequency effect to be smaller for the opaque compounds than for the transparent compounds. However, as will become apparent, this tendency was not confirmed in Experiment 3.

EXPERIMENT 3

In Experiment 3, an eye movement contingent display change technique was applied in yet another attempt to uncover effects of semantic transparency on compound word processing. In the experiment, there were two display change conditions. In one, all but the first two letters of the second constituent were replaced with visually similar letters before the second constituent was fixated (which made the second constituent initially a non-word), and in the other (a control condition), there were no display changes. An invisible 'boundary' was set at the constituent boundary; when the eyes crossed this boundary, the changed letters were replaced with the correct ones during the saccadic eye movement. As vision is reduced during saccades (so-called saccadic suppression), readers are not able to see the actual change taking place (provided that the change is completed before the end of the critical saccade). Thus, when the readers fixated on the second constituent, it always appeared in its correct form, and, as indicated above, they were unaware of the display change.

This boundary technique, which was employed previously with transparent compound words (Hyönä, Bertram, & Pollatsek, in press), allowed us to test whether the processing of opaque compounds would be more strongly affected by the display change than the processing of transparent compounds. In other words, if the identification of opaque compounds is less compositional than for transparent compounds and thus is more through the whole-word form, the processing of opaque compounds should be affected more by display change. That is, in the display change condition, the second constituent is initially obscured and the readers can only have access to the first constituent. As a result, the reader would be induced to adopt a compositional processing strategy, which should be less suitable for opaque compounds, if the reader prefers to access opaque compounds as wholes. Furthermore, as most of the opaque compounds in the present study had first constituents that were semantically opaque, such compositional processing may lead to 'garden-path' effects (if the meanings of constituents are being composed).

A second reason for conducting Experiment 3 was to see whether the suggestive trends involving transparency that were observed in gaze duration and in the duration of second and third fixations in Experiment 2 would obtain stronger empirical support. Experiment 3 employed the same materials as Experiment 2 (i.e., the pairwise matching was done between transparent and opaque compounds) with half of the target compounds appearing in the display change condition and the other half in the no change condition.

Method

Participants.   Twenty-three university students took part in the experiment for course credit. All were native speakers of Finnish.

Apparatus.   The apparatus used in Experiment 1 and 2 was updated to a second generation EyeLink tracker (EyeLink II, Toronto, Ontario, Canada), which runs at a sampling rate of 500 Hz (i.e., a new sample is recorded every 2 ms).

Materials and design.   The same target words were used as in Experiment 1 and 2. The target sentences were the ones used in

Experiment 2, which means that each transparent compound was matched pairwise with an opaque compound. The target compound appeared initially either unchanged (i.e., the second constituent was present throughout the sentence presentation) or the last letters of the second constituent were replaced with visually similar letters (i.e., *vaniljakastike* = 'vanilla sauce' would initially appear as *vaniljakaeflha*). In the change condition, the second constituent was always a non-word prior to the display change. An invisible boundary was set at the morpheme boundary. In the display change condition, when the eyes crossed this boundary, the word was changed to its correct form during the saccade across this boundary. A crucial design feature of the experiment was that we wanted to make the display change as unobtrusive as possible. Accordingly, we experimented with various possibilities for how much of the second constituent to preserve. If none of the second constituent was preserved in the display change condition, the display change was often quite noticeable. However, when the first two letters of the second constituent were preserved, the display change was rarely, if ever, detectable. Thus, in the display change condition, the first two letters of the second constituent were kept intact before the boundary crossing and the last letters of the second constituent were replaced by visually similar letters.

The target sentences were presented in Courier font (so that each character position was of equal width). The sentences occupied a maximum of 2 lines of text, and the critical word always appeared on the first line but it never was the initial or final word of the line. With a viewing distance of about 60 cm, each character subtended approximately 0.3 degrees of visual angle. There were four blocks of sentences; each member of the matched quadruplet appeared in a separate block. However, each participant only saw two of the four blocks so that he or she saw all the target words only once (i.e., either in the Change or No Change condition). There were 10 items in each condition per participant. The order of the blocks was counterbalanced across participants, and the order of the target sentences was randomised within each block. There were 96 filler sentences among the critical sentences. The text was presented on a 17" ViewSonic (P775) monitor as white against a dark background. The refresh rate of the monitor was set at 150 Hz.

Procedure. The experimental procedure was identical to that of Experiment 1 and 2.

Results and discussion

The experimental design included three variables, transparency (transparent vs. opaque), display change (change vs. no change), and first constituent frequency (low vs. high) that were all within-participant variables and all except frequency were within-item variables. In the display change condition, 21.4% of the trials were excluded from the analyses due to the change taking place after a fixation had already started on the second constituent (these were trials where the eyes crossed the invisible boundary just before the end of the critical saccade).[5] We start by reporting the gaze duration, followed by more detailed analyses of the eye movement pattern. The means of the eye movement measures are given in Table 4.

Gaze duration. There were reliable effects of both first constituent frequency and display change on gaze duration. Gaze durations on compounds with a low-frequency initial constituent were 64 ms longer than gazes on compounds with a high-frequency initial constituent, $F_1(1, 22) = 47.78, p < .001, F_2(1, 38) = 5.01, p < .05$, and gazes were 105 ms longer when there was a display change than when there was no display change, $F_1(1, 22) = 59.49, p < .001, F_2(1, 38) = 77.23, p < .001$. However, averaged over the other two variables, the mean gaze duration on transparent compounds was actually 6 ms greater than the mean gaze duration on opaque compounds ($Fs < 1$). There was, as in Experiment 2 but not as in Experiment 1, a somewhat bigger frequency effect for the opaque compounds (71 ms vs. 59 ms). However, this interaction, as well as all the other interactions of transparency with the other two variables were far from significant ($Fs < 1$). Moreover, there was no evidence in the gaze duration measure to suggest that opaque compounds were more strongly affected by the display change than transparent compounds: the effect of the display change manipulation was 104 ms for transparent compounds and 107 ms for opaque compounds. There was a suggestion that the display change effect was slightly greater for compounds with low-frequency first constituents than for those with high-frequency first constituents (114 ms vs. 96 ms), but, as indicated above, this difference was not close to significant. This robust display change effect indicates that readers did process the orthographic information of the second constituent while fixating on the first constituent and subsequently utilized it regardless of the transparency of the compound word and the frequency of its first constituent. The effect size is very similar to that observed by Hyönä *et al.* (in press).

---

[5] The percentages of excluded trials were 17.0, 20.9, 27.0, and 23.5, for the transparent high-frequency first constituent, opaque high-frequency first constituent, transparent low-frequency first constituent, and opaque low-frequency first constituent condition, respectively.

TABLE 4

Experiment 3: Various reading indexes on the target word as a function of semantic transparency, first constituent frequency and display change

| | Transparent compounds | | | | Opaque compounds | | | |
| | Low-frequency 1st constituent | | High-frequency 1st constituent | | Low-frequency 1st constituent | | High-frequency 1st constituent | |
Eye movement measure	Change	No change	Change	No change	Change	No change	Change	No change
Gaze duration (in ms)	652	535	580	490	649	538	574	472
First fixation duration (in ms)	224	215	203	209	222	208	212	218
Subgaze on the 1st constituent (in ms)	266	272	234	228	271	245	244	235
Subgaze after change	439	339	435	361	461	367	424	359
Probability of refixating 1st constituent	0.19	0.23	0.12	0.07	0.17	0.14	0.1	0.07
Duration of first fixation on the 2nd constituent (in ms)	241	225	248	226	241	217	244	225
Probability of more than 2 fixations	0.59	0.41	0.48	0.35	0.63	0.41	0.52	0.31
Per cent of saccades leaving target word that are regressions	5.3	4.3	5.4	3.9	4.2	5.8	3.5	1.9
Per cent of forward saccades that skip word N + 1	46.1	48	43.8	51.8	49.4	40.5	49.5	45.1
Duration of first fixation on Word N + 1 (in ms)	214	207	224	216	197	196	209	213

More detailed measures on the target word. In order to get a more detailed picture of the time course of the effects, a set of early and later processing measures were analysed. Given that the detailed measures revealed little in the first two experiments, we concentrated on a 'rougher' division corresponding to the display change. That is, one can divide the gaze duration into the time spent on the word before the first saccade over the constituent boundary (i.e., before the display change in the display-change conditions) and the time spent on the word after that saccade. Accordingly, we defined *subgaze$_1$ duration* as the sum of the durations of all fixations that landed on the first constituent prior to the initial saccade to the second constituent (trials on which there was no initial fixation on the first constituent were excluded). The 29 ms main effect of first constituent frequency was nearly significant for this subgaze duration measure, $F_1(1, 22) = 31.46, p < .001, F_2(1, 35) = 3.33, p < .10$. Although this frequency effect was greater for transparent (38 ms) than for opaque (19 ms) compounds, the Frequency × Transparency interaction was significant only in the participant analysis, $F_1(1, 22) = 4.93, p < .05, F_2 < 1$. Most strikingly, subgaze$_1$ was only 9 ms greater when there was a display change than when there was not ($Fs < 2.1$).

A finer analysis of processing before the first fixation on the second constituent revealed little else of interest. The only effect on a more detailed measure that was significant was that the probability of making a second fixation on the first constituent prior to saccading to the second constituent was .18 for the low-frequency and .09 for the high-frequency first constituent targets, $F_1(1, 22) = 33.75, p < .001, F_2(1, 38) = 6.88, p < .01$. This difference accounts for most of the subgaze$_1$ effect above. The only other effect that came close to reaching significance was the Frequency × Display Change interaction on the first fixation duration, $F_1(1, 22) = 4.16, p < .10, F_2(1, 35) = 4.19, p < .05$, which suggested that the frequency effect was larger in the display change condition than in the control condition.

To summarise, the most striking thing about processing before the constituent boundary is crossed is that there was virtually no early effect of display change in spite of the large effect of this manipulation on gaze duration. In contrast, there were early effects due to the frequency of the first constituent. Although the effect was not quite significant over items for the subgaze$_1$ measure, it was quite reliable in the probability of making a second fixation prior to fixating the second constituent. In addition, consistent with the overall null effects, there were no reliable early effects related to semantic transparency.

As indicated above, we defined a summary measure of later processing which we called the *subgaze$_2$ duration*. It was the sum of the durations of all fixations on the compound word (i.e., on either constituent) after the initial saccade over the constituent boundary (i.e., after the display change in the display change condition). Trials with no fixations on the target word after the display change were excluded from the analysis. Here the only reliable effect was the 83 ms main effect of display change, $F_1(1, 22) = 52.70, p < .001, F_2(1, 38) = 44.51, p < .001$. Thus, the bulk of the overall change effect observed in gaze duration appeared as a relatively late effect (i.e., when the second constituent appeared in its correct form). There was a slight hint in the participant analysis of a Frequency $\times$ Transparency interaction, $F_1(1, 22) = 2.65, p > .10, F_2 < 1$. Perhaps surprisingly, the first constituent frequency only had a 7 ms effect on the subgaze$_2$ duration ($Fs < 1$).

The display change effect occurred early during subgaze$_2$, as the duration of the first fixation on the second constituent was 21 ms longer in the display change than in the no change condition, $F_1(1, 22) = 14.81, p < .001, F_2(1, 38) = 28.37, p < .001$. It should be noted that at this point the compound word appeared in its correct form, so the change effect is due to processing done during earlier fixations. In addition, unsurprisingly, the probability of making at least three fixations on the target compound word was affected both by the first constituent frequency, $F_1(1, 22) = 16.08, p < .001, F_2(1, 38) = 3.54, p < .10$, and display change, $F_1(1, 22) = 106.52, p < .001, F_2(1, 38) = 40.79, p < .001$. There were no significant effects on later measures involving transparency.

To summarise the results of later processing measures, two findings came out very clearly. First, the display change effect that was quite absent during the early processing is large and significant in later processing. Second, the first constituent frequency effect that was present in the early measures also had some effects in the later measures, although the overall effect of first constituent frequency on later measures, as measured by the subgaze$_2$ duration, was quite small and not close to significant. In addition, there was little effect of semantic transparency even on later measures.

Measures after leaving the target word ('spillover').   We also examined fixations made immediately after leaving the target word, especially to see if there were any later effects due to transparency. As in Experiment 2, the sentence frames containing the pairs of matched transparent and opaque words were identical up to the word following the target word. Thus, we analysed the duration of first fixation made on the word N+1 as a function of the manipulated variables. One participant was removed from the participant analysis and eight items were removed from the item analysis due to missing data. There was a non-significant trend for a transparency effect, $F_1(1, 21) = 2.52, p > .1, F_2(1, 30) = 4.42, p < .05$, but the trend was 11 ms in the wrong direction (i.e., the transparent condition was associated with a longer fixation duration than the opaque condition). There was a tendency for a frequency effect in the participant analysis, $F_1(1, 21) = 3.63$, $p < .10$, $F_2 < 1$, but again in the wrong direction (i.e., the high-frequency condition was associated on average with a 12 ms longer fixation than the low-frequency condition). It is very likely that the trend reflects the fact that Word N + 1 was not identical between the two frequency conditions.

The probability of leaving the target compound with a regression showed no reliable effects, all Fs < 1.5 (see Table 4). Another measure indexing late processing, the probability of skipping word N + 1 yielded an almost significant Transparency × Display Change interaction, $F_1(1, 22)$ = 3.95, $p < .10$, $F_2(1, 38) = 3.88$, $p < .10$. The nature of this marginal interaction is that with opaque compounds, word N + 1 was skipped more often in the change than in the no change condition, whereas an opposite trend was evident for transparent compounds.

GENERAL DISCUSSION

Our data indicate that there was no effect of transparency for the global 'first pass' processing time on a word (i.e., gaze duration). In Experiment 1, there was virtually no main effect of transparency (1 ms) nor any interaction with frequency. In Experiment 2, although there was a suggestion of a transparency effect (a main effect of 11 ms), the pattern of the effect is counter to what would be predicted by most views of how transparency would affect the processing of compound words. That is, there was virtually no transparency effect for the words with high-frequency first constituents, and the entire transparency effect occurred for the words with low frequency first constituents. If composition of the meanings of the constituents was an important part of recognising a compound word, one would have expected that this process would be particularly important when the first constituent was frequent, as the compositional process would have a head start over a direct look-up process. Moreover, in Experiment 3, the transparency main effect on gaze duration was actually 6 ms in the 'wrong direction' (i.e., opaque words having shorter gaze durations than transparent ones).

In addition, the more detailed analyses of 'first pass' processing also provided no convincing evidence for transparency effects. There were a few suggestions of transparency effects on other measures, but they were not consistent across experiments nor were they in places where one would expect to find them. Most notably, the effect of transparency on the first fixation duration in Experiment 1 was not replicated in either Experiment 2 or Experiment 3. As mentioned earlier, the comparison in Experiment 1 was across different sentence frames (and thus may have been due to a confounding of the difficulty of the sentence frames with transparency) whereas the designs in Experiments 2 and 3 did not have this confounding.

Moreover, the duration of the first fixation would seem like a strange place to find a transparency effect, as one would expect transparency to only affect later processing (e.g., second and third fixation durations) — presumably only after the meaning of the second constituent had been identified. This argument is bolstered by the finding that the display change manipulation in Experiment 3 (where the second constituent was either visible at the outset or only when it was fixated) had no effect on first fixation duration or other measures of early processing. In Experiment 2, where main effects of transparency would be picked up more reliably than in Experiment 1, there was a suggestion of a transparency effect on the third fixation duration—but a suggestion of an opposite effect on the duration of the second fixation. There were also four transparency by frequency effects that were reliable or marginally reliable over participants but not close to reliable over items, all in the direction of a greater frequency effect for transparent compounds. However, their locus was not consistent: in Experiment 2, these interactions were found in second and third fixation duration, whereas in Experiment 3, they were on first fixation duration and subgaze$_1$ duration (the latter two measures are not independent). Thus, besides being not reliable over items, these effects were not consistent across experiments and were opposite to the direction of the (non-significant) interaction observed in the gaze duration. Moreover, as indicated above, early measures are implausible places to find a transparency effect, as it is unlikely that the meaning of the second constituent is processed quickly. Thus, we think that the best conclusion one can draw from the three experiments is that there is no transparency effect on 'first-pass time' for processing Finnish compound words, or if there is an effect, it is so small to be of no real importance in understanding how compound words are processed in context.[6]

We should also comment briefly on the results of our display change manipulation, although that was not the primary focus of the present study. Essentially, these results replicated those of Hyönä et al. (in press) in finding: (a) a strong effect of the first morpheme frequency before the second constituent is fixated, but virtually no effect of the display change; and (b) a strong effect of the display change manipulation after the second constituent is fixated, but only weak effects of the first constituent frequency on these later measures.[7] This pattern of results suggests that

---

[6] It is possible that the processing of opaque compounds receives benefit from a sentence context (even a neutral one).

[7] This points to another reason that it is unlikely that transparency would affect early measures. That is, if early measures do not even pick up whether a meaningful second constituent is present or not, they are quite unlikely to be sensitive to whether the composition of the meanings computes semantically.

these long Finnish compounds are processed quite serially, with the initial fixations reflecting processing of the first constituent and the later fixations reflecting processing of the second constituent. They also indicate that constituents yet to be fixated (i.e., material in the parafovea) have little influence on the duration of the initial fixation.

We think it is fair to say that our data indicate that the transparency has little or no effect on the processing of long compound words in reading Finnish and that the compositional processes exposed by manipulating the frequency of the constituents involve 'glueing together' something like the constituent lexemes rather than composing the meanings of those lexemes. The one caveat we need to make is that it is possible that there are 'later' transparency effects that our paradigm failed to pick up. That is, our sentences were only matched up to the word after the target word. Thus it is possible that there might be more later regressions back to the target word for opaque words, indicating some sort of 'double take'. Analyzing such later measures with our materials would be fruitless, as the putative transparency effects would be hopelessly confounded with differences in the sentence frames. However, our design did permit analysis of some earlier 'spillover' effects, and again, there was little or no effect of transparency on these measures.

Another possible caution we should mention in interpreting our data is that the pattern of results may be restricted to Finnish compound words. However, we think it is quite unlikely that there is anything special about Finnish that would produce a reduced effect of transparency. In fact, most plausibly the opposite is true, as Finnish compounding is very productive. As a result, Finnish readers frequently need to put together the meanings of constituents of novel compound words in order to understand them. Thus, the fact that transparency has virtually no effect on the understanding of already existing compounds is indeed quite remarkable. It suggests that the composition process may exist in two stages: first a composition of entities that does not involve composing the meanings followed by a composition of meanings, if that is needed for novel compounds.

Basically, our results are consistent with most of the work using the priming techniques we reviewed earlier. That is, a large majority of the lexical decision experiments that used variations on the constituent priming paradigm (i.e., priming the compound with a constituent or vice versa) failed to obtain a transparency effect either. However, in one of these studies and in two of the semantic priming experiments we reviewed, there was an indication that there might have been a smaller priming effect for completely opaque words such as *cocktail*, where the relation of the parts to the whole would be known only to specialists of the language. Our opaque words were a mixture of such completely opaque words and those that were partially opaque (i.e., where the meaning of one of the constituents was related to the meaning of the compound). Given our overall null results, we were sceptical that the relative opaqueness would make any difference. Nonetheless, we decided to perform a post-hoc item analysis where we predicted the difference in gaze duration between each matched transparent-opaque target pair of Experiment 2 by the relative difference in the transparency rating of the target pair. In this analysis, the correlation between the difference in transparency rating with gaze duration was small ($r = -.137$, $F < 1$) and was in the 'wrong' direction; a bigger difference in rated transparency between the transparent and opaque words predicted a somewhat smaller difference in gaze duration.

What kind of processing model could explain the observed pattern of data? There seem to be two types of model that would be plausible. The first is the one that we have implicitly been assuming. That is, the lexical entries of the components are accessed, which then are glued together to 'look up' the lexical entry of the whole word. For example, in English, one would first access the lexical entry for 'straw' and then the entry for 'berry', which in turn would look up a lexical entry for 'straw–berry' from which the meaning of the compound would be looked up. Such a componential process is likely to be going on in parallel with a direct look-up process, where the entire string of letters is accessing 'strawberry' directly. These two processes could either be independent processes or could be working interactively. Either version of such a dual-route model would be consistent, at least qualitatively, with both constituent frequency effects and whole-word frequency effects.

The second type of model is something like Taft and Forster's (1976) two-stage model, where the first constituent accesses a first stage 'file drawer' that contains all the entries that have the initial constituent as a first constituent. The second stage of the access would then be 'finding' the compound word in the 'file drawer'. However, the second stage needs not be serial, as Taft and Forster originally posited, but, as in Lukatela, Gligorijevic, Kostic, and Turvey's (1980) 'satellite-entries' model, could be a parallel process which is determined by both the number of competitors in the file drawer and/or their frequency relative to the frequency of the word actually seen. Such a model is also consistent with both first constituent frequency effects (the ease of finding the 'file drawer') and whole word frequency effects (whole word frequency will be confounded with the position of the item in the file drawer assuming first constituent frequency has been equated).

What do the two types of models predict about transparency effects? For the file drawer model, the meanings of the two constituents seem besides the point; the access of the meaning is through the whole-word entry. In contrast, the dual route model could make any prediction, depending on whether the components that are activated and combined are 'lexical' or 'semantic''. Thus, the present results are consistent either with a two-stage model, such as Taft and Forster (1976), or with a dual-route model in which there is no significant activation of meaning by the access of the constituents in the combination process. However, a critic may argue that possible processing differences between transparent and opaque compounds may be obscured by differences in the number of competitors in the file-drawer (the size of the morphological family) and/or the relative ranking of the transparent and opaque compounds in the file-drawer. To examine this possibility, we did some post-hoc analyses to determine whether these variables significantly affected processing in the present experiments.

We computed a measure of the morphological family size for each target word by counting the number of compound words that existed in our computerised corpus (Laine & Virtanen, 1999) given the first constituent (possible allomorphic variation was taken into consideration; the so-called positional family size, see De Jong, Feldman, Schreuder, Pastizzo, and Baayen, 2002). We also computed the relative ranking of each target word in the family. As expected, the family size was clearly bigger for the compounds in the high-frequency than in the low-frequency first constituent condition. It was also somewhat bigger for transparent than opaque compounds. The mean sizes were 314, 218, 48, and 27 for the high-frequency transparent, high-frequency opaque, low-frequency transparent, and low-frequency opaque conditions, respectively. As one might expect, the relative ranking in the family was higher in the low-frequency than in the high-frequency condition. It was somewhat higher for transparent than opaque compounds. The mean rankings were 27.3, 15.3, 2.1, and 1.4 for the high-frequency transparent, high-frequency opaque, low-frequency transparent, and low-frequency opaque conditions, respectively. In the low-frequency conditions, the ranking was 1 or 2 for all but five words.

The prior data suggest that a big family facilitates compound word processing (De Jong et al., 2002). This would imply that our present confounding of transparency with family size should have produced a transparency effect. In contrast, the prior data suggest that a high ranking within the family facilitates processing; this confounding with transparency should work against a transparency effect. Thus, it is not obvious that there is a confounding problem. However, we did post-hoc correlational analyses on the item means for each of the experimental conditions of Experiment 2 and 3 to examine whether family size and relative ranking within the family had any effect on the pattern of data. We first computed the bivariate correlation of family size and ranking, and the correlation of each with gaze duration and the two sub-gaze measures and found that (a) family size and ranking correlated quite highly, and (b) family size produced stronger correlations with the eye fixation measures than ranking. As a result, in the subsequent analyses, we used family size to predict the fixation time measures. As word frequency and first constituent length might be confounded with family size in these analyses, these variables were also entered as predictors.

The multiple regression analyses demonstrated that for all other conditions except for the opaque low-frequency first constituent condition the relationship between family size and gaze duration is depicted by a small negative slope that was non-significant. In other words, the bigger the family the shorter the gaze duration is. However, for the opaque compounds having a low-frequency first constituent the slope was clearly positive. The slope was statistically significant ($p < .05$) for the gaze duration of both the no-change and the change condition of Experiment 3; for the gaze duration of Experiment 2, the slope was positive, but did not reach significance. For these opaque compounds, there appears to be an inhibition effect due to family size: the bigger the morphological family, the longer the gaze duration is. To examine the time course of this inhibition effect, we then computed the regression analyses on the two sub-gaze measures of Experiment 3 (separately for the no-change and the change conditions). In Subgaze$_1$ (i.e., the summed duration of first-pass fixations on the first constituent) there was no indication of an early inhibition effect, whereas Subgaze$_2$ yielded a significant positive slope for family size in both the change and no change conditions, indicating that the effect appears relatively late.

These regression analyses thus suggest that, although there is no evidence that opaqueness exerts any overall effect of slowing identification of compound words, opaqueness may play some role in compound word processing if the frequency of the initial constituent is relatively low. We are not sure why opaqueness played a role only for the compounds with low first constituent frequency, however. Here is one speculation. As the frequency of the compound word was held constant across conditions, the low-frequency first constituent conditions had a much smaller family size (see above) and also the compound word was more often close to the most frequent member of the family. In a recent paper (Hyönä et al., in press) we found suggestive evidence that there was a late facilitation effect suggestive of a predictability effect on processing the second constituent when the family size was low. What may be critical is whether the word that is seen is the most frequent member of the family or not. That is, if the observed word is the most frequent, it may be 'predicted' and thus there would be little interference, whereas if it is not, some other compound word (which is presumably usually transparent) will be predicted, and its activation will cause interference with obtaining the correct meaning for an opaque compound when the word is ultimately identified. If this analysis is correct, it suggests that there may be transparency effects, but for a very limited set of compound words. Of course, one should treat these analyses with some caution, as they were post-hoc and thus there could be some other variable confounded with family size that was the real underlying variable.

One question that our experiments leaves open is whether the entity that starts either of these hypothetical compositional processes needs to be a constituent or a morpheme. For example, perhaps any reasonable syllable or common orthographic pattern will do. Although there may be different answers in different languages, there is evidence in Finnish that morphemically defined constituents have a privileged status. Laine, Vainio, and Hyönä (1999) observed no difference in lexical decision times between pseudo-inflected words and their monomorphemic controls, whereas inflected words consistently produced longer decision times than their monomorphemic controls. These data may be taken as evidence against the view that all letter clusters within a word that can potentially form a morpheme would be automatically activated. Further corroborative evidence against this view comes from an eye-tracking study of Bertram, Pollatsek, and Hyönä (in press) on compound word processing. In Experiment 1, there was a set of compounds that contained a pseudo-morpheme within a two-constituent compound. The identification of these compounds took no longer than for compounds that did not contain a pseudomorpheme. Moreover, the finding reported by Bertram and Hyönä (2003) that there was no constituent frequency effect for short compounds (7–9 characters) indicates that the constituent frequency effect is unlikely to be a general orthographic effect. If it were, the constituent frequency effect should show up for short and long compounds alike.

Some of the priming studies discussed in the Introduction also have addressed the question about the nature of the constituent effect observed for opaque and transparent compounds. Zwitserlood (1994) was able to rule out an orthographic explanation, as she failed to find a priming effect for a letter string that was not a compound word constituent (in her orthographic prime condition of Experiment 1, the prime was a compound and the target was a word or a pseudoword; *kerstfeest* → *kers*). The masked priming study of Longtin, Segui, and Hallé (2003) observed a priming effect of similar magnitude for semantically transparent, opaque and pseudo-derived words (not compounds), whereas no priming was obtained for orthographic controls. This study points to an early parsing mechanism that is blind to semantic transparency and blind to whether or not the two morphemes actually combine to form an existing complex word. This seems consistent with Monsell's (1985) constituent priming results, as he found that there was no significant difference in priming for pseudo-compounds (*boy* → *boycott*) and priming for real compounds (although the priming effect was somewhat smaller for pseudo-compounds than for real compounds).

The bulk of the existing evidence thus points to a morphological interpretation for the constituent frequency effect observed in the present study. Hence, we suggest that, in reading text, lexical entries for the constituents of both transparent and opaque long compound words are used in a compositional mechanism that is part of the word encoding process. However, the lack of a transparency effect indicates that the composition of meaning is not an important part of this process, at least in the initial identification of the compound word.

REFERENCES

Andrews, S. Miller, B., & Rayner, K. (2004). Eye movements and morphological segmentation of compound words: There is a mouse in the mousetrap. *European Journal of Cognitive Psychology, 16*, 285–311.

Bertram, R., & Hyönä, J. (2003). The length of a complex word modifies the role of morphological structure: Evidence from eye movements when reading short and long Finnish compounds. *Journal of Memory and Language, 48*, 614–634.

Bertram, R., Pollatsek, A., & Hyönä, J. (in press). Morphological parsing and the use of segmentation cues in reading Finnish compounds. *Journal of Memory and Language.*

De Jong, N. H., Feldman, L. B., Schreuder, R., Pastizzo, M., Baayen, R. H. (2002). The processing and representation of Dutch and English compounds: Peripheral morphological and central orthographic effects. *Brain and Language, 81*, 555–567.

Hyönä, J., Bertram, R., & Pollatsek, A. (in press). Are long compound words identified serially via their constituents? Evidence from an eye-movement contingent display change study. *Memory and Cognition.*

Hyönä, J., & Pollatsek, A. (1998). Reading Finnish compound words: Eye fixations are affected by component morphemes. *Journal of Experimental Psychology: Human Perception and Performance, 24*, 1612–1627.

Hyönä, J., & Pollatsek, A. (2000). Morphological processing of Finnish compound words in reading. In A. Kennedy, R. Radach, D. Heller, & J. Pynte (Eds.), *Reading as a perceptual process* (pp. 65–87). Oxford: Elsevier.

Jarema, G., Busson, C., Nikolova, R., Tsapkini, K., & Libben, G. (1999). Processing compounds: A cross-linguistic study. *Brain and Language, 68*, 362–369.

Juhasz, B. J., Starr, M. S., Inhoff, A. W., & Placke, L. (2003). The effects of morphology on the processing of compound words: Evidence from naming, lexical decisions and eye fixations. *British Journal of Psychology, 94*, 223–244.

Laine, M., Vainio, S., & Hyönä, J. (1999). Lexical access routes to nouns in a morphologically rich language. *Journal of Memory and Language, 40*, 109–135.

Laine, M., & Virtanen, P. (1999). *WordMill Lexical Search Program.* Center for Cognitive Neuroscience, University of Turku, Finland.

Libben, G. (1998). Semantic transparency in the processing of compounds: Consequences for representation, processing, and impairment. *Brain and Language, 61*, 30–44.

Libben, G., Gibson, M., Yoon, Y., & Sandra, D. (1997). Semantic transparency and compound fracture. *CLASNET Working Papers, 9*, 1–13.

Libben, G., Gibson, M., Yoon, Y. B., & Sandra, D. (2003). Compound fracture: The role of semantic transparency and morphological headedness. *Brain and Language, 84*, 50–64.

Longtin, C.-M., Segui, J., & Hallé, P. A. (2003). Morphological priming without morphological relationship. *Language and Cognitive Processes, 18*, 313–334.

Lukatela, G., Gligorijevic, B., Kostic, A., & Turvey, M. T. (1980). Representation of inflected nouns in the internal lexicon. *Memory and Cognition, 8*, 415–423.

Monsell, S. (1984). Repetition and the lexicon. In A. W. Ellis (Ed.), *Progress in the psychology of language* (Vol. 2). Hove, UK: Lawrence Erlbaum Associates Ltd.

Pollatsek, A., Hyönä, J., & Bertram, R. (2000). The role of morphological constituents in reading Finnish compound words. *Journal of Experimental Psychology: Human Perception and Performance, 26*, 820–833.

Pollatsek, A., Reichle, E., & Rayner, K. (2003). Modeling eye movements in reading. In J. Hyönä, R. Radach, & H. Deubel (Eds.), *The mind's eye: Cognitive and applied aspects of eye movement research* (pp. 361–390). Amsterdam: Elsevier.

Rayner, K. (1998). Eye movements in reading and information processing: 20 years of research. *Psychological Bulletin, 124*, 372–422.

Sandra, D. (1990). On the representation and processing of compound words: Automatic access to constituent morphemes does not occur. *Quarterly Journal of Experimental Psychology, 42A*, 529–567.

Schreuder, R., Burani, C., & Baayen, R. H. (2003). Parsing and semantic opacity. In E. M. H. Assink & D. Sandra (Eds.), *Reading complex words: Cross-linguistic perspectives* (pp. 159–189). Dordrecht: Kluwer Academic.

Taft, M, & Foster, K. I. (1976). Lexical storage and retrieval of polymorphemic and polysyllabic words. *Journal of Verbal Learning and Verbal Behavior, 15*, 607–620.

Zwitserlood, P. (1994). The role of semantic transparency in the processing and representation of Dutch compounds. *Language and Cognitive Processes, 9*, 341–368.

LANGUAGE AND COGNITIVE PROCESSES
2005, 20 (1/2), 291–316

The role of interword spaces in the processing of English compound words

Barbara J. Juhasz
University of Massachusetts, Amherst, MA, USA

Albrecht W. Inhoff
Binghamton University, NY, USA

Keith Rayner
University of Massachusetts, Amherst, MA, USA

Four experiments are reported which examined the role of interword spaces in the processing of English compound words. Normally nonspaced compounds (e.g., softball) as well as normally spaced compounds (e.g., front door) were presented with either their correct spatial layout (softball, front door) or with an incorrect spatial layout (soft ball, frontdoor). Lexical decisions and first fixations on the compounds showed an advantage for interword spaces. However, when refixations on the compounds were taken into account, inserting a space into a normally nonspaced compound significantly disrupted processing. This disruption was larger for adjective-noun compounds than for noun-noun compounds. The results indicate that spatially segmenting compounds facilitates access to the constituent lexemes while spatial unification of compounds benefits the specification of full compound meaning.

Correspondence should be addressed to Barbara J. Juhasz, Department of Psychology, University of Massachusetts, Amherst, MA 01003, USA. Email: bjjuhasz@psych. umass.edu

This research was supported by a pre-doctoral fellowship on Grant MH16745 to the first author, and by grants HD17246 and HD26765. We thank Debra Machacek, Anna Doran, Kadian Leslie, Matt Starr, and Lars Placke with their help on various aspects of these experiments, and Kathy Rastle and two anonymous reviewers for their helpful comments on an earlier version of this paper. Portions of the data were presented at the 12th European Conference of Eye Movements and the 3rd International Conference on Morphology.

http://www.tandf.co.uk/journals/pp/01690965.html   DOI: 10.1080/01690960444000133

The English written language is a spatially rich orthography. That is, as compared with languages such as Chinese and Japanese, the vast majority of English words are separated by spaces. These interword spaces serve to make reading more efficient. Several eye movement studies (where a reader's eye position is monitored) have shown that when interword spaces are deleted (by either removing them altogether, or filling them in with other characters), reading is disrupted. Specifically, reading rates when the spaces between words are absent are slowed significantly relative to a standard condition where spaces are left intact (Fisher, 1976; Morris, Rayner, & Pollatsek, 1990; Pollatsek & Rayner, 1982; Rayner, Fischer & Pollatsek, 1998).

English does consist of certain instances where the space is deleted between two words, in order to create a single unified concept. For example, *dark room*, written as two free words (lexemes), refers to any room that may be dark. On the other hand, the spatially concatenated compound word *darkroom* refers to a specific type of room used for developing photographs. These spatially concatenated English compound words are usually relatively short, and rarely consist of more than two lexemes. Spatial concatenation is also usually only reserved for familiar, lexicalised two-word phrases. This is in contrast to other European languages, such as German, Finnish, and Dutch, which are more generative than English. These languages allow for the spatial concatenation of novel compound words. For example, in English a problem with data protection would be written as three separate words 'data protection problem' with interword spaces. In German, this would be written as a spatially concatenated novel compound, 'DatenSchutzProblem' (see Inhoff, Radach, & Heller, 2000). In addition, the spatial concatenation of compound words longer than two lexemes is much more common in these languages. It is plausible to suggest, therefore, that the processing of compound words may differ in English, which has specific instances of compound words, as compared to those other languages.

For instance, compound representations may be more closely tied to the representations of their lexemes in languages that permit the spatial concatenation of novel compound words, since readers would need to gain access to the meaning of the novel compound word's constituents to surmise its meaning. Therefore, lexical decomposition may be easily observed in such languages. In a language such as English, there are only a specific set of spatially concatenated compound words, many of which are not related to the meaning of their constituents (i.e., they have become opaque—such as the compound *deadline*). Therefore, the lexical entry for English compound words may have lost its connection to the entries for its constituents, and lexical decomposition may not be observed.

Recent research has suggested that this is not the case, however. Studies in both Finnish and English have manipulated the frequencies of a compound word's constituents, and monitored reader's eye movements while they read sentences containing these compounds. Past research has shown that how long readers fixate a word is influenced by the linguistic properties of the word, such as word frequency (Inhoff & Rayner, 1986; Rayner & Duffy, 1986; Rayner & Fischer, 1996; Rayner & Raney, 1996; Schilling, Rayner, & Chumbley, 1998). The logic behind these compound word studies is that if readers are decomposing the compounds into their constituents at some point during compound recognition, then the frequency of the component lexemes will affect fixation durations. If the compound is not being decomposed into its lexemes, no lexeme frequency effects will be observed. Evidence for lexical decomposition has been found in both a generative language such as Finnish (Bertram & Hyönä, 2003; Hyönä & Pollatsek, 1998; Pollatsek, Hyönä, & Bertram, 2000), as well as English (Andrews, Miller, & Rayner, 2004; Juhasz, Starr, Inhoff, & Placke, 2003). Therefore, it appears that even in English, lexical decomposition of compound words does occur.

The results of Hyönä and Pollatsek (1998) and Pollatsek et al. (2000) are particularly intriguing. They found an early but lasting effect of the first constituent frequency in Finnish bimorphemic compound words (effects were found on the first fixation on the compound, as well as when refixations on the compound were taken into account). The effect of second constituent frequency occurred only later, when refixations on the compound were taken into account. Similarly, the effect of whole compound frequency occurred at least as early as the effect of second constituent frequency. This suggests that processing of the first lexeme precedes processing of the second lexeme and that of the whole compound. A purely compositional model of compound word recognition (where the meaning of the compound is computed from the meaning of its lexemes) could not explain these results, as in these models whole compound frequency should not have an effect. Pollastek et al. (2000) interpreted their results in terms of a parallel race model of compound word recognition. In this model, there is a race between a whole-word lookup of the compound, and a compositional route. Access to the first constituent begins at least as early as access to the whole compound, with beginning lexeme effects occurring prior to whole word effects. Effects due to second lexeme frequency could overlap with effects due to whole word frequency and occur after access to the first constituent.

Inhoff et al. (2000) investigated a similar question as Hyönä and Pollatsek (1998) and Pollatsek et al. (2000). However, they took a different approach than the frequency manipulations previously described. Specifically, they manipulated the spacing of German trilexemic compound words in order to examine how it would affect compound processing. If compounds are decomposed into their constituent lexemes during processing, then interword spaces should facilitate this decomposition and result in faster compound recognition. There were several conditions, two of which consisted of the three lexemes in the compound written without interword spaces (which is grammatically regular in German) versus a condition where grammatically improper interword spaces were inserted between the three lexemes. Insertion of the unusual interword spaces resulted in significantly shorter naming latencies in a naming experiment and shorter first fixation durations and gaze durations in an eye movement experiment. However, if the compound was fixated three or four times, then the last fixation on the compound word was actually longer in the spaced condition. Inhoff et al. concluded that the spaces facilitated lexical decomposition (by providing a strong cue by which to segment the compound), but hindered readers' abilities to correctly compute the meaning of the compound word (which is essential for compound recognition).

Inhoff et al. (2000) noted that the effects they observed for German might not be observed in non-generative languages such as English. Since spatial concatenation of novel compounds is rare in English, interword spaces may not hamper proper meaning assignment to compound words, as novel spatially segmented compounds are often encountered and understood. However, they also offered the opposite prediction that the effects they observed are language-universal, much as lexical decomposition has been found to be.

The current study sought to determine whether sequential lexeme-to-compound processing also takes place during the reading of English compounds; that is, whether lexical decomposition precedes access to the whole compound form. The Hyönä and Pollatsek (1998) and Pollatsek et al. (2000) results suggest that decomposition of the compound precedes compound recognition, as beginning lexeme frequency effects were observed prior to whole compound frequency effects. Similarly, the Inhoff et al. (2000) study demonstrated an early effect of interword spaces, suggesting that interword spaces facilitate lexical decomposition of compounds, which precedes compound word meaning assignment.

The question of whether sequential lexeme-to-compound processing takes place in English is of theoretical interest as English differs from German and Finnish in that the generative forming of new spatially unified compounds is the exception rather than the rule. Furthermore, English differs from German and Finnish in that there is natural variation in the spacing of compounds; that is, the spatial composition of compounds can be manipulated without violating orthographic conventions. As mentioned previously, there is a specific set of familiar, lexicalised, spatially unified compound words in English (referred to as nonspaced compounds throughout the rest of the paper). English, unlike German or Finnish, also has cases of two-word phrases that refer to a single concept, are familiar, and which appear in dictionaries but which are always written with a space between the two words (referred to as spaced compounds throughout the paper). If lexeme-to-compound processing occurs in English, with segmentation preceding access to full compound meaning, then spacing should benefit the initial phase of compound processing, irrespective of the conventional form of these compounds. Spatial unification, by contrast, could benefit the specification of compound meaning, which may occur irrespective of the compound type (spaced vs. nonspaced).

In the following experiments both types of compounds (spaced and nonspaced) were presented to participants with either their correct spacing, or their incorrect spacing. Participants were asked either to make lexical decisions on these compounds (Experiments 1 and 2) or simply to read them in sentences, while their eye movements were monitored (Experiment 3 and 4). The use of the two tasks (lexical decision vs. sentence reading) allows a comparison between the role of spatial layout in a word-in-isolation task and normal silent reading. There are several reasons why the results may be different in these two tasks. For example, in lexical decision a word is presented in isolation, with no context, while in a sentence reading experiment the purpose is to combine each word in the sentence to form the meaning for the entire sentence. Also, in normal reading, parafoveal preview of the compound word is available. That is, readers obtain useful information to the right of the word that they are currently fixating (see Rayner, 1998 for a review of parafoveal preview effects). This thus speeds up processing of the parafoveal word once it is subsequently fixated. One type of parafoveal information that readers obtain is word length. Word length is a very important factor in determining where in a word readers' eyes will land. If the spaces between words are not available, saccade sizes are dramatically reduced (McConkie & Rayner, 1975; Pollatsek & Rayner, 1982; Rayner, 1986). The majority of first fixations on a word land somewhere between that word's beginning and middle (McConkie & Zola, 1984; O'Regan, 1981; Rayner, 1979). Therefore, whether a reader parafoveally identifies the upcoming word as long (in the case of a spatially unified compound) or short (the first lexeme in the case of a spaced compound) could affect their initial landing position on the compound, and thus processing time. This type of effect is not observable in lexical decision, but is very important during normal reading.

The final goal of this study was to compare the role of spatial layout for compounds in which both lexemes are nouns (e.g., *cornfield, earthquake*) with those in which the first lexeme is an adjective and the second lexeme is a noun (e.g., *highlight, softball*). The meaning of an adjective-noun compound may be more likely to change once a space is inserted between the two lexemes. For example, a *cornfield* means a field of corn whether it is written as '*cornfield*' or as '*corn field*'. On the other hand, *softball*, written as a spatially unified compound, refers to either a specific type of ball, or the sport in which the ball is used. A *soft ball*, with a space between the lexemes, can refer to any ball that happens to be soft. Since interword spaces could be more pivotal to the assignment of correct meaning for adjective-noun compounds, the pattern of results could be different for these compounds. Critically, spatial unification should not benefit compound reading when this hampers meaning specification, as may be the case for adjective-noun compounds.

EXPERIMENT 1: NOUN-NOUN COMPOUNDS IN LEXICAL DECISION

Method

Participants.   Thirty-two students from the Binghamton University community received credit for participating in this experiment, which went to fulfilling their psychology class requirements. All participants were native speakers of English and were naïve to the purpose of the experiment.

Apparatus.   The items were presented on a video monitor in white on a black background. If the letter string was word, participants were instructed to press the 'M' button on a QWERTY keyboard. If the letter string was a nonword, participants were instructed to press the 'Z' button on the same keyboard. Both buttons were labelled with either word or nonword, respectively. Lexical decision times were measured by the latency to push the correct button. Responses were recorded by a custom written program which measures reaction time, as well as which key the participant pressed for each trial. The temporal accuracy of the system is within 4 ms. Head position was not restrained but the monitor and keyboard were positioned so that a typical eye distance was around 80 centimeters and each character of text subtended approximately .33 degrees of visual angle.

Procedure.   Participants were tested individually. Participants rested their right index finger on the 'M' key that was labelled 'word' and they rested their left index finger on the 'Z' key that was labelled 'nonword'.

Each participant completed 105 trials. The nine initial trials were counted as practice trials and were not analysed. The practice consisted of both word compounds and nonword compounds. There were both spaced and non-spaced compounds that were shown with and without their proper spacing in the practice. Each trial began with a fixation marker '+' in the centre of the screen that lasted for 500 ms. After a 100 ms interval of blank screen, the target appeared. The target stayed on the screen until the participant made a decision. There was a 1500 ms intertrial interval. Participants were instructed that the dependent variables were accuracy and reaction time so they should respond as quickly and accurately as possible. They were also instructed that the only time they should classify a letter string as a nonword was when either the first or the second lexeme was actually a nonword. This instruction was needed to let the participants know that they should not respond 'nonword' if a compound looked awkward (e.g. when an item was presented with incorrect spatial layout).

Stimuli. There were 96 compound words in this experiment, 48 of which were normally nonspaced compounds and the remaining 48 were normally spaced compounds. In this experiment, both lexemes of each compound were nouns. All compounds were taken from the Celex English database (Baayen, Piepenbrock, & Gulikers, 1995). The 96 compounds were split into two lists so as to reduce the number of lexeme repetitions per list and to reduce the number of overall items that each participant would see. Each participant saw 48 compound words per list. Items that were presented with a space in lists 1 and 3 were presented without a space in lists 2 and 4. The opposite was also true. Twenty-four of the compound words per list were normally presented without a space in the English language (*bookcase*). The other 24 per list were normally presented with a space between the two lexemes in the English language but still represented a single concept (*rush hour*). Within each list, half of the compounds were presented with their proper spacing (*bookcase, rush hour*) and the other half were shown with improper spacing (*book case, rushhour*). The type of presentation (correct or incorrect) was counter-balanced between lists 1 and 2 and between lists 3 and 4.

The nonwords in this experiment consisted of compound words (spaced and nonspaced) where either the first or second lexeme was altered to form a new orthographically legal nonword. There were 48 compound nonwords in each of the lists. These nonwords were the same for each list. Twenty-four of the nonwords were created by changing a few letters in a nonspaced compound. Twelve of the non-spaced compounds had their beginning lexeme changed to a nonword (e.g., *birkbook*). The other 12 had their ending lexeme changed to a nonword (e.g., *doorklib*). The other 24 compounds were created by changing a few letters in a spaced compound. Again, in 12 of the nonwords, the first lexeme was changed into a nonword (e.g., *huke front*). The other 12 were created by changing the second lexeme into a nonword (e.g., *fruit bip*).

Results

The data were analysed using a 2 (compound type: spaced or nonspaced) × 2 (compound presentation: correct or incorrect) Analysis of Variance (ANOVA). Error variance was computed over participants (F_1) and over items (F_2). Compound type and compound presentation were both treated as within-participants variables in the F_1 analyses. In the F_2 analyses compound type was considered a between-items variable while compound presentation was considered a within-items variable. There were two dependent measures, lexical decision times (LDTs) to correctly identified items and error rates.

Table 1 shows the mean LDTs and errors as a function of the four conditions. There was a significant main effect of compound type, $F_1(1, 31) = 88.21, p < .001, F_2(1, 94) = 10.20, p < .003$. Compounds which are usually spelled without a space were responded to 78 ms faster than compounds which are usually shown with a space. There was also a significant main effect of correctness, $F_1(1, 31) = 6.10, p < .02, F_2(1, 94) = 15.36, p < .001$. Compounds presented in their correct spatial layout were responded to 32 ms faster than compounds shown in an incorrect spatial layout. However, these two main effects were qualified by a significant interaction $F_1(1, 31) = 35.56, p < .001, F_2(1, 94) = 20.94, p < .001$. While compounds that are normally spelled with a space were responded to 95 ms faster if they were presented correctly (i.e., with a space), compounds that are normally presented without a space were actually responded to with 30 ms shorter LDTs if they were presented incorrectly (i.e., with a space). Planned contrasts showed that while the 95 ms correctness effect was significant for the spaced compounds, $t_1(31) = -5.31, p < .001, t_2(47) = -4.60, p < .001$, the 30 ms reverse correctness effect for the nonspaced compounds was marginal in the participants analysis, $t_1(31) = 1.91, p = .065$, and was not significant in the items analysis, $t_2(47) = 1.29, p > .20$.

The results of the analysis on error rates mirrored those on the LDTs. There were 4.9% more errors to compounds which are usually spelled with

TABLE 1

Lexical decision times (LDT- in ms) and percentage of errors as a function of compound type and presentation for Experiment 1 (noun-noun compounds)

Type	Presentation	Example	LDT	Errors
Nonspaced	Correct	bookcase	669 (105)	5.47 (8.36)
Nonspaced	Incorrect	book case	639 (114)	4.17 (10.79)
Spaced	Correct	rush hour	685 (118)	4.17 (9.70)
Spaced	Incorrect	rushhour	780 (160)	15.36 (13.41)

Note: Numbers in parentheses represent the standard deviations.

a space, $F_1(1, 31) = 14.74, p < .002, F_2(1, 94) = 5.92, p < .02$. There was also a significant main effect of presentation correctness, $F_1(1, 31) = 16.88, p < .001, F_2(1, 94) = 10.18, p < .003$, with 4.95% more errors being made to incorrectly spaced compounds. The interaction between compound type and compound presentation was again significant, $F_1(1, 31) = 14.68, p < .002, F_2(1, 94) = 16.42, p < .001$. Compounds that are normally spelled with a space received 11% fewer errors if they were presented correctly, $t_1(31) = -4.95, p < .001$; $t_2(47) = -4.73, p < .001$. There was no significant difference in error rates for normally nonspaced compounds shown correctly versus incorrectly (both $ps > .4$).

Discussion

The results of Experiment 1 are straightforward. Interword spaces resulted in decreased noun-noun compound word recognition time, as well as fewer errors. This was even true if the compound word was supposed to be presented without a space (as evidenced by the significant crossover interaction between compound type and presentation correctness). These results therefore replicate Inhoff et al.'s (2000) finding that naming latencies decreased when spaces were inserted between the lexemes in long German compounds. However, when compounds that were supposed to be spaced were presented incorrectly (i.e., without a space), they became very difficult for participants to distinguish from the nonwords, as shown by the inflated error rates in this condition.

EXPERIMENT 2: ADJECTIVE-NOUN COMPOUNDS IN LEXICAL DECISION

Method

Participants.   An additional 32 students from the Binghamton University community participated in this experiment.

Apparatus.   Same as in Experiment 1.

Procedure.   Same as in Experiment 1.

Stimuli.   As in Experiment 1, there were 96 compound words in this experiment, half of which are normally nonspaced and half of which are normally spaced. In this experiment, the first lexeme of all compounds was an adjective while the second lexeme was a noun. The assignment of items to lists was the same as in Experiment 1. Also, the same nonwords were used as in Experiment 1.

TABLE 2
Lexical decision times (LDT- in ms) and percentage of errors as a function of
compound type and presentation for Experiment 2 (adjective-noun compounds)

Type	Presentation	Example	LDT	Errors
Nonspaced	Correct	softball	688 (105)	6.25 (8.98)
Nonspaced	Incorrect	soft ball	674 (107)	2.63 (5.80)
Spaced	Correct	front door	659 (108)	6.27 (7.34)
Spaced	Incorrect	frontdoor	723 (117)	11.74 (10.55)

Note: Numbers in parentheses represent the standard deviations.

Results

The data were analysed in the same manner as in Experiment 1. Table 2 shows the mean LDTs and errors as a function of the four conditions. For adjective-noun compounds, there was no significant difference between type of compounds ($ps > .1$). There was a significant main effect of presentation correctness, $F_1(1, 31) = 6.97, p < .02, F_2(1, 94) = 4.97, p < .03$. Compounds presented in their correct spatial layout were responded to 25 ms faster, on average, than compounds shown in an incorrect spatial layout. There was also a significant interaction between compound type and presentation correctness, $F_1(1, 31) = 16.72, p < .001, F_2(1, 94) = 6.87, p < .02$. Compounds that are normally spelled with a space were responded to 64 ms faster if they were presented correctly, $t_1(31) = -4.24, p < .001$; $t_2(47) = -3.37, p < .003$. Compounds that are normally presented without a space were actually responded to 15 ms slower if they were presented correctly (i.e., without a space), although this difference did not reach significance ($ps > .2$).

There were 4.6% more errors to compounds that are usually spelled with a space. This difference was significant in the participants analysis, $F_1(1, 31) = 23.43, p < .001$), but not by items ($p > .1$). The main effect of presentation correctness was not significant ($ps > .1$). However, the interaction between compound type and compound presentation was again significant, $F_1(1, 31) = 15.02, p < .001, F_2(1, 94) = 3.93, p = .05$. Compounds that are normally spelled with a space received 5% fewer errors if they were presented correctly, $t_1(31) = -3.14, p < .005$; $t_2(47) = -2.48, p < .02$. Compounds which are normally spelled without a space received approximately 4% more errors if they were presented correctly, this difference was significant by participants, $t_1(31) = 2.59, p < .02$, but not by items.

Discussion

The results of Experiment 2, using adjective-noun compounds, were remarkably similar to those of the noun-noun compounds in Experiment 1. One difference was that there was no effect of compound type for adjective-noun compounds. However, the most important finding, a crossover interaction between compound type and presentation correctness, was again significant. Therefore, the role of interword spaces appears to benefit lexical decision performance for both noun-noun and adjective-noun compounds. However, since the nonwords used in both experiments were compounds where only one of the lexemes was changed into a nonword, participants may have evaluated each lexeme individually to see if it made up a word before making their decision. This can be seen as an advantage, as the task provides insight into one hypothesised stage of compound processing, the accessing of constituent (lexeme) meaning. However, note that if this is the case, participants would not need to combine the meaning of the two lexemes into the compound and interword spaces should definitely facilitate this strategy. Thus, the lexical decision task may produce a different pattern of results than that seen in sentence reading. The motivation for Experiment 3 and 4 was to determine if the pattern of results from the two lexical decision experiments would generalise to sentence reading.

EXPERIMENT 3: NOUN-NOUN COMPOUNDS AND EYE MOVEMENTS

Method

Participants.   Thirty-two members of the University of Massachusetts community participated. They either received extra credit for a psychology class or were paid 5–8 dollars for their participation. All participants were native speakers of American English, were naïve to the purpose of the experiment, and had 20/20 vision or contacts.

Apparatus.   A Fourward Technologies Dual Purkinje eye tracker (Generation VI) was used to record participants' eye movements. Eye movements were only measured from the right eye but viewing was binocular. The eye tracker has a resolution of less than 10 minutes of arc and was interfaced with an IBM compatible computer. Participants were seated 61 cm from the computer. One degree of visual angle equalled approximately 3.8 characters. The sentences were displayed on a 15-inch NEC MultiSync 4FG monitor.

Procedure. Before the experiment, participants had a bite bar prepared for them that served to reduce head movements. Instructions detailing the procedure were provided to each participant. A single-line calibration routine was performed. The accuracy of the calibration was checked after each sentence and where necessary a new calibration routine was performed. Comprehension was checked on approximately 10–15% of trials during the experiment by presenting the participant with a question that they could answer yes or no. Accuracy was over 95%.

Stimuli. Individual sentences were written for each of the 96 noun-noun compounds used in Experiment 1. The compound never occupied the beginning or last two words in the sentence. A group of 10 students from the University of Massachusetts rated how well each compound fit into the sentences on a 1–7 scale, with higher numbers signalling a better fit. The mean goodness-of-fit was 6.19 for nonspaced compounds and 6.04 for spaced compounds. These means did not differ significantly from each other ($p > .3$). A separate group of 10 raters from the University of Massachusetts was provided with the beginning of each sentence and was asked to provide a word (or two-word phrase) that could fit as the next word in the sentence. The average compound predictability was 2.1% for nonspaced compounds and 1.7% for the spaced compounds, which did not differ significantly from each other ($p > .3$).

Results

As with the lexical decision data, 2 (compound type: spaced or nonspaced) × 2 (compound presentation: correct or incorrect) ANOVAs were conducted separately for participants (F_1) and items (F_2). Compound type and compound presentation were again both treated as within-participants variables in the F_1 analyses. In the F_2 analyses compound type was considered a between-items variable while compound presentation was considered a within-items variable.

Eye tracking data yield many interesting measures that give a detailed picture of how word processing unfolds over time. For this experiment, four dependent measures were analysed, all of which deal with how the compound is processed the first time it is fixated (called first-pass measures). First fixation duration is the duration of the first fixation on the target region, irrespective of how many fixations the target receives. Gaze duration is the sum of all fixations on the target region prior to the eyes leaving the word. Two additional measures that are reported are the number of first pass fixations and the landing position of the first fixation in

TABLE 3

First fixation duration (FF), gaze duration (GD), number of first-pass fixations (NF) and the landing position of the first fixation (FFP) as a function of compound type and presentation for Experiment 3 (noun-noun compounds)

Type	Presentation	Example	FF	GD	NF	FFP
Nonspaced	Correct	bookcase	286 (42)	363 (66)	1.32 (.22)	3.59 (.57)
Nonspaced	Incorrect	book case	265 (37)	438 (84)	1.66 (.24)	3.23 (.61)
Spaced	Correct	rush hour	267 (41)	450 (72)	1.76 (.21)	3.22 (.61)
Spaced	Incorrect	rushhour	290 (47)	432 (113)	1.54 (.31)	3.80 (.50)

Note: Numbers in parentheses represent the standard deviations.

the target region.[1] Table 3 shows the means for these dependent measures as a function of the four conditions.

For first fixation duration, neither main effect was significant (all $ps > .2$). The interaction between type of compound (spaced or nonspaced) and presentation (correct or incorrect) was significant, $F_1(1, 31) = 39.40$, $p < .001$; $F_2(1, 94) = 48.10$, $p < .001$. First fixations on compounds that should normally be nonspaced were 21 ms shorter if they were shown incorrectly (i.e., with a space), $t_1(31) = 5.47$, $p < .001$; $t_2(47) = 4.42$, $p < .001$. First fixations on compounds that should normally be spaced were 24 ms shorter if they were shown correctly (i.e., with a space), $t_1(31) = -4.67$, $p < .001$; $t_2(47) = -5.45$, $p < .001$.

For gaze duration, there was a main effect of type of compound, $F_1(1, 31) = 48.28$, $p < .001$; $F_2(1, 94) = 11.75$, $p < .002$. Compounds that should be nonspaced received 40 ms shorter gaze durations. There was also a main effect of presentation, $F_1(1, 31) = 11.21$, $p < .003$; $F_2(1, 94) = 15.46$, $p < .001$. On average, correctly spaced compounds received 28 ms shorter gaze durations. However, these main effects were qualified by a significant crossover interaction, $F_1(1, 31) = 21.97$, $p < .001$; $F_2(1, 94) = 43.97$, $p < .001$). The nature of this interaction was opposite of that found in first fixation duration. If a compound is supposed to be nonspaced, gaze durations were 75 ms shorter if it was shown in its correct spacing (i.e., without a space), $t_1(31) = -7.06$, $p < .001$; $t_2(47) = -7.58$, $p < .001$. However, if the compound is supposed to be spaced, gaze durations were actually shorter if it was shown incorrectly (i.e., without a space). However, this 19 ms difference did not reach significance ($ps > .05$).

---

[1] Single fixation duration (the duration of the first fixation on the compound if it receives only a single fixation) was also analysed. It showed a significant crossover interaction that was in the same direction as first fixation duration for both the noun-noun and adjective-noun compounds.

Number of first pass fixations showed the same pattern of results as gaze duration. There was a main effect of type of compound, $F_1(1, 31) = 49.54$, $p < .001$; $F_2(1, 94) = 15.50$, $p < .001$. Compounds which should be nonspaced received fewer first pass fixations. There was also a main effect of presentation, $F_1(1, 31) = 4.85$, $p < .04$; $F_2(1, 94) = 5.83$, $p < .02$. On average, correctly spaced compounds received fewer first pass fixations. However, these main effects were again qualified by a significant interaction, $F_1(1, 31) = 51.59$, $p < .001$; $F_2(1, 94) = 124.88$, $p < .001$. If a compound was supposed to be nonspaced, it received fewer first pass fixations if it was shown in its correct spacing, $t_1(31) = -7.86$, $p < .001$; $t_2(47) = -9.24$, $p < .001$. However, if the compound is supposed to be spaced, it received fewer first pass fixations if it was shown incorrectly (i.e., without a space), $t_1(31) = 3.91$, $p < .001$; $t_2(47) = 6.46$, $p < .001$.

Finally, for initial landing position, there was only a significant interaction, $F_1(1, 31) = 31.30$, $p < .001$; $F_2(1, 94) = 48.10$, $p < .001$. If a compound was supposed to be nonspaced, first fixations landed further into it if it was shown in its correct spacing, $t_1(31) = 3.77$, $p < .002$; $t_2(47) = 4.42$, $p < .001$. However, if the compound was supposed to be spaced, first fixations landed further into it if it was shown incorrectly (i.e., without a space), $t_1(31) = -4.78$, $p < .001$; $t_2(47) = -5.45$, $p < .001$.[2]

ANCOVAs.   It is possible that other properties either of the compound words themselves, or of the way the compound words fit in the sentence influenced the observed pattern of results. In order to assess the robustness of the preceding results, ANCOVAs were performed on the item means. Three measures were covaried out simultaneously. These were compound transparency (rated by 20 Binghamton University undergraduates on a 1–7 scale with higher ratings indicating more transparency), compound familiarity (rated by 15 University of Massachusetts undergraduates on a 1–7 scale with higher numbers indicating more familiarity), and the

---

[2] Correct spatial presentation for these items was defined as how the compounds appeared in the Celex English database (Baayen et al., 1995). However, the results of this study could be compromised if the participants did not agree with how the compounds are supposed to be spaced. Therefore, 13 University of Massachusetts students who did not participate in any aspect of any of the experiments reported were provided with each compound, both with and without a space, and asked to circle how the compound was supposed to spaced. Items in which 50% or more of the participants did not agree with how correct spatial layout was defined in this study were removed. In addition to this, some compounds were removed due to a familiarity rating of less than 4 on a 7 point scale. In all, this led to the removal of 28 items (20 nonspaced and 8 spaced). Participants and items analyses were then rerun on the subset of stimuli. Importantly, the main result (a crossover interaction between compound type and presentation) was still significant for this restricted subset of items.

plausibility of the compound's first lexeme given the beginning of each sentence (rated by 17 University of Massachusetts undergraduates on a 1–7 scale with higher numbers indicating greater plausibility).

For first fixation duration, the interaction was still significant in the ANCOVA, $F_2(1, 91) = 37.39$, $p < .001$. As in the original analysis, compounds received shorter first fixation durations if they were shown with a space (irregardless of how they were supposed to be spaced). For gaze duration, both main effects were no longer significant when the covariates were included in the analysis. However, the interaction between compound type and presentation was still significant, $F_2 (1, 91) = 37.96$, $p < .001$. Compounds that were presented without a space received shorter gaze durations (irregardless of how they were supposed to be spaced). For the number of first pass fixations, the only significant effect in the ANCOVA was the interaction between compound type and presentation, $F_2(1, 91) = 107.03$, $p < .001$. Compounds received fewer first pass fixations if they were shown without a space (irregardless of how they should have been spaced). Finally, there was still a significant interaction for initial landing position, $F_2(1, 91) = 31.10$, $p < .001$. First fixations landed further into the compound if it was presented without a space (irregardless of how it is supposed to be spaced).

Supplemental analyses.   In more than half of the cases readers did not fixate both lexemes in the compound word. This fact can be obscured when looking at the whole compound as the region of analysis. Therefore, analyses were performed using the second lexeme as the region of analyses and only including cases where the first lexeme of the compound was fixated. Means from these analyses can be found in Table 4.

If the first lexeme was fixated, the probability of fixating the second lexeme was 7% higher if the compound was supposed to be spaced, $F_1(1, 31) = 13.31$, $p < .001$; $F_2(1, 94) = 5.58$, $p < .03$. This main effect was also qualified by a significant interaction, $F_1(1, 31) = 87.98$, $p < .001$; $F_2(1, 94) =$

TABLE 4
First fixation duration (FF), gaze duration (GD), and the probability of fixating (Prob.) the second lexeme, given that the first lexeme was fixated as a function of compound type and presentation for Experiment 3 (noun-noun compounds)

Type	Presentation	Example	FF	GD	Prob.
Nonspaced	Correct	bookcase	231 (62)	236 (67)	33 (18)
Nonspaced	Incorrect	book *case*	261 (44)	276 (50)	69 (17)
Spaced	Correct	rush *hour*	250 (45)	261 (46)	74 (16)
Spaced	Incorrect	rush*hour*	256 (50)	268 (60)	43 (25)

Note: Numbers in parentheses represent the standard deviations.

318.01, $p < .001$. For both types of compounds, the probability of fixating the second lexeme was much lower if the compound was presented without a space, as opposed to with a space.

First fixations on the second lexeme of the compound were 18 ms longer if the compound was presented incorrectly, $F_1(1, 31) = 7.73$, $p < .01$; $F_2(1, 93) = 18.22$, $p < .001$. The interaction between compound type and presentation was marginally significant in the participants analysis, $F_1(1, 31) = 3.47$, $p = .072$, but not significant by items ($p > .2$). The nature of the interaction was that for nonspaced compounds there was a large effect of presentation correctness (30 ms), while for spaced compounds the effect was smaller (5 ms).

The analyses for the gaze duration on the second lexeme, given that the first lexeme was fixated, mirrored those above. There was a significant 24 ms effect of presentation correctness, $F_1(1, 31) = 13.23$, $p < .001$; $F_2(1, 93) = 14.46$, $p < .001$. There was also a significant interaction between compound type and compound presentation in the participants analysis, $F_1(1, 31) = 4.18$, $p < .05$, showing a larger (40 ms) correctness effect for nonspaced compounds as compared with spaced compounds (7 ms). This interaction failed to reach significance in the items analysis ($p > .3$).

Discussion

The results from Experiment 3 are very interesting, as they demonstrate a complex relationship between compound spacing and compound recognition during the course of normal reading. The most important findings were the crossover interactions between compound type and presentation. The first fixation on a compound was shorter if the compound was shown with a space, irrespective of whether the compound was supposed to be spaced or not. This finding replicates the lexical decision data, as well as the first fixation data of Inhoff et al. (2000) in German. It is possible that first fixations may tap into an earlier process than gaze duration, when refixations are taken into account (Inhoff & Radach, 1998; Rayner, 1998). First fixation durations thus show that the accessing of constituent meaning is a functional stage of compound processing during normal sentence reading.

However, the story changes when refixations on the compound are taken into account. Gaze durations on both types of compounds were actually shorter if the compound was presented without a space (irrespective of how it should be spaced). This finding is similar to Inhoff et al.'s (2000) finding that the last fixation on spatially unified German compounds was shorter than if the spaces were inserted between the lexemes. This effect most likely occurred earlier during the current study as compared to Inhoff et al.'s study due to the fact that the current compounds were shorter (only consisting of two lexemes) compared to Inhoff et al.'s German compounds (which consisted of three lexemes).

If the compound word was presented as spatially unified, readers landed further into the word, more towards its centre, or optimal viewing position (O'Regan, 1981; Rayner, 1979). They were therefore less likely to refixate the word in these cases. This is evidenced by fewer first pass fixations when the compound was written without spaces. Also, readers were much less likely to fixate the second lexeme, once the first lexeme had been fixated, if the compound was written as a spatially unified compound.

Another interpretation of the results is that including interword spaces in a normally nonspaced noun-noun compound results in significant disruption in reading, when refixations on the compound are taken into account. However, whether a space was provided between a normally spaced noun-noun compound did not seem to matter much. It resulted in significantly fewer first pass fixations. This led to shorter gaze durations, but the difference was not significant. When only time spent on the second lexeme was taken into account, there was a slight effect of spatial correctness for the normally spaced compounds, but this difference was small (5 ms in first fixations and 7 ms in gaze). Therefore, while readers appear sensitive to the correct spatial layout of normally nonspaced noun-noun compounds, the same is not true of normally spaced compounds.

Experiment 4 addressed the question of whether the pattern of results would be the same for adjective-noun compound words. As mentioned in the introduction, more disruption for the insertion of interword spaces into normally nonspaced adjective-noun compound could occur, because interword spaces are more important for determining correct compound meaning in the case of adjective-noun compounds.

EXPERIMENT 4: ADJECTIVE-NOUN COMPOUNDS AND EYE MOVEMENTS

Method

Participants.   An additional 28 members of the University of Massachusetts community, who did not participate in any aspect of Experiment 3, participated. They either received extra credit for a psychology class or were paid 5–8 dollars for their participation. All participants were native speakers of American English, were naïve to the purpose of the experiment and had 20/20 vision or contacts.

Apparatus.   The apparatus was identical to that used in Experiment 3.

Procedure.   The procedure was identical to Experiment 3.

Stimuli. Individual sentences were written for each of the 96 adjective-noun compounds used in Experiment 2. The compound never occupied the beginning or last two words in the sentence. A group of 10 students from the University of Massachusetts rated how well each compound fit into the sentences on a 1–7 scale, with higher numbers signalling a better fit. The mean goodness-of-fit was 5.94 for nonspaced compounds and 6.09 for spaced compounds. These means did not differ significantly from each other ($p > .3$). A separate group of 10 raters from the University of Massachusetts was provided with the beginning of each sentence and was asked to provide a word (or two-word phrase) that could fit as the next word in the sentence. The average compound predictability was .63% for nonspaced compounds and .42% for the spaced compounds, which did not differ significantly from each other ($p > .6$).

Results

The data for the adjective-noun compounds were analysed in the same manner as the noun-noun compounds. Means can be seen in Table 5.

For first fixation duration there was a significant effect of presentation, $F_1(1, 27) = 7.32, p < .015; F_2(1, 94) = 6.86, p < .02$. Compounds presented correctly received 8 ms shorter first fixation durations on average. The interaction between type of compound (spaced or nonspaced) and presentation (correct or incorrect) was also significant, $F_1(1, 27) = 29.65, p < .015; F_2(1, 94) = 46.35, p < .001$. First fixations on compounds that should normally be nonspaced were 15 ms shorter if they were shown incorrectly (i.e., with a space), $t_1(27) = 2.72, p < .015; t_2(47) = 2.80, p < .01$. First fixations on compounds that should normally be spaced were 33 ms shorter if they were shown correctly (i.e., with a space), $t_1(27) = -6.11, p < .001; t_2(47) = -7.09, p < .001$.

For gaze duration, there was a main effect of presentation, $F_1(1, 27) = 30.92, p < .001; F_2(1, 94) = 37.60, p < .001$. On average, correctly spaced

TABLE 5
First fixation duration (FF), gaze duration (GD), number of first-pass fixations (NF) and the landing position of the first fixation (FFP) as a function of compound type and presentation for Experiment 4 (adjective-noun compounds)

Type	Presentation	Example	FF	GD	NF	FFP
Nonspaced	Correct	softball	303 (41)	401 (84)	1.38 (.31)	3.62 (.70)
Nonspaced	Incorrect	soft ball	288 (36)	497 (84)	1.80 (.29)	3.08 (.72)
Spaced	Correct	front door	276 (36)	463 (89)	1.73 (.30)	3.15 (.65)
Spaced	Incorrect	frontdoor	308 (40)	462 (121)	1.57 (.40)	3.69 (.66)

Note: Numbers in parentheses represent the standard deviations.

compounds received 48 ms shorter gaze durations. However, this main effect was qualified by a significant interaction, $F_1(1, 27) = 18.17, p < .001$; $F_2(1, 94) = 37.82, p < .001$. If a compound was supposed to be nonspaced, gaze durations were 96 ms shorter if it was shown in its correct spacing (i.e., without a space), $t_1(27) = -7.57, p < .001; t_2(47) = -9.69, p < .001$. However, there was no difference for correctly and incorrectly presented spaced compounds ($ps > .9$).

For number of first pass fixations there was a main effect of type of compound that was significant in the participants analysis, $F_1(1, 27) = 5.01$, $p < .035$, but not in the items analysis, $F_2(1, 94) = 2.57, p > .10$. Compounds which should be nonspaced received fewer first pass fixations. There was also a main effect of presentation, $F_1(1, 27) = 17.31, p < .001; F_2(1, 94) = 19.52, p < .001$. On average, correctly spaced compounds received fewer first pass fixations. However, these main effects were qualified by a significant interaction, $F_1(1, 27) = 31.65, p < .001; F_2(1, 94) = 103.23, p < .001$. If a compound is supposed to be nonspaced, it received fewer first pass fixations if it was shown in its correct spacing, $t_1(27) = -6.97, p < .001$; $t_2(47) = -11.56, p < .001$. However, if the compound is supposed to be spaced, it received fewer first pass fixations if it was shown incorrectly (without a space), $t_1(27) = 2.56, p < .02; t_2(47) = 3.70, p < .002$.

Finally, for initial landing position, there was only a significant interaction, $F_1(1, 27) = 20.09, p < .001; F_2(1, 94) = 44.97, p < .001$. If a compound was supposed to be nonspaced, first fixations landed further into it if it was shown in its correct spacing, $t_1(27) = 3.66, p < .002; t_2(47) = 5.38, p < .001$. However, if the compound was supposed to be spaced, first fixations landed further into it if it was shown incorrectly (without a space), $t_1(27) = -3.56, p < .002; t_2(47) = -4.29, p < .001$.[3]

ANCOVAs. As with the noun-noun compounds, ANCOVAs were used to covary out any effects due to familiarity, transparency, and first lexeme plausibility. For first fixation duration, the interaction was still significant in the ANCOVA, $F_2(1, 91) = 40.22, p < .001$. As in the original analysis, compounds received shorter first fixation durations if they were shown with a space (irregardless of how they are supposed to be spaced). For gaze duration, the interaction between compound type and presentation was the only significant effect in the ANCOVA, $F_2(1, 91) = 33.76$, $p < .001$. Normally nonspaced compounds received shorter gaze durations

---

[3] A separate group 20 University of Massachusetts undergraduates were asked to circle the correct spacing for the 96 adjective-noun compounds used in Experiments 2 and 4. Using the same criteria as for the noun-noun compounds, 16 items were removed (9 nonspaced and 7 spaced). As with the noun-noun stimuli, the crossover interactions were still significant for this restricted set of stimuli.

if they were presented correctly, while there was almost no difference between correctly and incorrectly presented spaced compounds. For the number of first pass fixations, the main effect of type of compound (spaced or nonspaced) was significant when the three variables were covaried out, $F_2(1, 91) = 4.76, p < .035$. Compounds which should be nonspaced received fewer first pass fixations, on average, compared with compounds that should be spaced. There was also a significant interaction between compound type and presentation, $F_2(1, 91) = 93.53, p < .001$. Compounds received fewer first pass fixations if they were shown without a space (regardless of how they should have been spaced). Finally, there was still a significant interaction for initial landing position, $F_2(1, 91) = 34.37, p < .001$. First fixations landed further into the compound if it was presented without a space (irregardless of how it is supposed to be spaced).

Supplemental analyses. As with the noun-noun compounds, supplemental analyses were performed. The second lexeme was treated as the unit of analysis and only trials where the first lexeme was fixated were analysed. The means from these analyses can be seen in Table 6.

If the first lexeme was fixated, the probability of fixating the second lexeme was 5% higher if the compound was supposed to be spaced, $F_1(1, 27) = 5.67, p < .03$. However, this effect was not significant in the items analysis ($p > .1$). There was also a main effect of presentation that was not significant in the participants analysis, but was significant by items, $F_2(1, 94) = 4.14, p < .05$. These main effects were also qualified by a significant interaction, $F_1(1, 27) = 130.13, p < .001; F_2(1, 94) = 367.50, p < .001$. For both types of compounds, the probability of fixating the second lexeme was much lower if the compound was presented without a space, as opposed to with a space.

For first fixation durations on the second lexeme, the interaction between compound type and presentation was significant, $F_1(1, 23) = 18.42, p < .001; F_2(1, 91) = 21.16, p < .001$. For compounds that are

TABLE 6

First fixation duration (FF), gaze duration (GD), and the probability of fixating (Prob.) the second lexeme, given that the first lexeme was fixated as a function of compound type and presentation for Experiment 4 (adjective-noun compounds)

Type	Presentation	Example	FF	GD	Prob.
Nonspaced	Correct	soft*ball*	248 (50)	264 (68)	30 (18)
Nonspaced	Incorrect	soft *ball*	271 (36)	283 (32)	68 (23)
Spaced	Correct	front *door*	262 (42)	274 (44)	70 (21)
Spaced	Incorrect	front*door*	239 (44)	251 (56)	38 (19)

Note: Numbers in parentheses represent the standard deviations.

supposed to be nonspaced, the second lexeme received 23 ms shorter first fixation durations if it was presented correctly, $t_1(23) = -3.02, p < .007$; $t_2(46) = -4.42, p < .001$. For compounds that are supposed to be spaced, the second lexeme received 23 ms shorter first fixation durations if it was presented incorrectly, $t_1(23) = 3.46, p < .003$; $t_2(45) = 2.10, p < .05$.

Gaze durations on the second lexeme were 12 ms shorter if the compound was supposed to be spaced. This difference was marginally significant by participants, $F_1(1, 23) = 3.80, p = .064$, but not significant by items ($p > .1$). There was also a significant interaction, $F_1(1, 23) = 7.48, p < .015$; $F_2(1, 91) = 11.48, p < .002$. Gaze durations on the second lexeme were 18 ms shorter for nonspaced compounds presented correctly, as compared to incorrectly, $t_1(23) = -1.83, p = .080$; $t_2(46) = -4.47, p < .001$. For spaced compounds, gaze durations on the second lexeme were shorter if the compound was presented incorrectly, $t_1(23) = 2.66, p = .014$; $t_2(45) = 1.51$, $p = .138$.

Discussion

Similar to the noun-noun compounds, interword spaces resulted in shorter first fixation durations for adjective-noun compound words. However, interword spaces also resulted in an earlier initial landing position and thus a greater number of first pass fixations. For adjective-noun compounds that are supposed to be nonspaced, insertion of interword spaces resulted in inflated gaze durations, suggesting that people are sensitive to the correct spatial layout of these compounds. In fact, as predicted, the size of this disruption (96 ms in gaze duration) was larger than that observed for normally nonspaced noun-noun compounds (75 ms). This suggests that readers find it more difficult to combine the meaning of a normally nonspaced adjective-noun compound once a space has been inserted between its lexemes compared to the noun-noun compounds.

As with the noun-noun compounds, insertion or deletion of the interword spaces for normally spaced adjective-noun compounds did not seem to matter too much. While first fixations did land significantly farther into normally spaced compounds if they were presented incorrectly, there was almost no difference between correct and incorrect presentations for spaced compounds in gaze duration. When only the second lexeme was analysed, a small advantage was seen for the deletion of interword spaces in the case of spaced compounds.

GENERAL DISCUSSION

Our discussion of the results of the studies will be divided into four parts: (1) comparison of the results from lexical decision and eye movement experiments, (2) comparison of the results from noun-noun and adjective-noun compounds, (3) comparison of the results from the use of spaces for English compound words and German, and (4) implications for processing of compound words.

Comparison of the results from the two tasks

For both types of compounds, lexical decision reaction times as well as error rates showed an advantage for the insertion of interword spaces. Due to the nature of the compound nonwords used in the lexical decision experiments, participants needed to assess both constituents of each compound in order to make a correct lexical decision. The demands of constituent processing are thus exaggerated in such a task. However, it is clear by examining the lexical decision data that spatial segmentation facilitates constituent processing. If constituent processing is the first step in compound word recognition, one should also see a benefit for spatial segmentation the first time a compound word is fixated in the sentence reading task. This is exactly what was found for first fixation durations on both noun-noun and adjective-noun compounds. Thus, the lexical decision data and the first fixation data converge in demonstrating a beneficial role of spatial segmentation in constituent processing. However, other processing measures during sentence reading (such as gaze duration) showed a cost to spatial segmentation that was not apparent by examining the lexical decision data. These results will be interpreted in more detail below.

Comparison of the results from noun-noun and adjective-noun compounds

Overall, the qualitative pattern of results was remarkably similar between noun-noun and adjective-noun compounds. Both types of compounds showed a benefit for the insertion of interword spaces for lexical decision and first fixation durations. For both types of compounds, fixations landed further into the compound if it was presented without a space, irrespective of how it should be spaced. For both types of compounds, normally spaced compounds were not benefited or disrupted too much by the insertion or deletion of interword spaces. The processing of normally nonspaced compounds was disrupted when a space was inserted between its lexemes in gaze duration for both types of compounds.

What differed between noun-noun and adjective-noun compounds was the size of the disruption observed in gaze durations that resulted from inserting a space into a normally nonspaced compound. This disruption was larger for adjective-noun compounds. Spatial segmentation should only benefit compound processing when it does not disrupt meaning assignment for the entire compound. As discussed in the introduction, inserting a space into a normally nonspaced noun-noun compound does not change the meaning of the compounded expression nearly as much as inserting a space into a normally nonspaced adjective-noun compound. Therefore, the fact that the size of the disruption was larger for adjective-noun compounds fits with our predictions. The larger spacing effect for adjective-noun compounds also fits the overall pattern of results according to which spatial configuration serves as a cue for the specification of compound meaning. Future research should address other differences and/or similarities between adjective-noun and noun-noun compounds.

Comparison of the results to German

The pattern of results observed for normally nonspaced compounds was very similar to that observed by Inhoff et al. (2000) in German. Insertion of interword spaces was seen to facilitate lexical decision and first fixation duration, but hindered later aspects of processing, once refixations were taken into account. While Inhoff et al. only found interword spaces to hinder very late first-pass processing (when the third or fourth fixation was taken into account), it is not surprising that we observed it earlier as our compounds were on average shorter (only two lexemes as opposed to Inhoff et al.'s which had three lexemes). Inhoff and Radach (2002) also report a similar study examining the use of hyphens for the processing of bilexemic noun-noun German compounds. The compound could either be presented in sentences as spatially unified, or else with a hyphen between the two lexemes. In the spatially unified condition, the location of the first fixation on the compound was further towards the middle of the compounds, relative to the hyphenated condition. This result is very similar to our initial landing position effects discussed above, namely that reader's eyes land further into a spatially unified compound compared with a spaced compound.

Implications for compound word processing

As mentioned in the introduction, Pollatsek et al. (2000) interpreted their eye movement data in terms of a race between a compositional route and a direct look-up of the entire compound. The present results for normally nonspaced compounds fit nicely into such a model so we will direct our attention to the results from those compounds first.

When the compound is fixated for the first time, an advantage is seen for normally nonspaced compounds presented with a space, indicating that accessing the first constituent meaning is important in normal compound processing (as suggested by the Pollatsek et al. model). The interword spaces thus served as an important segmentation cue where the first constituent was easier to isolate from the entire compound. However, while segmentation was easier when the compounds were presented with spaces, spatial unification was beneficial to accessing the compound's meaning. This may be due to the fact that when the compound was spatially unified, the direct look-up of the whole compound was able to begin in parallel to accessing the first constituent of the compound. The direct route may have 'won' the race more often when the normally nonspaced compound was presented correctly, as opposed to when it was spaced. When the compound was presented with a space, the direct route to compound meaning may not have begun until the second lexeme was identified. This pattern of results thus provides evidence for both a functional role of lexemes in compound word identification, as well as the fact that there also exists a lexical entry for the entire compound.

The same explanation cannot be given for the normally spaced compounds, however. As mentioned in the introduction, these spaced compounds are familiar to the typical college age students. However, participants are also aware that these types of compounds are not supposed to be spatially unified (see footnotes 2 and 3). Therefore, there should not be a direct route to compound meaning for these words. Due to this fact, one might expect to find a large disadvantage for a normally spaced compound when it is presented incorrectly. While a disadvantage was seen on first fixation durations, gaze durations showed either no disadvantage for incorrect spatial unification (in the case of adjective-noun compounds) or a small advantage (in the case of noun-noun compounds). This could be due to the fact that when the compound was spatially unified, readers' eyes landed further into the word and were closer to the onset of the second lexeme. Readers may thus have attained a better parafoveal preview of the second lexeme, resulting in less chance of a refixation.[4] While this is certainly true, one would then expect that deletion of interword spaces might always benefit reading (or at least not hinder it). This is simply not the case; previous eye movement studies have found disadvantages when interword spaces are deleted from normal text (Fisher, 1976; Morris et al., 1990; Pollatsek & Rayner, 1982, Rayner et al., 1998).

In fact, the gaze duration data for the normally spaced compounds fits nicely into the framework introduced by Inhoff et al. (2000) where spatial unification benefits conceptual unification. This is especially evident given that while a small, non-significant advantage was seen for the noun-noun spaced compounds, where meaning should not change when spaces are deleted, no advantage was found for adjective-noun compounds where, we have argued, spaces are more important for identifying correct compound meaning. Importantly, according to this theory, advantages for interword

---

[4] We would like to thank an anonymous reviewer for suggesting this interpretation.

spaces (or the lack of a disadvantage) on gaze durations should only be seen for what we have called spaced compounds in this article. Similar results should not be found when any two words in text are written together. The important factors are that the two-word expression represents a single concept and is familiar to readers.

REFERENCES

Andrews, S., Miller, B., & Rayner, K. (2004). Eye movements and morphological segmentation of compound words: There is a mouse in mousetrap. *European Journal of Cognitive Psychology, 16*, 285–311.

Baayen, R. H., Piepenbrock, R., & Gulikers, L. (1995). *The CELEX Lexical Database.* [CD-ROM]. Philadelphia: Linguistic Data Consortium, University of Pennsylvania.

Bertram, R., & Hyönä, J. (2003). The length of a complex word modifies the role of morphological structure: Evidence from eye movements when reading short and long Finnish compounds. *Journal of Memory and Language, 48*, 615–634.

Fisher, D. (1976). Spatial factors in reading and search: The case for space. In A. Monty & W. Senders (Eds.), *Eye movements and psychological processes.* Hillsdale, NJ: Lawrence Erlbaum Associates, Inc.

Hyönä, J., & Pollatsek, A. (1998). The role of component morphemes on eye fixations when reading Finnish compound words. *Journal of Experimental Psychology: Human Perception and Performance, 24*, 1612–1627.

Inhoff, A. W., & Radach, R. (1998). Definition and computation of oculomotor measures in the study of cognition processes. In G. Underwood (Ed.), *Eye guidance in reading and scene perception* (pp. 29–53). Oxford: Elsevier Science Ltd.

Inhoff, A. W., & Radach, R. (2002). The biology of reading: The use of spatial information in the reading of complex words. *Comments on Modern Biology. Part C., Comments on Theoretical Biology, 7*, 121–138.

Inhoff, A. W., Radach, R., & Heller, D. (2000). Complex compounds in German: Interword spaces facilitate segmentation but hinder assignment of meaning. *Journal of Memory and Language, 42*, 23–50.

Inhoff, A. W., & Rayner, K. (1986). Parafoveal word processing during eye fixations in reading: Effects of word frequency. *Perception and Psychophysics, 40*, 431–439.

Juhasz, B. J., Starr, M., Inhoff, A. W., & Placke, L. (2003). The effects of morphology on the processing of compound words: Evidence from naming, lexical decisions, and eye fixations. *British Journal of Psychology, 94*, 223–244.

McConkie, G. W., & Rayner, K. (1975). The span of effective stimulus during a fixation in reading. *Perception & Psychophysics, 17*, 578–586.

McConkie, G. W., & Zola, D. (1984). Eye movement control during reading: The effect of words units. In W. Prinz & A. F. Sanders (Eds.), *Cognition and motor processes* (pp. 63–74). Berlin: Springer-Verlag.

Morris, R. K., Rayner, K., & Pollatsek, A. (1990). Eye movement guidance in reading: The role of parafoveal letter and space information. *Journal of Experimental Psychology: Human Perception and Performance, 16*, 268–281.

O'Regan, J. K. (1981). The convenient viewing position hypothesis. In D. F. Fisher, R. A Monty, & J. W. Senders (Eds.), *Eye movements: Cognition and visual perception* (pp. 289–298). Hillsdale, NJ: Lawrence Erlbaum Associates, Inc.

Pollatsek, A., Hyönä, J., & Bertram, R. (2000). The role of morphological constituents in reading Finnish compound words. *Journal of Experimental Psychology: Human Perception and Performance, 26*, 820–833.

Pollatsek, A., & Rayner, K. (1982). Eye movement control in reading: The role of word boundaries. *Journal of Experimental Psychology: Human Perception and Performance, 8,* 817–833.

Rayner, K. (1979). Eye guidance in reading: Fixation locations within words. *Perception, 8,* 21–30.

Rayner, K. (1986). Eye movements and the perceptual span in beginning and skilled readers. *Journal of Experimental Child Psychology, 41,* 211–236.

Rayner, K. (1998). Eye movements in reading and information processing: 20 years of research. *Psychological Bulletin, 124,* 372–422.

Rayner, K., & Duffy, S. A. (1986). Lexical complexity and fixation times in reading: Effects of word frequency, verb complexity, and lexical ambiguity. *Memory and Cognition, 14,* 191–201.

Rayner, K., & Fischer, M. H. (1996). Mindless reading revisited: Eye movements during reading and scanning are different. *Perception and Psychophysics, 58,* 734–747.

Rayner, K., Fischer, M., & Pollastek, A. (1998). Unspaced text interferes with both word identification and eye movement control. *Vision Research, 38,* 1129–1144.

Rayner, K., & Raney, G. E. (1996). Eye movement control in reading and visual search: Effects of word frequency. *Psychonomic Bulletin and Review, 3,* 245–248.

Schilling, H. E., Rayner, K., & Chumbley, J. I. (1998). Comparing naming, lexical decision, and eye fixation times: Word frequency effects and individual differences. *Memory and Cognition, 26,* 1270–1281.

LANGUAGE AND COGNITIVE PROCESSES
2005, 20 (1/2), 317–339

Are stem homographs and orthographic neighbours processed differently during silent reading?

Manuel Carreiras, Ambrosio Perdomo and
Enrique Meseguer

Universidad de La Laguna, Tenerife, Spain

The aim of this research was to investigate the inhibitory effect of stem homographs—words that share stems but are morphologically unrelated—during reading. In Experiment 1 eye movements of participants were recorded while reading sentences that contained a target word preceded either by a stem homograph, an orthographically related or an unrelated control word. Target words were more difficult to read when preceded by stem homographs and orthographically related controls than when preceded by unrelated control words. However, no differences were found between stem homographs and unrelated controls. Two further priming experiments, one using the same stimuli as in Experiment 1 and the other using the same stimuli as in Allen and Badecker's (1999) failed to show an inhibitory effect of stem homographs distinguishable from the inhibitory effect of orthographic controls.

In recent years, one of the major topics of interest in the literature on lexical access has been the role played by morphology during word recognition. One of the debates still open on this question concerns whether obligatory morphological mediation is necessary for lexical access (see Alvarez, Carreiras, & Taft, 2001; McQueen & Cutler, 1998), in other words, whether morphological processing occurs at a prelexical or at a postlexical stage. One type of model assumes that morphological decomposition precedes access to word representation. In the earlier

Correspondence should be addressed to Manuel Carreiras, Departamento de Psicología Cognitiva, Universidad de La Laguna, 38205-Tenerife, Spain.
Email: Manuel.Carreiras@ull.es.

This research was partially supported by grants BSO2003-01135 (Spanish Ministry of Science and Technology) and PI2001/058 (Canary Islands Government). We would like to thank Manuel Perea, Wayne Murray, and an anonymous reviewer for comments to previous versions of this manuscript.

http://www.tandf.co.uk/journals/pp/01690965.html   DOI: 10.1080/01690960444000179

versions of these models, stems were the keys for lexical entries (e.g., Taft & Forster, 1975); whereas in more recent formulations, words are posited to be accessed via activation of their morphemes in connectionist-type architecture with a morpheme level between letter and word units (e.g. Taft, 1991; Taft & Zhu, 1995). Other proposals have claimed that morphologically complex words are represented as whole undecomposed forms, morphology thus being at a postlexical level. Morphologically related words are interconnected through morphological links, so that they will be closer to each other than to other words in the lexicon (Butterworth, 1983; Fowler, Napps, & Feldman, 1985; Lukatela, Gligorijevic, Kostic, & Turvey, 1980; Grainger, Cole, & Segui, 1991; Schreuder et al., 1990; Schriefers, Friederici, & Graetz, 1992; Schriefers, Zwitserlood, & Roelofs, 1991; Giraudo & Grainger, 2000). A third type of models combines decomposed accounts of lexical access with whole-word accounts. (e.g., Caramazza, Laudanna, & Romani, 1988; Schreuder & Baayen, 1995; Frauenfelder & Schreuder, 1992).

Empirical evidence favouring the morphological decomposition account has been obtained in experiments using nonwords with different degrees of decomposability (Taft & Forster, 1975, 1976; Henderson, Wallis, & Knight, 1984; Caramazza, Laudanna, & Romani, 1988). The logic behind these experiments is that if the processor tries morphological parsing as a routine, it should be more difficult to reject nonwords that contain legal stems and/or affixes than nonwords that contain pseudostems and/or pseudoaffixes or no morphemic units at all. However, it has been argued (Henderson, 1985) that the mechanisms involved in the recognition of familiar words could be different from those involved in the rejection of nonwords (see Grainger & Jacobs, 1996 for a computational account of word and nonword recognition).

Other results cannot be taken to unequivocally support decompositional models that assume prelexical morphological access, because these results can also be explained by models that assume postlexical morphology or by dual route models. For instance, experiments that have compared the effects of surface frequency and root frequency (e.g., Baayen, Burani, & Schreuder, 1997; Baayen, Dijkstra, & Schreuder, 1997; Burani & Caramazza, 1987; Colé, Beauvillain, & Segui, 1989; Taft, 1979) have not been critical in distinguishing between models. The combined stem frequency effect on word recognition could be either because the stem acts as the access representation for all words with that stem, or because representations of stems are linked to those for whole-word forms in a cluster within a shared entry or in a network—so that lexical entries belonging to the same cluster would be sensitive both to combined stem frequency and their own surface frequency. Probably, the most solid piece of evidence that morphological units mediate early stages of word identification has been provided in Hebrew (Frost, Forster, & Deutsch, 1997; Frost, Deutsch, & Forster, 2000; Deutsch, Frost, Pollatsek, & Rayner, 2000; Deutsch, Frost, Pelleg, Pollatsek & Rayner, 2003). However, it remains to be seen to what extent these effects are also obtained in other languages in which the salience of morphemic composition is less relevant than in Hebrew (see Longtin, Seguí, & Halle, 2003 for French data partially supporting a morphological decomposition).

It is important to indicate that morphological relatedness is, to a large extent, confounded with orthographic, phonological and semantic similarity, because of the natural co-occurrence of all of these variables. To establish that there is an independent morphological dimension, that is not just a byproduct of orthography, phonology, or semantics, it is necessary to show that morphological relatedness has a different impact with respect to these variables. Thus, there has also been some research devoted to isolating a purely morphological effect by comparing it to semantic, phonological and orthographic conditions, mainly using priming paradigms. Feldman and Moskovljevic (1987) compared morphological priming effects when visual similarity was very low—when prime and targets were in two different alphabets of Serbo-Croatian: Roman and Cyrillic—and when it was very high—when prime and targets were presented in the same alphabet. They obtained priming effects of similar size. A similar type of result was found by Feldman and Bentin (1994) in Hebrew. Other studies have revealed that morphological effects are facilitatory, usually comparable to those obtained with repetition priming, independently of what sort of priming paradigm is used, either long-term priming, masked, or unmasked priming (e.g., Fowler, Napps, & Feldman, 1985; Kempley & Morton, 1982; Stanners, Neiser, Hernon, & Hall, 1979; Drews & Zwitserlood, 1995). In contrast, orthographic priming produces inhibitory, facilitatory, or null effects, depending on the particular experimental conditions, the relative frequency of prime and target, the priming procedure—masked or unmasked, the SOA, etc. (Seguí & Grainger, 1993). For instance, form priming produces inhibition when a word is primed by a higher frequency neighbour in masked priming, and results in a null effect in unmasked priming; while inhibition is obtained when a word is primed by a lower frequency neighbour in unmasked contiguous presentation (Grainger, 1990; Segui & Grainger 1990), but facilitatory effects of form priming have also been obtained under masked conditions (Forster et al., 1987). Perhaps the most important evidence concerning the differences between morphologcial and orthographical priming has been gathered by Drews and Zwitserlood (1995). They presented a series of experiments using masked and unmasked priming for lexical decision and naming in Dutch and German. Morphologically related pairs (kersen-KERS, cherries-cherry) produced a facilitatory effect across the different intervals of prime presentation and the type of task used. In contrast, the orthographically related pairs (kerst-KERS, Christmas-cherry) showed inhibition in lexical decision tasks (masked and unmasked priming) and facilitation in naming tasks. Further experiments in which morphological, semantic and orthographic relationships between primes and targets were varied at different SOAs showed that morphology has an independent influence from semantic and orthographic relatedness (Domínguez, Cuetos, & Seguí, 2002; Domínguez, de Vega, & Barber, 2004; Rastle, Davis, Marslen-Wilson, & Tyler, 2000).

All these findings showing differential effects of morphological information provide evidence in favour of an independent dimension of morphological structure. Nonetheless, we are faced again with the central question that has not been answered yet: When and where does morphological similarity play a role in word recognition? Is lexical access mediated by morphological decomposition? Negative priming effects of words which share homographic stems (Allen & Badecker, 1999, 2002; Badecker & Allen, 2002; Laudanna, Badecker, & Caramazza, 1989, 1992) seem to provide important evidence in favour of models which posit a prelexical decomposition (see however, McQueen & Cutler, 1998; Stolz & Feldman, 1995). Stem homographs are words with stems that are orthographically identical but morphologically unrelated. For example, in Spanish the stems of mor-ir (to die) and mor-os (moors) are orthographically the same but are not morphologically related. According to a prelexical account, if decomposition is taking place in lexical access, both stem homograph entries first become activated and then, after competing with each other, the inappropriate entry is suppressed. Laudanna et al. (1989) carried out three experiments with Italian materials to investigate whether words which share their stems but are morphologically unrelated inhibit each other. In the first two experiments they presented pairs of words simultaneously for a double lexical decision task. They showed a facilitatory effect for morphologically related words, but more importantly, an inhibitory effect for stem homograph pairs. Thus, lexical decisions to pairs which were morphologically related (e.g., porta "door" and porte "doors") were faster than those to orthographically related pairs which shared neither morphological relationship nor homographic stems (e.g., collo "neck" and colpo "blow" with the stems coll- and colp-), which were also faster than those of pairs with homographic stems that were morphologically unrelated (e.g., portare "to carry" and porte "doors" with the stem port-). Furthermore, they found no differences between orthographically related and unrelated pairs (e.g., causa "cause," ponte "bridge"). In their Experiment 3, in which a priming technique was used, they found that lexical decisions to target words preceded by word primes which shared homographic stems were slower than those to target words preceded by unrelated primes. However, this third experiment did not include a condition with orthographically related primes. Thus, Laudanna et al. (1992) replicated the inhibitory effect of stem homographs relative to unrelated controls for word targets.

Recently, Allen and Badecker (1999) carried out two experiments in Spanish to investigate whether the inhibitory effect of stem homographs was caused by orthographic similarity alone (see Stolz & Feldman, 1995 objection). Lexical decisions to target words (e.g., moros "moors", with the stem mor-) preceded by words that were morphologically unrelated but shared homographic stems (morir "to die", with the stem mor-) took longer than when preceded by orthographically related primes (e.g., moral "moral", with the stem moral), which in turn were slower than those to unrelated pairs (e.g., silla). See Allen and Badecker, 2002; Badecker and Allen, 2002 for further empirical evidence.

Allen and Badecker claimed that this inhibitory stem-homographic effect suggests that words are represented in a morphologically decomposed form, as predicted by the AAM model (Caramazza et al., 1988), so that, even if the access system has supplementary whole-word procedures, the stem homograph effect suggests that the decomposition approach still contributes to the recognition process. While morphological relatives facilitate each other through repeated access to the same stem, when two morpheme homographs are presented sequentially, the entry for one will be competitively inhibited by the previous activation of its homograph. That is, the inhibitory effect for stem-homograph primes would reflect a competition between two lemma entries (e.g., to die and moors) that are accessed by the same stem form (mor-). Moreover, they suggest that even assuming that morphological decomposition may be computationally more demanding than whole word access, the morphological decomposition may produce important benefits during sentence processing and higher levels of language comprehension, so that it may be preferred. For instance, decomposition of complex words may allow the comprehension system to exploit natural interfaces between complex lexical representations and the structure-building operations at higher linguistic processing levels, taking advantage, for instance, of inflectional morphology to integrate information in the syntactic context (see Badecker & Allen, 2002).

However, more recently, Laudanna, Voghera, and Gazzellini (2002) suggested that the stem homograph effect may not be as general as was initially claimed. Laudanna et al. found that the inhibitory effect of stem homographs was restricted to the use of verbs as targets. In particular, they presented noun and verb targets in a priming task preceded by noun and verb primes. They found that the effects on stem homographs occurred only in the two conditions in which a verbal form was used as target, either preceded by a verb or a noun. However, noun targets were not inhibited when preceded by verb primes, and when preceded by noun primes the inhibitory effect of stem homographs was strictly comparable to the effect observed in the orthographic control condition. They suggested that the inhibitory effects of stem homographs may only occur with verbs, since they are morphologically more productive than nouns. In addition, they noticed that the use of nouns as targets was under-represented in their previous studies.

The aim of this paper is to investigate the inhibitory effect of words that share homographic stems, and trace its time course during reading by using an eye tracking methodology. According to Badecker and Allen (2002), morphological decomposition is an important mechanism for comprehension operations such as syntactic structure and conceptual model building, since it allows extraction of the morpho-syntactic and conceptual information that is encoded separately in affixes and stems. Therefore, the stem homograph effect may be even more visible during reading than during lexical decision tasks, because the goal during reading is to build a sentence representation, while the lexical decision task may be solved looking for a match in the lexicon. In addition, from Laudanna et al.'s (2002) study, it would seem that the stem homograph effect may be restricted to verbs, which are more productive than nouns. Therefore, only verbs were used as targets in order to maximise the probability of capturing the effect. In Experiment 1 the participants' eye movements were recorded while they read sentences that contained a target word preceded earlier in the sentence by another word that could either be a stem homograph word, an orthographic neighbour or an unrelated control word. In Experiment 2 the same experimental stimuli that were used in Experiment 1 were now presented with a priming procedure similar to that used by Allen and Badecker (1999). Finally, in Experiment 3 we used the same stimuli and procedure as those used by Allen and Badecker in order to replicate their results.

EXPERIMENT 1

It is assumed that access to underlying morphologically decomposed levels of representation has occurred when the recognition of target words is hampered by the previous presentation of word primes with homographic stems. The rationale is that both stem homograph entries first become activated and then, after competing with each other, the inappropriate entry is suppressed. Thus, responses to target words (*moros*, with the stem mor-) should be slower when preceded by a word prime which shares a homographic stem (*moría*, with the stem mor-) than when preceded by an orthographically related word (moral). Allen and Badecker (1999) showed that at long SOAs (300 ms) the conflict between *"moros"* as target when preceded by *"moría"* as prime caused more interference than when preceded by *"moral"*, which caused also more interference than when preceded by *"silla"*. In the first case there is a conflict between two underlying lexical entries, which are not only associated with different semantic contents, but also share the stems linked to a different set of suffixes, while in the second case there is a conflict between two lexical entries with some formal (orthographic) overlap. It is important to note that to infer that the effect is purely morphological, the critical comparison is the stem homograph condition (*moría*) against the orthographically related condition (*moral*).

Badecker and Allen (2002) claimed that decomposition, although more costly computationally, offers some advantages for integrating information during comprehension. Therefore, the use of an advanced technique such as the recording of eye movements during reading should allow us to capture the inhibitory stem homographic effect during information integration in sentences, as well as to trace its time course. To this end, we created sentences that contained a target word preceded in earlier parts of the sentence by a stem homographic word or an orthographic neighbour or an unrelated control word. Two to four words separated the "primes" and the target word to avoid any type of parafoveal benefit during reading of the primes. According to the stem homograph hypothesis put forward above, more difficulty should be expected during the reading of the target word or/and subsequent words when the target word is preceded by stem homographic words as compared with orthographic neighbours and to unrelated control words. Note that the critical comparison is between stem homographs and orthographic neighbours. In addition, the recording of eye movements will allow us to observe whether effects of the manipulated variables on the target and subsequent words occur in early measures (e.g., the duration of the first fixation) or/and in later measures (e.g., the total time spent in a particular word), which will shed light on the nature and the time course of the stem homograph effect. Finally, it is important to note that since Laudanna et al. (2002) only obtained stem homograph effects when verbs were used as targets, only verbs were used as targets in the present experiment.

Method

Participants. Forty-two undergraduate students of the Universidad de La Laguna participated in the experiment for course credit. All were native speakers of Spanish.

Materials and design. Thirty Spanish words were selected from the Spanish word pool (Sebastián, Martí, Carreiras, & Cuetos, 2000) based on a count of 5,600,000 Spanish words. All the target words were verbs of low frequency. We also selected 90 low-frequency words of the same length (same number of letters and same number of syllables) sharing all letters, except one, with their corresponding target (see Table 1). Of those 90 prime words, 30 were orthographic neighbours—words similar in form but unrelated in meaning—and 30 were stem homographs: words similar in form because they shared a homographic stem with the target, but again unrelated in meaning. Thus, like the orthographic neighbours, stem homograph primes were unrelated in meaning to the targets, but, in contrast to the orthographic neighbours, they shared with the targets a stem which was similar in form but different in meaning. In addition, 30 primes were unrelated controls. None of the unrelated primes shared any letters (in any position) with their corresponding targets.

Thirty sets of three matched sentences like those displayed in Table 2 were constructed with the selected word. Target words were preceded by stem homographs, orthographic neighbours, or unrelated control words. After the prime word, the sentences were the same in all three conditions. Two to four words separated the primes and the targets in all experimental sets of sentences in order to prevent parafoveal preview of the target while reading the prime. In addition, two to three words were included after the target word so that wrap-up effects would not occur on the target.

Ninety additional sentences with different types of structures were written to serve as fillers, as well as ten sentences for practice trials. Three sets of materials were created, each containing the 30 experimental sentences and 90 fillers. Each experimental sentence occurred in each of the three experimental conditions. The assignment of a sentence to one of the three conditions was counterbalanced across participants.

TABLE 1

Means of printed lexical frequency (per million), standard deviations (within parentheses) log frequency (in italics), and means of length for the target and prime words in the three experimental conditions in Experiments 1 and 2

	Stem homograph moros	*Orthographic neighbour* noria	*Unrelated control* calles	*Target* moría
Lexical frequency	18 (35)	13 (25)	27 (38)	20 (34)
	1.24	*1.11*	*1.43*	*1.29*
Length	5.17	5.17	5.17	5.17

TABLE 2
Example of materials used in Experiment 1. Slashes indicate how regions were divided only for the purposes of the analyses. Participants read the sentences without slashes

---

Stem homograph
En el barrio de los / **moros**/ algunas horas / antes /**moría**/ un joven / atropellado
In the Moorish quarter some hours before a youth died run over

Orthographic neighbor
En el parque de la /**noria**/ algunas horas / antes /**moría**/ un joven / atropellado
In the park of the big wheel some hours before a youth died run over

Unrelated control
En aquellas céntricas /**calles**/ algunas horas / antes /**moría**/ un joven / atropellado
In those central streets some hours before a youth died run over

---

Apparatus and procedure. The sentences were presented in lowercase letters on a video screen interfaced with a PC compatible computer. The monitor displayed up to 80 characters per line. All the sentences had less than 80 characters, so they were displayed in one line. Participants were seated 73 cm away from the monitor, and three characters equalled 1 degree of visual angle. Participants' eye movements were monitored by a Forward Technologies Dual Purkinje Image Eye-tracker which was interfaced to the computer. The eye-tracker has a resolution of 10 min of arc (half a character). Viewing was binocular, with eye position recorded from the right eye. The signal from the eye-tracker was sampled every millisecond by the computer.

Participants were seated in front of the monitor with their head on a chin rest to cancel head movements. The initial calibration of the eye-tracking system generally required about 5 minutes. The participants were asked to read silently the sentences displayed on the monitor and were told that they would be questioned about the sentences and should read them for comprehension. Questions were asked on approximately one third of the trials. Prior to reading each sentence, the participants were instructed to look at a fixation box which outlined the first character position of the sentence. A red dot within the square indicated to the participants that they were correctly looking at the first square and ready to start reading, so he/she could press a button to display the sentence. When they pressed the button, a sentence appeared immediately on the screen. After reading the sentence, the participants again pressed a button that could cause the presentation of a question or a row of squares. When a question appeared on the screen, participants had to press one of two buttons to answer yes or no. Each participant initially read 10 practice sentences to become familiar with the procedure. Then he/she read the 30 experimental sentences intermixed randomly with the 90 filler sentences.

Norming study

In order to test whether sentences belonging to the three experimental conditions were equally comprehensible, 27 participants, none of whom participated in the eye movements experiment, rated the comprehensibility of the sentences. They were asked to read the sentences and rate the degree of comprehensibility in a 1 to 7 point scale, 1 indicating nonsense and 7 completely understandable. Three questionnaires were created, each containing 30 experimental sentences and 40 fillers. The assignment of a sentence to one of the three questionnaires was counterbalanced across participants so that each experimental sentence occurred in each of the three experimental conditions, but each participant was only presented with one condition of each sentence. Comprehensibility means were very similar in the three conditions: stem homograph (6.32), orthographic neighbour (6.1), and unrelated control (6.27). The overall ANOVA showed that there were no significant differences between the three conditions, $F_1(2, 52) = 1.55$, $MSE = 0.23$, $p > .1$ $F_2 < 1$. Thus, sentences in the three conditions seem to be similarly comprehensible.

Data analysis

We will report results for six different eye-movement measures. *First fixation duration* is defined as the duration of the first fixation the participants made when they looked for the first time at a region. *First-pass reading times* are the sum of all fixations from when the reader first enters a region from the left to the time when the region is first exited either to right or left. This measure is usually considered as reflecting first-pass difficulty. *First pass regressions out* includes the percentage of trials in which at least one regression was made from a given region to previous parts of the sentence prior to leaving that region in a forward direction. *Regressions-in* includes the percentage of trials in which a given region received at least one regression from later parts of the sentence. *Regression path time* is the summed fixation duration from when the region is first fixated until the eyes first move past the region; this includes first pass time, time spent in previous parts of the sentence following any regressive eye movements, and time due to refixations coming from the left before the eyes move past the region. *Total reading times* are the sum of all fixations that occurred in a particular region.

Results

For the purpose of the analyses, the texts were segmented as shown with slashes in Table 2: The first region contained all the material up to the prime; the second comprised the prime; the third contained the first half of the words between the prime and the target; the fourth contained the second half of the words between the prime and the target; the fifth the target; the six one or two words after the target, and the seventh was the final region. ANOVAs by participants and by items were carried out for Regions 4 to 7 in the previously defined eye movement measures. The mean first fixation duration, first pass reading times, first pass regressions, regressions into the region, regressions path time and total reading times are shown in Table 3.

TABLE 3

Means and standard deviations (within parentheses) for first fixation duration, first pass reading times, first pass regressions, regressions into the region, and total time reading times on regions of sentences with stems homographs, orthographic neighbours and unrelated control primes

		Pre-target Region 4 antes	Target Region 5 moría	Post-target Region 6 un joven	Final Region 7 atropellado
First fixation	SH	244 (43)	259 (48)	260 (60)	257 (39)
duration	ON	241 (43)	263 (46)	250 (55)	254 (45)
	UR	242 (47)	260 (47)	236 (61)	251 (43)
First pass	SH	299 (73)	320 (77)	294 (71)	668 (226)
reading times	ON	295 (77)	318 (76)	274 (67)	660 (126)
	UR	295 (82)	319 (93)	265 (77)	624 (180)
First pass	SH	14.4 (16)	12 (13)	20.5 (20)	53.6 (24)
regressions	ON	17.5 (17)	10.8 (14)	21.6 (22)	54 (22)
	UR	14.3 (13)	10.5 (13)	21.4 (22)	53.6 (22)
Regressions into	SH	18.0 (15)	27.2 (16)	31.4 (22)	
the region	ON	15.2 (15)	23.2 (16)	33.6 (22)	
	UR	14.2 (12)	28.4 (16)	33.5 (25)	
Regression	SH	380 (138)	381 (122)	417 (154)	1596 (845)
path time	ON	410 (146)	404 (139)	393 (177)	1651 (761)
	UR	378 (146)	377 (129)	371 (138)	1521 (717)
Total reading	SH	390 (144)	493 (182)	377 (116)	937 (311)
times	ON	397 (110)	457 (155)	358 (100)	938 (253)
	UR	385 (130)	466 (164)	351 (102)	885 (232)

Note: SH, stem homograph; ON, orthographic neighbour; UR, unrelated control.

Duration of the first fixation.   There were no significant effects for Regions 4, 5 and 7 (all $Fs < 1$). However, the ANOVA showed significant effects for Region 6 in the analysis by subjects, $F_1(2, 82) = 3.13$, $MSE = 2039$, $p < .05$, $F_2 (2, 58) = 1.04$, $MSE = 1274$, $p > .1$.

Pairwise contrasts showed that in Region 6—post-target—the stem homographs were 24 ms. slower than the unrelated controls, $F_1(1, 41) = 5.74$, $MSE = 2193$, $p < .05$, $F_2(1, 29) = 2.59$ $MSE = 932$, $p > .1$, but no differences were found between stem homograph and orthographic controls, $F_1 < 1$, $F_2 < 1$, or between the orthographic neighbour and the orthographic control, $F_1(1, 41) = 2.4$, $MSE = 1953$, $p > .1$, $F_2(1, 29) = 1.08$, $MSE = 1348$, $p > .1$.

First pass time.   The ANOVAs revealed no differences for Region 4 ($F_1 < 1$, $F_2 < 1$) and for Region 5 ($F_1 < 1$, $F_2 < 1$), and marginally significant effects in the analyses by participants in Region 6, $F_1(2, 82) = 2.95$, $MSE = 3093$, $p < .06$, $F_2(2, 58) = 1.17$, $MSE = 1693$, $p > .1$, and in Region 7, $F_1(2, 82) = 2.96$, $MSE = 15128$, $p < .06$, $F_2(2, 58) = 2.17$, $MSE = 15236$, $p > .1$.

Pairwise contrasts showed that in Region 6—post-target—the stem homographs were 29 ms. slower than the unrelated controls, $F_1(1, 41) = 5.42$, $MSE = 3208$, $p < .05$, $F_2(1, 29) = 2.20$, $MSE = 1637$, $p > .1$, but no differences were found between stem homographs and orthographic controls, $F_1(1, 41) = 2.45$, $MSE = 3410$, $p > .1$, $F_2(1, 29) = 1.29$, $MSE = 1698.34$, $p > .1$, or between the orthographic neighbours and the orthographic controls, ($F_1 < 1$ $F_2 < 1$). In Region 7 the stem homograph condition was 44 ms. slower than the unrelated control condition, $F_1(1, 41) = 4.71$, $MSE = 18982$, $p < .05$, $F_2(1, 29) = 3.60$, $MSE = 18398$, $p < .07$. No differences were found between the stem homographs and the orthographic controls, $F_1(1, 41) = 1.28$, $MSE = 13884$, $p > .1$, $F_2(1, 29) < 1$, nor between the orthographic control and the unrelated condition, $F_1(1, 41) = 2.19$, $MSE = 2418$, $p > .1$, $F_2(1, 29) = 1.73$, $MSE = 9468$, $p > .1$.

First pass regressions.   The ANOVAs did not show any significant differences for any region: Region 4, $F_1(2, 82) = 1$, $MSE = 191$ $p > .1$, following regions all $Fs < 1$.

Regressions in.   The ANOVAs did not show any significant effects: Region 4, $F_1(2, 82) = 1.53$ $MSE = 105$, $p > .1$, F_2 1; Region 5, $F_1(2, 82) = 1.51$, $MSE = 205$ $p > .1$, $F_2 < 1$; Region 6, $Fs < 1$.

Regression path time.   The ANOVAs did not show any significant effects for any region: Region 4, $F_1(2, 82) = 1.11$, $MSE = 12571$, $p > .1$, $F_2 < 1$; Region 5, $F_1 < 1$, $F_2 < 1$; Region 6, $F_1(2, 82) = 1.05$, $MSE = 20819$,

$p > .1$, $F_2(2, 58) = 1.02$, $MSE = 15649$, $p > .1$; Region 7, $F_1(2, 82) = 1.42$; $MSE = 145100$, $p > .1$, $F_2 < 1$.

Total reading time. The ANOVAs did not show any significant effects for any region: Region 4 ($F_1 < 1$; $F_2 < 1$); Region 5, $F_1(2, 82) = 1.60$, $MSE = 9434$, $p > .1$, $F_2(2, 58) = 1.88$, $MSE = 5568$, $p > .1$; Region 6, $F_1(2, 82) = 1.06$, $MSE = 7110$, $p > .1$, $F_2 < 1$; and Region 7, $F_1(2, 82) = 1.93$, $MSE = 20130$, $p > .1$, $F_2(2, 58) = 1.85$, $MSE = 14093$, $p > .1$.

Discussion

The effects indicate that participants experience more difficulty after reading the target word in the post-target region and in the last region— when preceded by a stem homographic than when preceded by an unrelated word, as was shown in the duration of the first fixation and in the first pass time measures. However, no differences were found between the stem homograph and the orthographic neighbour conditions. It is important to notice that no differences between stem homographs and orthographic controls were found in any measure for any region.

In sum, the present results seem to suggest that stem homograph interference effects are the results of mutual inhibitory links between lexical representations similar to those postulated to explain orthographic similarity effects. Targets were inhibited when preceded by stem homographs as compared with unrelated words, but the effect was comparable to that observed in the orthographic control condition. Thus, the most parsimonious explanation for both effects is that they are orthographic (as opposed to morphological) in nature.

It is important to stress that to be able to conclude that there are genuine stem homograph effects, stem homographs should produce more inhibition than orthographic controls. It is not sufficient to show that stem homographs produce more inhibition than unrelated controls. However, it could be argued that the lack of genuine stem homograph effects in this study could be due to the particular paradigm: the recoding of eye movements while participants read primes and targets inserted in sentences. Stem homograph effects have been obtained in Spanish using a priming task (e.g., Allen & Badecker, 1999, 2002). Therefore, it is necessary to test whether genuine stem homograph effects can be obtained with the same materials using a priming task. This was the goal of Experiment 2.

EXPERIMENT 2

Experiment 1 did not show any pure effects of stem homographs compared to orthographic controls. However, it could be argued that such an effect has not been obtained because primes and targets were not presented one after the other, as they are in the priming technique. Even though this argument would drastically reduce the scope of the stem homograph phenomenon, it is important to investigate whether this could be the case. To that end, the same primes and targets used in Experiment 1 were employed in the present experiment with the same priming procedure used by Allen and Badecker (2002). Again, in their Experiment 3 they found a differential activation of targets preceded by stem homograph primes as compared with that of orthographically related control primes (see also Allen & Badecker, 1999, Expt 1). Thus, if the effect depends on the paradigm used, inhibitory priming effects of stem homographs, compared with their orthographically related prime controls, are expected.

Method

Participants.   A total of 24 undergraduate students from the Universidad de La Laguna took part in the experiment for course credit. All were native speakers of Spanish. None of them had participated in the previous experiment.

Materials and design.   The experimental materials and design were the same as those used in Experiment 1. In addition to the 30 sets of experimental materials, the 168 pairs of filler prime-target pairs used by Allen and Badecker (1999) were included. Of the 168 fillers, 96 had targets that were nonwords so that participants were presented with 102 "yes" trials and 96 "no" trials. Items were presented randomly in three counterbalanced experimental lists such that each participant would see each target only once and each target would be presented once in each priming condition across the three lists.

Procedure.   The procedure was similar to that used by Allen and Badecker (1999), with the only exception that participants were not asked about the primes. Therefore, a trial started with a fixation cross in the centre of the screen for 400 ms. Fifty milliseconds after the fixation cross disappeared, the (unmasked) prime stimulus appeared for 250 ms in the same location. The target appeared immediately after the offset of the prime in the location occupied by the prime, and remained on the screen until the participant made a response. Prime and target stimuli were presented in lowercase font and included all of the diacritical marks of standard Spanish orthography. Participants were instructed to respond only to the target by pressing one designated response key if the target was a real word and another if it was a nonword. The trial ended either with the participant's response or after 3000 ms if no response occurred. In the latter case, the trial was considered as an error. After the end of each trial there was an interval of 1500 ms before starting the new trial.

Results and discussion

Incorrect responses were excluded from the latency analysis. In addition, in order to avoid the influence of outliers, reaction times more than 2.5 standard deviations above or below the mean for that participant in all conditions were also excluded.

Mean reaction times and error rates on words were submitted to an ANOVA with type of relation between prime and target as a factor. The mean lexical decision times and the error rates on words in each experimental condition are displayed in Table 4. The ANOVA of the latency data showed that there were significant differences between the three conditions in the analysis by participants, $F_1 (2, 40) = 5.07$, $MSE = 2190$, $p < .05$, $F_2 < 1$. The pairwise contrasts showed that stem homographs were 40 ms. slower than the unrelated controls, $F_1 (1, 23) = 13.42$, $MSE = 1236$, $p < .05$, $F_2 (1, 29) = 1.96$, $MSE = 3266$, $p > .1$. Similarly, the orthographic controls were 40 ms slower than the unrelated controls, $F_1 (1, 23) = 5.93$, $MSE = 2821$, $p < .05$, $F_2 < 1$. No differences whatsoever were found between the stem homographs and the orthographic controls. The ANOVA of error rates did not show significant differences between type of primes ($F_1 < 1$, $F_2 < 1$).

The results of this experiment are similar to those obtained in Experiment 1 with eye movement methodology, but do not replicate those obtained by Allen and Badecker (1999, 2002). Therefore, again the most parsimonious explanation for both effects is that they are orthographic (as opposed to morphological) in nature. Bear in mind that we have used the same experimental procedure as Allen and Badecker (2002) with a different set of stimuli. Thus, it could be the case that even though we carefully select stimuli that maximised the chance of obtaining

TABLE 4

Mean lexical decision times and standard deviations (in ms) as well as percentage of errors of target words in Experiment 2

	Prime	Target	RTs	Error rates
Stem homograph	moros	moría	697 (87)	10%
Orthographic neighbour	noria	moría	697 (119)	10%
Unrelated control	calles	moría	657 (93)	8%

an inhibition of the stem homographs relatively to the orthographic controls, some characteristics of our stimuli may be responsible for the lack of this effect. However, there are reasons to think that this is not the case. Some other studies in Spanish that have used different stimuli but similar priming tasks have also failed to obtain a genuine stem homograph effect in reaction times distinguishable from an orthographic similarity effect, or even significantly different from unrelated controls in some cases (e.g., Domínguez et al., 2002, 2004; García-Albea, Sánchez-Casas, and Igoa, 1998). Nonetheless, Dominguez et al. (2004) have reported a difference in N400 peak latencies between a stem homograph condition and an unrelated control condition, although they did not directly compare the stem homograph and the orthographic similarity condition. Laudanna et al. (2002), on the other hand, failed to obtain a genuine stem homograph effect when using nouns as targets, the stem homograph effect being restricted to the cases in which verbs were used as targets.

Even though the present experiments, among others, failed to replicate Allen and Badecker's results, all these studies have used different sets of materials and in some cases similar stimuli but not the same procedure. Thus, the importance of replicating Allen and Badecker's findings by using their materials and the same procedure is clear. This was the goal of Experiment 3.

EXPERIMENT 3

Method

Participants.   A total of 27 undergraduate students from the Universidad de La Laguna took part in the experiment for course credit. All were native speakers of Spanish. None of them had participated in the previous experiment.

Materials and design.   The materials and design were the same as those used by Allen and Badecker (1999, Expt 1).

Procedure.   The procedure was the same as that used by Allen and Badecker (1999) in their Expt 1, except that the participants were not asked about the primes.

Results and discussion

Incorrect responses were excluded from the latency analysis. In addition, in order to avoid the influence of outliers, reaction times more than 2.5 standard deviations above or below the mean for that participant in all conditions were also excluded. The mean lexical decision times and the error rates on the target words in each experimental condition are displayed in Table 5. Mean reaction times and error rates on words were submitted to an ANOVA, with type of relation between prime and target as a factor.

The ANOVA on the latency data showed that the effect of type of prime was significant, F_1 (2, 58) = 3.53, MSE = 8640, p < .05, F_2 (2, 46) = 3,05 MSE = 10351, p < .06. The pairwise contrasts showed that stem homographs were 43 ms slower than the unrelated controls, $F_1(1, 29)$ = 3.24, MSE = 8586, p < .09, $F_2(1, 23)$ = 3.42, MSE = 7190, p < .08. Similarly, the orthographic controls were 62 ms slower than the unrelated controls, F_1 (1, 29) = 7.23, MSE = 8032, p < .01, $F_2(1, 23)$ = 5.50, MSE = 11242, p < .05. The differences between the stem homographs and the orthographic controls were not significant (F_1 < 1, F_2 < 1). The ANOVA of the error data did not show any significant difference, $F_1(2, 58)$ < 1, $F_2(2, 46)$ < 1.

Again, inhibitory effects of stem homographs and orthographic controls as compared with the baseline (unrelated controls) were found in the present data. However, no inhibitory effects of stem homographs over orthographic controls were found. Thus, the most parsimonious explanation for both effects is still that they are orthographic in nature.

Allen and Badecker (1999) obtained substantially longer reaction times to those of the present experiment. This could have been caused by the fact that participants in their experiment were asked to remember the prime 20% of the time. Thus, it could be argued that some strategic effects of this request could have contributed to the stem homograph effects they found. However, Allen and Badecker (2002, Experiment 3) replicated their previous findings obtaining an inhibitory effect of stem homographs (73 ms) that was larger than the inhibitory effect obtained for the orthographic controls (23 ms). Both effects were significantly different from the unrelated controls, but more importantly, the 50 ms difference between the stem homographs and the orthographic controls was also significant. In this case, they did not ask participants to remember the prime, and reaction times were slightly shorter than those obtained in the present

TABLE 5

Mean lexical decision times and standard deviations (in ms) and percentage of errors of target words in Experiment 3

	Prime	Target	RTs	Error rates
Stem homograph	moría	moros	815 (207)	22%
Orthographic neighbour	moral	moros	834 (174)	21%
Unrelated control	silla	moros	772 (136)	20%

experiment. Why we were unable to observe a genuine stem homograph effect while Allen and Badecker (1999, 2002) did is still unclear. A careful examination of Allen and Badecker's (2002) procedure did not reveal potentially important differences except, of course, that the participants were different. In any case, the present data casts some doubts about the reality of a stem homograph effect in Spanish, which should be resolved before the effect is further considered in the elaboration of models of morphological processing.

GENERAL DISCUSSION

The aim of this research was to investigate the stem homograph effect in reading and to ascertain whether this effect, which has important implications for models of morphological processing, is different from the orthographic neighbourhood effect also reported in the literature. To that end, we carried out one reading experiment in which the eye movements of the participants were recorded during the reading of sentences that contained a target word preceded earlier in the sentence by a stem homograph word, an orthographic neighbour, or an unrelated control. In none of the different measures of reading time or regressions did we find significant differences between the stem homograph and the orthographic neighbour conditions, while the stem homograph differed from the unrelated condition. Two additional priming experiments, one with the same materials as in Experiment 1 and the other with the same materials as those used by Allen and Badecker (1999) were carried out to discard the possibility that differences in procedure or in materials were causing the lack of effects between stem homographs and orthographic neighbors. Again, in neither of the two experiments were there significant differences between the stem homographs and the orthographic neighbours, although each of these two conditions differed from the unrelated control condition. Taken together, the results of the three experiments showed that stem homographs, even though they were always more difficult to process than the unrelated controls, never produced inhibitory effects greater than the inhibitory effects produced by the orthographic neighbours. Therefore, the simplest and most parsimonious explanation is that differences between stem homographs and unrelated controls are orthographic and not morphological in nature. In other words, the results of the three experiments do not support the hypothesis that the inhibitory effects of stem homographs are determined by morphological interference mechanisms.

The stem homograph priming effect (e.g., Allen & Badecker, 1999, 2002; Laudanna et al., 1989, 1992) strongly suggests that lexical processing does not operate exclusively in terms of whole-word recognition procedures for familiar words with ambiguous morphological constituents, but that decomposition contributes to the recognition process for these forms. However, in none of the three experiments did we obtain a stem homograph priming effect. With a reading task (Experiment 1), in which we tried to maximise the chances of obtaining the effect by using only verbs as targets, with a priming task with the same materials as Experiment 1, and again with a priming task with Allen and Badecker's materials (Experiment 3) we consistently failed to replicate the effect found in their studies. Therefore, our results suggest that the stem homograph effect is not a reliable effect and should be considered cautiously in the elaboration of models of morphological processing.

The stem homograph inhibitory effect was first reported by Laudanna et al. (1989) using a double lexical decision task (Experiments 1 and 2) and a priming task (Experiment 3). Unfortunately, they did not include an orthographic control condition in their Experiment 3. Targets were preceded by stem homographs or by unrelated words, and each participant was presented with only 3–4 items per condition. Furthermore, from the description of their Experiments 1 and 2, it seems that different targets were used in each condition (see page 539), and that each participant saw only 7–8 stimuli in each category. Finally, no orthographic control condition was included in the Laudanna et al. (1992) experiments, either. In addition, they had very few data points for each participant per experimental condition (3–4), accompanied by a high error rate (17.3 in Experiment 2 and 11.3 in Experiment 3) that could compromise the stability of reaction times, as well as the generalisation of the effects. More recently, Laudanna et al. (2002) failed to replicate these earlier effects when nouns were used as target words. The effect only appeared when verbs were used as targets. Targets which were mostly verbs were also used in Allen and Badecker's (2002) Experiment 3, in which they found an inhibitory effect of stem homographs greater than the inhibitory effect of orthographic controls. Nonetheless, the effect was also obtained in Allen and Badecker (1999, Experiment 1) using mostly nouns as targets, although reading times in this experiment were rather long, perhaps due to the fact that they asked participants to remember the prime in 20% of the trials.

It is important to stress that our results are similar to those obtained by other researchers in Spanish (Domínguez et al., 2002; García-Albea, Sanchez-Casas, & Igoa, 1998; Sanchez-Casas, Igoa, & García-Albea, 2003). For instance, García-Albea et al. (1998) compared priming effects for inflected, derived, and orthographically related pairs, matching syntactic category, word length, and the degree of orthographic similarity of the members of each pair, within and across the three types of word relations. They had inflected pairs such as (niña-NIÑO), derived pairs such as (rama-

RAMO), and orthographic pairs such as (*foca-FOCO*). For each pair they constructed two controls: one unrelated control such as (*celo-NIÑA*; *cita-RAMO*; *suma-FOCO*) and one orthographic control in which the first letter was changed (*piña-NIÑA*; *gamo-RAMO*; *loco-FOCO*). The interesting question is that what they call orthographic pairs (*foca-FOCO*) are in fact words that share homographic stems, whereas the other orthographic control condition, in which the first letter was changed, acts as a true orthographic neighbour control condition. Lexical decision latencies in the masked priming task revealed that while facilitatory effects were found for inflected and derived words, no significant differences were obtained for pairs such as *foca-FOCO*, that are stem homographs.

Why the present experiments (see also Dominguez et al., 2002; García-Albea et al., 1998, Sanchez-Casas et al., 2003) were unable to observe a stem homograph effect in Spanish while Allen and Badecker (1999, 2002) did is still unclear. As indicated above, Laudanna et al. (2002) were only able to observe the stem homograph effect in Italian when they used verbs as targets but not when they used nouns as targets. To our knowledge, the three most important differences between the different experiments are: (a) the experimental procedure—e.g., participants were asked to remember the prime; (b) the targets—verbs or nouns—since verbs can be more prone to decomposition than nouns; (c) the orthographic control condition—the amount of orthographic overlap between primes and targets, since primes and targets are not always orthographic neighbours. The orthographic control condition is important because the effect cannot be considered genuinely morphological unless there is a significant difference with an orthographic control condition. Differences in the definition of what is an orthographic control may account for part of the discrepancies. For instance, in Experiments 1 and 2 we tried to maximise the orthographic overlap between primes and targets (e.g., vendar (SH) tender (ON) vender (target), whereas Laudanna et al. (2002) used a different strategy (e.g., ardiva (SH), armare (OC), ardere (target)). The orthographic overlap in their study for target verbs with primes was approximately 60%, whereas this percentage was clearly higher in our case.

In sum, we are led to conclude that the stem homograph effect is not a reliable effect and should be considered cautiously in the elaboration of models of morphological processing. Our data seem to further complicate the conflictive field of morphology by challenging an effect which has been regarded as providing support for a decompositional or indirect route during word recognition in the dual route models. To sustain the hypothesis of prelexical decomposition will require other empirical demonstrations. Clearly, more empirical evidence is necessary in order to determine under what conditions the stem homograph effect can or cannot be observed.

REFERENCES

Allen, M., & Badecker, W. (1999). Stem homograph inhibition and stem allomorphy: Representing and processing inflected forms in a multi-level lexical system. *Journal of Memory and Language, 41*, 105–123.

Allen, M. & Badecker, W. (2002) Stem homographs and lemma level representations. *Brain and Language, 81* (1,2,3), 79–88.

Alvarez, C., Carreiras, M., & Taft, M. (2001). Syllables and morphemes: Contrasting frequency effects in Spanish. *Journal of Experimental Psychology: Learning, Memory and Cognition, 27*, 545–555.

Baayen, R. H., Burani, C., & Schreuder, R. (1997). Effects of semantic markedness in the processing of regular nominal singulars and plurals in Italian. In G. Booij & J. van Marle (Eds.), *Yearbook of morphology 1996*. Dordrecht: Kluwer.

Baayen, R. H., Dijkstra, T., & Schreuder, R. (1997). Singulars and plurals in Dutch: Evidence for a parallel dual-route model. *Journal of Memory and Language, 37*, 94–117.

Badecker, W., & Allen, M. (2002) Morphological parsing and the perception of lexical identity: A masked priming study of stem homographs. *Journal of Memory and Language, 47*, 125–144

Burani, C., & Caramazza, A. (1987). Representation and processing of derived words. *Language and Cognitive Processes, 2*, 217–227.

Butterworth, B. (1983). Lexical representation. In B. Butterworth (Ed.), *Language production. Vol. 2: Development, writing and other language processes* (pp. 257–294). London: Academic Press.

Caramazza, A., Laudanna, A., & Romani, C. (1988). Lexical access and inflectional morphology. *Cognition, 28*, 297–332.

Colé, P., Beauvillain, C., & Segui, J. (1989). On the representation and processing of prefixed and suffixed derived words: A differential frequency effect. *Journal of Memory and Language, 28*, 1–13.

Deutsch, A., Frost, R., Pollatsek, A., & Rayner, K. (2000). Early morphological effects in word recognition in Hebrew: Evidence from parafoveal preview benefit. *Language and Cognitive Processes, 15*, 487–506.

Deutsch, A., Frost, R., Pelleg, S., Pollatsek, S., & Rayner, K. (2003). Early morphological effects in reading: Evidence from parafoveal preview benefit in Hebrew. *Psychonomic Bulletin and Review, 10*, 415–422.

Domínguez, A., Cuetos, F., & Seguí, J. (2002) The time course of inflexional morphological priming. *Linguistics, 40* (2), 235–259.

Domínguez, A., de Vega, M., & Barber, H. (2004). Event related brain potentials elicited by morphological, homographic, orthographic and semantic priming. *Journal of Cognitive Neuroscience, 16*, 598–608.

Drews, E., & Zwitserlood, P. (1995). Morphological and orthographic similarity in visual word recognition. *Journal of Experimental Psychology: Human Perception and Performance, 21*, 1098–1116.

Feldman, L. B., & Bentin, S. (1994). Morphological analysis of disrupted morphemes: Evidence from Hebrew. *Quarterly Journal of Experimental Psychology, 47A*, 407–435.

Feldman, L. B., & Moskovljevic, J. (1987). Repetition priming is not purely episodic in origin. *Journal of Experimental Psychology: Learning, Memory and Cognition, 15*, 1–12.

Fowler, C. A., Napps, S. E., & Feldman, L. B. (1985). Relations among regular and irregular morphologically related words in the lexicon as revealed by repetition priming. *Memory and Cognition, 13*, 241–251.

Forster, K. I., Davis, C., Schoknecht, C., & Carter, R. (1987). Masked priming with graphemically related forms: Repetition of partial activation. *Quarterly Journal of Experimental Psychology: Human Experimental Psychology, 39*, 211–251.

Frauenfelder, U. H., & Schreuder, R. (1992). Constraining psycholinguistic models of morphological processing and representation: The role of productivity. In G. Booij & J. van Marle (Eds.), *Yearbook of morphology 1991* (pp. 165–183). Dordrecht: Kluwer.

Frost, R., Forster, K. I., & Deutsch, A. (1997). What can we learn from the morphology of Hebrew? A masked priming investigation of morphological representation. *Journal of Experimental Psychology: Learning, Memory and Cognition, 23*, 829–856.

Frost, R., Deutsch, A., & Forster, K. I. (2000). Decomposing morphologically complex words in a nonlinear morphology. *Journal of Experimental Psychology: Learning, Memory and Cognition, 26*, 751–765

García-Albea, J. E., Sanchez-Casas, R. M., & Igoa, J. M. (1998). The contribution of word form and meaning to language processing in Spanish: Some evidence from monolingual and bilingual studies. In X. X. Hillert (Ed.), *Sentence processing: A cross-linguistic perspective*. New York: Academic Press.

Giraudo, H., & Grainger, J. (2000). Effects of prime word frequency and cumulative root frequency in masked morphological priming. *Language and Cognitive Processes, 15*, 421–444.

Grainger, J. (1990). Word frequency and neighborhood frequency effects in lexical decision and naming. *Journal of Memory and Language, 29*, 228–244.

Grainger, J., Colé, P., & Segui, J. (1991). Masked morphological priming in visual word recognition. *Journal of Memory and Language, 30*, 370–384.

Grainger, J., & Jacobs, A. M. (1996). Orthographic processing in visual word recognition: A multiple read-out model. *Psychological Review, 103*, 518–565.

Henderson, L. (1985). Towards a psychology of morphemes. In A. W. Ellis (Ed.), *Progress in the psychology of language* (Vol. 1, pp. 15–72). Hove, UK: Lawrence Erlbaum Associates Ltd.

Henderson, L., Wallis, J., & Knight, D. (1984). Morphemic structure and lexical access. In H. Bouma & D. G. Bowhuis (Eds.), *Attention and perfomance X* (pp. 221–226). Hove, UK: Lawrence Erlbaum Associates Ltd.

Kempley, S. T., & Morton, J. (1982). The effects of priming with regularly and irregularly related words in auditory word recognition. *British Journal of Psychology, 73*, 441–445.

Laudanna, A., Badecker, W., & Caramazza, A. (1989). Priming homographic stems. *Journal of Memory and Language, 28*, 531–546.

Laudanna, A., Badecker, W., & Caramazza, A. (1992). Processing inflectional and derivational morphology. *Journal of Memory and Language, 31*, 333–348.

Laudanna, A., Voghera, M., & Gazzellini, S. (2002). Lexical representations of written nouns and verbs in Italian. *Brain and Language, 81*, 250–263

Longtin, C. M., Segui, J., & Halle, P. (2003) Morphological priming without morphological relationship. *Language and Cognitive Processes, 18*, 313–334

Lukatela, G., Gligorijevic, B., Kostic, A., & Turvey, M. T. (1980). Representation of inflected nouns in the internal lexicon. *Memory and Cognition, 8*, 415–423.

McQueen, J. M., & Cutler, A. (1998). Morphology in word recognition. In A. Spencer & A. M. Zwicky (Eds.), *The handbook of morphology*. Oxford: Blackwell Publishers.

Rastle, K., Davis, M. H., Marslen-Wilson, W. D., & Tyler, L. K. (2000). Morphological and semantic effects in visual word recognition: A time-course study. *Language and Cognitive Processes, 15*, 507–537.

Sanchez-Casas, R. M., Igoa, J. M., & García-Albea, J. E. (2003). On the representation of inflections and derivations: Data from Spanish. *Journal of Psycholinguistic Research, 32,* 621–668.

Schreuder, R., & Baayen, H. (1995). Modeling morphological processing. In L. B. Feldman (Ed.), *Morphological aspects of language processing.* (pp. 131–154). Hillsdale, NJ: Lawrence Erlbaum Associates Inc.

Schreuder, R., Grendel, M., Poulisse, N., Roelofs, A., & Voort, M. van der (1990). Lexical processing, morphological complexity and reading. In D. A. Balota, G. B. Flores d'Arcais, & K. Rayner (Eds.). *Comprehension processes in reading* (pp. 125–141). Hillsdale, NJ: Lawrence Erlbaum Associates Inc.

Schriefers, H., Friederici, A., & Graetz, P. (1992). Inflectional and derivational morphology in the mental lexicon: Symmetries and asymmetries in repetition priming. *Quarterly Journal of Experimental Psychology, 44A,* 373–390.

Schriefers, H., Zwitserlood, P., & Roelofs, A. (1991). The identification of morphologically complex spoken words: Continuous processing or decomposition? *Journal of Memory and Language, 30,* 26–47.

Segui, J., & Grainger, J. (1990). Priming word recognition with orthographic neighbors: Effects of relative prime-target frequency. *Journal of Experimental Psychology: Human Perception and Performance, 16,* 65–76.

Segui, J., & Grainger, J. (1993). An overview of neighbourhood effects in word recognition. In G. Altmann & R. Shillcock (Eds.), *Cognitive models of speech processing.* Hove, UK: Lawrence Erlbaum Associates Ltd.

Sebastián, N., Martí, M. A., Carreiras, M., & Cuetos, F. (2000). *LEXESP: Una base de datos informatizada del español.* Barcelona: Servicio de Publicaciones de la Universitat de Barcelona.

Stanners, R. F., Neiser, J. J., Hernon, W. P., & Hall, R. (1979). Memory representation for morphologically related words. *Journal of Verbal Learning and Verbal Behavior, 18,* 399–412.

Stolz, J. A., & Feldman, L. B. (1995). The role of orthographic and semantic transparency of the base morpheme in morphological processing. In L.B. Feldman (Ed.). *Morphological aspects of language processing.* Hillsdale, NJ: Lawrence Erlbaum Associates Inc.

Taft, M. (1979). Recognition of affixed words and the word frequency effect. *Memory and Cognition, 7,* 263–272.

Taft, M. (1991). *Reading and the mental lexicon.* Hove, UK: Lawrence Erlbaum Associates Ltd.

Taft, M., & Forster, K. I. (1975). Lexical storage and retrieval of prefixed words. *Journal of Verbal Learning and Verbal Behavior, 14,* 638–647.

Taft, M., & Forster, K. I. (1976). Lexical storage and retrieval of polymorphemic and polysyllabic words. *Journal of Verbal Learning and Verbal Behavior, 15,* 607–620.

Taft, M., & Zhu, X. (1995). The representation of bound morphemes in the lexicon: A Chinese study. In L. B. Feldman (Ed.), *Morphological aspects of language processing.* (pp. 293–316). Hillsdale, NJ: Lawrence Erlbaum Associates Inc.

LANGUAGE AND COGNITIVE PROCESSES
2005, 20 (1/2), 341–371

Ψ Psychology Press
Taylor & Francis Group

Morphological parafoveal preview benefit effects in reading: Evidence from Hebrew

Avital Deutsch and Ram Frost

The Hebrew University, Jerusalem, Israel

Alexander Pollatsek and Keith Rayner

University of Massachusetts, Amherst, MA, USA

Hebrew words are composed of two interwoven morphemes: a three-consonantal root and a word-pattern (a nominal or a verbal pattern). Previous research has revealed that a parafoveal preview of a word derived from the same root morpheme as the foveal target word facilitated first-pass reading (as indexed by first fixation duration and gaze duration). In the current study we extended our research on parafoveal preview effects to other derivational morphemes in Hebrew and also examined whether context has an influence on these early morphological effects. We found that a parafoveal preview which had a common verbal pattern with a target word facilitated processing, but a preview with a common nominal pattern did not. These results are similar to previous results obtained using the masked priming paradigm with single words, and suggest that masked priming and parafoveal preview tap similar cognitive processes in word recognition. Furthermore, a preview of a verbal form (that was syntactically incongruent with the prior sentence context) inhibited the identification of a nominal form. However, biasing semantic context did not affect the first-pass reading time for target words which were previewed by a word derived from the same root. These results suggest that morphological information extracted from the parafovea in the initial phases of word recognition in Hebrew may be affected by syntactic contextual processes.

Correspondence should be addressed to: Avital Deutsch, The School of Education, The Hebrew University, Jerusalem, 91905 Israel. Email: msavital@mscc.huji.ac.il.

This study was supported by the Israel Science Foundation, Grant 0322253 granted to the first two authors, and by grant HD26765 from the National Institute of Health to the third and fourth authors. We wish to thank Yuval Ziv, Alonit Ranya, Noga Sagiv, and Tamar Gvor for their extensive help and assistance in running the experiments,

http://www.tandf.co.uk/journals/pp/01690965.html   DOI: 10.1080/01690960444000115

The identification of morphologically complex words has usually been investigated in the context of studies of single-word identification. A typical experiment involves making responses to target words (either a naming or lexical decision response), and morphological processing is probed by presenting primes that are either morphologically related or unrelated to the target word. Morphological involvement in the encoding of the target is inferred if there is greater priming from a morphologically related prime than from an unrelated control prime when the primes are equated on a number of attributes (such as orthographic and/or phonological similarity to the target). This paradigm has provided substantial evidence, that component morphemes are involved in the encoding of morphologically complex words (Taft & Forster, 1975 in English; Laudana, Cermele, & Caramazza, 1997 in Italian; Grainger, Cole, & Segui, 1991 in French; Drews & Zwitserlood, 1995 in German and Dutch; Frost, Forster, & Deutsch, 1997 in Hebrew; Boudelaa & Marslen-Wilson, in Arabic 2001).

The priming paradigm has been generally employed in tasks that involve the identification of isolated words. However, readers usually do not encounter isolated words. Words are usually identified when people read text, which involves the rapid, on-line integration of the words into syntactic structures and semantic representations of discourse (Rayner & Pollatsek, 1989). Indeed, a fundamental question in research on word recognition concerns the role of sentential context in the process of word recognition—whether higher level contextual information can interact with lexical processes of word identification, or whether sentential effects are restricted to post-lexical phases of lexical selection and sentence integration. This question is especially important in investigating the involvement of morphological factors in the process of word recognition because the semantic and grammatical characteristics of words are related to their morphological structure. As a result, the on-line processes of syntactic parsing and sentence integration may influence the morphological analysis of an upcoming word during reading. Accordingly, it seems important to determine the role of morphemes in the process of word identification in conditions that mimic natural reading as closely as possible, namely in identifying morphologically complex words within sentential context. Thus, an important challenge for research that deals with the process of morphological decomposition during word identification is to find an experimental setting that reflects early processes of lexical access but is also sensitive to other on-line contextual factors that may affect lexical access.

Much of the evidence for early morphological decomposition occurring during single-word identification is based on priming under masked presentations. These include findings in various Indo-European languages

(Dutch: Drews & Zwitserlood, 1995; English: Forster & Azuma, 2000, Rastle, Davis, Marslen-Wilson, & Tyler, 2000, but see Masson & Isaak, 1999; French: Grainger et al., 1991; German: Drews & Zwitserlood, 1995), as well as in Hebrew, in which all derivational morphemes have been studied (Frost et al., 1997; Frost, Deutsch, & Forster, 2000; Deutsch, Frost, & Forster, 1998). The masked-priming paradigm is particularly useful for exploring early processes of word recognition because the brief presentation of the prime combined with forward and backward masking prevents the full conscious identification of the prime. Consequently, the priming effect obtained in this procedure is not influenced by the participants' appreciation of the prime-target morphological relation, as is the case with some long-term morphological priming effects. However, for technical reasons, this procedure has not been applied to investigating word recognition within sentential context.

Recently, converging evidence for morphological decomposition was obtained in Hebrew by measuring preview benefit effects induced by presenting morphological information in the parafovea. This effect was demonstrated both in single-word identification tasks (Deutsch, Frost, Pollatsek, & Rayner, 2000) and when people (silently) read sentences (Deutsch, Frost, Pelleg, Pollatsek, & Rayner, 2003). In particular, it was found that the parafoveal presentation of a letter string derived from the same root morpheme as the foveal target word shortened the processing time of the word when it was later fixated. As this method reveals early processes of word recognition on the one hand, and can be applied for identifying words in sentential context on the other hand, we made use of this methodology in the present research. We will briefly discuss the results of research using the masked priming and the parafoveal preview paradigm in the domain of morphology and will focus on findings obtained in Hebrew. First, however, we provide some general information regarding Hebrew morphology.

BASIC FEATURES OF HEBREW DERIVATIONAL MORPHOLOGY

In Hebrew, as in other Semitic languages, all verbs and the vast majority of nouns and adjectives consist of two basic derivational morphemes: (a) the root, and (b) either a nominal or verbal pattern. The root usually consists of three consonants, while the word-pattern consists of either vowels or a mixture of vowels and consonants. Whereas the root usually carries the core semantic meaning of the word, the word-pattern defines its word-class and other grammatical characteristics, such as gender, the verb's mode (active or passive) and the verb's transitivity. Thus, the specific meaning of a word is determined by both the root and the word-pattern. It should be noted, however, that even though the word-pattern shapes the meaning of the root for any specific word, the exact meaning of a word cannot be unequivocally predicted by considering its constituent morphemes (the root and the word-pattern) independently. This semantic fuzziness is much greater for the more than 100 word-patterns in the nominal system than for the verbal system, which contains only seven word patterns in Modern Hebrew (see Deutsch et al., 1998, for a more detailed description).

A fundamental feature of derivational morphology of Semitic languages is the non-concatenated manner in which the two derivational morphemes are interwoven to form words. For example, the root xbr (meaning 'to assemble') may intertwine with the nominal pattern ma - - e - et (a feminine nominal form) to form the word /maxberet/ ('notebook') or with the word-pattern ta - - i - (a nominal masculine form) to form the word /taxbir/ ('syntax'). The same principle also applies to conjugations in the verbal system: the root xbr may intertwine with the verbal pattern - i- - e - (an active verbal form) to form the word /xibber/,[1] a causative transitive verb ('he combined'), or with the verbal-pattern - u- - a - (a passive form) to form the word /xubbar/ ('was combined').

This nonlinear structure often obscures the phonological and orthographic transparency of the two constituent morphemes as two independent units. Furthermore, the position of the root and the word-pattern letters within the orthographic sequence of a word is not fixed, and depends on the structure of the word-pattern. For instance, in the above examples, whereas the root consonants, xbr, constitute the second, third, and fourth letters within the five-letter word mxbrt, /maxberet/, they constitute the second, third, and fifth letters in the five-letter word txbyr pronounced as /taxbir/. (In unpointed Hebrew script, which is the common way of writing, the vowel marks are often omitted from print, except for some vowels which are sometimes denoted by 'vowel letters', such as the letter 'y' for the vowel /i/ in the word taxbyr. The same 'vowel letters', however, may represent consonants in other contexts.) Thus, unlike concatenated linear morphological systems, Hebrew morphemes are not spatially contiguous.

MORPHOLOGICAL DECOMPOSITION IN HEBREW WITH THE MASKED PRIMING PARADIGM

Previous experiments in Hebrew that used the masked priming procedure have consistently obtained two principal findings. First, there is a robust priming effect induced by the root morpheme. One way this was

---

[1] The double b represents germination of the second consonant of the root.

demonstrated was using the isolated root as the prime. These root primes facilitated lexical decision and naming of nouns and verbs derived from them, both in the nominal and verbal systems (Deutsch et al., 1998; Frost et al., 1997). Another way this was demonstrated was by using primes derived from the same root as the target. In this paradigm, a similar pattern of facilitation was observed even though the root was not presented explicitly as a unit in the prime. Furthermore, this facilitation was found to be independent of semantic transparency (Deutsch et al., 1998; Frost et al., 1997). Second, there was a robust priming effect induced by verbal patterns (Deutsch et al., 1998), whereas no priming was obtained for nominal patterns (Frost et al., 1997). Thus, even though word patterns are basically the same types of morphological unit in the nominal and verbal systems, the two types of patterns seem to have a different role in lexical organisation and in lexical access.

In an attempt to explain these differences, we (Deutsch et al., 1998; Deutsch & Frost, 2003; Frost et al., 2000) have suggested that they stem from differences in the specific linguistic characteristics of the nominal and the verbal patterns. Whereas there are only seven different verbal patterns in Hebrew, there are more than 100 different nominal patterns into which any root can be embedded to form a noun or an adjective. Furthermore, each conjugated verbal form must be derived using one of the verbal patterns, whereas there are numerous examples of foreign nouns in Hebrew which are used in the language almost in their original form. Consequently, for most cases, any verbal pattern appears much more frequently than any nominal pattern. Another difference between the nominal and the verbal patterns concerns the linguistic information they convey. First, a verbal pattern conveys grammatical information beyond identifying the word as a verb (such as active/passive mode) which is important for syntactic analysis. In addition, the variation in the meaning conveyed by any specific nominal pattern is usually much higher than any specific verbal pattern. In sum, verbal patterns have both the advantage of being more frequent in the language and conveying more semantic and grammatical information than nominal patterns. Our findings thus suggest that the role of a given morpheme in mediating lexical access may reflect a fine tuning among the morpheme's distributional properties, semantic transparency, syntactic role, and structural properties.

PARAFOVEAL PREVIEW BENEFIT EFFECTS

A good procedure for monitoring the early processes of lexical access that is similar to masked priming, is measuring how the information extracted from a word before the eyes land on it affects the identification of that word. We will refer to this information as parafoveal because this information is typically about 5–10 characters from fixation and thus is near, but not in, the foveal region. A large body of research on eye movements in reading (see Rayner, 1998, for a review) has revealed that although the perceptual span from which readers extract information is small, it is not restricted to the fixated word, and readers can extract information from the next word or two. The common finding is that reading is significantly slowed if the parafoveal information about the word to the right of the fixated word is withheld. In addition, the perceptual span is asymmetric, being extended further to the right of the fixation point when reading from left to right and to the left when reading from right to left (Pollatsek, Bolozky, Well, & Rayner, 1981). This asymmetry is probably due to an attentional shift from the currently fixated word to the following words in the text, before the initiation of the actual eye movement (Morrison, 1984; Reichle, Pollatsek, Fisher, & Rayner, 1998). Subsequent experiments have attempted to discover, in more detail, what kind of information is extracted from a word before it is fixated, and how this information is combined with the information extracted when the word is fixated.

A detailed assessment of the benefit from a parafoveal preview can be provided using the boundary technique (Rayner, 1975). This technique involves rapidly changing a single word during the saccade in which the eyes move to fixate the word. (The display change is triggered when the eyes cross an invisible boundary just prior to the target word.) An important feature of the boundary technique is that readers are virtually unaware of the display change, and are also unable to identify the stimulus in the parafovea. Nevertheless, the parafoveal information is apparently integrated with the subsequent activation of the foveal word, as parafoveal information was found to facilitate the identification of the foveal target word (Rayner, McConkie, & Zola, 1980). Using the boundary technique, it has been shown that both orthographic (Inhoff, 1989b; Rayner, Well, Pollatsek, & Bertera, 1982) and phonological information (Henderson, Dixon, Peterson, Twilley, & Ferreira, 1995; Pollatsek, Lesch, Morris, & Rayner, 1992) are extracted from the parafovea, while the exact visual shape of the letters is irrelevant (i.e., whether the case of the letter in the parafovea matches the case of the letter when fixated; Rayner et al., 1980). The explanation for parafoveal benefit resembles the one for masked priming effects: information extracted from the parafovea causes partial activation of the lexicon, and this activation is integrated with the later activation due to accessing information from the foveal word (Rayner, 1998; and see Forster & Davis 1984, for masked priming).

When preview benefit is assessed during sentence reading, the fixation time on the target word is the primary dependent measure. Thus, participants are not required to perform any external task aside from naturally reading the text. This procedure has three fundamental advantages in studying word identification in reading. First, it is based on a natural phenomenon that takes place in reading (extracting information from the parafovea), and therefore does not require the introduction of additional experimental procedures that affect the visual system, such as masking. Second, the dependent variable, fixation duration, registers an inherent element of the reading process, rather than being based on the reaction time to specific artificial tasks external to the process of reading. Furthermore, because a word is often fixated more than once, this procedure makes it possible to monitor the time course of lexical processing. Finally, since the target word is embedded in a sentential context, it is possible to manipulate contextual factors and assess their effects on the early on-line processes of word identification.

Interestingly, only a few studies have manipulated morphological factors in the parafovea while measuring preview effects. These consist of a few studies in English (Inhoff, 1989a; Kambe, 2004; Lima, 1987) and Hebrew (Deutsch et al., 2000, 2003). The studies in English used previews that shared a morpheme with the target word and found no greater benefit from these previews than from control previews that shared as many letters with the target (in the same positions) as the morphemic previews. However, in contrast to the findings in English, consistent morphemic effects have been obtained in Hebrew. Deutsch et al. (2003) demonstrated that a preview of a word derived from the same root morpheme as the foveal target word shortened processing of the target word, compared with a preview that was as orthographically similar to the target as the morphemic preview. (The measure employed in this study was *gaze duration*, the sum of the durations of all fixations made on a target word from the first time the reader's eyes land on the word until the eyes move to preceding or following parts of the sentence.) These results replicated previous results observed for single-word identification in the masked priming paradigm in Hebrew (Frost et al., 1997), with one interesting exception. Whereas an identical prime always provided the most priming in single-word identification reaction time paradigms using masked priming, a preview containing the same root morpheme provided as much preview benefit as an identical prime in the reading studies.

THE PRESENT RESEARCH

The Deutsch et al. (2000, 2003) studies that used parafoveal preview to assess morphological processing in Hebrew examined only the root morpheme. The present study extends our investigation by examining morphological preview benefit for all other derivational morphemes, thereby providing a more complete picture of early morphological processes in reading Hebrew. The first part of our study assessed the effects of parafoveal previews of the verbal pattern (Experiment 1) and the nominal pattern (Experiment 2). Consistent with our previous research on the root morpheme (Deutsch et al., 2003), we kept the semantic context of the sentences neutral in these two experiments, manipulating only the morphological relatedness of the preview. The second aim of our study was to examine whether morphological processing during word recognition, which presumably involves the semantic and the syntactic role of the word, is affected by contextual information in reading. This is related to the more general issue of the role of contextual processes in word recognition. That is, if contextual processes actually affect lexical access (rather than influencing post-lexical processes), they are likely to interact with any morphological parafoveal preview effects that are observed. Thus, in the second part of the present study, we investigated the interaction between early morphological effects and contextual processes in the semantic (Experiment 3) and syntactic (Experiment 4) domains. The use of parafoveal preview benefit to assess possible interactions between contextual effects and the early processes of lexical access is possible since the gaze duration (i.e., first-pass time) on the target word can reflect not only aspects of the word in isolation (such as its frequency), but also the influence of prior context, such as its predictability from the prior text (Rayner & Pollatsek, 1989). Given that the root mainly carries semantic information, while the verbal pattern contains the grammatical information relevant to syntactic processes, we manipulated contextual effects in the semantic domain with respect to the root morpheme, and contextual syntactic effects with respect to the verbal-pattern morpheme.

EXPERIMENT 1

The aim of Experiment 1 was to examine whether a parafoveal preview of a verbal pattern can facilitate the encoding of a verb conjugated with this pattern. In line with the facilitation effects obtained for the root in masked priming and parafoveal preview experiments (Frost et al., 1997; Deutsch et al., 2003), we expected a morphological preview benefit effect to be induced by a verbal-pattern preview similar to the verbal-pattern effect observed in masked priming (Deutsch et al., 1998). As with the masked priming study, we employed three experimental conditions: (1) an identical condition—the parafoveal preview was identical to the foveal target word; (2) a morphologically related condition—the parafoveal preview and the foveal target words were two verbs conjugated with the same verbal pattern, but with a different root; (3) an orthographic control condition—the parafoveal preview and the foveal target words were two verbs with the same number of shared letters as in the morphologically related condition, but with different verbal patterns and with different roots. In all conditions, previews and targets had the same number of letters. Facilitation in both the related and the identical conditions was assessed relative to the orthographic control condition.

As indicated above, in this experiment we attempted to keep the semantic context of the sentences neutral, manipulating only the morphological relatedness of the preview and target. Thus, the foveal targets were coherent with the semantic context of the sentence, but neither had a close semantic relation to any of the preceding words, nor formed a highly predictable continuation of the preceding part of the sentence.

The primary dependent variables employed for assessing the effects of a morphologically related preview in all the reported experiments were the following two first-pass reading-time measures: (1) the *first fixation duration* on the target word (this includes first fixations that are the only fixation on the target word and those that are followed by a refixation on the target word), and (2) the *gaze duration* on the target word (i.e., the sum of the durations of all fixations made on a target word from the first time the reader's eyes land on the word, until the eyes move to the preceding or following parts of the sentence). Both measures are means conditional on the word being fixated; that is, a trial in which the target word was skipped was excluded from the analysis rather than counted as zero fixation time. We anticipated that if morphological information from a verb's verbal pattern is extracted from the parafovea and influences early phases of lexical access during reading, its effects would be seen in at least one of these two measures. Two other commonly used measures to assess processing of a word are *total time* (i.e., the total fixation time on the target including regressive fixations), and *second-pass time*, (i.e., the fixation time on the word after it is left for the first time).[2] Although these measures were also calculated, we focus on the first pass measures, since the latter measures are associated with later processes of sentence integration.

Method

Participants. The participants were 36 undergraduate students at the Hebrew University. All were native speakers of Hebrew who participated in the experiment for course credit or payment. All had normal vision or wore corrective lenses.

---

[2] The statistical analysis will be carried out only on the second pass measure, as it is a cleaner measure than total time which includes also first-pass duration.

Stimuli and design.   There were 48 target words, all verbal forms (4–5 letters long) that were inflected on the past, singular, masculine base form. All targets were conjugated with one of three different verbal patterns. (Note that there are only seven different verbal patterns in Hebrew.) Each target word was paired with three different previews to form the identical, related, and control conditions (see Figure 1 for an example of the materials). Each target word and its two non-identical preview words were equated for length. Both the morphologically related previews and the control previews shared, on average, 2.3 letters with the target, and the shared letters in the non-identical previews and the target always appeared in the same order. However, the original position of the common letters was not necessarily preserved, except for the first or first two letters. Since most verbal patterns in Hebrew include a prefix of one or two letters, all morphological previews shared the first or the first two letters with the target. Because past research has found that the initial letters of a word have special importance in inducing parafoveal preview benefit (see Rayner, 1998), we ensured that the number and the position of the common initial letters within each triple were equated.

All the target words were embedded in sentences of 7–10 words, each of which had a simple structure of subject, predicate, and object. The sentences also included attributive phrases attached to the noun phrases of the subject and the object. Each target word was the predicate of the sentence and was the fourth or fifth word in the sentence. The target word was never the last word on a line. Another 12 filler sentences were included, in which the display change took place in a different syntactic

Target Sentence

לאכזבת הילד המפונק התירס <u>התבשל</u> (/hitbaʃel/) יתר על המידה

(To the disappointment of the spoiled child the corn **was cooked** too long)

Preview Sentences:

Identical Preview Condition:

<u>התבשל</u> (/hitbaʃel/)

Morphological Preview Condition:

<u>התרשם</u> (/hitraʃem/) was impressed)

Orthographic Control Condition:

<u>התחיל</u> (/hitxil/ started)

Figure 1. Example of the stimuli used in Experiment 1. Target and preview words are underlined.

component of the sentence (the nominal object rather than the verbal predicate). We added these filler sentences to try to prevent participants from developing special strategic process for processing the verb if they happened to see a flicker caused by the display change.

The predictability of the target word was assessed with a rating procedure. Twenty participants were asked to assess the predictability of the predicate phrase for each of the sentences given the beginning of the sentence, on a 1 (low)–7 (high) scale. In the rating procedure, another eight filler sentences (in which the verb was in the same position in the sentence but was not predictable) were added to the experimental sentences to increase the range of predictability in the list of sentences to be scored. Only sentences that scored between 3 and 6 were included in the experiment. (Sentences that had a score of 7 were not included because a highly predictable completion increases the probability of skipping the predictable word; Rayner & Well, 1996.)

The sentences were divided into three lists. Each list contained 60 sentences: 16 sentences in each of the three experimental conditions and the 12 filler sentences. The stimuli were rotated within the three conditions in each list by a Latin square design. Twelve participants were tested on each list, allowing each participant to provide data in each condition, yet avoiding stimulus repetition effects. The stimuli were ordered randomly for each subject.

Procedure and apparatus.   Eye movements were monitored by an SR RESEARCH Ltd. (Canada) EYLINK eyetracker. The eyetracker is an infra-red video-based tracking system with two cameras (one for each eye), with two infra-red LEDs for illuminating each eye mounted on a headband (which weighs 450 g). The cameras sample pupil location at a rate of 250 Hz. The sentences were presented on a video monitor (EIZO FlexScan F56 /T) that was interfaced with a 586 computer, which in turn was interfaced with another 586 computer which was interfaced to the eyetracking system. Although viewing was binocular, only data from the right eye were used for analysis. The spatial resolution of the eyetracking system is less than half a degree. Participants were seated 57 cm from the video monitor and 1.8 characters subtended one degree of visual angle.

Each trial started with a fixation point on the right-hand side of the monitor, the location of which coincided with the location of the first letter in the sentence. Once the participant focused on the fixation point, the calibration was verified and the preview screen, which consisted of the complete sentence with one of the three preview words in the target location, was displayed. An invisible boundary was located before the last letter of the word preceding the target word. Participants were instructed to read the sentences for comprehension. When the participant's eyes crossed the invisible boundary, the preview screen was replaced by the target screen, which was identical to the preview screen for all words except the target word (Rayner, 1975). This display change was accomplished within 16 ms, and thus always took place during the saccade. The target screen was displayed until participants finished reading the sentence and moved their eyes towards a green square at the bottom left corner of the screen. Seeing the participant's eyes fixed on the green square signalled the experimenter to bring up the next trial. Twenty-five per cent of the sentences were followed by a yes/no question to ensure that the sentences were being read for meaning. The experiment began with 9 practice sentences, which were immediately followed by the 48 experimental sentences and 12 filler sentences.

RESULTS

All trials in which the word preceding the target word was skipped were eliminated from the analysis, as there would have been little processing of the preview on those trials. Cut-off points of 140 ms and 800 ms were used to eliminate very short or very long single fixations. Twenty-eight per cent of the total observations were excluded on the basis of these criteria. (Most were excluded because of skipping the prior word.) Separate means were calculated for each participant and each item for each of the measures: first fixation duration, gaze duration, total time, and second-pass time. For each of the four measures, outliers more than 2.5 SD above the mean (for each participant in each condition) were replaced by the cut-off value and the mean was recalculated. The same procedures were used for Experiments 2–4.

We first examined the percentage of times the target word was skipped, which would be the earliest plausible effect of the preview manipulation. As indicated in Table 1, the target words were rarely skipped, and there was little effect of the preview on the skipping rate (F < 1). There was virtually no difference between the morphemically related and control conditions, and for some reason, the skipping rate was actually a bit lower in the identical preview condition than in the other two conditions. In contrast, for the earliest fixation measure, the first fixation duration, there was a significant effect of preview condition, $F_1(2, 70) = 18.11$, $MSE = 120$, $p < .001$, $F_2(2, 94) = 10.55$, $MSE = 228$, $p < .001$ (see Table 1). Of greatest interest in the planned comparison analysis is that the 9 ms advantage of the morphologically related condition over the orthographic control condition was significant, $F_1(1, 35) = 8.67$, $MSE = 293$, $p < .01$, $F_2(1, 47) = 5.13$, $MSE = 479$, $p < .05$. The 7 ms difference between the identical and morphologically related conditions was also significant, $F_1(1, 35) = 13.53$, $MSE = 136$, $p < .001$; $F_2(1, 47) = 7.12$, $MSE = 332$, $p < .01$.

TABLE 1
Percentage of time the target word was skipped and mean (and SD) of first fixation duration, gaze duration, and second-pass time (in ms) on the target word for the three preview conditions in Experiment 1

Dependent variable	Identical preview	Morphologically related preview	Orthographic control preview
Percent of trials target word was skipped	3.1%	3.7%	3.5%
First fixation duration	225 (14.7)	232 (14.6)	241 (22.5)
Preview effect	**16**	**9**	–
Gaze duration	274 (22.0)	279 (23.5)	295 (25.3)
Preview effect	**21**	**16**	–
Second pass	54 (26.7)	49 (32.0)	48 (26.3)
Preview effect	**−6**	**−1**	–

A similar pattern of results was found for gaze duration. There was a significant effect of preview condition, $F_1(2, 70) = 14.61$, $MSE = 288$, $p < .001$; $F_2(2, 94) = 9.71$, $MSE = 405$, $p < .001$. The 16 ms advantage of the morphologically related preview condition over the orthographic control was significant, $F_1(1, 35) = 14.27$, $MSE = 617$, $p < .001$, $F_2(1, 47) = 9.62$, $MSE = 819$, $p < .01$. However, the 5 ms difference between the identical and the morphologically related preview conditions was not significant, $F_1(1, 35) = 1.56$, $MSE = 607$, $p > .20$, $F_2(1, 47) = 1.24$, $MSE = 839$, $p > .20$.

In contrast to the robust preview effects on the first pass measures, there were no significant preview effects on second pass times ($Fs < 1$). Indeed, as can be seen in Table 1, the largest difference in second pass measures is that the identical condition was actually 6 ms slower than the control condition (which is implausible as a real effect), and there was only a 1 ms difference between the morphologically related and the orthographic control conditions.

Discussion

The results of Experiment 1 demonstrated a benefit induced by presenting a parafoveal preview word that had the same verbal pattern as the target. These results replicate the morphological priming effect observed in the masked priming paradigm (Deutsch et al., 1998), but in the context of sentence reading in conditions which simulate the natural conditions of reading quite closely. Furthermore, the 16 ms parafoveal preview effect in gaze duration obtained here was similar to both the 12 ms effect obtained in masked priming and the 12 ms parafoveal preview benefit effect induced by the root morpheme (Deutsch et al., 2003). As expected, the effect was observed in first-pass measures only. This is the same pattern that we observed in an earlier study when the parafoveal preview shared the root with the target (Deutsch et al., 2003). As this effect was early—reflecting information extracted prior to the initial fixation on the word and measured within 200–300 ms of the initial fixation on the target word—the likely locus for our morphemic preview effect is in the process of word identification.

An interesting outcome is that the effect of the morphological condition was similar to that of the identical condition. The advantage of the identical over the morphological preview reached statistical significance in first fixation duration, but not in gaze duration. This outcome is different from the clear advantage of the identical over the morphologically related condition in masked priming, but resembles the pattern in our earlier experiment using the root as the preview, where there was no advantage of the identical over the morphological condition in either of the first-pass measures. We will postpone further discussion of these results to the general discussion.

EXPERIMENT 2

In Experiment 2, we investigated whether a parafoveal preview of a nominal pattern can facilitate the reading of nouns derived from that pattern. Thus, in the morphologically related condition, the preview and the foveal word were two nouns with the same nominal pattern but with different root morphemes. Note that in the masked priming paradigm nominal patterns did not produce any priming (Frost et al., 1997).

Method

Participants.   The participants were 42 undergraduate students at the Hebrew University, all native speakers of Hebrew, who participated in the experiment for course credit or payment. All had normal vision or wore corrective lenses.

Stimuli.   The 48 target words were 4–6 letters long. They were all nouns, whose word patterns represented a variety of common word patterns in Hebrew. As in Experiment 1, each target word was paired with three different previews to form the identical, related, and control conditions. All previews were equated in length with the targets (see Figure 2 for examples of the stimuli). The preview in the related condition shared the same nominal pattern as the target but had a different root, whereas the preview in the control condition had both a different nominal pattern and different root. Both the morphologically related previews and the control previews shared, on average, 2.1 letters with the target, and the

Target Sentence:

הפקיד המפוזר חיפש <u>מחברת</u> (/maxberet/)   חשבון ריקה במגירה

(The absent-minded clerk looked for **a notebook** in the drawer)

Preview Sentences:

Identical Preview Condition:

<u>מחברת</u>(/maxberet/)

Morphological Preview Condition:

<u>מדפסת</u>(a printer /madpeset/)

Orthographic Control Condition:

<u>מזמרה</u>(pruning shears /mazmera/)

Figure 2. Example of the stimuli used in Experiment 2. Target and preview words are underlined.

shared letters in the non-identical previews and the target always appeared in the same order, and in most cases (45 out of 48) in the same position within the word.

All the target words were embedded in sentences of 7–10 words which had the same syntactic structure as the sentences used in Experiment 1. Each target word was an object completion of the sentential predicate and was the fourth or fifth word in the sentence. The target word was never the last word on a line. There were also 12 filler sentences, in which the display change took place in a different syntactic element of the sentence (the predicate rather than the object).

These target words, as well as the sentences in which they were embedded, are the same as those that had previously been used to investigate the benefit induced by presenting a parafoveal preview word derived from the same root as the foveal target word (Deutsch et al., 2003). In that experiment we kept the semantic context of the sentence neutral. As the root carries the core semantic meaning of the word, we applied two preliminary procedures to ensure that there was little or no contextual semantic bias. The first was a completion task: 21 participants who did not take part in the reading experiment were asked to read the beginning of each of the experimental sentences (i.e., the words preceding the target) and complete them. Any sentential context that was completed with the target word by at least four participants was replaced (six sentences were replaced for this reason). The second was a predictability rating procedure. These ratings were gathered after the completion task to ensure that no odd sentences were included: 20 participants who had not participated in the completion task were asked to assess the target's predictability for each of the sentences, on a 1 (low)–7 (high) scale. Only sentences that scored between 3 and 6 were included in the experiment. Since all sentences included in this semantic scoring procedure were moderately predictable, another eight filler sentences, in which the noun that was located in the same position as in the target sentences was not predictable, were added to the final list to increase the variability in predictability within the list of sentences to be scored.

Design and procedure.   The design and procedure were identical to those of Experiment 1.

Results

Twenty-eight per cent of the total observations were excluded on the basis of the same exclusion criteria described in Experiment 1: (a) skipping the word prior to the target word, and (b) fixation duration distribution cutoffs. As can be seen in Table 2, the per cent of times that the target word was skipped was somewhat higher than in Experiment 1. However, again, there were no significant differences among the conditions ($Fs < 1$).

The pattern of results in the first pass measures was different from that in Experiment 1, as the identical preview condition differed from the other two conditions, but there was no facilitation from the morphemically related prime. For first fixation duration, there was a significant effect of preview condition, $F_1(2, 82) = 4.98$, $MSE = 192$, $p < .01$, $F_2(2, 94) = 5.12$, $MSE = 214$, $p < .008$, which was due to fixation times in the identical preview condition being 9 ms shorter than in the orthographic control

TABLE 2

Percentage of time the target word was skipped and mean (and SD) of first fixation duration, gaze duration, and second-pass time (in ms) on the target word for the three preview conditions in Experiment 2

Dependent variable	Identical preview	Morphologically related preview	Orthographic control preview
Percent of trials target word was skipped	11.0%	9.6%	9.7%
First fixation duration	222 (15.3)	230 (17.1)	231 (21.7)
Preview effect	**9**	**1**	–
Gaze duration	250 (24.1)	263 (24.6)	262 (38.0)
Preview effect	**12**	**−1**	–
Second pass	61 (42.5)	52 (39.9)	57 (38.6)
Preview effect	**−4**	**5**	–

condition, $F_1(1, 41) = 8.59$, $MSE = 382$, $p < .01$, $F_2(1, 47) = 9.28$, $MSE = 399$, $p < .01$, and 8 ms shorter than in the morphologically related condition, $F_1(1, 41) = 8.78$, $MSE = 271$, $p < .005$, $F_2(1, 47) = 9.27$, $MSE = 299$, $p < .005$. The 1 ms difference between the morphologically related and orthographic control conditions was clearly not close to significance ($Fs < 1$). The pattern was the same for gaze duration, as there was a main effect of preview condition, $F_1(2, 82) = 4.49$, $MSE = 534$, $p < .01$, $F_2(2, 94) = 6.50$, $MSE = 424$, $p < .005$, with first fixation duration in the identity condition being 12 ms shorter than in the orthographic control condition, $F_1(1, 41) = 6.57$, $MSE = 1045$, $p < .001$; $F_2(1, 47) = 9.64$, $MSE = 806$, $p < .005$, and 13 ms shorter than in the morphologically related condition, $F_1(1, 41) = 10.04$, $MSE = 747$, $p < .005$, $F_2(1, 47) = 9.94$, $MSE = 879$, $p < .005$. Again, the 1 ms difference between the morphologically related and orthographic control conditions was not close to significant ($Fs < 1$). As in Experiment 1, there was no main effect of morphological preview condition in second pass time, $F_1(2, 82) = 1.56$, $MSE = 551$, $p > .20$, $F_2(2, 94) = 1.46$, $MSE = 672$, $p > .20$. The small differences in second pass times would be hard to interpret (even if reliable) as the second pass times in the morphologically related condition were less than the control condition, but the second pass time in the identical condition was actually greater than in the control condition.

Discussion

In Experiment 2, previews that were morphologically related to the foveal target words, in that they shared a nominal pattern, did not facilitate first pass processing of the target word. This outcome replicates the results obtained in the masked priming paradigm for single-word identification (Frost et al., 1997). In both paradigms, no effect was observed for nominal patterns. The null priming effect for nominal patterns was previously explained as anchored in some salient characteristics of the nominal patterns, which are (a) low frequency of most patterns relative to the frequency of each verbal pattern, (b) vague semantic characteristics, and (c) no specific prominent structural property such as the three-consonantal structure that most roots have. Thus, as a group, nominal patterns do not have any prominent property that would assist lexical access (for a detailed discussion, see Deutsch et al., 1998). It should be noted that a dissociation between two types of morphemes was recently observed in French. Using the masked priming paradigm, Giraudo and Grainger (2003) obtained a significant facilitation effect for primes that shared a prefix with the target, but no hint of an effect for primes that shared a derivational suffix with the target. The results may be parallel because, like the difference between verbal and nominal patterns in Hebrew, prefixes in French are more limited in number and have more systematic meanings than derivational suffixes in French.

EXPERIMENT 3

In the next two experiments we moved to examine the effect of contextual factors on morphological preview benefit. The aim of Experiment 3 was to assess whether prior semantic context influences the extraction of morphological information in reading. The parafoveal preview technique allows one to assess the influence of prior context on the initial phases of extraction of information from a word before it is actually fixated. In particular, previous studies have shown that there was greater benefit in extracting orthographic information from a parafoveal preview when the target word was predictable from the preceding context (Balota, Pollatsek, & Rayner, 1985). In the current experiment we investigated whether morphological processing is also more efficient when the meaning of a morpheme is predictable from the prior sentence context. This was tested by employing a preview in the morphologically related condition that was derived from the same root as the foveal word, and embedding it in either a semantically neutral or in a biasing context. The key question was whether the size of the benefit from a preview of the root morpheme would be larger when the meaning of that morpheme was predictable from prior sentence context than when the prior context was neutral with respect to the target word (and hence the meaning of the root morpheme was not predictable). We focused on the interaction between *semantic* contextual effects and the morphological parafoveal preview benefit induced by the root morphemes, as the root carries the core meaning of a word.

Method

Participants. The participants were 56 undergraduate students at the Hebrew University. All were native speakers of Hebrew, who participated in the experiment for course credit or payment. All had normal vision or wore corrective lenses.

Stimuli and design. The 64 target words were nominal forms that were 4–5 letters long. Each target word was paired with two different previews to form the morphologically related and orthographic control conditions. (There was no identical preview condition in this experiment.) The morphologically related preview had the same root morpheme as the target. The target and the two non-identical previews in each set of sentences were equated for length. The morphologically related previews and control previews both shared, on average, 2.3 letters with the target, and the shared letters in the non-identical previews and the target always appeared in the same order. However, the original position of the common letters and their contiguity was not necessarily preserved, as it is close to impossible to control all these aspects within each set of stimuli, when the root morpheme is under investigation. No previews had the same initial letter as the target. (See Figure 3 for an example of the stimulus materials.)

All target words were embedded in sentences of 7–10 words that had the same syntactic structure as the previous experiments. Each target word was embedded in two different sentential contexts—one was semantically neutral and the other was semantically biased. The semantically biased context was constructed by replacing one (or sometimes more) of the content words preceding the target with a word that was semantically related to the target.

The semantic biasing manipulation was assessed by two preliminary procedures. The first was a predictability completion task: 40 participants who did not take part in the reading experiment were asked to read the beginning of each of the experimental sentences (i.e., the words preceding the target) and complete them. Half of the sentences were candidates for the semantically neutral condition, and half were candidates for the semantically biasing condition. For the former, any sentential context that was completed by at least 10 participants with the actual target word was replaced. For the latter, only sentences that were completed with the actual target word by at least 10 participants were included. After this step, the sentences were rated for semantic plausibility by 40 participants who had not participated in the completion task, on a 1 (low)–7 (high) scale. Only pairs of sentences that scored between 3 and 6 in the semantically neutral context, and not less than 4 in the semantically biased context, were included in the experiment. These ratings were gathered after the completion task to ensure that no odd sentences were included. As in Experiment 1 and 2, we included another eight filler sentences with very low predictability.

The sentences were divided into four lists. Each list contained 64 sentences: 32 provided a semantically neutral context and 32 provided a semantically biased context. Each of these sentences in the list had either a morphologically related or an orthographic control preview. Each list thus contained 16 sentences in each of the four experimental preview conditions: (1) Semantically neutral—Morphologically related, (2) Semantically neutral—Orthographic control, (3) Semantically biased—Morphologically related, (4) Semantically Biased—Orthographic Control. The stimuli were rotated within the four conditions in each list by a Latin Square design. Fourteen participants were tested in each list, allowing each participant to provide data in each condition, yet avoiding stimulus repetition effects.

Semantically neutral context:

Target Sentence:

משטרת הגבולות תפסה **מרגלת** (/mragelet/) בביקורת הדרכונים

(The border police caught **a spy** at passport control)

Preview Sentences:

Morphological Preview Condition:

ריגול (spying /rigul/)

Orthographic Control Condition:

רוכלת (a peddler /roxelet/)

Semantically biasing context:

Target Sentence:

סוכנות הביון תפסה **מרגלת** (/mragelet/) בביקורת הדרכונים

(The intelligence agency caught **a spy** at passport control)

Preview Sentences:

Morphological Preview Condition:

ריגול (spying /rigul/)

Orthographic Control Condition:

רוכלת (a peddler /roxelet/)

Figure 3. Example of the stimuli used in Experiment 3. Target and preview words are underlined.

Procedure. The procedure was identical to that of the previous experiments.

Results

Thirty-one per cent of the total observations were excluded on the basis of the same exclusion criteria described in Experiment 1: (a) skipping the word prior to the target word, and (b) fixation duration distribution cut-offs. As in Experiment 1, the target word was rarely skipped (see Table 3) and there was little difference among the four conditions.

There were significant effects of a morphemically related preview in both measures of first pass processing, and the apparent modulation of this effect by the prior context was not consistent across the two measures. For first fixation duration, there was a 7 ms effect of preview condition, $F_1(1, 55) = 4.98$, $MSE = 169$, $p < .001$, $F_2(1, 63) = 11.73$, $MSE = 245$, $p < .001$, and the main effect of context was 0 ms. The preview effect appeared to be bigger in the semantically neutral condition, but the interaction between the preview and the context condition was not close to significant, $F_1(1, 55) = 1.82$, $MSE = 197$, $p > .10$, $F_2(1, 63) = 1.90$, $MSE = 223$, $p > .10$. Planned comparisons revealed that the 9 ms preview effect in the semantically neutral context was significant, $F_1(1, 55) = 13.65$, $MSE = 367$, $p < .001$; $F_2(1, 63) = 11.95$, $MSE = 461$, $p < .001$, but the 4 ms preview effect in the semantically biased context was not, $F_1(1, 55) = 2.47$, $MSE = 385$, $p > .10$, $F_2(1, 63) = 2.29$, $MSE = 476$, $p > .10$. For gaze duration, there was a 13 ms effect of preview condition, $F_1(1, 55) = 13.70$, $MSE = 608$, $p < .001$, $F_2(1, 63) = 17.27$, $MSE = 551$, $p < .001$, and the main effect of context was again 0 ms. This time the preview effect was larger in the semantically biased condition, but again the interaction between the preview and the context condition was not close to significant, $F_1(1, 55) = 1.87$, $MSE = 532$, $p > .10$, $F_2(1, 63) = 1.81$, $MSE = 629$, $p > .10$. Planned comparisons revealed that the 9 ms preview effect in the semantically neutral context was close to significant, $F_1(1, 55) = 4.36$, $MSE = 818$, $p < .05$, $F_2(1, 63) = 3.88$, $MSE = 1050$, $p = .053$, and the 17 ms preview effect in the semantically biased context was significant, $F_1(1, 55) = 10.32$, $MSE = 1462$, $p < .005$, $F_2(1, 63) = 13.16$, $MSE = 1309$, $p < .001$.

TABLE 3

Percentage of time the target word was skipped and mean (and SD) of first fixation duration, gaze duration, and second-pass time (in ms) on the target word for the four preview conditions in Experiment 3

Dependent variable	Semantically neutral prior context		Semantically biased prior context	
	Morphologically related	Orthographic control	Morphologically related	Orthographic control
Percent of trials target word was skipped	1.4%	1.4%	1.7%	1.9%
First fixation duration	224 (19.1)	233 (20.8)	227 (19.0)	231 (23.4)
Preview effect	9	–	4	
Gaze duration	279 (32.7)	288 (30.1)	275 (34.2)	292 (39.3)
Preview effect	9	–	17	–
Second pass time	98 (58.3)	105 (65.6)	75 (50.4)	90 (64.3)
Preview effect	7	–	15	–

There was also an 11 ms preview effect on second pass time, $F_1(1, 55) = 6.28$, $MSE = 1081$, $p < .05$, $F_2(1, 63) = 4.66$, $MSE = 1666$, $p < .05$. In addition, second pass times were smaller in the semantically biased condition than in the control condition, $F_1(1, 55) = 16.33$, $MSE = 1201$, $p < .001$, $F_2(1, 63) = 9.00$, $MSE = 2490$, $p < .01$, which indicated that when target words were easier to relate to the prior context, it facilitated the reading of the ensuing text. Again, the interaction between the preview and the context condition was not significant, $Fs < 1$, but planned comparisons revealed that in the semantically biased context the 15 ms preview effect on second-pass time in the morphologically related condition was significant, $F_1(1, 55) = 6.2$, $MSE = 2050$, $p < .05$, $F_2(1, 63) = 5.12$, $MSE = 2837$, $p < .05$, but that the 7 ms preview effect on second pass time in the semantically neutral condition was not, $Fs < 1$.

Discussion

The results of Experiment 3 revealed a significant morphological preview effect induced by the root morpheme in the first pass, but that there was no consistent effect of a semantically biasing context either on the overall duration of first pass fixations or on the size of the benefit from a morphologically related preview. The results for a semantically neutral context replicated previous results in Hebrew, where the morphological preview effect induced by the root morpheme was investigated for semantically neutral sentences (Deutsch et al., 2003). In contrast, both factors had an effect on second pass times: both a semantically biased context and a morphemically related preview shortened second pass time. This indicates that prior semantic contextual factors did not affect the initial morphological processes in word identification, but only came into play later, in post-lexical processing.

EXPERIMENT 4

In Experiment 4, we investigated the interactions between early morphological processes and on-line *syntactic* processes in reading. The key question was whether seeing a preview that contained a verbal form in a syntactically constraining context that required the target word to have a nominal completion, would inhibit processing of the word, and moreover, whether this inhibition effect would occur in first-pass reading measures. We focused on verbal patterns because they provide important grammatical information for syntactic analysis. The expectation that a syntactically constraining context may affect the reader sensitivity to parafoveal information is supported by the well documented phenomenon of a higher skipping rate for function words (Gautier, O'Regan, & LaGargasson, 2000; O'Regan, 1979). As this higher skipping rate cannot be solely attributed to perceptual factors such as word length (Brysbaert & Vitu, 1998), or orthographic familiarity (Koriat & Greenberg, 1994), it may imply, given an appropriately constraining syntactic context (Reichle, Rayner, & Pollatsek, 2003), that function words are identified quickly because of their high predictability and/or easy assimilation into the on-line process of building syntactic structures. In the present experiment we wanted to investigate whether on-line syntactic processes, which apparently affect the speed of word identification, may also affect the extraction of morphological information from the parafovea which is relevant to these analyses, and/or its impact on lexical access of the foveal word.

Method

Participants. The participants were 42 undergraduate students at the Hebrew University. All were native speakers of Hebrew, who participated in the experiment for course credit or payment. All had normal vision or wore corrective lenses.

Stimuli. The sentences used in this experiment were the same as in Experiment 2 with the same (4–6 letter) nominal target words. Thus the target words were nominal completions required by the preceding verbs. Each target word was coupled with three different previews forming three experimental conditions: (1) identical, (2) syntactically incongruent, with a preview of a word containing a verbal rather than a nominal pattern, and (3) syntactically congruent control, with a preview of a word having a different root and a different nominal pattern from the target word, but sharing the same number of letters with the target as the syntactically incongruent preview (see Figure 4). Neither the syntactically congruent nor the syntactically incongruent previews were at all semantically related to the target word. The third preview condition served as an orthographic control condition for the syntactically incongruent condition. The target and the two non-identical previews within each triple were equated for length. Both the syntactically congruent and control previews shared, on average, 1.6 letters with the target, and the shared letters in the non-identical previews and the target always appeared in the same order, and in most cases (45 out of 48) in the same position within the word. Another 12 filler sentences, in which the display change took place in a different syntactic element of the sentence (the predicate rather than the object), were included.

Results

Thirty five percent of the total observations were excluded on the basis of the same exclusion criteria described in Experiment 1: (a) skipping the word prior to the target word, and (b) fixation duration distribution

Target Sentence

סוכן הביטוח קיבל (.Pred)   <u>תשלום</u> (/ta∫lum/)בעבור שרותיו הנאמנים

(The Insurance agency received **payments** for his loyal service)

Preview Sentences

Identical Preview Condition:

<u>תשלום</u> (/ta∫lum/)

Syntactically Incongruent Context

<u>השחים</u> (/hi∫xim/) (browned)

Syntactically Congruent Context – Control Condition

<u>אילוף</u> (/∫iluf / (training of animals

Figure 4. Example of the stimuli used in Experiment 4. Target and preview words are underlined.

cutoffs. The skipping rates for the target word were again low, and there were no significant differences among the three preview conditions (see Table 4).

However, the type of preview did affect first pass processing times. As can be seen from Table 4, having an identical preview speeded processing of the target word relative to a control preview that shared several letters and which was syntactically congruent with the target word. Of greatest interest was that a syntactically incongruent preview slowed processing relative to a syntactically congruent preview, even though neither preview shared any morphemes with the target. For first fixation duration, there was a significant effect of preview condition, $F_1(2, 82)$ = 5.91, $MSE = 210$, $p < .01$, $F_2(2, 94) = 4.14$, $MSE = 342$, $p < .05$. Planned comparisons indicated that the 8 ms facilitation due to having an identical preview (compared to the orthographic control condition) was significant, $F_1(1, 41) = 7.06$, $MSE = 405$, $p < .01$; $F_2(1, 47) = 7.47$, MSE = 4.37, $p < .05$, but that the 5 ms inhibition due to having an incongruent verbal preview (compared to the orthographic control condition) was not, $Fs < 1$. For gaze duration, the effect of preview condition was also significant, $F_1(2, 82) = 16.25$, $MSE = 377$, $p < .001$; $F_2(2, 94) = 11.09$, $MSE = 632$, $p < .001$, and both the 12 ms facilitation in the identity condition (relative to the orthographic control condition), $F_1(1, 41) = 7.85$, $MSE = 723$, $p < .01$; $F_2(1, 47) = 5.74$, $MSE = 1131$, p < .05, and the 13 ms inhibition effect in the verbal preview condition (relative to the orthographic control condition), $F_1(1, 41) = 8.86$, $MSE =$ 743, $p < .01$; $F_2(1, 47) = 4.71$, $MSE = 1599$, $p < .05$, were significant.

TABLE 4

Percentage of time the target word was skipped and mean (and SD) of first fixation duration, gaze duration, and second-pass time (in ms) on the target word for the three preview conditions in Experiment 4

Dependent variable	Identical preview	Syntactically incongruent preview	Syntactically congruent control preview
Percent of trials target word was skipped	3.6%	2.9%	1.8%
First fixation duration	226 (21.6)	239 (22.2)	234 (28.7)
Preview effect	**8**	**−5**	–
Gaze duration	258 (45.1)	282 (43.3)	269 (42.1)
Preview effect	**12**	**−13**	–
Second pass ime	73 (58.6)	91 (64.8)	66 (52.4)
Preview effect	**7**	**−25**	–

The pattern of results was somewhat different in the second-pass times. There was a significant effect of preview condition, $F_1(2, 82) = 7.19$, $MSE = 937$, $p < .001$; $F_2(2, 94) = 6.38$, $MSE = 1207$, $p < .01$, and planned comparisons indicated that although the 7 ms difference between the identical condition and control condition was not close to significant, $F_1 < 1$, $F_2(1, 47) = 1.18$, $MSE = 1686$, $p > .20$, the 25 ms inhibition induced by the syntactically incongruent preview was significant, $F_1(1, 41) = 13.25$, $MSE = 1892$, $p < .001$, $F_2(1, 47) = 9.19$, $MSE = 3117$, $p < .01$.

Discussion

The results of Experiment 4 revealed a clear inhibition effect induced by presenting a preview of a verbal form that was syntactically incongruent, because it was in a syntactically constraining context that required a nominal form. The gaze duration on the nominal foveal word was lengthened as was the second pass measure. This supports our claim, based on Experiment 1, that verbal pattern information is indeed extracted from the preview. Furthermore it indicates that whether or not this information is congruent with on-line syntactic processing has a fairly immediate impact on processing the foveal target word. This outcome contrasts with the findings of Experiment 3 which did not reveal early contextual effects in the semantic domain on morphological processing. However, note that the inhibitory effect on first fixation duration was not significant, so that the morphological information that was extracted from the parafovea, and was relevant for the construction of the syntax of the sentence, did not seem to affect the earliest stages of word recognition when the word is initially fixated.

GENERAL DISCUSSION

In the present experiments, we investigated the effects of morphological information in the parafovea on the identification of an up-coming Hebrew word in the course of sentence reading. In the first two experiments, we examined whether there would be a benefit from presenting a preview that was a word that shared either a verbal or a nominal pattern with the target word. We found a clear benefit from having a preview of the verbal pattern in Experiment 1, but no benefit from presenting a preview of the nominal pattern in Experiment 2. These results complement previous studies which demonstrated a morphological preview benefit effect induced by the root morpheme (Deutsch et al., 2003). Thus, it appears that of the three derivational morphemes that exist in Hebrew—the root, the verbal pattern, and the nominal pattern—only a preview of the nominal pattern fails to provide any benefit. In all cases, a significant benefit from the preview only occurred in first-pass reading measures. These findings parallel those in single-word identification in masked priming, where a priming effect was observed for roots and verbal-pattern primes, but not for nominal patterns. Furthermore, the size of the effects observed in masked priming was very similar to the effects found on gaze duration in the sentence reading studies (about 12 ms), suggesting that the two paradigms tap similar encoding processes. This is in spite of obvious differences in the paradigms, such as differences in the exposure duration of the 'prime' and differences in the location of the 'prime'. Perhaps this means that information extraction in the parafovea is not fundamentally different than in the fovea. It should also be noted that although most of the parafoveal preview experiments cited here involved reading words in sentence context, there is a variant of the parafoveal preview paradigm involving naming of isolated words that has obtained quite similar results as the sentence reading version with respect to obtaining benefit from orthographically and phonologically previews but not obtaining benefit from semantically similar previews (Altarriba, Kambe, Pollatsek, & Rayner, 2001; Pollatsek et al., 1992; Rayner, 1975).

One difference between the masked priming and the parafoveal preview experiments should be noted, however. In masked priming the priming effect for identical primes is typically about twice as large as for morphologically related primes (Frost et al., 1997, 2000). In contrast, for parafoveal previews, there was no advantage of an identical preview over a root preview in Deutsch et al. (2003) and a significant advantage of an identical preview over a verbal pattern preview in Experiment 1, but only for the first fixation measure. This indication of a difference between root previews and verbal pattern previews suggests that the root morpheme is identified earlier than the verbal-pattern morpheme, at least in the parafovea. That is, if the completion of encoding the root occurs prior to the completion of the encoding of the verbal pattern, one might observe no advantage for seeing the whole word in the parafovea (i.e., the identical preview condition) over seeing only the root, but observe an advantage of the identical preview over the verbal-pattern preview early in processing (indexed by the first fixation duration). However, this advantage should diminish later in processing.

The present results thus indicate that extraction of the root morpheme precedes the extraction of the verbal pattern, although both are extracted relatively early in the process of identifying a word. Another study (Frost et al., 2000) suggested that extraction of the root morpheme not only precedes the extraction of the verbal pattern, but that the extraction of the verbal pattern depends on extracting the root morpheme. Frost et al. investigated the extraction of the verbal-pattern morpheme from verbs derived from *weak roots* (Frost et al., 2000). (Weak roots are roots that do not possess the regular structure of a three-consonantal root.) Using the masked priming paradigm, they obtained no evidence for a verbal pattern priming effect, in contrast to the robust verbal pattern priming effect observed for other verbal forms in Hebrew. They concluded that extraction of the verbal pattern from the prime failed because the extraction of the root morpheme failed (probably because of violation of structural constraints) and thus the whole process of decomposition could not proceed. Thus, there are several converging clues for the time course of decomposing the root and the verbal pattern. However, it should be noted that our suggestion that the verbal pattern lags behind the root, in the present research, is a post-hoc explanation based on fairly subtle differences between the identical and the morphologically related conditions in first fixation and gaze duration in Experiment 1. This issue deserves further investigation.

Experiments 3 and 4 investigated whether prior semantic or syntactic context can interact with early morphological processing. The answer was different in the two cases: a semantically biasing context did not influence the processing of a parafoveal preview of the root morpheme in the first pass. In contrast, a preview of a verbal pattern in a syntactically incongruent context lengthened the fixation duration of a nominal word even on the first pass. The latter findings suggest that contextual syntactic constraint can modulate the use of parafoveal morphological information in the process of identifying the foveal word. In contrast, there was no clear indication of such an interaction with prior semantic context. That is, if the meaning of the root morpheme seen in the parafovea was more easily recognised and/or more quickly utilised given a strongly biasing semantic context, then one would have expected a larger preview benefit from this information in the biasing context than in a more neutral context.

Although there was a hint of such an effect in the gaze duration data, it was far from significant, and the effect in the first fixation data actually went in the opposite direction. The absence of any contextual effect on early morphological processes in the semantic domain supports bottom-up models for word recognition, where the process of word recognition is not affected by higher contextual processes. Thus it seems that the process of root extraction is an initial and thus fast process that is not affected by on-line higher semantic processing. However, the findings from manipulating syntactic contextual effect do suggest a top-down influence in which information from higher levels feeds back and interacts with processing at lower levels.

This discrepancy between the semantic and syntactic effects, however, could be because the syntactic domain is much more highly constrained than the semantic domain. It could also reflect the linguistic characteristics of the root and the verbal-pattern morphemes. That is, there are many roots, each of them with a global (i.e., not very precise) semantic meaning, and each having a large number of homonyms. In contrast, there are only seven verbal patterns, each of them with fairly well-defined syntactic characteristics, such as transitivity and mode. Accordingly, the preview of a verbal pattern provides well-defined syntactic information whereas the semantic information provided from the root preview morpheme is vague. Thus, the way prior context interacts with early morphological decomposition processes may depend not only on the type of contextual factor (semantic or syntactic), but on the linguistic characteristics of the specific morpheme. This issue should, however, be investigated further, where the next step would be to examine whether contextual effects in the semantic domain can interact with early morphological processes of nominal patterns, which usually reveal no morphological effects. The critical question is whether supporting contextual semantic context can enhance early morphological effects of decomposing nominal patterns that are usually not expressed in single word identification paradigms or in a semantically neutral context.

Finally, our results contrast with studies in English, where no morphological preview effects have been observed in sentence reading (Inhoff, 1989a; Kambe, 2004; Lima, 1987). Similarly, as indicated earlier, although morphological priming effects in Hebrew are very robust in masked priming paradigm, they are more fragile in English (Forster & Azuma, 2000; Rastle & Davis, 2003). However, interestingly, the opposite pattern is observed with form priming in the two languages. That is, in English (as well as in other Indo-European languages) pure *orthographic similarity* between prime and target (i.e., matching letters in the same letter positions) strongly facilitates the identification of written words both in the masked priming paradigm (Forster, Davis, Schoknecht, & Carter,

1987; Forster & Veres, 1998) and in parafoveal preview (Altarriba et al., 2001, Rayner, 1975). In contrast, there is recent evidence that there is no form priming in Hebrew (Frost, Kugler, Deutsch, & Forster, 2004). This discrepancy between the two languages could reflect differences in the principles by which the two lexicons are organised: lexical organisation guided primarily by orthographical principles based on letter sequentiality and letter position as opposed to lexical organisation primarily guided by morphological principles. (See Frost et al., 2004, for a detailed discussion.). In the latter case, the organising units are morphological units with non-concatenated repeated structures. The differences in the principle of lexical organisation may be anchored in the linguistic differences between Hebrew and English both with respect to morphological structure and to the role of morphology in the grammar. If so, this suggests that the organisation of the lexicon may differ depending on many aspects of the language one is studying.

REFERENCES

Altarriba, J., Kambe, G., Pollatsek, A., & Rayner, K. (2001). Semantic codes are not used in integrating information across eye fixations: Evidence from fluent Spanish-English bilinguals. *Perception and Psychophysics, 63*, 875–891.

Balota, D. A., Pollatsek, A., & Rayner, K. (1985). The interaction of contextual constraints and parafoveal visual information in reading. *Cognitive Psychology, 17*, 364–390.

Boudelaa, S., & Marslen-Wilson, W. D. (2001). Morphological units in the Arabic mental lexicon. *Cognition, 81*, 65–92.

Brysbaert, M., & Vitu, F. (1998). Word skipping: Implications for theories of eye movement control in reading. In G. Underwood (Ed.), *Eye guidance in reading and sentence perception* (pp. 125–148). Oxford: Elsevier.

Deutsch, A., & Frost, R. (2003). Lexical organization and lexical access in a non-concatenated morphology. In J. Shimron (Ed.), *Language processing and acquisition in languages of semitic, root-based, morphology* (pp. 165–186). Amsterdam: John Benjamins Publishing Company.

Deutsch, A., Frost, R., & Forster, K. (1998). Verbs and nouns are organized and accessed differently in the mental lexicon: Evidence from Hebrew. *Journal of Experimental Psychology: Learning, Memory, and Cognition, 24*, 1238–1255.

Deutsch, A., Frost, R., Pelleg, S., Pollatsek, A., & Rayner, K. (2003). Early morphological effects in reading: Evidence from parafoveal preview benefit in Hebrew. *Psychonomic Bulletin and Review, 10*, 415–422.

Deutsch, A., Frost, R., Pollatsek, A., & Rayner, K. (2000). Early morphological effects in word recognition in Hebrew: Evidence from parafoveal preview benefit. *Language and Cognitive Processes, 15*, 487–506.

Drews, E., & Zwitserlood, P. (1995). Morphological and orthographic similarity in visual word recognition. *Journal of Experimental Psychology: Human, Perception and Performance, 21*, 1098–1116.

Forster, K. I., & Azuma, T. (2000). Masked priming for prefixed words with bound stems: Does submit prime permit? *Language and Cognitive Processes, 15*, 539–561.

Forster, K. I., & Davis, C. (1984). Repetition priming and frequency attenuation in lexical access. *Journal of Experimental Psychology: Learning, Memory, and Cognition, 10,* 680–698.

Forster, K. I., Davis, C., Schoknecht, C., & Carter, A. (1987). Masked priming with graphemically related forms. Repetition or partial activation. *Quarterly Journal of Experimental Psychology, 30,* 1–25.

Forster, K. I., & Veres, C. (1998). The prime lexicality effect: Form-priming as a function of prime awareness, lexical status, and discrimination difficulty. *Journal of Experimental Psychology: Learning, Memory, and Cognition, 24,* 498–314.

Frost, R., Deutsch, A., & Forster, K. (2000). Decomposing morphologically complex words in a nonlinear morphology. *Journal of Experimental Psychology: Learning, Memory, and Cognition, 26,* 751–765.

Frost, R., Forster, K. I., & Deutsch, A. (1997). What can we learn from the morphology of Hebrew: A masked priming investigation of morphological representation. *Journal of Experimental Psychology: Learning Memory, and Cognition, 23,* 829–856.

Frost, R., Kugler, T., Deutsch, A., & Forster, K. I. (2004). *Orthographic structure versus morphological structure: Principles of lexical organization in a given language.* Manuscript submitted for publication.

Gautier, V., O'Regan, J. K., & LaGargasson, J. F. (2000). "The skipping" revisited in French: Programming saccades to skip the article "les". *Vision Research, 40,* 2517–2531.

Giraudo, H., & Grainger, J. (2003). On the role of derivational affixes in recognizing complex words: Evidence from masked priming. In R. H. Baayen & R. Schreuder (Eds.), *Morphological structure in language processing* (pp. 209–232). Berlin: Mouton de Gruyter.

Grainger, J., Cole, P., & Segui, J. (1991). Masked morphological priming in visual word recognition. *Journal of Memory and Language, 30,* 370–384.

Hadley, J. A., & Healy, A. F. (1991). When are reading units larger than the letter? Refinement of the unitization reading model. *Journal of Experimental Psychology: Learning, Memory, and Cognition, 17,* 1062–1073.

Henderson, J. M., Dixon, P., Peterson, A., Twilley, L. C., & Ferreira, F. (1995). Evidence for the use of phonological representation during transaccadic word recognition. *Journal of Experimental Psychology: Human Perception and Performance, 21,* 82–97.

Inhoff, A. W. (1989a). Lexical access during eye fixations in reading: Are word access codes used to integrate lexical information across interword fixations? *Journal of Memory and Language, 28,* 444–461.

Inhoff, A. W. (1989b). Parafoveal processing of words and saccade computation during eye fixations in reading. *Journal of Experimental Psychology: Human Perception and Performance, 15,* 544–555.

Kambe, G. (2004). Parafoveal processing of prefixed words during eye fixations in reading: Evidence against morphological influences on parafoveal preprocessing. *Perception and Psychophysics,* in press.

Koriat, A., & Greenberg, S. N. (1994). The extraction of phrase structure during reading: Evidence from letter detection errors. *Psychonomic Bulletin and Review, 1,* 345–356.

Laudana, A., Cermele, A., & Caramazza, A. (1997). Morpho-lexical representations in naming. *Language and Cognitive Processes, 12,* 49–66.

Lima, S. D. (1987). Morphological analysis in sentence reading. *Journal of Memory and Language, 26,* 84–99.

Masson, M. E. J., & Isaak, M. I. (1999). Masked priming of words and nonwords in a naming task: Further evidence for a nonlexical basis for priming. *Memory and Cognition, 27,* 399–412.

Morrison, R. E. (1984). Manipulation of stimulus onset delay in reading: Evidence for parallel programming of saccades. *Journal of Experimental Psychology: Human Perception and Performance, 10*, 667–682.

Musseler, J., Koriat, A., & Nißlein, M. (2000). Letter-detection patterns in German: A window to the early extraction of sentential structure during reading. *Memory and Cognition, 28*, 993–1003.

O'Regan, K. (1979). Saccade size control in reading: Evidence for the linguistic control hypothesis. *Perception and Psychophysics, 25*, 501–509.

Pollatsek, A., Bolozky, S., Well, A. D., & Rayner, K. (1981). Asymmetries in the perceptual span for Israeli readers. *Brain and Language, 14*, 174–180.

Pollatsek, A., Lesch, M., Morris, R. K., & Rayner, K. (1992). Phonological codes are used in integrating information across saccades in word identification and reading. *Journal of Experimental Psychology: Human Perception and Performance, 18*, 148–162.

Rastle, K., & Davis, M. H. (2003). Reading morphologically complex words: Some thoughts from masked priming. In A. Kinoshita & S. J. Lupker (Eds.), *Masked priming: The state of the art* (pp. 279–308). New York: Psychology Press.

Rastle, K., Davis, M. H., Marslen-Wilson, W., & Tyler, L. K. (2000). Morphological and semantic effects in visual word recognition: A time-course study. *Language and Cognitive Processes, 15*, 507–537

Rayner, K. (1975). The perceptual span and peripheral cues in reading. *Cognitive Psychology, 7*, 65–81.

Rayner, K. (1998). Eye movements in reading and information processing: 20 years of research. *Psychological Bulletin, 124*, 372–422.

Rayner, K., McConkie, G. W., & Zola, D. (1980). Integrating information across eye movements. *Cognitive Psychology, 12*, 206–226.

Rayner, K., & Pollatsek, A. (1989). *The psychology of reading*. New Jersey: Prentice Hall.

Rayner, K., & Well, A. D. (1996). Effects of contextual constraint on eye movements in reading: A further examination. *Psychonomic Bulletin and Review, 3*, 504–509.

Rayner, K., Well, A. D., Pollatsek, A., & Bertera, J. H. (1982). The availability of useful information to the right of fixation in reading. *Perception and Psychophysics, 31*, 537–550.

Reichle, E. D., Pollatsek, A., Fisher, D. L., & Rayner, K. (1998). Toward a model of eye movement control in reading. *Psychological Review, 105*, 125–157.

Reichle, E. D., Rayner, K., & Pollatsek, A. (2003). The E-Z Reader model of eye movements control in reading: Comparisons to other models. *Behavioral and Brain Sciences, 26*, 445–476.

Saint-Aubin, J., & Klein, R. A. (2001). The influence of parafoveal processing on the missing-letter effect. *Journal of Experimental Psychology: Human, Perception and Performance, 27*, 318–334.

Taft, M., & Forster, K. I. (1975). Lexical storage and retrieval of prefixed words. *Journal of Verbal Learning and Verbal Behavior, 14*, 638–647.

LANGUAGE AND COGNITIVE PROCESSES
2005, 20 (1/2), 373–394

Changing morphological structures: The effect of sentence context on the interpretation of structurally ambiguous English trimorphemic words

Roberto G. de Almeida

Department of Psychology, Concordia University, Montreal, Canada

Gary Libben

Department of Linguistics, University of Alberta, Edmonton, Canada

Morphological parsing has often been studied with words in isolation. In this study we used sentence context to investigate how structural analyses of morphologically complex words are affected by the semantic content of their carrier sentences. Our main stimuli were trimorphemic ambiguous words such as *unlockable* (meaning either "not able to be locked" or "able to be unlocked"). We treat these words as structurally ambiguous such that the meaning of the words is determined by the perceived organisation of their constituent morphemes. The effect and malleability of this structural organisation were examined in one offline rating experiment and one cross-modal priming experiment with ambiguous words embedded in sentence context. The results of the study suggest that morphologically

Correspondence should be addressed to either author. Gary Libben, Department of Linguistics, 4-36 Assiniboia Hall, University of Alberta, Edmonton, Alberta, Canada T6G 2E7. Email: gary.libben@ualberta.ca or Roberto G. de Almeida, Department of Psychology, Concordia University, 7141 Sherbrooke St. West, Montreal, QC, Canada, H4B 1R6. Email: almeida@alcor.concordia.ca

Authors are listed in alphabetical order. This research was supported by research grants from the Social Sciences and Humanities Research Council of Canada (SSHRC) and the Fonds québécois de la recherche sur la société et la culture to Roberto G. de Almeida and a Major Collaborative Research Initiative Grant from SSHRC to Gary Libben (Director) Gonia Jarema, Eva Kehayia, Bruce Derwing, and Lori Buchanan.

We would like to thank Julie Turbide for her help in the preparation of the materials and for recording the sentences for Experiment 2. We also thank our research assistants for helping with data coding and running the experiments: Julie Turbide, Heather Wilcox, and Sally Cooper. Finally, we would like to thank Harald Baayen, Jonathan Grainger, and an anonymous reviewer for many helpful comments and suggestions.

http://www.tandf.co.uk/journals/pp/01690965.html   DOI: 10.1080/01690960444000232

ambiguous words do show two interpretations and that the balance of these interpretations can be affected by the semantics of the sentence in which they are embedded. We interpret the pattern of data to suggest that when structurally ambiguous words are presented in isolation, word-internal factors determine which interpretation is to be preferred. However, in strongly constraining sentence contexts, these preferred parses are modified online to be consistent with the semantics of the entire sentence structure.

Ambiguity in language has delighted poets and annoyed philosophers for centuries. Aristotle (Rhetoric, Book 3) states that "Words of ambiguous meaning are chiefly useful to enable the Sophist to mislead his hearers". However, it is possible that Aristotle may have failed to note the manner in which linguistic ambiguity also reveals the intricate connectedness of language levels—the connectedness that allows us to achieve communicative precision despite the widespread ambiguity that characterises the system itself.

The key to the human ability to resolve linguistic ambiguity is undoubtedly the use of higher-level contexts to resolve lower-level equivocality. By this means, the phonetic values of graphemes are resolved by their realisations within words, the ambiguities that characterise words are resolved in their sentence contexts, and ambiguous sentences are resolved by the discourse contexts within which they are embedded.

Ambiguity in human language is routine. Indeed, the title of this paper is ambiguous. The phrase *changing morphological structures* may refer to structures that have the property of changeability (under the adjectival reading of *changing*), or it may refer to structures that are changed by an unspecified subject (under the verbal reading of the word *changing*).

In the investigation that we report in this paper, it means both. We concentrate on prefixed and suffixed trimorphemic words that can change meanings by virtue of the manner in which their constituent morphemes are construed to be organised. We also investigate whether the perceptions of the morphological structure of these words can be changed by sentence context.

Our core stimuli are words such as *unlockable,* which can be interpreted either as "not able to be locked" or as "able to be unlocked". For these two interpretations to be obtained, it is necessary that the reader or hearer compute two different morphological organisations of the constituent morphemes. Thus, for the meaning "able to be unlocked" to be obtained, it is necessary that the word be represented such that the adjective-marking suffix *able* is attached to the morphologically complex verb *unlock* (see Figure 1a). On the other hand, for the meaning "not able to be locked" to be obtained, *unlockable* needs to be represented such that the prefix *un-* is attached to a morphologically complex adjective *lockable* (see Figure 1b). These alternative structural organisations within the word may

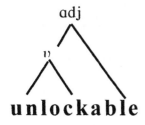

"able to be unlocked"

(a) LEFT-BRANCHING

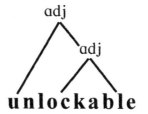

"not able to be locked"

(b) RIGHT-BRANCHING

Figure 1. Two morphological trees corresponding to two interpretations of the ambiguous word *unlockable*.

be represented diagrammatically as left-branching (Figure 1a) and right-branching trees respectively (Figure 1b).

Words such as *unlockable* possess the minimum morphological complexity required to probe the psycholinguistic consequences of hierarchical morphological structure and structural ambiguity within words (Libben, 2003). They also allow us to probe the interaction (or lack thereof) between morphological parsing and sentence interpretation processes because, in order for the ambiguous trimorphemic word to be interpreted properly, the meaning that best fits the semantic context needs to be determined. For example, the sentence context (1a) biases the interpretation of *unlockable* as "able to be unlocked"—an interpretation that is consistent with the left-branching analysis presented in Figure 1a. Sentence (1b), on the other hand, biases the interpretation of the ambiguous trimorphemic word to be consistent with the right-branching structure represented in Figure 1b.

(1) a. *When the zookeeper tried to unlock the birdcage he noticed that the birdcage was unlockable.*

b. *When the zookeeper tried to lock the birdcage he noticed that the birdcage was unlockable.*

The potential interaction between the morphological structure of ambiguous words such as *unlockable* and the semantics of sentences such as (1a) and (1b) may be best understood as a question of time course. Although it is clear that at some point in time the proper meaning of the ambiguous word is selected, it is of fundamental importance to understand when this interpretation is achieved. As is summarised in Table 1, one possibility (Option A) is that the very process of establishing a constituent

TABLE 1
Three alternatives for the influence of sentence context on the morphological structure
of ambiguous trimorphemic words

	Option A	Option B	Option C
Step 1.	Decompose strings into morphemes, but do not produce a morphological structure	Produce two morphological structures	Produce a single morphological structure
Step 2.	Create a morphological structure on the basis of sentence context	Use the appropriate morphological structure on the basis of sentence context	Revise that structure if required by the sentence context

structure for the trimorphemic word is a process influenced by the semantics of its carrier sentence. This would mean that the morphological system is not autonomous, but rather is influenced by the semantic or conceptual system during its computations, thus constituting evidence against the view that morphological processes are encapsulated. Two other possibilities, however, can be taken as evidence that the morphological system is in fact encapsulated. One (Option B) is that the system produces outputs that are consistent with its two constituent structures. That is, given an ambiguous input, the output of the system would be two parsing trees with the proper one then selected by the demands of the context. A third possibility (Option C) is that the system produces only one output which is independent of the contextually appropriate interpretation. This would mean that the morphological system produces its own preferred parsing analysis—which could be determined by the frequency of a given analysis or by the morphological system's own principles of analysis of morphologically complex strings.

These views regarding the nature of the workings of the morphological system find parallels in the sentence parsing literature. While there are researchers who believe that the parsing mechanism interacts freely with processes of semantic interpretation (e.g., MacDonald, Perlmutter, & Seidenberg, 1994; Trueswell & Tanenhaus, 1994), others believe that sentence parsing is relatively isolated from semantic interpretation. Proponents of the multiple-output parsing analyses (e.g., Gibson, 1998), for instance, claim that all possible syntactic analyses of a given phrase or sentence are made available for selection by semantic and pragmatic systems. Proponents of single-output parsing analyses (e.g., Frazier & Clifton, 1996) claim that the sentence parsing system commits itself to one analysis—usually the simplest in terms of parsing nodes—for later revising if the analysis is incongruent with the semantic context of the sentence.

It is also important to note that these views on syntactic analysis have been at the forefront of disputes regarding the nature of the cognitive architecture of the language system. In the last two decades or so, a great deal of psycholinguistic work has investigated the hypothesis that the language system and some of its subcomponents are computationally encapsulated or modular (Fodor, 1983; Chomsky, 1984). Many of the studies supporting or refuting the modularity hypothesis have also investigated the influence of semantic context in the process of lexical access. Thus, for instance, in the study conducted by Swinney (1979), in sentence contexts biasing towards one meaning of an ambiguous prime word such as *bug*, priming was obtained for targets related to both meanings of the ambiguous word (e.g., *spy* and *ant*) when these targets were presented for lexical decision at the offset of the prime. When the targets were presented three syllables after the offset of the prime, however, only the contextually relevant target word was primed. Tanenhaus, Leiman, and Seidenberg's (1979) study produced a similar effect, suggesting that the process of accessing the meaning of an ambiguous word is relatively immune to the demands of the sentence context, with all meanings being initially accessed in parallel (or ordered by frequency; see Onifer & Swinney, 1981) with the selection of the appropriate meaning by the context coming a few hundred milliseconds later. However, in a study similar to that of Swinney (1979), Tabossi (1988) found that contextual information affected the proper interpretation of the ambiguous word. Tabossi varied the strength of the semantic contexts of her sentences and obtained priming effects only for the appropriate meaning of ambiguous words when contexts were strong (i.e., when sentence contexts were created based on "features" of one meaning of the ambiguous word) and priming for targets related to both meanings when contexts were weak. Tanenhaus, Dell, and Carlson (1987) proposed that the strength of the context (couched in terms of feedback from higher to lower levels of processing) should be predictive of the nature of the lexical access process, with weak contexts (or words in isolation) producing representations consistent with both meanings of an ambiguous word—thus, compatible with the encapsulation assumption—and strong contexts producing selective outputs—thus, compatible with an interactive view of the language system. In a meta-analysis of the influence of context on lexical ambiguity resolution, Lucas (1999) found that the evidence weighs in favour of the interactive, non-modular view of the lexical access process. The picture that emerges from these studies is that the strength of the semantic context may determine the nature of the lexical access process—with weaker contexts leading to the production of multiple interpretations for the ambiguous word to be activated and stronger contexts pre-selecting the proper semantic interpretation.

The present study, then, can be seen as an investigation of the nature of the architecture of the lexical processing system and how it interacts with semantic representations built during sentence comprehension. We reasoned that if morphological computations were influenced by the demands of the sentential-semantic context, then they would produce contextually appropriate parsing trees for morphologically ambiguous items. If, by contrast, the morphological system produces a parsing tree that is initially *incompatible* with the context of the sentence, then this could be taken as evidence for the encapsulation of the lexicon.

EXPERIMENT 1: SEMANTIC PLAUSIBILITY RATINGS

The first step in this study was to investigate whether putatively ambiguous trimorphemic strings such as *unlockable* can indeed receive two interpretations and whether sentences can be constructed that effectively bias toward one interpretation or the other. In this initial experiment, these questions were addressed by examining semantic plausibility rating as the dependent variable and by manipulating sentence context with both ambiguous trimorphemic words and their paraphrases. We reasoned that if ambiguous words such as *unlockable* could indeed be assigned two interpretations, they would show roughly equal plausibility when embedded in sentences such as (1), repeated as (2a) and (2b) below.

(2) a. *When the zookeeper tried to unlock the birdcage he noticed that the birdcage was unlockable.*
   b. *When the zookeeper tried to lock the birdcage he noticed that the birdcage was unlockable.*

Crucially, we reasoned that sentences with *lock* would bias toward the right-branching interpretation of *unlockable* (i.e., "not able to be locked") whereas sentences with *unlock* would bias toward the left-branching interpretation of *unlockable* (i.e., "able to be unlocked"). In order to test whether the contexts were indeed semantically biasing in this manner, we replaced the trimorphemic words with exactly those corresponding paraphrases, as in examples (3a) and (3b) below.

(3) a. *When the zookeeper tried to lock the birdcage he noticed that the birdcage was not able to be locked.*
   b. *When the zookeeper tried to lock the birdcage he noticed that the birdcage was able to be unlocked.*

Thus, if indeed the sentence contexts were semantically constraining, we expected to find sentence (3a) to be judged as more plausible than sentence (3b).

Method

Participants. Forty-two native speakers of English, all students at Concordia University, participated in this study. They either received course credit or $7 for participation in this and other unrelated experiments in a one-hour session. They were all naïve as to the main hypotheses under investigation.

Design and materials. Twenty-four ambiguous trimorphemic words were used in this experiment. Twenty-three of these were taken from Libben's (2003) study of lexical ambiguity, to which one stimulus item (*uninstallable*) was added.

For each word, six sentences were constructed (see Appendix). Two of these sentences biased the ambiguous trimorphemic word to be interpreted either as "able to un-*X*" or "unable to *X*". Thus, for instance, for the word *unlockable*, two contexts were created (as in (2) above): one biasing towards the right-branching analysis of the trimorphemic word (e.g., *When the zookeeper tried to lock the birdcage he noticed that the birdcage was unlockable*) and one biasing towards its left-branching analysis (e.g., *When the zookeeper tried to unlock the birdcage he noticed that the birdcage was unlockable*). In addition, there were four other sentences corresponding to each of the 24 trimorphemic words. These sentences were created with periphrastic versions of the two possible interpretations of the trimorphemic words. Thus, for instance, for sentences that contained the word *unlockable*, two other sentences were created with the expression *able to be unlocked* (e.g., *When the zookeeper tried to lock/unlock the birdcage he noticed that the birdcage was able to be unlocked*) and two sentences were created with the expression *not able to be locked* replacing the ambiguous word (e.g., *When the zookeeper tried to lock/unlock the birdcage he noticed that the birdcage was not able to be locked*). This way, two semantically consistent (*lock ... not able to be locked, unlock ... able to be unlocked*) and two semantically inconsistent (*lock ... able to be unlocked, unlock ... not able to be locked*) sentences were created from each one of the sentences with the trimorphemic words, forming six sentence types. In the present study, we refer to the periphrastic sentences that contain the root form of the verb in the first clause (e.g., *lock*) as *positive* and those that contain the *un-* prefixed form (e.g., *unlock*) as *negative*.

Thus, in summary, stimulus sentences had two types of first clauses—(1) those with a positive critical stimulus (e.g., *lock*) and (2) those with a negative critical stimulus (e.g., *unlock*). These were crossed with three types of second clauses—(a) those with an ambiguous trimorphemic stimulus (e.g., *unlockable*), (b) those with a paraphrase of the left-branching interpretation of the trimorphemic stimulus (e.g., *able to be unlocked*) and (c) those with a paraphrase of the right-branching interpretation of the trimorphemic word (e.g., *not able to be locked*). As is shown in Table 2, if indeed the presence of the positive and negative stimuli in the first clause constrains the interpretation of the sentence as a whole, then half of the second-clause paraphrases would be inconsistent with the meaning of the first clause.

Materials were counterbalanced across six booklets, with each booklet containing 24 sentences, four of each of the six types, and with only one sentence corresponding to one of the 24 trimorphemic words in each booklet.

Procedure.   Participants were given one of each of the six booklets and asked to rate how plausible each sentence was using a scale between 1 (*not plausible at all*) and 5 (*completely plausible*). They were instructed to rely on their first instinct and not to revise their ratings, proceeding from start to finish as quickly as they could.

Results and discussion

Figure 2 presents the mean plausibility ratings and standard errors for all sentence types. A 2 (first-clause word type: positive vs. negative) × 2

TABLE 2
Conditions and sample materials employed in Experiment 1

First clause word type	Second clause word/expression	Semantic consistency	Sample sentence
(1) Root (*positive*)	(a) Trimorphemic	consistent	*When the zookeeper tried to lock the birdcage he noticed that the birdcage was unlockable*
	(b) Periphrastic (*left-branching*)	inconsistent	*When the zookeeper tried to lock the birdcage he noticed that the birdcage was able to be unlocked.*
	(c) Periphrastic (*right-branching*)	consistent	*When the zookeeper tried to lock the birdcage he noticed that the birdcage was not able to be locked*
(2) Un + Root (*negative*)	(a) Trimorphemic	consistent	*When the zookeeper tried to unlock the birdcage he noticed that the birdcage was unlockable*
	(b) Periphrastic (*left-branching*)	consistent	*When the zookeeper tried to unlock the birdcage he noticed that the birdcage was able to be unlocked*
	(c) Periphrastic (*right-branching*)	inconsistent	*When the zookeeper tried to unlock the birdcage he noticed that the birdcage was not able to be locked*

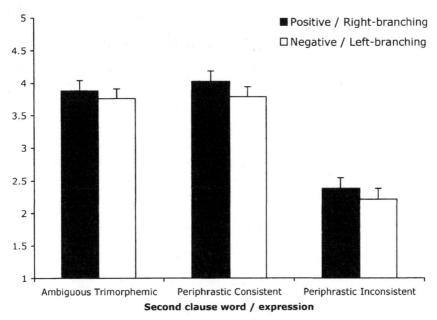

Figure 2. Mean plausibility judgements for sentences as a function of first clause context word (positive/right-branching: *root*; negative/left-branching: *un* + *root*) and second clause word or expression (trimorphemic or periphrastic). 1 = not plausible; 5 = completely plausible.

(semantic consistency: consistent vs. inconsistent) repeated measures ANOVA showed a main effect of consistency, $F_1(1, 41) = 75.68$, $p < .0001$, $F_2(1, 92) = 87.33$, $p < .0001$, but not word type effect, $F_1(1, 41) = 2.38$, $p = .13$, $F_2(1, 92) = 1.17$, $p = .28$, and no interaction between these two variables, $F_1(1, 41) = 0.55$, $p = .82$, $F_2(1, 92) = 0.70$, $p = .40$. These results suggest that participants compute correctly the interaction between the meaning of the first clause word (*lock* or *unlock*) and the second-clause periphrastic expression (*not able to be locked* or *able to be unlocked*). In the analyses for sentence types with trimorphemic words in the second clause, there was no significant difference in plausibility rating, $F_1(1, 41) = 0.43$, $p = .51$, $F_2(1, 47) = 1.88$, $p = .18$, indicating that both left- and right-branching contexts did not differ in terms of plausibility. In the comparison between the two trimorphemic sentences and their respective consistent periphrastic sentences, the difference between positive contexts was non-significant in the analysis by participants, $F_1(1, 82) = 0.39$, $p = .53$, and failed to reach significance in the analysis by items, $F_2(1, 45) = 3.66$, $p = .062$. In the comparison between negative contexts, there were no significant differences by participants nor by items, $F_1(1, 82) = 0.013$, $p = .91$, $F_2(1, 48) = 1.39$, $p = .25$.

Taken together, the results of Experiment 1 indicate that the sentence contexts that we constructed were indeed sufficiently constraining so that inconsistent paraphrases of the critical ambiguous words were judged to be less plausible than their consistent counterparts. No plausibility differences, however, were found for the ambiguous words themselves. This suggests that the ambiguous words were able to shift interpretations in order to adjust to the overall meaning of the sentences. That is, the word *unlockable* was assigned a right-branching structure in sentences containing *lock*, but a left-branching structure for sentences containing *unlock* in the first clause. Did the morphological structure of the word then actually change as a result of sentence context? This question was at the core of our cross-modal priming study reported in Experiment 2 below.

EXPERIMENT 2: ON-LINE MORPHOLOGICAL PARSING IN CONTEXT

The purpose of this experiment was to test if sentential context would influence the *online* parsing of the ambiguous trimorphemic words. Although ambiguous words can acquire two interpretations in strongly biasing sentence contexts, as we have seen in Experiment 1, it is not clear how this is achieved in online processing. One possibility is that the structure of the ambiguous trimorphemic word is assigned online, at the offset of the word, if not before. This prediction is consistent with an interactive language processing system in which syntactic, morphological, semantic, and background-knowledge representations interact online during linguistic input. However, as we discussed in the introduction, we can also raise two other possible outcomes in the process of parsing and interpreting those ambiguous words: one is that interpretation may occur only after the proper morphological parsing analysis is selected, among the two activated candidate parsing trees. Another is that the language comprehension system (and more specifically, the morphological parser) may commit itself to one possible analysis, leaving the interpretation that is relevant for the context for a later stage in the language comprehension process. These two last possible outcomes are consistent with a modular language processing system which takes the computation of different linguistic components to be independent of each other and, in particular, independent of the influence of semantic or conceptual representations.

In this experiment, we used a cross-modal lexical decision task on the assumption that it would allow us to tap parsing processes as participants were listening to sentences carrying ambiguous trimorphemic words. This technique has been widely used in the investigation of lexical access, in particular with ambiguous words (e.g., Swinney, 1979; Tanenhaus et al., 1979; Tabossi, 1988). Our stimuli were built upon the sentences employed in Experiment 1. We manipulated the priming obtained between the ambiguous trimorphemic word (the prime; e.g., *unlockable*) and a visual target composed of *root + able* morphemes (e.g., *lockable*). We predicted that *unlockable* would prime *lockable* regardless of sentence context because of their shared morphemes. However, we predicted that the priming between *unlockable* and *lockable* would be of a greater magnitude in the case where the context biases towards the right-branching analysis of *unlockable*. This is because the adjective *lockable* is a constituent of the right-branching negative adjective $[_{Adj}[un][_{Adj}lockable]]$ but not a constituent of $[_{Adj}[_{V}unlock][able]]$. Thus, if context determines the immediate parsing analysis of the ambiguous trimorphemic string, there should be an advantage for the target *lockable* when it is preceded by an analysis of *unlockable* in which the target behaves as a major constituent of the prime.

Method

Participants. A total of 94 Concordia University undergraduate students participated in this experiment. They were all native speakers of English and had normal or corrected-to-normal vision and no known reading or cognitive disabilities. They received either credit for a Psychology course or were paid between $6 and $7 for an hour session that included this and other unrelated experiments.

Materials and design. Our main stimuli were the 24 morphologically and semantically ambiguous trimorphemic words used in Experiment 1, all with the basic structure [un + *root* + able]. All 24 words allowed either a left- or right-branching parsing analysis, as discussed above. For each word, six sentence contexts were created, as shown in Table 3 (see Appendix for a list of materials). The sentences were similar in structure, all containing two clauses, the first with a context word and the second with the main trimorphemic prime word. In the context clause, the difference between sentences was in the presence of either the root verb (e.g., *lock*) related to the trimorphemic derived adjective (e.g., *unlockable*), the un-prefixed verb (e.g., *unlock*) or a neutral verb (e.g., *clean*). In the prime clause, the sentences contained either a trimorphemic prime word (e.g., *unlockable*) or another unrelated trimorphemic unambiguous word (e.g., *unapproachable*). Thus, all context-prime combinations formed six different sentences (e.g., *When the zookeeper tried to lock/unlock/clean the birdcage he noticed that the birdcage was unlockable/unapproachable*). For all these combinations, the target was composed by *root + able* morphemes (e.g., *lockable*) corresponding to the two last morphemes of the experimental prime (e.g., *unlockable*). Six lists of materials were

TABLE 3
Main context and prime conditions for Root + suffix targets (e.g., *lockable*) in Experiment 2

Context type	Prime type	Example (context and prime words in italics)
Root (e.g., *lock*)	Related (e.g., *unlockable*) Unrelated (*unapproachable*)	When the zookeeper tried to *lock* the birdcage he noticed that the birdcage was *unlockable* When the zookeeper tried to *lock* the birdcage he noticed that the birdcage was *unapproachable*
Un + root (*unlock*)	Related (*unlockable*) Unrelated (*unapproachable*)	When the zookeeper tried to *unlock* the birdcage he noticed that the birdcage was *unlockable* When the zookeeper tried to *unlock* the birdcage he noticed that the birdcage was *unapproachable*
Neutral (*clean*)	Related (*unlockable*) Unrelated (*unapproachable*)	When the zookeeper tried to *clean* the birdcage he noticed that the birdcage was *unlockable* When the zookeeper tried to *clean* the birdcage he noticed that the birdcage was *unapproachable*

created. The lists were counterbalanced so that all six contained an equal number of context and prime types, with one context-prime combination for each one of the main experimental trimorphemic words. In addition to the 24 experimental trials, each list contained 120 filler trials. These consisted of simple sentences (e.g., *Inactive people can get overweight*) and complex sentences (e.g., *When the skier reached the bottom of the slope, he noticed that he was the first one down*), with a mixture of morphologically simple (e.g., *load*) and complex (e.g., *repayment*) word targets. The nonword targets were also complex (e.g., *unmithable*) and simplex (e.g., *mirk*). They were constructed by changing characters or morphemes in actual English words, but preserving their phonotactic properties. There were 144 trials in total, 96 of which had word targets (*yes* responses; including the 24 experimental trials) and 48 had nonword targets (*no* responses).

Apparatus and procedure.   We used a cross-modal priming with lexical decision technique. Participants sat in front of a Macintosh G3 computer which had a CMU response box and a pair of headphones attached to it. The response box had two main buttons, one labelled *yes* and the other labelled *no*. We used PsyScope 1.2.5b (Cohen, MacWhinney, Flatt, & Provost, 1993) to present the stimuli (both auditory and visual) and to collect response times.

Participants were instructed that in each trial they would hear a sentence, and that for each sentence, they would see a string of letters appearing in the middle of the computer screen. They were told that the string of letters would appear at any time during the presentation of each sentence. They were also instructed that they had to pay attention to the sentences because after the experimental session they would be given a task in which they would have to remember some of the sentences they heard during the experiment. In addition, participants were instructed that they had to pay attention to each string of letters presented on the screen and to decide as fast and as accurately as possible whether or not it formed an English word. If the string of letters formed an English word, they had to press *yes* on the button box; otherwise they had to press *no*.

For the 24 experimental trials, the visual targets (always words) were presented 500 ms after the offset of the aurally presented final word in the sentence (always a trimorphemic prime such as *undoable*). For all the filler trials, the targets were presented at different points in the sentences, including 12 that were presented 500 ms after the offset of the sentences. Participants were run individually in a dark room. Visual stimuli (strings of letters) were presented on white Times 24 font over black background. Auditory stimuli were recorded by a female student at a normal pace and were presented at a comfortable volume over the headphones. The experimental session started with instructions presented on the screen and reinforced by the experimenter, followed by a series of 10 practice trials, a reinforcement of the instructions also presented on the screen, and the 144 main trials. The experimental session lasted about 20 min.

Results and discussion

Raw data points above 3000 ms or below 300 ms were discarded from the analyses (2.9% of all data). Two participants who committed errors (i.e., responded *no*) in all experimental trials were eliminated. In the remaining data from 92 participants, there were 29.6% errors (including data from 17 participants who committed errors in over 50% of the experimental trials).

Our analyses focused on two primary variables: context type and prime type. A 3 (context type: left-branching biasing, right-branching biasing, neutral) $\times$ 2 (prime type: trimorphemic related vs. unrelated) repeated measures ANOVA showed a main effect of context in the participants analysis only, $F_1(2, 142) = 3.07, p = .049, F_2(2, 40) = 1.39, p = .26$, and a main effect of prime, $F_1(1, 71) = 15.91, p = .0002, F_2(1, 20) = 5.63, p = .028$. There was no interaction between the two factors.

Although the overall ANOVA showed no interaction between the context and prime factors, we note that analyses taking the neutral prime and related primed conditions separately as one-way ANOVAs showed that context had an effect only when the trimorphemic prime was present in the stimulus sentence, $F_1(2, 156) = 4.17, p = .017$. For the unrelated prime condition, context had no effect, $F_1(2, 156) = 0.45, p = .65$.

TABLE 4
Target response times in milliseconds (standard errors, in parentheses) and per cent errors for each of the core conditions in Experiment 2

Prime type	Context type		
	Root	Un + Root	Neutral
Response Times (ms)			
Related *(un + root + able)*	835 (37)	926 (49)	925 (48)
Unrelated	964 (40)	1007 (46)	1000 (46)
Errors (%)			
Related *(un + root + able)*	24	22	24
Unrelated	35	34	39

Given the high number of errors in the dataset, we also analysed the error rates for participants and items. These analyses produced no effect of context type, $F_1(2, 180) = 1.33$, $p = .27$, $F_2(2, 40) = 1.45$, $p = .25$, but a significant effect of prime type, $F_1(1, 90) = 35.4$, $p < .0001$, $F_2(1, 20) = 20.6$, $p = .0002$. Table 4 shows RTs and error rate data for all conditions.

In summary, the results of Experiment 2 indicate that the presence of trimorphemic ambiguous words in sentence final position increased response speed to their respective bimorphemic substrings as targets. In contrast, the effect of context on target response times was weak. To the extent that it did play a role, its effect must be seen as semantic, rather than purely lexical. Target response times in the neutral and *un + root* contexts were virtually identical. It was the *root* context that resulted in reduced response times as compared to the neutral context. Because only the *root* context (e.g., *lock*) is semantically compatible with the bimorphemic target (e.g., *lockable*), we conclude that it is not simply the presence of the corresponding lexical root in the sentence context that affects response latencies to the target, but rather the meaning of the word containing that lexical root. Finally, our analyses treating the related and unrelated prime conditions separately revealed that an effect of context is only reliable when the ambiguous trimorphemic word is present as the last word of the sentence. The implication of this observation is taken up in the General Discussion below.

GENERAL DISCUSSION

This investigation has focused on the question of whether structurally ambiguous words can be disambiguated by sentence context.

In Experiment 1, we probed the extent to which the interpretation of ambiguous trimorphemic words such as *unlockable* would be adjusted to fit the alternative meanings of sentence frames. We concluded that this was indeed the case, based on the finding that the trimorphemic words were judged to be equally plausible in sentences that biased toward either left-branching or right-branching interpretations. The critical evidence in support of this conclusion was that, although the ambiguous words were judged to be equally plausible, their paraphrases (*able to be unlocked* or *not able to be locked*) were not judged to be equally plausible across sentence contexts. Thus, although the paraphrases showed fixed meanings that affected the plausibility of the sentence as a whole, the ambiguous words showed interpretive malleability. This malleability appears to be inconsistent with the view that their morphological structure is insulated from the effects of sentence context.

Experiment 2 probed the extent to which the pattern of metalinguistic ratings found in Experiment 1 would be manifested in a task in which morphological parsing and interpretation were implicit rather than explicit. The behavioural task in this experiment was a lexical decision on a target such as *lockable*, which is a morphological constituent of the right-branching structure *un-lockable*, but not of the left-branching structure *unlock-able*. We reasoned that if sentence context influenced the constituency structure that participants would implicitly assign to ambiguous trimorphemic words, then those effects would be evident in the magnitude of the sentence's facilitative effect on the ambiguous word's root + suffix substring.

The results of Experiment 2 bring us back to the alternative hypotheses stated at the outset of this paper. We argued that there are three main ways in which the assignment of morphological constituency within a trimorphemic word could interact with sentence semantics.

The first (Option A) is that sentence context directly affects how a morphologically ambiguous word will be structured. The second (Option B) is that a computationally encapsulated morphological parser produces two candidate parses. Finally, it may be the case (Option C) that there is an initial preferred parse that is then revised, if necessary, on the basis of sentence context.

If we accept that sentence context played some role in the related prime condition, but no role in the unrelated prime condition, then the strong modularity position (Option B) cannot be supported. This option would predict lexical priming to be completely uninfluenced by sentence context because both morphological parses are always available.

This leaves Options A and C as viable alternatives. Option A, which suggests full interactivity between syntax and morphology, would account for the effect of context in the related prime condition by claiming that when *unlockable* is preceded by the *lock* context, it becomes *un-lockable*, thus serving as a more effective prime for its morphological constituent *lockable*.

A context effect in Experiment 2, however, does not rule out the possibility that an initial parse, based solely on lexical factors is initially constructed and then revised in accordance with the semantics of sentence context (Option C). We assume that this analysis would be a right-branching one, following the findings of Libben (2003) and Popescu (2004) who found that, all other things being equal, the morphological processing system seems to prefer a right-branching analysis for prefixed and suffixed trimorphemic words presented in isolation.

This leaves us then with the following conclusion based on the results of this study. Trimorphemic ambiguous words do indeed have two potential parses and interpretations. However, in normal language processing, only one of those potential meanings appears to be used. When ambiguous words are presented in isolation, the morphological parsing system shows an overall propensity to prefer prefix-stripping (see Taft, 1981). However, in sentence context, we see strong evidence that the sentence affects the interpretation of the ambiguous word which it contains. The extent to which this change in interpretation affects the actual morphological structure of the trimorphemic word and the time course of such a structural change are less clear. Although we see some evidence in Experiment 2 that sentence context can penetrate morphological priming effects, the fact that morphological priming effects in the inappropriate semantic context (81 ms) were not less than those for the neutral sentence context (75 ms) suggests to us that there is an independent level of morphological analysis in the on-line processing of sentences that cannot be inhibited by a sentence context that biases toward an incompatible parse (e.g., *unlockable* with respect to the target *lockable*).

It is important to also note that our data support the view that morphological decomposition is a fundamental property of the processing of words both in isolation and in sentence context. If individual morphemes were not available to the cognitive system throughout lexical processing, they could not be arranged (or rearranged) on-line in accordance with the semantics of a sentence. This brings us finally to the observation with which we began this paper—the almost ubiquitous ambiguity found in language. The results of Experiment 1 show that participants seem to effortlessly resolve this ambiguity. Elsewhere, we have also found that participants are almost completely unaware of morphological ambiguity, even under conditions in which they are asked directly whether strings such as *unlockable* can have two meanings (Popescu, 2004; Popescu, de Almeida & Libben, 2004). But, whether or not participants are aware that ambiguous strings can have two meanings, the key finding in this study is that they can *use* two meanings, and that it is the human ability to reorganise existing elements into new configurations that allows them to do so.

REFERENCES

Aristotle. (n.d.). Rhetoric, Book 3, Chapter 2. In R. Maynard (Ed.). *Great Books of the Western World* (Vol. 9, 1404–[39], p. 655). Chicago: Encyclopedia Britannica Inc. [1952].

Chomsky, N. (1984) *Modular approaches to the study of the mind.* San Diego: San Diego State University Press.

Cohen, J., MacWhinney, B., Flatt, M., & Provost, J. (1993). PsyScope: An interactive graphic system for designing and controlling experiments in the psychology laboratory using Macintosh computers. *Behavior Research Methods, Instruments, and Computers, 25,* 257–271.

Fodor, J. A. (1983). *The modularity of mind.* Cambridge, MA: MIT Press.

Frazier, L., & Clifton, C. Jr. (1996). *Construal.* Cambridge, MA: MIT Press.

Gibson, E. (1998). Linguistic complexity: Locality of syntactic dependencies. *Cognition, 78,* 1–76.

Libben, G. (2003). Morphological parsing and morphological structure. In A. Egbert & D. Sandra (Eds.), *Reading complex words* (pp. 221–239). Amsterdam: Kluwer.

Lucas, M. (1999). Context effect in lexical access: A meta-analysis. *Memory and Cognition, 27,* 385–398.

MacDonald, M. C., Pearlmutter, N. J., & Seidenberg, M. S. (1994). The lexical nature of syntactic ambiguity resolution. *Psychological Review, 101,* 676–703.

Onifer, W., & Swinney, D. A. (1981). Accessing lexical ambiguities during sentence comprehension: Effects of frequency of meaning and contextual bias. *Memory and Cognition, 9,* 225–236.

Popescu, A. (2004). *Structural ambiguity in trimorphemic English words: Morphological processing and lexical access in structurally ambiguous words presented in isolation.* Unpublished MSc thesis. University of Alberta, Edmonton, Canada.

Popescu, A, de Almeida, R. G., & Libben, G. (2004). *What can we learn from morphological ambiguity?* Manuscript in preparation.

Swinney, D. (1979). Lexical access during sentence comprehension: (Re)consideration of context effects. *Journal of Verbal Learning and Verbal Behavior, 18,* 645–659.

Tabossi, P. (1988). Accessing lexical ambiguity in different types of sentential contexts. *Journal of Memory and Language, 27,* 324–340.

Taft, M. (1981). Prefix stripping revisited. *Journal of Verbal Learning and Verbal Behavior, 20,* 289–297.

Tanenhaus, M., Leiman, J. M., & Seidenberg, M. S. (1979). Evidence for multiple stages in the processing of ambiguous words in syntactic contents. *Journal of Verbal Learning and Verbal Behavior, 18,* 427–440.

Tanenhaus, M. K., Dell, G. S., & Carlson, G. (1987). Context effects in lexical processing: A connectionist approach to modularity. In J. L. Garfield (Ed.), *Modularity in knowledge representation and natural-language understanding* (pp. 83–108). Cambridge, MA: MIT Press.

Trueswell, J. C., & Tanenhaus, M. K. (1994). Toward a lexicalist framework of constraint-based syntactic ambiguity resolution. In C. Clifton Jr., L. Frazier, & K. Rayner (Eds.), *Perspectives on sentence processing* (pp. 155–179). Hillsdale, NJ: Lawrence Erlbaum Associates Inc.

APPENDIX

Materials used in Experiments 1 and 2

All sentences (a) and (b) were employed in Experiment 1 together with the periphrastic versions of the ambiguous trimorphemic words. Thus, for example, for the word *unbendable,* four other sentences were formed by replacing the trimorphemic word in each sentence (a) and (b) with either *not able to be bent* or *able to be unbent.* All sentences (a) to (f) were employed in Experiment 2.

1. Unbendable
a. The painter wanted to bend the board and he was told that the board was unbendable
b. The painter wanted to unbend the board and he was told that the board was unbendable
c. The painter wanted to bend the board and he was told that the board was unremovable
d. The painter wanted to unbend the board and he was told that the board was unremovable
e. The painter wanted to take the board and he was told that the board was unremovable
f. The painter wanted to take the board and he was told that the board was unbendable

2. Unbucklable
a. When the driver tried to buckle the belt he realised that the belt was unbucklable
b. When the driver tried to unbuckle the belt he realised that the belt was unbucklable
c. When the driver tried to buckle the belt he realised that the belt was uncomfortable
d. When the driver tried to unbuckle the belt he realised that the belt was uncomfortable
e. When the driver tried to adjust the belt he realised that the belt was uncomfortable
f. When the driver tried to adjust the belt he realised that the belt was unbucklable

3. Unbuttonable
a. The shopper wanted to button the dress and realised that the dress was unbuttonable
b. The shopper wanted to unbutton the dress and realised that the dress was unbuttonable
c. The shopper wanted to button the dress and realised that the dress was unsuitable
d. The shopper wanted to unbutton the dress and realised that the dress was unsuitable
e. The shopper wanted to try on the dress and realised that the dress was unsuitable
f. The shopper wanted to try on the dress and realised that the dress was unbuttonable

4. Uncoilable
a. When the electrician tried to coil the wire he realised that the wire was uncoilable
b. When the electrician tried to uncoil the wire he realised that the wire was uncoilable
c. When the electrician tried to coil the wire he realised that the wire was unmanageable
d. When the electrician tried to uncoil the wire he realised that the wire was unmanageable
e. When the electrician tried to connect the wire he realised that the wire was unmanageable
f. When the electrician tried to connect the wire he realised that the wire was uncoilable

5. Uncorkable
a. The waitress tried to cork the bottle and realised that the bottle was uncorkable
b. The waitress tried to uncork the bottle and realised that the bottle was uncorkable
c. The waitress tried to cork the bottle and realised that the bottle was unusable
d. The waitress tried to uncork the bottle and realised that the bottle was unusable
e. The waitress tried to recycle the bottle and realised that the bottle was unusable
f. The waitress tried to recycle the bottle and realised that the bottle was uncorkable

6. Undoable
a. The clerk that attempted to do the job was convinced that the job was undoable
b. The clerk that attempted to undo the job was convinced that the job was undoable
c. The clerk that attempted to do the job was convinced that the job was unchangeable
d. The clerk that attempted to undo the job was convinced that the job was unchangeable
e. The clerk that attempted to evaluate the job was convinced that the job was unchangeable
f. The clerk that attempted to evaluate the job was convinced that the job was undoable

7. Undressable
a. When the child wanted to dress the doll she realised that the doll was undressable
b. When the child wanted to undress the doll she realised that the doll was undressable
c. When the child wanted to dress the doll she realised that the doll was uncontortable
d. When the child wanted to undress the doll she realised that the doll was uncontortable
e. When the child wanted to play with the doll she realised that the doll was uncontortable
f. When the child wanted to play with the doll she realised that the doll was undressable

8. Unfastenable
a. When the jeweler tried to fasten the brooch, the jeweler realised the brooch was unfastenable
b. When the jeweler tried to unfasten the brooch, the jeweler realised the brooch was unfastenable
c. When the jeweler tried to fasten the brooch, the jeweler realised the brooch was unfashionable
d. When the jeweler tried to unfasten the brooch, the jeweler realised the brooch was unfashionable
e. When the jeweler tried to appraise the brooch, the jeweler realised the brooch was unfashionable
f. When the jeweler tried to appraise the brooch, the jeweler realised the brooch was unfastenable

9. Unfoldable
a. When the janitor tried to fold the table, he saw that the table was unfoldable
b. When the janitor tried to unfold the table, he saw that the table was unfoldable
c. When the janitor tried to fold the table, he saw that the table was unstable
d. When the janitor tried to unfold the table, he saw that the table was unstable
e. When the janitor tried to paint the table, he saw that the table was unstable
f. When the janitor tried to paint the table, he saw that the table was unfoldable

10. Unhookable
a. The fisherman tried to hook the bait and he realised that the bait was unhookable
b. The fisherman tried to unhook the bait and he realised that the bait was unhookable
c. The fisherman tried to hook the bait and he realised that the bait was unpiercable
d. The fisherman tried to unhook the bait and he realised that the bait was unpiercable
e. The fisherman tried to use the bait and he realised that the bait was unpiercable
f. The fisherman tried to use the bait and he realised that the bait was unhookable

11. Unloadable
a. The courier wanted to load the packages by hand and was told that the packages were unloadable
b. The courier wanted to unload the packages by hand and was told that the packages were unloadable

c. The courier wanted to load the packages by hand and was told that the packages were unavailable
d. The courier wanted to unload the packages by hand and was told that the packages were unavailable
e. The courier wanted to deliver the packages by hand and was told that the packages were unavailable
f. The courier wanted to deliver the packages by hand and was told that the packages were unloadable

12. Unlockable
a. When the zookeeper tried to lock the birdcage he noticed that the birdcage was unlockable
b. When the zookeeper tried to unlock the birdcage he noticed that the birdcage was unlockable
c. When the zookeeper tried to lock the birdcage he noticed that the birdcage was unapproachable
d. When the zookeeper tried to unlock the birdcage he noticed that the birdcage was unapproachable
e. When the zookeeper tried to clean the birdcage he noticed that the birdcage was unapproachable
f. When the zookeeper tried to clean the birdcage he noticed that the birdcage was unlockable

13. Unpackable
a. When the mover asked if he could pack the furniture, he was told that the furniture was unpackable
b. When the mover asked if he could unpack the furniture, he was told that the furniture was unpackable
c. When the mover asked if he could pack the furniture, he was told that the furniture was unmovable
d. When the mover asked if he could unpack the furniture, he was told that the furniture was unmovable
e. When the mover asked if he could carry the furniture, he was told that the furniture was unmovable
f. When the mover asked if he could carry the furniture, he was told that the furniture was unpackable

14. Unpluggable
a. When the repairman attempted to plug the old appliance, he noticed that the old appliance was unpluggable
b. When the repairman attempted to unplug the old appliance, he noticed that the old appliance was unpluggable
c. When the repairman attempted to plug the old appliance, he noticed that the old appliance was unadaptable
d. When the repairman attempted to unplug the old appliance, he noticed that the old appliance was unadaptable
e. When the repairman attempted to service the old appliance, he noticed that the old appliance was unadaptable
f. When the repairman attempted to service the old appliance, he noticed that the old appliance was unpluggable

15. Unrollable
a. The architect wanted to roll the blueprints and the blueprints were unrollable
b. The architect wanted to unroll the blueprints and the blueprints were unrollable
c. The architect wanted to roll the blueprints and the blueprints were unreadable
d. The architect wanted to unroll the blueprints and the blueprints were unreadable
e. The architect wanted to copy the blueprints and the blueprints were unreadable
f. The architect wanted to copy the blueprints and the blueprints were unrollable

16. Unscrewable
a. When the carpenter tried to screw the parts, he realised the parts were unscrewable
b. When the carpenter tried to unscrew the parts, he realised the parts were unscrewable
c. When the carpenter tried to screw the parts, he realised the parts were unreliable
d. When the carpenter tried to unscrew the parts, he realised the parts were unreliable
e. When the carpenter tried to assemble the parts, he realised the parts were unreliable
f. When the carpenter tried to assemble the parts, he realised the parts were unscrewable

17. Unscramblable
a. When the hacker tried to scramble the message he noticed the message was unscramblable
b. When the hacker tried to unscramble the message he noticed the message was unscramblable
c. When the hacker tried to scramble the message he noticed the message was unavailable
d. When the hacker tried to unscramble the message he noticed the message was unavailable
e. When the hacker tried to decipher the message he noticed the message was unavailable
f. When the hacker tried to decipher the message he noticed the message was unscramblable

18. Unsealable
a. The postman wanted to seal the package and was told the package was unsealable
b. The postman wanted to unseal the package and was told the package was unsealable
c. The postman wanted to seal the package and was told the package was unalterable
d. The postman wanted to unseal the package and was told the package was unalterable
e. The postman wanted to inspect the package and was told the package was unalterable
f. The postman wanted to inspect the package and was told the package was unsealable

19. Untieable
a. When the sailor attempted to tie the knot, he noticed the knot was untieable
b. When the sailor attempted to untie the knot, he noticed the knot was untieable
c. When the sailor attempted to tie the knot, he noticed the knot was unattainable
d. When the sailor attempted to untie the knot, he noticed the knot was unattainable
e. When the sailor attempted to displace the knot, he noticed the knot was unattainable
f. When the sailor attempted to displace the knot, he noticed the knot was untieable

20. Untwistable
a. When the gardener tried to twist the hose, he noticed that the hose was untwistable
b. When the gardener tried to untwist the hose, he noticed that the hose was untwistable
c. When the gardener tried to twist the hose, he noticed that the hose was unfreeable
d. When the gardener tried to untwist the hose, he noticed that the hose was unfreeable
e. When the gardener tried to drag the hose, he noticed that the hose was unfreeable
f. When the gardener tried to drag the hose, he noticed that the hose was untwistable

21. Unwindable
a. When the clocksmith started to wind the antique watch, he realised that the antique watch was unwindable
b. When the clocksmith started to unwind the antique watch, he realised that the antique watch was unwindable
c. When the clocksmith started to wind the antique watch, he realised that the antique watch was unsaleable
d. When the clocksmith started to unwind the antique watch, he realised that the antique watch was unsaleable
e. When the clocksmith started to fix the antique watch, he realised that the antique watch was unsaleable
f. When the clocksmith started to fix the antique watch, he realised that the antique watch was unwindable

22. Unwrapable
a. When the florist tried to wrap the bouquet, she thought that the bouquet was unwrapable
b. When the florist tried to unwrap the bouquet, she thought that the bouquet was unwrapable
c. When the florist tried to wrap the bouquet, she thought that the bouquet was unbearable
d. When the florist tried to unwrap the bouquet, she thought that the bouquet was unbearable
e. When the florist tried to arrange the bouquet, she thought that the bouquet was unbearable
f. When the florist tried to arrange the bouquet, she thought that the bouquet was unwrapable

23. Unzipable
a. When the computer programmer wanted to zip the file, he realised that the file was unzipable
b. When the computer programmer wanted to unzip the file, he realised that the file was unzipable
c. When the computer programmer wanted to zip the file, he realised that the file was unfindable
d. When the computer programmer wanted to unzip the file, he realised that the file was unfindable
e. When the computer programmer wanted to the copy the file, he realised that the file was unfindable
f. When the computer programmer wanted to copy the file, he realised that the file was unzipable

24. Uninstallable
a. When the technician tried to install the program he noticed that the program was uninstallable
b. When the technician tried to uninstall the program he noticed that the program was uninstallable
c. When the technician tried to install the program he noticed that the program was unobtainable
d. When the technician tried to uninstall the program he noticed that the program was unobtainable
e. When the technician tried to transfer the program he noticed that the program was unobtainable
f. When the technician tried to transfer the program he noticed that the program was uninstallable

LANGUAGE AND COGNITIVE PROCESSES
2005, 20 (1/2), 395–415

Psychology Press
Taylor & Francis Group

Priming morphologically complex verbs by sentence contexts: Effects of semantic transparency and ambiguity

Pienie Zwitserlood

University of Münster, Germany

Agnes Bolwiender

Max Planck Institute for Psycholinguistics, Nijmegen, the Netherlands

Etta Drews

University of Sunderland, UK

Semantic priming of morphologically complex Dutch verbs was investigated in two cross-modal experiments. Spoken sentences served as primes to visual target words, presented for lexical decision. Targets were either simple verbs (e.g., *brengen*, bring) or particle verbs, consisting of a simple verb plus a separable prefix (e.g., *meebrengen*, bring along). Particle verbs were either semantically transparent or opaque. Transparent particle verbs are semantically related to their constituent verb (e.g., *meebrengen*, bring along), opaque verbs are not (e.g., *ombrengen*, exterminate). In Experiment 1, facilitation was consistently obtained when verb targets were semantically congruent with the content of the sentence primes. But priming was also found in incongruent conditions, when opaque verbs served as targets with sentences constructed to prime the meaning of their embedded verbs. Post-hoc analyses and data from Experiment 2, however, showed that this was due to the ambiguous nature of some opaque particle verbs. Whereas the dominant opaque and the subordinate transparent meaning of ambiguous particle verbs could both be primed, truly opaque verbs were not facilitated by the

Correspondence should be addressed to Pienie Zwitserlood, Psychologisches Institut II, Fliednerstr. 21, D-48149 Münster, Germany. Email: zwitser@psy.uni-muenster.de

All experiments were carried out in the Netherlands, at the Max Planck Institute for Psycholinguistics. We thank the Institute and the members of the technical group for their support. We are grateful to Ram Frost and two anonymous reviewers, for their valuable comments. This research was supported by a grant (Dr. 229/2) from the Deutsche Forschungsgemeinschaft (DFG) to Drews and Zwitserlood.

http://www.tandf.co.uk/journals/pp/01690965.html   DOI: 10.1080/01690960444000160

semantic field of their constituent verbs. Given abundant evidence for a close association, at a morphological level, of transparent and opaque complex words to their constituents, the data demonstrate a dissociation between connections at lexical and conceptual levels of representation.

Words that share free morphemes are very often also related in form and in meaning. As with *smallish* and *small*, such words not only share graphemes and phonemes and root morpheme, they also represent strongly related concepts. This can pose problems for the view that the morphological make up of words is explicitly represented in the language system (Burani & Caramazza, 1987; Feldman & Fowler, 1987; Frauen-felder & Schreuder, 1992; Schreuder & Baayen, 1995; Schriefers, 1999, for an overview). To validate such claims, it has to be shown that morphological complexity has a role of its own, independent of form and meaning. As a matter of fact, many recent models of word recognition do not implement morphology but regard it as a by-product of the language system, emerging from semantic and formal similarity (Plaut & Gonnerman, 2000; Rueckl, Mikolinski, Raveh, Miner, & Mars, 1997; Plunkett & Marchmann, 1993).

In the last decade, evidence has accumulated that effects of morpho-logical relatedness cannot be reduced to mere formal similarity, for example between primes and targets in priming studies (Drews & Zwitserlood, 1995; Feldman & Andjelkovic, 1992; Marslen-Wilson, Tyler, Waksler & Older, 1994; Napps, 1989; Stolz & Feldman, 1995; Zwitserlood, Bölte & Dohmes, 2000, 2002). It is not easy to disentangle semantic and morphological similarity, since the two are confounded in a natural way. But here also, a growing number of studies demonstrate that effects of morphology and semantics can be separated (Dohmes, Zwitserlood, & Bölte, 2004; Feldman, Barac-Cikoja, & Kostic, 2002; Frost, Deutsch, Gilboa, Tannenbaum, & Marslen-Wilson, 2000; Laudanna, Badecker, & Caramazza, 1989; Zwitserlood, 1994).

Although morphological complexity is an issue in the research reported here, the focus is not on lexical representation or on morphological parsing per se, but on the interface between morphology and semantics. A major question is whether complex words are always activated by the semantic fields of their constituent morphemes. We investigated verbs that are equal as far as their morphological structure is concerned, but that differ in the semantic relation to their verbal root morphemes. Such verbs were used in cross-modal priming, with spoken sentences serving as semantic primes. To facilitate a discussion of the questions at issue, we first introduce the particular verbs used, because these come from Dutch and are not common to many languages. We couch our research questions in a working model of lexical and conceptual representation, illustrated below.

Dutch particle verbs, the materials used here, are morphologically complex verbs consisting of three morphemes: a root, an inflectional suffix and a separable prefix, commonly labelled particle (cf. Booij, 1990, 2002; Lüdeling, 1999). Particle verbs always contain simple verbs (e.g., *plakken*, paste).[1] Particles may function elsewhere as prepositions or adverbs (e.g., *op*, on, in *opplakken*, paste onto, or *vast*, tight, in *vastplakken*, paste together). Thus, simple verbs as well as particles are free morphemes. What makes particle verbs different from other complex words is the separability of their components in speech or text. In infinitival form, simple verb and particle are firmly attached, written as one word. With particle verbs in finite form, simple verb and particle are separated, and any number of words may come in between (e.g., 'Max *plakte* de nieuwe postzegels van zijn verzameling *in*', literally: Max pasted the new stamps of his collection in). This is not the case for prefixed verbs, because bound prefixes and roots are never separated (e.g., *beplakken*, paste over). Below, we argue that this separability might have consequences for the conceptual/semantic representation of particle verbs.[2]

Whereas prefixed words are often used in experiments on morphological issues (e.g., Bergman, Hudson, & Eling, 1988; Taft, Hambly, & Kinoshita, 1986; Tyler, Marslen-Wilson, Rentoul, & Hanney, 1988), little is known about verbs with separable particles. Schriefers, Zwitserlood and Roelofs (1991) found no differences between prefixed and particle verbs, using spoken complex verbs in their infinitival form in gating and phoneme monitoring. However, data from Schreuder, Grendel, Poulisse, Roelofs, and van de Voort (1990) suggest differences between the two types of verb. They obtained facilitation of naming responses due to a brief preview of morphological components for particle verbs, but not for prefixed verbs (see also Frazier, Flores, d'Arcais, & Coolen, 1993; Schreuder, 1990; Zwitserlood, 1990). For the present purposes, it is important that particle verbs are morphologically complex and that morphological priming is evident for their constituent morphemes (cf. Roelofs & Baayen, 2002; Zwitserlood, Drews, Bolwiender, & Neuwinger, 1996). Based on such findings, we assume connections between complex verbs and their constituents in our working model illustrated in Figure 1.

Particle verbs provide an interesting testing ground to tackle the relation between morphology and semantics. Dutch (as well as German) is rife with

---

[1] We use the term 'simple verb' throughout to refer to the combination of a root (e.g., plakk-) and the infinitival inflection (-en). Simple verbs contained in particle verbs are also referred to as 'constituent verbs' or 'embedded verbs'.

[2] We use semantic and conceptual interchangeably and consider this information to be outside of, but closely linked to, the language system proper.

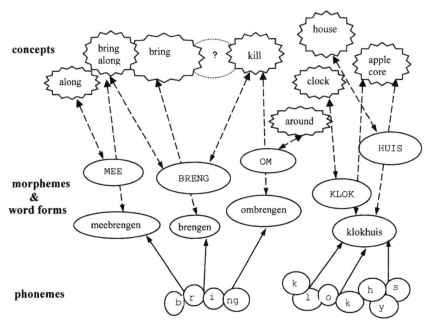

Figure 1. Illustration of representations and connections at the lexical and conceptual stratum. Note: The bi-directionality of arrows represents the flow of information in comprehension and production and is neutral with respect to feedback between nodes. Translations are provided in the 'concept nodes'.

particle verbs. Simple verbs may be combined with many particles, each time creating a different (or slightly different) word sense for the combination. Although the semantic relation between particle verb and constituent simple verb is transparent for most verbs, some particle verbs are semantically non-compositional or opaque. Thus, their meaning cannot be derived from the meaning of the constituents. There exist quite a number of so-called transparent/opaque pairs: Whereas *meebrengen* (bring along) is transparently related in meaning to *brengen* (bring), *ombrengen* (kill or exterminate) clearly is not. We used such pairs here to investigate their representation in semantic-conceptual memory.

There is ample evidence that semantically opaque complex words reveal a sensitivity, in lexical processing, to their morphological make up, in the same way that transparent complex words do (Boudelaa, & Marslen-Wilson, 2001; Feldman, & Soltano, 1999; Frost, Forster, & Deutsch, 1997; Longtin, Segui, & Halle, 2003; Rastle, Davis, Marslen-Wilson, & Tyler, 2000; Roelofs, & Baayen, 2002). Thus, our working model treats semantically transparent and opaque complex words alike at morphological-lexical levels of representation (see Figure 1). But although opaque words apparently are related to their constituent free morphemes at a morphological level, this seems not to extend to semantic-conceptual memory. For example, Zwitserlood (1994), with semantic priming, showed close semantic links between transparent Dutch compounds such as *kerkorgel* (church organ) and their constituent morphemes. But this was not the case for truly opaque compounds such as *klokhuis* (apple core, literally: clock house; see also Sandra, 1990; but see Shillcock, 1990). Similarly, Marslen-Wilson et al. (1994) obtained priming for semantically transparent derived word pairs such as *friendly-friend*, but not for opaque pairs such as *casualty-casual*. These findings are incorporated in our model in terms of a lack of overlap or connections between representations at the conceptual stratum.

The core question here is, whether the lack of semantic priming due to semantic opacity, observed for compounds and for derived words, will also hold for particle verbs. For the following reasons, we expect particle verbs to behave differently. The separation of their constituents in sentences often creates a temporary semantic ambiguity, as in: *Jan **brengt** niet alleen zijn moeder, maar ook zijn vriendin en zijn hond (1) **mee** (2) **om**.* In (1), with the transparent particle verb *brengt ... mee*, the sentence means: John not only takes along his mother, but also his female friend and his dog. In (2), with the opaque verb *brengt ... om*, the sentence means: John not only kills his mother but also his female friend and his dog.

Such local (morphological and semantic) ambiguities arise as a consequence of the unique separability of particle verbs. Upon hearing the simple verb (*brengt*), the listener does not know whether this, by itself, is the main verb, whether a particle is going to follow, and if so, which particle. Such ambiguities occur regularly in normal speech; they just do not arise with compounds or with derived words with bound suffixes. In fact, evidence for the existence of such ambiguities comes from crossmodal priming. Semantically neutral spoken sentence fragments containing the verb stem, but not the particle ('John brings his mother ...') primed both transparent and opaque particle verb targets containing the verb stem (*meebrengen*, bring along; *ombrengen*, kill), when these were presented visually for lexical decision (Zwitserlood, 1996). The question pursued here is whether such temporary ambiguities have an impact on the ways in which conceptual information of complex verbs is organised. We tested the idea that, as a consequence of frequent situations of ambiguity, the connectedness between such verbs that is attested at a lexical-morphological level is carried over to semantic-conceptual levels (see Figure 1). Perhaps paradoxically, in terms of priming, we expect opaque complex verbs to be primed by semantic information pertaining to their embedded verb—with which they bear no semantic relation.

The assumptions with respect to lexical and conceptual representation, illustrated in our model, can be summarised as follows. As a preamble, the model is designed to capture both language comprehension and production, hence the bidirectional links between representations. The model incorporates whole-word representations for complex words. Such unitary representations are needed to code grammatical information (such as word class or gender) that cannot be unequivocally derived from a combination of constituents (cf. Levelt, Roelofs, & Meyer, 1999; Zwitserlood et al., 2002). Whole-word representations might also be important for spoken-word recognition (cf. Schriefers et al., 1991). Based on the evidence cited above, we believe that these whole-word units are connected to their constituent morphemes within the lexical level, independent of semantic transparency. This implies morphological parsing in comprehension, and construction processes in production. In the model, semantically transparent complex words and their constituents share overlap in semantic-conceptual space, whereas completely opaque words do not.

So far, this is a relatively uncontroversial view of lexical and conceptual representation. The specific assumption put to test here is less obvious: Semantically opaque complex verbs become activated when the semantic domain of their embedded verb is activated. In the model, this is implemented by connections at the conceptual stratum (question-marked in Figure 1). Crucially, this assumption does not apply to every type of complex word, only to particle verbs, because of the separability of constituents.

EXPERIMENTAL CONSIDERATIONS AND PREDICTIONS

We investigated whether particle verbs are primed by semantic information pertaining to their embedded simple verb, independent of semantic transparency. Given that the constituent verb is always encountered first when particle verbs are read or heard in finite form, we surmised that semantic activation of this simple verb would spread to the conceptual representation of its particle verbs, even in the absence of semantic transparency (Yantis & Meyer, 1988).

We used cross-modal semantic priming, with spoken sentences as primes, and verbs as targets, visually presented for lexical decision. A sample set of the materials is given in Table 1. We constructed the spoken sentences such that they should home into the semantic representation of verbs in conceptual memory. If, for example, the sentence is about a wet raincoat creating puddles of rain in the hallway, we expected the conceptual representation of the verb 'drip' to be activated. The way in which we probed for activation of the verbs' conceptual information was by presenting them visually, as targets at the offset of the spoken sentences.

TABLE 1
A sample set of materials used in Experiment 1

Primes	Targets
Simple Verb	
Anja ging enorm tekeer tegen haar baas	SCHELDEN
(Anja worked herself into a rage as she confronted her boss)	(call names)
Transparent	
Hij slingerde haar de meest gemene dingen naar het hoofd	UITSCHELDEN
(he shouted all sorts of mean things when talking to her)	(abuse)
Opaque	
Gelukkig hoeft het geld niet te worden terugbetaald	KWIJTSCHELDEN
(fortunately we may keep the money)	(remit payment)
Control	
Alle heesters werden voor de winter nog een keer gesnoeid	
(all shrubs were pruned once more before the winter)	

Sentence primes were combined with triplets of targets: a transparent and an opaque particle verb, as well as their shared constituent verb. Separate sentence primes were constructed for each target verb, expecting that such primes would activate the verb's conceptual representation. When spoken sentence and target were semantically congruent, we expected facilitation of decision times to the targets, relative to an unrelated control sentence prime. Since transparent particle verbs and constituent simple verbs largely overlapped in meaning, we expected the sentences constructed for simple verbs to prime transparent particle verb targets and vice versa. Of course, sentences constructed for opaque verbs should prime the opaque targets.

For incongruent conditions we expected the following. Given that only simple verbs, as constituent of particle verbs, temporarily create ambiguities, we assume that prime sentences for simple verbs also activate their particle verbs—transparent and opaque ones alike. However, particle verbs, when encountered in the full in a sentence, never create ambiguities (e.g., Jan heeft zijn moeder *meegebracht / omgebracht*, John has brought along / killed his mother). We therefore expected asymmetric effects in incongruent conditions, with no facilitation of simple verb targets—or of transparent verb targets—after opaque verb primes.

EXPERIMENT 1: PRIMING SEMANTICALLY TRANSPARENT AND OPAQUE VERBS

In general, verb meaning is more flexible than noun meaning (Gentner, 1981). Many verbs have more than one sense and are thus fairly polysemous. Moreover, the meaning of a simple verb may be slightly altered by combining it with a specific particle. It was important, therefore, to establish the most dominant or frequent meaning of simple verbs before determining the appropriate particle with which it was to be combined to form a semantically transparent combination. A free association test for the simple verbs was carried out to establish an empirical basis for choosing between word senses.

Method

Participants

A total of 166 participants were tested in the experiment, 58 in the association pretest, and 108 in the main experiment. All participants were native speakers of Dutch, mainly students from Nijmegen University, between 19 and 28 years of age. They were paid for their participation.

Material

Association pretest. The dominant sense of simple verbs was established in a free association test. Participants had to write down, for every written stimulus word, the first three words that spontaneously came to mind. One hundred and fifty simple verbs were divided over three lists, which were presented to 19, 20, and 19 participants respectively. Participants' responses were attributed to the various senses of each word. For example, the verb *drukken* can mean print or push. Associations like *PRESS*, *PAPER*, *INK*, and *BOOK* were scored under the first meaning; associations such as *ARM* or *PULL* were scored under the second. The word sense to which at least 80% of the associations could be attributed was considered to be the dominant meaning. For 18 verbs, a proper dominant sense could not be established, and these verbs were discarded.

Test material. A total of 132 material sets were used in the main experiment. Each set included four spoken sentence primes and three targets (see Table 1): a simple verb without particle (e.g., *schelden*, call names), a semantically transparent particle verb (*uitschelden*, verbally abuse), and a semantically opaque particle verb (*kwijtschelden*, remit a payment). The transparent particle verbs were chosen such that their meaning, as established with the aid of a dictionary (Van Dale, 1995), was close to the dominant sense of their constituent verbs. Opaque verbs were selected on the basis of a semantic relatedness pretest carried out in the context of other experiments. Opaque complex verb—simple verb pairs (e.g., *kwijtschelden—schelden*) were mixed with completely unrelated pairs (e.g., *weglopen—snijden*, run away—cut) and transparent pairs. Using a five-point scale (1: completely unrelated; 5: completely related), the median relatedness score for opaque verbs was 1.5, close to the score for completely unrelated verb pairs (1.3). Simple verb and particle verb targets differed in length (simple verbs were 3 to 5 letters shorter). Frequency of occurrence could not reliably be established, but we can be fairly sure that simple verbs were more frequent.[3] Because of this lack of control over target length and frequency, all targets served as their own control when paired with control sentences.

There were four sentence prime conditions, one for each of the three target verbs and one control sentence. Sentences primes were labelled according to the targets for which they were constructed: Simple Prime, Transparent Prime, and Opaque Prime. Given their conceptual proximity, simple verb and transparent verb targets were congruent with Simple and Transparent Prime sentences, but opaque targets were not. Moreover, only the opaque verbs were congruent with the meaning of Opaque Prime sentences, simple verb and transparent particle verbs were not. In the control condition (Control Prime), the three verbs of each set were combined with a sentence prime that was semantically completely unrelated to each of the three targets. For a sample set, see Table 1.

To reduce the relatedness proportion to 33%, 99 filler sentences were added with unrelated verb targets (particle and simple verbs). In addition, 231 trials were constructed for the lexical decision task, in which spoken sentences were combined with orthographically legal pseudo-word targets. These pseudo-words were derived from existing simple or complex verbs (e.g., *krussen* from *krassen*, scratch, *uitblezen* from *uitblazen*, blow out). A further 30 trials, mirroring test and pseudo-word trials, served as practice.

Design

Within each material set, every sentence prime was combined with all targets, resulting in 12 conditions: 4 (Sentence Primes) × 3 (Targets). Materials were rotated over 12 experimental lists with a Latin Square design, so that participants were presented with only one condition of each material set. Each list contained 11 different material sets in each of the 12 conditions. Nine participants were tested on each list. Pseudo-word and filler trials were the same on all lists.

---

[3] Word frequency is difficult to assess for particle as well as for simple verbs. In the CELEX database for Dutch (see Baayen, Piepenbrock, & van Rijn, 1993), every occurrence of a verb in the text corpus adds to the lemma of the simple verb. This implies that particle verbs in finite form add to the count of their constituent simple verbs, leading to an overestimation of their frequency and an underestimation of the frequency of particle verbs. The frequency count of particle verbs is based only on those cases in which the verb was written as one word.

Procedure

Two to four participants were tested simultaneously. The experiment was run with NESU software (Baumann, Nagengast, & Klaas, 1993). Spoken sentences were presented over closed headphones (Sennheisser HD224). Targets were presented in upper case, centred on CRT screens, for 500 ms immediately after the acoustic offset of the sentence. Participants had to decide whether visual targets were Dutch words or not (lexical decision). They used their preferred hand for word decisions. Latencies were measured from the onset of target presentation to the participants' response. The experiment lasted about 50 minutes.

Results

Mean error rates were 7.7% for word targets and 4.5% for pseudo-word targets. Data for correct answers were submitted to analyses of variance, (ANOVA), with subjects and items as random factors. The data are presented in Table 2.

The ANOVAs on latencies showed a significant main effect of the factor Target, $F_1(2, 214) = 359.94, p < .001, MSE = 2092; F_2(2, 262) = 104.37, p < .001, MSE = 8820$. Simple verb targets produced overall faster reactions (464 ms) than transparent (541 ms) or opaque (529 ms) target verbs. This was expected, because simple verbs are shorter and of higher frequency than complex verbs. There was also a main effect of Prime Type (Simple Verb, Transparent, Opaque, and Control Prime), $F_1(3, 321) = 95.71, p < .001, MSE = 1384; F_2(3, 393) = 51.94, p < .001, MSE = 3118$. Compared to Control Prime (534 ms) mean RTs were faster in the Simple Verb (492 ms) and Transparent (497 ms) prime conditions, but not in the Opaque Prime condition (522 ms).

More interesting is the significant interaction between the two factors: $F_1(6, 642) = 14.46, p < .001, MSE = 1099; F_2(6, 786) = 7.6, p < .001, MSE = 2558$. Opaque targets showed clear priming effects in all sentence prime

TABLE 2

Mean lexical decision latencies, priming effects, and error percentages (in brackets), as a function of Prime Type and Verb Target, Experiment 1

	Verb target					
	Simple verb		Transparent verb		Opaque verb	
Prime type	RT (error)	effect	RT (error)	effect	RT (error)	effect
Simple Prime	446 (1.9)	32	511 (4.6)	62	520 (5.1)	32
Transparent Prime	454 (2.3)	24	516 (5.3)	57	520 (5.6)	32
Opaque Prime	477 (4.6)	1	564 (12.2)	9	525 (6.1)	27
Control Prime	478 (4.4)		573 (13.5)		552 (8.1)	

conditions, while Simple Verb and Transparent targets were not facilitated in incongruent conditions, that is, when preceded by sentence primes belonging to opaque verbs. To establish which conditions had actually led to significant facilitation, mean reaction times for each target type in the simple verb, transparent and opaque sentence prime condition were compared with their Control condition (two-tailed t-tests; see Table 2 for effects). Transparent and simple verb primes produced reliable facilitation in congruent conditions (all $p < .05$). The overall largest priming effects were observed for transparent particle verb targets. This seems in part to be due to the latencies for the corresponding control condition, which were quite slow and error-prone. As expected, simple and transparent verb targets were not facilitated after incongruent sentences constructed for the opaque targets (1 and 9 ms). Comparisons for the opaque verb targets clearly showed a different pattern. There was significant priming with all three sentence primes, that is, in congruent and incongruent conditions (all $p < .05$).

The ANOVAs on errors showed similar patterns of effects as the analyses on latencies. A main effect of Target revealed more errors for Transparent (8.9) and Opaque (6.2) targets than for short and frequent simple verbs (3.3), $F_1(2, 214) = 62.09, p < .001, MSE = .0055; F_2(2, 262) = 22.15, p < .001, MSE = .0187$. Prime Type also affected error rate: $F_1(3, 321) = 32.12, p < .001, MSE = .0056; F_2(3, 393) = 30.82, p < .001, MSE = .0072$, with about twice as many errors after Control and Opaque prime sentences than after Transparent and Simple Verb primes. The interaction between the two factors was also significant: $F_1(6, 642) = 8.94, p < .001, MSE = .0048; F_2(6, 786) = 8.45, p < .001, MSE = .0062$. The highest error rates were observed in the incongruent and control prime conditions for the transparent particle verbs. These high error rates were paired with the longest mean RTs in the experiment; so, speed-accuracy trade-off effects were not observed.

Discussion

The most interesting part of the results resides in the interaction between the factors sentence prime and target. As expected, facilitation was found whenever the content of the sentence was congruent with the meaning of the target verb. This held for all three verb types. Incongruity, however, affected transparent and opaque verb targets differentially.

Overall, a context sentence activates the semantic field of a target that is congruent with the information in the sentence. On subsequent presentation of that target, less processing time suffices for its recognition. The data show that the sentence contexts constructed for simple verbs prime those simple verbs as well as transparent particle verbs. Similarly, contexts for transparent particle verbs also facilitate reactions to simple verbs. Not surprisingly given the choice of material, our semantically transparent complex verbs and their constituent simple verbs seem to be close neighbours in conceptual space, and to share semantic features. In contrast, incongruent sentences—those constructed for opaque verbs— did not prime simple and transparent verbs.

As expected, opaque targets were primed by their own congruent sentences. But unlike for simple and transparent verbs, facilitation was also found in incongruent conditions. Thus, the sentences favouring simple verbs and transparent particle verbs were also effective primes for opaque targets. This facilitation seems to indicate that the semantic field of the simple verb, which is contained in the opaque one, serves to activate the opaque verb, although there is merely morphological but no conceptual similarity between the two.

There is, however, a potential alternative explanation for at least some of our results. We treated semantic transparency versus opacity as an all-or-none phenomenon, based on the data from the semantic rating test. We only selected verbs that were rated as clearly opaque; in fact, they were considered to be almost as unrelated to their constituent simple verb (1.5 on a 7-point scale) as completely unrelated pairs (1.3). However, closer inspection of the material showed that some of these opaque particle verbs indeed had a dominant opaque meaning, but also an additional transparent sense, derivable from the meaning of the simple verb. The particle verb *uitroeien*, for example, with its constituent verb *roeien* (row), most prominently means 'exterminate' or 'annihilate', but it can also mean 'to finish by rowing', as in *Jan roeide de regatta uit* (John finished the regatta by rowing). So, although participants in the semantic relatedness pretest apparently were not consciously aware of the existence of secondary, infrequent transparent senses, some particle verbs turned out to be semantically ambiguous.[4] This is reminiscent of other semantically ambiguous words, such as *bank* (Cottrell, 1988; Kawamoto, 1988; Seidenberg, Tanenhaus, Leiman, & Bienkowski, 1982; Simpson, 1994; Swinney, 1979; Tabossi, 1988).

So, effects could well be contaminated by those opaque verbs in the set that turned out to have multiple senses. To assess whether the facilitation of opaque particle verbs in incongruent contexts reflects priming of the subordinate transparent sense, we performed a post-hoc analysis on the data. The selection criteria for deciding on the ambiguity of the verbs in

---

[4] The clear dominance of the opaque meaning of these verbs is evident from the semantic pretest data and from the fact that none of us had ever reckoned with a secondary transparent sense before we started close-reading the dictionary.

the opaque set are described in detail below, with Experiment 2. From the original 132 sets, 24 were selected with truly opaque participle verbs and 24 with ambiguous particle verbs, which had a dominant opaque and a subordinate transparent meaning. An ANOVA on items was performed, with item sets nested under the factor Ambiguity (truly opaque vs. ambiguous) and with all four sentence primes (Simple Verb, Transparent, Opaque, and Control Prime), excluding data from simple verbs and transparent particle verbs.

There was a significant interaction between Ambiguity and Sentence Prime: $F_2(3, 138) = 3.14$, $p < .05$, $MSE = 2631$, indicating a differential pattern of priming for the two verb types. Truly opaque particle verbs were facilitated only by their own opaque sentence primes, not by transparent and simple verb sentences. Ambiguous verbs, on the other hand, were primed by all sentence primes, thus providing evidence for multiple activation.

Since we were not aware of the ambiguity of a subset of opaque verbs by the time that Experiment 1 was run, we decided to corroborate the results of the post-hoc analysis in Experiment 2, explicitly manipulating the ambiguity factor.

EXPERIMENT 2: TRULY OPAQUE AND AMBIGUOUS PARTICLE VERBS

We established the semantic ambiguity of verbs that were included in the original opaque set by means of a dictionary (Van Dale, 1995), at the same time using a criterion of 'morphological integrity'. Almost all verbs and particles can be used in a transparent way when the particle's morpheme is not part of a morphologically complex verb but serves another function in the sentence. For example, *Jan brengt de krant om de hoek* (John takes the newspaper around the corner), contains the same two words that make up an opaque particle verb in *Jan brengt de man om in de tuin* (John kills the man in the garden). The first sentence, however, does not contain the particle verb *ombrengen*, but rather the simple verb *brengen* and a prepositional phrase with the preposition *om* (around), thus violating morphological integrity of the two elements. All selected verbs were indeed particle verbs, even if their particles can be used as prepositions. Importantly, the number of verbs with 'prepositional' particles was very similar for truly opaque (19) and ambiguous (17) particle verbs.

Thus, truly opaque particle verbs were defined as verbs that exclusively had an idiosyncratic sense, unrelated to the meaning of the embedded simple verb. Ambiguous particle verbs had an opaque as well as a transparent sense, while keeping the status of particle verb. Examples are 'uitroeien': *Jan roeit de regatta uit* (John finishes the regatta by rowing) and

Jan roeit de tijgers uit (John exterminates the tigers) and 'aftuigen': *Jan tuigt zijn schip af* (John unrigs his ship) and *Jan tuigt zijn broer af* (John beats his brother). With a reduced number of prime and target conditions, Experiment 2 contrasted effects of truly opaque, ambiguous, and fully transparent particle verbs. With the above criteria, 24 of the opaque particle verbs used in Experiment 1 were considered truly opaque. Next, another 24 verbs were selected for which the dictionary listed at least two meanings—the original opaque meaning and a transparent sense that was close to the meaning of the constituent simple verb.

The reduction of the number of material sets to 48 forced us to reduce the number of conditions, to keep enough observations per condition and participant. A first reduction concerned the exclusion of simple verb targets. Second, only two of the original four sentence primes were included: the transparent and the control sentence. Simple Verb prime sentences were excluded, because the data from Experiment 1 showed no important differences between simple verb and transparent sentence primes with respect to their impact on opaque verb targets. The exclusion of the opaque sentence primes was the next obvious choice, since evidence for the facilitation of opaque targets—whether truly opaque or ambiguous—by their own sentences was already obtained in Experiment 1.

The purpose of Experiment 2 was to assess the activation of opaque particle verbs with and without a secondary transparent meaning, as a function of sentences that primed the meaning of the embedded verb. Combining transparent, truly opaque and ambiguous targets with the transparent sentences and unrelated control sentences suffices to test this question.

Method

Participants

Twenty-four native speakers of Dutch, students from Nijmegen University, were tested. They had not taken part in Experiment 1 or in any pretest and were paid for their participation.

Material

The critical material consisted of 48 sets. Half of these had opaque particle verbs with an additional transparent sense; the other half had truly opaque particle verbs. These targets were paired with their transparent counterparts, so that the material contained 48 target pairs. Each target pair was combined with two sentences primes: Transparent and Control sentence. Pseudoword trials, fillers, and practice items were similar to Experiment 1.

Design

The design had the following within-materials factors: Sentence Prime (Transparent and Control Sentence) and Target (Transparent Verb and Opaque Verb). Ambiguity (truly opaque vs. ambiguous) was a between-materials factor, with 24 item sets in each level. Unlike in Experiment 1, where all prime conditions of a material set were allocated to separate lists, some conditions were tested within-subjects. Two lists were constructed, each divided into two blocks. Participants received each material set in two of the four combinations of the factors Target by Sentence Prime, one in each block. It was ensured that they never heard the same prime or saw the same target twice. So, if block 1 contained the Transparent Target and Transparent Prime of a given material set, block 2 had the Opaque Target and Control Prime. Participants thus saw all 96 targets, and an additional 48 unrelated filler items with word targets, to reduce the relatedness proportion. The 144 pseudo-word sets were taken from Experiment 1. They were the same on both lists, as were the 16 practice items.

Procedure

The procedure was the same as in Experiment 1. An experimental session lasted about 30 minutes.

Results

Mean error rates were 4.9% for words and 4.2% for pseudo-word targets. The highest error rates were paired with the slowest mean RTs; so, no speed-accuracy trade-off effects were observed. Reaction times in Experiment 2 were much longer than in Experiment 1. This could be due to a different population of participants and/or to the specific selection of 48 out of 132 item sets. Analyses of Variance (ANOVA), by subjects and by items, were performed on error and latency data. The results are presented in Table 3.

In the ANOVAs on latencies there were main effects of Ambiguity and Target, but both factors involve different sets of targets that were not matched on any criterion. There was a main effect of Prime Type, with overall faster latencies after transparent (655 ms) than after control primes (676 ms), $F_1(1, 23) = 15.75, p < .001, MSE = 1443, F_1(1, 46) = 10.72, p < .002, MSE = 2120$. The most important finding was a three-way interaction between Sentence Prime (Transparent vs. Control Sentence), Target Type (Transparent vs. Opaque) and Ambiguity (Truly Opaque vs. Ambiguous). This interaction was significant by subjects, $F_1(1, 23) = 7.10, p < .02, MSE = 834$, but just failed significance by items, $F_1(1, 46) = 3.14, p = .07, MSE = 1884$. This could in part be due to the nesting of item sets under the factor Ambiguity in this analysis.

TABLE 3

Mean lexical decision times, priming effects, and error percentages (in brackets) as a function of Prime Type and Verb Target, Experiment 2

	Verb target				
Prime type	Transparent verb			Opaque verb	
	RT (error)	effect		RT (error)	effect
Transparent prime	631 (4.2)	33		699 (8.3)	−9
Control prime	664 (5.6)			690 (6.2)	
	Transparent verb			Ambiguous verb	
	RT (error)	effect		RT (error)	effect
Transparent prime	655 (0.7)	31		634 (3.8)	33
Control prime	686 (5.2)			667 (5.2)	

Planned comparisons (t-tests) of mean latencies in test and control prime conditions showed that there was facilitation in all conditions except one. As expected, latencies for the transparent targets were facilitated when paired with transparent sentence primes, as compared with control primes (see Table 3). This was the case in each of the two material subsets (33 and 31 ms, all $p < .05$). Ambiguous verb targets paired with transparent primes also showed significant priming (33 ms: both $p < .05$). In stark contrast, reactions to truly opaque verb targets were virtually the same, whether paired with transparent primes or with control primes (9 ms interference trend, NS).

Some conditions show the same effects as in Experiment 1: Reactions to transparent particle verbs are facilitated by congruent sentences. There is a healthy semantic priming effect that amounts to 30 ms or more. Moreover, the data clearly replicate the post-hoc analysis of Experiment 1. Truly opaque verbs are not primed by the context favouring the transparent verb. But when 'opaque' verbs have two meanings, we find congruency effects for both. The same target verb is facilitated by two sentences with completely different content. One sentence primes the verb's idiosyncratic, opaque meaning, which is unrelated to the meaning of the embedded verb. The other sentence that favours the transparent verb also causes facilitation, because it is related to the subordinate meaning of the ambiguous verb — which happens to be very close to the meaning of the embedded verb.

These results are reminiscent of what is often reported in the literature on semantic ambiguity: Both meanings of ambiguous words can be primed, even subordinate ones (Simpson, 1981, 1994; Tabossi, Colombo, & Job, 1987). The way we looked at ambiguity is the reverse from what is common in the semantic ambiguity literature. Normally, the ambiguous words themselves are used as primes for their distinct semantic fields, as with *bank* priming 'money' or 'river'. We reversed this by using sentences to evoke two different semantic fields, and presenting the ambiguous word as target. Of course, we never planned to investigate ambiguity; it just happened to come our way.

Perhaps the most important finding is the lack of facilitation of the meaning of the constituent verb, if the embedding particle verb is truly opaque. There is no trace of an effect here. Data from Experiment 1 showed that the idiosyncratic, opaque meaning can be primed by an adequate sentence context — which is not at all surprising. The results from Experiment 2 unequivocally show that this is the only meaning that is primable for such verbs.

CONCLUSIONS

Cross-modal priming was used in two experiments, with prime sentences constructed to activate the conceptual-semantic representations of (particle) verbs, which were subsequently presented as targets. Clear facilitation was found whenever sentences that were meant to prime the transparent meaning of a (simple or complex) verb were followed by those verbs as targets. Similarly, sentences that were designed to prime the idiosyncratic meaning of opaque particle verbs facilitated lexical decision latencies to such opaque targets. Thus, as expected, facilitation was obtained in all congruent conditions.

But we also found priming in conditions that we believed to be incongruent, with opaque verbs preceded by the prime sentence of their constituent verb. We hypothesised that such effects could occur, under the assumption that the semantic representation of the simple verb is always activated, whatever complex verb it is embedded in. This seemed a plausible option, because the simple verb is often encountered before the particle. However, this assumption clearly turned out to be wrong. In the post-hoc analysis of Experiment 1 and in Experiment 2, a distinction between verbs that are truly opaque and verbs that are ambiguous became evident. We found ambiguity effects for particle verbs that we had erroneously considered to be completely opaque. Reactions to these verbs were facilitated by primes for the dominant idiosyncratic meaning as well as for the subordinate transparent meaning. Taken together, semantic priming consistently occurred whenever a target had at least one meaning that is congruent with the sentence prime. But if the meaning of a target was truly incongruent with the preceding sentence, no priming was found.

As is often the case with language phenomena, semantic transparency and opacity are hard to operationalise. It is certainly no all-or-none phenomenon, and it is hard to find good instances of the tail-end of the distribution, even though our own intuitions and data from off-line tasks had lured us into thinking otherwise.

What do our data reveal about the interface between morphological and conceptual levels of representation? There is, by now, ample evidence for the existence of genuine morphological effects in the absence of semantic transparency (Bentin & Feldman, 1990; Feldman et al., 2002; Frost et al., 2000; Zwitserlood, 1994; Zwitserlood et al., 1996, for particle verbs). This means that morphological relatives are in some way closely linked at a lexical level. One possibility is in terms of morphemes, not words, as the core elements of representation in (some part of) the lexicon. Based on work in speech production (Zwitserlood et al., 2002; Dohmes et al., 2004), this is what we adopt in our working model, including a level of morphemes, connected to whole-word representations for complex words. An alternative implementation is in terms of whole-word entries that share morphemes, closely huddled together in lexical space, living in morphological families. For those who prefer other metaphors, hidden layers may surely code such similarities even in the absence of information that is explicitly labelled 'morphological'.

What we have shown here is that all this is not necessarily mirrored in conceptual memory. We obtained semantic priming in all congruent conditions, even for semantically ambiguous, unbalanced particle verbs. But crucially, we also demonstrated that truly opaque verbs cannot be semantically primed through their constituent simple verbs, although these are clearly part of their morphological make-up. What we see is a dissociation between lexical and conceptual systems. Thus, Dutch equivalents of *guard* and *blackguard*, or *bring* and *bring about*, whose relatedness, at a morphological level, is honoured within the language system, live separate lives in conceptual memory — as much as *red wine* and *frost*, or *grain* and *befuddle*.

REFERENCES

Baayen, H., Piepenbrock, R., & van Rijn, H. (1993). *The CELEX lexical database*. Philadelphia, PA: Linguistics Data Consortium, University of Pennsylvania.

Baumann, H., Nagengast, J., & Klaas, G. (1993). *New experimental set up (NESU)*. The Netherlands: Max-Planck-Institute for Psycholinguistics.

Bentin, S., & Feldman, L. B. (1990). The contribution of morphological and semantic relatedness to repetition priming at long and short lags: Evidence from Hebrew. *Quarterly Journal of Experimental Psychology, 42A*, 693–711.

Bergman, M., Hudson, P. T. W., & Eling, P. E. (1988). How simple complex words can be. *Quarterly Journal of Experimental Psychology, 40A*, 41–72.

Booij, G. (1990). The boundary between morphology and syntax: Separable complex verbs in Dutch. In G. Booij & J. van Marle (Eds.), *Yearbook of morphology, 3* (pp. 45–63). Dordrecht: Foris Publications.

Booij, G. (2002). *The morphology of Dutch*. Oxford: Oxford University Press.

Boudelaa, S., & Marslen-Wilson, W. D. (2001). Morphological units in the Arabic mental lexicon. *Cognition, 81*, 65–92.

Burani, C., & Caramazza, A. (1987). Representation and processing of derived words. *Language and Cognitive Processes, 2*, 217–227.

Caramazza, A., Laudanna A., & Romani, C. (1988). Lexical access and inflectional morphology. *Cognition, 28*, 297–332.

Cottrell, G. W. (1988). A model of lexical access of ambiguous words. In S. L. Small, G. W. Cottrell, & M. K. Tanenhaus (Eds.), *Lexical ambiguity resolution: Perspectives from psycholinguistics, neuropsychology and artificial intelligence* (pp. 179–194). San Mateo, CA: Morgan Kaufmann.

Dohmes, P., Zwitserlood, P., & Bölte, J. (2004). The impact of morphological complexity and semantic transparency on picture naming. *Brain and Language, 90*, 203–212.

Drews, E., & Zwitserlood, P. (1995). Effects of morphological and orthographic similarity in visual word recognition. *Journal of Experimental Psychology: Human Perception and Performance, 21(5)*, 1098–1116.

Feldman, L. B. (1990). Morphological relationships revealed through the repetition priming task. In M. Noonan, P. Downing, & S. Lima (Eds.), *Linguistics and literacy* (pp. 239–254). Amsterdam: John Benjamins.

Feldman, L. B., & Andjelkovic, D. (1992). Morphological analysis in word recognition. In R. Frost & L. Katz (Eds.), *Orthography, phonology, morphology, and meaning* (pp. 343–360). Amsterdam: North Holland.

Feldman, L. B., Barac-Cikoja, D., & Kostic, A. (2002). Semantic aspects of morphological processing: Transparency effects in Serbian. *Memory and Cognition, 30*, 629–636.

Feldman, L. B., & Fowler, C. A. (1987). The inflected noun system in Serbo-Croatian: Lexical representations of morphological structure. *Memory and Cognition, 15*, 1–12.

Feldman, L. B., & Soltano, E. G. (1999). Morphological priming: The role of prime duration, semantic transparency, and affix position. *Brain and Language, 68*, 33–39.

Frauenfelder, U. H., & Schreuder, R. (1992). Constraining psycholinguistic models of morphological processing and representation: The role of productivity. In G. Booij & J. van Marle (Eds.), *Yearbook of morphology, 1991* (pp. 165–183). Dordrecht: Foris Publications.

Frazier, L., Flores d'Arcais, G. B., & Coolen, R. (1993). Processing discontinuous words: On the interface between lexical and syntactic processing. *Cognition, 47*, 219–249.

Frost, R., & Bentin, S. (1992). Processing phonological and semantic ambiguity: Evidence from semantic priming at different SOAs. *Journal of Experimental Psychology: Learning, Memory and Cognition, 18(1)*, 58–68.

Frost, R., Deutsch, A., Gilboa, O., Tannenbaum, M., & Marslen-Wilson, W. (2000). Morphological priming: Dissociation of phonological, semantic, and morphological factors. *Memory and Cognition, 28*, 1277–1288.

Frost, R., Forster, K. I., & Deutsch, A. (1997). What can we learn from the morphology of Hebrew? A masked-priming investigation of morphological representation. *Journal of Experimental Psychology: Learning, Memory, and Cognition, 23*, 829–856.

Gentner, D. (1981). Some interesting differences between verbs and nouns. *Cognition and Brain Theory, 4*, 161–178.

Kawamoto, A. H. (1988). Distributed representations of ambiguous words and their resolution in a connectionist network. In S. L. Small, G. W. Cottrell, & M. K. Tanenhaus (Eds.), *Lexical ambiguity resolution: Perspectives from psycholinguistics, neuropsychology and artificial intelligence* (pp. 195–228). San Mateo, CA: Morgan Kaufmann Publishers.

Laudanna, A., Badecker, W., & Caramazza, A. (1989). Priming homographic stems. *Journal of Memory and Language, 28*, 531–546.

Levelt, W. J. M., Roelofs, A., & Meyer, A. S. (1999). A theory of lexical access in speech production. *Behavioral and Brain Sciences, 22*, 1–75.

Longtin, C.-M., Segui, J., & Hallé, P. A. (2003). Morphological priming without morphological relationship. *Language and Cognitive Processes, 18*, 313–334.

Lüdeling, A. (1999). *On particle verbs and similar constructions in German.* Doctoral dissertation, University of Tübingen.

Lukatela, G., Gligorijevic, B., Kostic, A., & Turvey, M. T. (1980). Representation of inflected nouns in the internal lexicon. *Memory and Cognition, 8*, 415–423.

Marslen-Wilson, W., Tyler, L. K., Waksler, R., & Older, L. (1994). Morphology and meaning in the English mental lexicon. *Psychological Review, 101*, 3–33.

Napps, S. E. (1989). Morphemic relations in the lexicon: Are they distinct from semantic and formal relationships? *Memory and Cognition, 17*, 729–739.

Plaut, D., & Gonnerman, L. G. (2000). Are non-semantic morphological effects incompatible with a distributed connectionist approach to lexical processing? *Language and Cognitive Processes, 15*, 445–485.

Plunkett, K., & Marchmann, V. (1993). From rote learning to system building: Acquiring verb morphology in children and connectionist nets. *Cognition, 48*, 21–69.

Rastle, K., Davis, M. H., Marslen-Wilson, W. D., & Tyler, L. K. (2000). Morphological and semantic effects in visual word recognition: A time-course study. *Language and Cognitive Processes, 15*, 507–537.

Roelofs, A., & Baayen, R. H. (2002). Morphology by itself in planning the production of spoken words. *Psychonomic Bulletin and Review, 9*, 132–138.

Rueckl, J. G., Mikolinski, M., Raveh, M., Miner, C. S., & Mars, F. (1997). Morphological priming, fragment completion, and connectionist networks. *Journal of Memory and Language, 36*, 382–405.

Sandra, D. (1990). On the representation and processing of compound words: Automatic access to constituent morphemes does not occur. *Quarterly Journal of Experimental Psychology, 42A*, 529–567.

Schreuder, R., & Baayen, R. H. (1995). Modeling morphological processing. In L. B. Feldman (Ed.), *Morphological aspects of language processing* (pp. 131–154). Hillsdale, NJ: Lawrence Erlbaum Associates Inc.

Schreuder, R. (1990). Lexical processing of verbs with separable particles. In G. Booij & J. van Marle (Eds.), *Yearbook of morphology, 3* (pp. 65–79). Dordrecht: Foris Publications.

Schreuder, R., Grendel, M., Poulisse, N., Roelofs, A., & van de Voort, M. (1990). Lexical processing, morphological complexity and reading. In D. Balota, G. B. Flores d'Arcais, & K. Rayner (Eds.), *Comprehension processes in reading* (pp. 125–141). Hillsdale, NJ: Lawrence Erlbaum Associates Inc.

Schriefers, H. (1999). Morphology and word recognition. In A. D. Friederici (Ed.), *Language comprehension: A biological perspective* (pp. 101–132). Berlin: Springer.

Schriefers, H., Zwitserlood, P., & Roelofs, A. (1991). The identification of morphologically complex words: Continuous processing or decomposition? *Journal of Memory and Language, 30*, 26–47.

Seidenberg, M. S., Tanenhaus, M. K., Leiman, J. M., & Bienkowski, M. (1982). Automatic access of the meanings of ambiguous words in context: Some limitations of knowledge-based processing. *Cognitive Psychology, 14*, 489–537.

Shillcock, R. (1990). Lexical hypotheses in continuous speech. In G. Altmann (Ed.), *Cognitive models of speech processing* (pp. 24–49). Cambridge, MA: MIT Press.

Simpson, G. B. (1981). Meaning dominance and semantic context in the processing of lexical ambiguity. *Journal of Verbal Learning and Verbal Behavior, 20*, 120–136.

Simpson, G. B. (1994). Context and the processing of ambiguous words. In M. A. Gernsbacher (Ed.), *Handbook of psycholinguistics* (pp. 359–374). San Diego, CA: Academic Press.

Stolz, J. A., & Feldman, L. B. (1995). The role of orthographic and semantic transparency of the base morpheme in morphological processing. In L. B. Feldman (Ed.), *Morphological aspects of language processing* (pp. 109–129). Hillsdale, NJ: Lawrence Erlbaum Associates Inc.

Swinney, D. A. (1979). Lexical access during sentence comprehension: (Re)considerations of context effects. *Journal of Verbal Learning and Verbal Behavior, 18*, 645–659.

Tabossi, P. (1988). Accessing lexical ambiguity in different types of sentential contexts. *Journal of Memory and Language, 27*, 324–340.

Tabossi, P., Colombo, L., & Job, R. (1987). Accessing lexical ambiguity: Effects of context and dominance. *Psychological Research, 49*, 161–167.

Taft, M., Hambly, G., & Kinoshita, S. (1986). Visual and auditory recognition of prefixed words. *Quarterly Journal of Experimental Psychology, 38A*, 351–366.

Tyler, L. K., Marslen-Wilson, W. D., Rentoul, J., & Hanney, P. (1988). Continuous and discontinuous access in spoken-word recognition: The role of derivational prefixes. *Journal of Memory and Language, 27*, 368–381.

Van Dale (1995). Groot Woordenboek der Nederlandse Taal. Utrecht/Antwerpen: Van Dale Lexicografie, Nijhoff.

Yantis, S., & Meyer, D. E. (1988). Dynamics of activation in semantic and episodic memory. *Journal of Experimental Psychology: General, 117(2)*, 130–147.

Zwitserlood, P. (1989). The locus of the effects of sentential-semantic context in spoken-word processing. *Cognition, 32*, 25–64.

Zwitserlood, P. (1990). Comments on the paper by Schreuder. In G. Booij & J. van Marle (Eds.), *Yearbook of morphology, 3* (pp. 81–85). Dordrecht: Foris Publications.

Zwitserlood, P. (1994). The role of semantic transparency in the processing and representation of Dutch compounds. *Language and Cognitive Processes, 9(3)*, 341–368.

Zwitserlood, P. (1996). *Processing Dutch equivalents of "bring along" and "bring about" in sentence contexts.* 37th meeting of the Psychonomic Society, Chicago, November 1996.

Zwitserlood, P., Bölte, J., & Dohmes, P. (2002). Where and how morphologically complex words interplay with naming pictures. *Brain and Language, 81*, 358–367.

Zwitserlood, P., Drews, E., Bolwiender, A., & Neuwinger, E. (1996). Kann man Geschenke umbringen? Assoziative Bahnungsexperimente zur Bedeutungsheterogenität von Verben. In C. Habel, S. Kanngießer, & G. Rickheit (Eds.), *Perspektiven der kognitiven Linguistik.* Opladen: Westdeutscher Verlag.

Language and Cognitive Processes
Index

For Product Safety Concerns and Information please contact our EU
representative GPSR@taylorandfrancis.com Taylor & Francis Verlag GmbH,
Kaufingerstraße 24, 80331 München, Germany

Batch number: 08153825

Printed by Printforce, the Netherlands